MW01040844

THE OXFORD HANDBOOK OF

MORMONISM

THE OXFORD HANDBOOK OF

MORMONISM

Edited by

TERRYL L. GIVENS

and

PHILIP L. BARLOW

OXFORD

UNIVERSITY PRESS

OXFORD
UNIVERSITY PRESS

Oxford University Press is a department of the University of
Oxford. It furthers the University's objective of excellence in research,
scholarship, and education by publishing worldwide.

Oxford   New York
Auckland   Cape Town   Dar es Salaam   Hong Kong   Karachi
Kuala Lumpur   Madrid   Melbourne   Mexico City   Nairobi
New Delhi   Shanghai   Taipei   Toronto

With offices in
Argentina   Austria   Brazil   Chile   Czech Republic   France   Greece
Guatemala   Hungary   Italy   Japan   Poland   Portugal   Singapore
South Korea   Switzerland   Thailand   Turkey   Ukraine   Vietnam

Published in the United States of America by
Oxford University Press
198 Madison Avenue, New York, NY 10016

© Oxford University Press 2015

Library of Congress Cataloging-in-Publication Data
The Oxford handbook of Mormonism / edited by
Terryl L. Givens and Philip L. Barlow.
pages cm
Includes index.
ISBN 978-0-19-977836-2 (cloth : alk. paper)
1. Mormon Church.   2. Church of Jesus Christ of Latter-day Saints.   I. Givens, Terryl, editor.
II. Barlow, Philip L., editor.
BX8635.3.O94 2015
289.3—dc23
2015002338

3 5 7 9 8 6 4
Printed in the United States of America
on acid-free paper

To Eugene and Charlotte England
for creating an environment conducive to the best in Mormon Studies

Contents

PART V MORMON SOCIETY

PART VI MORMON CULTURE

PART VII   THE INTERNATIONAL CHURCH

PART VIII   MORMONISM
IN THE WORLD COMMUNITY

Acknowledgments

We are indebted to Mssrs. Chase Kirkham, Scott Marianno, Cory Nani, and Christopher Blythe at Utah State University for editorial and other assistance in preparing the essays for publication. We also thank Theo Calderara at Oxford University Press for patiently and expertly shepherding this project along.

Contributor Biographies

Paul L. Anderson is head of design and curator of the Brigham Young Museum of Art, which he helped launch in 1992. He has been active in restoration projects for the LDS Church's historical buildings and was president of the Mormon History Association from 2007 to 2008.

Michael Austin is Provost and Vice-President of Academic Affairs at Newman University in Wichita, Kansas. He is the author or editor of eight books, including (with Mark T. Decker) *Peculiar Portrayals: Mormons on the Page, Stage, and Screen* (2010).

Philip L. Barlow is the Leonard J. Arrington Professor of Mormon History and Culture at Utah State University. He is the author of such works as *Mormons and the Bible: The Place of the Latter-day Saints in American Religion* (updated ed., 2013) and (with Edwin Scott Gaustad) *The New Historical Atlas of Religion in America* (2001).

Hal R. Boyd studied philosophy under coauthor David Paulsen at Brigham Young University. He has written professionally for both the *Deseret News* and the LDS Church, where his writing has appeared in a variety of journalistic and scholarly venues. His most recent work (coedited with Susan Easton Black) is *Psalms of Nauvoo: Early Mormon Poetry* (forthcoming). He is a JD candidate at Yale Law School.

R. Lanier Britsch was vice-president for academics at BYU-Hawaii and director of the David M. Kennedy Center for International Studies at Brigham Young University and is now professor emeritus of history and Asian studies at BYU. He has published on Latter-day Saint history in Asia and the Pacific.

Samuel Morris Brown is Assistant Professor of Pulmonary/Critical Care Medicine and Medical Ethics and Humanities at the University of Utah School of Medicine, based at Intermountain Medical Center. He is the author of *In Heaven as It Is on Earth: Joseph Smith and the Early Mormon Conquest of Death* (2012).

Claudia L. Bushman is a social and cultural historian and former professor at several universities, including Columbia University. Her many publications include *Building the Kingdom: A History of Mormons in America* (2001), *Contemporary Mormonism: Latter-day Saints in Modern America* (2006), and *Mormon Sisters: Women in Early Utah* (1997).

Richard Lyman Bushman is Gouverneur Morris Professor of History, Emeritus, at Columbia University in New York City. His first book, *From Puritan to Yankee: Character* *and the Social Order in Connecticut, 1690–1765* (1967), was awarded the Bancroft Prize. Among other books, he also published *Joseph Smith: Rough Stone Rolling* (2005).

Kathryn M. Daynes is associate professor emerita of history at Brigham Young University. She has published a number of works on Mormon plural marriage, including the award-winning book *More Wives than One: Transformation of the Mormon Marriage System, 1840–1910* (2001).

Wilfried Decoo is professor emeritus of applied linguistics at the University of Antwerp (Belgium) and at Brigham Young University. His published books include *Systemization in Foreign Language Teaching* (2010) and *Crisis on Campus: Confronting Academic Misconduct* (2001). He has a special interest in Mormon Studies, in particular as it pertains to Europe.

Eric A. Eliason is professor of folklore at Brigham Young University. His books include *The J. Golden Kimball Stories* (2007), *Mormons and Mormonism: An Introduction to an American World Religion* (2001), and (edited with Tom Mould) *Latter-day Lore: Mormon Folklore Studies* (2007).

James E. Faulconer is a professor of philosophy and a former Richard L. Evans Professor of Religious Understanding at Brigham Young University. He is the author of works including *The Life of Holiness* (2012), and coeditor (with Mark A. Wrathall) of *Appropriating Heidegger* (2000).

Noah R. Feldman is Felix Frankfurter Professor of Law at Harvard Law School, and a Senior Fellow of the Society of Fellows at Harvard. He specializes in constitutional studies, with particular emphasis on the relationship between law and religion, constitutional design, and the history of legal theory. He is the author of seven books.

J. Spencer Fluhman is associate professor of history at Brigham Young University, where he teaches American religious history and Mormon history. He is the author of *"A Peculiar People": Anti-Mormonism and the Making of Religion in Nineteenth-Century America* (2012) and is editor of the *Mormon Studies Review*.

Richard V. Francaviglia is professor emeritus of history and the former director of the Center for Southwestern Studies and Cartography at the University of Texas Arlington. He is the author of *Believing in Place: A Spiritual Geography of the Great Basin* (2003), and *The Mapmakers of New Zion: A Cartographic History of Mormonism* (2015).

Van C. Gessel is Professor of Japanese at Brigham Young University, where he served as chair of the Department of Asian and Near Eastern Languages and as the Dean of the College of Humanities. His academic specialty is modern Japanese literature, particularly Japanese Christian writers, and he has translated seven literary works by the Japanese Catholic novelist Endō Shūsaku.

Terryl L. Givens is James A. Bostwich Chair of English and Professor of Literature and Religion at the University of Richmond. He is the author of several books, including

When Souls Had Wings: Pre-Mortal Existence in Western Thought (2010), and *Wrestling the Angel: The Foundations of Mormon Thought: Cosmos, God, Humanity* (2014).

Sarah Barringer Gordon is Arlin M. Adams Professor of Constitutional Law and professor of history at the University of Pennsylvania. She is author of multiple books and articles on religion and law in American history including, *The Mormon Question: Polygamy and Constitutional Conflict in Nineteenth-Century America* (2002) and *The Spirit of the Law: Religious Voices and the Constitution in Modern America* (2010). She also serves as coeditor of Studies in Legal History, a book series published in association with the American Society for Legal History.

Darius Aidan Gray is former president of the Genesis Group and codirector of the Freedman's Bank Records Project, a genealogy database containing the marriage, birth, and family records of more than 480,000 freed slaves.

Mark L. Grover is a librarian emeritus from Brigham Young University. His library responsibilities included Latin American and Africa collection development and reference. His research publications have ranged from Latin American librarianship to the history of the LDS Church in South America.

Matthew J. Grow is the director of publications at the LDS Church History Department and a general editor of the Joseph Smith Papers. He is the author of *"Liberty to the Downtrodden": Thomas L. Kane, Romantic Reformer* (2009) and the coauthor (with Terryl L. Givens) of *Parley P. Pratt: The Apostle Paul of Mormonism* (2011).

Tona J. Hangen is associate professor of US History at Worcester State University. She is the author of *Redeeming the Dial: Radio, Religion and Popular Culture in America, 1920–1960* (2002), and other works on media and religion in American history. She teaches courses in historical methods, social history, and cultural studies.

Grant Hardy is Professor of History and Religious Studies at the University of North Carolina at Asheville. In addition to books and articles on early Chinese history and historiography, he has published *The Book of Mormon: A Reader's Edition* (2003) and *Understanding the Book of Mormon: A Reader's Guide* (2010).

Tim B. Heaton holds a Camilla Kimball chair in the Department of Sociology at Brigham Young University. His research focuses on demographic trends in the family. He has coedited a volume in Mormon studies entitled *Revisiting Thomas F. O'Dea's The Mormons: Contemporary Perspectives* (2008).

Michael D. Hicks is professor of music composition and theory at Brigham Young University. He is the author of six books, including *Mormonism and Music: A History* (1989) and *The Mormon Tabernacle Choir: A Biography* (forthcoming).

Kate Holbrook is Specialist in Women's History for the LDS Church History Department. She is coeditor of two forthcoming books: *Selected Relief Society Documents, 1842–1892* (2016) and *Women and the Mormon Church: Historic and*

Contemporary Perspectives (2016). She also coedited *Global Values 101: A Short Course* (2006). Kate was the first recipient of the Eccles Fellowship in Mormon Studies at the University of Utah.

David F. Holland is Associate Professor of North American Religious History at Harvard Divinity School. His work has appeared in the *New England Quarterly, Gender and History,* and *Law and History Review.* His first book, *Sacred Borders: Continuing Revelation and Canonical Restraint in Early America,* was published in 2011.

Daniel Walker Howe is Rhodes Professor of American History Emeritus at Oxford University and Professor of History Emeritus at UCLA. His book *What Hath God Wrought: The Transformation of America, 1815–1848* (2007) won the Pulitzer Prize.

Valerie M. Hudson is professor and George H. W. Bush Chair at the Bush School of Government and Public Service at Texas A&M University. Hudson is coauthor of *Bare Branches: The Security Implications of Asia's Surplus Male Population* (2004), *Sex and World Peace* (2012), and *Women in Eternity, Women of Zion* (2004). She was named one of *Foreign Policy* magazine's Top 100 Global Thinkers for 2009.

Cardell K. Jacobson is professor of sociology at Brigham Young University. His work *Modern Polygamy in the United States* (2011) centers on social issues in religion. Another work, *White Parents, Black Children: Experiencing Transracial Adoption* (2011), focuses on race and ethnicity in adoption. He teaches courses on social psychology and current social problems.

Laurie F. Maffly-Kipp is Archer Alexander Distinguished Professor at the Danforth Center on Religion and Politics at Washington University in St. Louis. Her recent publications include *Proclamation to the People: Nineteenth-Century Mormonism and the Pacific Basin Frontier* (2008); *Setting Down the Sacred Past: African-American Race Histories* (2010); and *American Scriptures: An Anthology of Sacred Writings* (2010). Currently she is working on a survey of Mormonism in American life.

Armand L. Mauss is professor emeritus of sociology and religious studies at Washington State University. He is the author or *The Angel and the Beehive: The Mormon Struggle with Assimilation* (1994) and *All Abraham's Children: Changing Mormon Conceptions of Race and Lineage* (2003). More recently, he has been an adjunct faculty member in Mormon Studies at Claremont Graduate University.

James M. McLachlan is professor of philosophy and religion at Western Carolina University. He is past Co-Chair of the Mormon Studies Group at the American Academy of Religion and past President of the Society for Mormon Philosophy and Theology. His research interests focus on European personalism and existentialism, process theology, and Mormon theology.

Richard J. Mouw is distinguished professor of Faith and Public Life and the former president of Fuller Theological Seminary. Among his many books is *Talking with*

Mormons: An Invitation to Evangelicals (2012), a reflection on his years of dialogue with members of the faith.

Reid L. Neilson is Assistant Church Historian and Recorder of The Church of Jesus Christ of Latter-day Saints. He is the author and award-winning editor of over two-dozen books, including *Exhibiting Mormonism: The Latter-day Saints at the 1893 Chicago World's Fair* (2011) and Early Mormon Missionary Activities in Japan, 1901-1924 (2010). He serves on the editorial boards of the Joseph Smith Papers and the Deseret Book Company.

David L. Paulsen is emeritus professor of philosophy at Brigham Young University. A graduate of BYU, he holds a JD from the University of Chicago and a PhD in philosophy from the University of Michigan. His scholarly work has appeared in the *Harvard Theological Review, International Journal for the Philosophy of Religion*, and *Faith and Philosophy*. With Donald Musser, Paulson edited *Mormonism in Dialogue with Contemporary Christian Theologies* (2007).

John Durham Peters is A. Craig Baird Professor of Communication Studies and Professor of International Studies at the University of Iowa, and has written on diverse topics in media theory and cultural history, including *Speaking into the Air: A History of the Idea of Communication* (2001).

Daniel Peterson is professor of Islamic Studies and Arabic at Brigham Young University, and founder and editor-in-chief of BYU's Middle Eastern Texts Initiative (METI). He is also the founder and editor of *Interpreter: A Journal of Mormon Scripture*, and was for many years editor of the *FARMS Review*. His many publications include *Muhammad, Prophet of God* (2007).

Gregory A. Prince is a scientist whose four-decade career has focused on the prevention and treatment of viral pneumonia in infants. His has published two books in Mormon studies: *Power from on High: The Development of Mormon Priesthood* (1995), and (with William Robert Wright) *David O. McKay and the Rise of Modern Mormonism* (2005). He is currently writing the biography of Leonard J. Arrington, Church Historian of the LDS Church in the 1970s.

W. Paul Reeve is associate professor of history at the University of Utah. He currently teaches Utah history, Mormon history, and history of the US West. He is the author of *Making Space on the Western Frontier: Mormons, Miners, and Southern Paiutes* (2006) and *Religion of a Different Color: Race and the Mormon Struggle for Whiteness* (2015).

Jana Riess is an acquisitions editor and the former Religion Book Review Editor for *Publishers Weekly*. She is the author or coauthor of many books, including *Flunking Sainthood* (2011), *The Twible* (2013), and *Mormonism for Dummies* (2005). She blogs about Mormonism and other topics for Religion News Service.

William D. Russell is professor emeritus of American history and government at Graceland University in Lamoni, Iowa. He served previously as president of the Mormon History Association (1982–83) and the John Whitmer Historical Association (1977). He is editor of the volume *Homosexual Saints: The Community of Christ Experience* (2008) and is published widely in Mormon studies.

Jan Shipps is professor emerita of religious studies and history at Indiana University-Purdue University, Indianapolis. She has long been the most widely acclaimed non-Mormon specialist in Mormon studies. She is the author of *Mormonism: The Story of a New Religious Tradition* (1985) and *Sojourner in the Promised Land: Forty Years among the Mormons* (2000).

David J. Whittaker was Curator of Western and Mormon Manuscripts, L. Tom Perry Special Collections, Harold B. Lee Library, and Associate Professor of History, Brigham Young University, Provo, Utah. His research and publications focused on Mormon History, Mormon Historiography, Mormon Bibliography, and Early Mormon Print Culture.

Margaret Blair Young coauthored with Darius Gray the award-winning trilogy of historical novels about early Black Mormon pioneers *Standing on the Promises*. They also coproduced two documentary films, *Jane Manning James: Your Sister in the Gospel* and *Nobody Knows: The Untold Story of Black Mormons*. Margaret Young teaches in the English Department at Brigham Young University.

THE OXFORD HANDBOOK OF

MORMONISM

INTRODUCTION

TERRYL L. GIVENS AND PHILIP L. BARLOW

THE *Oxford Handbook of Mormonism* concerns more than history. Yet the study of the Mormon past has always been an imperative for the Mormon people themselves. On the day the church was formed, a revelation directed that a record be kept (Doctrine and Covenants [D&C] 21:1). Smith's scribe Oliver Cowdery at first assumed responsibility, then in March 1831 John Whitmer was officially designated historian and recorder of the church. Mormons have been assiduous at record keeping ever since. As a consequence of their tumultuous nineteenth-century conflicts with their neighbors, and their sense of being a persecuted minority in a supposedly tolerant and pluralistic democracy, Mormon record keeping often emphasized their sufferings at the hands of hostile outsiders. In fact, they considered themselves under divine command in 1839 to "gather . . . up a knowledge of all the facts, and sufferings, and abuse put upon them by the people of [Missouri]" (D&C 121:1). As a consequence, the story of the Mormon people, their beliefs, practices, and history, was for most of the past narrated by the Saints themselves. The story of their religion's founding, their repeated expulsions from their homes, and their epic trek to the Great Basin of Utah were the stuff of faith-promoting Sunday sermons and official history as well. To other Americans who knew of the movement, Mormons served—if notice was taken—as a foil for American self-fashioning: unrepublican, polygamous, theocratic, secretive, and perhaps dangerous. A whole array of famous visitors ventured into their mountain fastness to regale the wider public with impressions that ranged from admiration to bemusement to outrage.

In the early twentieth century, little changed, though much was changing within the religion itself as it adjusted to statehood for Utah and accommodation to American social and political ways. The country's academics by and large omitted Mormonism from accounts of the American religious experience, even if historians took note of their role in colonizing the intermountain West. So for the first half of the century, Mormon historians occupied with Mormon history typically told their story to an audience of religious peers or a few curious outsiders, as an act of devotion and even defense. But in the years after the Second World War, Mormonism became a subject of interest to far more people than the Saints and their record keepers. Growing scrutiny from outside, and intellectual pressures from within, combined to challenge the narratives of the past.

In 1945, Fawn Brodie published *No Man Knows My History: The Life of Joseph Smith*. It was not the first biography of Joseph Smith by a skeptic or dissenter from the faith—but it had the greatest impact. Brodie was a gifted writer and historian, and unlike past exposés and critiques of the Prophet, Brodie's account acknowledged a high level of intellectual and creative capacity on the part of Smith. Her extremely popular treatment was thus taken seriously by historians and general readers, and added a new dimension—a credible, book-length, scholarly dimension—to attacks on the truthfulness and legitimacy of Mormonism's orthodox rendering of its own history. Such a widely read and plausible challenge was something the church had never confronted to any significant degree.

Then in 1950, Juanita Brooks published an account of the 1857 Mountain Meadows Massacre, which blew the lid off the darkest chapter in Mormonism's history, assigning unambiguous blame to Mormons for the tragedy, while offering context for the traumatized and exiled people's paranoid action. This same decade, Mormonism received one of its first serious treatments from a nonhistorian. Thomas O'Dea, a sociologist, produced a balanced and insightful study in 1957 (*The Mormons*) and the next year, LDS historian Leonard Arrington published his *Great Basin Kingdom: An Economic History of the Latter-day Saints, 1830–1900*. O'Dea and Arrington were important figures for expanding the study of Mormonism to fields and disciplines beyond history. But they were also important harbingers of a new middle ground in writing about Mormonism. O'Dea as a Catholic and Arrington as a Mormon were part of a growing wave of academics to rise above hostility and apologetics alike, and expose the richness of Mormon history, culture, and theology to a public largely nurtured on caricature and stereotype—not to say a narrowly circumscribed range of topics that usually started and ended with polygamy.

Still, the study of Mormonism remained largely a Mormon enterprise. In 1965, Arrington and other progressive scholars in the church formed the Mormon History Association (MHA), with the explicit goal of rendering the faithful study of Mormon history more professionalized.[1] What might have been a cause for unalloyed celebration was complicated in Mormon eyes by the group's decision to execute Mormon history in more "human or naturalistic terms."[2] Given the organization's concurrent goal "to include Reorganized LDS members, non-Mormons, [and] lapsed Mormons" as well as believers,[3] the forum for uninhibited discussion and exploration of Mormonism outside the bounds of orthodox control would clearly be a potentially explosive experiment.

Initially, the surge of scholarly interest in the Mormon past ushered in a vibrant era of intellectual inquiry and productive work that received official praise and support. In fact, staunch conservative Joseph Fielding Smith, who in the 1960s was Church Historian as well as a senior apostle, was a prime mover in efforts to professionalize the office.[4] Membership in professional associations was urged on employees, trained archivists and librarians were hired, and upgraded facilities were planned. By 1969, the changes in approach to the Mormon past taken by LDS scholars were marked enough that professor of history Moses Rischin, not himself a Latter-day Saint, concluded that developments constituted a "new Mormon history."[5] The era of Camelot, as Arrington's associate Davis Bitton later called the next years, would mark unprecedented access to church archives, and surging scholarly production of high quality and volume. Outside official channels, developments were just as dramatic. By 1974, the Mormon History Association would have almost a thousand members, with enough scholars, interested public, and resources to launch the *Journal of Mormon History*. But it was a painfully short-lived Camelot. Within a decade, Arrington had been released and he and his colleagues reassigned to disparate programs and locations. Access to church archives was no longer as open, and signals from the church leadership suggested concern over the new trends.

These setbacks, however, were temporary, and insufficient to stem the currents that have become a tidal wave of new scholarship on Mormonism. A number of events, within and outside the academy, coalesced to give impetus to a field now commonly referred to as Mormon Studies. In 1984, sociologist Rodney Stark controversially predicted that Mormonism stands on the threshold "of becoming the first major faith to appear on earth since the Prophet Mohammed rode out of the desert."[6] In 2001, the LDS Historical Department began a multivolume, multimillion dollar project to publish the Joseph Smith Papers, a series with nationally prominent non-Mormon advisors that aspires to put into print all documents created by or under the direction of Joseph Smith. Chairs and programs in Mormon Studies were established at the University of Durham, in the UK (originally in Nottingham), Utah State University, Claremont Graduate School, and the University of Virginia. Monographs on Mormon topics that were in the past the province of the University of Illinois Press or a few Utah presses are now regularly published by Oxford, the University of North Carolina, Harvard, Columbia, and other prestigious presses. Journals and blogs devoted to Mormon Studies have proliferated (including the *Mormon Studies Review*, launched in 2013), and venues like the American Academy of Religion and the American Historical Association hold regular sessions on Mormon themes. The media have continued, meanwhile, to provide a steady diet—of uneven quality—of Mormon images: from the serious to the comic to the absurd, from PBS documentaries (*The Mormons*, 2007) to exploitative series about polygamy (*Big Love, Sister Wives*) to Broadway musicals (*The Book of Mormon*). Finally, in 2012, a Mormon almost won the race to the White House, forcing many Americans to consider as never before the relevance of Mormonism in American public life.

In the present collection, no attempt is made to provide comprehensive coverage of this field coming to be called Mormon Studies. The *Handbook* is not an encyclopedia. Geographic coverage, for example, is selective and illustrative rather than global. What the editors have attempted to do is provide a number of chapters by leading scholars in their fields, to convey the range of disciplines and subjects where Mormonism might enrich and recontextualize any number of academic conversations. Seeking to go beyond the traditional coverage that is largely concerned with history and sociology, we have included essays on various aspects of theology, lived religion, cultural studies, communication studies, philosophy, the arts, the law, and other fields. Together, they suggest not just the present status, but the future possibilities of an exciting new field still in process of definition.

Notes

1. Arrington gives his account of the founding and early years of the MHA in *Adventures of a Church Historian*, 58–61.
2. Arrington, "Scholarly Studies of Mormonism in the Twentieth Century," 28.
3. Arrington, *Adventures of a Church Historian*, 59.
4. In the 1960s, Smith directed his assistant's involvement in professional organizations and oversaw the hiring of employees with professional credentials, the implementation of more professional cataloguing practices, and the planning of new facilities. See Arrington, *Adventures of a Church Historian*, 69.
5. Rischin, "New Mormon History," 49, cited in Walker, Whittaker, and Allen, *Mormon History*, 60. This chapter is the best overview of the New Mormon History; chap. 2 provides an authoritative account of LDS historiography from 1900 to 1950.
6. According to sociologist Rodney Stark, some now living may see it grow from its eleven million in the year 2000 to the neighborhood of 267 million by the year 2080. See his "Rise of a New World Faith," 19, 22–23. Though criticized as extravagant by some sociologists, Stark argues more recently that his estimate may have been too conservative. As of 1999, "membership is substantially higher than my most optimistic projection." "Extracting Social Scientific Models from Mormon History," *Journal of Mormon History* 25, no. 1 (Spring 1999): 176.

Bibliography

Arrington, Leonard J. *Adventures of a Church Historian*. Urbana: University of Illinois Press, 1998.

Arrington, Leonard J. "Scholarly Studies of Mormonism in the Twentieth Century." *Dialogue: A Journal of Mormon Thought* 1, no. 1 (Spring 1966): 15–28.

Rischin, Moses. "The New Mormon History." *American West* 6 (March 1969): 49.

Stark, Rodney. "The Rise of a New World Faith." *Review of Religious Research* 26, no. 1 (September 1984): 18–27.

Stark, Rodney. "Extracting Social Scientific Models from Mormon History." *Journal of Mormon History* 25, no. 1 (Spring 1999): 174–94.

Walker, Ronald W., David J. Whittaker, and James B. Allen, eds. *Mormon History*. Urbana: University of Illinois Press, 2001.

PART I

HISTORY
OF MORMONISM

CHAPTER 1

....

AN INTERPRETIVE
FRAMEWORK
FOR STUDYING THE
HISTORY OF MORMONISM

....

JAN SHIPPS

A strange book made its appearance in Palmyra, New York, in March 1830. Its title page proclaimed it to be a history of Near Eastern Hebrews whom God had led to the Western hemisphere before the beginning of the Babylonian captivity in 587 BCE. It was a record preserved and edited by a later ancient prophet, Mormon, then completed and buried for posterity by his son, Moroni. More than two millennia later, a twenty-five-year-old farmer, Joseph Smith Jr., said he found Mormon's book in a box buried in a hill near his home. The book, Smith said, was engraved in hieroglyphics on gold plates. He also reported finding "interpreters": stones called Urim and Thummim like the ones used by Old Testament priests to determine God's will. With the help of scribes, especially school teacher Oliver Cowdery, these stones functioned supernaturally, allowing Smith to translate the hieroglyphics into English. The result was the Book of Mormon, which members of the translator's family and other Smith followers began to sell or give away.[1]

A prophecy that "a marvelous work [was] about to come forth among the children of men" had heightened the aura of anticipation around Smith as the book neared completion (Doctrine and Covenants [D&C] 4:1). This prediction convinced his family and supporters that he was a prophet as well as a seer and translator. Their conviction deepened when Smith and Cowdery reported that God had restored the ancient Aaronic priesthood to them—an authority essential to the restoration of the Church of Christ, which was organized only weeks after the publication of the Book of Mormon.

During the first third of the nineteenth century, spiritual conflagrations seared the area along New York's newly opened Erie Canal as Protestants experienced revivals and religious seekers—set free by disestablishment to experiment—followed unconventional religious figures who moved through the region offering unconventional faiths. Charles Finney, the famed revivalist preacher, remembered antebellum western New York as the "burnt district" because of the recurrent heating and cooling of religious fervor there. Although the Second Great Awakening was by no means over when Mormon's opus appeared, it might have seemed that it would fall on deaf ears in a region already so singed by religious enthusiasm.[2] But the revelation that predicted the coming forth of the "marvelous work" also said that the field was "white to the harvest" (D&C 4:4). And so it proved to be.

The editor of the *Palmyra Reflector* and many others called the Book of Mormon "Smith's Gold Bible." Despite much derision, the curious work attracted the attention of readers who accepted it as truth—enough of them for Mormon's story to become the basis of a new religious movement. The volume itself was Bible-like, and those who distributed it were certain of its legitimacy. Its extraordinary religious claims, including the account of its origin, told readers that divine communication with humanity had not ceased with the New Testament.

These new religious claims were analogous to those of early Christianity in another way. First-century Palestinian Christians had pointed to the identity of Jesus as the long-awaited Messiah, declaring him a clear fulfillment of Old Testament prophecy. Early Mormons accepted this notion while extending the method behind it: they presented the Book of Mormon itself as a fulfillment of Old Testament prophecy. Ezekiel 37:19, for example, foretells that "the stick of Joseph which is in the hand of Ephraim" (i.e., the Book of Mormon, as an early Mormon revelation made clear) will be linked "with the stick of Judah" (i.e., the Hebrew Bible). Made into one stick, "they shall [saith the Lord] be one in thine hand." These new-world descendants of Abraham thus completed the biblical story of the patriarch's descendants in the ancient Near East without the intruding filter of European religious history. The Book of Mormon's narrative also included a visit Christ paid to these Hebraic peoples in the western hemisphere during the interim between his crucifixion and resurrection. This made the gold bible a third testament, one that bequeathed to the Americas a new and pure Christianity free of the creeds and conflicts that marked the stories of Catholicism, Orthodoxy, and Protestantism.

Descriptions of Mormon beginnings typically start with Joseph Smith's First Vision, which came to him as a teenager when he saw God and Jesus, who told him that he would have an important part in the imminent restoration of the true Church of Christ. Smith's story continues with accounts of several additional visions, of his discovery of the gold plates, and describes his role in the coming forth of the Book of Mormon. Such narratives are important, especially as they provide a picture of Smith's early prophetic career. They point to him as a charismatic figure whose claim to a position of leadership was embedded in his report of finding gold plates.

What such portrayals do not recognize is that the Book of Mormon legitimates Joseph Smith as much as Smith's prophetic charisma legitimates the book. The third chapter of the original edition of the Book of Mormon is devoted to the prophesied history of the book that would come forth in the latter days. It quotes the angel of the Lord as connecting a seer—whose name, like that of his father, would be Joseph—to the coming forth of this "Book of the Lamb of God." Consequently, such accounts underplay the dominant role of the Book of Mormon in the birth of the movement. Smith's leadership was crucial in founding Mormonism and decisive as well in generating the movement's institutional embodiment. But in Mormonism's earliest generation, more members joined the movement as a result of reading or even merely hearing about the Book of Mormon than by getting to know the movement's charismatic leader. In accounts of the earliest missionary sermons (1831–1834) the Book of Mormon was always mentioned, if only as a sign that "the heavens are no longer brass," whereas Smith's role in the new movement was not always a part of the missionaries' sermonic subject matter.[3] As Mormonism came together in Ohio and Missouri, however, the crucial nature of Smith's role as prophet and church president became increasingly visible, the importance of his revelations increased, and, by comparison, the role of the movement's new scripture gradually receded.

This chapter considers the critical significance of a new scripture in the initiation of this new religious movement, along with the century and a half of Mormonism's history when the scripture's content was far less consequential than its status. The book was essential, to be sure, but primarily as an indicator that God continued to be in touch with humanity. The recent return of the book's textual content as an indispensable scriptural resource for the faith is also considered. Likewise contemplated is the Book of Mormon's prediction that the "seer" whose appearance it foretold would "do much good both in word and deed . . . [to] bring forth much restoration unto the House of Israel" (2 Nephi 3:24). Of even greater importance in what follows is the weightiness in the life of this new religious movement of the 1831 revelation that called for a gathering of those who accepted the Book of Mormon as scripture and Joseph Smith Jr. as prophet.

In conjunction with the revelation on gathering, stress is placed on an accompanying Mormon conception that believers shared kinship as descendants of the Old Testament patriarch Abraham. Other foci include how the gathering set the Mormons apart from non-Mormons wherever they went and the almost inevitable conflict their separationist stance produced; the institution of peoplehood when the gathering engendered the materialization of a literal kingdom which had four decades of life; and the subsequent transformation from existence as a people to becoming an ethnicity when the kingdom became a client state of the American nation. Finally, the chapter suggests the process through which converts became a part of nineteenth-century Mormon peoplehood and how more recent converts adopt twentieth- and twenty-first-century Mormon ethnicity. Motifs throughout are this movement's connections to the biblical story and "drivings," as the early Saints described the instances when non-Mormon settlers used threats, force, or physical violence to compel them to leave areas where they had gathered, established homes, and organized the church. Predictably, these dreadful experiences drove the Mormons ever closer to each other.

New religious movements generally take one of two configurations: a schismatic group that regards itself as a "saving remnant" separates itself from an existing religious body due to disagreements over liturgy, ritual, basic beliefs, or, as is often the case, a conviction that the members of the body they were leaving had gone too far in accommodating to the world. Such movements are sects. The other configuration is a diverse group that forms around a charismatic figure *and* radical new religious claims. These are cults; and just as Christianity started as a cult, so did Mormonism. Sadly, from very early on, the word "cult" took on a negative connotation in popular usage, suggesting that the people involved were not just unconventional, but that they had weird or dangerous beliefs. Trying to avoid derogatory designations such as "Mormonites" or "Smithites," Mormons stressed their Christian connection: aware that early followers of Jesus called themselves saints, they called themselves Latter-day Saints (LDS). Nevertheless, in nineteenth-century Ohio—and in every place Mormons have established a place for themselves ever since—they have found it almost impossible to steer clear of being described as a cult.

At first the newly restored Church of Christ was simply identified as another primitivist Christian church. It was seen as a theological body different from the Campbellites and other primitivist groups mainly in being led by a prophet and having an additional scripture. Still, it began as merely one more competitor in the Protestant marketplace. Smith's ongoing revelations soon carried his followers so far from evangelical Protestantism, however, that the following decades were marked by "drivings," persecution, and the murder of Joseph Smith.

Scholars generally agree that while several Mormon groups followed other contenders for Smith's prophetic mantle, Brigham Young, the second president of the LDS Church, was responsible for the survival of the hardy and vigorous form of Mormonism that is found throughout the world today. Young led a large body of LDS from the Midwest to the Great Basin, the land sitting between the two great north-south western ranges. In the process, he became an "American Moses," a "pioneer prophet."[4] Yet Young's initial introduction to the new movement was not a response to Smith's charisma. He was one of a host of "Book of Mormon converts."[5]

Young's conversion story is just one example of what happened to many people living across western and northern New York, New England, and southern Canada who joined the new movement after they became acquainted with the Book of Mormon. As recounted in John Turner's biography, Young, a struggling artisan, was a member of a large family attempting to survive on the New York frontier. During his early years, the Young family belonged to the Methodist Episcopal Church, but as adults Brigham and his wife, as well as several members of his birth family, became Reformed Methodists. That change, however, did not fully satisfy their seeking for a nurturing religious community in which such gifts of the spirit as speaking in tongues and interpretation, as well as healing, were regularly present.

Virtually on the morrow of the organization of the Church of Christ with Joseph Smith at its head, the Prophet's younger brother Samuel traveled to Mendon, New York. There he either gave or sold a copy of the new Mormon scripture to Brigham Young's brother Phineas who agreed to read it, intending to demonstrate its errors. Instead Phineas, convinced the book was true, was converted to the new movement. Young's father and his sister Fanny read the book as well; his father said it was as clear of error as the Bible, while Fanny declared it to be a revelation. Brigham also read the Book of Mormon—this would have been in the spring of 1830—but he did not immediately accept it as scripture. Some months later, he concluded that there was something in Mormonism and this conclusion was intensified after he heard some traveling Mormon elders preach what he later described as the "everlasting gospel." Many of those who heard members of the new church preach would be baptized soon afterward. Brigham, however, traveled to Pennsylvania to visit and worship with a Mormon congregation and even then put off joining until he had carefully reflected on the new scripture in the light of the Bible. His baptism came a full two years after he first read the Book of Mormon. Following his uniting with the movement, he spent several months spreading word of the new gospel before traveling to Ohio to meet the man responsible for the book's coming forth.

By the time Brigham Young met the Prophet Joseph Smith in the fall of 1832, the Mormon movement was a going concern. An early revelation had called four male members of the new church to fulfill their new scripture's title-page assignment to carry the message of the Book of Mormon to Native Americans. Revelation further specified that these missionaries were to identify land appropriate for a New Jerusalem when they reached the border between civilization and the land of the "Lamanites" (the Book of Mormon name for Native Americans).

On their way west, these missionaries stopped in Mentor, a small Ohio settlement. There they converted Sidney Rigdon, a Campbellite preacher, who, in turn, converted most of the members of his local congregation. Following their baptism into the new Church of Christ, Rigdon left for Fayette, New York, where Smith was living. He carried with him an invitation to the Mormon leader to transfer his headquarters to Ohio.

Joseph Smith accepted the invitation. With his wife Emma and many members of his extended family, Smith left New York, moving west to Ohio in late January 1831. They were not alone.

Perhaps desiring to live within the prophetic ambience, numbers of members of the new church had moved to the general area where the Smiths lived. Naturally, this congregating of his followers was affected by the Mormon prophet's decision to leave. Consequently their leaders asked whether assembling near their prophet should continue. The answer was "the gathering revelation" that told them to "listen to the voice of Jesus Christ . . . who will gather his people, even as a hen gathereth her chickens under her wing." Smith's adherents were "called to bring to pass the gathering of mine elect." They shall, the revelation continued, "be gathered in unto one place" to prepare their hearts for the ending of time (D&C 29:1–8).

In a different arena, Smith started a new translation of the Bible not long after the church was organized. He was assisted in this task by three scribes: Oliver Cowdery, John Whitmer, and, in particular, the convert Sidney Rigdon, who had ten years of experience as, first, a Regular Baptist preacher and, afterward, a Campbellite minister. Although not completed in Smith's lifetime, this translation effort was reflected in numerous sections in the LDS Doctrine and Covenants.[6] Smith and his colleagues were required to suspend their work on the Bible until the move to Ohio was accomplished.

When work on the translation resumed, Smith and Rigdon experienced a vision in February 1832 that had a powerful impact on Mormon soteriology in its precise description of three degrees of glory, or kingdoms (the telestial, the terrestrial, and the celestial), where resurrected individuals will experience the afterlife.

The Saints' acceptance of an open canon, reverence for the Book of Mormon, and devotion to a living prophet set them apart from their new neighbors in an Ohio town called Kirtland. But those were *beliefs*. The gathering was something else again; this response to revelation was *behavior* initially engendered by a collective anticipation of Christ's Second Coming. Not surprisingly, increasing numbers of Saints arrived in the region with the intent of settling. The Prophet's presence there became the center of a Kirtland "stake" in the tent of Zion.

Three major developments that would have profound effects in different Mormon arenas stemmed from events that occurred in Kirtland and revelations Smith received there. One was a maturing of the way authority would be exercised within Mormonism as both institution and movement. Another was further elaboration of Smith's narrative theology issuing from his work on the inspired translation of the Bible. This includes a now-canonized prologue to the story of creation and the fall and material from Smith's revision of Genesis with the addition of prophecies of Enoch. The third development was recognition of the significance of *restoration* to Mormonism.

All three of these developments are crucial parts of the story of the nearly seven years that Smith and many of his followers were in Kirtland—and ever afterward. But two of them were essentially internal to the movement. The first was not as straightforward as the receipt of a coherent revelation that spelled out church structure. The issue of the flow of authority within that structure caused multiple problems during the church's earliest years and would lead to a rift within the movement that would result in the creation of several different Mormonisms following the Prophet's death. Yet, although sometimes challenged, Smith's strong personality and his multiple positions as "Seer, Translator, Revelator, High Priest, and Church President" meant that authority remained in his hands in spite of the many distressing experiences the Saints lived through during his lifetime. Furthermore, ever afterward, the position of church president has carried with it the role of prophet, seer, and revelator.

The second of these developments was likewise internal to the faith. From the time of his immersion in bringing the Book of Mormon into existence, Smith was intellectually as well as spiritually captivated by learning and language, especially Hebrew and—after a traveler sold his mother two mummies and a papyrus—Egyptian. He established a "School of the Prophets" for church leaders and missionaries. At times, this school incorporated reading, writing, and arithmetic, but it also included theology and even a class in Hebrew taught by a visiting rabbi. One product of this educational effort that became known as the Temple School was a series of "Lectures on Faith" that was published in all the issues of the church's Doctrine and Covenants between 1835 and 1921. These provide a basic summary of Mormon belief. Smith's inspired translation of the Bible and the two newly translated scriptures, the books of Moses and Abraham which were canonized much later as a part of an additional scripture called the Pearl of Great Price, would assume greater importance in the later history of Mormonism than they proved to have in Kirtland.

A more extravagant understanding of restoration was the third major Kirtland development. While there, the Saints' knowledge of the restoration of the priesthood was augmented by their comprehension of the distinction between the Aaronic (lower) priesthood and the Melchizedek (higher) priesthood. This came as the internal organization of the restored Church of Christ was being worked out according to Joseph Smith's and other LDS leaders' understanding of the biblical pattern. Also in Kirtland, yet another element of restoration was emphasized as the gathered Saints were reminded that, in addition to being the restored Church of Christ, they were the restoration of Israel. Recognition of this additional identity came as Joseph Smith Sr., called as "Church Patriarch," gave individual Saints patriarchal blessings that, among much else, informed them of the particular Abrahamic tribe from which they were descended. That they were the restoration of Israel also registered when they realized that their Abrahamic legacy was very visible to outsiders because it turned all non-Mormons into "Gentiles." This became ever more apparent as the Mormon gathering created a ghetto-like atmosphere in the Kirtland area and in every other place where they gathered in the nineteenth century. Even more obviously to insiders and outsiders, Smith's Kirtland followers constructed an imposing temple, not a church.

Their emergence as an Abrahamic people was at least as potent in setting the Saints apart in Missouri. In the summer of 1831, a group of Saints, accompanied by Smith who had traveled from Kirtland, assembled on land in Jackson County. There twelve men representing the tribes of Israel laid the foundation for Zion's "Center Place." This special section of land was not immediately settled and the temple the Mormon prophet anticipated constructing was not built during his lifetime. (The area is now the site of the architecturally striking Community of Christ Temple, a handsome Church of Jesus Christ of LDS "Visitor's Center," and the house of worship of the Church of Christ, Temple Lot, representing three of the multiplicity of Mormonisms that now exist).

While their prophet returned to Ohio, the Saints who had traveled to the Mormon Zion with their families settled in the frontier town of Independence, Missouri. One of the new movement's printing presses (an absolute necessity for new religious movements before the coming of the Internet) was also situated there. For a year, the editor William Wines Phelps issued *The Evening and Morning Star* without incident. During those twelve months, many converts made by Mormon missionaries gathered in the area, thereby establishing a second stake in Zion's tent. But when, in July 1833, non-Mormons construed an article Phelps published in the *Star* as a welcome to free blacks to join the Saints, this gave them an ostensible reason to destroy the printing press and drive the Mormons from the area.

Smith talked of persecution as the reason he left New York, but he left there on his own initiative. In Independence, it was different. Whereas Smith's followers salvaged a few printed copies of the Book of Commandments and while they were able to escape with some of their possessions, this move, this first "driving," was a matter of Saints fleeing for their lives. They managed to find refuge in nearby Clay County, but most reached there with either very few or no belongings.

Upon learning about the happenings in Jackson County, Smith organized a military body of Mormon men that traveled to Missouri under his command with the goal of reestablishing the Independence Stake. This expedition, known as "Zion's Camp," was unsuccessful. But it brought a number of valiant Saints to Smith's attention, one of whom was Brigham Young. After the Zion's Camp participants returned to Kirtland, some of them would be called as members of the first Quorum of Twelve Apostles—or as they were called at the time, the Traveling High Council—a body that played an ever more significant role in the leadership of the movement. Early on, however, Smith sent several of the Twelve as missionaries to Britain, where they, along with missionaries later sent to Denmark and other northern European countries, made so many converts that their gathering with the Saints from the United States and Canada ultimately altered the all-American character of the movement.

Their being driven from Independence was only the first of a series of drivings the gathered Saints experienced between 1833 and 1847. Yet all was not persecution in either Missouri or Ohio. The Jackson County refugees were soon joined in Clay County by other Mormons, including new converts, who were responding to the revelation to gather. This, however, was but a temporary haven. As the Saints were struggling into the Clay County seat, their leaders reached an agreement with county officials that their settlement in the county would not be permanent. Although their stay was not marked by persecution, by 1836 it became obvious that the time for them to leave had come. The reason: the state established Caldwell County in the northwest part of the state, designed essentially as a Mormon county. The main town where the headquarters of the church would be located in 1838 was known as Far West.

Also in 1836, the dedication of the completed Kirtland Temple was the occasion of a powerful transcendent event, sometimes described as a Mormon "Pentecost." Contemporaries described the introduction of the washing of the feet at the beginning of the dedicatory services as a group mystical experience. When the temple was filled for the Sunday morning service that was the climax of the three-day dedication, Joseph Smith and Oliver Cowdery retired to the temple's central pulpit. As the structure's literal veils dropped around them, "the veil was taken from [their] minds" and together they visualized Christ who forgave their sins, accepted the temple, and promised that he would manifest himself there. Yet the spiritual zenith of the temple dedication reflected not the New but the Old Testament as Moses appeared and committed to these two leaders of the Saints "the keys of the gathering of Israel from the four parts of the earth." Elias also appeared and committed to them "the dispensation of the gospel of Abraham" that through them and their seed all generations would be blessed. Finally, in a "great and glorious vision," the prophet Elijah said he had been sent to "turn the hearts of the fathers to the children and the children to the fathers." These promises were entrusted to them and their people, assuring them that they were indeed Abraham's progeny singing to the Lord a new song as they waited for the "great and dreadful day of the Lord" (D&C 110:1–16).

This Abrahamic linkage with its deep and distinctive valuing of family would lead to yet another restoration that the Mormon prophet called "the restoration of the ancient order of things." This included the establishment of a widespread family network, including a system of adult adoption and the practice that most identified the Saints for the remainder of the nineteenth century—plural marriage (or, as the Gentiles called it, polygamy). Although not publicly revealed until 1852, scholars agree that this distinctive marriage practice was initially revealed to Smith in the 1830s in Kirtland. In any event, the Mormons' rapidly developing distinctiveness as a people would have profound consequences in Ohio and in their subsequent lives in Missouri, Illinois, and Utah.[7]

After the spiritual zenith of the temple dedication, the situation in Ohio deteriorated rapidly. Kirtland's population tripled in the years between 1831 and 1838 as nearly 2,000 LDS gathered to the area, many of them poor and needy. The new temple was impressive, but the town (which at the beginning of the decade had appeared to be losing its frontier character as frame and brick structures replaced small log homes) had regressed to a marginal state. Unpretentious cabins and small log huts undercut the town's original residents' aspirations to sophistication. To make matters worse, the Panic of 1837 led to economic catastrophe. Just prior to the Panic, Ohio had refused to authorize a Mormon bank whose primary assets would be land holdings, but the desperate Saints went ahead and established a financial institution anyway. They called it an "anti-bank"; almost immediately it collapsed. The combination of this failure and the flood of new Mormons gathering to the area led to another "driving."

This one, however, started with the tarring and feathering of Smith and other Mormon leaders who escaped from their tormentors and fled west to join the Saints in their Missouri Zion. The movement's members were not driven collectively from Kirtland, but most followed the Mormon prophet to northwestern Missouri where the Clay County Saints and many of the church members who had not gathered to Kirtland had gone.

A certain logic supported the Saints' claim that this land was their divine "inheritance": the state had created Caldwell County specifically for the Mormons; almost 5,000 Saints had gathered around the church headquarters in Far West and elsewhere in the western part of the state; and despite problems generated by some of the leaders who made personal profits on land sales, Smith and virtually all of the movement's leaders were there. In view of all this, the Zionic gathering created a consciousness among the Saints that they were living in times comparable to those in the Old Testament when God had given Abraham's family a land of promise. Therefore they made no secret of their belief that northwestern Missouri was or would be their "inheritance," whether or not they held title to it.

Again the gathering of the members of this new religious movement triggered the opposition of non-Mormons, initially because the numbers seemed so overwhelming that Missourians feared the Saints would gain political control of the area, but also because, in very public sermons, Sidney Rigdon proclaimed that the Saints would meet "mobocracy" with force and "exterminate" those who tried to take their inheritance from them. Hostility, involving the arrest of Smith and other Mormon leaders, and an "Extermination Order" issued against the Mormons by the Missouri governor, as well as violence epitomized by a massacre in which all the LDS men in the entire Haun's Mill settlement were shot and even a young child was killed because "nits make lice," led to another "driving" and scarred the Mormon psyche.[8]

With Brigham Young assuming responsibility, the Saints fled back across the state and over the Mississippi River to Quincy, Illinois. They were made welcome there, but again, not as permanent settlers. Smith and several other key LDS leaders were still in jail in Missouri when the Mormons—closely bonded by suffering, dashed hopes, and shared belief—moved northward on the east side of the river and put roots down in a region surrounding a small town called Commerce. This area, renamed Nauvoo by the Saints, included a beautiful bluff overlooking the Mississippi and land far enough away from the river to be verdant and healthful, but the lowlands were malarial swamps. The wetlands would have to be drained so that households could be established in that part of the town, yet so many Saints were without shelter that families built huts or cabins on the "flats." As a consequence, malaria infected nearly all the households established in that part of Nauvoo.

This made the first year in Illinois particularly difficult. Moreover, as the gathering continued, in subsequent years overcrowding remained a problem, even though gathered Mormons settled land across the river in Iowa. Yet in the next seven years, this part of Illinois became, as historian Robert Flanders called it, a "Kingdom on the Mississippi," inhabited by the men and women who had been Smith's early followers, the hosts of converts they made, and, by now, a second generation of young adult LDS who understood outsiders as Gentiles and themselves as God's chosen people.[9]

No wall was built around Nauvoo, but a virtual barrier separated its interior and exterior as the city grew to such an extent that, for a brief period between the censuses of 1840 and 1850, it was probably the largest town in Illinois. In light of its population growth, Nauvoo Saints proposed to the state legislature that the town and its surrounding periphery should be given county status. As might have been expected, the legislature ignored the petition, leaving this densely populated region to remain a part of Hancock County. This practically guaranteed formidable competition for LDS votes among the outside candidates for the US House of Representatives, including Abraham Lincoln and Stephen A. Douglas, as well as the animosity of non-Mormon policymakers in Carthage, the county seat.

The liturgical and theological elaboration that occurred in Nauvoo amplified the Saints' identity as a peculiar people. Once more they set about building a temple wherein "ancient ordinances," including "endowments" (ceremonies that prepared participants to become kings and queens, priests and priestesses in the afterlife), and plural celestial marriages could be celebrated. Smith did not delay enactments of these singular ordinances until the temple could be completed, however. Between 1842 and 1844 in the upper room of his red brick store, Smith revealed the endowment ordinance to some fifty Saints. Initially he shared with the Quorum of the Twelve the gist but not the wording of the revelation regarding marriages for time and eternity, including plural marriages. But as he put this revelation into practice by marrying a sister of an apostle, and the daughters and even some of the others' wives, he described this revelation in detail to most of his ecclesiastical colleagues.

During the last year of his own life, Smith clarified and added more about marriage and family to church doctrine. He said that men and women who enter into an everlasting covenant, that is, who are married for time and eternity "by the power and authority of the Holy priesthood," will dwell in the highest reaches of the celestial kingdom. Then, in a sermon preached at the burial of his friend King Follett, Smith publically introduced three of the most distinctive aspects of Mormon theology. First, he rejected *ex nihilo* creation, saying that the cosmos was organized out of existing elements. Second, he said that God was once a man and third, that men and women can become gods. This has commonly been interpreted to mean that in the resurrection men and women who are married for eternity as well as time will continue to give birth to spirit children and at some future (but unspecified) point they will become gods and will rule over their own kingdoms.[10]

After Joseph Smith and his brother Hyrum were murdered in 1844, life within the Mormon world changed dramatically. The contention for leadership was not finally settled, but, except for Smith's first wife, Emma, and his children, who followed James J. Strang for a time, the great majority of prominent Saints remained in Nauvoo. Leadership was exercised by the Quorum of the Twelve which, by that time, was headed by Brigham Young. Although the Saints were aware that the non-Mormons in the area were so anxious for them to go that staying in Illinois indefinitely would not be possible, they stayed long enough to finish the Nauvoo Temple and delayed their departure in order to celebrate the temple ordinances within its walls.

This final "driving" came almost as much from the inside as the outside. The shared sorrow of their prophet's death and the realization that, as his people, life could not continue as they had hoped drove the Saints ever closer together. Considering possible destinations where they could set about kingdom building once more, their leaders decided on the Great Basin, then Mexican territory. The Saints were encouraged to sell, if they could, their farms, meadows, and homesteads, and to prepare for a hazardous journey.

Young made plans for moving what amounted to an embryonic realm, peopled by individuals who believed they had a common ancestor in Father Abraham, across the plains and mountains to a new Zion. Yet the members of the procession crossing the Mississippi to make up one of history's larger migrations were by and large still New England or Southern or Canadian or British Saints. The trek west changed that. It became a journey through the wilderness that recapitulated the Old Testament exodus to the Promised Land. This so altered the way Mormons thought of themselves that the pioneers were transformed into Saints first and foremost. When they arrived, they established the state of Deseret and set about building the kingdom of God in the tops of the mountains in fulfillment, they believed, of the prophecy in Isaiah 2:1–5.

In the year following their 1847 arrival, the Great Basin became US territory as a result of the treaty following the Mexican War. For the Mormons who had joined the movement early on, living in land that belonged to the United States would change things. The gatherings in Ohio, Missouri, and Illinois had been grounded on shared belief; now what they had in common as they struggled to survive in what at first seemed desert land became much more experiential. During the Saints' first decade of residence in their mountain domain, civic leaders in their communities, towns, cities, and territory were also their church leaders. Following the Utah War in 1857–58, a campaign in which President James Buchanan sent the US Army to install a non-Mormon governor and other territorial officers to govern the Mormons, the State of Deseret continued as a shadow government comprising God's chosen people. In Mormon minds Young remained the governor, but Gentile civil officers, including judges and growing numbers of non-Mormon inhabitants, as well as the coming of the railroad in 1869, meant that the LDS kingdom had to function in US territory. For many, this change reminded them of the persecution they had gone through before they left the United States, the land they more and more thought of as Babylon.[11]

The shift in sovereignty from Mexico to the United States made little difference to new Mormon emigrants from Europe. Bodies of believers traveled across the Atlantic in crowded and uncomfortable ships; then in crowded and uncomfortable wagons they struggled west to the kingdom the Saints were building. Their journey was also an initiation. As Young said, "The trek is for making Saints." Their arrival and living in Deseret where the "ancient order of things" was openly restored engulfed them with a deeper perception of their identity as a Zionic people.

For the thirty years that Young presided as church president, prophet, and sometime governor, the saintly kingdom welcomed these new inhabitants from England, Wales, and northern Europe, especially Denmark. The newcomers, too, had moved through an experiential pathway, coming across the ocean, then across the plains and mountains to reach the Great Basin. But the violent history of the Saints in Ohio, Missouri, and Illinois was not part of the personal history of these new converts. Yet when the newcomers heard about those devastating encounters from the Saints who had lived through them, their identity as peculiar people was nurtured. In surprising ways their route to peoplehood replicated the earlier pattern. Rather than being Saints first when they arrived in Deseret, they were Welsh Saints or German Saints or Danish Saints. In time, their primary identity was simply Saints.

Generations made a difference in this transference of identity. Children born in the valleys or in the tops of the mountains did not remember the land from which their parents had come. Those whose parents had come from Europe might speak a different language at home and, for a decade or so, in their meetings at church. But the children spoke English and participated in the public and economic life of the Mormon kingdom. At the same time, this second generation of emigrants matured in a world that set them apart, for if they were not a part of a polygamous family, many of their contemporaries were. Sermons reminded them of the *Principle* (plural marriage) and told them that they all had the blood of Abraham running in their veins. This religious relatedness was reinforced by the intricate lines of blood connection that resulted from plural marriages, in which a father's kindred became a part of the kinship lines of all his wives. Indeed, it would be difficult to find a social system better suited to the development of an actual kindred people.

Mormon peoplehood was buttressed by active involvement in the life of the church and citizenship in Deseret (later Utah Territory). But the presence of Gentile civil officers and growing numbers of non-Mormon inhabitants among the Saints meant that the privacy that distance and the mountains had once afforded the Saints was increasingly attenuated. By the time of Brigham Young's death in 1877, Mormondom was faced with reentering American life.

In 1862, Congress had turned its attention away from the Civil War long enough to pass the Morrill Act making bigamy a crime in US territory. The Supreme Court upheld this statute in *Reynolds v. United States* (1879), rejecting the defendant's claim that plural marriage should be protected under the free exercise clause of the First Amendment. Despite the statute's being upheld by the highest court in the land, charges brought in Utah Territory had to be tried there; finding a jury who would convict a Mormon defendant of bigamy proved practically impossible. In the 1880s, Congress passed two major statutes punishing plural marriage. The Edmunds Act of 1882 prohibited polygamous cohabitation, behavior much more difficult to hide. Five years later, the Edmunds-Tucker Act confiscated church property and enforced for the first time a provision of the Morrill Act that revoked the church's legal status as a corporation, based on the grounds that the church promoted polygamy. An Idaho territorial Test Act disenfranchised LDS. Other legal and law enforcement efforts made it clear to LDS leaders that the continued public restoration of the "ancient order of things" could not continue if Mormonism wished to come to terms with the nation and to protect its kingdom by having Utah join the Union as one of the states.[12]

Aware of what retaining plural marriage would cost the people he led, church president Wilford Woodruff issued a "manifesto" in 1890 that told the world that the church would no longer sustain the practice of plural marriage. So committed had previous generations been to the practice that it required decades for the church fully to eliminate the practice among members who wished to remain in good standing. Today, "the Principle" is carried on by schismatic Mormon sects.[13]

The sense of being peculiar people persisted among the Saints long after the demise of plural marriage, the coming of Utah statehood in 1896, and the suspension of the gathering in the first two decades of the twentieth century.[14] However, their status as a people, not unlike the Jews, subtly shifted. Despite the accommodations to American law and culture as the twentieth century began, the Mormons held onto their understanding of the LDS priesthood as the *restoration* of the ancient priesthoods of Aaron and Melchizedek and to their conviction that their religious institution is the *restored* church of Jesus Christ. By contrast, their sense of being the "restoration of Israel" and their confidence that the "ancient order of things" had been restored were no longer expressed overtly and construed as literal and present. Instead, they were seen as more future-oriented, and were privately and symbolically retained by being embedded in the ordinances celebrated in LDS temples. Because the temples are open only to members of the church in good standing as verified by "recommends" from the bishop (pastor) of members' local wards, that part of Mormonism is no longer transparent to the world. In the minds of many outsiders, this element of privacy amounts to secrecy and makes Mormonism suspect. In spite of its fifteen million adherents, many nonmembers—unaware that when a cult becomes a culture, it is no longer a cult—still use "cult" as a way of denigrating Mormonism as non-Christian.

During the half-century before the Second World War, Mormonism became an ethnicity. With a shared history—but not necessarily shared beliefs or shared behavior, since not every individual Mormon or every LDS family continued to believe that Joseph Smith was a prophet or stayed active in the church—its people remained intimates who shared a land, an idiosyncratic understanding of the formation of time and the universe, and a history of persecution and of making the desert bloom "as a rose." Separated geographically and culturally long enough to become distinctive, this shift from peoplehood to ethnicity came during a time when the LDS Church grew more by natural increase than conversion. Better transportation and communication within the mountain west reinforced internal kinship and friendship ties as the Saints lived through the last possible period for collective identity development before radio, television, and digital technology imposed the world onto Mormon culture.

Mormon ethnicity became a possession and a memory. Just as the stories of persecution told by the Saints who had lived in Ohio, Missouri, and Illinois became the possession and memory of the converts who later gathered to Zion from Europe, so Mormon ethnicity was adopted by millions of the new LDS converts who joined the Church of Jesus Christ of LDS in the half-century following the Second World War. The process was modernized, but not so very different than enacted previously. For example, the church inaugurated the *Ensign* as an official magazine in 1971. Many issues during its first decade focused on descriptions of the heroic suffering, valiant struggles, and victories of Mormon pioneers. At the same time, the Church History Department—concerned with producing legitimate academic works—was turning out narrative accounts of the Mormon past that placed the Saints inside the ongoing-ness and ordinariness of life, thereby portraying them as a part of the all-too-human history of the American west and the history of the United States. The Museum of Church History and Art and the restoration of Mormon historic sites had a different task. They created exhibits that portrayed pioneer Saints as heroes and heroines, bringing them to life for new converts and long-time church members, as well as introducing them to tourists. Each historic site had a film that recounted what had happened there from the LDS perspective. Moreover, the first film to be shown in Salt Lake City's Joseph Smith Building, *Legacy*, was a sentimental rendering of the beginnings of Mormonism and the story of how courageous LDS pioneers reached the "Promised Land." From the outside, all this attention to persecution, struggle, and accomplishment might have appeared to be directed toward making conversions. Upon reflection, however, it is obvious that the *Ensign* accounts, the museum exhibits and historic sites, and the idealized historical films were also a means of allowing new converts to adopt a past that would become their own.

The half-century after the Second World War was a time of extraordinary growth in numbers of individual and family converts to Mormonism. As the history of these years reveals and as the history of twenty-first-century Mormonism continues to demonstrate, however strong a convert's conviction of the truth of LDS religious claims, the adopting of an identity as a LDS is critical to remaining active in the church. Since gatherings have already become more electronic than physical, the role they played in the nineteenth century cannot be replicated. Moreover, as Mormonism has become a universal faith, present all across the globe, the belief that all Mormons have the blood of Abraham running in their veins either has or is becoming more metaphorical than literal. Similarly, because there are now Saints from virtually every region in the world, if Mormon ethnicity persists—and it has proved to be such a potent supplement to the LDS belief structure that Mormon leaders are likely to encourage its preservation—the church will have to find effective ways to connect Saints from one part of the world to all the others.

Such realities prompt an important query: what is it that all Mormons have in common? The obvious answer is the firm conviction that Joseph Smith was a prophet and that the Book of Mormon is modern scripture. While compelling and inspirational, Smith's life story is all that is left of his charisma. He is not regarded as a deity who continues to be influential in the lives of those who believe he was a prophet. But what about the Book of Mormon today?

In the beginning of this new religious movement, this scriptural work was, as noted earlier, at least as important as the charismatic leadership of the Prophet Joseph Smith. As the movement came together, the book continued to signal that the "heavens were no longer brass," that God had not ceased communicating with humanity when the New Testament was completed and canonized. But its content—its story—was not as significant or powerful or exciting as the lives the Saints themselves were living through during the movement's early growth and as the Mormon canon was indisputably open during the lifetime of the first Mormon prophet. Gradually, in the same way as the Bible became for Protestants in the Progressive era, Mormon's book became an icon. Every saintly family owned a copy, often prominently displayed in their homes. But as their church was institutionalized and their culture brought into being, that is, through their long pioneer period and the explosion of church growth, Smith's revelations and the words of their current prophet seemed more pertinent to their lives.

In the 1980s, however, what had been icon became text once again. When, in 1981, a new edition of the Book of Mormon was published, it had a new subtitle: Another Testament of Jesus Christ. That this was more than a reiteration that the LDS Church is the Church of Jesus Christ became clear when church president Ezra Taft Benson, in a pivotal talk in 1986, resurrected Joseph Smith's statement that this central modern scripture is "The Keystone of Our Religion." Benson added that it is "the keystone of our testimony, the keystone of our doctrine, and the keystone in the witness of our Lord and Savior." As such, the church president, speaking prophetically, told the Saints to read and study the Book of Mormon so that it could become the keystone of their lives. In the years since, Mormon's book has not entirely reclaimed the place it occupied in the early 1830s. But it is read and studied and used in Sunday school and Gospel Doctrine classes. Furthermore, from time to time it is the testimony that makes Book of Mormon converts to a religious movement that is no longer new.

Notes

1. Several works offer a reasonably complete look into the origins of the Smith family and the coming forth the Book of Mormon. Eminent among them is Bushman, *Joseph Smith: Rough Stone Rolling*, which represents the most complete and respected scholarship on the founding Prophet to date. Eclipsed in its scholarship, yet still important in the Prophet's historiography, is Brodie, *No Man Knows My History*; see also Hill, *Joseph Smith: The First Mormon*; Vogel, *Joseph Smith: Making of a Prophet*.
2. Cross, *Burned-Over District*. This work is more than sixty years old, yet remains valuable for studies of western New York during the early nineteenth century.
3. Baer, "Charting the Missionary Work of William E. McLellin."
4. Arrington, *Brigham Young*; Turner, *Brigham Young*. Both authors offer compelling, yet not always compatible, views of the controversial Mormon prophet. Both works, however, are necessary reading for understanding the origin, character, and life of the "lion of the Lord."
5. This reality is based on a systematic reading of the entries about early Mormons in Jenson's *Latter-day Saint Biographical Encyclopedia*.
6. Barlow, *Mormons and the Bible*, 67; Harper, *Making Sense of the Doctrine and Covenants*.
7. Gordon, *Mormon Question*; Hales, *Joseph Smith's Polygamy*; Smith, *Nauvoo Polygamy*.
8. LeSueur, *1838 Mormon War in Missouri*; Spencer, *The Missouri Mormon Experience*.
9. Flanders, *Nauvoo*.
10. Flake, "Translating Time"; Ostler, *Exploring Mormon Thought*, vol. 3.
11. McKennon, *At Sword's Point*; Walker, Turner, and Leonard, *Massacre at Mountain Meadows*; Alexander, *Utah*.
12. Gordon, *Mormon Question*; Melville, *Conflict and Compromise*.
13. Bennion, "History, Culture, and Variability of Mormon Schismatic Groups."
14. Shipps, "Scattering of the Gathering and the Gathering of the Scattered," 259–61; Alder, "German-Speaking Immigration to Utah, 1850–1950," 114–18.

Bibliography

Alder, Doug. "The German-Speaking Immigration to Utah, 1850–1950." Master's thesis, University of Utah, 1950.
Alexander, Thomas G. *Utah: The Right Place*. Rev. ed. Salt Lake City: Gibbs Smith, 2003.
Arrington, Leonard J. *Brigham Young: American Moses*. New York: Alfred A. Knopf, 1985.
Baer, Teresa. "Charting the Missionary Work of William E. McLellin: A Content Analysis." In *The Journals of William E. McLellin, 1831–1836*, ed. Jan Shipps and John W. Welch, 379–405. Urbana: University of Illinois Press, 1994.
Barlow, Philip L. *Mormons and the Bible: The Place of the Latter-day Saints in American Religion*. Rev. ed. New York: Oxford University Press, 2013.
Bennion, Janet. "History, Culture, and Variability of Mormon Schismatic Groups." In *Modern Polygamy in the United States: Historical, Cultural, and Legal Issues*, ed. Cardell Jacobson and Lara Burton, 101–24. New York: Oxford University Press, 2011.
Brodie, Fawn M. *No Man Knows My History: The Life of Joseph Smith*. 2nd ed. New York: Vintage, 1995.
Bushman, Richard L. *Joseph Smith: Rough Stone Rolling*. New York: Alfred A. Knopf, 2005.

Cross, Whitney R. *The Burned-Over District: The Social and Intellectual History of Enthusiastic Religion in Western New York, 1800–1850*. Ithaca, NY: Cornell University Press, 1950.

Flake, Kathleen. "Translating Time: The Nature and Function of Joseph Smith's Narrative Canon." *Journal of Religion* 87, no. 4 (October 2007): 497–527.

Flanders, Robert Bruce. *Nauvoo: Kingdom on the Mississippi*. Urbana: University of Illinois Press, 1965.

Gordon, Sarah Barringer. *The Mormon Question: Polygamy and Constitutional Conflict in Nineteenth-Century America*. Chapel Hill: University of North Carolina Press, 2002.

Hales, Brian C. *Joseph Smith's Polygamy*. 3 vols. Salt Lake City: Greg Kofford, 2013.

Harper, Steven Craig. *Making Sense of the Doctrine and Covenants: A Guided Tour through Modern Revelation*. Salt Lake City: Deseret, 2008.

Hill, Donna. *Joseph Smith: The First Mormon*. Salt Lake City: Signature, 1998.

Jenson, Andrew. *Latter-day Saint Biographical Encyclopedia: A Compilation of Biographical Sketches of Prominent Men and Women in the Church of Jesus Christ of Latter-day Saints*. Charleston, SC: BiblioBazaar, 2011.

LeSueur, Stephen C. *The 1838 Mormon War in Missouri*. Columbia: University of Missouri Press, 1987.

MacKinnon, William P. *At Sword's Point: A Documentary History of the Utah War to 1858*. Norman, OK: Arthur H. Clark, 2008.

May, Dean L. "Mormons." In *Harvard Encyclopedia of American Ethnic Groups*, ed. Stephan Thernstrom. Cambridge, MA: Belknap Press of Harvard University Press, 1980.

Melville, J. Keith. *Conflict and Compromise: The Mormons in Mid Nineteenth-century American Politics*. Provo, UT: Political Science Department, BYU Printing Service, 1974.

Ostler, Blake T. *Exploring Mormon Thought*. 3 vols. Salt Lake City: Greg Kofford, 2008.

Shipps, Jan. "The Scattering of the Gathering and the Gathering of the Scattered: The Mid-Twentieth-century Mormon Diaspora." In *Sojourner in the Promised Land: Forty Years Among the Mormons*, 258–78. Urbana: University of Illinois Press, 2000.

Smith, George D. *Nauvoo Polygamy: ". . . But We Called It Celestial Marriage"*. Salt Lake City: Signature, 2008.

Spencer, Thomas M. *The Missouri Mormon Experience*. Columbia: University of Missouri Press, 2010.

Turner, John G. *Brigham Young: Pioneer Prophet*. Cambridge, MA: Harvard University Press, 2012.

Vogel, Dan. *Joseph Smith: The Making of a Prophet*. Salt Lake City: Signature, 2004.

Walker, Ronald W., Richard E. Turley Jr., and Glen M. Leonard. *Massacre at Mountain Meadows: An American Tragedy*. New York: Oxford University Press, 2008.

CHAPTER 2

....

EMERGENT MORMONISM IN CONTEXT

....

DANIEL WALKER HOWE

To many people, the Mormon religion seems unique; its doctrines, whether properly understood or not, very strange and startling. The Mormons have scriptures besides the Old and New Testaments; they are famous for having once practiced polygamy; they believe in continuing revelation and regard the head of their church as a prophet. Indeed, the distinctiveness of Mormonism is commonly emphasized both by Mormons themselves and their Gentile critics. Yet, if one examines the context in which the Latter-day Saint Church first appeared and spread, much that might seem unique about it will come to appear characteristic of the time and place of its origin.

In 1830, the publication year of the Book of Mormon, Americans enjoyed almost complete freedom of religion, making theirs an unusual country at the time. The First Amendment to the Constitution had forbidden the federal Congress to establish religion or limit its free exercise. This provision, actually noncontroversial when adopted in 1791, recognized a pluralist religious situation that rendered any nationwide establishment unworkable. At the state level there had been several religious establishments, but only one, that of Massachusetts, remained in 1830. It permitted towns to choose which Protestant denomination they wished to support with tax money; in practice they always chose either Congregationalism or its theologically liberal offshoot, Unitarianism. Dissenters (that is, followers of other religions) could often arrange to divert their religious tax to their own local congregation—so long as they were Protestants. Already perceived as anachronistic, the religious "standing order" in Massachusetts would be abolished three years later. Foreign observers who visited in the 1830s marveled that the United States displayed a giant free marketplace in religions.

Not only did the United States accord freedom to the many varieties of Western European Christianity (including Catholics, Lutherans, Anglicans, Presbyterians, Congregationalists, Methodists, Baptists, Quakers, Shakers, Huguenots, Dutch Reformed, Moravians, Amish, and Swedenborgians), but new religious bodies continually cropped up. Prominent among these were the heirs of the "Christian Movement," which sought to transcend the divisions of denominationalism but ended, ironically, by founding several new denominations: the Christian Connection, the Disciples of Christ, and the Churches of Christ. The Unitarians who shared in the religious standing order of Massachusetts proudly represented a native New England development rather than an importation from overseas. Sometimes denominations preserved a racial or ethnic basis; thus, the Dutch Reformed remained distinct from Congregationalists despite their common Calvinist theological background. When free black Methodists rebelled against discrimination from white Methodists, they founded not just one but two new denominations: the Philadelphia-based African Methodist Episcopal (AME) Church and the New York-based African Methodist Episcopal Zion (AME Zion) Church. Throughout Joseph Smith's lifetime, the church he founded could always lay claim to American freedom of religion, no matter how unpopular it might become with neighbors in New York, Ohio, Missouri, or Illinois.

America's religious pluralism manifested and nurtured American democracy. Ordinary people felt free to express themselves on religious subjects, free to join institutions and organize new ones. In the America of 1830, religious life was in some ways actually more democratic than political life. Women, African Americans, and newly arrived poor immigrants could participate in religion, often in leadership roles, earlier than they participated in American politics. Throughout most Protestant denominations, the role of lay men and women expanded in comparison with the traditional role of ordained and specifically educated professional clergy. The Latter-day Saints took what one might call this laicism a step further: all male church members shared in the priesthood, and at least officially there was no professional clergy at all.

Of all the religions in America, perhaps the Baptists exemplified local-based democracy most strongly. Their practice of adult baptism by immersion founded their faith on freely consenting equal agents. The Baptists splintered into innumerable factions, often reflecting disagreements over fervently held theological opinions: Separate Baptists, Regular Baptists, United Baptists, General Baptists, Particular Baptists, Calvinist Baptists, Free-Will Baptists, Primitive Baptists, Anti-Mission Baptists, Two-Seed-in-the-Spirit Baptists. The Mormons too would base their faith on conscious reasoned consent and practice dramatic baptisms by immersion, restricting the rite to persons old enough to make their own commitment. And although the Mormons did not accord their local wards the degree of autonomy typical of Baptist congregations, they still experienced schisms of their own, most notably the one between Josephites and Brighamites after the death of Joseph Smith.

Western New York State, where the Book of Mormon was published in Palmyra, was famously the scene of religious enthusiasm during the 1820s and '30s—so much so, in fact, that it has become known as "the burned-over district"—burned over, metaphorically, by the fires of religious zeal. Preachers sought to "revive" the true spirit of religion by holding well-publicized meetings in temporary shelters; these became known as "camp meetings" because the attendees brought tents to camp out and stay for several days. Revivalists like Lyman Beecher and Charles Finney became famous for particular styles of Christian piety and particular innovations in evangelism. Evidence has come to light that Joseph Smith attended a Methodist camp meeting as early as 1820. In this atmosphere of religious questing and a myriad of religious options, the young Joseph's First Vision provided an authoritative admonition: "Join none of them." Instead, Smith followed the supernatural instructions of his own visions and produced a new scripture.[1]

What historians call "the Second Great Awakening" of American Christianity (by analogy to the First Great Awakening in eighteenth-century colonial New England) manifested a fervent zeal for the conversion of the world. Missionaries included a wide variety of traveling preachers from many denominations, including the Catholics, who employed members of religious orders as itinerants. Several Protestant denominations cooperated in 1826 to form the American Home Missionary Society. Other interdenominational organizations engaged in proselytizing included the American Bible Society, the American Tract Society, and the American Board of Commissioners for Foreign Missions. The American Colonization Society envisioned resettling emancipated slaves in West Africa, who were then expected to help spread Christianity in that region. Although it did not participate in such ecumenical missionary organizations, the Latter-day Saint Church initiated its own well-organized missionary activity from its very inception. Mormons proved among the most successful missionaries, carrying their restored gospel to England and Scandinavia, as well as across the United States. The missionary hymn "From Greenland's Icy Mountains to India's Coral Strand," written by an Anglican bishop in 1819 and set to music by Lyman Beecher's future choirmaster Lowell Mason in 1823, became a favorite of Mormons. Though most of the other denominations involved in the missionary activity of the nineteenth-century Second Great Awakening have long since lost enthusiasm for it, the Mormons carry on their overt missionary effort with more dedication than ever. Today, most young Mormon males contribute two years of their lives, and many females eighteen months, to foreign or domestic mission work.

Along with their proselytizing for Christ, the evangelists of the Second Great Awakening often espoused a number of moral reforms. Sometimes they were able to cooperate in these causes across denominational lines in what contemporaries called the Evangelical United Front. Typically their reforms involved the imposition of some kind of personal discipline serving a redemptive goal. For example, the prison reform movement founded "penitentiaries" (that is, places of penance and reform) to replace prisons that simply punished in order to deter others. Dorothea Dix sought to create "insane asylums" where the mentally ill could be treated, instead of just locking them up in basements and jails. Evangelical antislavery had as its goal the transformation of slaves into responsible agents, able to marry, negotiate wage contracts, and obtain credit. Second only to antislavery in controversy and consequences among the moral reforms of the Second Great Awakening came the Temperance Movement.

The intemperate abuse of alcohol constituted a genuine and severe social problem in antebellum America, comparable to drug abuse in later generations. In 1825, the average American over fifteen years of age consumed seven gallons of alcohol a year, mostly in the form of whiskey and hard cider. (The corresponding figure in the early twenty-first century is two gallons, most of it from wine and beer.) Then, people commonly drank alcohol with every meal, as well as at mid-morning and mid-afternoon breaks. Although socially tolerated, drunkenness frequently generated violence, especially domestic violence. Temperance, not surprisingly, had a special appeal to wives and mothers.

The temperance movement, as the word "temperate" implies, originally promoted moderation in the use of alcohol. Starting with Lyman Beecher in 1812, temperance advocates urged people to shift away from consuming hard liquor to wine and beer. Temperance evangelists operated the same way revivalists did: They called on people to come forward and sign a temperance pledge, just as revivalists demanded an overt decision for Christ. By 1825, evangelists had discovered the effectiveness of a stronger call: to promise *total* abstinence rather than just moderation, they asked pledgers to put a capital "T" after their signature, and become "teetotalers."

In February 1833, Joseph Smith received his revelation called "the Word of Wisdom," enjoining abstinence from "wine or strong drink." Like other dietary reformers of the time, such as Sylvester Graham and Ellen G. White, the Prophet also warned against tobacco and "hot drinks" (interpreted to mean tea and coffee). Meat and poultry should be eaten only "sparingly." Echoing the biblical book of Proverbs, chapter 3, verse 8, keepers of the Word of Wisdom were promised "health to their navel and marrow to their bones." As the wider temperance movement gradually became stricter in its demands (culminating in nationwide Prohibition between 1919 and 1933), so the Word of Wisdom, at first considered advisory, became mandatory for Latter-day Saints in the early twentieth century.

A prominent theological feature common to several denominations of the Second Great Awakening was restorationism, that is, the effort to restore authentic New Testament Christianity. The goal of restoration went back at least as far as the Protestant Reformation of the sixteenth century, which had written off purgatory, indulgences, and the invocation of saints as unscriptural innovations. The Baptists went farther than other Protestants by restoring baptism by immersion (rather than by pouring or sprinkling water) and rejecting the baptism of infants as a corruption. The Christian Movement of Barton Stone, Elias Smith, and Alexander Campbell (among others) carried restorationism a step farther. They sought to transcend denominational lines and bring an end to the scandal of divisions among followers of Christ. To this end, they rejected all creeds, and theological formulations like the Trinity, as postbiblical. They hoped that if Christians confined themselves to affirming the language of the New Testament, it would eliminate occasion for disagreement. But their quest for unity through restoration proved illusory. The words of scripture require interpretation, and even the followers of the Christian Movement couldn't help disagreeing with each other about their meaning.

Joseph Smith's revealed religion was avowedly restorationist, even while also presenting a whole new set of scriptures in the form of the Book of Mormon. The faith of the Latter-day Saints asserts both a new dispensation and the "restitution of all things, which God hath spoken by the mouth of his holy prophets since the world began" (Acts 3:21). Smith's followers included many won over from other restorationist movements, most notably the Campbellite minister Sidney Rigdon. Alexander Campbell himself, no doubt recognizing in Smith a powerful restorationist rival, published one of the most influential early critiques of the Book of Mormon. When, near the end of his life, the Prophet confided to intimates his revelation concerning polygamy, he justified it as a restoration of Old Testament practice.

Millennialism constituted a feature of the Second Great Awakening even more widespread and conspicuous than restorationism. The New Testament book of Revelation prophesies a thousand-year reign of peace and justice on earth in connection with the Second Coming of Christ. Christian commentators over the centuries have identified this "millennium" with the messianic age foretold by the Hebrew prophets, and have developed two different theories of how it will come about. One version holds that Christ's miraculous return will initiate the millennium; this is called "premillennialism," because Christ returns at the start of it. The other version holds that the thousand-year millennium must occur first, so as to prepare the world to receive Christ's Second Coming afterwards; theologians term it "postmillennialism." In the latter understanding, the millennium is the glorious climax of a historical process, the fruit of human effort. Postmillennial speculations and expectations flourished in the nineteenth century, in connection with widespread enthusiasm for progress in all its forms—technological, scientific, social, economic, and political. The great evangelist, reformer, and educator Charles G. Finney once told his audience that if Christians applied themselves fully to the works of mission and reform, they could bring about the millennium in three years.[2] Many of the varied interdenominational charitable and reform organizations of the Second Great Awakening enlisted postmillennial energies, among them the American Peace Society, the American and Foreign Anti-Slavery Society, the Society for the Promotion of Theological Education at the West, and the American Sunday School Union. The Roman Catholic Church rejected Protestant millennialism along with the literal interpretation of the book of Revelation on which it was based. Postmillennial Protestants accordingly looked forward to the destruction of Catholicism as part of the lead-up to the millennium. Some of them organized the Evangelical Alliance to Overthrow the Papacy; other Protestants joined mobs to burn Catholic churches and convents.

Alongside the broad appeal of postmillennialism, the Second Great Awakening also witnessed a dramatic outburst of premillennialism. William Miller, a Vermont farmer, pondered the vision of the Prophet Daniel: "Unto two thousand and three hundred days; then shall the sanctuary be cleansed" (Daniel 8:14). Miller interpreted "days" to mean "years," and the cleaning of the sanctuary to mean the Second Coming of Christ. Calculating the time from (what he thought) the date of Daniel's prophecy, Miller concluded that the Second Advent would occur sometime between March 1843 and April 1844. In 1831, Miller felt God's call to start sharing this breathtaking news with the world.

Miller and his publicity agent Joshua Himes exploited the methods of other evangelicals; by the time of the fateful year, some half million people had attended their camp meetings. When the year expired in April 1844, Miller apologized for his evident mistake. But one of his followers, Samuel Snow, reworked the calculations and decided Jesus must come on the next Jewish Day of Atonement, October 22, 1844. A specific day aroused the Millerite crowds even more urgently. Estimates of their numbers run to twenty-five thousand or more. Expecting the end of the world, some quit their jobs, closed their businesses, left their crops unharvested in the fields. On October 22 they gathered in many locations to watch the sky. But Jesus did not appear to them, and the Adventists have remembered the date as their Great Disappointment. Only then did the general public heap scorn on them; before that, most people had hedged their bets by treating Millerite predictions respectfully.

But neither the Great Disappointment nor the ridicule of others put an end to Miller's movement. Many of them having been expelled from their previous affiliations, the faithful eventually organized a denomination of their own. They decided that Jesus had entered a new "heavenly sanctuary" on October 22. They began to observe Saturday rather than Sunday, a restoration of the Jewish Sabbath which gave them the name Seventh-Day Adventists. Following the visions of Ellen G. White, they adopted dietary reforms banning alcohol, tobacco, coffee, and meat. When the Civil War came, they declared themselves conscientious objectors, and so the Seventh-Day Adventists have remained in subsequent conflicts to this day.

At least one prominent abolitionist had participated in the Millerite movement. Isabella Baumfree, a New York slave liberated when the state implemented general emancipation in 1827, got involved with Miller's movement and became an itinerant preacher. During this time she adopted the pseudonym Sojourner Truth, signifying a traveling herald of the Divine Word. After the Great Disappointment she continued preaching millenarianism and abolitionism, both with great urgency. The majority of abolitionists, however, like Charles G. Finney, Lewis Tappan, and William Lloyd Garrison, were postmillennialists.

Like William Miller, Joseph Smith and his family had been farmers in Vermont. The early Mormons came from backgrounds similar to Miller's followers: mostly of Yankee extraction living in New England or upstate New York, small to medium-size farmers and small-town artisans, religious seekers, generally of Baptist, Methodist, or other non-Calvinist evangelical background. The year of the Miller's Great Disappointment, 1844, proved pivotal for the Mormons too: Smith and his brother Hyrum were murdered on June 27, succeeded by Brigham Young as president of the LDS Church. Like the Millerites, the Mormons were premillennial, or "millenarian," to use a common synonym. Like them too, the Mormons were chiliasts, believers that the Second Coming will occur soon. "Behold and lo I come quickly," declared Jesus Christ in Joseph Smith's First Vision.[3] The Mormons took their name "Latter-day Saints" from their belief that the end of history is nigh, though they did not presume to set a date. Mormons and Millerites both believed in a literal, personal, sudden Second Advent, but Millerites relied simply on human calculations, while the Mormons proclaimed new, modern revelations. Contemporaries took note of the parallels between Millerites and Mormons. The two movements viewed each other as rivals and exchanged mutual denunciations.

In an important other respect, the Mormons resembled the postmillennialists. They believed the Second Coming for which they longed required efforts on their part to prepare the way for the Lord. Constructing temples, instituting sacraments, converting and gathering the saints, founding the American Zion—each represented a stage in a process, at once mandatory and inescapable, in building up the Kingdom of God for Christ's return. When Mormons rejected Miller's imminent predictions, they pointed out that necessary precursors to Christ's return had not yet occurred—notably, the restoration of the Jews to the Holy Land.

The faith in progress expressed by a multitude of antebellum reform movements and associations also appeared in the numerous utopian communities of the time. The British industrialist Robert Owen, an enthusiastic Enlightenment rationalist, came to the United States to implement his vision of perfecting social relations based on analogy with the technological improvements he had so successfully applied in industry. Notwithstanding the sympathetic interest of many opinion makers, Owen's experimental community of New Harmony, Indiana, recruited few experienced farmers or skilled artisans and lasted only two years (1825–27). Owen soon returned to Britain to pursue his communitarian experiments there (likewise unsuccessfully), but some eighteen other short-lived utopian communities in the United States also drew in varying degrees upon Owenite principles. Another form of utopian socialism, the Associationism of Albert Brisbane, based on the theories of the Frenchman Charles Fourier, aroused a measure of support from working people.[4] Twenty-eight phalanxes, as the Associationists called their communes, sprang up during the economic hard times of the early 1840s. Brisbane's utopianism attracted more followers than William Miller's millenarianism. Like Owen, Brisbane envisioned his communities setting such a compelling example that society at large would voluntarily follow them. Unlike Marx and Engels, these utopian socialists expected to revolutionize the Western world peacefully. Although the phalanxes pioneered some good ideas in architecture and town planning, none of them lasted more than a dozen years. Lack of investment capital and the difficulty of sustaining commitment among the residents proved fatal.

Some of the religious utopian communities proved more enduring than the secular ones, for they mobilized precisely the lasting sense of commitment that eluded their secular counterparts. One of the most celebrated of the communitarian religions in antebellum America was the United Society of Believers in Christ's Second Appearing, better known as the Shakers, a name derived from their ritual dance. They considered their founder, Ann Lee, a second incarnation of Christ. Just as Jesus was the Son of God, Ann was the Daughter of God. Ascetic millenarians, Shakers renounced "the world," held their property in common, and lived simple lives in communities of their own, preparing themselves for the final Advent of Christ. They practiced celibacy; to perpetuate their sect they relied on converts and the adoption of orphan children. The Shakers grew gradually from 1774, when Ann Lee came to America, and by 1840 had about six thousand members in nineteen communities. Across the twentieth century the Shakers underwent a long slow decline; by 2009 there were only three members still alive. The furniture, buildings, handicrafts, and music of the Shakers remain, revered today as masterpieces of American folk art.

Several pietistic groups migrated from the German lands to the United States. In colonial times came the Mennnonites, a strict form of Baptists (then called Anabaptists) who settled in Pennsylvania; later Mennonite immigrants established communities west of the Appalachians. Mennonites followed a lifestyle even simpler than that of the Quakers, retained their German language, and practiced nonviolence, refusing military service in wartime. A particularly strict variety of Mennonites, the Amish, regard modern technology as potentially corrupting and refuse to use it. The Amish and other Mennonites respect family life, have large families, and flourish still in growing numbers. On the other hand, the Rappites, who came to Pennsylvania from Germany in 1804, practiced celibacy like the Shakers and looked for the imminent Second Coming. The Rappite communities held their property in common, prospered economically, and made donations to other millenarian groups, including the Shakers and Mormons. Disappointed by the failure of Christ to return, they allowed their celibate community to die out at the end of the nineteenth century. The Amana Society, another group of German pietists, migrated to western New York State in 1843 and moved from there to Iowa in the 1850s. They held their property in common until 1932, to a considerable extent keeping economically self-sufficient. Their seven communities continue to flourish in Iowa, combining agriculture with tourism and the manufacture of Amana refrigerators and air conditioners.

Looked at in this context, Mormon communities ("Stakes of Zion" in LDS terminology) including Kirtland, Nauvoo, Salt Lake City, and many other settlements in Missouri, Utah, and elsewhere, can be seen as examples of a utopian communalism that had many versions in antebellum America, both secular and religious. Like the others, the Mormon communities reflected the ideology of their founders and modeled social relationships for the instruction of the world at large as well as for the inhabitants themselves. Some of the Mormon communities, like some of the other utopias, practiced the law of "all things [in] common," a restoration of New Testament practice recorded in Acts 2:44 and 4:32. Utah under Brigham Young undertook a policy of economic self-sufficiency intended to preserve independence from the outside world. Individual Mormon settlements were not necessarily successful; some, such as Nauvoo and Far West, Missouri, were victimized by the hostility of neighbors. Nevertheless, by comparison with the other communitarians of antebellum America, the Mormons stand out as the most conspicuously successful by far. Although Mennonites, Amish, and Amanas still exist, they have not done much to win converts, while the Mormons have been spectacularly successful in this regard.

Several agricultural communities were established for Jews in the nineteenth-century United States, even before the wave of Jewish immigration that began in the 1880s. They looked forward to the liberation of the Holy Land from the Ottoman Empire as the fulfillment of God's promise. One of the earliest of these was the abortive effort of Mordecai Noah in 1825 to establish a Zionist haven called Ararat in western New York state. The Jewish settlements may be considered relevant to the LDS ones, since the Mormons considered themselves Children of Israel (among the Ten Lost Tribes) and were also preparing for their restoration in Zion.

Contemporaries viewed not only the various utopian communities but the whole United States as an experimental society, an example to the world of democratic government. More than just a passive model for others, America actively fostered the democratization of the world. This was how Alexis de Tocqueville and many other foreign observers interpreted America, and this was how Americans themselves regarded their country, most eloquently in the words of Lincoln's Gettysburg Address. As ancient Israel had a providential mission to nurture ethical monotheism among the pagan nations, the United States seemed to her Protestant patriots to have a providential mission to promote democratic government. Mormon theology elaborated on the exceptional, providential role of the United States in world history. The Mormons saw themselves restoring both Israel and the primitive Christian Church in America. According to Joseph Smith's revelations, both Zion and the Garden of Eden were located in the New World (specifically, in Independence, Missouri) and there Christ's Second Coming would occur.

How America should best carry out her providential mission provoked passionate political disagreement among antebellum citizens. Jacksonian Democrats foresaw the country remaining largely agricultural. They stressed the realization of the nation's "Manifest Destiny" to expand across the North American continent. Opening up new lands for cultivation while keeping tariff duties and other taxes low would ensure economic opportunity for coming generations of white farmers and planters, including slaveowners. Government should play a role narrowly confined to military security and the closely related task of maintaining white American supremacy over blacks, Native Americans, and foreign powers such as Mexico and Britain. The opposition party, the Whigs, endorsed economic development and diversification. Less eager for territorial expansion, they urged the benefits of public education, a national bank, investment in infrastructure like railroads, canals, and lighthouses, and a protective tariff to encourage infant industries. These projects implied a more active role for government (both state and federal) and therefore required a willingness to levy taxes.

Although the Whigs envisioned a more economically diverse America than the Democrats did, they strongly supported cultural uniformity. The Whigs were predominantly Protestant, postmillennial, and supportive of the Evangelical United Front and its reform causes like temperance. Democrats often resented what they considered the presumptuousness of the evangelical reformers; although they envisioned an America more economically uniform than the Whigs, they tolerated more cultural diversity. As a result, immigrant voters generally found the Democratic party more congenial, especially if they were Catholics. Americans tended to vote in blocs, as much ethnoreligious as economic. The fact that voting was not secret reinforced this tendency. Democratic voting blocs included Roman Catholics, Dutch Reformed, Antimission Baptists, and freethinkers. Whig voting blocs included Congregationalists, African Americans (in places where blacks could vote), "New School" Presbyterians, and "Low Church" Episcopalians.

Early Mormon men, whether in Ohio, Missouri, or Illinois, generally voted the way Joseph Smith urged, more often Democratic but occasionally Whig. Voting for the party of Jackson made sense in light of its broader tolerance of religious diversity; besides, most Mormons came from the small farming and artisan background common within the Democratic party. After Missouri governor Lilburn Boggs, a Democrat, called for the "extermination" of the Mormons, they understandably turned toward the Whigs. Joseph Smith led a delegation to Washington to ask for federal protection. The Whig leader Henry Clay supported their cause in the Senate, but Democratic president Martin Van Buren, a firm state-righter, told the Mormon delegation, "Your cause is just, but I can do nothing for you."[5] Not surprisingly, Mormon voters cast their ballots for the Whig presidential electors in 1840. Then agents from Missouri came to Illinois demanding the extradition of Joseph Smith (who had escaped from custody in that state). An Illinois state judge named Stephen Douglas, a prominent Democrat, ruled in the Prophet's favor and set him free. The grateful Saints returned to the Democratic fold in 1842. The Illinois Whig party leaders felt betrayed; the Democratic ones knew they could not really depend on the Mormons. The fact that the Mormons voted as a bloc did not surprise people, accustomed as they were to such political behavior. But contemporaries were not accustomed to a voting bloc that would go either way, as instructed. The Mormons seemed politically dangerous, because unreliable. Their prophet's temporal power aroused suspicion.

When the election of 1844 approached, Joseph Smith decided to run for president. (If the abolitionists could field a candidate, why not the Mormons?) The campaign seems to have had a place in the Prophet's vision of an earthly Kingdom of God that would precede and prepare for the Second Coming of Christ. If it failed, emigration might be necessary to establish the kingdom.[6] Such millennial expectations did not preclude policies sensible in secular terms. Smith's program included federal protection for civil liberties abridged by states and mobs; the reestablishment of a national bank; abolition of imprisonment for debt; the acquisition of not only Texas and Oregon but all of Mexico and Canada—provided the inhabitants peacefully consented; and encouragement for states to enact emancipation by providing masters compensation from federal land revenues.[7] The program combined moderate antislavery with Whig federal activism and Democratic expansionism. Whatever his program's merits, Smith's campaign persuaded many Gentiles that the Prophet had fallen into megalomania. In the event, of course, he did not live to participate in the election.

Joseph Smith was not the only American of his time to assert the gift of prophecy or teach the power of direct inspiration from God. Even after the publication of the Book of Mormon, the Saints could still affirm, in words Smith published in 1842, "We believe that He [God] will yet reveal many great and important things pertaining to the Kingdom of God," leaving it open whether this would be in the form of new books of scripture or other forms of inspiration (Article of Faith 9, Pearl of Great Price). The Quakers had long emphasized the Inner Light of divine guidance "which lighteth every man that cometh into the world" (John 1:9). While Joseph Smith prepared the Book of Mormon for publication, an elderly Quaker named Elias Hicks split the Society of Friends by declaring that the Inner Light, the inspiration of the individual, took precedence even over the scriptures. Hicks's followers, known as Hicksites, saw themselves reviving the spirit of the original seventeenth-century Quakers and rejecting compromise with modern worldliness. Theodore Parker, a radical antebellum Unitarian preacher, took the same line that the individual conscience superseded the authority of scripture, but based his argument on Transcendentalist romanticism rather than Quaker tradition. Closer to the role of Joseph Smith was the Seventh-Day Adventist prophet Ellen G. White. She had visions containing revelations, and her prolific writings are still revered by her community as divinely inspired, if not quite the equal of the scriptures.

One of the most dramatic American prophetic figures during Joseph Smith's generation was Nat Turner. This charismatic enslaved preacher worked in the fields by day, prophesying and healing by night and on weekends. His parents having taught him to read, Turner applied the teachings of the Hebrew prophets to the situation of his own people. He listened to "the Spirit that spoke to the prophets in former days" and heard the Spirit direct him to "proclaim liberty to the captives" and "the day of vengeance of our God" (Isaiah 61:1–2). This Spirit of the Lord instructed him that a millennium was "fast approaching" and that then the "first shall be last; and the last shall be first" (Matthew 19:30). Turner interpreted his visions as a call to rebellion. Starting on Monday, August 22, 1831, he led an unknown number of fellow blacks (mostly slaves, but a few of them free men) in a bloody uprising that killed some fifty-seven whites, mostly women and children, before being suppressed. More than twice as many blacks were killed in the fighting or massacred afterwards. Thirty rebels were tried and convicted, of whom twenty, including Turner himself, were executed. While in jail, Turner was interviewed by a white journalist, to whom he explained his premises and eschatological vision. "Do you not find yourself mistaken now?" asked the journalist. Turner's faith remained unshaken. He responded, "Was not Christ crucified?"[8]

The possession of a newly revealed scripture is often regarded as a distinctive attribute of Mormonism. Yet, even in this case, the Latter-day Saints are not completely unique. The historian can find other examples among the religions prevalent in the United States during the era of emergent Mormonism. A Shaker named Philemon Stewart published *A Holy, Sacred, and Divine Role and Book* in 1843, an addition to scripture that he claimed had been revealed to him by an angel who led him to a hillside where ancient plates were buried and who then supervised their translation into the idiom of the King James Bible over a two-week period. The work basically recapitulated the existing content of Shaker theology, including the place of Ann Lee as the Daughter of God. One cannot help wondering whether accounts of Joseph Smith's experiences influenced Stewart. In any case, Stewart did not enjoy the primacy in his community that Smith did in his; on the contrary, he gradually alienated the other Shakers. His scripture, originally well received by them, fell into disuse after a generation.[9] Nevertheless, the Shakers firmly retained and propagated the doctrine of individual inspiration. One exemplar was the free black woman evangelist Rebecca Cox Jackson; she started out as a Methodist exhorter and ended up leading an urban community of black Shaker women in Philadelphia.

Other claims to the miraculous translation of ancient plates, surely derived from the example of the Prophet Joseph Smith, came from the leaders of Mormon schismatic groups. James Colin Brewster published *A Warning to the Latter-day Saints: An Abridgment of the Ninth Book of Esdras in 1842*, with later amplifications. He predicted the fall of Nauvoo and the end of the world in 1878. James J. Strang published

The Book of the Law of the Lord in 1856. The Spiritualist lecturer Andrew Jackson Davis illustrates a different form of divine revelation. Davis went into trances. When in this altered state of consciousness he not only communicated with the spirits of dead persons but also received messages from God. In 1842, he published a collection of these inspirations: *The Principles of Nature, Her Divine Revelations, and a Voice to Mankind*. Davis long remained prominent in the Spiritualist movement, which has never entirely died out.

More powerfully influential was Mary Baker Eddy's *Science and Health with Key to the Scriptures* (1875 and later editions), continually revised by the author and still revered by the Christian Science denomination. Eddy did not claim a miraculous revelation, but her magnum opus is nevertheless considered inspired and a supplement to the Bible; she characterized her role in its creation as that of a scribe. As context for emergent Mormonism, the most important element in nineteenth-century American religious culture besides its sheer diversity was an openness to the prospect of continuous revelation or inspiration. Quakers, Shakers, Unitarians, Transcendentalists, African-American visionaries, Seventh-Day Adventists, Christian Scientists, Spiritualists, and others all agreed that God had not stopped communicating with humanity in ancient times.

Some of the religious communities of the young American republic did not shrink from experimenting with novel gender relationships. Mormons are famous for practicing plural marriage, which the Gentiles called polygamy, until 1890. Less well known is their pioneering of woman suffrage. The Perfectionist Community led by John Humphrey Noyes in Oneida, New York, practiced "complex marriage," in which every man was the husband of every woman, and every woman the wife of every man. Couples had to gain permission of the community as a whole before consummating their relationships. The Shakers, who worshipped Anne Lee as the Daughter of God, combined the practice of celibacy with a measure of feminism, according their women leadership roles. The Quakers, who separated the sexes during worship like Orthodox Jews, taught gender equality, approved women as ministers, and provided a host of early suffragists.

Consideration of the context of emergent Mormonism must take account of more than the religious environment. Critically important to that context were the revolutionary improvements in communications. The Book of Mormon could not have circulated so widely without the steam-powered printing press and the improvements in paper manufacturing that were also facilitating the rise of the novel. News of the Mormon movement and its persecutions could attract wide attention because of the proliferation of newspapers and, after 1844, telegraph lines. Mormon missionaries took advantage of inexpensive mass-produced tracts and the shorter times of transatlantic packet ship crossings.

In retrospect, early Mormonism seems very successfully adapted to the environment within which it originated. It emerged from a democratic culture characterized by freedom of expression, widespread literacy, absence of deference, and extreme religious pluralism. Religious movements sprang up from a populace accustomed by the Protestant Reformation to personal Bible reading. It was an innovative culture, in which startling claims and big ambitions did not put off audiences. Although Americans prided themselves on their individualism, in practice they readily followed revivalist preachers, joined associations both civil and religious, and enlisted in cooperative utopias. They took a lively interest in civic affairs and voted *en masse* along with their neighbors. The Latter-day Saints participated in such undertakings characteristic of antebellum America, and their leaders displayed an effective understanding of that culture.

NOTES

1. Jessee, *Papers of Joseph Smith*, 273. The two most detailed accounts of the First Vision are this 1838–39 version (272–75) and an 1832 version (5–7). See also Quinn, "Joseph Smith's Experience of a Methodist 'Camp Meeting.'"
2. Finney, *Lectures on Revivals of Religion*, 306.
3. Jessee, *Papers of Joseph Smith*, 7.
4. Guarneri, *Utopian Alternative*.
5. Arrington and Bitton, *Mormon Experience*, 50.
6. Hansen, *Quest for Empre*, 72–79; Hansen, "Metamorphosis of the Kingdom of God," 221–46.
7. Smith, *Views on the Powers and Policy of the Government of the United States*, 15–22.
8. Gray, *Confessions of Nat Turner*, 6, 10, 11.
9. Stein, "Story of the Shaker Bible," 347–76.

BIBLIOGRAPHY

Arrington, Leonard J., and Davis Bitton. *The Mormon Experience: A History of the Latter-day Saints*. New York: Alfred A. Knopf, 1979.

Brooke, John. *The Refiner's Fire: The Making of Mormon Cosmology, 1644–1844*. Cambridge: Cambridge University Press, 1994.

Finney, Charles G. *Lectures on Revivals of Religion*. Ed. Wiliam McLoughlin. Cambridge, MA: Harvard University Press, 1960.

Gray, Thomas. *Confessions of Nat Turner . . . Fully and Voluntarily Made to Thomas Gray*. Petersburg, VA: 1881. (Originally published in 1831.)

Guarneri, Carl. *The Utopian Alternative: Fourierism in Nineteenth-Century America*. Ithaca, NY: Cornell University Press, 1991.

Hansen, Klaus J. "The Metamorphosis of the Kingdom of God." In *The New Mormon History*, ed. D. Michael Quinn, 221–46. Salt Lake City: Signature, 1992.

Hansen, Klaus J. *Mormonism and the American Experience*. Chicago: University of Chicago Press, 1981.

Hansen, Klaus J. *Quest for Empire*. Lansing: Michigan State University Press, 1967.

Holland, David F. *Sacred Borders: Continuing Revelation and Canonical Restraint in Early America*. New York: Oxford University Press, 2011.

Howe, Daniel Walker. *What Hath God Wrought: The Transformation of America, 1815–1848*. New York: Oxford University Press, 2007.

Jessee, Dean C., ed. *Papers of Joseph Smith*. Vol. 1, *Autobiographical and Historical Writings*. Salt Lake City: Deseret, 1989.

Maffly-Kipp, Laurie F., ed. *American Scriptures: An Anthology of Sacred Writings*. New York: Penguin, 2010.

Oates, Stephen. *Fires of Jubilee: Nat Turner's Fierce Rebellion*. New York: New American Library, 1976.

Quinn, D. Michael. *Early Mormonism and the Magic World View*. Salt Lake City: Signature, 1987.

Quinn, D. Michael. "Joseph Smith's Experience of a Methodist 'Camp Meeting' in 1820." *Dialogue Paperless*, E-Paper #3, Expanded Version (Definitive). December 20, 2006. http://www.dialoguejournal.com/wp-content/uploads/2010/04/QuinnPaperless.pdf.

Smith, Joseph. *Views on the Powers and Policy of the Government of the United States*. Salt Lake City, 1886; written in 1844.

Stein, Stephen J. "America's Bibles: Canon, Commentary, and Continuity." *Church History* 64 (1995): 169–84.

Stein, Stephen J. *The Shaker Experience in America: A History of the United Society of Believers*. New Haven, CT: Yale University Press, 1992.

Stein, Stephen J . "The Story of the Shaker Bible." *Proceedings of the American Antiquarian Society* 105, no. 2 (October 1995): 347–76.

Underwood, Grant. *The Millenarian World of Early Mormonism*. Urbana: University of Illinois Press, 1993.

CHAPTER 3

··

THE MORMON CHURCH
IN UTAH

··

W. PAUL REEVE

THE Mormon abandonment of Nauvoo, Illinois, in 1846, comprised a mass migration of an entire people. Roughly 12,000 religious refugees deliberately, and with considerable pathos, walked away from brick homes, log cabins, fences, barns, outbuildings, and community structures. It was an exodus of biblical proportions which stretched across an eight-month period culminating in the violent expulsion of the remaining poor Saints by September of that year. Some were leaving their second or third home since joining this upstart and unpopular religion. But even more than hard-won homes, it was leaving their temple that most fully embodied a collective sense of sacrifice and sorrow.

It was the most substantial religious edifice the Mormons had constructed to date, a stately structure with a limestone exterior perched on a bluff overlooking the Mississippi River and the town of Nauvoo. When the Mormons arrived at the site of their future city in 1839 they did so as refugees, fleeing a violent expulsion from Missouri and a state-sanctioned extermination order. At Nauvoo they rebuilt their homes, their lives, and their faith. Their leader Joseph Smith introduced new ideas about the corporeal nature of God, humankind's potential to be like Him, new temple rituals patterned after Masonic rites, and most controversially he introduced polygamy to a select inner circle of followers, a new doctrine that would ultimately lead to his martyrdom in June 1844. In the background to these events, but central to the Saints' expanding cosmology, the temple reached slowly heavenward, a product of sweat, sacrifice, financial donations, and communal labor.

Although Smith did not live to see it completed, for the Saints he left behind, the temple stood as a solid and imposing witness of their devotion to their God and even more deeply, it represented their longings to be in His presence. Above the temple's single tower rose a weather vane which featured a horizontal angel sounding a trump. It was an artistic rendering that for some Mormons symbolized Moroni, the same angel whom Joseph Smith claimed led him to buried gold plates from which he translated the Book of Mormon. In a vigorous east wind, the angel's trump would have pointed the way west for the beleaguered Saints, across the Louisiana Purchase territory, still mostly Native American controlled, and from there outside the political boundaries of the United States, into Northern Mexico.

More than sounding a message of gospel outreach in 1846, the angel's trump signaled the call for retreat and a search for refuge. It was a decided Mormon withdrawal from the outside world and a flight from secular time. As the Mormons trekked west across Native American territory and breached an international boundary, they simultaneously inserted themselves into the biblical narrative. They became ancient Israelites, born anew as sons and daughters of Abraham, heirs to a literal lineage upon covenanting to follow Jesus. Their removal was both geographic and spiritual, withdrawing into the isolation of the Great Basin and also into sacred time and space.

Soon after arriving in the Great Basin, the Mormons made plans to build a new temple at the heart of their desert Zion, a structure so grand that it took forty years to complete. The Salt Lake Temple and the surrounding Temple Square quickly became the spiritual, emotional, and geographic center of Mormonism and the iconic symbol of their religious kingdom in retreat. When the temple was completed in 1893, a standing angel Moroni faced east atop its highest spire, in symbolic welcome to the returning Jesus whom the premillennial Mormons anticipate will come from the east at His second advent and usher in a thousand years of peace. Yet Moroni also looked east that year in a hopeful gaze back toward the United States, the nation that the Mormons had fled only forty-seven years earlier. It was a dramatically different geopolitical view than the Saints encountered on their trek to the Great Basin. The railroad and telegraph now permanently connected them to the outside world and new states and territories had been carved out of the Louisiana Purchase and Mexican cession to crowd the Mormons and even whittle away at Utah's borders. With strict geographic isolation no longer possible and federal pressure nearly crushing in its weight, Moroni's trump this time sent a conciliatory signal of a newfound Mormon willingness to reenter secular time and space, and to abandon the two elements of Mormonism that Protestant America found most anathema to American values, polygamy and theocracy. In 1893, Moroni trumpeted that intent to a still-skeptical but hopeful nation. Three years later, Utah was admitted into the sisterhood of states and a rocky Mormon assimilation process was under way.

The westward-facing Nauvoo Temple and the eastward-facing Moroni at Salt Lake City signal both the Mormon withdrawal and subsequent reengagement with the world that serve as bookends for this chapter. In the period between, Mormonism developed the policies, practices, attitudes, and cultural attributes that came to typify the Utah Church in the nineteenth century and impact its form and function into the twentieth and twenty-first centuries. The Utah church that emerged from this crucible was in many ways in transition as it entered the twentieth century, from communalism to capitalism, from polygamy to monogamy, from Old Testament Israelites to New Testament Christians, and from despised outcasts and racialized un-Americans to flag-waving, apple-pie-eating, teetotaling, über-Americans with a racial policy of their own. The transformation was gradual but stunning.

EXODUS, GATHERING, AND WITHDRAWAL

When the Mormons abandoned Nauvoo in 1846 they left not just their homes; they left the country whose ideals of religious pluralism and freedom were enshrined in the free-exercise clause of the First Amendment. The Mormons had already forced Protestant America to test the boundaries of that clause in frontier practice, and eventually they would force Congress and the Supreme Court to test it in legal principle. As the Mormons trudged across Iowa and Indian country, the lessons of their short history must have resonated with every step, that contact with the outside world worked decidedly to their disadvantage. They would therefore sever ties with the outside world and establish a religious kingdom isolated from Euro-American settlement and anchored in a restorationist cosmology.

The Great Basin became sacred space for Mormons and the new gathering place for its global missionary outreach. It was an isolated desert Zion, which included some of the driest expanses in the continental United States. In Brigham Young's mind it was "a good place to make Saints." He saw the benefit of an inhospitable region in both keeping outsiders away and sifting the wavering from the devout: "My soul feels hallelujah, it exults in God, that He has planted this people in a place that is not desired by the wicked; for if the wicked come here they do not wish to stay, no matter how well they are treated, and I thank the Lord for it. I want hard times," Young insisted, "so that every person that does not wish to stay, for the sake of his religion, will leave." Young was satisfied with the Great Basin as "the place the Lord has appointed," and announced his intent to "stay here" until Jesus told the Saints "to go somewhere else."[1]

The first pioneers arrived in July of 1847 and by the spring of 1848 Young announced the Salt Lake valley as the new gathering place for Mormon proselytes: "To all saints in England, Scotland, Ireland, Wales and adjacent islands and countries, we say emigrate as speedily as possible to this vicinity."[2] A follow-up announcement tapped into an Israelite identity: "The long looked for time of gathering has come. Good tidings from Mount Zion! The resting place of Israel, for the last days, has been discovered."[3]

The nineteenth-century doctrine of gathering became a central tenet of the faith and proved a crucial element in unifying Mormonism's scattered flock. Conversion to Mormonism meant much more than changing where one worshipped on Sunday. For many Mormons it dictated an international migration, a new climate and culture, and a conscious decision to abandon the perceived corrupting influences of Babylon. It brought together disparate Saints from a largely northern and western European harvest and made them into Mormons. It was an important element in forging a group identity, especially in distinguishing Latter-day Saints from Gentiles. The doctrine tightened internal bonds in direct correlation to seemingly constant opposition from without. As some historians have argued, it forged a new ethnicity out of a multicultural and polyglot people.

Mormon leaders urged a new identity upon a sometimes divided flock. In 1852, for example, two Mormon apostles, Erastus Snow and Franklin Richards, visited a struggling economic mission sent to southern Utah to produce iron. They reported "considerable excitement" among the iron missionaries over problems of integrating former iron workers from Wales and Pennsylvania. To the visiting authorities it seemed that the missionaries were divided along cultural lines and lacked unity and a common purpose. Snow wrote: "we found a Scotch party, a Welch party, an English party, and an American party, and we turned Iron Masters and undertook to put all these through the furnace, and run out a party of Saints for building up the Kingdom of God." Although Snow does not specify the means for such a process, broadly speaking it included the elevation of a Mormon identity above any other.[4]

It was a process that continued throughout the nineteenth century and signaled the Mormon effort to unify its people. In 1856, Jedediah M. Grant put it succinctly: "I like to see the English, the Scotch, Welsh, French, Danes, and men from every nation, kindred, tongue, and people, come forth and unite under the standard of truth, obey God and be one."[5] In the sermons at least, the Saints' Mormon identity transcended former national and cultural ties and created a new sense of peoplehood.

Still, the failed Deseret alphabet, foreign-language worship services and newspapers, nationalistic celebrations and holidays, as well as public services available in foreign languages, all suggest that the desired assimilation had its limits. It raises intriguing questions about the development of a distinctive Mormon identity and the impact that it might have had upon foreign immigrants. What impact did immigrants have upon a developing Mormon ethnicity? Did they view themselves as Mormons first or did their Scotch, Irish, Swedish, or English cultural roots dominate? In what ways did Mormonism shape the immigrant populations and in what ways did the immigrants shape Mormonism?

Because the gathering has dominated the story of the Utah church, the history of post-1847 Mormonism focuses on Salt Lake City and the Mormon colonization of the intermountain West. It is a focus, however, that leaves the story of the ungathered Saints unexplored. What did it mean to be a Mormon in the nineteenth century if one stayed in Wales or Denmark or Scotland, or New Jersey or in the postbellum American South? Was it possible to forge a Mormon identity in small and isolated settings? What impact did staying behind have upon ritual, worship, and unity with those in the Great Basin? What did it mean for the international church when the significant strength of a congregation had gathered to Utah? Telling the story of the ungathered will deepen the traditional story and further complicate the ways in which historians think about the emergence of a Mormon ethnicity.

Gathering and colonizing the Great Basin was intimately intertwined with concern for the poor and less fortunate. Public works projects, economic missions, such as the Iron and Cotton missions, Zion's Cooperative Mercantile Institution (ZCMI), United Order efforts, and monthly fasts with corresponding offerings to the poor were all facets of an economic withdrawal and evidence of ways in which Mormons attempted to insulate themselves from harsh market fluctuations. These initiatives were also components of the Mormon effort to achieve economic self-sufficiency and create an egalitarian society with no poor among them. Of course their efforts met with varying success, but even failures serve as evidence of a commitment to communitarian ideals.

Those ideals insisted that even the unfit, the poor, and the needy should gather to Zion and if they could not afford to do so, communal concern would provide a solution. For the gathering, that solution took the form of the Perpetual Emigrating Fund Company (PEF), a revolving micro lender. It provided financial assistance to poor Saints gathering to Zion with the understanding that they would pay back the loan after arrival. Repayment would then fund a new immigrant's opportunity.

Although the PEF ran heavily in debt due to the failure of many to repay, it nonetheless assisted thousands of Mormon converts to make their way to the Great Basin. To cut expenses, Mormon leaders in 1856 launched a new and subsequently storied version of emigration via handcarts. In lieu of more expensive horses or oxen the converts would walk to Zion pulling their meager possessions in the two-wheeled carts. Ten handcart companies made their way to Utah between 1856 and 1860, bringing roughly 3,000 Mormons to the Salt Lake Valley, only a small fraction of the estimated 70,000 Mormon immigrants who traveled to Utah before the completion of the transcontinental railroad in 1869.

In Mormon memory, however, the handcart migration has grown to occupy a disproportionate position. Handcarts have come to stand in for all forms of migration, and the two handcart tragedies, those of the James G. Willie and Edward Martin companies, have come to stand in for all migrant companies. In 1856, the Willie and Martin companies left late in the season with green handcarts and were subsequently caught in an early Wyoming blizzard. Around 200 members of the two companies died before rescuers arrived.

In Mormon memory, the suffering and privation of those handcart pioneers symbolize faith in adversity and fortitude against great odds. In the twenty-first century, Mormon youth groups and congregations go on scripted handcart pulls, and during summer months as many as 3,000 Mormons a week travel to Martin's Cove, Wyoming, to camp, square dance, and pull handcarts in an effort to connect to a constructed version of sacred history. Handcart treks have become nearly universal rites of passage for youth groups in the United States and sometimes internationally, even though the vast majority of nineteenth-century Mormons emigrated via other means and even though the majority of those who came via handcart did not endure tragedies like those of the Willie and Martin companies.

ENGAGEMENT AND INTEGRATION

For as much as the Mormons sought isolation, it was never fully possible. The dynamic that most powerfully shaped the Mormon Utah experience involved a complex and shifting tension between isolation and separation on the one hand and the desire for

acceptance, belonging, and inclusion on the other. The one demanded severing of political, economic, social, and geographic ties, the other dictated engagement and contact in
a protracted search for self-determination and religious liberty, a search that included
seven applications for statehood and considerable wrangling with the federal government as well as with "Gentiles" or non-Mormons.

The first evidence of the impossibility of complete separation came even as the
Mormons fled the United States in 1846. The US war with Mexico erupted as the
Mormons were stretched in camps across Iowa. Reaction to its outbreak offers a unique
glimpse into Mormon views of the nation they were then leaving. One Mormon, Hosea
Stout, learned in May of the outbreak of war with Mexico and recorded his feelings in his
diary: "I confess that I was glad to learn of war against the United States and was in hopes
that it might never end until they were entirely destroyed for they had driven us into the
wilderness & was now laughing at our calamities."[6]

To add insult to injury, Captain James Allen, a US Army recruiter, appeared with
authorization to enlist 500 men to serve in the US war against Mexico. When Stout
learned of this development, he saw it as a plot to harm the Mormons. If they did not
join, it would reinforce suspicions of their disloyalty and brand them "as enemies to our
country," and if they did enlist, Stout surmised, "they would then have 500 of our men in
their power to be destroyed as they had done our leaders at Carthage."[7] Other Mormons
expressed similar reactions, with Abraham Day perhaps the most succinct when he
wrote, "Here is one man who will not go, dam'um."[8]

Unbeknown to those on the ground, Allen's recruitment efforts were actually the fruit
of negotiations between President James K. Polk and Mormon agent Jessie Little. Little
had requested federal aid to assist the Mormon exodus, and the enlistment opportunity
resulted from his efforts. Brigham Young recognized the financial boon the enlistment
represented and he in turn ensured that Mormons filled the 500-man quota.

Here then, at the very moment of their flight from the United States, the Mormons
agreed to enlist in the US Army. It is a moment that captures the central paradox of
the Mormon experience in the Great Basin, the desire for autonomy coexisting with the
desire for belonging. To be sure there was a significant amount of self-interest bound
up in the Mormon enlistment, but the Mormons nonetheless were fond of reminding
federal officials of their service in the war with Mexico as evidence of their loyalty to
the nation, especially when they felt the crushing weight of federal power bearing down
upon them. Ultimately, those competing forces found expression in multiple applications for Utah statehood. Statehood offered sovereignty, especially in the antebellum
period, and autonomy to define marriage laws. Statehood also meant equal footing in
the sisterhood of states.

Historians debate the degree and nature of Mormon desires for separation, with some
suggesting it was a full-blown effort at political and religious independence, an independent Mormon theocracy, or even an effort at "world dominion."[9] Others view a more
nuanced and complex relationship with federal authority, one that captures both the
Mormon desire to establish a godly kingdom in preparation for Christ's imminent return,
and the Mormons' vision of themselves as the true preservers of republican principles. In

1852, Brigham Young expressed his devotion to the Declaration of Independence and Constitution as "the safe guard of our liberties, and for our protection. We not only cordially support its principles, but will defend it with our utmost endeavors, physical, or otherwise, whenever required."[10] By 1856, however, Young grew dissatisfied with the federal territorial system, announcing to a Mormon congregation, "I say, as the Lord lives, we are bound to become a sovereign State in the Union, or an independent nation by ourselves, and let them drive us from this place if they can; they cannot do it."[11]

Too frequently such statements are taken out of context, both from the entirety of a speech, and from the broader history of the US West. Young's speech in 1856, for example, was laced with Mormon millenarian references suggesting that in due course earthly power did not matter because Jesus would return and assume control: "Those who vote for Jesus will be on the right hand, and those who vote for Lucifer on the left. . . . We are going to vote for the sovereign we believe in; and when he comes behold he will go into the chair of state and take the reins of government." Young predicted that "Jesus Christ will be the President, and we are his officers."[12] It was Jesus to whom Young swore final loyalty. Republicans and Democrats were irrelevant in his cosmic vision. Young viewed his call as a divine mandate to preserve an embattled people, mold them into Saints, and with them establish God's kingdom on earth in anticipation of Jesus' return.

From the outside looking in, however, the sometimes fiery Mormon rhetoric sounded alarm bells and touched off fears of treason and rebellion. Mormon William I. Appleby had difficulty understanding that response. He wrote to Brigham Young from New York, in October 1857, as federal troops marched on Utah and a reported Mormon rebellion commanded national attention: "There is a great excitement here in relation to Utah, and any news from that quarter is sought after with great anxiety by press and people, and the cry is *down with the Mormons, use them up,* *blot them out*' &c." What perplexed Appleby most was a lack of understanding about Mormon devotion to the United States. "They do not know the Mormons[;] they are the best friends of this Government, its constitution, and its laws, and feel willing to protect and defend them," he explained. Appleby made a distinction between the Constitution and those who administered it and, like Young, placed his utmost trust in God: "I love my country and its constitution, but I hate and despise demagogues. Come what will, all is well and all is right with those who put their trust in their god, and relies upon his Almighty arm."[13] In essence, Mormons swore allegiance to the Constitution and the United States even as they saw its governments as corrupt and oppressive.

Because the Mormon desire for self-determination was frequently couched in religious language, historians have sometimes exaggerated its exceptional aspects and failed to situate the Mormon experience within the broader history of the US West. In fact, the American West was rife with calls for self-rule, especially as many westerners viewed the territorial system as oppressive, little better than the British colonialism that Americans had overthrown. The appointment of outsiders to territorial positions was particularly troubling in the West. In 1869, for example, when James M. Ashley, former congressman from Toledo, Ohio, was appointed governor of Montana Territory, *The Independent* of Deer Lodge, Montana, called Ashley a "carpet-bagger" and a "broken down political hack." The newspaper wondered "how long are the people to be scorned and insulted by being told, by implication at least, that there is not one among the thirty thousand free-men of Montana who is capable of discharging the functions of the executive office?"[14] That same year, in a more general criticism about the territorial system, the *Idaho Statesman* expressed frustration over political neglect and ignorance of the West: the "Committee on Territories is composed of men, who with one or two exceptions, never saw a Territory, much less lived in one long enough to appreciate its peculiar necessities."[15] Mormons, in other words, were far from unique in their desire for self-rule or in their frustration with the territorial system. It was when the Mormons mixed their frustrations with sometimes bombastic religious rhetoric and strident defenses of polygamy that politicians in Washington, DC, and the Protestant majority in America resisted.

In no case was this truer than that of the Utah War. By 1857, United States president James Buchanan became convinced that Utah Territory under Governor Brigham Young was in a state of rebellion. Without communicating his intent, Buchanan determined to replace Young as governor, send a 2,500-man army to Utah to suppress rebellion, and install new territorial officials. Young, in turn, viewed the advancing army through a glass darkly and filtered through previous persecution. He treated the troops as an invading army. The result was an avoidable episode that grew into the most extensive and expensive military operation between the US war with Mexico and the Civil War, and it was aimed at American citizens. Cooler heads eventually prevailed and the conflict ended with no pitched battles between Mormons and federal forces, but the heightened atmosphere proved deadly for groups whom the Mormons became convinced were allied with government forces or whom they demonized as the enemy.

The Mountain Meadows Massacre was the most bloody of the violent episodes to grow out of the Utah War. Southern Utah Mormons induced members of the Baker-Fancher party, a group of immigrants passing through Utah on their way to California, to give up their weapons under a flag of truce and then murdered them after promising protection. Mormons killed 120 innocent men, women, and children, on September 11, 1857. Postmassacre justifications focused upon the provocative nature of the Baker-Fancher party's interactions with Mormons at Cedar City. They included accounts of the emigrant party insulting Mormon leaders, speaking provokingly of prior atrocities committed against Mormons, or suggesting that they would send an army to Utah from California after they arrived. Those stories, if nothing else, only confirm the heightened sense of fear that permeated southern Utah in the face of an impending federal invasion. Those fears led southern Utah leaders from one bad decision to the next until they became convinced that the Baker-Fancher party was a threat to their continued safety and needed to be destroyed.

Since 1857, Mormons, government investigators, descendants of the victims and of the perpetrators, as well as historians have struggled to understand such horrific violence, made more difficult to explain because it involved whites killing whites, with no easy racial answer self-evident. Adding to the complexity of the issue, especially for subsequent generations of Mormons, is the effort to understand how their pioneer co-religionists could violate fundamental aspects of the Christian gospel, the divine mandate to "renounce war and proclaim peace" (Doctrine and Covenants [D&C] 98:16), to rescue and aid the less fortunate, to turn the other cheek, and to "forgive all men" (D&C 64:10). Instead, Mormons at Mountain Meadows lied and murdered in a cowardly manner and then attempted to cover their crimes with silence and blame shifting.

While historians generally agree on a timeline, their interpretations and explanations of events vary widely. Where Juanita Brooks described the massacre as a tragic byproduct of the Utah War and an overzealous response to the impending federal invasion, Will Bagley sees it as the natural outgrowth of a Mormon "culture of violence."[16] More recently Ronald Walker, Richard Turley, and Glen Leonard situate the decisions for the massacre in southern Utah. They see events spiraling out of control as hot-headed southern leaders linked the Baker-Fancher party with federal troops and dehumanized them as an enemy in need of elimination.[17]

Much of the contention animating massacre historiography centers upon the extent of Young's involvement. Historians also debate the nature of Southern Paiute participation in the siege and at the massacre. Those controversies, however, cloud more difficult questions, especially because no single narrative will satisfy the various constituencies who are so heavily invested in the event. Although no evidence to date implicates Young in ordering the massacre, the full complexity of moral responsibility and the heightened sense of obedience to authority that created an atmosphere ripe for deterioration into fanaticism remains underexplored. The bombastic sermons from the Mormon Reformation of 1856–57 hung heavily in the air, especially talk of blood atonement and harsh language aimed at apostates and backsliders. Factor in the failure to hold accountable the perpetrators of the Santa Clara ambush and the Parish-Potter murders, or at the very least to denounce those events as clear violations of the standards expected of Latter-day Saints, and then add in an impending federal invasion with Mormon memories of previous persecutions, and the stage was set.

Why did not more southern Utah Mormons refuse the order to murder? What did the Mormon culture of obedience look like and what did those in southern Utah believe that disobedience might mean? Questions also remain regarding the postmassacre cover-up. How might the impact of the massacre been different if justice stern and severe had been meted out to the perpetrators? John D. Lee was the only participant held accountable for the massacre when he was tried and then executed by firing squad in 1877. While Mormon-federal tension complicated the issue, a clear denunciation of the massacre from LDS leaders could have sent a strong message that those involved not only violated the law, but the standards of what it meant to be a Latter-day Saint. Absent such decisive messages, the massacre remained a taboo topic, at least until Juanita Brooks wrote about it in 1950, to the discomfort of some Latter-day Saints. It was not until 2007 that the LDS Church officially addressed the event in its publications. In 2011 the massacre site was designated a National Historic Landmark, a move that may neutralize ongoing tension over who controls the land and how to memorialize the victims.

Following the Utah War, federal troops remained in Utah. Although those troops were quickly called east at the outbreak of the Civil War, President Abraham Lincoln did not fully trust the Mormons. Replacement forces, volunteers from California, established Fort Douglas on the bench overlooking Salt Lake City and formed a permanent federal presence in the territory. Still, the end of the Utah War marked a shift in federal policy toward the Mormons, away from a military solution to a legislative and judicial solution. Congress largely viewed Mormon polygamy and theocracy as a two-headed monster and was intent upon severing both heads. The first antipolygamy legislation passed Congress in 1862. Over the ensuing nearly three decades, Congress proposed and sometimes passed legislation designed to force a Mormon surrender and ultimately to make the Latter-day Saints into acceptable Americans. The Mormons in turn claimed protection for polygamy as a religious principle under the free-exercise clause of the Constitution. Congress maintained its role as gatekeeper, making it clear that Mormonism did not fit prevailing ideals about what it meant to be an American.

The Supreme Court weighed in on the matter in 1879, in *United States v. Reynolds*, a decision which denied a constitutional shield for polygamy. The court held unanimously that the Constitution protected religious belief, not practice, and thereby paved the way for increasingly stringent federal action.

The Reynolds decision ushered in an era of Mormon civil disobedience, which pushed polygamists into hiding in an elaborate "underground" network of safe houses designed to shield them from arrest. It was only in 1890, after the Supreme Court opened the door for the confiscation of LDS temple properties, that Mormon resolve weakened. LDS president Wilford Woodruff articulated the difficult choice he faced between two important elements of Mormon religious life, temples and polygamy. For Mormons temples represent the highest manifestation of their devotion to their God, and when the government threatened to confiscate the St. George, Manti, and Logan temples, Woodruff blinked. On September 24, 1890, he announced the Manifesto, declaring his intention to submit to the law of the land and to use his influence with his Mormon flock to "have them do likewise" (D&C Official Declaration 1). Mormon leadership also adopted the national two-party political system. In the wake of these reforms, two US presidents issued successive proclamations of amnesty and in 1896 President Grover Cleveland proclaimed Utah the forty-fifth state.

Linking the abandonment of polygamy to statehood, however, obscures the real tradeoff. There was no quid pro quo agreement between the federal government and Mormon leaders, no trading polygamy for statehood. For almost forty years after they outlawed polygamy, Congress had consistently impressed upon the Mormons the necessity of abandoning it, but Mormons still clung tenaciously to "the Principle." Even after Woodruff issued the Manifesto, statehood was still almost six years away. The most immediate tradeoff was internal, the abandonment of polygamy to preserve temple worship.

Even with temples hanging in the balance, the abandonment of polygamy was wrenching, especially for individual Mormons who had sacrificed to defend it and who now had to find new paths forward. The federal government was generally willing to let existing plural marriages die out so long as new marriages did not take place. Although federal authorities did expect Mormons to stop "cohabitating" with plural wives, they did not punish offenders with the same zeal as before the Manifesto.

For polygamous Mormons it was a bewildering new world without clear directives from LDS leaders. Some Mormons breathed a sigh of relief that the long tension with the federal government was coming to an end. Others viewed Woodruff's manifesto as a capitulation to political pressure and labeled him a fallen prophet; they refused to abandon polygamy. B. Carmon Hardy has documented over 200 cases of post-Manifesto plural marriage, including those of seven members of the Quorum of Twelve Apostles. Still others refused to abandon existing families and continued to cohabit with plural wives. Even church president Joseph F. Smith pled guilty to unlawful cohabitation in 1906, and was fined $300. The transformation was dramatic, from monogamy to polygamy and back to monogamy in less than seventy years.

The Americanization process was still not complete and polygamy still not fully ended. When Utahns elected polygamist B. H. Roberts to the US House of Representatives in 1898, Congress refused to seat him. The real test came, however, in 1903 when Reed Smoot, a monogamist and sitting LDS apostle, was elected to the US Senate. Charges of continuing plural marriage, devotion to priestly rule over devotion to the Constitution, and church control of politics in Utah promoted Senate hearings that stretched over three years and put the entire Mormon church on trial. In the end Smoot retained his seat, but the hearings forced the hand of LDS leadership. Joseph F. Smith ducked and weaved in his testimony before the Senate and then issued what historians refer to as the "Second Manifesto." He proclaimed excommunication as the penalty for future plural marriages. Two particularly determined defenders of polygamy, sitting LDS apostles Matthias Cowley and John W. Taylor, were dropped from the Quorum, and after 1910 the church actively excommunicated those entering plural marriage, a policy it continues in the twenty-first century. Splinter groups committed to the continuation of polygamy emerged from this context, forming their own churches.

Polygamy, once preached as the ideal marriage system and taught as a sacrament essential for exaltation, was difficult to leave behind. Contemporary Mormon sensitivity to polygamy stems from a variety of concerns. Feminist sensibilities, genuine abhorrence of the practice, and the ever-present concern among Mormon leaders for the public image of the faith cultivate a desire to dismiss lingering misperceptions that Mormon men in the twenty-first century have more than one wife. The HBO series *Big Love*, which ran from 2006 to 2011, along with reality television shows, add to the confusion, as does news attention given to fundamentalist splinter groups which continue to practice polygamy outside of the LDS Church.

A STRUGGLE FOR WHITENESS

Historians most frequently characterize the nineteenth-century Utah experience as an Americanization process, whereby Mormons shed polygamy and theocracy in a struggle for statehood and broader acceptance. While that characterization is accurate, it obscures the ways in which the Mormon story can be recast as a struggle for whiteness. Like other marginalized groups in the nineteenth century, the Protestant white majority racialized Mormons as somehow less than white. The racialization that Mormons endured never reached the same level as that employed against African Americans, but fell somewhere between hard racism and full acceptance.

Whiteness in the nineteenth century meant access to power, acceptability, and the full privileges of citizenship. Senator John C. Calhoun, in late 1847, asserted on the floor of the US Senate that America "is the Government of a white race."[18] It was a sentiment consistently reinforced in policy and practice even after the Civil War and the end of Reconstruction, when white Southerners reinstated racial supremacy through Jim Crow laws and the Supreme Court stamped its approval on the idea of "separate but equal." Within that broader and shifting racial context, outsiders looked at the Mormon body and concluded that Mormons were not just religiously, but physically different; as such they were unfit for the blessings of democracy.

The most explicit and provocative enunciation of this racialization came from two medical doctors whose reports were widely distributed in medical journals. In 1860, Dr. Roberts Bartholow, a US Army doctor, argued that Mormon polygamy was giving rise to a "new race," so degraded, deformed, and degenerate that one could "distinguish" it "at a glance."[19] Three years later, Dr. Charles C. Furley likewise described the Mormon body as "mean and sensual to the point of absolute ugliness."[20] Other observers conflated white Mormons with Indians, blacks, and Asians in a process designed to justify discriminatory policies against Mormons and suggest that they were more like the other "undesirable" groups than they were white.

Mormons were aware of these assertions and responded with a racialized rhetoric of their own. In 1868, Mormon leader George Q. Cannon insisted that "here in these [Utah] valleys, we shall raise a race of men who will be the joy of the earth, whose complexions will be the complexions of angels."[21] Neither side questioned that a marriage system could give rise to a new race, they only debated its outcome. It is a powerful commentary on race as a social construct and on the shifting, fluid, and frequently illogical way in which nineteenth-century Americans imagined it.

The racialization of Mormons places Mormonism's own troubled history with race in a different light. When the Mormons arrived in the Great Basin in 1847 there was no racial priesthood policy in place. Blacks were among the earliest converts to Mormonism and at least two black men were ordained to the Mormon priesthood prior to 1847. One of the ordinations, that of Elijah Abel, was sanctioned by Joseph Smith, himself. Abel served at least three proselytizing missions for the church and remained devout throughout his life.

It was Brigham Young in 1852 who publicly announced a priesthood restriction based upon his belief that blacks belonged to a divinely cursed lineage traceable through Cain and Ham. In doing so, Young borrowed from long-standing Judeo-Christian ideas that predated Mormonism by several centuries. Young and other Mormon leaders employed those ideas to their own ends. In a self-reinforcing process that stretched across the course of the nineteenth century they created and then reinforced race-based priesthood and temple restrictions. In 1908 LDS president Joseph F. Smith solidified those restrictions with a false memory that forgot the black priesthood holders of the early church and wrongly suggested that the ban had always been in place. LDS leaders thereby distanced the institutional church from its own black converts. It was a process that repeated itself outside Mormonism in a variety of ways as white Americans across the nation reasserted supremacy in the wake of black freedom.

Fear of interracial mixing also permeated nineteenth-century America and took form in a variety of miscegenation laws. Utah's 1852 "servant" code included a clause prohibiting "any white person" from "sexual intercourse with any of the African race." Brigham Young further declared to a Mormon audience in 1863 that "If the white man who belongs to the chosen seed mixes his blood with the seed of Cain, the penalty, under the law of God, is death on the spot." Such alarm over race mixing made Young more American than uniquely Mormon, especially as Americans moved to enforce racial separation in the aftermath of the Civil War and black freedom. In Arkansas, as legislators there contemplated the issue, one lawmaker argued for a provision that stipulated "if any white man shall be found cohabiting with a negro woman, the penalty shall be death." Even some Native American tribes distanced themselves from blacks. The Choctaw General Council declared it a felony for a Choctaw to marry a black, while Creek leaders stated that it was "a disgrace to our nation for our people to marry a Negro."

In essence, marginalized groups across the nation clamored for position on America's hierarchical racial ladder, Mormons included. The Mormon struggle for whiteness occurred in the face of its own racialization at the hands of outsiders, especially as outsiders came to view polygamy as not just a threat to the traditional family, but a threat to the white race. Political cartoons featured a black wife among a Mormon man's "harem," or black children as the offspring of polygamy. One antipolygamy writer even turned the mark of Cain back on the Mormons, a sign of the degenerative effects of polygamy upon women: "Especially do the first wives seem to carry the signs of care and sorrow,—a mark of Cain, as it were, which separates them from the rest of their kind. It is perceptible to even the most transient visitors, and those who tarry for any length of time can readily distinguish a Mormon woman from an outsider."

The irony here is that by the turn of the century Utah had already adopted its own antimiscegenation law and Mormons barred black men from the priesthood and black women and men from LDS temple worship. While membership remained open to people of all races, the highest sacraments of Mormonism were in essence segregated. These internal policies took shape against a backdrop in which outsiders portrayed Mormons as racially impure. The Mormon response was an attempt to claim whiteness for Mormonism that solidified into a racial policy by the early twentieth century and did not end until 1978.

TEMPLES AND LIVED RELIGION

While Mormonism's ongoing tension with the United States offers a compelling way of viewing the major events engaging the Utah Church, it simultaneously neglects Mormonism's internal development: transitions and changes in ritual, the creation of new organizational programs, the shedding of doctrines, and aspects of Mormon lived religion, all of which directly impacted the average Saint in the nineteenth century.

Wilford Woodruff, for example, not only issued the Manifesto ending polygamy but also ended the law of adoption, a practice unfamiliar to most modern-day Mormons. In its place, Woodruff instituted genealogy and family history, something that grew into a central tenet of Mormonism in the twentieth century. Charismatic gifts of the spirit such as speaking in tongues also transitioned over time. Those gifts attracted some converts to early Mormonism and found continued and vibrant expression in the Great Basin. Their practice, however, diminished and all but disappeared after the turn of the twentieth century. Modern Mormons tend to think of the gift of tongues as divine help for missionaries learning a foreign language rather than a spiritual manifestation in worship. Female ritual healing also diminished, as did baptisms for health and rebaptisms in general. Brigham Young's ideas about blood atonement were formally rejected in an 1889 First Presidency manifesto, and Young's successors distanced themselves from his identification of Adam as humanity's God.

The Church also adopted new programs: it formalized its Sunday school initiative, added organizations for youth and children, and formally reinstituted the Relief Society. Perhaps the most important development in the territorial period had to do with the architectural and liturgical distinction between Sunday worship and weekday temple worship. Almost from the beginning, Mormons were a temple-building people but they did not routinely build chapels for Sunday worship before coming to the Great Basin. The Kirtland Temple was something of an anomaly, a hybrid between what would formalize as separate worship facilities in Utah. Joseph Smith's focus was so intent upon temple construction that Sunday worship facilities were an afterthought that only formally developed in the intermountain West. The temple ritual also developed over time. It was at St. George in 1877 that temple worship first included patrons performing all of the present rituals of the LDS temple, not just for the living but also by proxy for the dead.

In conjunction with these developments, Mormons began to build chapels for weekly Sunday services. As Mormons founded new communities spread across the intermountain West, the need for local meeting places prompted the building of chapels. These structures were much smaller and less elaborate than temples, and frequently served weekday functions, such as schoolhouse, a place for dances, meetings, celebrations, funerals, and dinners, in addition to Sunday worship. Chapels were always open to visitors of other faiths or of no faith, whereas after dedication temples are reserved for Mormons who meet specified standards of conduct.

Temple worship as a fully articulated proxy work for the dead and a corresponding focus upon family history are among the most enduring legacies of the Utah territorial phase. They represent a central component of the Mormon experience which passed into the twenty-first century and served to set Mormons apart from other Christian denominations. Temples captured the imagination and devotion of nineteenth-century

Mormon pioneers who sacrificed time, money, and labor to build them, and then sacrificed polygamy to keep them.

The Salt Lake Temple's completion in 1893 marked both the continued centrality of temples to Mormonism and important transformations then underway. Mormons were three years into their difficult extraction from polygamy, they were integrating themselves economically and politically into the national mainstream, and in other ways they demonstrated a willingness to shed their distinctiveness and to Americanize. Yet Mormons clung to certain aspects of peculiarity and withdrawal. The completed Salt Lake Temple represented a purely religious withdrawal, but a withdrawal nonetheless, a retreat into the solace of sacred space, and an ongoing desire to seek and encounter the divine. Rather than gather to the Great Basin, Mormons thereafter would gather to temples. The fiery rhetoric of blood and justice were gone, the millenarian fervor tempered, and the grandiose visions of a religious kingdom subsumed. Moroni's eastward-facing trump atop the tallest spire of the Salt Lake Temple sounded a call to all nations that primitive Christianity was restored and that Zion was established anew. It signaled an invitation to enter sacred temple space and therein experience a diminished but persistent Mormon desire to be in the world but not of it.

Notes

1. Young, "Holy Ghost Necessary in Preaching," 1856, 4: 32.
2. "General Epistle from the Council of the Twelve Apostles," *Latter-day Saints' Millenial Star* 10, no. 6, March 15, 1848, 84.
3. "Emigration!" *Latter-day Saints' Millenial Star* 10, no. 3, February 1, 1848, 40.
4. Erastus Snow, "To My Friend, 'The News':" *Deseret News*, December 25, 1852, 2.
5. Grant, "Present Scarcity of Food," 1856, 3: 202; see also Taylor, "Why the Saints Meet Together," 1883, 24: 2.
6. Stout, *On the Mormon Frontier*, 163–64.
7. Ibid., 172.
8. Yurtinus, " 'Here is One Man Who Will Not Go, Dam 'Um,' " 475–87.
9. Bigler and Bagley, *Mormon Rebellion,* 79; Bigler, *Forgotten Kingdom.*
10. Young to Bernhisel, May 27, 1852.
11. Brigham Young, "Testimony to the Divinity of Joseph Smith's Mission," 1857, 4: 33–42.
12. Ibid.
13. Appleby to Young, October 31, 1857.
14. "Our New Governor," *Deer Lodge Weekly Independent*, April 10, 1869, 2.
15. "Territorial Reformers," *Boise Idaho Tri-Weekly Statesman*, February 9, 1869, 2.
16. Bagley, *Blood of the Prophets*, 378; Brooks, *Mountain Meadows Massacre.*
17. Walker, Turley, and Leonard, *Massacre at Mountain Meadows.*
18. *Congressional Globe*, 98.
19. US Senate, *Statistical Report*, 301–2.
20. Furley, "Physiology of Mormonism," 1–4.
21. Cannon, "Word of Wisdom," 1868, 12: 224.

BIBLIOGRAPHY

Alexander, Thomas G. *Mormonism in Transition: A History of the Latter-day Saints, 1890–1930.* Urbana: University of Illinois Press, 1986.

Arrington, Leonard J. *Brigham Young: American Moses.* New York: Alfred A. Knopf, 1985.

Arrington, Leonard J. *Great Basin Kingdom: An Economic History of the Latter-day Saints, 1830–1900.* Lincoln: University of Nebraska Press, 1966.

Arrington, Leonard J., and Davis Bitton. *The Mormon Experience: A History of the Latter-day Saints.* New York: Alfred A. Knopf, 1979.

Appleby, William I. New York, to Brigham Young, Salt Lake City, October 31, 1857, Young Correspondence, CR1234/1, Box 25, folder 10 (reel 35). Church History Library, Church of Jesus Christ of Latter-day Saints, Salt Lake City, Utah.

Bagley, Will. *Blood of the Prophets: Brigham Young and the Massacre at Mountain Meadows.* Norman: University of Oklahoma Press, 2002.

Bigler, David L. *Forgotten Kingdom: The Mormon Theocracy in the American West, 1847–1896.* Logan: Utah State University Press, 1998.

Bigler, David L., and Will Bagley. *The Mormon Rebellion: America's First Civil War, 1857–1858.* Norman: University of Oklahoma Press, 2011.

Bowman, Matthew. *The Mormon People: The Making of an American Faith.* New York: Random House, 2012.

Bringhurst, Newell G. *Saints, Slaves, and Blacks: The Changing Place of Black People within Mormonism.* Westport, CT: Greenwood, 1981.

Brooks, Juanita. *The Mountain Meadows Massacre.* Norman: University of Oklahoma Press, 1950.

Bush, Lester E., Jr., and Armand L. Mauss, eds. *Neither White nor Black: Mormon Scholars Confront the Race Issue in a Universal Church.* Midvale, UT: Signature, 1984.

Campbell, Eugene E. *Establishing Zion: The Mormon Church in the American West, 1847–1869.* Salt Lake City: Signature, 1988.

Cannon, George Q. "Word of Wisdom" [April 7, 1868]. *Journal of Discourses* 12: 221–26.

Congressional Globe. 30th Congress, 1st Session. Washington, DC: Blair and Rives, 1848.

Daynes, Kathryn M. *More Wives than One: Transformation of the Mormon Marriage System, 1830–1910.* Urbana: University of Illinois Press, 2001.

Farmer, Jared. *On Zion's Mount: Mormons, Indians, and the American Landscape.* Cambridge, MA: Harvard University Press, 2008.

Flake, Kathleen. *The Politics of Religious Identity: The Seating of Reed Smoot, Mormon Apostle.* Chapel Hill: University of North Carolina Press, 2004.

Furley, Charles C. "The Physiology of Mormonism." *British Medical Journal* 2 (18 July 1863), 66.

Furniss, Norman F. *The Mormon Conflict, 1850–1859.* New Haven, CT: Yale University Press, 1960.

Givens, Terryl L. *The Viper on the Hearth: Mormons, Myths, and the Construction of Heresy.* New York: Oxford University Press, 1997.

Gordon, Sarah Barringer. *The Mormon Question: Polygamy and Constitutional Conflict in Nineteenth-Century America.* Chapel Hill: University of North Carolina Press, 2002.

Grant, Jedediah M. "The Present Scarcity of Food" [January 27, 1856]. *Journal of Discourses* 3: 199–202.

Hardy, B. Carmon. *Doing the Works of Abraham: Mormon Polygamy, Its Origin, Practice, and Demise*. Vol. 9 of *Kingdom in the West: The Mormons and the American Frontier*. Edited by Will Bagley. Norman, OK: Arthur H. Clark, 2007.

Hardy, B. Carmon. *Solemn Covenant: The Mormon Polygamous Passage*. Urbana: University of Illinois Press, 1992.

Journal of Discourses. 26 vols. Reported by G. D. Watt et al. Liverpool: F. D. and S. W. Richards et al., 1851–86; reprint., Salt Lake City: n.p.

Kerstetter, Todd M. *God's Country, Uncle Sam's Land: Faith and Conflict in the American West*. Urbana: University of Illinois Press, 2006.

Lyman, Edward Leo. *Political Deliverance: The Mormon Quest for Utah Statehood*. Urbana: University of Illinois Press, 1986.

MacKinnon, William P. *At Sword's Point: A Documentary History of the Utah War to 1858*. Norman, OK: Arthur H. Clark, 2008.

Mason, Patrick Q. *The Mormon Menace: Violence and Anti-Mormonism in the Postbellum South*. New York: Oxford University Press, 2011.

Mauss, Armand L. *All Abraham's Children: Changing Mormon Conceptions of Race and Lineage*. Urbana: University of Illinois Press, 2003.

Mauss, Armand L. *The Angel and the Beehive: The Mormon Struggle with Assimilation*. Urbana: University of Illinois Press, 1994.

Reeve, W. Paul. *Making Space on the Western Frontier: Mormons, Miners, and Southern Paiutes*. Urbana: University of Illinois Press, 2006.

Reeve, W. Paul. *Religion of a Different Color: Race and the Mormon Struggle for Whiteness*. New York: Oxford University Press, 2015.

Stout, Hosea. *On the Mormon Frontier: The Diary of Hosea Stout, 1844–1861*. Ed. Juanita Brooks. Salt Lake City: University of Utah Press and Utah State Historical Society, 1964.

Turner, John G. *Brigham Young: Pioneer Prophet*. Cambridge, MA: Harvard University Press, 2012.

Taylor, John. "Why the Saints Meet Together" [February 11, 1883]. *Journal of Discourses* 24: 1–8.

US Senate, *Statistical Report on the Sickness and Morality in the Army of the United States, compiled from the Records of the Surgeon General's Office; Embracing a Period of Five Years from January 1, 1855, to January, 1860*. Senate Executive Document 52, 36th Congress, 1st session.

Walker, Ronald W., Richard E. Turley Jr., and Glen M. Leonard. *Massacre at Mountain Meadows: An American Tragedy*. New York: Oxford University Press, 2008.

Young, Brigham. "The Holy Ghost Necessary in Preaching" [August 17, 1856]. *Journal of Discourses* 4: 20–32.

Young, Brigham. "Testimony to the Divinity of Joseph Smith's Mission" [August 31, 1856]. *Journal of Discourses* 4: 33–42.

Young, Brigham, to John M. Bernhisel, May 27, 1852, CR1234/1, Box 60, folder 2 (Reel 70), Brigham Young Correspondence. Church History Library, Church of Jesus Christ of Latter-day Saints, Salt Lake City, Utah.

Yurtinus, John F. "'Here is One Man Who Will Not Go, Dam 'Um': Recruiting the Mormon Battalion in Iowa Territory." *BYU Studies* 21, no. 4 (Fall 1981): 475–87.

···

CHAPTER 4

THE MODERN
MORMON CHURCH

···

MATTHEW J. GROW

In 1900, the membership of the Church of Jesus Christ of Latter-day Saints was overwhelmingly centered in Utah and in the surrounding regions of the Mormon corridor in the western United States. Ten years after the Manifesto announcing an end to plural marriage, nine years after the church disbanded its political party, and four years after Utah statehood, Mormonism remained far outside the mainstream of American culture. In the early years of the new century, the United States Senate vigorously debated whether it should seat an elected senator from Utah, Reed Smoot, who was a church apostle and a monogamist. By the early twenty-first century, the United States Senate Minority Leader, Democrat Harry Reid of Nevada, was a Mormon, while his co-religionist Mitt Romney was racing toward the Republican US presidential nomination. From 1900 to 2000, the membership of the church grew from under 300,000 to over eleven million. By 2000, Mormonism had spread across the globe; more members lived outside of the United States than within its borders. Even though Latter-day Saints continued to have a fraught relationship with American culture, they were far more mainstream and accepted than they had been a century earlier. Obviously, the Church of Jesus Christ of Latter-day Saints underwent profound changes over the course of the twentieth century.

Nevertheless, Mormonism's founding decades—the era in which, ironically, a small fraction of Latter-day Saints through history have lived—has received the lion's share of historians' attention. By contrast, comparably few historians and sociologists have studied twentieth-century Mormonism. The future of Mormon studies must involve a fundamental change in that dynamic, particularly in historians' understanding of the rise of global Mormonism. This chapter will, in a suggestive rather than comprehensive fashion, trace the developments within Mormonism over the past century, situate the existing historiography, and suggest some avenues for future scholarship.

ERA OF TRANSITION

Many of the best historical studies on twentieth-century Mormonism have focused on the late 1800s and early 1900s, as the church was leaving behind its polygamist, theocratic, and communal past for integration into monogamous, democratic, and capitalist America. Wilford Woodruff's Manifesto of 1890 signaled the beginning of the end of plural marriage within the church. The following year, the church disbanded its political party, the People's Party, and church members reorganized along the lines of the two major national parties, the Republicans and the Democrats. The Republican Party, partly as a result of its leadership in the antipolygamist national crusades of 1850s through the 1880s, initially lagged behind in recruiting Latter-day Saints. Church leaders, interested in promoting a rough parity between the two parties, encouraged many members to become Republicans. In 1896, Utah was admitted as a state, ending the nearly half-century of confrontations between outside territorial officials and local Latter-day Saints.

Statehood, which had been long sought by Latter-day Saints, did not end the tensions between the church and the federal government. In 1898, the House of Representatives refused to seat Brigham H. Roberts, a polygamist church leader, after his election from Utah as a Democrat. The struggle of Latter-day Saints to confront the decline of polygamy and their relationship with the US government was even more dramatically revealed in the US Senate hearings over Reed Smoot, a Republican, from 1904 to 1907. Protestants throughout the nation petitioned senators to bar Smoot from the Senate. The Senate hearings focused not only on Smoot's personal beliefs, but on a wide range of church policies, including the relationship between church leaders and politics and the continuing practice of plural marriage. Kathleen Flake's insightful book *The Politics of American Religious Identity* inserts the Smoot trials into the context of the Progressive era and developing notions of American denominationalism, demonstrating the value of integrating studies on Mormonism within broader debates in the historiography of US religion and politics. In her phrase, the hearings represented a battle "between the nation with the soul of a church and the church with the soul of a nation." After four years of hearings, a majority of senators, but not the required two-thirds, voted to expel Smoot, who then served in the Senate until 1933. According to Flake, "it can be said that the Mormon Problem was solved finally because the Mormons had figured out how to act more like an American church, a civil religion; the Senate, less like one."[1]

The Senate hearings on Smoot shone a bright spotlight on post-Manifesto polygamy. In 1904, church president Joseph F. Smith issued a second manifesto which threatened church discipline if individuals participated in new plural marriages. Soon thereafter, John W. Taylor and Matthias F. Cowley were dropped from the Quorum of the Twelve Apostles for their sanctioning of new plural marriages. Nonetheless, many Latter-day Saint men, including Joseph F. Smith, continued to cohabit with their already existing plural wives, meaning that the demographic decline of polygamy extended over decades. In response to the crackdown on new plural marriages, some believers in plural marriage split with the mainstream church and began developing their own polygamist movements. Opposition between these fundamentalists, as they came to be known, and the mainstream church has continued to the present.

The end of plural marriage and the gradual extrication of church leaders from partisan politics meant that new social boundaries were necessary to retain a distinctive Latter-day Saint identity. The Word of Wisdom became increasingly prominent as a marker of identity, becoming a prerequisite for temple worship in 1921. Family history research and temple ordinances likewise assumed an increasingly prominent role within Mormon life. Embrace of American patriotism—evident in the enthusiastic participation in military service by Latter-day Saints, beginning in the Spanish-American War and continuing throughout the twentieth century—also became a key component of identity for Saints in the United States. Likewise, Latter-day Saints reemphasized the founding events of the restoration, including the purchasing of historic sites such as Joseph Smith's birth site, celebrating Smith and his First Vision, while deemphasizing controversial aspects of LDS history. The end of geographic gathering and the beginning of an expanded presence outside of Utah was signaled by temples built in Laie, Hawaii (1919); Cardston, Alberta (1923); and Mesa, Arizona (1927).

Historians have approached this transformative era from a number of vantage points. In his landmark *Mormonism in Transition*, Thomas Alexander meticulously traces the changes within Mormonism over these decades. Influenced by the broader historiography of the Progressive Era, Alexander argues that standardization, bureaucratization, professionalization, and organization reshaped the church and Latter-day Saint culture. In *Transformation of the Mormon Culture Region*, cultural geographer Ethan Yorgason approaches the same topics, emphasizing to a greater extent cultural changes, particularly as reflected in attitudes toward women, economics, and family. In *On Zion's Mount*, an insightful study of Utah Valley's Mount Timpanogos and perceptions of place and environment, Jared Farmer suggests that this era also changed the relationship between the Saints and the physical and symbolic environment. The story of the Utah-Idaho Sugar Company, analyzed by Matthew Godfrey in *Religion, Politics, and Sugar*, demonstrates the deep involvement of early twentieth-century church leaders in economic affairs and the intense opposition this provoked in both local areas and in national politics in an era of trust-busting politicians. Church leaders gradually removed themselves from many economic enterprises over the course of the twentieth century, though the church's corporate holdings still differentiate it from most other American denominations. More studies on the relationship between the church and its complex ties to businesses, as well as scholarship on economic attitudes among its members, are needed.

On a personal level, the tensions felt by Latter-day Saints in this era are explored in William B. Smart's biography of his grandfather William H. Smart, a stake president in the Uinta Basin in northeastern Utah, who struggled to leave behind the ideals of nineteenth-century Mormonism, including communal economics and plural marriage. The two church presidents who presided over this era of transition—Joseph F. Smith (1901–18) and Heber J. Grant (1918–45)—both lack scholarly biographies. Biographies of later church presidents David O. McKay (by Gregory Prince and William Robert Wright) and Spencer W. Kimball (by his son Edward Kimball) demonstrate how such studies can illuminate an era and suggest that biographies of Smith and Grant would be major contributions. In addition, more scholarly work must be done on shifting notions of gender within Mormonism. David Hall's excellent article "A Crossroads for Mormon Women: Amy Brown Lyman, J. Reuben Clark, and the Decline of Organized Women's Activism in the Relief Society" demonstrates how studying the interactions of men and women, both in local congregations and in the church hierarchy, can yield significant results.

During the 1930s and 1940s, Mormons were becoming more accepted within American culture and Latter-day Saints were beginning to see the expansion of church membership overseas. Twentieth-century Mormonism lacks a coherent scholarly narrative not only because of the lack of studies but also because the narrative necessarily becomes more fragmented with the church's international expansion. As such, the remainder of this essay will examine the relationship of Mormonism with American culture from the 1940s to the present and then the rise of the international church.

Relationship with America: Demographics, Politics, Image

On June 4, 2011, *Newsweek* placed on its cover a cast member, in missionary attire, from the Tony Award–winning play *The Book of Mormon*. The magazine mixed the cultural with the political by replacing the cast member's head with that of presidential candidate Mitt Romney. The cover proclaimed: "The Mormon Moment: How the Outsider Faith Creates Winners." "They've conquered Broadway, talk radio, the U.S. Senate—and they may win the White House," *Newsweek* wrote as its justification for exploring the contemporary implications of Mormonism in the United States.[2] The cover illustrates both how the era of transition fundamentally changed Mormonism, making possible a significant rapprochement with American culture, and yet how Mormonism remains an "outsider faith" in the early twenty-first century.

Demographic and cultural shifts within U.S. Mormonism have shaped its relationship to American culture, including how Americans have perceived Mormons, as well as how Latter-day Saints in the United States have approached politics and history. In its use of the *Book of Mormon* musical—which demonstrates that Mormons are mainstream enough to be mocked by the wider culture (even if lovingly so, as the play's producers claim) but remain outsiders—the *Newsweek* cover article hints at the complicated and nonlinear "Americanization" of Mormonism. The relationship between American culture and Mormonism has always been a complex dance, characterized by both mutual suspicion and attraction, and involving moments of reconciliation and intense friction.

Indeed, Latter-day Saints have both approached and withdrawn from American culture over the course of the twentieth century. Sociologist Armand Mauss, in *The Angel and the Beehive*, has perceptively used the metaphors of the angel and the beehive to explore the dual impulses within Mormonism toward accommodation and toward separation. Within Mormon culture, the beehive is a "symbol of worldly enterprise," while the angel (that is, the Angel Moroni atop temple spires) represents the "other-worldly heritage of Mormonism, the spiritual and prophetic elements." Religious movements always struggle to balance their relationship with the broader culture; if they move too much toward "assimilation and respectability," they lose their "unique identity." On the other hand, if a religion goes too far toward "greater separateness, peculiarity, and militance," they "invite repression" which might threaten the movement's existence.[3]

During the first half of the twentieth century, Mauss argues, Latter-day Saint culture moved toward assimilation with the broader culture as it left behind its polygamist, theocratic, and communal past. Leaders such as James Talmage, John Widtsoe, and Brigham H. Roberts emphasized somewhat more the commonalities rather than the differences between Latter-day Saint theology and more traditional Christian theology. Roughly around 1960, according to Mauss, church leaders became concerned that members were losing their sense of being a "peculiar" people, prompting efforts toward retrenchment and increased distance from the surrounding culture. These efforts included increased attention toward unique Mormon activities such as genealogy and temple building; a more sophisticated and pervasive system of religious education including seminaries for high school students and institutions for college students; and a church-wide system of correlation, which brought previously autonomous organizations, such as the Relief Society, under stricter supervision by the First Presidency and the Twelve Apostles. In addition, concerned by shifting American practices and beliefs of sexuality, gender roles, and family structures, church leaders more strongly articulated a theology of family life and sought to defend the traditional nuclear family.

This retrenchment coincided with demographic changes within Mormonism which contributed to the faith's growing prominence within the United States. In a process that historian Jan Shipps has called "the scattering of the gathering and the gathering of the scattered," significant numbers of Latter-day Saints participated in a "diaspora" following the Second World War, leaving Utah and the intermountain West and spreading out across the United States in search of educational and employment opportunities. Settling in what was then known as the "mission field," these Utah exports combined with local converts to create centers of Mormons throughout the nation. Whereas Latter-day Saints were relatively isolated within the intermountain West during the 1800s and early 1900s, the growing concentrations of Latter-day Saints throughout the broader West (especially California) and in smaller numbers throughout the rest of the United States meant that many more Americans were likely to know Latter-day Saints on a personal level. In addition, it meant that many Latter-day Saints were increasingly comfortable with being Mormon in a largely non-Mormon setting, with negotiating their dual identities of Latter-day Saint and American. The Mormon diaspora, combined with the church's missionary program and Spencer W. Kimball's 1978 revelation removing priesthood and temple restrictions from men and women of black African descent, has also led to the increasing prominence within Mormonism of African Americans, Hispanic Americans, and Asian Americans. Jessie Embry has examined the racial and ethnic dynamics of contemporary Mormonism in books focused on each of these groups; in addition, Armand Mauss in *All Abraham's Children* has documented Latter-day Saints' developing ideas and theology of race.

This Latter-day Saint diaspora has led to increased participation in politics by Latter-day Saints outside of Utah, symbolized by George and Mitt Romney. In 1968, Michigan governor George Romney became a serious contender for the Republican nomination for the US presidency. Forty years later, his son Mitt also ran for the Republican nomination; in 2012, not only Mitt Romney but Utah governor Jon Huntsman Jr. contended for the nomination. Whereas George Romney's religious beliefs were mostly a nonissue in 1968, Mitt Romney's became a major issue in 2008 and, to a lesser extent, in 2012, suggesting the continued and perhaps increasing ambivalence about Latter-day Saints among large segments of the American population, especially the Protestant evangelicals who between 1968 and 2008 had become an increasingly dominant part of the Republican Party coalition. In addition, in his insightful dissertation (and award-winning book), J. B. Haws partially explains this phenomenon by highlighting the growing "perception paradox" around Mormonism, "between admiration for Mormons as individuals—often described as friendly, hard-working, family-oriented—and ambivalence for Mormonism as an institution—secretive, authoritarian, deceptive."[4] Strikingly, a century after the Senate voted to expel Reed Smoot in 1907, a Mormon became the Senate Majority Leader in 2007. Almost as strikingly, the senator did not fit the dominant Republican mold of recent Mormon politicians, but was a liberal Democrat from Nevada, Harry Reid.

Church leaders eschewed partisan politics with more rigor as the twentieth century progressed, though they maintained their right to speak publicly and politically on issues of morality. Shifting national political trends sparked controversy both between the church and the nation and within the church, including during the battle over the Equal Rights Amendment (ERA) in the 1970s. Church members played a decisive role in the amendment's defeat in several states, helping lead to its demise in 1982. The battle over the ERA, a story told in Martha Sonntag Bradley's *Pedestals and Podiums*, marked an important moment in which most church members identified with the cultural concerns expressed by conservative evangelicals and Catholics, helping pave the way for the often uneasy but nevertheless long-standing alliance among these groups in American conservative politics. Like other conservative Americans, many Mormons feared the effects of the ERA on the traditional family, saw it as part of a radical feminist agenda, and asserted that it would lead to unwanted social practices such as women being subject to the draft and coed college dorms. Some Latter-day Saints, most prominently Sonia Johnson, publicly disputed the church's stance in favor of absolute gender equality. Other Mormons, both women and men, were uncomfortable with the actions against the ERA but silently supported the church's stance in a gesture of solidarity with their people. The church's opposition to the ERA foreshadowed its aggressive stance against same-sex marriage in the 1990s and early 2000s. Most controversially, leaders asked church members in California in 2008 to support financially and participate actively in the successful referendum campaign to ban same-sex marriage. The Proposition 8 campaign again placed the church's actions at the center of American cultural politics and allied it with conservative evangelical and Catholic groups.

While the church's involvement in politics has shaped Mormon image in late twentieth-century and early twenty-first-century America, so has the increasing visibility of Mormon splinter groups (so-called Mormon fundamentalists)—believers in plural marriage who assert that the mainstream church has sold out to the broader society. Mormon fundamentalists are divided into myriad groups, the largest of which has been the Fundamentalist Church of Jesus Christ of Latter-day Saints (FLDS). Mormon polygamy attracted more attention in the first decade of the twenty-first century than it had since the Reed Smoot hearings. Successful TV shows, such as HBO's *Big Love* and TLC's *Sister Wives,* and best-selling books, including Jon Krakaeur's *Under the Banner of Heaven: A Story of Violent Faith* and many memoirs of women who had left polygamy, thrust the subject into the public eye. In addition, increasing clashes between polygamists and legal authorities—driven both by attempts of legal authorities to prosecute abuses among polygamist groups, most famously the prosecution in 2007 of Warren Jeffs and other FLDS authorities in Texas, and by the increasing assertiveness of defenders of polygamy—attracted international media attention. The controversy over Mormon fundamentalists seems likely to increase in the future.

The demographic and cultural shifts in US Mormonism also helped transform Mormon historiography. Leonard Arrington, an affable and entrepreneurial historian, published his ground-breaking economic analysis of nineteenth-century territorial Utah, *Great Basin Kingdom,* in 1958 with Harvard University Press. It signaled a dramatic shift away from the polemical and polarizing history that had been produced by both supporters and detractors throughout Mormon history. Led by Arrington, New Mormon Historians (as they called themselves) were often educated outside of Utah, sought objectivity, advocated reliance on archival manuscripts, and integrated the Mormon past within the broader currents of American historiography, including new fields such as women's history and social history. New Mormon Historians were drawn not only from the ranks of the mainstream LDS Church, but also from the Reorganized Church of Jesus Christ of Latter Day Saints (RLDS, now called the Community of Christ) and included outsiders like Jan Shipps. Cooperation between LDS and RLDS historians contributed to and reflected a gradual thaw in the relationship between the two denominations. More recently, Richard Bushman, who made his career among the Mormon diaspora as a distinguished and Bancroft Prize–winning historian of the colonial era, has become the most prominent interpreter of early Mormonism. His biography of Joseph Smith, *Rough Stone Rolling,* received both critical acclaim for its placing of the Prophet within his cultural context and attacks—from some within the church for its frank portrayal of Smith's weaknesses and from outside scholars who wanted a more critical appraisal of Smith's motivations and actions. Some New Mormon Historians, such as Thomas Alexander, focused in part on the twentieth century. Most, however, studied Mormonism's nineteenth-century origins, meaning that the next generation of scholarship on Latter-day Saints must grapple more intensely with twentieth-century Mormonism in the United States.

GLOBAL MORMONISM

The Church of Jesus Christ of Latter-day Saints has had a substantial international focus since its early days. Joseph Smith's revelations proclaimed the need to carry the Latter-day Saint message worldwide. Mormon missionaries began making significant inroads in England in the late 1830s and 1840s, in Scandinavia and other European nations in the 1850s, and in Hawaii and other Pacific islands in the 1850s. The strong call for converts to physically gather to Zion, however, resulted in an ethnically heterogeneous center to Mormonism but a perpetually weak periphery, as faithful members left their native homes for Illinois and then Utah. This gradually began to change in the late nineteenth and early twentieth centuries. By the 1890s, church leaders began to encourage converts to remain in their country of origin rather than emigrate to the United States, a policy that became more firm by the 1920s. The building of temples outside the United States, beginning in England, Switzerland, and New Zealand in the 1950s, signaled the expansion of global Mormonism. In 1977, Elder Bruce R. McConkie, an apostle, expressed the new vision of church growth, using the Mormon language of Zion, in a sermon in Peru: "The gathering place for Peruvians is in the stakes of Zion in Peru, or in the places which soon will become stakes. The gathering place for Chileans is in Chile; for Bolivians it is in Bolivia; for Koreans it is in Korea; and so it goes through all the length and breadth of the earth." Theologically, church leaders thus emphasized a spiritual gathering rather than a physical one.[5]

The policy that converts should remain in their homelands has led to the growth of church membership throughout the world. The experience of the church in Europe during the twentieth century shows some of the dynamics and complications of internationalization. Following the First World War, missionaries returned to Germany and Austria and experienced substantial success; by 1930, Germany boasted more Latter-day Saints than any other country besides the United States. Nevertheless, internal tumult and the rise of Nazism in Germany in the 1930s slowed growth, and missionaries were withdrawn from Germany and all of Europe in 1939 due to the Second World War. Following the war, church leaders supervised a substantial relief effort in Germany and other decimated European areas; missionaries soon returned as well. The building of a temple outside of Berne, Switzerland, dedicated in 1955, symbolized a growing institutional presence of the church throughout Europe. In East Germany, Latter-day Saints faced opposition from the communist government, but nevertheless maintained church meetings and eventually obtained legal status, a story told in Raymond Kuehne's documentary history. Dieter F. Uchtdorf, born in East Germany in 1940 and raised from the age of ten in West Germany, became the first German apostle and the first apostle born outside of North America in over a half century in 2004; in 2008, Uchtdorf became a member of the church's First Presidency. Even with the growing institutional presence of European temples and prominent leaders in the general church hierarchy, growth rates have atrophied in Germany and across Europe in more recent decades.

The strongest area of church growth internationally in the mid to late twentieth century has been in Latin America. Mormon missionary efforts in Latin America began inauspiciously in 1851, when Apostle Parley P. Pratt, along with another missionary and one of Pratt's plural wives, served a short-lived and unsuccessful mission to Chile. Mormon missionaries began proselytizing in Mexico in the mid-1870s, searching both for converts and for a potential refuge for American Mormons from the intensifying antipolygamy campaign in the United States. In the 1880s, Latter-day Saints founded a series of colonies in northern Mexico. During the Mexican Revolution of the 1910s, many Latter-day Saints returned to the United States. Nevertheless, in the 1920s, church leaders began to consider an expanded effort of missionary work throughout Latin America. In 1925–26, Elder Melvin J. Ballard, an apostle, visited South America to dedicate it for preaching. He stated, "The work of the Lord will grow slowly for a time here just as an oak grows slowly from an acorn. It will not shoot up in a day as does the sunflower that grows quickly and then dies. . . . The work here is the smallest that it will ever be. . . . The South American Mission will be a power in the Church."[6] Ballard's prediction proved correct: Mormon expansion in Latin America (outside of Mexico) began in the 1920s and continued relatively slowly until the 1960s and 1970s, when it accelerated dramatically. German converts who had immigrated to Argentina and Brazil served as the basis for the initial growth in Latin America. After establishing a base among these European immigrants, missionaries gradually expanded their efforts to others. The example of the growth in Brazil tells the demographic story: 3700 members in the late 1950s; 54,000 at the dedication of Brazil's first temple, in São Paulo, in 1978; 300,000 by 1990; more than 700,000 by the end of the twentieth century; and more than one million by 2010.[7]

By contrast, the growth of the church in Asia began later, after the Second World War, and has occurred more slowly. Earlier efforts—including short-lived missionary journeys to India and Hong Kong in the early 1850s and more sustained proselytizing in Japan from 1901 to 1924—yielded relatively few converts. In 1947, the church reopened its mission in Japan. Efforts soon spread to other Asian nations, including South Korea, Hong Kong, the Philippines, Thailand, and Singapore in the 1950s and 1960s. The world's two most populous nations have not yet experienced significant Latter-day Saint growth. A mission in India was organized officially in 1993, while missionaries have not yet been allowed to proselytize in China. The complex relationship of the United States with Asia—through the Second World War, the Korean War, the Vietnam War, and the Cold War—has both promoted and inhibited Mormon growth in the region. The interactions of LDS US servicemen and Japanese individuals led to some early conversions, for instance, but mistrust of American foreign policy has also raised questions about Mormon missionaries who are sometimes seen as ambassadors of US culture.

Rapid church growth has also occurred in recent decades in Africa, a situation unthinkable until Spencer W. Kimball's 1978 declaration extending the priesthood to all worthy males, thereby reversing the policy that had excluded those of African origins from holding the priesthood. Thus, from Germany to Brazil to the Philippines to Nigeria, the most striking historical trend about twentieth-century Mormonism has been its aggressive internationalization. To keep pace, the church has ambitiously built temples throughout the globe. In 2009, there were 130 temples, with another twenty-one announced or under construction; more than half had been completed in the previous dozen years.[8] In 2009, of the 13.5 million Latter-day Saints, 45 percent lived in the United States and Canada, 15 percent in Mexico, 28 percent in the rest of Latin America, 7 percent in Asia, 5 percent in Europe, and 2 percent in Africa.[9] The raw numbers alone may overestimate to some extent the strength of global Mormonism, as many converts leave Mormonism as quickly as they arrive; more studies are needed on this phenomenon, particularly in comparison with other religious movements.

A striking paucity of scholarship exists on the spread of global Mormonism, particularly when compared with the rich historiography of nineteenth-century Mormonism. Most writing on the international growth of the Church of Jesus Christ of Latter-day Saints has occurred within devotional or local contexts, without engagement with religious studies scholarship, and without significant historical context. But the rise of global Mormonism has paralleled a larger shift of Christianity to the global South, which has been compellingly described by religious studies scholar Philip Jenkins in *The Next Christendom: The Coming of Global Christianity*. Jenkins documents the dramatic shifts within Christianity as it declines in Europe, stagnates in the United States, and explodes in Latin America, Asia, and Africa. Mormonism is following a similar trajectory and few scholars have yet grappled with what this means for Mormonism's present and future. In addition, the lack of scholarship on international Mormonism means that college instruction about Mormonism—limited in any case—focuses on the founding decades of Mormonism (Joseph Smith, the trek to Utah), thus presenting Mormonism in terms of its nineteenth-century origins rather than its twenty-first-century realities.

The internationalization of the church has raised powerful questions for leaders, members, and academics about the relationship between Mormon culture, particularly as it exists in the United States, and the church. Just as Catholics, Anglicans, and Pentecostals in the United States and Europe are wrestling with the implications of growth in the global South, the expansion of Mormonism has already reshaped and will continue to alter the church both at its core and at its periphery. To what extent does Mormon faith become confused with its American cultural context in the minds of missionaries and converts alike? How will Latter-day Saints balance rapid growth with preserving a core sense of identity and theology? How will the growth of church members and the rise of leaders in the international areas change Mormonism within the United States?

Mormonism's record-keeping culture has ensured that a large body of primary materials—including missionary records, local church histories, oral interviews, and records kept by local Saints—exists with which scholars can begin to answer these questions. Most of these primary sources are housed in the Church History Department of the Church of Jesus Christ of Latter-day Saints in Salt Lake City. In addition, a recent initiative by the Church History Department to decentralize the gathering of historical documents promises even richer material in the future. Within the past few years, area historians have been designated by ecclesiastical leaders within each of the church's sixteen international areas (large ecclesiastical units of church governance); many country historians have also been called. These officials, who have included some American missionary couples but also many local members, have been charged with collecting materials, including conducting oral-history interviews, related to church history in their areas. In addition, recent attempts to establish scholarly organizations and a journal aimed at international Mormonism are a hopeful sign. These efforts include the organization of the European Mormon Studies Association in 2006; the establishment of the *International Journal of Mormon Studies*, published first in 2008; the attempted formation of an Association for Spanish and Portuguese Mormon Studies in 2007; and the organization of a Brazilian Association for Mormon Studies in 2009.

Clearly, the resources, in terms of primary sources and scholarly support, are beginning to coalesce for the study of global Mormonism. The primary materials will also continue to grow. Devotional and local histories on the expansion of the church, many written by church members in international areas and published in non-English languages and with limited distribution, will increase.[10] These histories can be cautiously mined with profit by scholars. What, then, should be the agenda of scholars of global Mormonism? I will suggest three possible starting points.

First, historians of both American and global Mormonism need to produce more and better studies of what it meant to be Mormon at a particular time and place. Just as Paul Reeve in his chapter of this volume calls for more scholarship on the "ungathered" in the nineteenth century, scholars of the twentieth century need to carefully study the different contexts and experiences of a Latter-day Saint in Brazil in the 1950s, Boston in the 1970s, and Nigeria in the 1990s. The rich collection of oral interviews being collected by the Church History Department will provide much of the necessary raw data for these studies. The Women's Oral History Project at Claremont University, directed by Claudia Bushman and focused on the lived experience of Mormon women in twentieth-century Southern California, provides an example of another approach, as does the LDS Ethnic Groups Oral History Project at the Charles Redd Center for Western Studies at Brigham Young University.

Second, scholarship on international Mormonism should examine the complex interactions between the core and the periphery. Events on the international periphery have often altered the trajectory of Latter-day Saint history, and attitudes brought from the Mormon core have deeply influenced the international expansion. In his history of Mormon missionary work in early twentieth-century Japan, for instance, Reid L. Neilson argues that the unwillingness of American missionaries to adapt to local circumstances led to the small success of Mormon missionary work compared to its Protestant contemporaries: "The Mormons, who basically imposed or translated their message, struggled to make headway in Japan, while the American Protestants converted tens of thousands of Japanese, due in large part to their greater willingness to adapt their missionary approach to the needs of East Asia."[11] In addition, Mark Grover has demonstrated how the church's growth in Brazil and the announcement of the construction of the São Paulo Brazil Temple in 1975, formed a critical part of the context for Spencer W. Kimball's 1978 revelation ending the ban on the priesthood for men of African descent. The history of racial mixing in Brazil meant that a large percentage of Brazilians were partially descended from Africans; the faithfulness of many Brazilian Saints and their desire to participate in the temple ordinances deeply impressed President Kimball and other Mormon leaders. The announcement of the priesthood revelation in June 1978 and the dedication of the São Paulo Temple five months later were thus linked, as both core and periphery deeply influenced each other.

Third, scholarship on international Mormonism must be deeply integrated into other scholarly contexts, particularly the spread of global Christianity. Within the last two decades, a vibrant field of research into global Christianity and missionary studies has sprung up within the broader academy. Historians of Mormonism, however, have done relatively little to engage with this scholarship. Nor have historians or sociologists of Mormonism yet studied to much extent the relationship between the spread of Mormonism and the spread of other forms of Christianity (particularly Pentecostalism and evangelicalism, but also Catholicism and smaller denominations such as Seventh-Day Adventists and Jehovah's Witnesses) in the global South. Latter-day Saint missionaries and members must be brought into this scholarly conversation, which will also deeply inform our understanding of global Mormonism.

Notwithstanding the fine historical studies on elements of the Mormon experience during the twentieth century, scholarship on the modern church remains in its infancy. Unlike nineteenth-century Mormonism, no coherent narrative has been established. Rich, often untapped documentary sources exist. The continuing evolution of Mormon studies must involve a significantly increased engagement with the twentieth century and, in particular, with the expansion of Mormonism across the globe.

Notes

1. Flake, *Politics of American Religious Identity*, 7, 158.
2. Kirn, "Mormons Rock!"
3. Mauss, *Angel and the Beehive*, 3–6.
4. Haws, "Mormon Image in the American Mind," iv.
5. McConkie, "Come: Let Israel Build Zion."
6. Ballard, *Melvin J. Ballard*, 84.
7. *Deseret News 2010 Church Almanac*, 434–35.
8. Ibid., 197–200.
9. Ibid., 5.
10. For a survey of the existing historiography, see Mehr et al., "Growth and Internationalization," 199–228.
11. Neilson, *Early Mormon Missionary Activities in Japan*, 119.

BIBLIOGRAPHY

Deseret News 2010 Church Almanac. Salt Lake City: Deseret News, 2010.

Alexander, Thomas G. *Mormonism in Transition: A History of the Latter-day Saints, 1890–1930.* Urbana: University of Illinois Press, 1986.

Ballard, Melvin J. *Melvin J. Ballard: Crusader for Righteousness.* Salt Lake City: Bookcraft, 1966.

Bradley, Martha Sonntag. *Pedestals and Podiums: Utah Women, Religious Authority, and Equal Rights.* Salt Lake City: Signature, 2005.

Embry, Jessie L. *Asian American Mormons: Bridging Cultures.* Provo, UT: Charles Redd Center for Western Studies, 1999.

Embry, Jessie L. *Black Saints in a White Church: Contemporary African American Mormons.* Salt Lake City: Signature, 1994.

Embry, Jessie L. *"In His Own Language": Mormon Spanish-Speaking Congregations in the United States.* Provo, UT: Charles Redd Center for Western Studies, 1997.

Farmer, Jared. *On Zion's Mount: Mormons, Indians, and the American Landscape.* Cambridge, MA: Harvard University Press, 2008.

Flake, Kathleen. *The Politics of American Religious Identity: The Seating of Reed Smoot, Mormon Apostle.* Chapel Hill: University of North Carolina Press, 2004.

Godfrey, Matthew C. *Religion, Politics, and Sugar: The Mormon Church, the Federal Government, and the Utah-Idaho Sugar Company, 1907 to 1921.* Logan: Utah State University Press 2007.

Grover, Mark L. "The Mormon Priesthood Revelation and the São Paulo, Brazil Temple." *Dialogue: A Journal of Mormon Thought* 23, no. 1 (Spring 1990): 39–53.

Hall, David. "A Crossroads for Mormon Women: Amy Brown Lyman, J. Reuben Clark, and the Decline of Organized Women's Activism in the Relief Society." *Journal of Mormon History* 36, no. 2 (Spring 2010): 205–49.

Haws, J. B. *The Mormon Image in the American Mind: Fifty Years of Public Perception.* New York: Oxford University Press, 2013.

Haws, John Ben. "The Mormon Image in the American Mind: Shaping Perception of Latter-day Saints, 1968–2008." PhD diss., University of Utah, 2010.

Jenkins, Philip. "Letting Go: Understanding Mormon Growth in Africa." *Journal of Mormon History* 35, no. 2 (Spring 2009): 1–26.

Jenkins, Philip. *The Next Christendom: The Coming of Global Christianity.* New York: Oxford University Press, 2002.

Kimball, Edward L. *Lengthen Your Stride: The Presidency of Spencer W. Kimball.* Salt Lake City: Deseret, 2005.

Kirn, Walter. "Mormons Rock!" *Newsweek*, June 4, 2011.

Krakauer, Jon. *Under the Banner of Heaven: A Story of Violent Faith.* New York: Doubleday, 2003.

Kuehne, Raymond. *Mormons as Citizens of a Communist State: A Documentary History of the Church of Jesus Christ of Latter-day Saints in East Germany, 1945–1990.* Salt Lake City: University of Utah Press, 2010.

Mauss, Armand L. *All Abraham's Children: Changing Mormon Conceptions of Race and Lineage.* Urbana: University of Illinois Press, 2003.

Mauss, Armand L. *The Angel and the Beehive: The Mormon Struggle with Assimilation.* Urbana: University of Illinois Press, 1994.

McConkie, Bruce R. "Come: Let Israel Build Zion." *Ensign* 7, no. 5 (May 1977): 115–118. http://www.lds.org/general-conference/1977/05/come-let-israel-build-zion?lang=eng.

Mehr, Kahlile B., Mark L. Grover, Reid L. Neilson, Donald Q. Cannon, and Grant Underwood. "Growth and Internationalization: The LDS Church since 1945." In *Excavating Mormon Posts: The New Historiography of the Last Half Century*, ed. Newell G. Bringhurst and Lavina Fielding Anderson, 199–228. Salt Lake City: Greg Kofford, 2004.

Neilson, Reid L. *Early Mormon Missionary Activities in Japan, 1901–1924*. Salt Lake City: University of Utah Press, 2010.

Prince, Gregory A., and William Robert Wright. *David O. McKay and the Rise of Modern Mormonism*. Salt Lake City: University of Utah Press, 2005.

Shipps, Jan. *Sojourner in the Promised Land: Forty Years among the Mormons*. Urbana: University of Illinois Press, 2000.

Smart, William B. *Mormonism's Last Colonizer: The Life and Times of William H. Smart*. Logan: Utah State University Press, 2008.

Yorgason, Ethan R. *Transformation of the Mormon Culture Region*. Urbana: University of Illinois Press, 2003.

CHAPTER 5

··

WOMEN IN MORMONISM

··

CLAUDIA L. BUSHMAN

JOSEPH SMITH, the founding Mormon prophet, had bad luck with many of his male acolytes. One after another they exhibited jealousy, disloyalty, weakness, and ambition. Many of his leaders, with whom he had shared the wondrous power of the priesthood, even the three witnesses privileged to see the golden plates, defected from his service, some crawling back later when their hopes did not work out. John C. Bennett was a major disappointment. Both Orson Hyde, the missionary to Jerusalem, and W. W. Phelps, the sweet singer of the restoration, left the fold. The resilient Smith was able to rebound from this desertion. He had many second acts. He found new leaders and carried on.

But Smith's women were true. He asked much of them and they delivered. During his lifetime, he received major service for the work of the kingdom and for building his image from three I will mention.

His mother Lucy Mack Smith loved and supported him. She bore this wonder child and watched him grow. Though she saw nothing of the magical events surrounding his life, she believed in them. After his death, she dictated an account of his activities and those of her family, preserving for all time her view of his background. Thanks to her, and to her alone, we can observe some of the memorable moments of his short life: Joseph, the brave little boy suffering the painful operation; Joseph, the leader of the first Family Home Evening, describing people from other places and other times; Joseph's triumphant reception of the plates at the Hill Cumorah, including his helping himself to a neighbor's buggy without permission. Lucy Mack, the devoted mother, experienced her son as a real human person. And her account is also the most important woman's voice we have from the early church.[1]

Emma Hale Smith, Joseph Smith's wife, was bright, observant, and better educated than he. Certainly no easily swayed young lady, she saw qualities in him that caused her to risk all for this unpromising laborer. She devoted herself to his work, she bore his children, she gave her life to him, and she was more faithful to him than he was to her. To her he pronounced the great blessing of Doctrine and Covenants (D&C) section 25, given in July 1830, in Harmony, Pennsylvania, four months after the church was organized.

In this brief section he expounds promises to her that he suggests are the model for all women of the restored church, a description broader and more comprehensive than could have been imagined in those earlier times. This section suggests that the Lord had expansive ideas for the women in the church. Emma Smith's devotion and example are unequalled.

In section 25, Emma Smith and other members of the church are first welcomed into the Lord's kingdom, forgiven of their sins, and told that they will be rewarded and their lives preserved if they are faithful.

But in the next part Emma Smith is assigned specific tasks of the sort that are now general callings in the church. She is to serve as her husband's scribe and to make a selection of hymns for a hymnbook. These assignments represent an awareness of her specific talents and abilities. These are jobs that she can do, for which her experience has prepared her. They reflect her knowledge and ability. Women in the church receive such callings today.

The next part, truly remarkable for its time and for any time, explains to Emma Smith that she will be ordained by her husband to "expound scriptures, and to exhort the church" under the direct inspiration of the Spirit of the Lord. She is to be a leader in church meetings. She will receive the Holy Ghost and is to prepare for her assignment by "writing, and [by] learning much." What is more, the leader of the church, her husband, will "support thee in the church." He will stand behind her and what she says, as she helps him reveal to the members "all things" "according to their faith." Here is the precedent for Mormon women today teaching and preaching.

As far as we know, Emma Smith did not exercise this active option until twelve years later, when she was elected presidentess of the Ladies Relief Society of Nauvoo in 1842. But Emma Smith could have exhorted and expounded. She was given that power as were all women by extension. This vision of female activity in church comes from 1830. Quaker women were traveling preachers, but the women in the Protestant sects with which Joseph was familiar did not speak from the pulpit.

Yet with this broad power, Emma Smith is also given a very personal responsibility in a very personal way. She is told that her calling is to be a "comfort unto my servant, Joseph Smith, Jun., thy husband, in his afflictions, with consoling words in the spirit of meekness." She is to hold up the arms of the Lord's anointed. With all his powers, Smith needed consolation and comfort. She is to fill this responsibility with humility and meekness. The word "meekness" is used twice, suggesting that she needed the further admonition and the instruction to "beware of pride." She is promised great things, but she needs warning against making too much of herself in comparison to her husband. She is to let her "soul delight in thy husband, and the glory which shall come upon him." She is not to "murmur" because she does not see all that he sees. Much is promised, but subordination is still asked of her, and a warning is given. Unless she follows this admonition, the Lord tells her, "where I am you cannot come."

What is remarkable in this list of duties is the absence of mundane tasks of "women's work." Emma Smith is not told to keep her house in order or to serve nutritious meals. There is nothing that indicates that child care is her primary task. Emma Smith, at this

point, had no living children. Although we know her to have been an excellent, inde-
fatigable housekeeper, no household tasks are listed. This list rises above basic chores to
deal with interpersonal relations, those with her husband, the church congregation, and
the Lord.

With this promise, Emma Smith served as her husband's scribe, when he needed her.
She did do her hymnbook, with the help of W. W. Phelps. She did exhort and expound,
though not until 1842, when Smith specifically read this document to the assembled
Relief Society sisters. She did comfort and console her husband, although she was
sorely tried by some of his teachings and behavior. And she was loyal and faithful to him
throughout their marriage and beyond.

Woman's role in the Church of Jesus Christ is effectively set out by this scripture even
unto today. Women are told that they are valiant, able creatures, expected to take on
significant responsibilities in the kingdom. At the same time they are to be comforting
and submissive wives. Mormon women have lived with this possible contradiction for
almost 200 years.

Fourteen years later in 1844 when Smith was on his way to his death, his wife asked
for his blessing, evidence of her enduring devotion. He was harried and suggested that
she write her own blessing which he would later sign. She wrote the blessing, but he was
no longer able to affix his signature. In the blessing, she shows attitudes reflecting those
suggested in section 25.[2]

Emma Smith asks first for wisdom, "bestowed daily," "from my Heavenly Father."
"I desire a fruitful, active mind, that I may be able to comprehend the designs of God,"
"I desire a spirit of discernment, which is one of the promised blessings of the Holy
Ghost." This emphasis on intelligence, wisdom, discernment, "on a fruitful, active
mind," on blessings from the Holy Ghost, continues the specific interest in activities
of the mind shown in section 25. She prays she will "comprehend the designs of God,
when revealed through his servants without doubting." She asks not for help in obedience, but in comprehension, understanding. In this prayer, there is the sense of daily
chores, of looking back at the close of each day and evaluating her performance.

Here she is specific about the care of children, seeking assistance in raising all the children "that are, or may be" given to her to raise. She had already been given children born
by others to bring up besides those born of her body. She would later take on the care of
others. She asks for two rather static blessings on her children—that they may be "useful
ornaments in the Kingdom of God" and that "in a coming day [they may] arise up and
call me blessed." She wants them, then, to be evidence of her good work. She says nothing of their earthly father.

The section on her health is perhaps unexpected. She wants to care for her body so
that she will be able to do her work. This comment may reflect the age of the health pioneers that she lived through. But her desire has strong religious overtones. She wants to
be able to perform the work that she "covenanted to perform in the spirit-world, to be
able to present a cheerful face to the world," and to meet any obligations which she may
encounter to do good. There is no sign of vanity in desiring that her body not become
"prematurely old and care-worn." It is all service and good works.

The final section of her blessing is all love and obedience to her husband and to the Lord. Her most adamant language and the climactic position of this section in her blessing underscore her "desire with all my heart to honor and respect my husband as my head, ever to live in his confidence and by acting in unison with him retain the place which God has given me by his side." She loves and obeys her husband and the Lord. She values her position as the wife of the prophet, at his side, "in his confidence," "acting in unison with him." She does not want to forfeit that place. She does not seek to improve her husband. She does not want independence, but a favored subservient position. She desires that she will always be "enabled to acknowledge the hand of God in all things." This again is a plea for comprehension and discernment, that whatever happens she will be able to understand what is required of her so that she may be obedient through understanding.

Emma Smith, then, is a valuable example of and for LDS women. She was given work to do to build the kingdom, work for which she was well suited and where she could make a serious contribution. She was offered broad ecclesiastical powers which she was hesitant to undertake. She obeyed, not easily, and not without effort, the teachings of the church, praying always for discernment, comprehension and understanding. She thought for herself, but she wanted to be convinced of the views of her leaders. She was faithful to Joseph Smith in his life and beyond. LDS women feel the power of that model to this day.

Eliza R. Snow is the third of the women faithful to Joseph Smith. She represents the collection of Mormon women who followed his teachings as well as his thirty or so plural wives, the Relief Society Sisters, and the writing women of the church. These women supported Joseph Smith's serious work.

Mormon pioneer women have long been praised for their foresight in choosing this new religion, for sacrificing much to leave home and family to follow its teachings, and for risking all in going against the accepted morals of the age in living a marital style foreign to them. They consecrated all to their church. The men, when they were asked to donate their goods and riches to the church and live in common with the other saints, failed the test. They were unwilling to share with the poor in a modest Utopian society. They failed to live the larger life. The women, when they were asked to give up their good names as pure and virtuous women, to live as secret or open wives of men already married to other women, rose to the challenge. They overcame their initial reluctance and revulsion, and pledged themselves to unions that they believed would bring future blessings to their families.

Eliza R. Snow was one of those women, a prim New England poetess who nevertheless married polygamously the first two presidents of the church. She later said that she had no reason to regret her decisions. She it was who recorded the beginnings of the Relief Society in Nauvoo in 1842, providing the document that the organization was based on. Again the role of faithful women was laid out. "The Society of Sisters might provoke the brethren to good works in looking to the wants of the poor—searching after objects of charity, and in administering to their wants—to assist, by correcting the morals and strengthening the virtues of the female community, and save the Elders the trouble of rebuking, that they [the Elders] may give their time to other duties &c. in their public teaching."[3] Much of this admonition can be seen in the current church. The sisters are strongly given to good works, assisting others, and being somewhat judgmental of the virtues of others. There is also the lingering sense that the women are to be faithful nudges, "provoking the brethren to good works," and doing basic tasks to free the men for more important things.

Eliza R. Snow was a cornerstone of the strong female society made up of the plural wives of the male leaders. Later in Utah, she reorganized the Relief Society which had become inactive in Nauvoo, traveling and preaching to the sisters in their efforts to be good wives and good Mormons. Under her direction the women organized to strengthen the economy as well as to share spiritual experiences. The Mormon women of the second half of the nineteenth century were financially useful to the economy. Brigham Young spoke positively of the value of women's work: "We believe that women are useful, not only to sweep houses, wash dishes, make beds, & raise babies, but they should stand behind the counter, study law or physic [medicine], or become good bookkeepers & be able to do the business in any counting house, and all this to enlarge their sphere of usefulness for the benefit of society at large. In following these things they but answer the design of their creation."[4]

He saw no question as to their ability. He saw the inclusion of working women for society's benefit, not for the pleasure or profit of the individual woman. Women's work would free men for harder physical labor. However, women were not to be excused from their traditional work in the home with children. They were to work together in areas requiring intelligence, learning, and skill to fulfill their promise and to move society forward.

The disjunction between images of oppressed plural wives and lady telegraphers and doctors was increased by the fact that they were the first women in the United States to vote in a regular election. Women were granted the franchise in the Utah Territory in 1870. Stringent anti-Mormon legislation, the Cullom Bill, introduced by Illinois Representative Shelby Moore Cullom, prompted the Utah Mormon women to hold mass meetings protesting against the passage of the bill. Here the women demonstrated themselves not only voters, but effective political speakers. These articulate and forceful women and the published, widely distributed versions of their remarks have been partially credited with the defeat of the bill. Mormon women exercised the franchise until 1887, when the privilege was snatched back by the passage of later antipolygamy legislation, the Edmunds-Tucker Act in 1887 in Washington, DC, preventing all Utah women from voting. Under extensive pressure, the Mormon Church discontinued plural marriage in 1890. The vote was returned to Utah women in 1896 in the new constitution when Utah became one of the United States.[5]

Back in 1870, Eliza R. Snow, in her speech to a large assemblage of gathered women, was quoted as saying:

> Our enemies pretend that in Utah woman is held in a state of vassalage; that she does not act from choice but by coercion; that we would even prefer life elsewhere were it

possible for us to make our escape. What nonsense! We all know that if we wished we could leave at any time—either to go singly or we could rise *en masse*, and there is no power here that could or would ever wish to prevent us.

I will now ask this intelligent assembly of ladies, Do you know of any place on the face of the earth where woman has more liberty and where she enjoys such high and glorious privileges as she does here as a Latter-day Saint? "No!" The very idea of women here in a state of slavery is a burlesque on good common sense. The history of this people, with a very little reflection, would instruct outsiders on this point; it would show at once that the part which woman has acted in it could never have been performed against her will. Amid the many distressing scenes through which we have passed, the privations and hardships consequent on our expulsion from State to State, and our location in an isolated, barren wilderness, the women in this church have performed and suffered what could never have been borne and accomplished by slaves. . . .

Were we the stupid, degraded, heart-broken beings that we have been represented, silence might better become us; but as women of God, women filling high and responsible positions, performing sacred duties, women who stand not as dictators but as counselors to their husbands, and who, in the purest, noblest sense of refined womanhood, being truly their helpmates, we not only speak because we have the right, but justice and humanity demand that we should.[6]

Eliza R. Snow's pungent rhetoric is marked by the same divide as earlier documents. She claims equality, even as she proudly notes that Mormon women "have performed and suffered what could never have been borne and accomplished by slaves." They are not only able and independent, they choose to abase themselves below slaves. But they only do so by choice, by their desire to serve their men and their God. They cannot be forced to take on such duties.

The contradictions of the Mormon women are described by Elizabeth Kane, an observer, who visited Utah in 1872. She found Mormon women "thousands of years behind" in some customs; but in others, "you would think these people the most forward children of the age." No career by which a girl could earn a living was closed to her. She could aspire to marry any husband.[7] Mormon women could do everything they cared to do, exercising equality with men, as long as they took their places in a patriarchal family structure and behaved themselves.

This independent, obedient, church-observant, maternal stance is the style by which the nineteenth-century Mormon women are known and celebrated. Certainly not all women were of that stamp, but many carried it on and were proud of it. It was the Relief Society style of independent, can-do women that carried over to the twentieth century. Given tasks to work hard, make money, and conserve resources, women gleaned in the fields, preserved food, saved grain, worked for wages, supported husbands on missions, spun and wove cotton and wool—while living frugally and raising large families.

The practice of and defense of polygamy faded in the twentieth century, as did the agricultural model of family life in which all family members worked together in a single place. As polygamy waned and urban life flourished, a very different style of ideal family was celebrated in the Mormon Church. The nuclear family with devoted father and mother and several children aimed for mutual emotional closeness, the parents practicing marital fidelity, eschewing divorce. The pioneer need for women to contribute directly to the economy also faded away, and women were expected to maintain the home as the center for virtue and for the nurturing of children. This seemed to be the American style, the ideal family life for most of the nation, particularly after the Second World War, when the fighting men returned home, moved to the suburbs, and practiced family togetherness. This LDS style, with the addition of the Relief Society style which promoted service, sacrifice, devotion, and good works, along with child rearing, became the Mormon model. The backs of LDS women were tilted to the burden of domestic labor.

Situations that are assumed are not described. Instruction only comes when the desired situation is threatened. Sociologist Laura Vance clocked mentions and instructions to women in the Latter-day Saint publication the *Improvement Era*. She found little mention of women's roles from the early years beginning in 1891. Mormon women were not instructed to restrict their activities to homemaking until the 1940s, when women began to move into the paid workforce to replace soldiers going to war. LDS apostle John A. Widtsoe, writing in 1942, said that women should devote themselves chiefly to the home, although they should learn marketable skills "should circumstances require" them to earn a living.[8]

That same year, an article from the First Presidency of the Mormon Church, Presidents Heber J. Grant, J. Reuben Clark, and David O. McKay issued a very strong statement that mothers should not work. Their article said that the "divine service of motherhood can be rendered only by mothers. It may not be passed to others. Nurses cannot do it; public nurseries cannot do it; hired help cannot do it. . . . The mother who entrusts her child to the care of others, that she may do non-motherly work, whether for gold, for fame, or for civic service, should remember that 'a child left to himself bringeth her mother to shame.'"[9] Mothering duties, which had not been included at all in section 25 of the Doctrine and Covenants because their importance and centrality were assumed, had to be strongly reemphasized. Nothing was said of fatherly responsibilities. There had seemed to be no need before to limit women's behavior.

So the social disruption of the 1960s was particularly distressing to leaders of the church who had taught the eternal identity of the nuclear family. One problem was that the membership increasingly did not reflect that style of family. Single females did not fit into the plan. The birthrate, with the rest of the United States, was steadily declining. Effective and available birth control and later legal abortion challenged the necessity of premarital chastity and alleviated some of the brutal consequences that had previously followed its lack. Housewives with smaller families and labor-saving devices became restless and bored. They felt that they no longer counted. The economy encouraged and for many required that women join the labor force. Female independence allowed divorce. The nuclear family as understood by the Mormons, the bedrock of civilization, the primal ecclesiastical unit, found itself crumbling under siege. What had seemed unchangeable became increasingly fragile.

As the woman's movement burst upon the scene, the issues multiplied. Did a woman's work upset the patriarchal hierarchy, the priesthood dominance that the male deserved and needed? What about a woman's desire for self-fulfillment, for meaningful work? How could the parents be equal when one was presiding over the other? Interesting here is that the church began to recognize that some mothers, deprived for whatever reason of their family breadwinners, had to work. The church provided no aid to help a woman stay at home.

Threatened by the rhetoric of the 1970s and the actions of women, the church worked against a proposed amendment to the United States Constitution which prohibited the abridgement of rights based on gender, the Equal Rights Amendment (ERA). The church had supported the initiative at first, but as the amendment moved toward ratification, the church took action against it and against LDS women involved in the ratification process. The church's participation was probably instrumental in the defeat of the initiative. After that furor broke down, the church began to moderate its stance against working women.

The church puts heavy pressure on its male breadwinners, requiring 10 percent of their income in tithing plus other expenses and many hours of involvement. Many children plus large family houses are expensive. Higher education and mission experiences, also expensive, are highly encouraged. Many families could not get by without the supplemental income of a working mother. While the clear desire of the church leaders is that women should stay home with their children, there has been an increasing understanding that sometimes this ideal cannot be met. Now permission for a woman to work outside her home is framed by recognition that some women need to work, that they need to seek divine guidance that working is the correct option, and that there exists the potential for judgment from other church women. All official statements now convey the preferred status of stay-at-home moms, often with the additional possibility that they may take up a job or a career when the children are grown.

A final document to be considered in this chapter is the *Proclamation on the Family*. Read to a Relief Society conference by President Gordon B. Hinckley in 1995, this document is not canonized scripture, but is generally treated as if it is. No claim has been made that the document is revelation from God, as is generally understood about the sections of the Doctrine and Covenants. Instead, the document seems to be a compilation of ideas from past talks and teachings of church authorities, neither attributed nor dated. Members are advised to read it carefully and prayerfully, to hang it on the wall as a reminder of virtuous action.

For our purposes here, we can note a strong effort to teach the equality of women, linking married couples as equals in marriage, as creations and children of God, with both possessing eternal gender, a teaching little noted before. Men and women are divided by divergent roles, not unequal status. Men are to have the outside leadership role, the responsibility of supporting the family. Women are to raise the children and tend the hearth. The only hint of hierarchy is the presence of the familiar word "preside." Fathers preside, provide, protect while mothers nurture children, but through fulfilling different functions, parents cooperate as equal partners. The *Proclamation on the Family* seeks to have it both ways, to write on both sides of the contradiction, as have the previous documents we have considered here.

This is a conservative document, harking back to family styles of yore, written in the solemn tones of Old Testament prophets, using strong language which affords little discussion. The document is "solemnly proclaim[ed]." "Marriage is ordained of God." "The family is central to the Creator's plan for the eternal destiny of His children." The language is strong throughout: "Divine nature and destiny," "Sacred ordinances and covenants," "Honor marital vows with complete fidelity." This vision of the family is endowed with religious certainly.

Unfortunately, the vision excludes the large number of women single for whatever reason. The significant number of gay Mormons is excluded. When the family becomes the unit for church membership, the individual is lost along the way. This vision of the family is imprinted and underscored and proclaimed. Yet, the proclamation stops short of ghettoizing women completely in their homes. The placement of the proclamation in historical perspective, with many examples of changes in authoritarian teachings, allows some variations. Church leaders acknowledge that sometimes two incomes may be necessary and that couples may engage in creative solutions where they "help one another" to raise and teach their children. Nothing is said of the strong doctrines preached in the past: early marriage, the evils of postponing and limiting families, or those of birth control. Families are told to pray and to make their own decisions on such important matters.

While efforts to standardize LDS families have been made over the years, there has been a recent effort to emphasize individuality, spearheaded by the church's public affairs department. To counter the strangeness, the lack of individuality, the roboticness of Mormons, individual vignettes on Latter-day Saints are being shown on the Internet. These list a series of unusual characteristics and then finish with, "And I'm a Mormon." These more hip and up-to-date Mormons include women who do colorful and ambitious things that, while not considered dangerous, would never have been encouraged by their church leaders. These are women who are active in careers, in civic volunteerism, in areas where their ambitions have been privileged against having another baby or along with another baby who might be waiting in heaven to join the family. Here are a couple of examples of women from the website, edited for length.

Shannon was born and raised in Texas. She participated in more than five religions before being baptized a Mormon.

> I am a 22 year old mother and just wrapped up my 1st year of marriage. I go to school full time and work part time. I will be graduating in my little community college soon just to start all over again so hopefully I can become a chiropractor someday. I have been in karate for over 15 years and won national champion when I was 16. Although working and going to school keep me busy my family means everything to me and I wouldn't be where I am without them.

Jessie is a former high school English teacher, married with three children.

> I am intrigued by all things worthy of my mental faculty—books, movies, music, traveling, etc. In fact, I do quite a bit of traveling with my family. I've been playing the piano since I was little, and I sure can sing at KTV![10]

In fact, there are all kinds of Mormon women, and always have been, even while an ideal shape is sketched out and promoted. The stereotypes are smudged and even erased by the subtle nuances of variety. The direction for women's lives so confidently set out by male leaders in the past grows regularly broader. For one thing, marriage and family are not an option for every woman. There aren't enough good men to go around. Women have to take potential careers more seriously than they used to do.

And as we might expect, even this effort to broaden the vision of possibilities for LDS women has come under attack. In the very active blogosphere operating in the realm of Mormonism, ZD Eve regrets the broad versions of women's lives allowed by the new rules. She finds the "I'm a Mormon" campaign painful to watch, thinking of the wasted lives and talents of past women who have tried hard to be obedient to the old models to which LDS women aspired. She sees, as do many, that the church is now willing to turn to the world the independent faces of hip women who are more than wives and mothers, faces that are "deeply at odds with the messages of our not so distant past."

> I know more than one woman of the generation ahead of mine who diligently, faithfully did as she was told—sacrificed her own education and interests and career possibilities, bore and raised the requisite large family, closely spaced, stayed in her marriage even if it was difficult or downright abusive, accepted every calling that came to her even if she could barely manage her family responsibilities—who now feels betrayed by the church. After the gut-wrenching sacrifices made by these women of their own dreams, it turns out that birth control isn't always evil, that it's acceptable to space your children and limit the number to what you can handle, that you shouldn't have to put up with being bullied and mistreated in your marriage, that you should get as much education as you can and maintain your own interests, and that working outside the home isn't necessarily evil.[11]

Mormon women have always had more space in which to act than they have cared to or believed they could exercise. That is becoming clearer as the balance of teachings has been shifting from service and sacrifice for women to making their own decisions and finding their own way with the help of good husbands, should they be fortunate enough to have them, and higher powers above. Mormonism has always taught that women, as well as men, have direct access to heavenly powers through prayer and revelation. Women who have felt their lives blighted by limitations can try again.

NOTES

1. Smith, *History of Joseph Smith by His Mother*. Lucy Mack Smith's biography of her son and family exists in many editions, some of them excellent. The most thorough critical version is Anderson and Bates, *Lucy's Book*.
2. This blessing is reproduced in Newell and Avery, *Mormon Enigma*, 190–91, n30, 344. The provenance of this document is complicated. A typescript is in the church vaults, but the original version has disappeared. The document came west with Joseph Smith's papers

and was in private hands for many years. The handwriting was authenticated by several sources before the original was misplaced. Newell and Avery think that there can be little doubt that the blessing, as follows, is authentic.

> First of all that I would crave as the richest of heaven's blessings would be wisdom from my Heavenly Father bestowed daily, so that whatever I might do or say, I could not look back at the close of the day with regret, nor neglect the performance of any act that would bring a blessing. I desire the Spirit of God to know and understand myself, that I desire a fruitful, active mind, that I may be able to comprehend the designs of God, when revealed through his servants without doubting. I desire a spirit of discernment, which is one of the promised blessings of the Holy Ghost.
>
> I particularly desire wisdom to bring up all the children that are, or may be committed to my charge, in such a manner that they will be useful ornaments in the Kingdom of God, and in a coming day arise up and call me blessed.
>
> I desire prudence that I may not through ambition abuse my body and cause it to become prematurely old and care-worn, but that I may wear a cheerful countenance, live to perform all the work that I covenanted to perform in the spirit-world and be a blessing to all who may in any wise need aught at my hands.
>
> I desire with all my heart to honor and respect my husband as my head, ever to live in his confidence and by acting in unison with him retain the place which God has given me by his side, and I ask my Heavenly Father that through humility, I may be enabled to over come that curse which was pronounced upon the daughters of Eve. I desire to see that I may rejoice with them in the blessings which God has in store for all who are willing to be obedient to his requirements. Finally, I desire that whatever may be my lot through life I may be enabled to acknowledge the hand of God in all things.

3. Snow, quoting from Joseph Smith in "Book of Records Containing the Proceedings of the Female Relief Society of Nauvoo," 7.
4. Young, "Obeying the Gospel" 1869, 13: 61; quoted in Bushman, *Contemporary Mormonism*, 112–13.
5. Bushman, *Mormon Sisters*, 157–75.
6. Snow, *Proceedings in Mass Meeting of the Ladies of Salt Lake City*, 4, 5.
7. Kane, *Twelve Mormon Homes*, 5; quoted in Bushman, *Mormon Domestic Life in the 1870s*, 114 (lecture originally given October 7, 1999).
8. Widtsoe, "What is the Place of Woman in the Church?," 161, 188.
9. Grant, Clark, McKay, "Message from the First Presidency," 601–12.
10. See http://mormon.org/me/2Z04/Jessie and http://mormon.org/me/34QZ/Shannon.
11. ZD Eve, response to Smith, "Does Gender Matter?"

Bibliography

Anderson, Lavina Fielding, and Irene M. Bates, eds. *Lucy's Book: Critical Edition of Lucy Mack Smith's Family Memoir*. Salt Lake City: Signature, 2001.

Beecher, Maureen Ursenbach, and Lavina Fielding Anderson, eds. *Sisters in Spirit: Mormon Women in Historical and Cultural Perspective*. Urbana: University of Illinois Press, 1987.

Bradley, Martha Sonntag. *Pedestals and Podiums: Utah Women, Religious Authority, and Equal Rights*. Salt Lake City: Signature, 2005. Available at http://mormon.org/me/2Zo4/Jessie, and http://mormon.org/me/34QZ/Shannon.

Bushman, Claudia L. *Contemporary Mormonism: Latter-day Saints in Modern America*. Westport, CT: Praeger, 2006.

Bushman, Claudia L. *Mormon Domestic Life in the 1870s: Pandemonium or Arcadia?* Collected Leonard J. Arrington Mormon History Lectures. Logan: Utah State University, 2005.

Bushman, Claudia L., ed. *Mormon Sisters: Women in Early Utah*. Cambridge, MA: Emmeline, 1976. New ed., Logan: Utah State University Press, 1997.

Cannon, Janath Russell, Jill Mulvay Derr, and Maureen Ursenbach Beecher. *Women of Covenant: The Story of Relief Society*. Salt Lake City: Deseret, 2002.

Grant, Heber J., R. L. Clark, and David O. McKay. "Message from the First Presidency." *Improvement Era* vol. 45 (1942).

Kane, Elizabeth Wood. *Twelve Mormon Homes: Visited in Succession on a Journey through Utah to Arizona*. Salt Lake City: University of Utah Library, 1974.

Newell, Linda King, and Valeen Tippetts Avery. *Mormon Enigma: Emma Hale Smith, Prophet's Wife, "Elect Lady," Polygamy's Foe, 1804–1879*. Garden City, NY: Doubleday, 1984.

Smith, Alison Moore. "Does Gender Matter?" *Times and Seasons*, May 24, 2011. http://timesandseasons.org/index.php/2011/05/does-gender-matter/.

Smith, Lucy Mack. *Biographical Sketches of Joseph Smith the Prophet, and His Progenitors for Many Generations*. Liverpool: Orson Pratt, 1853.

Snow, Eliza R. "A Book of Records Containing the Proceedings of the Female Relief Society of Nauvoo." March 17, 1842. http//josephsmithpapers.org/paperSummary/nauvoo-relief-society-minute-book?p=.

Snow, Eliza R. *Proceedings in Mass Meeting of the Ladies of Salt Lake City, to Protest against the Passage of Cullom's Bill, January 14, 1870*. Salt Lake City: n.p., 1870.

Widtsoe, John A. "What is the Place of Woman in the Church?" *Improvement Era* 45, no. 3 (March 1942): 161, 188.

Young, Brigham. "Obeying the Gospel—Recreation—Individual Development" [18 July 1869]. *Journal of Discourses* 13: 56–62.

ZD Eve. Response to Smith, "Does Gender Matter?" *Times and Seasons*, May 26, 2011. http://timesandseasons.org/index.php/2011/05/does-gender-matter/#comment-325922.

....

CHAPTER 6

UNDERSTANDING MULTIPLE MORMONISMS

....

WILLIAM D. RUSSELL

THE Mormon movement has experienced a remarkably large number (many dozens) of schismatic defections during its more than 180-year existence.[1] At least two factors appear to have prompted this. First, Mormon theology teaches that all believers are capable of receiving revelation from God. If these individuals believe they have received divine inspiration, and if their "revelation" is contrary to accepted church teachings, it is natural for some recipients of the inspiration to believe the church is in error.

Secondly, Mormons teach that Joseph Smith Jr. initiated a restoration of the ancient order of things or, at a minimum, a restoration of the New Testament church. This has inclined some Mormons to believe that periodic changes which have occurred in modern time constitute "apostasy," because the new beliefs represent departures from the initial inspired teachings that made up "the true church" restored by Joseph Smith Jr.

This fissive tendency in Mormonism may be discerned across its history, its geography, and among its variant organizational expressions, including the large Church of Jesus Christ of Latter-day Saints, whose headquarters are in Salt Lake City. This chapter, however, focuses on dissent that arose primarily in the American Midwest in the nineteenth century, along with the heirs of this dissent in the twentieth.

Joseph Smith's theology evolved significantly in his short fourteen-year career as the prophet and leader of his movement. His Book of Mormon (1830) and early revelations were reasonably consistent theologically with at least some versions of Protestantism in western New York at the time. His claim to modern revelation, a unique priesthood system, and publishing what amounted to a "second Bible" were his major variations from Protestant thinking at the beginning of the movement. By the end of his life in 1844 he had radically departed from or expanded upon the relative orthodoxy of the Book of Mormon and other early teachings.

Over the years of his leadership of the movement, Smith began to tell a story in which he claimed a miraculous and marvelous visitation from God in about 1820 in a grove near his home in Palmyra, New York. Later versions of the story added the attendance of a second divine personage: both God and Jesus Christ appeared in that sacred grove. One possible interpretation of some aspects of these changes is that the persecution which the Mormons experienced in New York, Ohio, and Missouri led him to expand upon his earliest story and to specify in later accounts that when he asked God which church he should join, God reportedly replied that he should join none of them, because their creeds were all "abominations."[2]

The most significant defection stemming from early developments in the faith came in the very early years when Joseph Smith quit using his "peep-stone"—a relatively flat stone with a hole in the middle—to obtain revelations from God. Since his peep-stone had been used to translate most of the Book of Mormon and to receive his first sixteen canonized revelations, David Whitmer, one of three special witnesses to Smith's gold plates and the Book of Mormon, as well as others, eventually concluded that Smith had erred in abandoning the use of his stone to receive divine truths. This led Whitmer and some others to believe that Smith erred in elaborating church governance by establishing a First Presidency and ordaining high priests, since neither is found as church offices in the Book of Mormon or the New Testament. One eventual dissenter who was led to similar views was William McLellin, one of the original twelve apostles ordained in 1835. For McLellin, Joseph Smith's only divine calling was as "translator," and not as a "prophet" or "church president." In his view, Smith translated the Book of Mormon by the power of God and correctly taught that God reveals himself in all ages. Smith's later teachings were unnecessary and wrong, at least when they differed from the Book of Mormon.[3]

The Nauvoo period, 1839–46, brought innovations by Smith that led to the creation, after his death, of several factions that did not accept some of these Nauvoo innovations. Ultimately, many people who had followed these defectors joined a new organization, believing that the mantle of leadership should fall on a son of Joseph the founder, preferably his oldest son, Joseph Smith III. Organizing in 1852, they ultimately persuaded young Smith to accept the leadership of the group in April 1860. In January of that year they had already begun publishing an official periodical, entitled *The True Latter Day Saints' Herald*, a not so subtle suggestion that the other factions, including the largest group, which had been led by Brigham Young to Utah, were false versions of the faith. They referred to themselves as the "New Organization" at first; eventually they adopted the name Reorganized Church of Jesus Christ of Latter Day Saints (RLDS), which became the largest and most influential alternative to the LDS Church based in Utah. The "Reorganites," as they were sometimes called, had their largest number of members and congregations in Illinois, Wisconsin, Michigan, Iowa, and, before long, Missouri. More recently (2001), the church changed its name to Community of Christ to reflect its evolved sensibilities toward a moderate or liberal Protestantism.

Over the course of the first century of its existence, the RLDS Church differed with the larger Utah Mormon church on six major issues, two of which were the dominant issues in the early years as the movement was getting established in the 1850s. Understandably, polygamy was the most important issue, as it conflicted with long-held moral views in Western Christian society. With Americans almost universally denouncing the

Mormons for this doctrine, it was a natural issue for the RLDS Church to exploit. Opposition to polygamy was a way to demonstrate its differences with the unpopular Mormons, and to attempt to gain respectability from its neighbors in the Midwest.

The second dominant issue in the early years was the matter of succession in the office of prophet-president of the church. This was often the most talked-about issue, because the question of religious authority—the authority to conduct religious affairs on behalf of God, including the authority to call and ordain clergy, to administer the sacraments, and to preach the gospel—was important in Mormon theology.[4]

The movement was a response in part to the revivals of the Second Great Awakening, which was at its peak in the decade of the 1820s when Joseph Smith was finding his religious voice. Mormonism was also partly a response to some of the excesses of the revivals. Since people could allegedly attend a revival, get caught up in the excitement and have an experience of "blessed assurance" that their soul had been saved, the question naturally arose: "But what is the role of the authority of the church, its authoritative ministry, the proper administration of its sacraments, its scriptures and long-held traditions, including the historic creeds?" The revivals, it seemed, bypassed these important matters.[5]

Part of the question of the authoritative calling and ordination to priesthood was the matter of how the successor to the church's president was to be chosen. Mormons who joined the New Organization came from virtually every faction of Mormonism that had developed during the sixteen years between the murder of Joseph Smith Jr. and the ordination of the first president-prophet of the New Organization. Various leaders had arisen, representing differing claims to authority. Brigham Young was the president of the Twelve Apostles; the majority of Saints believed that Joseph Smith's successor should be chosen from this quorum, identified in one of Smith's revelations as "the second presidency." On the other hand, a much smaller group was drawn to the authority of Sidney Rigdon, as the sole surviving member of the three-member First Presidency, since the third member was Joseph Smith's brother Hyrum, who also died in the gunfire at the Carthage, Illinois, jail on the night of June 27, 1844. Apostle Lyman Wight presented a third alternative. Wight was a prominent apostle, and had been commissioned by Joseph Smith to establish the church in the independent colony of Texas, which had declared its independence from Mexico in 1836 and would not be admitted to the United States until the year after the murder of the Smith brothers. James J. Strang, although a church member only four months before Smith's martyrdom, put forward yet another claim as Smith's proper successor, and a very creative case at that. So compelling was he that many of those who later joined and many even who came to lead the Reorganization had formerly followed Strang. Patterning his career closely after Joseph Smith, the would-be prophet allegedly received revelations, dug up and translated ancient documents, and claimed to have received a "letter of appointment" from Joseph Smith Jr.[6] Those who accepted Strang for a time included Jason W. Briggs, the eventual founder of the Reorganization. He had followed Strang just before forming the Reorganization, and as recently as 1849 had declared in the Strangite newspaper that he knew with certainty that James J. Strang was God's chosen successor to Joseph Smith.[7]

Strang's organization naturally gained a lot of followers because it was located in the Midwest, in southeast Wisconsin, not terribly far from where many Saints lived at the time of Smith's death. Those who were satisfied with the direction the Smith had taken the church during the Nauvoo period were more likely to have followed Brigham Young to what became Utah.

Probably because Joseph Smith Jr. had initiated polygamy and it was practiced by many in the leadership in Nauvoo,[8] several leaders of factions that claimed to succeed Smith after his death also engaged in what came to be called "the Principle." Sidney Rigdon, Lyman Wight, William Smith, and Alpheus Cutler were all among the Nauvoo elite who were polygamist during at least part of their time as leaders of successor organizations.

Jason W. Briggs was leader of a congregation of Mormons in Beloit, Wisconsin. As noted, he was, as late as 1849, certain about Strang's prophetic calling. Very likely Strang's clear preaching of monogamy as God's law of marriage was part of Briggs's certainty. But Strang reevaluated that teaching, perhaps influenced by his meeting Elvira Field, a nineteen-year-old school teacher from Michigan. When Strang returned from an eight-month missionary trip to the east with Elvira dressed as a boy, "Charlie Douglas," he probably realized he could not keep his polygamy secret any longer, so he announced it to his people. This was no doubt a shock for Briggs. And if polygamy wasn't enough of a problem, Strang had himself crowned "King" two months later, another action in which he copied Joseph Smith, whose "kingship" was far outside the American tradition.

A significant part of Emma Smith's resistance to invitations to move to Utah was her hatred of polygamy. She and her sons remained in Nauvoo. Perhaps Briggs's hatred of polygamy, and his knowledge that Emma did, too, and had kept her sons in Nauvoo, helped lead him to the conclusion that a son of the prophet should succeed his father. Lineage is significant in the Hebrew Bible and Joseph Smith Jr. had valued many Old Testament traditions. Additionally, lineal succession in the office of president was one of several ways in which Joseph Smith Jr. envisioned succession at one time or another.[9] Briggs's dream was fulfilled when Joseph Smith III accepted the presidency of the church on April 6, 1860.

A third major difference between the LDS and the RLDS churches soon emerged. "Young Joseph," as he was called, accepted the American principle of the separation of church and state, and urged his people not to gather into one location and seek political control of the secular government. He realized that the early church had continually brought trouble for itself by gathering into a central place, raising the animosity of those already settled there. There would be no RLDS theocracy, as had existed in Nauvoo and in Utah. Perhaps as a young lad he had seen too much persecution of his father and their religion because of the threat that Mormonism in gathered communities posed to the world around them. Joseph III would proceed very cautiously in the matter of gathering into "Zionic" communities. His major biographer, Roger Launius, appropriately labeled him a "pragmatic prophet."[10]

A fourth major difference emerged as the New Organization gradually rejected the secret temple rituals established at Nauvoo, especially the doctrine of the plurality of gods, with temple rituals reflecting this belief in the potential of eternal progression to godhood for especially worthy Mormon males. This was possibly the Mormon doctrine at the most variance from Christian orthodoxy, at least once polygamy was abandoned by the LDS Church in 1904. In the first decade of Joseph Smith III's presidency, a majority of church leaders believed the plurality of gods was correct doctrine, but young Smith apparently disagreed, and urged that the doctrine not be made a test of faith. Rather than possibly having a major battle with the older, far more experienced church leaders, the young "pragmatic prophet" wisely let this unusual doctrine die a slow death, as the members gradually found it unappealing. Eventually this doctrine was denied by the church, and cited as a doctrinal difference with the LDS Church.

A fifth major difference between the two churches in the first century of the existence of the RLDS Church involved the practice of baptizing for the dead. It appears that young Joseph also looked askance at this major temple ritual. Roger Launius has noted that Joseph Smith III gradually allowed this doctrine to fade into the background. By the 1950s, his son Israel A. Smith was church president, and he wanted to remove from the Doctrine and Covenants three revelations that supported the doctrine. But he was talked out of asking the church's General Conference to decanonize these revelations. The fear was likely that decanonizing some scripture would open a "can of worms" that might lead to a major battle within the church. Finally, at the World Conferences of 1970 and 1990, the church decanonized these revelations in a two-step process.

A sixth significant difference, which existed from 1865 until 1978, was the RLDS acceptance of African Americans into the priesthood, beginning with an 1865 revelation by Joseph III. Although the LDS Church did not abandon its priesthood exclusion policy until 1978, the RLDS Church rarely made an issue of this difference between the two churches until the modern civil rights movement, normally dated approximately 1954–68. As the RLDS people and its leaders became more aware of the tragic injustice in US race relations, it dawned on them that this was a significant difference which the RLDS could exploit in their missionary work, showing the world that they did not have this racist practice of the LDS Church.[11]

The RLDS Church was centered in the Midwest, first in Illinois, then Iowa, and by 1920 the headquarters was in Independence, Missouri. While the LDS Church in the intermountain West was relatively isolated from the outside world and its influences, the RLDS members were relatively few and concentrated in the Midwest, where they were more affected by the Protestant culture around them. The RLDS people sought to be legitimately Mormon but also legitimate in the eyes of their Protestant neighbors.[12]

A major schism occurred in the RLDS Church in the 1920s when Joseph Smith III's successor, his son Frederick M. Smith, centered significantly more power in the office of the president-prophet, leading to serious challenges by some of the apostles and several of the leading bishops. Several thousand people left the church in that decade, most of them joining the Church of Christ (Temple Lot), a small group which owned the choice piece of land which Joseph Smith Jr. had called the "Temple Lot."[13]

More significant RLDS defections occurred in the last two decades of the twentieth century, during which about one-fourth of the active members affiliated with dissenting groups. Three factors seem to have caused these defections. First was that, beginning in the 1960s, a critical mass of church members began to obtain graduate degrees in religion from Protestant seminaries and secular universities. This led to a rethinking of many of the church's tradition teachings about scripture, history, theology, and Christian ethics.[14]

A second factor was the movement of the church, after the Second World War, into many societies around the world whose population was primarily non-Christian. Led by Apostle Charles Neff, church missionaries began to regard many of the church's traditional teachings as not being universal truths but, rather, ideas emerging from American culture. While the RLDS people and missionaries had traditionally regarded their religion as something "other" than the various Christian denominations, Neff and others, operating in Asia and Africa, soon saw other missionaries as friends with whom they could work cooperatively.[15]

A third factor was the movement of a significant number of the RLDS membership from the working class into the middle class after the Second World War, with a significant increase in the number of church members going to college and becoming more "respectable" citizens of their communities. These middle-class people were more inclined than their forebears to want to fit in with the surrounding culture and tended to see their church as inclusive rather than exclusive.

All three of these factors led the church to a more ecumenical approach, but it caused serious dissatisfaction among more traditional members. They deplored the abandonment or deemphasis upon some traditional Mormon doctrines, including the idea of being the "one true church." Traditional teachings about the Bible and the Book of Mormon and the unique RLDS interpretation of history and theology were similarly being denied because modern scholarship made many of the traditional claims about the Book of Mormon and the RLDS interpretation of history untenable to them.

Significant dissent was being expressed by the latter part of the 1960s, and increased until it came to a head in 1984, when church president Wallace B. Smith presented to that year's World Conference a document which a majority of the delegates accepted as revelation for the church. The document proposed that women be eligible for ordination. Approximately 20 percent of the delegates voted against accepting it as revelation. Over the next six years at least 200 dissenting organizations came into existence. Most of them have remained only local congregations to this day, not yet affiliating with any new church. Collectively, these groups are "independent restoration branches," which remain separate from the RLDS church organization and teach what they regard as the true restoration gospel. In their view, a branch can call and ordain deacons, teachers, priests, and elders, but only a "general church," with a prophet, apostles, and so forth, can call and ordain the higher officers such as high priests, seventies, bishops, evangelist/patriarchs, apostles, and a president.

A minority of those who joined schismatic groups have formed new church organizations, complete with the higher officers. The most successful of these is the Remnant Church of Jesus Christ of Latter Day Saints, organized in 2000 and led by a prophet, Frederick N. Larsen, who is a direct descendant of Joseph Smith Jr. and the grandson of the second RLDS President, Frederick M. Smith. As of this writing, the Remnant Church has a membership consisting of about 10 percent of the approximately 20,000 members of these dissenting groups. A larger group, but still a minority of the total number of dissenters, is part of an organization called the Joint Conference of Restoration Branches. These branches have decided to move ahead and organize "districts" and empower them to call seventies and high priests. But they have not yet created a complete "general church" organization with apostles and a prophet.

Applying the definitions of "sect" and "cult" used by Jan Shipps,[16] almost all of the known dissenting groups can be understood as "sects," which have merely tried to recover a tradition they believe endangered. They have tried to carry on church life without the new teachings that developed in the Reorganized Church (Community of Christ) during the past fifty years, which they regard as apostate. By contrast, there developed two known groups that can be viewed as "cults," wherein a charismatic leader has promulgated "new truths" that guide the movement in a different direction than the religious tradition from which it emerged.

These two groups represented differing types of survivalist organizations. One type gathers weapons and prepares to do battle with the evil world. Jeffrey Don Lundgren led such a group. At one point he planned to kill RLDS leaders in Kirtland, Ohio, including the stake president and his family. Lundgren changed his plans and instead murdered a family of five that was part of his group, on the notion that they were hopelessly unrepentant and were standing in the way of the return of Christ and the establishment of Zion. He was convicted in 1990 and executed by the state of Ohio in 2006. He has no known disciples intent upon carrying on his work.

The other type of survivalist group withdraws rather than confronting the wider "evil" society, and seeks to live as independently as possible from the outside world. Ronald E. Livingston from Oregon settled in Lamoni, Iowa, in the early 1970s and developed a following of devout believers. In 1989, he and about sixty of his followers settled on 200 acres four miles east of Lamoni, where they sought to live free from wicked "Babylon," that is, the heavily RLDS town of Lamoni. This group remained fairly stable, suffering only minor defections, until the spring of 2011, when about one-half of the approximately sixty group members defected, most of them moving back into Lamoni, where they have been well received by the more traditional community, contrary to Livingston's claim that they would never be accepted if they moved back to Babylon.

Many RLDS Church members had been wanting to change the church's name for at least half a century before it occurred. Being located in the Midwest in communities where their numbers were few, and disliking, often intensely, the label "Mormon," they found the long name discomforting. When the church underwent dramatic changes in the last four decades of the twentieth century, creating even greater theological distance from the LDS Church, support for a new name intensified. The leadership settled on "Community of Christ," focusing on the centrality of Christ and the Zionic ideal of creating Christian communities.[17] After at least six years of testing the name, the delegates at the 2000 World Conference officially changed the name, to be effective on April 6, 2001.

In the twenty-first century, the Community of Christ is clearly an ecumenical Protestant church. By 2010, the church had been admitted into the National Council of Churches, an organization of mainline Protestant churches that is moderately liberal in its approach to theology and Christian ethics, and is to be distinguished from those American Protestant churches that are fundamentalist or evangelical in theology. In many localities the church is involved in ecumenical activities. In some cases this has been going on for decades.

Informed by a belief in personal revelation as well as a desire to restore the singular "true church of Jesus Christ," Mormons from their earliest days have been susceptible to schism. Perhaps the Reorganized, Midwestern wing of the movement was especially susceptible. When serious disagreements emerged in later years, those who were profoundly disillusioned were prone to participate in schism, an inclination made easier because dissent was an intrinsic part of their tradition from the time of their (re)organization as a schismatic church in 1852.

NOTES

1. Arrington, "Centrifugal Tendencies in Mormon History," 165–77. Shields, *Divergent Paths of the Restoration.*
2. Howard, "Joseph Smith's First Vision," 95–117.
3. Larson and Passey, *William E. McLellin Papers.*
4. De Pillis, "Quest for Religious Authority and the Rise of Mormonism," 68–88.
5. Russell, "Latter Day Saint Priesthood," 232–41.
6. Speek, *God Has Made Us a Kingdom.*
7. Bringhurst and Hamer, *Scattering of the Saints*: seventeen essays on schisms throughout Mormon history.
8. Smith, *Nauvoo Polygamy.*
9. Quinn, *Mormon Hierarchy.*
10. Launius, *Joseph Smith III.*
11. Launius, *Invisible Saints.*
12. Vlahos, "Moderation as a Theological Principle in the Thought of Joseph Smith III," 3–11.
13. Addams, *Upon the Temple Lot.*
14. Launius and Spillman, *Let Contention Cease.*
15. Bolton, *Apostle of the Poor.*
16. Shipps, *Mormonism.*
17. Russell, "LDS Church and Community of Christ," 177–90.

BIBLIOGRAPHY

Addams, R. Jean. *Upon the Temple Lot: The Church of Christ's Quest to Build the House of the Lord.* Independence, MO: John Whitmer, 2010.

Arrington, Leonard J. "Centrifugal Tendencies in Mormon History." In *To the Glory of God: Mormon Essays on Great Issues*, ed. Truman G. Madsen and Charles D. Tate Jr., 165–77. Salt Lake City: Deseret, 1972.

Basic Beliefs Committee (Clifford A. Cole, chair). *Exploring the Faith*. Independence, MO: Herald House, 1970.

Bolton, Matthew. *Apostle of the Poor: The Life and Work of Missionary and Humanitarian Charles D. Neff*. Independence, MO: John Whitmer, 2005.

Bringhurst, Newell G., and John C. Hamer, eds. *Scattering of the Saints: Schism within Mormonism*. Independence, MO: John Whitmer, 2007.

Brunson, L. Madelon. *Bonds of Sisterhood: A History of the RLDS Women's Organization, 1842–1983*. Independence, MO: Herald House, 1985.

Cheville, Roy A. *The Bible in Everyday Living*. Independence, MO: Herald House, 1945.

Cole, Clifford A. *The Prophets' Speak*. Independence, MO: Herald House, 1954.

Conrad, Larry. "Dissent among Dissenters: Theological Dimensions of Dissent in the Reorganization." In Launius and Spillman, *Let Contention Cease*, 125–51.

De Pillis, Mario S. "The Quest for Religious Authority and the Rise of Mormonism." *Dialogue: A Journal of Mormon Thought* 1, no.1 (Spring 1966): 68–88.

Earley, Pete. *Prophet of Death: The Mormon Blood-Atonement Murders*. New York: William Morrow, 1991.

Edwards, Paul M. *Our Legacy of Faith: A Brief History of the Reorganized Church of Jesus Christ of Latter Day Saints*. Independence, MO: Herald House, 1991.

Flanders, Robert Bruce. *Nauvoo: Kingdom on the Mississippi*. Urbana: University of Illinois Press, 1965.

Ham, Wayne. "Problems in Interpreting the Book of Mormon as History." *Courage: A Journal of History, Thought, and Action* 1, no. 1 (September 1970): 15–22.

Hiles, Norma. *Gentle Monarch: The Presidency of Israel A. Smith*. Independence, MO: Herald House, 1991.

Howard, Richard P. *Restoration Scriptures: A Study of Their Texture Development*. Independence, MO: Herald House, 1969; rev. ed. 1995.

Howard, Richard P. "Joseph Smith's First Vision: An Analysis of Six Contemporary Accounts." In *Restoration Studies 1*, ed. Maurice L. Draper and Clare D. Vlahos, 95–117. Independence, MO: (RLDS) Temple School, 1980.

Howard, Richard P. *The Church through the Years*. 2 vols. Independence, MO: Herald House, 1992–93.

Jorgensen, Danny L., and Joni Wilson, eds. *Religion and the Challenge of Modernity: The Recognized [recte Reorganized] Church of Jesus Christ of Latter Day Saints in the United States Today*. Binghamton, NY: Global, 2001.

Judd, Peter A., and Clifford Cole. *Distinctives: Yesterday and Today*. Independence, MO: Herald House, 1983.

Koury, Aleah G. *The Truth and the Evidence: A Comparison between Doctrines of the Reorganized Church of Jesus Christ of Latter Day Saints and the Church of Jesus Christ of Latter-day Saints*. Independence, MO: Herald House, 1965.

Lancaster, James E., Jr. "By the Gift and Power of God: The Method of Translation of the Book of Mormon." *Saints' Herald*, November 15, 1962, 798–802, 806, 817.

Lancaster, James E., Jr. "The Method of Translation of the Book of Mormon." *John Whitmer Historical Association Journal* 3 (1983): 51–61. [Rev. ed. of Lancaster "By the Gift and Power of God"].

Lancaster, James E., Jr. "The Translation of the Book of Mormon." In *The Word of God: Essays on Mormon Scripture*, ed. Dan Vogel, 97–112. Salt Lake City: Signature, 1990. [Rev. ed. of Lancaster "By the Gift and Power of God"].

Larson, Stan, and Samuel J. Passey, eds. *The William E. McLellin Papers, 1854–1880*. Salt Lake City: Signature, 2007.

Launius, Roger D. *Invisible Saints: A History of Black Americans in the Reorganized Church*. Independence, MO: Herald House, 1988.

Launius, Roger D. *Joseph Smith III: Pragmatic Prophet*. Urbana: University of Illinois Press, 1988.

Launius, Roger D. "The Contemporary RLDS Identify Crisis: A Decade of Decision." In Jorgensen and Wilson, *Religion and the Challenge of Modernity*, 91–135.

Launius, Roger D., and W. B. (Pat) Spillman, eds. *Let Contention Cease: The Dynamics of Dissent in the Reorganized Church of Jesus Christ of Latter Day Saints*. Independence, MO: Graceland/Park, 1991.

Launius, Roger D., and Linda Thatcher, eds. *Differing Visions: Dissenters in Mormon History*. Urbana: University of Illinois Press, 1994.

McKiernan, F. Mark, Alma R. Blair, and Paul M. Edwards, eds. *The Restoration Movement: Essays in Mormon History*. Lawrence, KS: Coronado, 1973.

McMurray, W. Grant. "'True Son of a True Father': Joseph Smith III and the Succession Question." In *Restoration Studies 1*, ed. Maurice L. Draper and Clare D. Vlahos, 131–45. Independence, MO: Herald House, 1980.

Newell, Linda King, and Valeen Tippetts Avery. *Mormon Enigma: Emma Hale Smith, Prophet's Wife, "Elect Lady," Polygamy's Foe, 1804–1879*. Garden City, NY: Doubleday, 1984. 2nd ed. Urbana: University of Illinois Press, 1994.

Olson, Kathryn. "A Reappraisal of Canonization in the Doctrine and Covenants." *Courage: A Journal of History, Thought, and Action* 2, no. 2 (Winter 1972): 345–52.

Palmer, Grant. *An Insider's View of Mormon Origins*. Salt Lake City: Signature, 2002.

Price, Richard. *The Polygamy Conspiracies: How the Latter Day Saints Were Betrayed by Men Nearest the Prophet*. Independence, MO: Cumorah, 1984.

Price, Richard. *The Saints at the Crossroads*. Independence, MO: Cumorah, 1974.

Price, Richard. *Restoration Branches Movement*. Assisted by Larry Harlacher. Independence, MO: Price, 1986.

Price, Richard, and Pamela Price. *The Temple of the Lord*. Independence, MO: Price, 1982.

Prince, Gregory A. *Having Authority: The Origins and Development of Priesthood during the Ministry of Joseph Smith*. Independence, MO: Independence, 1993.

Quinn, D. Michael. *Early Mormonism and the Magic World View*. Salt Lake City: Signature, 1987; rev. ed., 1998.

Quinn, D. Michael. *The Mormon Hierarchy: Origins of Power*. 2 vols. Salt Lake City: Signature, 1994.

Ralston, Russell. *Fundamental Differences between the LDS and RLDS Churches*. Independence, MO: Herald House, 1960.

Russell, William D. "Defenders of the Faith: Varieties of RLDS Dissent." *Sunstone* (June 1990).

Russell, William D. "History and the Mormon Scriptures." *Journal of Mormon History* 10 (1983): 53–63.

Russell, William D. "The Latter Day Saint Priesthood: A Reflection of 'Catholic' Tendencies in Nineteenth Century American Religion." In *Restoration Studies 1*, ed. Maurice L. Draper and Clare D. Vlahos, 232–41. Independence, MO: (RLDS) Temple School, 1980.

Russell, William D. "The LDS Church and the Community of Christ: Clearer Differences, Closer Friends." *Dialogue: A Journal of Mormon Thought* 36, no. 4 (Winter 2003): 177–90.

Russell, William D. "Reorganized Mormons Beset by Controversy." *Christian Century*, June 18, 1970.

Scherer, Mark A. "'Called by a New Name': Mission, Identity, and the Reorganized Church." *Journal of Mormon History* 27, no. 2 (Fall 2001): 40–63.

Shields, Steven. *Divergent Paths of the Restoration*. 4th ed. Los Angeles, CA: Restoration Research, 1990.

Shipps, Jan. *Mormonism: The Story of a New Religious Tradition*. Urbana: University of Illinois Press, 1985.

Smith, George D. *Nauvoo Polygamy: ". . . But We Called It Celestial Marriage."* Salt Lake City: Signature, 2008.

Smith, Joseph, III, Heman C. Smith (vols. 1–4), and F. Henry Edwards (vols. 5–8). *The History of the Reorganized Church of Jesus Christ of Latter Day Saints*. Independence, MO: Herald House, 1896, 1897, 1900, 1903, 1969, 1970, 1973, 1976.

Speek, Vickie Cleverley. *"God Has Made Us a Kingdom": James Strang and the Midwest Mormons*. Salt Lake City: Signature, 2006.

Spillman, W. B. "Pat." "Dissent and the Future of the Church." In Launius and Spillman, *Let Contention Cease*, 125–51.

Vlahos, Clare D. "Moderation as a Theological Principle in the Thought of Joseph Smith III." *John Whitmer Historical Association Journal* 1 (1981): 3–11.

Whitmer, David. *An Address to All Believers in Christ by a Witness to the Divine Authenticity of the Book of Mormon*. Richmond, MO: David Whitmer, 1888.

CHAPTER 7

··

MORMON STUDIES AS AN ACADEMIC DISCIPLINE

··

DAVID J. WHITTAKER

FROM their beginnings, Mormons have been a record-keeping people. Such a documentary record must lie at the heart of any effort in Mormon Studies. Religious purposes were central to such record keeping. Covenant making and covenant renewing in serious efforts to become better people were core concerns of this keeping of documents. Taking the news of the restoration to others was a serious activity, and in many ways Mormon history is missionary history; hence a large number of the personal journals Mormons have kept have been focused on their missionary experiences. The records of meetings, conferences, and other such gatherings (also kept from the earliest years) have functioned primarily as providing a record of institutional management and growth.[1] Such record keeping has proven both a curse and a blessing: a blessing because so much of the Mormon experience has been recorded in some form, a curse because any scholar who wishes to study Mormonism will have mountains of records to conquer.

The first generations of Latter-day Saints were not introspective in the modern sense. When early Mormons published their histories or autobiographies, they were primarily defensive, turned outward rather than inward. These early works were not analytical or interpretive as academic study has come to demand. This was to be expected as they were the center of much persecution and prosecution in the nineteenth century. Much of this began to change in the early years of the twentieth century. The emergence of more serious scholarly work on the Mormon experience, especially since the 1930s, has resulted in a significant increase in publications containing serious research on Mormonism, and more recently in the study of Mormonism in non-Mormon academic settings. It is the purpose of this chapter to provide a perspective on the history and current state of the study of Mormonism.

MORMON ANTIQUARIANISM

The keeping of historical records by the Latter-day Saints dates from their organized beginnings.[2] Reinforced and broadened by both their biblical heritage and record keeping in the early American republic, their Book of Mormon constantly referred its readers to the record-keeping activities of the peoples whose story is told in its pages—records that both kept their knowledge of their Redeemer and their sacred covenants alive, and also reinforced the cultural significance of language for the survival of civilization itself (Omni 1:17). In the Book of Mormon, history writing was a sacred responsibility.

Mormons maintain that Joseph Smith received a revelation on the day the church was organized, commanding him and his followers to keep a record of their activities. In time, specific individuals were assigned the duties of keeping the church history. While these early efforts were fitful and incomplete by modern standards, they did begin the process of record creation and interpretation in Mormonism. Because these early accounts were recorded by the participants, their value remains high. Additional directions from Joseph Smith broadened and deepened the responsibilities of these initial historical assignments, and these early directives also help in understanding the direct involvement of church leaders in the process of creating and maintaining a history of the church, an involvement that continues to the present day.

Forced moves, growing criticism, and active persecution assured that the earliest histories would be brief, incomplete, and polemical. Some records were lost or stolen, and some of the individuals assigned to keep the history proved incapable or incompetent. By the end of the first decade, following their expulsion from Missouri, Joseph Smith democratized Mormon historical efforts by inviting all those who had suffered losses in Missouri to prepare accounts of their own experiences. Such efforts, early members were told, constituted an "imperative duty" they owed to both their own generation and future generations (Doctrine & Covenants [D&C] 123). It was in these Missouri histories that a real defensiveness emerged in Mormon historiography. Feeling that they had been denied their personal and property rights, these authors left an imprint that colored Mormon historical writing for at least a century.

Significant pamphlet histories and hundreds of petitions for redress became important records of the Mormon Missouri experience. But the most significant historical project to emerge during this period was directed by Joseph Smith. Ironically, just as historical writing was democratized among the faithful, the real focus of Mormon history became the telling of Joseph Smith's life and revelations. This was primarily the work of the Church Historian, Willard Richards, and those assigned to work with him, especially George A. Smith and Wilford Woodruff. Titled the "History of Joseph Smith" in manuscript, it was in reality a documentary history of the main events of the church over which he presided. Primarily based on Joseph Smith's journals, including those kept by individuals he assigned, the history has a subjective first-person format. The project was not finished until ten years after his death, but this series was the most important historical work in the early church. It was serialized in the church's newspapers (both in the United States and in England) and was eventually edited into a multivolume work entitled the *History of the Church*. In an age when there was no real distinction between historian, editor, or compiler, such a work was really an antiquarian effort in a time before this word took on a pejorative meaning.

Thus, like so many early Mormon historical efforts, these were compilations of documents rather than crafted historical works. They did gather key documents upon which later interpretive works could be built, and such efforts at record keeping were at their heart document preservation. These foundational efforts help us to understand the reasons for the survival of rich manuscript sources for contemporary historians of the Mormon experience.

Mormon historical writing essentially remained in this documentary tradition throughout the nineteenth century. The individual who carried it the furthest was Andrew Jenson. A convert from Denmark, Jenson eventually found his calling in historical work. By the time he was called to be an Assistant Church Historian in 1891, he had already published several newspapers and periodicals, in addition to several other historical projects. After being called as "a historian in Zion," several main projects provided the focus of his work. The first was the preparation of biographies of the founders and officers of the church, many of which were published in his four-volume *LDS Biographical Encyclopedia* (1901–36). The *Encyclopedic History of the Church* (1941) did for church organizations and missions what the *Biographical Encyclopedia* did for individuals.

Jenson's most important project was the compilation of a multivolume scrapbook of church history. Eventually known as the "Journal History," this work of some 518 volumes of legal-size scrapbooks, ranging in size from three to five inches in thickness, is a gold mine of source material on Mormon history. It represents the apex of the documentary tradition in Mormon historical writing. Though never published, the "Journal History" has been indexed and microfilmed and is available in a number of Utah libraries.

Jenson was also a key figure in the attempts to modernize the church's archives at the turn of the century. His concerns for better and more systematic record keeping led church leaders to establish the Committee on Church Records, which encouraged local units to keep historical and statistical records and which also gave Jenson church support for his many travels to various Mormon communities and historic sites to gather documents of historical value. Jenson also worked to gather records and publications about the church in areas beyond the United States, making him a pioneer in documenting the growing internationalization of Mormonism.

TOWARD A SYNTHESIS

By the 1870s, a different approach was emerging in Mormon historiography. Still grounded in documentary efforts, some authors began to synthesize these into more interpretive narratives. T. B. H. Stenhouse's *Rocky Mountain Saints* was published in

New York in 1873. His work began as a defense of the church, and he was given access to the church's archives, but by the time he was writing his history he had left the church and joined the Reform Church of William S. Godbe. Thus his volume came to offer an anti–Brigham Young and pro-Godbe view of the Mormon experience. It was reprinted five times by 1905 and was the most read history outside Mormon Utah. The first volume to treat the handcart tragedies of 1856 and the Mountain Meadows Massacre of 1857, it was also the first interpretive history to suggest better ways of viewing Mormon history, arguing, for example, that the conflicts and persecutions of the Latter-day Saints in Missouri might be better understood as cultural conflicts, with both sides contributing to the problems; that the Mormon troubles in Illinois were as much related to politics as to religion; and that the Mormon frustration with governmental leaders in their attempts at redress ought to be considered within the growing conflict of states-rights struggles with the federal government. Thus Mormon issues were often placed at the mercy of the larger conflicts and compromises in nineteenth-century American politics.

Another historian who tried to move beyond just publishing documents was Edward W. Tullidge (1829–94). He held Mormon religion in low esteem but he admired Mormon culture. While his lifetime ambition was to create the "epic" of the Mormon experience, he generally wrote in the documentary tradition. His most important work was his *History of Salt Lake City* (1886), but like his other works, he offered documents with little analysis and synthesis.

An important attempt at synthesis appeared under the direction of non-Mormon Hubert Howe Bancroft. Bancroft's *History of the Pacific States*, eventually covering the areas from Alaska to Mexico, with volumes devoted to the Native Americans, grew to thirty-nine volumes. Wishing to include Utah in his project, he sought and eventually obtained church approval and assistance. His *History of Utah*, volume 26 in the series, covered the years from 1540 to 1886 and was published in 1889. Much of it was actually the work of Alfred Bates, an employee of Bancroft who assembled his histories as Henry Ford would assemble his cars. The volume's format told the Mormon story in the main text with sources and other points of view in the extensive footnotes. The lengthy bibliography at the front of the volume is still a valuable guide to the contemporary sources he and his coauthors used.

A Mormon version of Bancroft's *History* found its author in Orson F. Whitney (1855–1931), whose four-volume *History of Utah* (1892–1904) provided Latter-day Saints with a major narrative history of their own region by one of their own. His interest in poetry and theater gave his history a sense of the grand epic, but he gave to his people a story that was their story. He smoothed out the more critical parts, but as the Mormons were coming through a time of intense persecution and forced readjustment to American culture, he presented a stirring epic of this pioneering adventure.

The most important historian of this genre and period was Brigham Henry Roberts (1857–1933), an English convert whose poverty prevented him from learning to read until he was twelve. He eventually was called to be a church leader, and by his death in 1933 had become the most prolific author in the church. In addition to biographies and histories, he edited the earlier *History of Joseph Smith* into its multivolume format

(1902–1912). But his most extensive historical work was the *Comprehensive History of the Church of Jesus Christ of Latter-day Saints: Century 1*. Clearly influenced by the nineteenth-century Romantic historians he loved to read, Roberts painted the history of his people, both their triumphs and their tragedies. He was not afraid to treat events like the Mountain Meadows Massacre (see chapters 100 and 101) and he did not hide from addressing the criticism leveled at the church and its doctrines. This history is still essential reading for serious students of Mormon history.

PROFESSIONALIZATION
OF MORMON HISTORY

Even as Roberts was drafting his historical works, Mormon history was moving in new directions. By the 1880s, Mormon students had begun leaving Utah to seek higher education in various graduate schools in America. At first interested in law, education, and the sciences, these students eventually turned to studying in the social sciences. By the 1910s and '20s, Latter-day Saints were studying history and related subjects. Such outmigration for education was bound to have an effect on the way they understood their own history.

A number of trends seem obvious as one looks back on the early years of the twentieth century. Mormon history was clearly becoming an interesting subject for non-Mormon scholars. The Mormon involvement in the western American experience was one reason their history could not be ignored by American historians. After 1893, the popularity of the Frontier Thesis of Frederick Jackson Turner seemed to make the Mormon experience the ideal test case for its validity. Studies by Mormon students like Dean D. McBrien, Joel E. Ricks, and especially Milton R. Hunter suggested the Mormon experience proved Turner's ideas by focusing on the frontier phases of its history. Others found their topics by looking at Utah and its regional history. Thus Levi Edgar Young, Andrew Neff, and Leland Creer were important early students of these topics.

From the 1930s to the 1960s the study of Mormon history was also influenced by several individuals who were not trained historians (they were English majors for the most part), but who nevertheless researched and wrote books and reviews that helped bring Mormon history to a national audience. All had roots in small Mormon communities, but most left the faith of their youth. These individuals included Bernard DeVoto, Dale L. Morgan, Juanita Brooks, and Fawn M. Brodie.

Bernard DeVoto (1897–1955) was born in Ogden, Utah. He taught English at Northwestern University following his graduation from Harvard University. He became an editor of the *Saturday Review* and wrote a regular column for *Harper's*. His early published articles poked fun at his Utah origins. For example, in 1926 he wrote cruelly that "The Mormons were staid peasants whose only distinguishing characteristics were their servility to their leaders and their belief in a low-comedy God." By 1945, as national attitudes about the Mormons had softened, DeVoto repudiated his earlier Menchenesque tone. He said of his earlier comments, "they were ignorant, brash, prejudiced, malicious, and, what is worst of all, irresponsible."[3] DeVoto wrote three volumes on the history of the West in which he treated the Mormons with great sympathy. His trilogy remains an important study, one of which, *The Year of Decision, 1846* gave the Mormon's westward trek national attention.

Another scholar with Utah roots was Dale L. Morgan (1914–71). He found employment with the Historical Records Survey of the Works Progress Administration during the Depression. His assignment as the administrator of Utah State Records firmly established his path toward bibliography and history. Before long, few people could match his knowledge of the primary sources, first of Utah and then of the American West. In Mormon history he published a number of works that reflected his broad interests. While not a Mormon, he wrote with skill and fairness when he treated the Latter-day Saints. His major works included histories of Ogden, Provo, and Salt Lake City, and the 1941 *Utah, A Guide to the State* which he oversaw. In 1947, he published *The Great Salt Lake*, an interdisciplinary study of a major landmark in Utah and the West. His documentary compilation "The State of Deseret" in the *Utah Historical Quarterly* in 1940 is the essential work on the initial efforts of the Mormons to achieve statehood in 1849. His own history of the Mormons, originally planned for three volumes, never progressed beyond a few chapters. A lesser-known role Morgan played in the story of Mormon historiography was his work as a correspondent and reviewer of others' work. And he regularly reviewed books for the *Saturday Review*, calling national attention to works on Mormon and Utah history.

One of Morgan's correspondents was Juanita Brooks (1898–1989), a Mormon woman of independent spirit with great integrity. Remaining an active Latter-day Saint, she was trained in English and sought her whole life to better understand her southern Utah and southern Nevada roots. While best known for her pioneering study *The Mountain Meadows Massacre* (1950), she also wrote a sympathetic biography of John Doyle Lee, the only individual executed for his participation in the massacre; she also edited Lee's diaries and those of Hosea Stout, to mention only the most important. She also helped collect Mormon manuscripts for the Henry E. Huntington Library in San Marino, California, and she was a regular contributor to the *Utah Historical Quarterly*. Her work helped push the quest for truth in Mormon history to new levels, even when she was ostracized by her Mormon neighbors for treating controversial topics they felt would be better left covered and forgotten. But her historical work, by confronting hard and painful realities of early Mormon history, helped in the healing process and prepared the way for the next generation of Mormon historians who could build on her insights and her compassionate approach.

Another correspondent of Morgan was Fawn M. Brodie (1915–81), niece of church President David O. McKay. Best known for her 1945 biography of Joseph Smith, *No Man Knows My History*, it was, as Morgan noted, her act of "liberation and exorcism," her intellectual attempt to be rid of the founder of the religion of her youth. It was, at its heart, a naturalistic biography of a religious man. Brodie was also trained in English and clearly one of the enduring qualities of her biography is its literary grace. But it was, at its heart, a psychobiography that presented Joseph Smith as a fraud, a "myth-maker of prodigious talent," and man with an eye for young maidens, whose practice of polygamy was just a cover for his lust. Such an explanation was in the tradition of I. Woodbridge Riley's 1902 *The Founder of Mormonism* based on a Yale University dissertation of the same year that sought an explanation of Smith in his environment and especially in the inner workings of his mind. Religion was a mask for other, darker desires. Thus the Book of Mormon was really an autobiography of the young man and could provide insights into the Smith family, its strengths and weaknesses. Like Freud, Brodie treated religion as a negative force in her subject's life. But she failed to consult important manuscript collections that would have altered her account.

Brodie's biography was, however, a watershed in Mormon studies. While it offered a secular explanation for Mormon origins, and a naturalistic handling of the sources, it did suggest an agenda for the next generation of Mormon historians. For Latter-day Saints, it cried out for response and thus more research. For non-Mormons, many felt at last they had an explanation for Joseph Smith, and with that, no more work was necessary. In a second edition (1972) the volume continues in print and is, unfortunately, often the most recommended biography.

Scholars like DeVoto, Morgan, Brooks, and Brodie wrote in an age of growing secularism and modernity. Such secular scholarship took its toll on Mormons and some of their historians; one student of the period has referred to "Mormondom's Lost Generation," and indeed, other writers with Mormon roots, like Vardis Fisher, Maurine Whipple, and Virginia Sorenson turned their interest in history to writing historical fiction.

THE NEW MORMON HISTORY

In the 1950s, additional changes were becoming obvious in Mormon history. By 1969, these changes were being labeled "the New Mormon History." Whether the label is really the best one, it was clear new kinds of historical studies were appearing, which treated Mormon history in ways never imagined by earlier practitioners. Of course these new histories did not appear in a vacuum, and most were really building upon earlier scholarship. One benchmark for these changes was the 1958 publication of Leonard J. Arrington's *Great Basin Kingdom: An Economic History of the Latter-day Saints, 1830–1900.* Issued by Harvard University Press, it was the revision of his 1952 dissertation. Idaho-born and raised, Arrington eventually went east to study at the University of North Carolina. Arrington was aware of the important work being published by southern historians, as they focused on the South as a region. In time, Arrington decided to apply the same approach to the Mormon region in the Great Basin. He eventually accepted a job teaching economics at Utah State University in Logan. There he learned much from S. George Ellsworth, a colleague in the history department, who critiqued various drafts of the work, drawing upon his own extensive knowledge of Utah and Mormon history.

When *Great Basin Kingdom* appeared in 1958, it was both a summation of earlier Mormon scholarship and also a model of what could and should be done. Arrington continued to publish extensively in Utah, Mormon, and Western history. He was one of the founders of the Mormon History Association in 1965, and in 1972 was called to serve as the Church Historian of the LDS Church. Serving in that capacity for the next ten years, his Historical Department became staffed with scholars with academic training and given an extensive research and writing agenda. Arrington and his Assistant Church Historians, Davis Bitton and James B. Allen, actively encouraged fuller access to the rich holdings of the church's archives. The scholarly production of these ten years was astonishing. They produced two one-volume histories of the church, commissioned a multivolume history of the church, began a documents series, initiated projects that opened research on new topics, began scholarly biographical projects of church leaders and others, and offered fellowships to others who could travel to Salt Lake City to research their own topics in the rich holdings of the church's archives. It was truly a renaissance in Mormon studies.

But given the religious underpinnings of the earlier historiography, it was apparent that not everyone would be pleased with the work of the Historical Department. Some church leaders occasionally voiced concern with its products; others thought the historians were moving too fast and too far ahead for church membership to keep up with. A lively discussion about the nature of Mormon historiography ensued; this produced its own literature. At the heart of much of the concern of church leaders were the issues of using secular language to describe sacred events and a growing concern that the religious center of the Mormon experience was not coming through these new histories clearly enough.[4] The Historical Department scholars with Arrington were transferred in 1982 to Brigham Young University as the renamed Joseph Fielding Smith Institute for Latter-day Saint History, where many felt their scholarship would find a more congenial home. Since Arrington's death in 1999, some of the Smith Institute scholars have retired, moved into academic departments, or returned to the Historical Department in Salt Lake City to assist in the preparation of the multivolume Joseph Smith Papers project.

The issues, of course, did not go away. In the 1990s, several LDS scholars were excommunicated from the church, in part for their historical writings, but also for lifestyle choices or for public criticisms of church leaders. One of those disciplined was D. Michael Quinn. He worked with Arrington's Historical Department, and completed his PhD at Yale University in 1976, wrote a dissertation on the history of the Mormon hierarchy, and returned to Utah to accept a position in Brigham Young University's history department. He produced a number of important, deeply researched studies, but in each there seemed to be a subversion of how the traditional Mormon story was told. While he has denied he was following any one model in his work, one could argue that his work was gradually "Foucaulting" Mormon history. Like Michel Foucault, Quinn's major works examined power and authority, folk beliefs and magic, issues of gender and sexuality, and violence. While students of Mormon history must read his historical studies, they can be interpreted as subversive attempts to "deconstruct" the traditional interpretation of Mormon past. They are also representatives of the religious studies approach that has moved beyond the old Church History model. Of course, not all Mormon historical scholarship was produced by Arrington's Historical Department. But since the 1960s, Mormon scholarship has gone from a small stream to a river.

Religious Studies, Mormonism, and the Academy

Until fairly recently, the academic study of the Latter-day Saint experience was not given much of a priority, either by Latter-day Saints or by those outside the faith. Part of the problem was prejudice; part, taxonomy and methodology. Dismissed from its beginning as a fraud, Mormonism was not to be taken as a subject worthy of serious consideration. The real American religion was both Protestant and evangelical, a position articulated by Robert Baird in 1844 and followed, with few exceptions, by most Protestant church historians until the 1950s. The claims of Joseph Smith to heavenly visitations from God and subsequent new scripture were so patently absurd to the church historians of the Protestant evangelical school that to take the movement seriously would be to suggest you were as daft as your subject. One of the first critics of the church actually said that it was not necessary to read the Book of Mormon to know it was without merit! And almost no outsider thought the church would survive its founders.

But the church grew and prospered, helped settle a significant portion of the American West, and its missionaries continued to attract to its membership those whom Charles Dickens called, after a personal visit to a ship containing Mormon converts bound for the New World, the "pick and flower of England."[5] Its economic programs, colonization efforts, and its governmental system continued to attract public attention, and plural marriage brought constitutional challenges to the American legal system. The church just would not die. By the end of the nineteenth century, American politicians moved their tactics from destroying to regulating the LDS Church. Mormon leaders shifted their positions also (ended polygamy, downplayed millennialism and the quest for Zion, moved to realign its membership politically along national party lines, and adopted many of the approaches of the Progressive Movement), and a rough accommodation with the nation was achieved. Utah became a state of the union in 1896.

The twentieth century gave the church many opportunities to demonstrate its loyalty to the nation and with its accommodation to the political and economic realities, it has seen its membership grow from about 300,000 in 1900 to over fourteen million in 2012. Its members have moved out of Utah's Wasatch Front into most all the states in the nation. Missionary work has brought in many people from outside the United States;

today, more members have Spanish as their primary language, with a significant membership in Latin and South America. With growth and public acceptance has come more attention. There has been a shift from nineteenth-century polemical literature attacking the church to literature seeking to understand the church.

Mormon Studies have primarily been historical, following the emphasis on denominational histories that were the emphasis of the founders of the American Society for Church History (ASCH). Philip Schaff and those who followed him in the ASCH wrote histories of American denominations. Mormons themselves have generally followed this model. But the study of Mormonism never fit this model, and by the time Sydney Ahlstrom published his *A Religious History of the American People* in 1972, it was clear the old taxonomies just would not work. Ahlstrom himself recognized this when he concluded his discussion of the Mormons by noting how rich and complex a subject Mormonism was and that the old denominational categories just would not suffice in studying it: was it "a sect, a mystery cult, a new religion, a church, a people, a nation, or an American subculture?" For him, "at different times and places it is all of these."[6] Such a conclusion was an honest evaluation of the complex evidence, and if students want to try to understand the Mormon experience they will have to take Ahlstrom's frustration seriously and approach Mormonism from many different angles. Jan Shipps has suggested that Mormonism is a "New Religious Tradition" that cannot be fit into the old denominational categories.[7] This means that there must be many Mormon Studies, not just one. The alternative is to become bogged down in the quagmire of apologetics that the old Church History paradigm seems to encourage.

Since Ahlstrom's time it has become increasingly clear that there couldn't be a Mormon Studies, just like there could not be Lutheran or Methodist or Shaker or Seventh-Day Adventist studies. Rather, like in the approaches of the American Academy of Religion, the emphasis has been on applying the methodologies of the social sciences to the study of various religious traditions. How do the methodologies of anthropology, sociology, psychology, political science, economics, history, and the broader field of Religious Studies (including but not limited to ritual, ecclesiology, phenomenology, and missiology) offer tools to better understand the history of various religions? In addition, the field of comparative religion (both US and World) and the impact of scholars like William James helped move the study of religion into the academy. Such approaches are at their core secular, as the tools of the social sciences do not have the capacity to deal with spiritual experience, even though scholars like James sought to study the religious experiences of real people, where real religion was at its core. These tools do have the advantage of illuminating the history of various religious bodies to better understand what they have to say about the complex human experience. Non-Mormons are not likely to read books about the Mormons unless these larger matters are addressed; the same is increasingly true of Mormons, who generally do not read denominational histories beyond their own.

Scholars have been applying various approaches to understanding Mormonism. Mormon scholarship reached its maturity just as the Church History School and the Religious Studies schools were parting company. This helps in understanding why there remains a bifurcation in the way Mormons study themselves or react to others trying to explain their religion and its history. Jan Shipps had noted this shift in her essay-review of Richard Bushman's recent biography of Joseph Smith, even suggesting that *Rough Stone Rolling* might be the last study of the Old-New Mormon history, even though it was a "cultural biography" that addressed some of the harder issues in early Mormon history.[8] The mixed reactions to the biography within Mormonism suggest that most Mormons remain uncomfortable with methodologies that depart from the more traditional Church History model. As a religion with historical claims that are anchored in specific episodes, it is likely that the primary emphasis on historical studies will remain central to Mormon Studies. A recent doctoral dissertation probes in depth the growing application of religious studies methodologies to the study of the origins of Mormonism, suggesting both the value and the challenges entailed by such approaches as deprivation theories, economic change, status anxiety, political change, urbanization, modernization, social mobilization, and various theories of cultural change.[9]

The interdisciplinary nature of the more recent scholarship on Mormonism also suggests the need for various approaches. Armand Mauss, using his training in sociology, has carefully studied Mormon notions of ethnicity and has also used the accommodation model to better understand how the church has adjusted to the various cultural challenges it has faced in the second half of the twentieth century.[10] The study of women in the Mormon experience is another topic that cries out for interdisciplinary approaches. The same can be said for one of the most controversial topics in Mormon history, plural marriage. The careful study of the Book of Mormon has hardly mattered to non-Mormons, and Mormons themselves usually see the volume only as a devotional text, in spite of its rich literary structure and complex relationship to the Mormon faith community. Grant Hardy has wondered out loud just how such a volume, with its sad narrative (a tragedy large writ), could be the foundational text of such a happy people.[11] Daniel Walker Howe has noted the "Book of Mormon should rank among the great achievements of American literature."[12] Both observations cry out for more study.

In the age of the Internet, it is no longer possible for any one person or organization to control how the history of the Church of Jesus Christ of Latter-day Saints is either studied or written about. The larger body of secondary scholarship is available to anyone who wishes to research this complex topic, and with such projects as the Joseph Smith Papers being published in scholarly editions by the Church History Library, a large number of Mormon manuscripts will be available either in print or online. Websites both positive and negative that are devoted to Mormonism and Mormon history have grown over the years. A recent synthesis of the Mormon experience by Matthew Bowman, based almost entirely on secondary scholarship, suggests how accessible the subject is.[13] With Mormon Studies programs, chairs now established at Claremont Graduate University in California and at Utah State University, and with others being planned, the future of the study of things Mormon looks very bright indeed—even if it still needs to find a surer footing in the academy.

NOTES

1. Whittaker, "Mormon Organizational and Administrative History."
2. This section draws from my chapter "Mormon Historiography," in *American Denominationalism*, 146–72. More fully, see Walker, Whittaker, and Allen, *Mormon History*.
3. DeVoto, "Utah," 319; Fetzer, "Bernard De Voto and the Mormon Tradition."
4. Packer, "The Mantle Is Far, Far Greater than the Intellect."
5. Dickens, "Uncommercial Traveller," 444–49.
6. Ahlstrom, *Religious History of the American People*, 500.
7. Shipps, *Mormonism*.
8. Shipps, "Richard Lyman Bushman."
9. Helfrich, "Idols of the Tribes," 185–243.
10. Mauss, *Angel and the Beehive*.
11. Hardy, *Understanding the Book of Mormon*, 8.
12. Howe, *What Hath God Wrought*, 314.
13. Bowman, *Mormon People*.

BIBLIOGRAPHY

Adams, Charles P., and Gustive O. Larson. "A Study of the LDS Church Historian's Office, 1830–1900." *Utah Historical Quarterly* 40 (Fall 1972): 370–89.

Ahlstrom, Sydney. *A Religious History of the American People*. New Haven, CT: Yale University Press, 1972.

Allen, James B., Ronald W. Walker and David J. Whittaker. *Studies in Mormon History, 1830–1997: An Indexed Bibliography with a Topical Guide to the Published Social Science Literature on the Mormons* by Armand L. Mauss and Dynette Ivie Reynolds. Urbana: University of Illinois Press, 2000.

Arrington, Leonard J. "The Founding of the LDS Historical Department, 1972," *Journal of Mormon History* 18 (Fall 1992): 41–56.

Beecher, Maureen Ursenbach, and Lavina Fielding Anderson, eds. *Sisters in Spirit: Mormon Women in Historical and Cultural Perspective*. Urbana: University of Illinois Press, 1987.

Bitton, Davis. "Ten Years in Camelot: A Personal Memoir." *Dialogue: A Journal of Mormon Thought* 16, no. 3 (Autumn 1983): 9–33.

Bitton, Davis, and Leonard J. Arrington. *Mormons and Their Historians*. Salt Lake City: University of Utah Press, 1988.

Bowman, Matthew. *The Mormon People: The Making of an American Faith*. New York: Random House, 2012.

Bradford, M. Gerald. "The Study of Mormonism: A Growing Interest in Academia," *FARMS Review* [Foundation for Ancient Research and Mormon Studies, Neal A. Maxwell Institute, Brigham Young University] 19, no. 1 (2007): 119–74.

Bringhurst, Newell G., and Lavina Fielding Anderson, eds. *Excavating Mormon Pasts: The New Historiography of the Last Half Century*. Salt Lake City: Greg Kofford, 2004.

Bushman, Richard L. *Believing History: Latter-day Saint Essays*. Ed. Reid L. Neilson and Jed Woodworth. New York: Columbia University Press, 2004.

Bushman, Richard L. *Joseph Smith: Rough Stone Rolling*. New York: Alfred A. Knopf, 2005.

Daynes, Kathryn M. *More Wives than One: Transformation of the Mormon Marriage System, 1840–1910*. Urbana: University of Illinois Press, 2001.

DeVoto, Bernard. "Utah." *American Mercury* 7 (March 1926): 319.

DeVoto, Bernard. *The Year of Decision, 1846*. Boston: Little, Brown, 1943.

Dickens, Charles. "The Uncommercial Traveller." *All the Year Round* 9 (July 4, 1863): 444–49.

Fetzer, Leland, "Bernard DeVoto and the Mormon Tradition." *Dialogue: A Journal of Mormon Thought* 6, nos. 3–4 (Autumn/Winter 1971): 23–38.

Flake, Kathleen. *The Politics of American Religious Identity: The Seating of Reed Smoot, Mormon Apostle*. Chapel Hill: University of North Carolina Press, 2003.

Hardy, Grant. *Understanding the Book of Mormon: A Reader's Guide*. New York: Oxford University Press, 2010.

Helfrich, Ronald G. Jr. "Idols of the Tribes: An Intellectual and Critical History of 19th and 20th Century Mormon Studies." PhD diss., University of Albany, State University of New York, 2011.

Howe, Daniel Walker. *What Hath God Wrought: The Transformation of America, 1815–1848*. New York: Oxford University Press, 2007.

Jensen, Robin Scott, " 'Rely upon the things which are written': Text, Context, and the Creation of Mormon Revelatory Records." MLIS thesis, University of Wisconsin-Milwaukee, 2009.

Jessee, Dean C. "Joseph Smith and the Beginnings of Mormon Record Keeping." In *The Prophet Joseph: Essays on the Life and Mission of Joseph Smith*, ed. Larry C. Porter and Susan Easton Black, 138–60. Salt Lake City: Deseret, 1988.

Mauss, Armand L. *All Abraham's Children: Changing Mormon Conceptions of Race and Lineage*. Urbana: University of Illinois Press, 2003.

Mauss, Armand L. *The Angel and the Beehive: The Mormon Struggle with Assimilation*. Urbana: University of Illinois Press, 1994.

Packer, Boyd K. "The Mantle Is Far, Far Greater than the Intellect." *BYU Studies* 21, no. 3 (Summer 1981): 259–78.

Quinn, D. Michael. *The Mormon Hierarchy*. 2 vols. Salt Lake City: Signature, 1994–97.

Quinn, D. Michael, ed. *The New Mormon History: Revisionist Essays on the Past*. Salt Lake City: Signature, 1992.

Rischin, Moses. "The New Mormon History." *American West* 6 (March 1969): 49.

Searle, Howard C. "Early Mormon Historiography: Writing the History of the Mormons, 1830–1858." PhD diss., University of California, Los Angeles, 1979.

Shipps, Jan. *Mormonism: The Story of a New Religious Tradition*. Urbana: University of Illinois Press, 1985.

Shipps, Jan. "Richard Lyman Bushman, the Story of Joseph Smith and Mormons, and the New Mormon History." *Journal of American History* 94, no. 2 (September 2007): 498–516.

Simpson, Tom. "Mormons Study Abroad: Latter-day Saints in American Higher Education, 1870–1940." PhD diss., University of Virginia, 2006.

Smith, George D., ed. *Faithful History: Essays on Writing Mormon History*. Salt Lake City: Signature, 1992.

Turner, James. *Religion Enters the Academy, The Origins of the Scholarly Study of Religion in America*. Athens: University of Georgia Press, 2011.

Walker, Ronald W., David J. Whittaker and James B. Allen. *Mormon History*. Urbana: University of Illinois Press, 2001.

Whittaker, David J. "Mormon Historiography." In *American Denominational History: Perspectives on the Past, Prospects for the Future*, ed. Keith Harper, 146–72. Tuscaloosa: University of Alabama Press, 2008.

Whittaker, David J., ed. *Mormon Americana: A Guide to Sources and Collections in the United States*. Brigham Young University Studies Monograph Series. Provo, UT: Brigham Young University Press, 1995.

Whittaker, David J. "Mormon Organizational and Administrative History: A Guide to the Sources." In *A Firm Foundation: Church Organization and Administration*, ed. David J. Whittaker and Arnold K. Garr, 611–95. Provo, UT: Brigham Young University Religious Studies Center; and Salt Lake City: Deseret, 2011.

PART II

REVELATION AND SCRIPTURE

CHAPTER 8

··

JOSEPH SMITH
AND HIS VISIONS

··

RICHARD LYMAN BUSHMAN

IN his study of prophetic figures in the time of Joseph Smith, the literary scholar Richard
Brodhead speculates about the inner experience of prophethood. "The embrace of prophetic identity," he proposes, "typically unleashes a flooding of the self with a sense of
authority, a sense that makes it feel compelled and entitled to announce a new right way
against the authority of worldly customs." Brodhead lines up a number of the figures
who seized a prophetic identity "circa 1830," men who felt the flooding of the self with
authority that entitled them to announce a new right way: Nat Turner, John Humphrey
Noyes, Ralph Waldo Emerson, Jemima Wilkinson, Handsome Lake, George Rapp.
Prophethood was one of the "repertoire of identities" waiting to be seized upon in this
biblical culture "as one idea of what a self can be."[1]

Brodhead could have named more if he had called up the scores of persons who
never claimed prophethood but who recorded visions of angels, ascents into heaven,
and glimpses of apocalyptic endings. They wrote about their dreams and open visions,
often in a single pamphlet, and then disappeared from history without attaining more
than local notoriety. Accompanied by an angel on a heavenly journey, Sarah Alley saw
a burning lake with "an abundance of people" in utmost misery and then passed on to a
happy place where she saw "Christ and the holy angels around him, and abundance of
people clothed in white robes." Norris Stearns in an 1815 account saw "God, my maker,
almost in bodily shape like a man," and "Jesus Christ my redeemer, in perfect shape
like man." Both reported their visions and went no further. They were not prophets but
merely visionaries who were afforded a glimpse into divine happenings but without a
call to announce a new right way.[2]

Charles Grandison Finney, the great nineteenth-century evangelist, fell somewhere
in between prophet and visionary. Finney began his long career as the most influential
preacher of his day with a vision in his law office. Known as a questioner and doubter in
his Presbyterian congregation in Adams, New York, Finney began to feel the pull of the
Bible on his skeptical nature. In October of 1821, he resolved to settle the state of his soul.

With some embarrassment, he prayed surreptitiously in the woods on the edge of town and felt an elevation of the spirit. That night he went into the dark back room of his law office to pray.

> As I went in and shut the door after me, it seemed as if I met the Lord Jesus Christ face to face. It did not occur to me then, nor did it for some time afterward, that it was wholly a mental state. On the contrary, it seemed to me that I met Him face to face and saw Him as I would see any other man. He said nothing, but looked at me in such a manner as to break me right down at His feet. I have always since regarded this as a most remarkable state of mind, for it seemed to me a reality that He stood before me and that I fell down at His feet and poured out my soul to Him. I wept aloud like a child, and made such confessions as I could with my choked utterance.[3]

The next day, overcome with joy and relief, he walked down the street telling the glad news to everyone he met. From then until the end of his life, Finney never stopped evangelizing. His visionary call flooded him with a store of energy that did not run out until the day he died, but he engaged only to preach the standard Christian gospel. He moderated Calvinism to suit his revivalistic preaching, but did not announce a new right way against the authority of cultural custom.

Joseph Smith certainly belongs among the visionaries of his time, but he was also perhaps the foremost example of the prophet, one who, as Broadhead put it, felt "singled out to enjoy special knowledge of ultimate reality" and to "enact that knowledge against the grain of worldly understanding."[4] He stands out because he left more of a mark on the world than any of his fellow prophets. Emerson appears more often in college syllabi, but he did not create a people who recognize one another as his followers. Emerson did not like churches, had no intention of forming one, and got his wish. Joseph Smith organized a church within weeks after publishing the Book of Mormon and devoted his life to augmenting and elaborating the organization he had brought into being. He considered the formation of the Church of Christ to be of equal importance with his revelation of doctrine. Smith was an activist visionary driven by his vision of a new right way.

Smith's views of heavenly beings began in 1820, the year before Finney's law office vision and not many miles away in Manchester, New York. Smith experienced a vision of God and Christ, soon followed by a series of angelic visitations: Moroni, a prophet from the Book of Mormon; John the Baptist; Peter, James, and John; Christ in the Kirtland Temple, followed by Moses, Elias, and Elijah. At the end of his life he referred to Michael, Gabriel, and Raphael as visitors.[5] The heavenly beings came not to reassure Smith or convert him like Finney's Christ; Smith's angels brought messages. They commissioned him. They imparted keys and power. He left their presence with work to perform—translate the Book of Mormon, organize a priesthood, begin temple work, establish Zion. Smith spoke of the "marvelous work" God was performing, and it was to be done through him and his followers (Doctrine and Covenants [D&C] 4:1).

Smith was strangely taciturn about the visions. He refused to tell his mother about his first vision in 1820 and likely never mentioned it to his family at the time. The night after Moroni appeared in his bedroom in September 1823 to inform him about the plates of the Book of Mormon, Smith said nothing about it at the breakfast table. Not until the angel appeared again to him in the fields and commanded him to open up to his family did he tell his father what had happened ("Joseph Smith—History," 1:20, 49–50, Pearl of Great Price [PGP]). The introduction in the first edition of the Book of Mormon made no mention of Moroni, saying only that "the plates of which hath been spoken, were found in the township of Manchester, Ontario County, New-York."[6] The same held true for subsequent visitors. The 1829 visit of John the Baptist to restore the Aaronic Priesthood did not appear in the Book of Commandments in 1833, or in the 1835 edition of the Doctrine and Covenants, or in any edition of his revelations while Joseph Smith lived. It was extracted from his written history and included for the first time in the 1876 edition of the Doctrine and Covenants.[7] The critical appearance of Peter, James, and John to restore the keys of the apostleship was never recorded and to this day the exact date is unknown (D&C 27:12, 13). Smith had his clerk enter an account of the 1836 Kirtland Temple visitations in his journal but is not known to have told anyone about them at the time.[8] Smith treated these visual revelations as private experiences, to be alluded to but not described.[9] They had a profound effect on what he did, but were not brought forward during his lifetime to authorize his actions. Until 1840 his followers had little idea of the visionary backdrop of his actions.[10] Allusions to what he called "his marvilous experience" leave no doubt that they had shaped his mentality (he wrote down the First Vision and the visit of Moroni in 1832 without showing the account to his followers), but they did not inform his followers' initial belief.[11] The first generation of Mormons joined the church without any idea that Joseph Smith believed he had seen God and Christ in vision.

Instead, Smith put forward his own distinctive form of revelation—a history. The Book of Mormon was a thousand-year-long story of a civilization wrought by a group of refugees from sixth-century Jerusalem who fled the city on the eve of its destruction to find a new promised land. From a tiny group of families, they raised up a people that spread across the land, built cities, conducted commerce, waged wars, heard prophecies, and eventually broke down into a civil war that destroyed the record-keeping segment of the population. Their last historian, Moroni, buried his account written on gold plates for safe-keeping, and as an angel, told Joseph Smith about the plates. They contained the fullness of the gospel and would help convert Gentiles and restore Israel. Smith's followers—and the world—were to learn God's purposes by reading this history!

Thus Smith began his public ministry with the premise that the present could learn from the past. It was a conception not unfamiliar to the Romantics of his time. If the Enlightenment had looked to the future in the confidence that reason could construct a better world, Romanticism sought a deeper wisdom by turning to the past. In 1819, eleven years before the publication of the Book of Mormon, the British Museum had erected the colossal head of the younger Memnon in the Egyptian Sculpture room. The arrival of the head from the Theban ruins, one product of the looting of Egypt following the Napoleonic conquest, had inspired Shelley to write "Ozymandias."

> I met a traveller from an antique land
> Who said: "Two vast and trunkless legs of stone
> Stand in the desert . . . Near them, on the sand,
> Half sunk, a shattered visage lies, whose frown,
> And wrinkled lip, and sneer of cold command,
> Tell that its sculptor well those passions read
> Which yet survive, stamped on these lifeless things,
> The hand that mocked them and the heart that fed:
> And on the pedestal these words appear:
> "My name is Ozymandias, king of kings:
> Look on my works, ye Mighty, and despair!"
> Nothing beside remains. Round the decay
> Of that colossal wreck, boundless and bare,
> The lone and level sands stretch far away.

The mystery of how this mighty lord of creation, whose very visage brought despair to all who looked, had fallen and sunk into the "lone and level" sand, thrilled the Romantics. The sight both humbled the viewers in reminding them of the transitory nature of human civilizations, even of mighty empires like the British, and exalted them in the knowledge that their empire had captured the mighty Ozymandias and brought him to stand in their museum like a lion in a zoo.[12]

Joseph Smith's Book of Mormon offered that kind of learning to its readers. He claimed to translate this long-lost and buried book just as the archeologists and curators brought Memnon before the gaze of the British public. Both sets of viewers were to learn from contemplating the passing of a civilization. Shelley's readers fell into a delicious awe in the presence of Ozymandias; Book of Mormon readers could ask what they might learn from the fall of a once great people who had pledged themselves to God and in the end abandoned him. Their bloody destruction could give the most exuberant American reason to pause.

Smith completed the Book of Mormon before he was twenty-four. In a peculiar reversal, he wrote his master work at the beginning of his career rather than as a culmination at the end. But it was not the end of his encounter with history. In the summer of 1830, three months after the publication of the Book of Mormon, he opened another window on the past. The Book of Moses, dictated from June to December, turned out to be the beginning of an inspired revision of the Bible (Moses 1–27, in PGP).[13] Smith was to sit down with the text and alter sentences and phrases according to his sense of what they were originally intended to mean, a project that took him three years to complete. The Book of Moses, however, began not with small, sentence-by-sentence emendations, but with a grand vision purportedly received by Moses on the eve of writing Genesis. Here Moses sees the scope of God's creations and is moved to ask why. What is your purpose in making all things? God's answer became perhaps the most quoted passage in all of

Mormon scripture: "Behold, this is my work and my glory to bring to pass the immortality and eternal life of man" (Moses 1:39).

In the course of augmenting the early chapters of Genesis, Smith expanded the biblical account with long excursions into the life of Adam and even longer accounts of the sixth from Adam, Enoch. Enoch, who receives only scant reference in the Bible though a massive figure in pseudepigraphical literature, also interrogates God, but not in the context of the glorious creations but against the backdrop of a failed mortal experience. Humans have forgotten God, turned on each other, and hate one another's blood. God openly weeps before Enoch in regret and disappointment at his children's capacity for evil. Enoch tries at first to comfort God and then seeing the horrors wrought by humankind, he too breaks down and pleads with God to know when this will end. Enoch is led through the course of history where no respite is promised, not even with the coming of the Savior. Only at the end, when truth will sweep the earth, will the earth rest. A new Zion will be reared and Enoch's people will descend and throw themselves on the necks of the redeemed people (Moses 7:21–69). The history Smith revealed to his people in these early revelations had a somber coloration. It was a story of breakdowns, calamities, human failures, and God's despair and wrath, lightened only by the promise of ultimate redemption.

Smith's third and last history purported to be a translation of actual Egyptian scrolls that the church purchased from a traveling exhibitor who had obtained them from an Egyptian antiquities dealer. Smith began translating in 1835 and finished and published the first part in 1842 as the writings of ancient Abraham.

Abraham returned to the cosmic visions of the early Moses. Abraham appears in his astronomer role, a person who has the secrets of the heaven revealed to him and who describes the premortal doings of God when he organized the spirits before the world was. These were our spirits, the text implied; we were all called by God and organized to come to earth to be tested. Abraham wrote in the spirit of the early Moses, seeing the creations and asking God about his intent. They were prehistory histories, more given to exploring the mysteries of the universe than to reflecting on the failings of humankind in earthly history.

Thus these three revelations—Book of Mormon, Book of Moses, and Book of Abraham—opened the shutters on one patch of history after another. Abraham and the Book of Mormon were supposed translations; Moses was pure inspiration. None of the works were systematic theology. They seem less intent on putting across a new body of doctrine than on illustrating human dealings with God in concrete, historical situations. They offer a few excursions into theology but are more given to incidents where the human struggle with good and evil is acted out in real life. While the overarching message is the familiar biblical one—serve Jehovah and flourish; reject him and suffer—the settings and the characters differ widely from one text to the other. Like Memnon they invite the viewer to learn an old lesson anew with each example of fallen might.

The presumption that truth was to be learned historically pointed to Smith's intimate, almost organic connection with the past. The past was not a distant, obscure, and exotic place. The characters in Joseph's histories have not fallen face first into the sand, to lie there dead and lifeless forever. Smith's past urgently speaks to the present. Moroni quoted Isaiah in speaking of his own written words as a voice from the dust, spoken initially with a future audience in mind. All of Joseph's angelic visitors came with the same urgent appeal to modern readers. The past recruits and mobilizes the present.[14]

Smith's angels did not come out of traditional angelogies; they are a different breed entirely from the angels in paintings of the Annunciation or Mary's ascent into heaven. For Mormons, wings betoken a corruption of the true understanding of angels. Gabriel's glorious luminescent wings miss the point Mormons believe. The wings identify angels as another order of being, distinct from human kind. In the intricate angelogies of medieval times, angels stood somewhere between humans and Gods in the great chain of being. They floated between heaven and earth, bearing up Mary on her upward ascent, singing to the shepherds at Christ's birth. In Catholic lore, angels were supernal, unearthly beings.[15]

Joseph's angels come out of history. They are not anonymous delegates from a corps of transhuman beings; they all have human names. Each one is linked to a specific historic period: Moroni to the last days of the Book of Mormon; John the Baptist and Peter, James, and John to Christ's ministry; Elias, Moses, and Elijah to their times in the biblical narrative. To the ahistorical angels, Gabriel and Michael, Smith assigned earthly identities; Noah for Gabriel and Adam for Michael. All the angels, he said, had once been attached to the earth (D&C 130:5). They were all akin to the appearance of Moses and Elias on the Mount of Transfiguration (Matthew 17:3).

That earthly connection lay at the heart of Smith's notion of history and of restoration. The angels in their earthly time had not completed their missions. Moses failed to prepare his people to see the face of God at Sinai; because of human wickedness, Enoch's Zion did not remain on earth; never in human history had the earth been allowed to rest. The work of God had always been truncated; the angels had died unfulfilled. The work of the last dispensation was to complete and fulfill the work of all past epochs of human history. The angels came to return keys and powers with demands on the present (D&C 130:5).[16]

> And the voice of Michael, the archangel; the voice of Gabriel, and of Raphael, and of divers angels from Michael or Adam down to the present time, all declaring their dispensation, their rights, their keys, their honors, their majesty and glory, and the power of their priesthood, giving line upon line, precept upon precept; here a little, and there a little; giving us consolation by holding forth that which is to come, confirming our hope. (D&C 128:21)

The saints of the latter day were to round out the work that remained to be completed. The phrase, the dispensation of the fullness of times, captured the belief that this was more than the end of the world, the cessation of wickedness; it was the fulfillment of human history. The angels in their earthly incarnations did not die and fall into the sand. They sought to continue their life missions in Joseph Smith's time through the work of the people he could assemble in his church. Ozymandias was tragic or even pathetic; his glory perished with him as his head fell from his trunkless legs face down in the desert. Sad as were their days on earth, Adam and Enoch would live again at the last day.

The historical revelations took the name of a man—the Book of Moses, the Book of Abraham, the Book of Mormon. Each book inside the Book of Mormon was named for an individual. They implied that redemption history for Joseph Smith resembled redemption history in the Bible; it was essentially the history of prophets and kings—great men. We learn about the past from studying Moses's and Abraham's writings.

But the Book of Mormon balanced that conception with the idea of people. The revelations came from God to various peoples. Looking ahead to the present, the Book of Mormon rebuked our age for relying too completely on the Bible while failing to appreciate its true nature: "O fools, they shall have a Bible; and it shall proceed forth from the Jews, mine ancient covenant people. . . . O ye Gentiles, have ye remembered the Jews, mine ancient covenant people? Nay; but ye have cursed them, and have hated them, and have not sought to recover them" (2 Nephi 29:4, 5).

The Hebrew Bible was a revelation to a people—the Jews. Revelation and nationhood were interlocked and not just in the cases of one nation. In the Book of Mormon account, all peoples received revelations, just as the Jews did. All the branches of the House of Israel, including the migrants to the new promised land, had their revelations. Likewise, all the peoples of the earth received as much as they were ready for. The snippets of historical texts that Smith revealed in Moses and Abraham were but a small sampling of the total body of revelation to the earth.

> Know ye not that there are more nations than one? Know ye not that I, the Lord your God, have created all men, and that I remember those who are upon the isles of the sea; and that I rule in the heaven above and in the earth beneath; and I bring forth my word unto the children of men, yea, even upon all the nations of the earth? . . . For I command all men, both in the east and in the west, and in the north, and in the south, and in the islands of the sea, that they shall write the words which I speak unto them. (2 Nephi 29:7, 11)

At the end all these people will come together to read each other's histories and learn and marvel. That would mark the great unification of mankind, when they listened to the stories kept by each other's prophets and historians through the course of human history (cf. Alma 29:8).[17]

Joseph Smith's people in his own time were one more of these people, but one charged with fulfilling the lives and work of all their predecessors. One of the titles given to Joseph Smith at the beginning of the church was "translator." He seemed to have believed that ancient records would fall into his hands from then on, as the histories of one after another of the earth's peoples came to light. He was to be the collector and a curator of the world's religious texts.

At the same time, he was to be the prophet of his own people, to prepare them to perform the work God had ordained for them. This role required that he make his own record as Mormon and Moroni before him had made a record. This record keeping took two forms: the writing of histories and the compilation of revelations. The first eluded him for a number of years, though he made attempts from the first years of the church. Only in 1838 did he initiate a systematic account of the rise of the church. The second, the compilation of revelations, came to him more naturally. Unlike the visions which he held close to his chest, he freely broadcast the revelations to guide the church.

He began writing revelations in 1828, when he was just beginning work on the Book of Mormon and from then on he received inspiration on matters small and large, from the atonement to where the church was to locate its base of operations. All of these revelations, even personal words of inspiration to individual followers, Smith carefully preserved and published as soon as he could. He thought of the revelations as precious jewels given of God to the saints of the latter days. In 1831, the revelation manuscripts were compiled, recopied, edited, and sent off to the printer. The first batch came off the press in 1833, only to be scattered in the mud by the opposition party in Missouri where the Mormon press was located. They were once again brought together, reedited, and augmented with subsequent revelations in an 1835 edition titled the Doctrine and Covenants. He said the revelations were "to be worth to the Church the riches of the whole Earth speaking temporally."[18]

These revelations took a peculiar rhetorical form. From the first revelation on, Smith virtually disappears from the scene. The words come directly from God with nothing of Joseph in them. He does not hear from God and pass the word along to the people, as did Isaiah who regularly injected the prophetic "I." The only "I" in Smith's revelations is God. They typically begin: "Behold, I am God; give heed unto my word, which is quick and powerful, sharper than a two-edged sword" (D&C 6:1). Or "hearken unto the voice of the Lord your God, while I speak unto you, Emma Smith, my daughter" (D&C 25:1). Joseph is imagined among the hearers, sometimes the recipient of rebuke, but not a speaker or interpreter.

Smith in effect creates a rhetorical space where he is the silent listener and God the only speaker. His space is only imaginary, unlike the place at Lourdes, where the fourteen-year-old Bernadette Soubirous sat on a river bank opposite a grotto and saw a soft light emanating from the bank across the stream. A smiling little girl in white beckoned to her and made the sign of the cross. Although chastised by her parents and neighbors, Bernadette returned again and again to the river bank to meet the smiling apparition. For the most part, the girl in white was silent but on a few occasions called for penitence and prayers for sinners. She directed Bernadette to kiss the ground and there sprang up the fountain that was later to be the object of devotion.[19]

Smith's revelations to the church came to him as words not appearances, but they created a rhetorical space, like the river and the grotto where the child appeared to Bernadette. The child was there or not, depending on the day, smiling and occasionally speaking. She was experienced by Bernadette as a personage outside herself, a something in the space between her and the river. Smith's revelations leave the same impression. God stands outside of the prophet, and even though the words came from Joseph's mouth or pen, they sound like they were spoken by someone standing before him in a rhetorical space. The words made his followers feel like God had spoken, not Joseph. When he asked them to take on a duty, they would sometimes hold back until they had received a "commandment," meaning a revelation from the Prophet. Though the words came from the same mouth, they distinguished between the man speaking and God.[20]

Before 1835, the revelations came thick and fast as the Saints importuned their prophet for revelations on virtually every subject, from the interpretation of scripture to where they were to preach. Sometimes their requests overwhelmed him. He warned the petitioners that "it is a gre[a]t thing to enquire at the hand of God or to come into his presence and we feel fearful to approach him upon subject[s] that are of little or no consequence . . . especially about things the knowledge of which men ought to obtain in all cencerity before God for themselves."[21] One revelation specifically enjoined the saints to do many good things of their own free will without a revelation (D&C 58:26–29).

The constant drumbeat of revelations tapered off after 1835. The frequency declined precipitously from then until the end of Smith's life. This was not an indication that Smith's creativity was flagging or that the restoration had been completed. If anything, innovation sped up in the last years of Smith's life. Instead the decrease of revelations from him seems to have been calculated. There are signs that he intended the revelatory power to pass from himself to the councils of the church, which were organized in 1834 and 1835. He had always been generous about the inclusion of his friends in his experiences. A number of the most critical revelations came jointly to Smith and someone else, notably Oliver Cowdery and Sidney Rigdon. One scripture declared that all who spoke in church were to be moved by the Holy Ghost and write scripture (D&C 68:3–4). Smith jealously guarded the right to have the last word and receive governing revelation for the church as a whole, but he encouraged everyone to seek guidance from the Holy Spirit.

That instruction was directed most pointedly at the councils of the church. In the early years Smith had adopted the practice of conducting church business in conferences or councils, which consisted of trusted associates who happened to be on hand. At first they were informal, catch-as-catch-can assemblages, but gradually the boundaries were better defined. In 1834, he organized a high council to govern the church in Kirtland and similar councils for the other church centers. The organizing charter directed that in cases of difficulty, "if there is not a sufficiency written to make the case clear to the mind of the council, the president may inquire and obtain the mind of the Lord by revelation" (D&C 102:23). Whoever happened to occupy the office of council president was enjoined to seek revelation. In 1835, Smith formed the Quorum of the Twelve Apostles to govern in the broader world where missionaries were collecting converts into small branches. Smith told the apostles to keep careful minutes of their decisions, for the minutes would be as "doctrine and covenants" to the church, invoking the name of his own compilation of revelations. The implication was that decisions in council were to be of equal authority with revelations to the prophet.[22] In making these changes, Smith not only shifted the responsibility for revelation from himself to the councils, he moved the locus of revelation from the individual prophet to the church's administrative bureaucracy.

From the time of the council organization on, the frequency of Smith's revelations dropped as the councils took up the slack. Although he reserved the last word for himself, Smith did not attempt to monopolize the prophetic office. It was as if he intended to reduce his own role and infuse the church bureaucracy with his charismatic powers. Revelation would be interwoven in the ongoing administrative life of the church beginning with the Twelve. After Smith was shot at Carthage, Brigham Young could take control of the church in the name of the apostles, who came to be designated "prophets, seers, and revelators." The great bulk of the membership understood by then that councils were revelatory agencies. And the diffusion did not end there. The wide investment of the prophetic impulse that began with the apostles in time seeped into every church office. Every Bishop, every Relief Society President, every young priesthood holder in the modern church is now enjoined to listen to the Spirit for guidance in his or her calling. In Smith's mind, it was to be a revelatory church, its members a charismatic people. The original prophet was not a singular, isolated case in the church's history but a model for all who would officiate.

One reason Smith's revelations made a deeper mark on American culture than the words of the other prophets of his time was because he paid so much attention to the routinization and democratization of charisma. Among nineteenth-century prophetic figures, he stands out as one who declared a new right way; but as Mormonism developed, it appeared that the new right way was for all the Lord's people to be prophets. Revelation was institutionalized and democratized, the divine gift shared. An 1833 revelation announced that the time would come when "every man might speak in the name of God, the Lord, the Savior of the world"; it was a suitable goal for an American prophet (D&C 1:20).

NOTES

1. Brodhead, "Prophets in America circa 1830," 21, 18.
2. Bushman, "Visionary World of Joseph Smith," 189, 191; Winiarski, "Souls Filled with Ravishing Transport"; Kirchner, "Tending to Edify, Astonish, and Instruct."
3. Rosell and Dupuis, *Memoirs of Charles G. Finney*, chap. 2.
4. Brodhead, "Prophets in America circa 1830," 18.
5. For a listing of Smith's visions, see Baugh, "Parting the Veil."
6. The Book of Mormon (Palmyra: E. B. Grandin, 1830).
7. Woodford, "Historical Development of the Doctrine and Covenants," 1: 126.
8. Jessee, Ashurst-McGee, and Jensen, *Joseph Smith Papers: Journals*, 1: 219–22.
9. An allusion to the 1820 vision appears in D&C 20:5.
10. Pratt, *Interesting Account of Several Remarkable Visions*.
11. "History, 1832," in Jessee, *Personal Writings of Joseph Smith*, 9.
12. Colla, *Conflicted Antiquities*.
13. For the Joseph Smith translation, see Matthews, *Plainer Translation*; and Faulring, Jackson, and Matthews, *Joseph Smith's New Translation of the Bible*.
14. See Brown, *In Heaven as It Is on Earth*, chap. 5.
15. For example, Keck, *Angels and Angelology in the Middle Ages*; and Marshall and Walsham, *Angels in the Early Modern World*.
16. Ehat and Cook, *Words of Joseph Smith*, 10–11, 169.
17. Bushman, "Book of Mormon in Early Mormon History," 3–18.

18. Cannon and Cook, *Far West Record*, 31–32; Bushman, *Joseph Smith*, 172–73.
19. Harris, *Lourdes*, 1–6.
20. Bushman, "Little, Narrow, Prison of Language."
21. Joseph Smith to Brother Carter, April 13, 1833.
22. "Kirtland High Council Minutes," February 27, 1835.

BIBLIOGRAPHY

Baugh, Alexander. "Parting the Veil: Joseph Smith's Seventy-six Documented Visionary Experiences." In *Opening the Heavens: Accounts of Divine Manifestations, 1820–1844*, ed. John W. Welch, 265–326. Salt Lake City: Deseret, 2004.

Brodhead, Richard. "Prophets in America circa 1830: Ralph Waldo Emerson, Nat Turner, Joseph Smith." In *Joseph Smith Jr.: Reappraisals over Two Centuries*, ed. Reid L. Neilson and Terryl Givens, 13–30. New York: Oxford University Press, 2009.

Brown, Samuel Morris. *In Heaven as It Is on Earth: Joseph Smith and the Early Mormon Conquest of Death*. New York: Oxford University Press, 2012.

Bushman, Richard L. "The Book of Mormon in Early Mormon History." In *New Views of Mormon History: A Collection of Essays in Honor of Leonard J. Arrington*, ed. Davis Bitton and Maureen Ursenbach Beecher, 3–18. Salt Lake City: University of Utah Press, 1987.

Bushman, Richard L. *Joseph Smith: Rough Stone Rolling*. New York: Alfred A. Knopf, 2005.

Bushman, Richard L. "The Little, Narrow, Prison of Language: The Rhetoric of Revelation." *The Religious Educator: Perspectives on the Restored Gospel* 1 (Spring 2000): 90–104.

Bushman, Richard L. "The Visionary World of Joseph Smith," *BYU Studies* 37, no. 1 (1997–98): 183–204.

Cannon, Donald Q., and Lyndon W. Cook, eds. *Far West Record: Minutes of the Church of Jesus Christ of Latter-day Saints, 1830–1844*. Salt Lake City: Deseret, 1983.

Colla, Elliott. *Conflicted Antiquities: Egyptology, Egyptomania, Egyptian Modernity*. Durham, NC: Duke University Press, 2007.

Ehat, Andrew F., and Lyndon W. Cook, eds. *The Words of Joseph Smith: The Contemporary Accounts of the Nauvoo Discourses of the Prophet Joseph*. Orem, UT: Grandin, 1991.

Faulring, Scott H., Kent P. Jackson, and Robert J. Matthews, eds. *Joseph Smith's New Translation of the Bible: Original Manuscripts*. Provo, UT: Religious Studies Center, Brigham Young University, 2004.

Harris, Ruth. *Lourdes: Body and Spirit in the Secular Age*. New York: Viking Penguin, 1999.

Jessee, Dean C., ed. *The Personal Writings of Joseph Smith*. Rev. ed. Salt Lake City: Deseret, 2002.

Jessee, Dean C., Mark Ashurst-McGee, and Richard L. Jensen, eds. *The Joseph Smith Papers: Journals Volume 1: 1832–1839*. Salt Lake City: Church Historian's Press, 2008.

Keck, David. *Angels and Angelology in the Middle Ages*. Oxford: Oxford University Press, 1998.

Kirchner, Ann. " 'Tending to Edify, Astonish, and Instruct': Published Narratives of Spiritual Dreams and Visions in the Early Republic." *Early American Studies* 1 (2003): 198–229.

"Kirtland High Council Minutes." February 27, 1835. Church History Library, Salt Lake City, UT.

Marshall, Peter, and Alexandra Walsham, eds. *Angels in the Early Modern World*. Cambridge: Cambridge University Press, 2006.

Matthews, Robert J. *"A Plainer Translation": Joseph Smith's Translation of the Bible, a History and Commentary*. Provo, UT: Brigham Young University Press, 1975.

Pratt, Orson. *A[n] Interesting Account of Several Remarkable Visions, and of the Late Discovery of Ancient American Records*. Edinburgh: Ballantyne and Hughes, 1840.

Rosell, Garth M., and Richard A. G. Dupuis, eds. *Memoirs of Charles G. Finney: The Complete Restored Text*. Grand Rapids, MI: Zondervan, 1989.

"Smith, Joseph, to Brother Carter." April 13, 1833. Joseph Smith Collection, Church History Library, Salt Lake City, Utah.

Winiarski, Douglas L. "Souls Filled with Ravishing Transport: Heavenly Visions and the Radical Awakening in New England." *William and Mary Quarterly*, 3rd series, 61, no. 1 (January 2004): 3–46.

Woodford, Robert J. "The Historical Development of the Doctrine and Covenants." PhD diss., Brigham Young University, 3 vols., 1974.

....

CHAPTER 9

MORMONS AND THE BIBLE

....

LAURIE F. MAFFLY-KIPP

To talk about the relationship of Mormons to the Bible is to wade into the center of a controversy over the status of scriptures that can be traced to the beginnings of Christianity itself. The battles over canonization in the early years of the church, the skirmishes between Catholics and Protestants beginning in the Reformation with the Protestant insistence on "sola scriptura" (belief that the scriptures were the only and complete authority for the Christian life), and the proliferation of dozens of authoritative translations and formats of the biblical text since the dawn of the industrial revolution, all signal that concerns over the status of the Bible—what it is, what it means, and how it relates to other sacred texts—drive to the heart of Christian identity.

Even if it is tempting, then, to try to define a "Mormon way" of understanding the Bible, we must begin with the recognition that there is no single "traditional" Christian use of the scriptures against which to measure Mormon approaches. Further, Mormons themselves have employed and continue to employ the Bible in multiple ways. To comprehend Mormons and their relationship to the Bible necessitates a tour through official doctrines, revelatory statements, and ethnographic descriptions of the text in the lives of ordinary believers.

THE BIBLE IN MORMON HISTORY

....

The Mormon faith was born into American culture in the antebellum era, a period of intense interest in the Bible fueled by the growing dominance of evangelical Protestantism in public life. For most Americans of the day, the Bible shaped the most basic structures of language, social life, habits of mind, and views of the past and the future. School children learned to read by poring over its pages, families gathered around a common book for study and guidance, and many churches featured the pulpit, the site from which the words of the book were proclaimed and elaborated, as the center of liturgical practice. Both proslavery and antislavery activists, and other political actors of all sorts, pulled from its pages to argue the righteousness of their causes. While English was the young nation's primary language, the words and images of the Bible, and especially of the King James Version (KJV), framed its imaginings.[1]

As with many of the religious movements springing up in the 1820s and 1830s, Mormons understood their new faith not as a departure from the Bible but as the most complete way of enacting its sacred truths. Mormonism's founder and first prophet, Joseph Smith Jr., claimed to have had his first revelation while contemplating a passage from the New Testament Epistle of James, and thereafter the Bible became his touchstone for understanding the outpouring of divine instructions that he received. Indeed, Smith and his followers, in a more literal-minded way than most Americans, quickly came to see themselves as living within the world of the biblical story.[2] Guided by visitations from God, Jesus, and prophets and apostles mentioned in the scriptures, Smith took it as his task to restore to the earth the ordinances, rites, and beliefs of God's church, the blueprint for which could be found in a commonsense reading of the Bible.

Few American evangelicals would have taken issue with this approach to the scriptures. For Methodists, Baptists, and members of most other Protestant denominations, the Bible was, indeed, a plain text whose meaning was clear to ordinary believers. They may have argued vociferously over what that meaning called them to do, but all would have conceded that the life of a Christian ought to be shaped by the teachings and precepts, God's revealed word to humanity, found in the text. When Joseph Smith articulated the foundational principles of his new church in 1842, his eighth article of faith seemed to fit right in with the thinking of many Protestant Americans: "We believe the Bible to be the word of God as far as it is translated correctly."[3]

Most Protestants also took the Bible to be the complete and final record of divine intervention in the world. They assumed that the early years of the Christian Church, the era of Jesus's life and resurrection and of the acts of his apostles, signaled the final age of miraculous healings and direct revelation. Jesus's incarnation was, indeed, the ultimate sign from God, an action that fulfilled the promises of the Hebrew scriptures and stood as the sole route to human salvation. The task of the Christian Church for now, until a future date when Christ once again returned to reign over the earth, was to live out biblical precepts as they had been spelled out in the books of the Old and New Testaments.

This is where the Mormons veered away sharply from other Christian groups. Joseph Smith's publication of the Book of Mormon in 1830, later subtitled "Another Testament of Jesus Christ," stood as a stark refutation of these received views of the Bible. Smith claimed that the book he had translated from golden plates buried in a hillside near his upstate New York farm constituted another divine record, a further revelation of God's working in the world that overlapped with the narrative of the Bible itself. Smith and his followers believed that he had been called by God to communicate this additional revelation and to begin to restore all of the truths of the Bible to human life, many of which they asserted had been lost or misapprehended by generations of Christians. Most important, Mormons believed that Smith himself, as head of this restored Christian Church, would inaugurate the return of divine revelation to human beings; rather than awaiting the return of Christ, God would once again communicate directly with His creatures.

This new revelation intrigued some people and offended many more, particularly those who remained within Protestant churches. The Book of Mormon itself was not theologically objectionable: like many of the tales in the Hebrew scriptures, its pages narrate the story of several groups of people who migrate from Palestine to the New World in the centuries before Jesus's appearance. It traces the fate of two bands, the Nephites and the Lamanites, who alternately clash, unite, meet the risen Christ in scenes directly parallel to New Testament renderings of Jesus's resurrection appearances, and then engage in a final series of battles in which the last of the Nephites, Mormon and his son, Moroni, are killed. But its very existence and the claims made by Mormons that it was an extension of biblical teaching flew in the face of notions of the sufficiency of the Holy Bible and the cessation of revelation after the age of the apostles, as Smith spelled out in the remainder of his eighth article of faith: "we also believe the Book of Mormon to be the word of God." For Mormons, then, the Bible stands in a different relationship to believers not because they deny its authority, but because its teachings are confirmed and augmented by other scriptures and by divine revelation. While followers of Joseph Smith consider themselves to be a "Bible-believing people," other Christians assert that, by virtue of the fact that the Bible is not their sole source of divine authority, its power is, for practical purposes, diminished.

Nineteenth-century Mormons, by all accounts, took the Bible very seriously. Like the followers of Alexander Campbell and Methodists, religious groups out of which many early converts came, Mormons sought guidance from the Bible as they set up their church and organized their lives. In the 1830s, Mormon periodicals cited the Bible nearly twenty times as often as they did the Book of Mormon. John Codman, a prominent Protestant visitor to the "Mormon country" of Utah in the 1870s (and himself the son of a New England minister), noted that Mormons were "astonishing biblical students" who did not seem to spend nearly as much time reading the Book of Mormon. "They are perpetually flinging texts at your head," he mused.[4]

Some scholars have taken this early Mormon focus on the Bible as evidence that the Book of Mormon was significant more as a symbol of restored revelation rather than for its content.[5] It is certainly true that the Book of Mormon contains few doctrines unique to the Latter-day Saints, and it is likely the case that the characters and figures of the text were incorporated only gradually into the sacred imaginations of followers, so that by the time Mormons migrated to the Salt Lake Basin in Utah in the 1840s and 1850s, they readily christened towns such as Lehi and Nephi, drawing their new world scripture under the sacred canopy of their new Zion.[6] But pitting the two books against each other and gauging the relative importance of each misses an important point: the Bible and the Book of Mormon were ineluctably interrelated in the minds of believers. One primary appeal of the Book of Mormon to potential converts was precisely its similarity to the KJV. Its binding bore a striking resemblance to popular editions of that text, and its cadences repeated what was, by the 1830s, a quaint and unmistakably biblical set of phrases, such as "And it came to pass," and "Verily I say unto you." Its rendering of the appearance of Jesus, this time in the Americas, quoted directly from the biblical passages of Isaiah 2–14 and 48–54, as well as Matthew 5–7. Detractors criticized the book because they deemed it simply a "garbled" version of the Old and New Testaments, while believers found in its pages an inspiring companion to the Bible itself.[7]

Yet Mormons then and now also believe that the Bible is not inerrant. It contained mistakes of transmission and translation introduced by human scribes. Those errors meant that the text had to be understood with the aid of subsequent revelation and the divine guidance of the newly restored church. In 1830, the year that Joseph Smith formed the "Church of Christ" (later renamed the Church of Jesus Christ of Latter-day Saints), the young prophet embarked on his own translation of the Bible that would correct and clarify some of its passages. Smith was not equipped with the original languages of the texts, but he believed that, using the KJV, he could "translate" God's intentions through his own revelatory experiences. He worked on the project for much of the rest of his life, publishing excerpts in church publications, but it was never completed, nor did it become the authorized biblical translation of his church.[8] This labor of interpretation, deeply inflected by high Jacobean English echoing the KJV, resulted in additional written works that would also become canonized scripture for the Church of Jesus Christ of Latter-day Saints, including the Doctrine and Covenants (published in a first edition in 1835) and the Pearl of Great Price (originally compiled in 1851, and recognized as canonical in 1880). For some other Mormon groups, as we will see, Joseph Smith's translation of the Bible assumed a different status.

MORMON INTERPRETIVE STRATEGIES

Mormons, by definition, believe that Joseph Smith was a prophet called to restore divine authority to the world and that the Book of Mormon is a sacred text that elaborates on the sacred history contained in the Bible. The very existence of another record, however—indeed, a record that mentioned the existence of still other sacred scriptures yet to be discovered—opened up Mormons to a new way of understanding the Bible. If God had revealed himself to human beings on many occasions, and was now revealing himself once again, there were, in theory, endless numbers of scriptures that had been produced (and could continue to be produced). When late nineteenth-century biblical scholars announced the existence of multiple versions of early Christian manuscripts, their discoveries only confirmed for Mormons the belief that God had called on humans throughout time to create sacred records, and to interpret their words through the light of continuing revelation. Whereas for many Protestants the issue of variations in the biblical manuscripts contributed to an intellectual crisis that eventually would result in a split between modernists (who read the Bible more as metaphor and guide) and fundamentalists (who constructed elaborate theories of scriptural inerrancy), Mormons in the nineteenth and early twentieth centuries had little trouble with the notion that fallible human beings had written texts that needed to be treated with cautious reverence.

Some scholars have attributed the lack of a Mormon controversy over biblical inerrancy that paralleled that of Protestants to this wariness of literalism. As Terryl Givens has noted, believers, aided by the guidance of latter-day prophets and church leaders, and by the light of their own inspiration, could in theory rely on this world of "scriptural productions" without feeling threatened by the textual discrepancies or multiplicity of language.[9]

Mormons also read (and still read) the Bible as prophecies for later events within their collective story.[10] Thus, the Old and New Testaments served as a record that prefigured the eventual appearance of Smith's restoration of the church in the "latter days" of sacred history, much as early Christians read the Hebrew scriptures through the fulfillment of its promises in the life, death, and resurrection of Jesus. A prominent example of this interpretive frame is the elaboration, articulated by church leaders from Joseph Smith to twenty-first-century Saints, of Ezekiel 37: 15–17, which reads: "The word of the Lord came again unto me, saying, Moreover, thou son of man, take thee one stick, and write upon it, For Judah, and for the children of Israel his companions: then take another stick, and write upon it, For Joseph, the stick of Ephraim, and for all the house of Israel his companions: And join them one to another into one stick; and they shall become one in thine hand."

Smith, in a revelation from August 1830, declared that "the keys of the record of the stick of Ephraim" were connected to the Book of Mormon. Subsequent church leaders have continued to read Ezekiel as referring to the Book of Mormon and its promises, and the latest LDS-authorized and annotated version of the Bible, published in 1979, prefaces the chapter with this gloss: "Israel will inherit the land in the Resurrection—The stick of Judah (the Bible) and the stick of Joseph (the Book of Mormon) will become one in the Lord's hand—The children of Israel will be gathered and cleansed—David (the Messiah) will reign over them—They will receive the everlasting gospel covenant." The words of Ezekiel thereby confirm and corroborate the Book of Mormon, binding all of these texts together into a continuous record of God's dealings with his people.

Almost immediately differences in approach began to emerge among Mormons over precisely which of the practices described in the Bible should be reinstated in the young church. A significant number of believers, like many Protestants of the day, sought to restore the principles of the early Christian Church (those activities described in the New Testament), including foot washing, healing, receiving of the gifts of the spirit (those experienced on the day of Pentecost, such as speaking in tongues), and the calling of elders and apostles. Many early Mormons also believed that they were mandated by God to restore many elements of ancient Israelite worship, including the rebuilding of the temple, reinstatement of a priesthood, and the restoration of ordinances such as vicarious baptism for the dead (a rite mentioned in the New Testament book of 1 Corinthians 15:29, but which had not been practiced by major Christian groups since the fourth century AD). Using the Israelite Patriarchs as their model, Joseph Smith and his inner circle also began to practice plural marriage, a controversial rite that led to divisions among his followers. At least one important element of this dispute focused on how to interpret the reinstatement of biblical practices, and whether God intended for the restored church to include all of the ordinances and practices described in the Hebrew scriptures as well as those in the New Testament.

After Smith's death and the leadership struggle that ensued, those Mormons who followed Brigham Young from Nauvoo to what quickly became Utah Territory (estimated at perhaps two-thirds of the 15,000 Mormons gathered in Illinois and Iowa at the time) continued to believe that their church, the Church of Jesus Christ of Latter-day Saints (LDS), should model itself after ancient Israel and should include the temple ordinance of plural marriage and the literal rebuilding of Zion. At this point they were, quite literally, reading the Hebrew scriptures through a Christian lens. The 5000 or so who stayed behind in the Midwest, including Smith's widow, Emma, and his extended family, eventually helped pull together a smaller band known as the Reorganized Church of Jesus Christ of Latter Day Saints (RLDS, renamed in 2001 the Community of Christ). That organization interpreted biblical restoration on a New Testament model, rejecting many of the temple rituals that became so central to the Utah Mormons' understanding of salvation.[11] Eventually the RLDS interpretation of scripture moved away from a focus on the distinctive features of the Book of Mormon, resembling more closely the Protestant understandings of the time. Several other organizational offshoots of the crisis over authority in the late 1840s, including the much smaller Mormon Strangites and Cutlerites, occupied a middle ground, instituting some temple ordinances but not all of those practiced by the LDS. Mormons today, of which there are dozens of communities (although the LDS Church is by far the largest single group), continue to hold varying interpretations of the Bible as a model for the restored church. These range from a whole adoption of modern scholarly methods to a nearly complete spurning of academic approaches.

Two additional features of the Mormon tradition that have decisively shaped its understanding of the Bible are its ecclesiastical structure and fluid understanding of doctrine. Emerging from a culture that placed great emphasis on individual deliberation and inspiration, Mormonism leaves a great deal of interpretive agency in the hands of the believer. Nonetheless, the church is also hierarchical in structure: the LDS Church and most other Mormons groups are headed by a prophet and quorum of apostles who have been called to receive revelation on behalf of the church and to provide guidance for members. In practice, this means that other than the canonized scriptures and a handful of doctrines from the leadership that have been presented for a vote to the membership, most pronouncements, speculative statements, or opinions put forth by church leaders fall into a broad category of official statements of ambiguous authority.

This categorical ambiguity, combined with the belief in an open canon (wherein doctrines may, in theory, change over time), lends a distinctive approach to the interpretation of all scripture, including the Bible. Moreover, the LDS Church (and most of the smaller Mormon sects) does not train a clerical elite. Instead, all adult men in good standing are eligible members of the Mormon priesthood, a sacred office that enables them to perform particular rites and ordinances such as healing, anointing, and temple rituals. While the church supports an extensive educational structure that encourages all members to attend "seminary," and many adherents serve voluntary offices within their local and regional church communities (wards and stakes), there is no specific clerical training that would establish orthodox standards of scriptural interpretation or criticism. The professional church leadership (including the First Presidency and the Quorum of the Twelve Apostles, among others), constituted of men from a variety of educational backgrounds, including lawyers, businessmen, and educators, serves less as an arbiter of right belief and more as the facilitator of acceptable practice. This is not to say that correct beliefs are not significant and at times determinative for members: but in practice, the correct articulation of creedal statements is less important for LDS than for most Protestant churches.

These elements of Mormon interpretive practice allow considerable leeway for individual scriptural evaluation, since church authorities focus on correct practice and step into matters of interpretation only in situations where they conclude that errant beliefs may harm the entire community. As a result, Mormons by and large avoided the deep rifts over textual interpretation that wracked American Protestants in the late nineteenth and early twentieth centuries. At the same time, contemporary theologians might call popular Mormon readings of scripture "naïve," in the sense that believers, most of whom are not trained in textual analysis, see no problem in freely associating from passages in the Bible to contemporary life. All members, in effect, interpret the Bible and share their convictions in Sunday meetings and informal settings. Statements about the Bible (and other matters) made by general authorities are particularly subject to speculation about how binding they are for members. In recent decades a number of books written by leaders of the LDS Church, such as Bruce McConkie's *Mormon Doctrine* (1958) and Joseph Fielding Smith's *Man, His Origin and Destiny* (1954), based at least in part on biblical interpretation, have occasioned a great deal of debate, because believers have had divergent opinions about the authority and meaning of their statements.

In recent decades, the LDS Church has sought greater hermeneutical consistency and more exclusive focus on the reading of canonized texts. In the 1970s, church leaders began to call for the replacement of student manuals, written by church educational leaders, with the KJV and other scriptures in the educational curriculum, a development that necessitated uniformity in the scriptural versions that were being used. If all students were expected to read the Bible for themselves and discuss its meanings, it would help greatly to have everyone reading a single text with annotations authorized by church leaders. In 1979, the church published its own version of the KJV, complete with chapter summaries and extensive cross-references to other LDS scriptures. They included as notes many of the elaborations added by Joseph Smith in his own biblical translation. The Standard Works, the current LDS edition of its canonized texts, also contains maps, a topical index, a Bible dictionary with entries designed to clarify the texts, and other aids to study, in order to fulfill the charge of the publication committee "to assist in improving doctrinal scholarship throughout the Church."[12] In this way, the LDS Church can guide believers more closely in their scriptural study, suggesting, if not mandating, orthodox approaches and frameworks. Today the Bible and other scriptures are read in Sunday school classes by church members in a four-year rotation.

The RLDS Church, now the Community of Christ (CC), has followed a different path in its approach to scripture. Like the LDS Church, the CC adheres to belief in an open canon and rejects scriptural inerrancy, but it has moved in marked respects toward a liturgical use of the Bible similar to that of many liberal Protestant denominations. No one version of the Bible is prescribed, although newer versions are most often used liturgically. The CC, along with many Protestant churches, follows the format of the Revised Common Lectionary in its three-year cycle for public worship and personal study. The Book of Mormon and the Doctrine and Covenants are also considered scripture, although the versions used by the CC differ from those of the LDS Church, and the Book of Mormon is much less likely to be used in church or for individual devotion than is the Bible. In 1867, the church published Joseph Smith's unfinished revision of the KJV as the *Inspired Version* (the Smith family had retained the original manuscripts), and that text, once dominant, is now used occasionally alongside modernized translations in the lectionary cycle.

The KJV and the International Church

As previously noted, the LDS Church today uses the KJV in ritual settings and for private devotion. Philip Barlow has suggested, however, that objections to other versions were more pragmatic than principled until the late twentieth century. Because Mormons believe that all modern Bibles contain some level of human error, and many early members had come to Mormonism through Protestant churches that utilized the KJV, it seemed the most natural and simplest format to retain.[13] By the early twentieth century publishers began to produce new versions of the scriptures, and church leaders continued to encourage the exploration of multiple scriptural renditions, resisting an insistence on an orthodox version.

Diversity of biblical formats became more difficult to maintain as the LDS Church spread well beyond the American West in the decades after the Second World War. The advent of a full-bodied correlation program, designed to ensure uniformity of worship, practice, and belief throughout the church, resulted in the proliferation of standardized procedural manuals and study guides by the 1960s. Increasing focus on the KJV as the standard for LDS usage followed this pattern. The publication of the Revised Standard Version (RSV) in the early 1950s, accompanied by an active publicity campaign by its liberal Protestant sponsors, had met with considerable uproar among Protestant fundamentalists. Some Mormons, equally concerned about dramatic deviations from the KJV phrasing and intent on preserving usage of a Bible more in keeping with the language of other LDS scriptures, voiced active opposition to the new version. In 1956, J. Reuben Clark, a member of the First Presidency of the church and a lawyer by training, published a lengthy critique entitled *Why the King James Version*. Clark argued that the KJV was not only superior linguistically to the RSV, but it was doctrinally purer and far better for having been crafted by faithful believers. While his opinions did not constitute

official LDS doctrine, and his views met disagreement within the church, Clark's advocacy also reflected a growing effort to bring uniformity to Mormon encounters with
the Bible.[14] In 1992, the First Presidency released a letter that further clarified the privileged place held by the KJV: "While other Bible versions may be easier to read than the
King James Version, in doctrinal matters latter-day revelation supports the King James
Version in preference to other English translations."[15]

Sanctioned use of the KJV, though, presents potentially thorny problems as the
church expands more rapidly into non-English speaking countries. The LDS Church
had worked assiduously for decades to translate the Book of Mormon and other new
scriptures into a wide array of languages for newly baptized members. Until 2009,
the church used readily available Bible translations in local languages. In that year
the first Spanish-language edition of the Standard Works (the four canonized scriptural texts, including maps and a Bible dictionary), appeared. The Bible is based on
the *Reina-Valera* version, translated by a Lutheran theologian in sixteenth-century
Switzerland and revised in 1909. One of the chief architects of the translation project,
Elder J. E. Jensen, commented that the church had selected the 1909 edition because
of copyright issues surrounding the more recent versions of the text; but he concluded
that usage of the earlier version turned out to be a "blessing in disguise" because the
language fit better with the cadences of the KJV.[16] French church members use the
Louis Segond translation of 1910, another Protestant text thought of as the French
equivalent of the KJV.

Why does it matter which Bible translation is used in foreign countries? In theory, it
might not, since Mormons tend to believe that the meaning of the text is not connected
to the exact wording. Yet the example of the German Bible illustrates how closely issues
of translation are related to matters of interpretation and doctrine, and how attempts
at international correlation are complicated by uses of non-KJV scriptures. At the very
least, it makes the linguistic similarities between the Book of Mormon, the Doctrine
and Covenants, and the Bible more problematic if a non-KJV Bible is employed in
non-English speaking contexts.

In 1981, the LDS Church leadership produced a new version of the "triple combination" (the Book of Mormon, the Doctrine and Covenants, and Pearl of Great Price),
the first German translations since the 1920s, for its membership in German-speaking
areas. At the same time, the First Presidency authorized use of the Uniform Translation
of the Bible, a modern version published just a year earlier by the Roman Catholic
Bishops' Conference of Germany. LDS elder Robert D. Hales, the church executive
administrator in Frankfurt, advised church leaders that the new Uniform Translation
and triple combination would be used in all future church publications in German, and
that priesthood leaders should employ the new translations exclusively and advise other
members to do the same. Although it was a Catholic publication, one that included the
Apocrypha and extensive annotation unrelated to the LDS canon, the Quorum of the
Twelve announced that the version "came closest" to the KJV and would be a great help
to German-speaking members. Elder Hales cautioned, however, that the Bible translation was not published by the church and therefore readers ought to bear in mind the

article of faith asserting that "We believe the Bible to be the word of God as far as it is translated correctly."[17]

There are trade-offs in using a different version, however. As noted above, the Uniform Translation contains apocryphal texts beyond those that appear in the LDS version of the KJV. While their addition might not be a theological issue, since neither Joseph Smith nor subsequent presidents have ruled out the reading of the Apocrypha, their presence is not contextualized or interpreted for the LDS reader. Further, the Uniform Translation contains extensive annotations that don't always correlate with the English-version annotations, and even seem to contradict them at some points.[18] More generally, the matter of choosing Bible translations according to how well they correspond to the KJV, rather than anchoring them to the sense of the original language texts, seems strangely to enshrine that particular version rather than to demonstrate its potential for error; at the same time, the use of modernized versions in other languages raises the possibility of moving away from the KJV among English speakers. Ironically, at least one LDS scholar who has studied and admired the Uniform Translation and its modernized language, and who remarks that his family typically uses more contemporary English Bible translations in family study and church lessons, has been led to question whether the KJV should not be replaced for English speakers with something more up-to-date.[19] Obviously, though, the further that English-language speakers in the LDS Church move away from the KJV, the less obvious are the linguistic parallels with other canonized scripture.

Conclusion

Mormon traditions range widely in their uses of the Bible and their legitimation of particular translations. Like nearly all nineteenth-century Protestants, early Mormons looked to a common-sense reading of the KJV for their spiritual understanding. Unlike Protestants, Mormon traditions share the belief that the Bible is not inerrant, and is not a sufficient guide for the Christian life. It must be supplemented by the use of other sacred records (the Book of Mormon and the Doctrine and Covenants, although authorized versions of these books differ among Mormon groups), and interpreted with the help of church leadership and individual discernment. In recent years the introduction of the Standard Works in English and Spanish, and the articulation of the KJV and the official biblical translation, have encouraged greater uniformity of interpretation within the LDS Church, although in practice members do consult other versions of the Bible for personal use.

Still, questions arise in a time of swift international growth, a trend that has necessitated the use of already extant Bible versions in other languages. If the rule of thumb in measuring the accuracy of other translations is not to compare them to earlier extant versions in original languages, "but by comparison with the Book of Mormon and modern-day revelations," most of which are linguistically and conceptually anchored to origins in the KJV, then the LDS Church is linking its interpretation of the Bible closely to an Jacobean translation in a curious hermeneutic circle.[20] It remains to be seen whether future members in far-flung nations will continue to find translations such as the German Uniform Translation as relevant to their lives as was the KJV for early Mormon followers. Ironically, it may also be English speakers who vote with their feet, using the KJV in liturgical and communal contexts but looking to more contemporary versions for family and home use.

NOTES

1. See Hatch and Noll, "Introduction."
2. For more on this theme, see Shipps, *Mormonism*, especially chap. 4.
3. The Articles of Faith, as they came to be known, were first written in a letter written by Joseph Smith Jr. to John Wentworth, editor of the *Chicago Democrat*, and published in the Latter-day Saint newspaper, *Times and Seasons*. They were later included in the canonical text the Pearl of Great Price. See Welch and Whittaker, "We Believe."
4. Barlow, *Mormons and the Bible*, 44; Codman, *Mormon Country*, 15, 16.
5. On the notion of the Book of Mormon as a sign, see Barlow, *Mormons and the Bible*, chap. 2; Shipps, *Mormonism*, 41–66; and Givens, *By the Hand of Mormon*, chap. 3.
6. Cohen, "Religion, Print Culture, and the Bible before 1876," 8.
7. Maffly-Kipp, "Introduction."
8. Barlow, *Mormons and the Bible*, 49, 53. Barlow refers to Smith's version as an "interpretive expansion" of the text.
9. Givens, "Joseph Smith's American Bible," 15. See also Givens, *By the Hand of Mormon*, 185–208.

   A contemporary example of this can be found in the listing at the website of Mormon apologist Jeff Lindsay, detailing the many lost sacred records mentioned in the Bible ("Why Don't You Accept the Bible as Complete?" http://www.jefflindsay.com/LDSFAQ/FQ_Bible.shtml#lost). Lindsay concludes that these references prove that the Bible is not an isolated case, and that the notion of biblical inerrancy is misguided. He includes, among others:

   - The book of the covenant, through which Moses instructed Israel (Exodus 24:7)
   - The book of the wars of the Lord (Numbers 21:14)
   - The book of Jasher (Joshua 10:13; 2 Samuel 1:18)
   - The book of the manner of the kingdom (1 Samuel 10:25)
   - Possible books containing three thousand proverbs, a thousand and five songs, a treatise on natural history by Solomon (1 Kings 4:32,33)
   - The acts or annals of Solomon (1 Kings 11:41)
   - The book of Gad the Seer (1 Chronicles 29:29)
   - The book of Nathan the prophet (1 Chronicles 29:29; 2 Chronicles 9:29)
   - The prophecy of Ahijah, the Shilonite (2 Chronicles 9:29)
   - The visions of Iddo the Seer (2 Chronicles 9:29)
   - The book of Shemaiah the prophet (2 Chronicles 12:15)

- The story of the prophet Iddo (2 Chronicles 13:22)
- The book of Jehu (2 Chronicles 20:34)
- The Acts of Uzziah, by Isaiah, the son of Amoz (2 Chronicles 26:22)
- Sayings of the Seers (2 Chronicles 33:19).

10. See Barlow, *Mormons and the Bible*, 98, on this point.
11. Shipps, *Mormonism*, ch. 5.
12. Anderson, "Church Publishes," 9.
13. Barlow, *Mormons and the Bible*, 157.
14. Ibid., 159–161, 174.
15. Benson, Hinckley, and Monson, "First Presidency Statement," 80.
16. Scott Taylor, "LDS Church Publishes New Spanish-Language Bible," *Deseret News*, September 13, 2009.
17. Snow, "Challenge of Theological Translation," 134–35.
18. Ibid., 148. According to Marcellus Snow, texts included are Tobit, Judith, 1 and 2 Maccabees, the Wisdom of Solomon, Jesus Shirach, and Baruch.
19. Ibid., 149.
20. Church of Jesus Christ of Latter-day Saints, Handbook 2, Section 21.1.7. The First Presidency of the LDS Church discourages members from rendering the Book of Mormon into modern English, because, in their phrasing, "there are substantial risks that this process may introduce doctrinal errors or obscure evidence of its ancient origin" (First Presidency Letter, printed as "Modern-language Editions of the Book of Mormon Discouraged," *Ensign* 23, no. 4 [April 1993], 74).

BIBLIOGRAPHY

Anderson, Lavina Fielding. "Church Publishes First LDS Edition of the Bible." *Ensign* 9, no. 10 (October 1979). http://www.lds.org/ensign/1979/10/church-publishes-first-lds-edition-of-the-bible?lang=eng.

Barlow, Philip L. *Mormons and the Bible: The Place of the Latter-day Saints in American Religion.* Rev. ed. New York: Oxford University Press, 2013.

Benson, Ezra Taft, Gordon B. Hinckley, and Thomas S. Monson. "First Presidency Statement on the King James Version of the Bible." *Ensign* 22, no. 8 (August 1992). http://www.lds.org/ensign/1992/08/news-of-the-church/first-presidency-statement-on-the-king-james-version-of-the-bible?lang=eng&query=king+james.

Church of Jesus Christ of Latter-day Saints. "Bible." *Church Handbook of Instructions* handbook 2: "Administering the Church," section 21.1.7. Salt Lake City: Intellectual Reserve, 2010. http://lds.org/handbook/handbook-2-administering-the-church/selected-church-policies?lang=eng#21.1.7.

Clark, J. Reuben. *Why the King James Version*. Salt Lake City, UT: Deseret Book, 1956.

Codman, John. *The Mormon Country: A Summer with the "Latter-day Saints."* New York: United States, 1874.

Cohen, Charles L. "Religion, Print Culture, and the Bible before 1876." In *Religion and the Culture of Print in Modern America*, ed. Charles L. Cohen and Paul S. Boyer, 3–13. Madison: University of Wisconsin Press, 2008.

Givens, Terryl L. *By the Hand of Mormon: The American Scripture that Launched a New World Religion*. New York: Oxford University Press, 2002.

Givens, Terryl L. "Joseph Smith's American Bible: Radicalizing the Familiar." *Journal of the Book of Mormon and Other Restoration Scripture* 18, no. 2 (2009). http://maxwellinstitute. byu.edu/publications/jbms/?vol=18&num=2&id=496.

Gutjahr, Paul C. "The Golden Bible in the Bible's Golden Age: The Book of Mormon and Antebellum Print Culture." *ATQ: 19th Century American Literature and Culture*, new series, 12, no. 4 (1998): 275–93.

Hatch, Nathan O., and Mark A. Noll, eds. "Introduction." In *The Bible in America: Essays in Cultural History*, 3–17. New York: Oxford University Press, 1982.

Maffly-Kipp, Laurie F. "Introduction." In *The Book of Mormon*, vii–xxviii. New York: Penguin, 2008.

McConkie, Bruce. *Mormon Doctrine*. Salt Lake City, UT: Bookcraft, 1958.

Shipps, Jan. *Mormonism: The Story of a New Religious Tradition*. Urbana: University of Illinois Press, 1985.

Smith, Joseph Fielding. *Man, His Origin and Destiny*. Salt Lake City, UT: Deseret Book, 1954.

Snow, Marcellus S. "The Challenge of Theological Translation: New German Versions of the Standard Works." *Dialogue: A Journal of Mormon Thought* 17, no. 2 (Summer 1984): 133–49.

Welch, John W., and David J. Whittaker. "'We Believe. . . .': Development of the Articles of Faith." *Ensign* 9, no. 9 (September 1979). http://www.lds.org/ensign/1979/09/we-believe-development-of-the-articles-of-faith?lang=eng.

CHAPTER 10

THE BOOK OF MORMON

GRANT HARDY

MORMONISM is a religion named for, and founded upon, a book. The first public notice of this new scripture, in an 1829 upstate New York newspaper, was not promising:

> Just about in this particular region, for some time past, much speculation has existed, concerning a pretended discovery, through superhuman means, of an ancient record, of a religious and a divine nature and origin, written in ancient characters, impossible to be interpreted by any to whom the special gift has not been imparted by inspiration. It is generally known and spoken of as the "*Golden Bible.*" Most people entertain an idea that the whole matter is the result of a gross imposition and a grosser superstition. It is pretended that it will be published as soon as the translation is completed.[1]

The reporter was probably mildly surprised when the Book of Mormon, at nearly 600 pages, was actually published nine months later. He would have been astonished to learn that it would eventually become one of the most successful world scriptures of the last thousand years, at least in terms of the number of its adherents and its global distribution, with over 170 million copies printed since 1830, in more than 110 languages.

Yet the Book of Mormon remains a curious text—easily dismissible as a nineteenth-century hoax or delusion, yet still capable of inspiring reverence among some fifteen million believers almost two hundred years later; a classic of American religious history that many find nearly impossible to read all the way through; the core scripture of a modern faith whose most distinctive beliefs and practices (including temples, eternal families, premortal existence, multiple heavens, deification, polygamy, and a health code) are hardly mentioned therein; and a book that insists on its authenticity as an ancient record, miraculously preserved and translated, which is nevertheless notably lacking in standard archaeological support. For students of Mormonism, American history, religious studies, or world scripture, it is hard to know where to begin with this strange, influential, puzzling work.

CANONICAL AUTHORITY

It is useful to distinguish the terms *scripture* and *canon*. The former refers to writings that are regarded as authoritative within a particular religious community; they are "canonical" in the sense of providing a standard of behavior or belief. But a *canon*, in its technical meaning, is a definitive list of such writings. Typically, there is a long process of revision and augmentation before texts achieve their final forms and canonical boundaries are firmly established. In Judaism and Christianity, different groups of believers accepted diverse writings for hundreds of years before finally agreeing to rather limited lists of biblical books. As late as the fourth and fifth centuries, for example, copies of the New Testament included documents such as 1–2 Clement, the Epistle of Barnabas, and the Shepherd of Hermas. The Hindu, Buddhist, and Daoist canons have been even more fluid, with huge numbers of books added over time.

Gerald T. Sheppard has noted a corollary to the general pattern of scripture or canon formation:

> In examining religious scriptures as "canons," one may generalize that the founding leaders of religions almost never compose for their disciples a complete scripture. The one obvious exception is that of the third-century Mani, founder of Manichaeism. There are usually substantial periods after the death of a leader or founder when oral and/or written traditions function authoritatively as canonical, in the sense of representing a scripture without specific dimension. This dynamic process may be influenced greatly by later disciples, and the scripture may for long periods of time, if not indefinitely, lack the public form of a fixed list of books or a standardized "text."[2]

Mani argued for the superiority of his religion by noting that he had written down and collected his revelations personally rather than leaving this task to his disciples, but today the Manichaean canon of seven scriptures exists only in fragments. A better example of an exception, at least in terms of being more accessible, is the Book of Mormon.

As can be seen from the early newspaper article cited above, the new revelation was viewed from the beginning as a "Golden Bible," that is, a text claiming to stand on equal footing with the Old and New Testaments. Coming out of a religious tradition with a strong notion of a limited canon, which had been closed for fourteen hundred years, the Book of Mormon was proclaimed by believers to be a long-lost, third installment of the word of God, and it was always regarded as a complete, coherent revelation. Not only was its canonical status set from its first appearance, its form was relatively fixed as well. The textual history of the Book of Mormon is remarkably clear compared with most other sacred books.

Eyewitness accounts and manuscript evidence all indicate that Joseph Smith dictated the entire text to scribes, one time through, from April to June of 1829. The original manuscript was then copied to a printer's manuscript, and the book was immediately typeset from that, although textual analysis has shown that one-sixth of the 1830 edition, from Helaman 13:17 to Mormon 9:37, was set from the original manuscript.[3] For the 1837 and 1840 editions, Joseph Smith made several thousand changes, almost all of which were typographical or grammatical corrections. In fact, there are only eleven verses where changes modified either the narrative or doctrine.[4] Shorter chapters and versification were introduced in 1879, additional grammatical revisions in 1920, and the current official edition (1981) is essentially the 1920 edition with a few corrections based on the original and printer's manuscripts (about 28 percent of the former is still extant, mostly housed in LDS Church archives; virtually the whole of the latter is held by the Community of Christ). This means that the Book of Mormon today is, apart from grammar, essentially the same book that Joseph Smith first dictated, as can be seen from Royal Skousen's meticulous reconstruction of the earliest text.[5]

This situation is quite different for the Qur'an, the Adi Granth, and the scriptures of Bahá'í (to say nothing of the writings of Emanuel Swedenborg or Mary Baker Eddy), all of which took shape and acquired authoritative status over the course of decades. The Book of Mormon is also distinct from other LDS scriptures in this regard. For various editions of the Doctrine and Covenants from 1835 to 1981, decisions were made about which of Joseph Smith's revelations to include and exclude, sometimes with substantive revisions to the documents themselves. The writings in the Pearl of Great Price were first collected and published in England in 1851, with additions in 1878 followed by formal canonization by church vote in 1880. By contrast, in March of 1830, when the Book of Mormon was first published, there was no Mormon Church in existence (the church was formally organized about two weeks later). Instead of a community of believers coming to accept the book as authoritative, the book created a religious community—those who viewed the Book of Mormon as equivalent to the Bible joined the movement and were soon known as "Mormonites," named after their distinctive scripture. When missionaries spread the news of Joseph Smith's prophetic calling, they did not tell the story of the First Vision, as Mormon missionaries do today. Rather, they recounted how the angel Moroni first told Smith about the golden plates from which the Book of Mormon was translated.[6]

There is one more way in which the Book of Mormon is unlike most other sacred books. The Vedas, the Hebrew Bible, the New Testament, the Qur'an, and even the Doctrine and Covenants contain a variety of materials in different genres ranging from historical narratives, legal codes, and moral injunctions to revelations, prophecies, visions, and ecstatic poetry. The Book of Mormon also includes heterogeneous materials, but they are all embedded within a coherent, integrated narrative that tells a unified story from beginning to end, as recounted by three major narrators: Nephi, Mormon, and Moroni. The Book of Mormon, produced in a sudden blaze of revelation in a three-month period in 1829, was immediately presented to the world as a complete scripture worthy of inclusion in the Christian canon. It was a remarkable, monumental first book for a twenty-four-year-old, minimally educated farmer. Joseph Smith never produced anything like it again.

CONTENTS

New readers of the Book of Mormon often find the complex narrative, multiple voices, and plethora of characters somewhat bewildering, if not off-putting. (There are over two hundred distinct individuals in the text, along with about ninety specific locations mentioned.) This is in part because the book has been inadequately formatted. The printer's manuscript, like the original, was divided into internal books and chapters but otherwise consisted of long strings of words with no punctuation, sentences, or paragraphs. These grammatical demarcations were added by the non-Mormon typesetter John Gilbert, who did a credible job but generally treated the ubiquitous phrase "and it came to pass" as a signal to start a new paragraph. The erratic paragraphs of the early editions were transformed into Bible-style double-columned verses by 1920, but both the early paragraphs and the fragmenting verses tended to obscure the basic structure of the text, which is revealed over the course of the narrative.

The Book of Mormon presents itself primarily as the work of a fourth-century prophet/historian named Mormon who, writing near the demise of his thousand-year-old civilization, had edited and condensed the records of his predecessors into an abridged history of his people, the Nephites. The book consists of four major sections:

1. 1 Nephi to Omni: the Small Plates of Nephi, a first-person account of the earliest generations of the Nephites.
2. The Words of Mormon: a two-page editorial interruption in which Mormon explains how after abridging the first 550 years of Nephite history, he discovered the Small Plates and liked this primary source so much that he included it as an appendix.
3. Mosiah to Mormon 7: the majority of the text, which is Mormon's abridgment of the Large Plates of Nephi (a lengthy, official, lineage history), along with a few chapters of his own writing.
4. Mormon 8 to Moroni: some concluding comments added by Mormon's son, Moroni, including the book of Ether, which was Moroni's summary of a record of the Jaredites, a people who had come to the New World from the tower of Babel and then destroyed themselves about the time the Nephites arrived.

Mormon's inclusion of the Small Plates later turned out to be providential (or convenient) when Smith's scribe Martin Harris lost the first 116 pages of the manuscript. Rather than retranslating the missing material, Smith was able to substitute the Small Plates so that the current Book of Mormon provides a continuous narrative from about 600 BC to 420 AD. (It appears that Smith continued the translation from Mosiah to the end, and only afterwards produced 1 Nephi to Omni, so the book was dictated out of its present, chronological order.) Within the individual books there are numerous editorial comments; multichapter preaching tours, missionary journeys, and military campaigns; insertions of primary source documents such as sermons, letters, poems, and scriptural excerpts; and a few flashbacks necessitated by simultaneous narratives. All of this can be seen more easily in Hardy's *Reader's Edition*. It is also noteworthy that Joseph Smith's voice never appears in the text. Everything is attributed to ancient writers. Whether one regards the Book of Mormon as history or fiction, this is how the text is organized, and interpretations of specific verses need to take into account the often multilayered narrative contexts.

The story begins in the first year of Judah's King Zedekiah (597 BC), when Lehi, an otherwise unknown prophet in Jerusalem, was warned by God to flee with his family before the Babylonians destroyed the city. (Note that these people were *not* part of the fabled ten lost tribes, who would have left Israel more than a century earlier.) After wandering for eight years in the Arabian Peninsula, Lehi's family was guided by the Lord to a new promised land in the Americas. Once there, however, the family quickly divided into two antagonistic groups. The righteous Nephites stayed true to the Hebrew scriptures they had brought with them on the Brass Plates as well as to new, startlingly detailed prophecies of a coming Messiah, Jesus Christ. The Lamanites rejected both and thereupon became less civilized, though more numerous. The tale is narrated by Lehi's son, Nephi, and we eventually learn that we are reading a divinely mandated, more spiritual revision of his memoirs (2 Nephi 5). Nephi tells us almost nothing of life in the promised land, instead filling his record with sermons, prophecies, visions, and lengthy quotations from Isaiah as he tries to make sense of his family's fate in terms of the destiny of the house of Israel. His younger brother Jacob took over the record after Nephi's death, and then a series of minor narrators conclude the Small Plates about 150 BC. The most significant event of those later years was the discovery of another people who had originally come from Jerusalem under the leadership of King Zedekiah's son, Mulek. They had lost touch with their Hebraic heritage over the centuries, and ended up merging with the Nephites.

Mormon begins his role as narrator with the book of Mosiah, which, after a memorable sermon by the Nephite King Benjamin, focuses on the fortunes of a Nephite colony that had been established in Lamanite territory. After losing contact with the main body of Nephites, the colonists were subjugated by the Lamanites but managed to establish a church under $Alma_1$ that looked forward to the coming of Christ. Eventually, with divine assistance, they escaped and made their way back to the Nephite capital of Zarahemla where their church spread throughout the populace. The church began to falter at the beginning of the book of Alma, which features a preaching tour by its high priest, $Alma_2$, the son of the founder, $Alma_1$. At about the same time, the government shifted from a monarchy to a judgeship and four sons of the last king, Mosiah, undertook a seventeen-year mission among the Lamanites with considerable success. The last half of the book of Alma recounts a series of wars between the Nephites and Lamanites, precipitated to some extent by the loss of thousands of Lamanite converts to the Nephites, as well as by royalists who wished to restore the monarchy. Under $Helaman_2$ and chief captain $Moroni_1$—not to be confused with the last narrator, $Moroni_2$—the Nephites survived and even prospered. But typically in the Book of Mormon, prosperity leads to pride and moral laxity, which then results in political disaster.

In the book of Helaman (which begins about 50 BC), the Lamanites were still a worry for the Nephites, though the rise of the Gadianton robbers threatened both groups. The Lamanites responded to their predicament by turning to God and becoming more righteous than the Nephites. In a reversal of the common pattern, a Lamanite prophet named Samuel went to preach among the Nephites and foretold signs of the birth and death of Jesus. He was nearly killed for his efforts. Third Nephi begins with the predicted signs of Jesus's birth—a night without darkness followed by a new star—but the Nephites paid little heed as they fought with the robbers and then saw their own corrupt government collapse. Shortly thereafter, tremendous natural disasters heralded the death of Jesus in Jerusalem, followed by Christ's three-day postresurrection visit to the Nephites. He performed miracles, taught the Sermon on the Mount, introduced new liturgy, reorganized the church with twelve disciples as leaders, and prophesied of the last days. Thereafter the Nephites and Lamanites joined together and enjoyed two hundred years of peace and prosperity, recounted in just two pages.

The narrative quickly concludes with the return of old social divisions and the Lamanites exterminating the Nephites in protracted, all-out war. Moroni, the last of the Nephites, took over as narrator after Mormon's death. He briefly relates the story of the Jaredites, from records that had been found by the Nephite colonists mentioned in the book of Mosiah, adds a sermon and two letters from his father, and then closes with an exhortation to future readers to pray about the truthfulness of the book and come to Christ. Although not recounted in the Book of Mormon itself, Joseph Smith reported that the same Moroni, now an angel, appeared to him in 1823 and revealed the location of the gold plates on which he had written his history.

MESSAGE

The Book of Mormon is obviously a lengthy, complex work, but there is a main theme running throughout—the possibility of deliverance. Or as the first narrator explains to readers at the beginning: "Behold, I, Nephi, will show unto you that the tender mercies of the Lord are over all those whom he hath chosen, because of their faith, to make them mighty even unto the power of deliverance" (1 Nephi 1:20). From Lehi's flight from Jerusalem, to wars with the Lamanites, to widespread conversions, to hair's-breadth escapes by missionaries, the book is replete with sermons, stories, and prophecies demonstrating that by turning to God, and specifically to Christ, people can be delivered both spiritually (from sin, death, and hell) and also temporally (from enemies, oppression, and captivity in this life). Most of the major ideas of the Book of Mormon—covenants, salvation in Christ, the importance of scriptural records, prophecy and its fulfillment, personal revelation, moral agency, good government, repentance, rational belief, social justice, church administration, and miracles—play a role in some aspect of deliverance.

New Testament soteriology seems out of place in the centuries before Jesus was born, but revelations to Nephite prophets about Christ's coming were accompanied

140   GRANT HARDY

by explanations of the future atonement, often with specific details provided by angels. Yet the Book of Mormon does not offer a strictly evangelical version of Christianity; it also speaks in terms of salvation history, that is, of God's providential intrusion into the realm of history and politics. In other words, liberation comes to individuals as they repent, accept baptism, and obey God's commandments, but redemption is also offered to entire nations and peoples. So when Christ visits the Nephites, he seems as much a Jewish Jesus as a Protestant Jesus. He says very little about the crucifixion, the atonement, justification, or resurrection; instead, he speaks as a prophet about God's ongoing mission for Israel—which is not superseded by the new church that he organizes.

Echoing Nephi's earlier teachings, Jesus prophesies how the records of the Nephites, miraculously preserved (the Book of Mormon is referring to itself here), will someday convert the Gentiles, who will then play a role in gathering scattered Israel—that is, the Jews and the descendants of the Lamanites, traditionally understood to be American Indians—to their respective promised lands in Palestine and in America, so that Jerusalem will find its counterpart in a New Jerusalem in the Western Hemisphere. Gentiles who do not repent and believe will become embroiled in violence, while those who accept the Book of Mormon will be adopted into the house of Israel and share in the blessings that God has reserved for his chosen people. In explicating this vision of the future, Jesus quotes Isaiah 52 and 54, as well as Micah 4–5 and Malachi 3–4.

Here and elsewhere, the Book of Mormon is inextricably connected to the Bible, as can be seen immediately from its archaic, King James–like diction. As in Islam, the Old and New Testaments are believed to have been reduced and corrupted in transmission (a situation foreseen by Nephi in the fifth century BC; see 1 Nephi 14), but rather than replacing the Bible in the manner of the Qur'an, the Book of Mormon puts itself forward as a supplement that reaffirms and at times clarifies biblical teachings. Excerpts from a few lost texts are restored (such as the writings of Zenos; see Jacob 5, Alma 33); prophecies from Isaiah are interpreted; the doctrines of revelation, baptism, the Lord's Supper, spiritual gifts, atonement, resurrection, and the last judgment receive additional explication; and there are occasional explanations of specific biblical phrases such as "to fulfill all righteousness" (Matthew 3:15; 2 Nephi 31:5–6) and "other sheep" (John 10:16; 3 Nephi 15:11–16:3).

The Book of Mormon is also unlike the Qur'an in that it is not regarded as an eternal or divinely created text. Instead, it is presented as the work of inspired but human authors who write from different perspectives and admit the possibility of weakness and error (title page, Mormon 8:17, Ether 12:22–29). Yet at the same time, it is more consistent and controlled in its production than the Bible. By its own account, the Book of Mormon has come directly from the engraving tools of its narrators/editors, who at times received explicit instructions from God as to what they should or should not include (1 Nephi 14:24–26, 2 Nephi 5:29–33, 3 Nephi 26:6–12, Ether 12:22–41, 13:13). In addition, Nephi, Mormon, and Moroni each realized that they were ultimately writing for a latter-day audience many centuries in the future. Moroni explicitly addresses these readers saying, "The Lord hath shown unto me great and marvelous things . . . at that day when these things shall come forth among you. Behold, I speak unto you as if ye were present, and yet ye are not. But behold, Jesus Christ hath shown you unto me, and I know your doing" (Mormon 8:34–35). Coincidentally (or not), it appears that the sins of the Nephites often correspond to those of modern societies: pride, oppression of the poor, social inequality, secret combinations, corrupt churches, and denying the possibility of miracles and prophecy.

RECEPTION

Oddly enough, despite its religious and historical significance, there has never been a full-length academic study of the theology of the Book of Mormon. This is in part because the book's biblically based teachings have been overshadowed by later, more distinctive LDS theological developments, and also because believers have long preferred to read their scriptures devotionally rather than analytically. Perhaps most important, however, is that the mere fact of the Book of Mormon's existence has long been considered as significant as any of its specific teachings.

Early church leaders cited the Bible twenty times as often as the Book of Mormon, and rather than preaching extensively from the new scripture, they drew upon just a few verses concerning the restoration of Israel, prophecies relating to the Gentiles, and parallels with recent archaeological discoveries.[7] They regarded the book as a sign that the Second Coming was imminent and that the preparatory gathering of Israel would begin with the widespread conversion of the Indians. Neither of these events took place in the expected time frame, and believers began to focus instead on the Book of Mormon as tangible proof that Joseph Smith was a prophet and that God continued to speak in modern times. The book itself was the first miracle of the restoration, which Mormons argued fulfilled prophecies such as Isaiah 29 and Ezekiel 37. Missionaries encouraged people to put aside their doubts and pray for a spiritual witness of the truth of the new scripture. This tactic can be seen as early as Alexander Campbell's 1831 critical review essay, "Delusions," and was formalized in the late nineteenth century with Moroni 10:4–5 as a proof-text. The main issue then became whether the Book of Mormon was credible as a revelation from God. Not surprisingly, most of the religious and scholarly debate since 1830 has centered on the transmission and historicity of the Book of Mormon rather than on its message.

Smith's explanation of the book's origins was that an angel (actually, the resurrected last Nephite writer, Moroni) first told him of the record in 1823. Four years later, he was permitted to remove the plates from the stone box in which they had been buried, along with a pair of eyeglass-like seer stones, called "interpreters," that allowed him to translate the "reformed Egyptian" writings. Eyewitnesses to the translation reported that Smith more commonly used another seer stone placed in his hat, which he would look into as he dictated the text to scribes.[8] Somewhat confusingly, and undoubtedly in an attempt to downplay the treasure-seeking connotations of seer stones, early Mormons later referred to both devices as the "Urim and Thummim," even though that biblical object does not seem closely related. Smith said that he returned the plates to the angel after the translation was completed, though before doing so he showed them to eleven men who signed one of two affidavits that have been published as part of the Book of Mormon since 1830—the Testimonies of the Three and the Eight Witnesses. There is also a tradition that Mary Whitmer, the mother of one of the three witnesses, saw the plates, and Smith's wife, Emma, reported that she had handled the plates while they were wrapped in a cloth.[9]

It is a rather remarkable tale, which many dismissed out of hand. Early critics questioned the need for extrabiblical revelation, saw the book's awkward, repetitive, ungrammatical style as evidence against its divine origin, and detected veiled references to contemporary issues such as Universalism, anti-Masonry, and anti-Catholicism.[10] They attacked the credibility of the witnesses and especially of Joseph Smith himself, and when Mormons argued that the book was beyond Smith's natural capabilities, many skeptics agreed and accepted a theory that he had plagiarized an unpublished novel by Solomon Spaulding. However, after Spaulding's manuscript came to light in 1884—bearing little resemblance to the Book of Mormon—most outsiders reverted to naturalistic explanations of the Mormon scripture as a creative work of Joseph Smith, derived from contemporary religious and historical speculations, such as those in *View of the Hebrews*, published in 1823 by Ethan Smith (no relation).[11]

The first generation of Latter-day Saints greeted John Lloyd Stephens's archaeological discoveries in Central America as confirmation of the Book of Mormon's historical claims, but with the rise of more scientific studies it soon became clear that ancient American civilizations did not consist of immigrants from Palestine who flourished between 600 BC to 400 AD, and that there were serious historical improbabilities and anachronisms including iron, steel, silk, barley, wheat, horses, chariots, cattle, sheep, and goats, not to mention modern Christian theology, revival language, and nearly exact borrowings from the King James Bible. In 1922, B. H. Roberts, a highly respected church leader, wrote two unpublished essays on these issues in which he acknowledged the seriousness of the problems, though he continued to affirm his faith in the truth of the book.

Missionaries have always used the Book of Mormon as evidence of Joseph Smith's status as a modern prophet, but for the first half of the twentieth century the book did not figure prominently in Latter-day Saint preaching or education, perhaps because after the conflict over polygamy Mormons were in an assimilationist mode. The situation began to change in the 1950s with the work of Brigham Young University (BYU) professor Hugh Nibley, who turned away from ancient American evidences—which were not forthcoming—and devoted his considerable linguistic skills to the identification of ancient Near Eastern parallels in the Book of Mormon that would have been unknown to Smith, including proper names, New Year's rites, Arabian customs, and concepts from Jewish apocrypha. (His collected works were republished from 1986 to 2010, though much of the scholarship is now dated.)

Nibley's efforts have been continued by scholars associated with the Foundation for Ancient Research and Mormon Studies (FARMS), founded in 1979, which eighteen years later became part of Brigham Young University and is now a component of the Neal A. Maxwell Institute for Religious Scholarship. Prominent among Nibley's successors has been John W. Welch, who discovered the presence of elaborate chiasmus (the literary device of inverted parallelism) in the Book of Mormon. Other evidences for historicity that have been advanced by LDS scholars include Hebraisms, wordprints, internal complexity and consistency, as well as ancient patterns of warfare, law, and record-keeping. It has also been asserted that the geography of the Arabian Peninsula accommodates some of the unexpected details of the flight of Lehi's family, including the place name NHM, discovered on altars in the 1990s and dated to the right time and place for the Book of Mormon account, which mentions a place called "Nahom." More sophisticated defenses of the Book of Mormon have called forth sharper critiques, based on closer analyses of nineteenth-century culture, biblical scholarship (particularly given the presence of Second Isaiah in a purportedly pre-exilic text), population demographics, and the DNA analysis of Native American peoples. The Maxwell Institute has often responded to such criticisms through regular publications, including the *Journal of Book of Mormon Studies* and the *FARMS Review*. More recently the latter journal, reflecting a new direction at the Maxwell Institute, has been renamed the *Mormon Studies Review*. Editors of the new enterprise seem more interested in the study of Mormonism as such, and less interested in battles over truth claims.

While scholars were debating, there was a major shift in the way that ordinary Latter-day Saints thought of the Book of Mormon. In the 1960s, BYU began requiring a full year of Book of Mormon study for all freshmen. Starting in the 1970s, the Book of Mormon became a basic text, in a four-year rotation with other LDS scriptures, studied in Sunday school, Institute (religious instruction for college-age adults), and Seminary (daily classes for high school students). The book was gradually cited much more frequently in General Conferences, particularly after 1988, when church president Ezra Taft Benson strenuously urged Latter-day Saints to "flood the earth with the Book of Mormon" and make it the object of daily study.[12] As a result, a Mormon upbringing now includes a firm grounding in the stories and basic teachings of the Book of Mormon, aided by children's songs, picture books, Arnold Friberg's famous illustrations, popular summer pageants such as the one at the Hill Cumorah in New York, films, novelizations, games, and toy action figures. In fact, Book of Mormon themed products at church-owned Deseret Book closely track biblical merchandise available at Christian bookstores, and basic attitudes toward Mormon scripture similarly reflect conservative Protestant sensibilities.

In the 1930s, prominent church leaders including J. Reuben Clark and Joseph Fielding Smith decisively rejected modernism and secular biblical scholarship.[13] As a result, the increased attention given to the scriptures in recent decades tends to align with evangelical or even fundamentalist models. Latter-day Saints rarely read the Book of Mormon critically; instead, they retell familiar stories and cite favorite verses. Within contemporary Mormonism the scriptures are seen as functionally inerrant; literalism or at least maximal-conservatism is the norm for interpretation; academic expertise is viewed with suspicion; harmonization is valued, along with the inductive use of individual

verses organized by topic; and church-produced curriculum materials are almost completely insular in their avoidance of non-Mormon sources or scholarship. This basic
approach informs the current official editions of both the Bible (1979) and the Book of
Mormon (1981), both of which feature an authoritative text—uncluttered with textual
variants or alternative readings—and extensive cross-references that treat scriptural
verses equivalently regardless of narrative or historical context and foster the impression of God's word as a unified, correlated whole.[14]

The Book of Mormon is well suited to this type of study since the absence of
original-language texts or a clear historical setting makes it difficult to apply standard
philological or historical-critical tools, and its adoption of Jacobean English allows for
easy correspondence with the King James Bible. In general, Mormons do not give sustained, critical attention to the contents of the Book of Mormon; instead they believe
the best way to approach the text is to ask God for a witness of its truthfulness, and then
they draw spiritual strength and guidance from its broad teachings while subordinating
its message to gospel doctrines as they have been defined by church authorities over the
last century.

One way in which the Mormon Church is not fundamentalist, however, is in its
encouragement of higher education. An increase in educated Latter-day Saints, combined with an openness to science and scholarship (except for biblical studies), has led
to a reevaluation of some common understandings of the Book of Mormon. It was long
assumed that when the Book of Mormon spoke of the Land Northward and the Land
Southward, it was referring to North and South America. As this hemispheric model
of geography began to diverge from scientific assessments of New World history in the
early twentieth century, Joseph Fielding Smith counseled the Saints to ignore science.[15]
Yet pressure from critics, along with greater engagement with secular education, led to
closer readings of the book itself, showing that, given the distances described therein,
the majority of the narrative would have taken place within a limited geographical area
of about 500 miles by 200 miles.

John L. Sorenson has worked out the most thoughtful, consistent, and plausible theory of Book of Mormon geography, which he places in Southern Mexico and
Guatemala. Most Latter-day Saint scholars have followed his lead and now regard the
Nephites as a small ethnic minority within a vast array of native peoples whose ancestors came across the Bering Straits thousands of years earlier. This hypothesis miti-
gates much of the force of DNA studies and the lack of identifiable Nephite artifacts.
The preface to the 1981 edition included the assertion that the Lamanites were "the
principal ancestors of the American Indians." This statement—unlike many religious
claims that are by nature unfalsifiable—is demonstrably erroneous. The church, recognizing that the statement goes beyond what the Book of Mormon explicitly claims
for itself, has altered the wording in its 2013 revision (the Lamanites are now counted
as being "among" the ancestors of the Indians). Since 2013, the LDS Church has begun
to respond directly to common criticisms through a series of Gospel Topics essays
found at www.lds.org. These include "Book of Mormon and DNA Studies" and "Book
of Mormon Translation."

THE FUTURE

Mormonism is a young religion and Latter-day Saints are still working through the implications of having a new revelation as the primary marker of their distinctive faith. The Eucharist prayers from Moroni 4–5 have always been central to weekly worship services, and missionaries have long used the book as evidence of Joseph Smith's prophetic calling, but only in the last half-century has the study of the Book of Mormon been seen as the core of LDS religiosity (though in recent years the temple and family have shared that position). Most Mormons accept the book as a genuine ancient record, delivered to Joseph Smith by an angel and translated through supernatural means. They take at face value its stories of prophecies, miracles, and divine providence, and they respond to its clear instructions about how to come to Christ in the modern era. Historical anachronisms and the paucity of corroborating evidence are troublesome to some, yet these concerns are generally thought to be overshadowed by the spiritual witness that is promised to those who ask God about the truth of the book. Indeed, coming to accept the Book of Mormon as scripture is considered to be the paradigmatic conversion narrative.

Mormons who are interested in reconciling faith and scholarship continue to debate questions of geography and whether the translation was tightly controlled or relatively free. The former model seems necessary to account for many of the literary patterns and narrative consistencies put forward by apologists, while the latter more easily accommodates the poor grammar and nineteenth-century elements in the text. Some Latter-day Saints have wondered whether the book might have ancient origins without being accurate in every detail, others have seen the text as a combination of ancient and modern influences, and a few have come to regard it as an inspired, religiously authoritative work of fiction.[16] There are also some who believe that the issue of historicity is less important than the power of the narratives themselves. Church authorities, however, have generally looked unfavorably on attempts to read the book as anything other than an ancient text miraculously preserved and rendered into English. There is a feeling that any admission of error or human invention would undermine the faith's religious claims as a whole, and the sheer physicality of the plates makes it difficult to see Joseph Smith as a generically "inspired" author, or as a sincere but deluded mystic. For outsiders, of course, historicity is less of a concern, and it probably makes the most sense for them to read the Book of Mormon as religious fiction or an example of modern pseudepigrapha.[17]

For students of religious studies, the Book of Mormon is a fascinating example of a sacred text that has successfully, and recently, made the transition to world scripture. There is much work to be done analyzing its theology, its literary forms, its relationship to its canonical predecessors, its usage in worship and preaching (including non-English-speaking contexts), and its role in the formation of multiple religious communities, the second largest of which is the Community of Christ, based in Independence, Missouri. All of this can be done in comparison with other holy books from around the world. For students of American history and literature, the book can function as a primary source documenting spiritual and political concerns of the early national era, as well as a record of Joseph Smith's developing ideas and an intriguing, rather unusual example of nineteenth-century letters.

Obviously, Latter-day Saints themselves have the most at stake in the text, and it will be interesting, as the book approaches its two-hundredth anniversary, to see how they come to differentiate between what is central and peripheral in its message, and how it can serve as a tool for sanctification as well as conversion. The question of historicity will continue to bear on Joseph Smith's credibility, of course, but it seems limiting to reduce any discussion of "What does it mean?" to "Is this detail scientifically or historically verifiable?" More than ever before, believers have the motivation and the tools to explore the richness of their scripture—in terms of both scholarly analysis and phenomenological experience—as they seek to more fully understand a text that Joseph Smith once referred to as "the most correct of any book on earth, and the keystone of our religion." Smith continued by noting that "a man would get nearer to God by abiding by its precepts, than by any other book," which is a bold claim indeed.

NOTES

1. *Wayne Sentinel*, June 26, 1829.
2. Sheppard, "Canon," 1408.
3. Skousen, *Book of Mormon*, xxix–xxx.
4. 1 Nephi 11:18, 21, 32, 12:18, 13:40, 20:1; 2 Nephi 30:6; Mosiah 21:28; Alma 5:48, 13:9. In addition, Ether 4:1 was revised by Orson Pratt in 1849 to match Mosiah 21:28. The exact changes are specified in appendices in Hardy's *Book of Mormon* and Skousen's *Book of Mormon*. Each is carefully scrutinized in Royal Skousen, *Analysis of Textual Variants of the Book of Mormon*.
5. Royal Skousen, in his Critical Text Project, has single-handedly created the Book of Mormon equivalent of the *Biblia Hebraica* or *UBS Greek New Testament* (though, to be fair, his source materials consist only of the two early manuscripts and twenty significant printed editions). Volumes 1 and 2 of the project are typographical reproductions of the original and printer's manuscripts. Volume 4, in six book-length parts, contains detailed analyses of significant variants. The forthcoming volume 3 will be the definitive history of the text, including an examination of its nonstandard grammar. Skousen's 2009 Yale edition is his reconstruction of the earliest text and should be the basis for any scholarly treatment of the Book of Mormon.
6. Allen, "Emergence of a Fundamental," 52.
7. Underwood, "Book of Mormon Usage in Early LDS Theology."
8. Van Wagoner and Walker, "Joseph Smith."
9. Vogel, *Early Mormon Documents*, 1:542, 546, 5:52, 189, 261–63, or Hardy, *Book of Mormon*, 639–42.
10. See, for example, Campbell, "Delusions."
11. Bush, "Spaulding Theory Then and Now."
12. Reynolds, "Coming Forth of the Book of Mormon in the Twentieth Century."

13. Barlow, *Mormons and the Bible*, 103–81; Griffiths, "Chicago Experiment."
14. The only authorized Bible for English-speaking Latter-day Saints is the King James Version. The LDS edition includes a few footnotes that explicate archaic English renderings, but there is no accommodation for alternative translations of uncertain Hebrew words or phrases, for other ancient versions, or the findings of the last 400 years of textual criticism—which even conservative evangelicals have come to accept.
15. Smith, *Doctrines of Salvation*, 3:203, 232–43 (the latter pages are reprinted from a *Church News* article dated September 10, 1938). See also Sorenson, *Geography of Book of Mormon Events*, 23–24, 388–89.
16. Blake Ostler argues for the second option in his "Book of Mormon as a Modern Expansion of an Ancient Source."
17. Stendahl, "Sermon on the Mount and Third Nephi in the Book of Mormon."

BIBLIOGRAPHY

Allen, James B. "The Emergence of a Fundamental: The Expanding Role of Joseph Smith's First Vision in Mormon Religious Thought." *Journal of Mormon History* 7 (1980): 43–61.

Barlow, Philip L. *Mormons and the Bible: The Place of the Latter-day Saints in American Religion*. Rev. ed. New York: Oxford University Press, 1991.

Bush, Lester E., Jr. "The Spaulding Theory Then and Now." *Dialogue: A Journal of Mormon Thought* 10, no. 4 (Autumn 1977): 40–69.

Campbell, Alexander, "Delusions." *Millennial Harbinger* 2, no. 2 (February 7, 1831): 85–96.

Duffy, John-Charles. "Mapping Book of Mormon Historicity Debates, Part 1: A Guide for the Overwhelmed." *Sunstone* 151 (October 2008): 36–62.

Givens, Terryl L. *The Book of Mormon: A Very Short Introduction*. New York: Oxford University Press, 2009.

Givens, Terryl L. *By the Hand of Mormon: The American Scripture that Launched a New World Religion*. New York: Oxford University Press, 2002.

Griffiths, Casey Paul. "The Chicago Experiment: Finding the Voice and Charting the Course of Religious Education in the Church." *BYU Studies* 49, no. 4 (2010): 91–130.

Gutjahr, Paul C. *The Book of Mormon: A Biography*. Princeton, NJ: Princeton University Press, 2012.

Hardy, Grant. *The Book of Mormon: A Reader's Edition*. Urbana: University of Illinois Press, 2003.

Hardy, Grant. *Understanding the Book of Mormon: A Reader's Guide*. New York: Oxford University Press, 2010.

Metcalfe, Brent Lee, ed. *New Approaches to the Book of Mormon: Explorations in Critical Methodology*. Salt Lake City: Signature, 1993.

Ostler, Blake T. "The Book of Mormon as a Modern Expansion of an Ancient Source." *Dialogue: A Journal of Mormon Thought* 20, no.1 (Spring 1987): 66–123.

Parry, Donald W., Daniel C. Peterson, and John W. Welch, eds. *Echoes and Evidences of the Book of Mormon*. Provo, UT: FARMS, 2002.

Reynolds, Noel B., ed. *Book of Mormon Authorship Revisited: The Evidence for Ancient Origins*. Provo, UT: FARMS, 1997.

Reynolds, Noel B. "The Coming Forth of the Book of Mormon in the Twentieth Century." *BYU Studies* 38, no. 2 (1999): 6–47.

Sheppard, Gerald T. "Canon." In the *Encyclopedia of Religion.* 2nd ed. Ed. Lindsay Jones, 1408. Detroit: Macmillan Reference, 2005.

Skousen, Royal. *Analysis of Textual Variants of the Book of Mormon.* 6 vols. Provo, UT: FARMS, 2004–9.

Skousen, Royal, ed. *The Book of Mormon: The Earliest Text.* New Haven, CT: Yale University Press, 2009.

Skousen, Royal. "Translating the Book of Mormon: Evidence from the Original Manuscript." In Reynolds, *Book of Mormon Authorship Revisited,* 61–93.

Smith, Joseph Fielding. *Doctrines of Salvation: Sermons and Writings of Joseph Smith.* 3 vols. Ed. Bruce R. McConkie. Salt Lake City: Bookcraft, 1954–56.

Smith, Timothy L. "The Book of Mormon in a Biblical Culture." *Journal of Mormon History* 7 (1980): 3–21.

Sorenson, John L. *An Ancient American Setting for the Book of Mormon.* Salt Lake City: Deseret and FARMS, 1985.

Sorenson, John L. *The Geography of Book of Mormon Events: A Source Book.* Rev. ed. Provo, UT: FARMS, 1992.

Stendahl, Krister. "The Sermon on the Mount and Third Nephi in the Book of Mormon." In *Meanings: The Bible as Document and as Guide,* 99–113. Philadelphia, PA: Fortress, 1984.

Thomas, Mark D. *Digging in Cumorah: Reclaiming Book of Mormon Narratives.* Salt Lake City: Signature, 1999.

Underwood, Grant. "Book of Mormon Usage in Early LDS Theology," *Dialogue: A Journal of Mormon Thought* 17, no. 3 (Autumn 1984): 35–74.

Van Wagoner, Richard S., and Steven C. Walker. "Joseph Smith: The Gift of Seeing." *Dialogue: A Journal of Mormon Thought* 15, no. 2 (Summer 1982): 48–68.

Vogel, Dan, ed. *Early Mormon Documents.* 5 vols. Salt Lake City: Signature, 1996–2003.

Vogel, Dan, and Brent Lee Metcalfe, eds. *American Apocrypha: Essays on the Book of Mormon.* Salt Lake City: Signature, 2002.

Wayne Sentinel, June 26, 1829. In *19th Century Publications about the Book of Mormon (1829–1844).* http://contentdm.lib.byu.edu/cdm/compoundobject/collection/BOMP/id/188/rec/1.

Welch, John W. "The Miraculous Translation of the Book of Mormon." *In Opening the Heavens: Accounts of Divine Manifestations, 1820–1844,* ed. John W. Welch, 77–213. Salt Lake City: Deseret, 2005.

CHAPTER 11

REVELATION AND THE OPEN CANON IN MORMONISM

DAVID F. HOLLAND

TEMPTED by Satan in one of the New Testament's most dramatic scenes, Jesus Christ reached back for an old Mosaic passage: "Man shall . . . live," he declared to his adversary, "by every word that proceedeth out of the mouth of God" (Matthew 4:4; Deuteronomy 8:3). The challenge for Latter-day Saints who take that declaration seriously is that they find so many godly words in so many places. They study four distinct volumes of ancient scripture and also celebrate the revelations of living prophets. They admonish one another to obey the teachings of authoritative apostles and also place great emphasis on personal inspiration. They express faith in the inspired decisions of their local leaders, cling to the personalized prophecies contained in "patriarchal blessings," and even look for flashes of heavenly truth in the advice of parents and peers. The mechanisms of Mormon revelation vary widely, ranging from open vision to a quiet certainty of spirit. Latter-day Saints thus live and worship at the confluence of endless divine words: from the past and the present, from the institutional church and the individual soul, in the meetinghouse up the street and at their own hearth. "We believe," they declare as an article of faith, "all that God has revealed, all that He does now reveal, and we believe that He will yet reveal many great and important things pertaining to the Kingdom of God."[1] How they choose to approach this abundance of revelation—with a fundamentalist resistance to new truths, a progressive distaste for the old, or an orthodox effort to reverence it all—becomes a defining factor of their religious lives.

This revelatory profusion sets Mormonism apart from many Christian faiths. In William Chillingworth's famous phrase, "the Bible, and the Bible only, is the Religion of Protestants"—a formulation that does not do justice to the full richness of Protestant epistemology but does effectively convey a "sola Scriptura" ideal.[2] The very first article of the Westminster Confession of Faith announces the cessation of God's former revelatory ways and the second article carefully lists a finite number of canonical books. Even Roman Catholicism and Eastern Orthodoxy, with their multifaceted faiths in holy writ, apostolic tradition, patriarchal leadership, and saintly mystics, refuse to raise any postprimitive statements to scriptural status. The creeds of Christianity have thus quite consciously rejected the notion of ongoing streams of authoritative revelation. In the twenty-first century Richard John Neuhaus—a man thoroughly familiar with traditional Christianity in both its Protestant and Catholic forms—declared that "almost all Christians of all times subscribe to a normative view of what is Christian ... [which] includes the acceptance of the unique inspiration of the biblical canon and the end of public revelation with the apostolic era." That Latter-day Saints did not adhere to such a view, that they believed there were prophets today with as much inspiration and authority as the penmen of scripture, was Neuhaus's leading reason for defining them outside the limits of Christianity.[3] Revelation, it seems, makes Mormons different.

And yet Mormonism's revelatory complexity produces questions similar to those confronted by all devotees of the Christian Bible. Why does the concluding message of the Hebrew scriptures so ominously warn readers to remember the same Mosaic law that the first book of the New Testament appears to supplant? Why was circumcision described as a sign that "shall be in your flesh for an everlasting covenant," only to be done away with by later apostles? Why does Jesus emphasize good works while Paul privileges grace? On the relationship among various sources and moments of revelation, even single verses can have multiple meanings; the venerable biblical scholar Jaroslav Pelikan has repeatedly argued that John 5:39, a verse in which the Christ apparently refers his opponents to the scriptures, is actually a condemnation of those who were so intently focused on the historic texts that "they refused to listen to the living words that he, being the Word of God in the flesh, was speaking to them here and now."[4] Modern Mormons, therefore, are hardly the first people to deal with the tension between a well-established written revelation and the ongoing word. They and traditional Christians alike have had to grapple with a religion that has been revealed in parts and in places and whose pieces do not always fit in obvious ways. The Christian concept of the Trinity, for instance, serves to reconcile the monotheism emphasized in the Old Testament with the references to three deities in the New. Latter-day Saints likewise have to harmonize a Book of Mormon that explicitly identifies Jesus as both Father and Son with more modern revelations that place anti-Trinitarian weight on His distinctive and separate identity as Son. The open-ended chronology and various sources of Mormonism's revelations are unique, but their contrasts and the questions that result look strikingly familiar.

To point out this centuries-spanning complexity is not to minimize the immense amount of clarifying authority which Latter-day Saints recognize in the person of the Church's president, a figure they honor as "*the* prophet." Many Mormons believe the prophet's role is to bring order to the chaos, to cut through the clutter rather than add to it. In this view, the prophet's voice overrules all subordinate repositories of inspiration. Of the Prophet Joseph Smith, Mormon scripture quotes the Lord as saying, "[H]is word ye shall receive, as if from mine own mouth, in all patience and faith" (Doctrine and Covenants [D&C] 21:5). Reflecting a long-standing and widely held belief in the prerogatives of prophetic authority, a later LDS apostle, Ezra Taft Benson, parsed such scriptures and applied them to all subsequent presidents, declaring that the "prophet *is the only man who speaks for the Lord in everything.*" In that same address Benson also warned, "[b]eware of those who would pit the dead prophets against the living prophets, for the living prophets always take precedence."[5] Benson's words both represent and have shaped a prominent Mormon understanding of the prophet: one uniquely appointed oracle whose words shall be as if from God's own mouth—a man who can speak for heaven "in everything"—overruling both predecessors and contemporaries. Based on these sorts of statements, and a resulting denominational culture that produces such expressions of devotion as the frequently sung hymns "Praise to the Man" and "We Thank Thee O God for a Prophet," outside observers have occasionally compared the Mormon prophet to Muhammad. There are some parallels.

The analogy, however, breaks down at a few key points of contrast. First, mortal Mormon prophets are fully and fundamentally subordinate to the divine Christ, whereas Islam sees Muhammad as comparable to the prophetic Jesus. Second, such a comparison may suggest the culmination and exhaustion of all inspiration in the person of one prophet and thus fail to account for the fact that at any given time the Church of Jesus Christ of Latter-day Saints is actually led by several oracles at once (a First Presidency and Quorum of the Twelve Apostles, all sustained as "prophets, seers, and revelators"), by thousands of local authorities (whose decisions members are to reverence as "inspired"), and that every leader is succeeded by others (called to their office, however great or small, "by the spirit of prophecy"). Though the history of the church began with the ministry of one inimitably gifted prophet, that seems to have been only a starting point; long before Smith's death, and at his direction, Latter-day Saints began recognizing the authority of a series of governing councils filled with inspired officers. Unlike Islam, in which a historically dominant prophet and a unitary book of revelation cap the scriptural spring, superseding all that came before them, Mormonism continues a much more complicated revelatory tradition. One might find a closer analogy to the Mormon prophet in Moses, whose word was so authoritative among the children of Israel, who was also told his voice would be "instead of God," but who eventually shared that prophetic spirit with seventy elders and at least two other revelators during his lifetime, and was succeeded by the innumerable prophets who admonished Israel for more than a millennium after his death. Similarly, the same book of scripture that identifies Joseph Smith as the sole commandment-giver for the church tells a group of Mormon elders that "whatsoever they shall speak when moved upon by the Holy Ghost shall be scripture, shall be the will of the Lord, shall be the mind of the Lord, shall be the word of the Lord, shall be the voice of the Lord, and the power of God unto salvation" (D&C 68:4).[6]

Such a verse sits in tension with those clearer statements of the church president's singular authority; indeed, the strongest scriptural passages privileging the church hierarchy came in moments when an unrestrained belief in the wide distribution of revelatory power threatened the church with a kind of prophetic anarchy. Yet, notwithstanding their historical role in checking each other, both sentiments fully remain in the Mormon scriptures. The God of the Latter-day Saints—like the God of the Bible—seems determined to speak both with order and through multiple voices. As in the days of Moses, there is one and also many more than one.

At any of the twice-yearly gatherings that Mormons call General Conference, the congregated Saints will likely hear the following: speeches from fifteen living prophets who rarely coordinate their topics before delivering them; scriptural passages from numerous ancient prophets—pulled liberally out of the Old Testament, the New Testament, the Book of Mormon, and the Pearl of Great Price; and the statements of any number of more recently passed Latter-day Saint prophets. Meanwhile, the audience will believe that each of the speakers—male and female, usually around thirty in all—received personal inspiration in preparing their remarks. And most listeners will trust that the Holy Spirit can knit together a personalized message directly to them from the constituent pieces of these addresses. Revelation will thus be felt to pass through that conference from every angle—through the speakers, through the listeners, through the wide array of authorities from which any given speech may draw. Most participants in the conference will seem utterly unconcerned about how these inspired ideas may cross or collide. Some of these speeches will talk about sacrificing one's private interests in serving a broader humanity; others will admonish the believers to put the nuclear family first. Some will emphasize the grace of God in making up for what we innately lack; others will highlight the pious rites and moral works required of the Saints. Some will declare mercy; others will demand justice. Some will highlight the uniqueness of Mormon theology; others will look for common ground with other faiths. Some will sound like they belong in the Tanakh, others like they came from the Epistles, and still others will clearly reflect the influence of modern sentiment and culture.

Perhaps what is most remarkable about the Latter-day Saints is that a faith informed by the sacred words of so many epochs and the declarations of so many prophets is so well known—at least within its dominant mainstream—for a certain cultural and intellectual unity. Indeed, countless members of the audience in that conference will go home afterward expressing gratitude for the clarity and stability of a revelatory church. Belief in ongoing revelation, they will say, keeps the faith plain and intelligible. Some of that sentiment, no doubt, is simply a disinclination to think critically about the actual complexity of what they just heard. Much of it is certainly a reflection of the reverence members have for the church president, whose office and status offer the Saints a tremendous assurance that—complexity notwithstanding—they will hear all they need to hear in their quest for redemption. But there is, it seems, more to it than that.

Mormonism suggests the possibility that a great profusion of divine words, even with many of those words in tension with each other, might result in a greater unity of purpose and understanding than a smaller, more restrained set of revelations. At first blush, such a suggestion seems dubious. It is difficult to see how more complexity might result in more coherence. But like brushstrokes on a canvas, the endless marks of revelation that color the lives of Latter-day Saints may, in their multiplicity, resolve (or, more accurately, *dissolve*) some contradictions rather than intensify them. A few strokes of red crossing a few strokes of yellow convey the idea of conflict, but scores of red strokes crossing scores of yellow strokes convey the idea of orange. In like manner, Paul's emphasis on grace and James's celebration of works struck a reader like Martin Luther as incongruous and the relative preponderance of Paul's statements seemed to carry the day; but Mormons, living with endless statements in support of both human works and atoning grace, have over time watched their boundaries blur into one ineffably understood truth which they seem to demonstrate ever less interest in separating.

If an unending and variegated stream of prophetic declaration, including the repeated affirmation of contrapuntal principles, thus ushers believers (with varying levels of consciousness) past certain theological tensions, the continuousness of such declarations also helps Mormons distinguish doctrines that are timeless from those that are merely timely. A prophet in the nineteenth century may preach faith and hope and charity and the importance of church members gathering into geographical centers for mutual support; a prophet in the twentieth century may preach faith and hope and charity and the necessity of leavening far-flung non-Mormon communities with the lives and values of Latter-day Saints. In a Mormon context, a snapshot of either of these historical moments would artificially freeze a particular instant, obscuring the difference between the transient and the permanent. That, the Saints say, is precisely the problem with the closed New Testament; no matter how masterful the artists, too few strokes on the canvas may initially look like simplicity but will actually leave the painting too ambiguous, too prone to conflict, too frozen in time. By having many more such revealed points of reference, over an extended period of time, Latter-day Saints may watch the relationship of the eternal and the expedient come into sharper relief. In such ways—counterintuitive as it might seem to outside observers and as subconsciously absorbed as it often is by Mormons themselves—it could be the very profusion of LDS inspirations that generates a sense of confidence and clarity. But this unity-by-complexity works only if, in their hermeneutics, Latter-day Saints resist the proof-texting impulses to rip a particular statement out of the context of a larger historical fabric or highlight one theological theme to the exclusion of others. Without such restraint, the Mormon potential for conflict and schism is immense.

Many Latter-day Saints, from Joseph Smith on, have thought of their faith as the place where more and more truth will always be welcomed. A frequently cited verse in Mormon scripture declares, "That which is of God is light; and he that receiveth light, and continueth in God, receiveth more light; and that light groweth brighter and brighter until the perfect day. . . . that you may know the truth, that you may chase darkness from among you" (D&C 50:24–25). Contemporary Latter-day Saint scholars have argued that "[t]he perpetual unending character of the scripture, a corpus ever augmented by living witnesses in a setting of prophecy and testimony, is a sign and symbol of the inclusiveness of LDS faith. . . . No document or collection is 'all-sufficient' for redemption, for salvation, for complete enlightenment, or for the perfecting of the soul."[7] The openness of Mormon revelation is at the very center of the church's sacred history and sacred texts. They call the Book of Mormon "the keystone of our religion" and "the most correct of any book on earth," although it is largely silent on a remarkable number of the church's distinctive doctrines: celestial marriage, eternal progression, divine corporeality, vicarious work for the dead, and so on.[8] That the book at the core of their faith says so little on so many topics of vital importance to Mormons offers a striking—if often subliminal—message about both the nature of scripture and the endlessness of revelation. As a verse of LDS scripture explains, the book's existence proves "that God does inspire men and call them to his holy work in this age and generation, as well as in generations of old; Thereby showing that he is the same God yesterday, today, and forever" (D&C 20:11–12).[9] In its declarative statements, in its conspicuous silences, and in its very being, the Book of Mormon serves as a testament to the principle that revelation goes on and on. While certainly not all Latter-day Saints are comfortable with the full implications of an unending quest for "greater light and truth," their doctrine and history irresistibly orient toward a perpetual pursuit of more of God's mind, a belief that the grandeur of the divine revelation is still being painted onto the canvas of the church.

"Perfect analogies" never really are, and to compare the history of Mormon revelation to a painting may obfuscate as much as it illuminates, but for the sake of its virtues we might risk its flaws. In a painting, not every brushstroke is of equal weight, and likewise in Mormonism not every revelation is of equal authority. The official, unanimous statements of the presidency of the church and the canonized scriptures of the Mormons' "Standard Works" (the Holy Bible, Book of Mormon, Doctrine and Covenants, and Pearl of Great Price) leave wide, solid swaths of color. In contrast to the heavy lines of the presidency and the canonized scripture, the individual teachings of this or that apostle are made with a lighter hand. Those of a local leader or a parent may be finer still, though they remain very much part of the composition. In this grand and growing portrait there are even—depending on the personal feelings of each individual hearer—marks from great secular writers, from the framers of enduring constitutions, from scientific investigation, and from the religious thinkers of other traditions. Latter-day Saint theology sees the Holy Ghost as the source of all truth, regardless of the human instrument by whom it may have been revealed. But not all revelators have the same prerogatives.

Many Latter-day Saints seem almost intuitively to agree on how much weight to lend the various voices that come at them. Yet clearly there are some points of contention and even confusion in this process. One of the more intractable questions regards the relationship between the living prophet and the canonized scriptures. From one set of prophets, Latter-day Saints read,

> [W]hen compared with the living oracles [the scriptures] are nothing to me; those books do not convey the word of God direct to us now, as do the words of a Prophet or a man bearing the Holy Priesthood in our day and generation. I would rather have the living oracles than all the writing in the books.[10]

From another they read,

> It makes no difference what is written or what *anyone* has said, if what has been said is in *conflict* with what the Lord has revealed, we can set it aside. *My words, and the teachings of any other member of the Church, high or low, if they do not square with the*

revelations, we need not accept them. Let us have this matter clear. We have accepted the four *standard works* as the measuring yardsticks, or balances, by which we *measure every man's doctrine.*[11]

It would seem that even statements about how to interpret this revelatory portrait are themselves part of the complex image, to be weighed and balanced in relation to one another.

The process of learning how to interpret this emerging image, to understand the interplay of brushstrokes of various weights and contrapuntal significance, places a heavy burden on Latter-day Saints and has not always gone smoothly. Their failures have resulted in some of the ugliest moments in their history. The 1857 Mountain Meadows Massacre, in which a group of Mormons colluded to murder some 120 members of a passing wagon train, resulted from an interpretive approach in which the immediate direction of local congregational leaders was given tremendous weight, and recent rhetoric from the general authorities was placed under a particular construction, both of which seemed to tear a "duty" to retaliate against offensive "Gentiles" from the overall frame of the faith. Indeed, at a critical moment in the run-up to the massacre, a subordinate church councilor both cited ancient scripture and appealed to modern prophets while pleading with his stake president not to pursue the attack: "Do not our principles of right teach us to return good for evil and do good to those who despitefully use us?" he asked, before insisting that they seek Brigham Young's opinion on the matter. Tragically, the momentum of the Saints' murderous conspiracy was already carrying it forward before either this scriptural argument or Young's command to peacefully forbear could take effect.[12] Any Latter-day Saint familiar with that horrific incident, and the generations of agony that have flowed out of it, should resist again allowing any set of brushstrokes to blot out the rest of the inspired opus. History has at times angrily conveyed to the church the necessity of taking in the entire landscape of divine truth. There is safety as well as beauty in the whole. Perhaps Jesus intended to convey something like this when he thwarted Satan with a reminder to live by *every* word.

For Latter-day Saints that injunction includes those words that come directly to the souls of church members, which provide an indispensable complement to the public declarations of church leaders. In the mid-twentieth century, the apostle J. Reuben Clark repudiated prophetic infallibility, arguing that "even the President of the Church, himself, may not always be 'moved upon by the Holy Ghost,' when he addresses the people." Then Clark asked the obvious question: "How shall the Church know" if and when the prophet is really speaking for God? Clark answered, "The Church will know by the testimony of the Holy Ghost in the body of the members."[13] Well before Clark, Brigham Young demonstrated both the necessity of lay revelation and his frustration with the Saints that did not always embrace it:

> I am more afraid that this people have so much confidence in their leaders that they will not inquire for themselves of God whether they are led by Him. I am fearful they settle down in a state of blind self-security trusting their eternal destiny in the hands

of their leaders with a reckless confidence that in itself would thwart the purposes of God in their salvation, and weaken what influence they could give their leaders, did they know for themselves, by the revelations of Jesus, that they are led the right way. Let every man and woman know, by the whisperings of the Spirit of God to themselves, whether their leaders are walking in the path the Lord dictates or not.[14]

As Young's fears suggest, not all Latter-day Saints take their individual place in the revelatory composition. Some Saints obviously feel safer with an intermediary between themselves and the weight of revelation. Thus the lines made by each person's soul on the canvas of their faith may vary in width and opacity, depending on how much confidence one places in one's ability to hear the voice of God (the hubristic may make them fat and dark, the timid not at all) but—given the flurry of revelations around them—these personal strokes must carry the burden of bringing coherence to the constant flow of color. As the many voices of church leaders and the ongoing discoveries of human intellect present themselves to individual Mormons and claim their place in the portrait of their understanding, it is the personal ability to take up the revelatory brush that seems to promise Latter-day Saints the ability to make sense of it all. The LDS scholar Terryl Givens has shown how this is precisely the message of the Book of Mormon's most memorable prophet, Nephi, who finds favor with the Lord by seeking his own clarifying revelations "outside official channels."[15]

This, however, raises the question of whether it is possible that a theology which makes every member a prophet can also facilitate order in an institutional church. To resolve this potential problem, one has to comprehend the Mormons' strong and internalized sense of prophetic hierarchy. Both ancient and modern declarations—including at such significant moments as when the Mormon prophet Joseph F. Smith tried to explain his role before a committee of the United States Senate, or when President Spencer W. Kimball looked for the divine guidance on the matter of race—indicate that the *kinds* of revelations the highest church officials receive do not necessarily differ from those received by all of God's children. Heaven does not seem to speak to them more clearly than to any comparably faithful soul: both leader and layperson may have open visions, and both rely mostly on the silent impressions to their hearts. And Latter-day Saint doctrine recognizes neither apostolic nor personal revelation as infallible. What differs, then, is not the quality of the revelations but the arena in which those revelations apply. To return to our analogy, a master painter is entitled to insist that certain lines appear on the canvas of her students, but for even the most prodigious student to unbidden—mark up a peer's work would be unconscionable. Likewise, when the president of the church speaks he makes a strong, thick mark on the conceptions of the faith crafted by the devout membership, but when the laity feel God speaking to them they must limit themselves to their own particular portraits of understanding. It is a matter of office, not of inspiration. The former is exclusive; the latter is universal.

This interplay of personal revelation and prophetic authority lies at the heart of the Mormon experience. Practicing Latter-day Saints may find the ultimate result satisfying, but they cannot justly call the process simple. Take, for instance, the history of the church's stance on birth control. In a 1969 letter to local authorities, at the height of a sexual revolution, the First Presidency of the church reinforced the sentiment of past and contemporary prophets on the matter of human generation and laid down a solid line on the question of family planning. It is a mistake, they unequivocally declared, to curtail the blessing of posterity. Their statement continues to be reprinted and cited by Mormons and has never been repudiated by the institutional church. However, a decade later, the church's official monthly magazine, *Ensign*, published a somewhat different sentiment in an article by a devout obstetrician-gynecologist, Homer Ellsworth. (Appearance in that magazine did not raise the doctor's words to the status of doctrine, as the article itself made clear, but it did reflect a prophetic allowance to speak his piece.) In endorsing a prayerful, thoughtful, high-minded approach to contraception, Ellsworth's recommendation amounted to the following: take the prophets' counsel seriously and then take your personal circumstances to the Lord. Such a combination of the prophetic and the personal, he believed, had always been the essence of the faith. In making this point, Ellsworth even cited the tragic example of a mother who died because, in conceiving her eighth child, she followed ecclesiastical policy to the exclusion of her own inspiration. Ellsworth's essay has subsequently been published in an official Church manual on marriage, alongside that 1969 letter, and the sentiments of both are reflected in current instructions to local leaders.[16] Thus, earlier statements critical of contraception have never been completely obscured, far from it, but neither are they the only lines on the canvas. Their strong declarations in the name of life and selflessness have been complemented by subsequent strokes—lighter and finer, no doubt, but sitting atop the others—in defense of caution and consideration. By design the old and the new are bound together. And the prevailing message is an invitation for every woman and man to make sense of these contrapuntal principles by seeking their own inspiration on a matter of both existential and essential importance.

As this example demonstrates, not only are there different weights to the revelatory strokes within the church, there is also a temporal sequence to them, a layering of color. A devout Mormon would say that this reflects both a changing world and the unchanging goodness of God; the physical and emotional demands of parenting may be different in 1999 than they were in 1969, and thus a good and loving God continually speaks to present need. A more cynical explanation would characterize the church as merely bowing to cultural pressure and shadowing social trends. But, whatever one's view, it is clear that some lines come after others and therefore unavoidably lay over them. Thus a lighter stroke can have a major amending influence on a heavier line if it is more recent. Mormons are often and understandably focused on the current additions to the painting, the ones on top. They hold that the Saints, at any given point in this process, should be acutely attentive to the lines that the current generation of prophets contributes to the composition. To miss these would be to miss the immediacy and vitality of God's ongoing work and to lose one's place within it. In Latter-day Saint scripture, God's voice criticizes those unable to keep up with the current stroke: "I command and men obey not," He laments, "I revoke and they receive not the blessing" (D&C 58:32).[17]

As the arresting term *revoke* here may indicate, lines laid down in the current moment theoretically have the capacity to completely efface the strokes made previously—that is, as Elder Benson averred, the declaration of the living prophet may fully supplant the teachings of past prophets—but such an effort is rarely made, as the underlying colors of the past necessarily bleed through and jut out, especially if those past strokes were made adamantly and repeatedly. The historical lag between the official Mormon proclamation doing away with polygamy in 1890 and the actual cessation of recognized plural marriages around 1904 bears out this notion that bold prophetic teachings of the past can be counterbalanced only by an equal amount of color, and that the application of such color takes time and effort, of which the twentieth-century church spent an enormous amount to rework that issue. The past does matter.

A ham-fisted or incongruous effort to completely obliterate past images has the potential to damage the entire composition. If a modern church leader decided to deny the divinity of Jesus, to use the most extreme example, he would have to scribble over millennia of the most exquisite prophetic artistry while somehow preventing the ongoing devotional statements of his fellow ecclesiarchs and the irresistible witness in millions of Mormon souls. To say—as many Latter-day Saints undoubtedly do—that the latest prophetic stroke is the most vital one on the canvas, is not to say that there are no structural limitations to what that stroke can do. There are such limitations and they increase as the history of the church continues. Given the complexity of the composition process, mainstream Mormons have historically remained open to new inspirations that cross past doctrines or personal revelations or traditional practice, but one that ran counter *to all* of those would likely be resisted as the work of an uninspired hand.

Such a culture of revelation invites a high degree of historical attentiveness—both for a fully textured understanding of doctrinal content and for an awareness of revelatory process. For all the importance of the current application of color, to ignore the past strokes is not only to risk the threat of imposture but it is also to lose perspective on the image emerging. Background is as important as foreground in making full sense of a masterpiece. The Latter-day Saints are, accordingly, deeply invested in historical matters. And yet the proper nature of that historical consciousness is a source of passionate—and sometimes painful—debate. The institutional church's focus on its own history has often been subject to withering criticism as defensive at best, or dishonest at worst, for its tendency to view the past through the filter of present policy. This critique may evince an essential antagonism between the oracle and the historian, between the figures charged with adding paint and those determined to peer beneath it. "How," the scholar-critic might ask, "can people properly assess the opus without a true sense of the stages by which it came to be? *All* the underlying color matters." "The underlying color that matters," the prophet-artist may answer, "is that which has survived the transformative work of a living God. Anything else distorts the image emerging." Such is the dynamic discourse engendered by a living revelation, in which questions abound. The application of new color may draw the Saints closer to God's truth, but must those brushstrokes obscure aspects of the church's past in the process? When the Apostle John declared that God is love, was he dishonest in not also dealing with Jehovah's command to destroy the Midianites? As the church has made Joseph Smith's revelation on abstinence from alcohol the behavioral standard for saving ordinances, should it also promote histories that show Smith to have drunk wine and beer? When a new splash of pigment adds to the image, something is revealed, but something may also be covered; likewise, to scrape away pigment in pursuit of the past may do damage to the present message. History thus becomes a site of intense soul searching within the LDS community.

The distinctively compositional nature of Mormon revelation, and its particular relationship to history, can make interfaith dialogue challenging. Latter-day Saints—lay and leader alike—often seem nonplussed when asked to account for a particular statement or practice of this or that figure from this or that era. The words of apostolic leaders of any period cannot be easily dismissed, but such comments—be they Paul's statements on women or Brigham Young's teachings on Adam—have been so framed, blended, softened, and overwhelmed by countless other strokes around them that they make little sense in isolation. One might as well discuss Renoir's *Duck Pond* by reference to a solitary dash of black. For similar reasons, the institutional church bristles at comparisons to renegade polygamous sects. It accepts that the mainstream church and its fundamentalist rivals began with a shared sketch on plural marriage, but—on that issue at least—the church kept painting while the fundamentalists stopped. Paradoxically, for mainstream Mormons, to embrace the "faith of their fathers" is often to embrace the current composition—including the fact that some of their ancestors' strokes have been essentially transformed by the addition of pigment around them—rather than defend the static images of the past. To many critics that may look like convenient human whitewashing. To many Latter-day Saints it looks like continuing divine artistry.

Consider the case of the church's deeply troubled experience with race. In 1978, the Latter-day Saints added to their Standard Works a revelation that lifted a long-standing prohibition on men of African descent receiving the priesthood, thus taking a broad brush to a portrait of the faith that had historically included pronounced teachings on race. In one sense that stroke was a repudiation of the past; in another, it represented continuity. Both aspects appear when the 1978 revelation is set in context with the clearest early statement of a race-based prohibition on the priesthood, an 1852 speech by Brigham Young. Young's words grate painfully on a modern Mormon ear: "Now then in the kingdom of God on the earth, a man who has the Affrican blood in him cannot hold one jot nor tittle of preisthood; Why? because they are the true, eternal principals the Lord Almighty has ordained, and who can help it, men cannot, the angels cannot, and all the powers of earth and hell cannot take it off." Here Young seemed to speak of racial distinctions as "eternal" principles, yet in the very next breath he anticipated their revision. A living, sovereign God adamantly pushed into his discourse: "[B]ut thus saith the Eternal I am, what I am, I take [the curse] off at my pleasure, and not one partical of power can that posterity of Cain have, until the time comes he says he will have it taken away. That time will come when they will have the privilege of all we have the privelege of, and more."[18] Young's promised day of equality seemed impossibly far off, but his God was actively near, insistently reserving the right to act again and on His own terms. Young implied a timeline, but—Young himself conceding the lesson of Jonah—the

Almighty acts as He pleases. The Mormon prophet thus spoke of eternity while anticipating change. The 1978 revocation of the priesthood restriction may have come at a
politically expedient time, but in the eyes of the Saints it was based on unchanging doctrines: God's ways are not man's ways and His revelation will continue.

In recent decades, Young's teachings and those of his successors have been so overlaid and reworked by subsequent generations of prophets that what is increasingly left
on the portrait of Mormon understanding is a doctrinal emphasis on the blessing of
the priesthood, an increased expectation of historical change, and a present prophetic
demand for complete racial equality. In the process Latter-day Saints have also grown
more aware that their own scriptural tradition (2 Nephi 26:28, 33; Galatians 3:28) provided a dominant theme of equality that might have much more rapidly transformed
the implications of such nineteenth- and twentieth-century racialized preaching had
the Saints' view of the whole of God's work not been limited by their own prejudices.
Twelve decades of painting that overwhelmingly excluded people of African descent
from the portrait of the faith will now not revise easily; much more color is clearly
needed before those past brushstrokes can be fully converted into a lasting message of
universal inclusion. And yet too much repainting may obscure essential and illustrative stories of human suffering, revelatory process, black endurance, and white arrogance embedded in those earlier brushstrokes. New revelations and stubborn histories
are thus locked in a complicated embrace. The Mormon willingness to allow present
revelation to reshape but not simply jettison or condemn the past—bearing some similarities to the early apostles' engagement with Israel's animus toward Gentiles—gives
church leaders and members a wide but restrained range of motion in reworking the
composition toward a more complete whole.

This ongoing process of revelation—with both its latitudes and its limitations—also
raises an important question about the Mormon understanding of *canon*. Latter-day
Saints celebrate their "open canon" and, as the official 1978 declaration lifting racial
restrictions demonstrates, have put it into effect. However, that revelation on race is one
of only a very small handful of new chapters and proclamations that have been officially
added to their Standard Works since the 1844 death of Joseph Smith. Why, then, would a
faith make so much of a principle that seems so rarely invoked?

One possible answer to the question is that the emphasis on openness refers as much
to the perpetual *possibility* of new scripture as it does to the immediate *reality* of new
scripture—in the sense that a door is considered open regardless of whether anything
actually passes through it. In and of itself, the very possibility has the power to shape
a religious culture in complex ways. On one hand, the openness can be emboldening
and self-affirming: "If God were to speak again," a seeker might ask, "where would we
find His word?"; a Mormon might confidently answer, "In a church that is institutionally
arranged and culturally conditioned to receive a new chapter of holy writ." On the other
hand, that openness can be profoundly humbling, a testament to the fact that whatever
understanding we have now is incomplete. The principle of an open canon serves as
an inescapable reminder of Paul's apostolic admission to the Corinthians: "prophecies,
they shall fail . . . knowledge, it shall vanish away. For we know in part, and we prophesy

in part. But when that which is perfect is come, then that which is in part shall be done away." (1 Corinthians 13:8–10). To say repeatedly to the world "God will add to our scriptures" may sound like, and may often be intended as, a boast; but in reality, it is to say, again and again, we don't have it all.

Another possible answer to the question of canonization is that Mormon conceptions of canon refer to something more than the published historic scriptures of the Standard Works. If *canon* connotes, as it traditionally has in a religious context, the rule by which teachings and practices are validated, the Mormon canon comprises not just the officially published scriptures but the entire portrait of the faith, with all its historical, personal, and institutional brushstrokes. In that sense, the canon really is added to continually. Every glint of revelation reflecting off the pages of church magazines, every breath of inspired counsel whispered by a mother at the bedside of her child, every glimpse of heaven—however fleeting—received in an act of prayerful yearning adds to the rule, the actual canon, by which believers live their lives.

In such a culture, the process of formally "canonizing" a document by adding it to the published scriptures is always possible but to do so often may appear unnecessary as it merely thickens a stroke already on the canvas; it is not the only means of such thickening nor is the process irreversible. For instance, a set of prophetic teachings known as the Lectures on Faith remained in the LDS scriptures for over eight decades and then was abruptly removed; Saints still occasionally cite it in church and study it at home, but its place on the portrait of the faith was undeniably attenuated by its removal from the Standard Works. Conversely, a prophetic address like Joseph Smith's King Follett discourse has never been added to the scripture, but as its message was reaffirmed in subsequent prophetic discourse and in the hearts and minds of the congregation, its stroke has been both reinforced and revised by the ongoing brush marks around it. Published canonization has an impact, the Standard Works play a distinctive role in the matrix of Mormon revelation, but the effect is not absolute, exclusive, or unalterable.

As time unfolds and the Latter-day Saint composition of understanding develops, bold lines can be narrowed, thin lines can be underscored, new lines can reorient the eye. The fine stroke of an "uncanonized" statement can be strengthened by the reiteration of other public revelators and the promptings of the individual soul; the thick mark of a "canonized" verse can be softened by the sentiments of today's apostles and the revelatory experiences of the faithful. To watch this process play out can be both inspiring and demanding. Many Mormons seem determined neither to jettison the project because it is still in process nor to stop painting and claim completion. They seem resolved, rather, to stay, to listen, to pray, and to believe that the visage of God is emerging on the canvas before them.

Notes

1. Talmage, *Study of the Articles of Faith*, 5.
2. Chillingworth, *Religion of Protestants*, 290–99.
3. Neuhaus, "Mormons and (Other?) Christians."

4. Pelikan, *Whose Bible Is It?*, 17.
5. Benson, "Fourteen Fundamentals in Following the Prophet."
6. Doctrine and Covenants 68:4.
7. Davies and Madsen, "Scripture," 3:1278.
8. Book of Mormon, Introduction.
9. Doctrine and Covenants 20:11–12.
10. Woodruff, *Sixty-Eighth Semi-Annual Conference of the Church of Jesus Christ of Latter-day Saints*, 22.
11. Smith, *Doctrines of Salvation*, 3:203.
12. Walker, Turley, and Leonard, *Massacre at Mountain Meadows*, 155–57, 225–26.
13. Clark, *Selected Papers*, 102.
14. Davies, "Reflections on the Mormon 'Canon,'" 52.
15. Givens, *By the Hand of Mormon*, 222–23.
16. *Eternal Marriage Student Manual*, 14–18.
17. Doctrine and Covenants 58:32.
18. Brigham Young, February 5, 1852, *Reports of Speeches ca. 1845–1972* (LDS Church Historian's Office). My thanks to archivist Ron Watt for his invaluable assistance in locating the original transcript of this speech.

BIBLIOGRAPHY

Benson, Ezra Taft. "Fourteen Fundamentals in Following the Prophet." In *1980 Devotional Speeches of the Year*, 26–30. Provo, UT: Brigham Young University Press, 1981.
Chillingworth, William. *The Religion of Protestants: A Safeway to Salvation*. 4th ed. London: A. Clark, 1674.
Clark, J. Reuben. *Selected Papers: On Religion, Education, and Youth*. Ed. David H. Yarn, Jr. Provo, UT: Brigham Young University Press, 1984.
Davies W. D. "Reflections on the Mormon 'Canon.'" *Harvard Theological Review* 79, nos. 1–3 (1986): 44–66.
Davies, W. D., and Truman Madsen. s.v. "Scripture." *Encyclopedia of Mormonism*.
Eternal Marriage Student Manual. Salt Lake City: Church of Jesus Christ of Latter-day Saints, 2001.
Givens, Terryl L. *By the Hand of Mormon: The American Scripture that Launched a New World Religion*. New York: Oxford University Press, 2002.
Holland, Jeffrey R. "My Words . . . Never Cease." *Ensign* 38, no. 5 (May 2008): 91–94.
Morrison, Alexander B. "The Latter-day Saint Concept of Canon." In *Historicity and the Latter-day Saint Scriptures*, ed. Paul Hoskisson, 1–16. Provo, UT: Religious Studies Center, Brigham Young University, 2001.
Neuhaus, Richard John. "Mormons and (Other?) Christians." *First Things* 104 (June–July 2000): 2–12.
Oaks, Dallin H. "Scripture Reading and Revelation." *Ensign* 25, no. 1 (January 1995): 6–9.
Pelikan, Jaroslav. *Whose Bible Is It? A History of the Scriptures through the Ages*. New York: Viking, 2005.
Smith, Joseph Fielding. *Doctrines of Salvation: Sermons and Writings of Joseph F. Smith*. 3 vols. Ed. Bruce R. McConkie. Salt Lake City: Bookcraft, 1954–56.
Talmage, James E. *A Study of the Articles of Faith*. 1890. Salt Lake City, UT: Deseret, 1985.

Walker, Ronald W., Richard E. Turley Jr., and Glen M. Leonard, *Massacre at Mountain Meadows: An American Tragedy*. New York: Oxford University Press, 2008.

Welch, John W., and David J. Whittaker, "Mormonism's Open Canon: Some Historical Perspectives on Its Religious Limits and Potentials." Paper presented at meetings of the Society of Biblical Literature and American Academy of Religion, Atlanta, 1986. In *Preliminary Report: Foundation for Ancient Research and Mormon Studies*, Americana Collection, Special Collections, Harold B. Lee Library, Brigham Young University, Salt Lake City, 1987.

Woodruff, Wilford. *Sixty-Eighth Semi-Annual Conference of the Church of Jesus Christ of Latter-day Saints*. Salt Lake City: Deseret News, 1897.

Young, Brigham. Feb. 5, 1852, Reports of Speeches ca. 1845–1972. LDS Church Historian's Office.

PART III

ECCLESIASTICAL
STRUCTURE
AND PRAXIS

CHAPTER 12

···

MORMON PRIESTHOOD
AND ORGANIZATION

···

GREGORY A. PRINCE

PRIESTHOOD within the Church of Jesus Christ of Latter-day Saints is generally misunderstood by both church members and outsiders. The former tend to view it as a prepackaged entity, with Joseph Smith's role being to untie the bow on the package; while the latter tend to compare it to the professional priesthood of their own traditions, not realizing that it is a unique combination of a highly centralized, semiprofessional hierarchy at the top, and a volunteer, lay organization at the bottom.

LDS priesthood is defined officially as follows: "The priesthood is the power and authority of God. . . . Through the priesthood, God created and governs the heavens and the earth. . . . In mortality, the priesthood is the power and authority that God gives to man to act in all things necessary for the salvation of God's children." This definition is important for two reasons. First, God "gives to man" the priesthood, meaning that it is conferred legalistically; a man does not take it upon himself.[1] Second, it is bipartite, consisting of both power and authority. Although a single act of ordination subsumes both elements today, such was not the case in the earliest days of the Restoration. Authority came first, initially in the implicit form of Joseph Smith's calling to produce and publish the Book of Mormon, and later by direct, angelic ordination in a manner analogous to Jesus's ordination of his disciples anciently. Receiving "power from on high" (Luke 24:49), on the other hand, emulating the gifts of the spirit bestowed on those same disciples on the day of Pentecost (Acts 2), did not occur for another two years.

One of the earliest known documents relating to the church, a history written by Joseph Smith with the aid of scribe Frederick G. Williams during the latter half of 1832, succinctly describes the genesis of priesthood in the church.[2] The introductory paragraph of that history describes four key stages:

(1) "firstly he receiving the testimony from on high";
(2) "secondly the ministering of Angels";
(3) "thirdly the reception of the holy Priesthood by the ministering of Aangels [sic] to administer the letter of the Gospel—the Law and commandments

as they were given unto him—and the ordinencs [*sic*]" (thus, legalistic authority);

(4) "fourthly a confirmation and reception of the high Priesthood after the holy order of the son of the living God power and ordinance from on high to preach the Gospel in the administration and demonstration of the spirit" (thus, spiritual power).

Stage 1: Personal Salvation: "Receiving the testimony from on high"

The narratives of what later became known as Joseph Smith's First Vision went through an evolutionary process that began in the early 1830s and continued until Smith's death in 1844. The earliest detailed account, and the only account written in Smith's own hand, is contained in the 1832 history noted above. The key elements, which differ substantially from subsequent accounts that revised the history to conform to later theological concerns, are:

- *Smith became concerned for his salvation at an early age*: "At about the age of twelve years my mind became seriously imprest with regard to the all important concerns for the wellfare of my immortal Soul."
- *His study of the Bible over a period of three years convinced him that all churches then in existence had apostatized from the primitive Christian Church*: "By Searching the Scriptures I found that mankind did not come unto the Lord but that they had apostatised from the true and liveing faith and there was no society or denomination that built upon the Gospel of Jesus Christ as recorded in the new testament."
- *The absence of an authentic church, wherein he might have received relief from his sinfulness, was the motivation for the prayer that resulted in his epiphany*: "I cried unto the Lord for mercy for there was none else to whom I could go and obtain mercy."
- *The message from the Lord addressed the issue that led Smith to pray*: "I Saw the Lord and he Spake unto me Saying Joseph my Son thy Sins are forgiven thee. go thy way walk in my Statutes and keep my commandments."

This account is significant not only for what it says, but also for what it does not say: the epiphany gave no indication that Smith would have a public ministry.

Stage 2: The Book of Mormon: "The ministering of Angels"

At the end of his 1832 First Vision account, Smith lamented that he "could find none that would believe the hevenly vision." Claiming a vision of the Lord, while audacious to modern sensibilities, was not unusual at that time and place; however, Smith's youth ("in the 16th year of my age"), poverty, and lack of education limited his credibility.

In marked contrast, a second epiphany, about three years later, led him to gold plates and, subsequently, the publication of the Book of Mormon. The boldness of adding to biblical canon, rather than the claim of angelic visitation, elicited both widespread attention and a firestorm of disdain for Smith. Months before the publication of the book, a local newspaper belittled him:

> The greatest piece of superstition that has ever come within the sphere of our knowledge is one which has for sometime past, and still occupies the attention of a few superstitious and bigoted individuals of this quarter. It is generally known and spoken of as the "*Golden Bible*." ... Now it appears not a little strange that there should have been deposited in this western world, and in the secluded town of Manchester, too, a record of this description, and still more so, that a person like Smith (very illiterate) should have been gifted by inspiration to read and interpret it. (*Palmyra* [New York] *Freeman*, November 29, 1829)

The persecution quickly rose to such a level as to cause Smith to respond in a preface to the Book of Mormon, published in late March 1830, to the "many false reports [that] have been circulated respecting the following work, and also many unlawful measures taken by evil designing persons to destroy me, and also the work."

Publication of the Book of Mormon shifted Smith's ministry from personal (working out his own salvation) to public, "to the convincing of the Jew and Gentile that Jesus is the Christ, the Eternal God, manifesting Himself unto all nations." However, the verbal authorization by which he undertook this ministry differed from the formal ordination by which Jesus had authorized his disciples anciently. Likewise, the nature of this ministry differed from that of the ancient disciples. Whereas theirs included proselytizing efforts across the ancient Mediterranean world that led to the establishment of several regional churches, Smith's as yet was limited to producing and publishing a book.

Stage 3: "The reception of the holy Priesthood by the ministering of Aangels"

For a year and a half after gaining access to the gold plates, Smith struggled to produce the text of the Book of Mormon. He worked with a succession of scribes, but had little to show for it. One scribe, Martin Harris, caused a catastrophic setback when he borrowed, and then lost, 116 pages of the manuscript.

In April 1829, schoolteacher Oliver Cowdery met Smith. Two days after they met, Cowdery became Smith's scribe, and in three months they completed the manuscript. A section of the book that described baptism in the Nephite church led Smith and Cowdery to seek authority to perform the ordinance. This proved a major transitional point, for it was the first time that Smith sought formal ordination, rather than acting under the implicit authority by which he published the Book of Mormon. A revelation to Cowdery, written in his hand sometime in the latter half of 1829, is important both for what it says about the matter and for what it does not say:

> I speak unto you even as unto Paul mine apostle for ye are called even with that same calling with which he was called. Now therefore whosoever repenteth & humbleth himself before me & desireth to be baptized in my name shall ye baptize them. And after this manner did he command me that I should baptize them Behold ye shall go down & stand in the water & in my name shall ye baptize them And now behold these are the words which ye shall say calling them by name saying Having authority given me of Jesus Christ I baptize you in the name of the Father & of the Son & of the Holy Ghost Amen.[3]

The revelation, by equating Cowdery's calling to that of Paul, implied that he had received his authority as had Paul, whose ordination occurred when Ananias laid hands on him (Acts 9:17). It did not indicate that there were two gradations of authority, as described in the Book of Mormon, nor did it refer to the authority as "priesthood."[4] However, in stating that his authority was given him *of* Jesus Christ, Cowdery made it clear that he and Smith had not taken it upon themselves.

Six years elapsed between Cowdery's vague reference to ordination, and an explicit statement attributing two layers of ordination through visits from named angelic emissaries:

> John the son of Zacharias, . . . which John I have sent unto you, my servants, Joseph Smith, Jun., and Oliver Cowdery, to ordain you unto the first priesthood which you have received, that you might be called and ordained even as Aaron And also with Peter, and James, and John, whom I have sent unto you, by whom I have ordained you and confirmed you to be apostles and especial witnesses of my name, and bear the keys of your ministry. (Doctrine and Covenants [D&C] 27:7–12)

The six-year transition of the narrative included several significant developmental stages:

- *Smith and Cowdery called and ordained of God; dual-tiered authority of officers, April 1830*: The "Church Articles and Covenants" noted that Smith "was called of God & ordained an Apostle of Jesus Christ, an Elder of this Church," and Cowdery "was also called of God an Apostle of Jesus Christ, an Elder of this Church & ordained under his [Smith's] hand." That Smith was specified as having ordained Cowdery, but no one was specified as having ordained Smith, implies angelic ordination. The specification of elders as being the only officers authorized to confer the

Holy Ghost is consistent with the dual-tiered authority structure described in the Book of Mormon.

- *Use of the word "priesthood," November 1831*: While earlier records referred to the generic concept of authority or to named offices to which men had been ordained, a revelation in late 1831 that referred to several elders as having been "ordained unto this priesthood" is the earliest use of what became the umbrella term encompassing all ordained, male officers.
- *Reception of authority through angels, late 1832*: The early history by Joseph Smith, mentioned earlier, marked the first time that Smith referred to angelic messengers in connection with priesthood. The "reception of the holy Priesthood by the ministring [sic] of Aangels" was consistent with later accounts describing two episodes of angelic ordination.
- *Separate ordination to two priesthoods by separate angels, December 1833*: A blessing given by Smith to Cowdery spoke of the fulfillment of ancient prophecy by the two of them having been "ordained . . . by the hand of the angel in the bush, unto the lesser priesthood, and after receive [sic] the holy priesthood under the hands of those who had been held in reserve for a long season, even those who received it under the hand of the Messiah."
- *Description of the conferral of the lesser priesthood, October 1834*: The first published history of the church, written by Cowdery, stated that "we received under his hand [the angel of God] the holy priesthood, as he said, 'upon you my fellow servants, in the name of Messiah I confer this priesthood and this authority, which shall remain upon earth, that the sons of Levi may yet offer an offering unto the Lord in righteousness.'"
- *Naming of the two priesthoods, March 1835*: A revelation in the spring of 1835 named, for the first time, the two levels of priesthood: "There are, in the church, two priesthoods, namely: the Melchizedek, and the Aaronic, including the Levitical priesthood."

The fleshing out, over several years, of the details of the establishment of LDS priesthood has led some to question its authenticity. While it is not known why earlier versions of the story lacked the details of later ones, the later versions never contradict the earlier ones. No claims of angelic interaction are susceptible to objective validation, and yet it is instructive to note that such claims, albeit lacking the details of later accounts, were reported by non-Mormon newspapers within the first year of the church's existence:

- *November 16, 1830*: "The name of the person here, who pretends to have a divine mission, and to have seen and conversed with Angels, is Cowdray." (*Painesville Telegraph*, Ohio)
- *December 4, 1830*: "About two weeks since, Oliver Cowdry, David Whitmer and Martin Harris, arrived at Painesville, Ohio, with the Books. In the evening they preached in the Methodist Chapel, claiming to act under a commission written by the finger of God." (*Republican Advocate*, Ohio)

- *December 7, 1830*: "Those who are the friends and advocates of this wonderful book [the Book of Mormon], state that Mr. Oliver Cowdry has his commission directly from the God of Heaven, and that he has his credentials, written and signed by the hand of Jesus Christ, with whom he has personally conversed, and as such, said Cowdry claims that he and his associates are the only persons on earth who are qualified to administer in his name." (*Painesville Telegraph*, Ohio)
- *February 14, 1831*: "They then proclaimed that there had been no religion in the world for 1500 years,—that no one had been authorised to preach &c. for that period—that Jo Smith had now received a commission from God for that purpose. ... Smith (they affirmed,) had seen God frequently and personally—Cowdery and his friends had frequent interviews with angels." (*Palmyra Reflector*, New York)

STAGE 4: "A CONFIRMATION AND RECEPTION OF THE HIGH PRIESTHOOD . . . POWER AND ORDINANCE FROM ON HIGH"

Authority, just discussed, was but one of two dimensions eventually embodied in Latter-day Saint priesthood. To understand the other dimension, it is necessary to introduce Sidney Rigdon. Rigdon, a Baptist minister, joined a movement headed by Alexander Campbell (eventually the Disciples of Christ) in the mid-1820s and quickly became one of its most popular and prominent preachers. However, he differed with Campbell on several issues, particularly in believing "that a 'complete' restoration of the New Testament church would include such original supernatural gifts as faith healing, miracles, tongues and prophecy—and that these manifestations would validate 'authorization.'"[5] Their differences came to a head at an August 1830 church conference, resulting in Rigdon's departure from the movement.

Two months later, Parley P. Pratt, one of Rigdon's former congregants who had converted to Mormonism at the time of Rigdon's schism with Campbell, began to proselytize in the area of Rigdon's Ohio home. Within two weeks Rigdon joined Pratt in the new religion, an event chronicled in a local newspaper: "The Elder referred to, [Sidney Rigdon] is the famous Campbellite leader, who has made so much noise in the Reserve for a few months past. He has finally concluded to receive the new Revelation, and has actually been baptized, (now for the third time)" (*Observer and Telegraph* [Ohio], November 18, 1830).

While enamored of his new religion, Rigdon soon took exception to the failed attempts of church members (most notably Oliver Cowdery, who was a missionary companion of Pratt) to exercise the gifts of the spirit that he had advocated in the Campbellite movement. A local newspaper account, which referred to Cowdery and others, noted, "When Jesus sent his disciples to preach, he gave them power against all unclean spirits, to cast them out, to heal all manner of diseases, and to raise the dead. But these newly commissioned disciples have totally failed thus far in their attempts to heal, and as far as can be ascertained, their prophecys have also failed" (*Painesville Telegraph* [Ohio], December 7, 1830). The same paper later noted, "Mr. R[igdon] now blames Cowdery for *attempting* to work miracles, and says it was not intended to be confirmed in that way" (February 15, 1831). As Cowdery, Pratt, and two other missionaries continued their mission westward, Rigdon traveled east and met Joseph Smith only one month after his baptism.

Rigdon immediately became a central figure in the development of Latter-day Saint theology. A revelation dating perhaps to the day Smith and Rigdon met stated, "And now this calling & commandment give I unto all men, that as many as shall come before my Servent Sidney & Joseph, embracing this calling & commandment, shall be ordained & sent forth to preach the everlasting gospel among the Nation." Far more important was a revelation three weeks later, for which Rigdon acted as scribe. Drawing upon the Lucan scripture describing the resurrected Christ's instructions to his disciples and echoing Rigdon's assertion that supernatural power must accompany the true church, the revelation instructed, "Wherefore, for this cause I gave unto you the commandment, that you should go to the Ohio; and there I will give unto you my law and there you shall be endowed with power from on high" (D&C 38:32).

The reference to Luke is essential to an understanding of Latter-day Saint priesthood. The Lord's ancient audience was his disciples, whom he had ordained during his mortal ministry. Without question they were *authorized* to act in his name; and yet, he was now telling them that for their new task—wherein "repentance and remission of sins should be preached in his name among all nations"—something was missing. That *something*—divine empowerment—came to them on the day of Pentecost, as described in Acts 2. The latter-day counterpart, which began with the promise of an endowment of "power from on high," just mentioned, proceeded in a remarkably parallel fashion.

Within days of meeting Smith, Rigdon replaced Smith's previous scribe in an ambitious and never completed effort to revise the King James Bible.[6] In addition to revising verses, Smith also added many. Some of those described Melchizedek, an otherwise obscure Old Testament figure, ascribing to him and his order great powers over the elements:

> having been approved of God, he was ordained an high priest after the order of the covenant which God made with Enoch ... that every one being ordained after this order and calling should have power, by faith, to break mountains, to divide the seas, to dry up waters, to turn them out of their course; to put at defiance the armies of nations, to divide the earth. (Genesis 14:26–40)

Two concepts—endowment and ordination—merged over a period of several months. In May, an unpublished revelation to Ezra Thayer explicitly linked the two and related them to proselytizing in the same manner described in Luke: "let my servent Ezra humble himself & at the conference meeting he shall be ordained unto power from on high & he shall go from thence (if he be obedient unto my commandments) & proclaim my Gospel."

The "conference meeting" was scheduled for early June. Such was the enthusiasm and expectation of church members that the meeting was publicized, in advance, in a local newspaper: "In June they are all to meet, and hold a kind of jubille [sic] in this new 'land of promise,' where they are to work diverse miracles—among others that of raising the dead" (*Western Courier* [Ohio], May 26, 1831). A description of the meeting written by the Church Historian eight years later provides an account that, except for the anachronistic use of the term "Melchizedek priesthood," accurately summarizes the first-hand accounts:

> Previous to this there was a revelation received, requiring the prophet to call the elders together, that they might receive an endowment. This was done, and the meeting took place some time in June. About fifty elders met, which was about all the elders that then belonged to the church. The meeting was conducted by Smith. Some curious things took place. The same visionary and marvellous spirits spoken of before, got hold of some of the elders; it threw one from his seat to the floor; it bound another, so that for some time he could not use his limbs nor speak; and some other curious effects were experienced, but, by a mighty exertion, in the name of the Lord, it was exposed and shown to be from an evil source. The Melchizedek priesthood was then for the first time introduced, and conferred on several of the elders. In this chiefly consisted the endowment—it being a new order—and bestowed authority. However, some doubting took place among the elders, and considerable conversation was held on the subject. The elders not fairly understanding the nature of the endowments, it took some time to reconcile all their feelings.[7]

Not all recipients of the endowment felt that the results matched the expectations. Ezra Booth, disappointed by an unsuccessful attempt to raise a dead child, left the faith and wrote a series of critical letters published in a nearby newspaper (*Ohio Star*, November 3, 1831). Most participants, however, remained in the faith, and some viewed the endowment as authentic and tangible. Jared Carter, for instance, wrote of a church member who sustained injuries feared to be fatal, and of his brother, who had received the endowment:

> In my conversation with her, I told her that she need not have any more pain, and also mentioned my Brother Simeon who was endowed with great power from on high, and that she might be healed, if she had faith. Brother Simeon also conversed with her, and after awhile took her by the hand, saying, "I command you in the name of Jesus Christ to arise and walk." And she arose and walked from room to room.

In a conference in October 1831, Smith introduced a new dimension to "power from on high," and simultaneously took the first step in the development of the unique Latter-day Saint theology of afterlife, by stating "that the order of the High-priesthood is that they have the power given them to seal up the Saints unto eternal life. And said it was the privilege of every Elder present to be ordained to the Highpriesthood."

Initially, the endowment of power from on high occurred in a schoolhouse and was restricted to men who were designated as missionaries. (Only men were allowed to serve as missionaries at that time.) With the completion of the Kirtland Temple in 1836, the endowment was reserved for "sacred space," meaning temples and, on occasion, other venues consecrated for the purpose. Beginning in 1843, the endowment was extended to women, as well as to men who were not designated as missionaries, an implicit recognition of the fact that women are fully capable of exercising gifts of the spirit. Indeed, a 1931 statement prepared under the direction of the Council of the Twelve Apostles elaborated on this point:

> Men, women and children who do not hold the Priesthood have had their prayers answered millions of times in the history of Christianity the world over and in the history of this dispensation. . . . One may pray, have his [and her] prayers answered, may have the Holy Ghost bestowed upon him [and her], and may exercise many of its gifts, without holding any Priesthood.[8]

Despite these changes, a continual thread that connects the earliest LDS endowment with current temple practice is the empowerment of missionaries. Throughout the world today, one of the final steps in the preparation of newly minted missionaries is participation in the endowment ceremony in an LDS temple, with the hope that the missionary will subsequently gain access to and use power from on high in the course of his or her missionary endeavors.

With the introduction of the endowment of power from on high, the essential elements of Latter-day Saint priesthood were completed. On the one hand, priesthood included divine authority that was originally bestowed on Joseph Smith and Oliver Cowdery through angelic administration and subsequently passed on to the present day from person to person, such that every priesthood bearer in the church can trace an unbroken "line of authority" back to Smith and Cowdery. On a day-to-day basis, the authority element of priesthood is the more common. The 1931 statement previously cited notes:

> Chiefly Priesthood functions in connection with organization. That is, the greatest need of Priesthood is where there is a service to be performed to others besides ourselves. Whenever you do anything [legally] for, or in behalf of, someone else, you must have the right to do so. . . . Now, when it comes to earthly power to perform a definite service, we call it the power of attorney in the case of acting legally for someone else, or the court and the judge where it is a question of acting for the government. But in the Church of Christ this authority to act for others is known as Priesthood.

And on the other hand, priesthood includes the endowment of power from on high or, simply stated, power; and it differs substantially from authority. Authority is automatic. For example, an ordinance such as baptism that is performed by a man holding the requisite priesthood will be recognized by the church even if the officiator is subsequently found to have been unworthy—"mired in sin"—at the time he performed it. By contrast, the ability to draw on supernatural power is linked to personal worthiness. One of the most eloquent of Joseph Smith's revelations discussed this linkage:

> Behold, there are many called, but few are chosen. And why are they not chosen? Because their hearts are set so much upon the things of this world, and aspire to the honors of men, that they do not learn this one lesson—That the rights of the priesthood are inseparably connected with the powers of heaven, and that the powers of heaven cannot be controlled nor handled only upon the principles of righteousness. That they may be conferred upon us, it is true; but when we undertake to cover our sins, or to gratify our pride, our vain ambition, or to exercise control or dominion or compulsion upon the souls of the children of men, in any degree of unrighteousness, behold, the heavens withdraw themselves; the Spirit of the Lord is grieved; and when it is withdrawn, Amen to the priesthood or the authority of that man.

When a priesthood holder is able to draw upon "the powers of heaven," miraculous things can happen. Indeed, the records of the church, particularly the diaries written over a period of nearly two centuries, are replete with such accounts. However, even personal righteousness, coupled with worthy desires, can fall short of delivering the desired outcome. Smith and his colleagues, in the immediate aftermath of the June 1831 conference at which the endowment occurred, were certain that their newly acquired power would allow them to raise a child from the dead. They failed, as did others in the early church.[9]

Church members have always struggled when the promises of priesthood blessings fall short of the outcomes. Two high church officials offered remarkably candid suggestions for those who struggle, both based on their own encounters with failed expectations. The first was Apostle Abraham H. Cannon, from the late nineteenth century:

> Bro. L. F. Moench traveled [with me] from Ogden to my destination where we arrived at 9.45 p.m. and were met by Bp. Wm. C. Parkinson and Presdts. Geo. C. Parkinson and M. F. Cowley. We were entertained at the home of the former. His wife here told me that when I was here last in blessing her new born babe I had promised it should live to manhood. Several weeks thereafter it was taken sick with pneumonia and while in this condition the Elders who administered to it promised it continued life. Yet it died, and being their first and only son out of several children the blow was a severe one. I could not account for the failure of our promises that it should live except that sympathy instead of the Spirit of God prompted the utterances. (Abraham Cannon diary, July 25, 1891)

The second was David O. McKay, who wrote in his diary only six months after being sustained as church president:

My son Robert called—said that he was going to be faced with some questions tonight that would be hard to answer without advice from me. A young man in Robert's Ward who has been suffering with cancer, and to whom I administered sometime ago, has just passed away, and the father and members of the family, converts to the Church, do not feel resigned to his having been taken after having been administered to. Robert said a number of the young people will no doubt face him with the answer to this seeming tragedy.

I told Robert that it is our right to ask the Lord to bless the sick, for He has said that if there be any sick among us to call in the Elders. However, the Lord does not always answer our prayers affirmatively; sometimes the answer comes negatively. If we always had an affirmative answer, there would be no death at all. Sometimes the power of faith is not sufficient to overcome the law of nature, but it is always our right to ask for a restoration to health, or to rebuke the disease, or whatever it is, and leave the rest for the operation of faith. (David O. McKay diary, October 17, 1951)

ORGANIZATION

Form followed function. Although one of the church's Articles of Faith states, "We believe in the same organization that existed in the Primitive Church," its structure and governance have undergone continual evolution. Consisting of a handful of converts at its founding in 1830, the church initially functioned under the sole leadership of Joseph Smith. While Smith remained the undisputed leader until his death fourteen years later, the organization over which he presided grew and developed as its numbers swelled, and it continues to grow and develop to the present day.

The earliest organization duplicated that described in the Book of Mormon and consisted of three ordained offices—elder, teacher, and priest—whose functions were more pastoral than hierarchical. Within a year, two other offices—bishop and deacon—were added, their inclusion in the new church coinciding with the conversion of Sidney Rigdon, Edward Partridge, and other members of the Disciples of Christ, a tradition that recognized only two offices within its own organization: bishop and deacon. The office of patriarch was introduced in 1833, followed in 1835 by the final two ordained offices, apostles and seventies. While all of these offices are mentioned in the New Testament, their function in the modern church has continually moved into new directions in response to ever-changing needs.

The basic congregational unit in today's LDS Church, the ward, began in Illinois in the early 1840s, but initially served more as a political ward might function today. Following the exodus of the church to the Great Basin in 1847, wards assumed the ecclesiastical form and function that they retain today, with each ward presided over by a bishop who serves both as administrative and pastoral leader. Ward membership, unlike in most Christian congregations, is defined by rigid geographical boundaries rather than social or philosophical preferences of congregants.

As Mormon society in the Great Basin gradually prospered in a harsh environment, concerns shifted from hand-to-mouth existence to increased quality of physical and spiritual life. Whereas the initial structure of the church was defined at the top, the fleshing out of auxiliary organizations and programs almost always began as grassroots initiatives in response to unmet local needs. Stated differently, "trickle-up revelation" grew to have a larger role in shaping both the structure and the flavor of the church than did "trickle-down." Indeed, *all* of the auxiliary organizations that flavor today's church—Relief Society, Sunday school, Young Men's Mutual, Young Women's Mutual, and Primary—began as local initiatives that, once successful at the local level, were appropriated by the central church and institutionalized church-wide.

While governance at the local level has changed little since the latter half of the nineteenth century, the central church has undergone a major transformation since 1970. Until this latter period, the church president functioned both as a spiritual leader speaking in a prophetic voice and as the administrative head of an increasingly large and complex organization known legally as the Corporation of the President. The Quorum of the Twelve served only staff functions, with no supervision of auxiliary organizations or departments.

With the death of church president David O. McKay in 1970, the process known as Correlation, which began a decade earlier to coordinate overlapping functions of organizations and eliminate duplication, moved in a new direction that shifted governance increasingly toward the Quorum of the Twelve. The shift was, in part, responsive to the fact that several church presidents, beginning with Heber J. Grant in the early 1940s, underwent periods of failing or failed health that lasted up to five years, during which time the counselors in the First Presidency often chose inaction rather than preempt their ailing leader. Today, nearly all auxiliary organizations and departments are under the direct supervision of one or more designated members of the Quorum of the Twelve, rather than the First Presidency. The church president, while still the chief executive officer of the church, serves primarily in the prophetic role; while the president (senior-tenured member) of the Quorum of the Twelve largely directs the day-to-day administrative functions of the church.

Church ecclesiology consists of a small group of semiprofessional clergy at the top and a large cadre of laity at the bottom. The "semiprofessional" clergy are so named because all come from other professions and are called to full-time—and financially compensated—church service upon the direction of the church president. There is no LDS equivalent of the professional seminaries of other Christian traditions, nor is there a professional ecclesiastical career track.

The First Presidency consists of the church president and two counselors, all drawn from the Quorum of the Twelve, who serve for life. Since the death of Joseph Smith in 1844, and as distinct from what became the much smaller Reorganized Church of Jesus Christ of Latter Day Saints, the senior-tenured apostle has become the new church president when a sitting president has died.

Members of the Quorum of the Twelve, who also serve for life, are generally chosen from the third group of general officers, the Seventy, although on occasion they have come directly from nonecclesiastical vocations. Virtually all elements of the church bureaucracy ultimately report to one or more members of the Quorum of the Twelve.

The Seventy who serve as general officers give full-time church service but do not have lifetime tenure. Most operate from church headquarters in Salt Lake City, while some are deployed to regional church headquarters throughout the world. They function both as line officers who are the link between the local and the central church; and as directors of general church departments and organizations, in each instance reporting to the Quorum of the Twelve.

Throughout its history, the church's local leadership has been laity serving voluntarily and without salary or theological training. The key office is bishop, who presides over a congregation (ward) and is responsible for both the administration of the ward and its component organizations and, more importantly, the spiritual well-being of its members. The bishop is generally chosen at an age when he is at the peak of his professional career, and yet he will often devote as many hours to his church calling as to his profession. While nearly all churchgoing members are asked to serve voluntarily in the various organizations comprising the ward, the week-in, week-out religious life of the typical Latter-day Saint is generally influenced more by his or her bishop than any other church officer, from the blessing of babies (christening), to the baptism of youth, to the marriage of young adults, to the funerals of the deceased.

Two groups of lay volunteers assist the bishop by visiting church members in their homes, ideally once a month, assessing their needs and offering spiritual and temporal guidance and assistance as needed. The Home Teachers are adult and young adult men who are assigned to each family unit within the ward, and the Visiting Teachers are adult women who are assigned specifically to the adult women.

Notes

1. Since the revelation of 1978 that ended the century-plus ban on ordination of males of black African ancestry, which is the subject of chapter 24 in this *Handbook*, priesthood is conferred upon all males of twelve years and older who desire ordination and who are determined by ecclesiastical leaders to be worthy of it.
2. This history, in the manuscript known as "Joseph Smith Letterbook 1," is housed in the LDS Church Library. It was published in Jessee, *Personal Writings of Joseph Smith*, 3–8.
3. The complete text of the revelation is in Faulring, "Examination of the 1829 'Articles,'" 76–79.
4. Aside from ordinances performed in LDS temples, only three in use today—baptism, blessing of bread, and blessing of water for the Sacrament of the Lord's Supper—have prescribed wording, all three of which were described in the Book of Mormon. None of the three uses the word "priesthood." By contrast, prayers in all other ordinances in today's

LDS Church explicitly state that the officiator is acting by virtue of the priesthood that he possesses, generally the Melchizedek Priesthood.

5. Foster et al., *Encyclopedia of the Stone-Campbell Movement*, 653.
6. The initiative, commonly referred to as the "Inspired Version," "New Translation," or "Joseph Smith Translation," is more accurately characterized as a redaction of the King James Bible, for it involved no foreign-language manuscripts of the Bible.
7. Corrill, *Brief History of the Church of Christ of the Latter Day Saints*, chap. 10.
8. "Why Priesthood at All?"
9. A notable example was the attempt to raise from the dead Joseph Brackenbury, an early LDS missionary, in 1832. Newspapers made much of the failure of his fellow missionaries (*Burlington Sentinel* [VT], March 23, 1832; *Wayne Sentinel* [NY], April 11, 1832; *Ohio Star*, April 12, 1832). Two decades later, LDS Church Historian George A. Smith wrote to Brackenbury's widow asking "the circumstances of his death, burial, and attempted resurrection" (Smith to Brackenbury, August 29, 1855).

BIBLIOGRAPHY

Backman, Milton V., Jr. *Joseph Smith's First Vision: The First Vision in its Historical Context*. Salt Lake City: Bookcraft, 1971.

Bushman, Richard L. *Joseph Smith: Rough Stone Rolling*. New York: Alfred A. Knopf, 2005.

Cannon, Donald Q., and Lyndon W. Cook, eds. *Far West Record: Minutes of the Church of Jesus Christ of Latter-day Saints, 1830–1844*. Salt Lake City: Deseret, 1983.

Church Handbook of Instructions. Handbook 2: Administering the Church. Salt Lake City: Church of Jesus Christ of Latter-day Saints, 2010.

Corrill, John. *A Brief History of the Church of Christ of the Latter Day Saints (Commonly Called Mormons): Including an Account of Their Doctrine and Discipline; With the Reasons of the Author for Leaving the Church*. St. Louis: Author, 1839.

Faulring, Scott H. "An Examination of the 1829 'Articles of the Church of Christ' in Relation to Section 20 of the Doctrine and Covenants." *BYU Studies* 43, no. 4 (2004): 57–91.

Foster, Douglas A., Paul M. Blowers, Anthony L. Dunnavant, and D. Newell Williams. *The Encyclopedia of the Stone-Campbell Movement*. Grand Rapids, MI: William B. Eerdmans, 2004.

Hartley, William G. *My Fellow Servants: Essays on the History of the Priesthood*. Provo, UT: Brigham Young University Studies, 2010.

Jessee, Dean C., ed. *The Personal Writings of Joseph Smith*. Salt Lake City: Deseret, 1984.

Jensen, Robin Scott, Robert J. Woodford, and Steven C. Harper, eds. *The Joseph Smith Papers: Revelations and Translations. Volume 1: Manuscript Revelation Books*. Salt Lake City: Church Historian's Press, 2011.

Marquardt, H. Michael. *Early Patriarchal Blessings of the Church of Jesus Christ of Latter-day Saints*. Salt Lake City: Smith-Pettit Foundation, 2001.

Matthews, Robert J. *"A Plainer Translation": Joseph Smith's Translation of the Bible, a History and Commentary*. Provo, UT: Brigham Young University Press, 1975.

Prince, Gregory A. *Power from on High: The Development of Mormon Priesthood*. Salt Lake City: Signature, 1995.

Smith, George A. to Elizabeth Brackenbury, August 29, 1855, Henry Stebbins Collection, P24/F1, Community of Christ Archives, Independence, MO.

Staker, Mark Lyman. *Hearken, O Ye People: The Historical Setting of Joseph Smith's Ohio Revelations*. Salt Lake City: Greg Kofford, 2009.

Van Wagoner, Richard S. *Sidney Rigdon: A Portrait of Religious Excess*. Salt Lake City: Signature, 1994.

"Why Priesthood at All?" *Improvement Era* 34, no. 12 (October 1931): 735.

CHAPTER 13

....

MORMON MISSION WORK

....

REID L. NEILSON

THE history of Christian missions is enjoying a renaissance of popularity among historians and religious studies scholars. By virtue of its size alone, the proselytizing program of the Church of Jesus Christ of Latter-day Saints (hereafter cited as "the church") should be an important field within the discipline. Despite the growing body of literature on Christian missionary work, however, non-Mormon scholars have made almost no effort to integrate the Latter-day Saint evangelistic experience into the larger field of mission studies. Mormon missionary work is the elephant in the mission studies room that is apparent to all but discussed by few.

To complicate matters, most Mormon scholars have written their evangelistic studies in a scholarly vacuum. "Seldom has the study of Latter-day Saint missionary work been put into a broader historical or cultural context. Mormons themselves could learn from the experiences of other Christian missions as could students of Mormon missionary work," historian David J. Whittaker laments in his historiographical survey of Latter-day Saint evangelism.[1] Although hagiographic and devotional missionary chronicles are plentiful, they typically lack historical perspective and a relationship with the larger American missionary community. As a result, the existing articles and book chapter histories of the Mormon missionary experience continue to float outside of the larger historical and academic world. This chapter, then, is designed to flesh out major themes of the Latter-day Saint evangelistic initiative, treating important similarities to and differences from their Protestant counterparts.

The American Protestant foreign missionary enterprise had its beginnings in outreach to the Native Americans during the colonial era. But it would not be until the First Great Awakening that the missionary impulse would play an increasing role in Protestant thought. By the Civil War, American Protestants were evangelizing in the nations of South Asia, Southeast Asia, the Pacific Islands, Latin America, East Asia, the Middle East, Africa, and Catholic Europe. Most Protestant denominations were driven by the sense of American Manifest Destiny, or the notion that American Christians were responsible for not only the salvation of North America but also the entire world.[2]

Like other antebellum American Christians, early Latter-day Saints believed that the resurrected Jesus Christ had commanded his disciples in the Old World to "teach all nations, baptizing them in the name of the Father, and of the Son, and of the Holy Ghost" (Matthew 28:19). Although nearly two millennia had passed since the earliest Christians attempted to meet this obligation, their counterparts in the New World still sought to share the Christian gospel with every nation, kindred, and tongue. The Mormons, despite their poverty, persecution, and eventual displacement to North America's Great Basin region, helped shoulder the ever-present burden of fulfilling the biblical Great Commission. As theological restorationists, in the most literal sense, the Latter-day Saints attempted to recapitulate biblical history. Mormon missionaries saw themselves walking in the footsteps of earlier evangelists like Paul and Timothy.[3]

Latter-day Saints in America shared much of the same Christian worldview as their Protestant colleagues. Millenarianism, for example, influenced the thought and decision making of Mormon leaders and laity alike. In the months leading up to the formal organization of the church in April 1830, Joseph Smith dictated a number of revelations that signaled that end-of-times evangelism would soon play a major role in his new religious movement. In February 1829, for example, he dictated a revelation addressed specifically to his father, Joseph Smith Sr., calling him to preach the gospel (Doctrine and Covenants [D&C] 4). Over the next several years the church's founding prophet dictated similar inspired callings for numerous members of his growing flock. It soon became clear that all baptized members were responsible for spreading the news of the "restoration." Once they were converted they were responsible for warning their neighbors (D&C 88). Latter-day Saints were promised great spiritual blessings, including eternal joy, if they fulfilled their missionary duties and helped save souls (D&C 18). As a result, members of the growing Mormon movement felt the need and desire to share what they believed to be the restitution of primitive Christianity.

During the 1830s and 1840s, while the Latter-day Saints gathered and scattered throughout New York, Ohio, Missouri, and Illinois, Joseph Smith continued to encourage evangelism. New converts, the products of missionary work themselves, embraced their missionary responsibilities and went forth on their own, sharing the good news with their family and friends with no formal missionary training. Although some were called directly to the work by revelation, the vast majority simply opened their mouths and shared their message with anyone who would listen. During these early decades, men continued to engage in their own economic pursuits and occupations, as the church had no paid clergy. They took sabbaticals from their worldly responsibilities and devoted themselves to short preaching tours, relying on the financial generosity of others. These early missions usually lasted for several weeks but sometimes as long as a few months, depending on the time of year and the missionaries' professional obligations.

In his classic study of North American Mormon missionary work, historian S. George Ellsworth labeled this early evangelism model the freelance missionary system. This corps of nonprofessional missionaries preached wherever they could get a hearing. They evangelized in both public and private spaces. Town squares and street corners, as well as barns and cabins, became the sites of Mormon preaching. Untrained by the Protestant divinity schools of the East Coast, they preached a homespun message, noteworthy for its simplicity and biblical underpinnings. Latter-day Saint missionaries typically worked through their existing social networks, approaching family and friends, with whom they already had a tie and, therefore, a better chance of being successful. Nevertheless, these men, like representatives of other Christian faiths, endured the lack of interest and often the antagonism of their audiences. Even so, freelance Mormon missionaries were remarkably successful in antebellum America and Canada.[4]

As the years rolled by, church leaders increasingly called Mormon men to serve specific missions beyond their own neighborhoods and kin. Joseph Smith assigned apostles from his newly created Quorum of the Twelve to evangelize up and down the Eastern seaboard and in Great Britain. (The British Mission soon became the church's largest growth center: at one point there were more church members in western Europe than in North America.) With many of the apostles abroad, by the end of the 1830s members of the Quorum of the Seventy assumed the duty of calling missionaries. Nevertheless, freelance missionaries continued to staff Mormon missionary fields into the 1840s. When the majority of the apostles returned from Great Britain in July 1841, they assumed the Seventy's responsibility to administer the calling of missionaries. From this point on, the number of formally called missionaries grew and the number of self-called freelance missionaries shrank. Even so, both systems of evangelism—freelance and appointed—continued through the Nauvoo, Illinois, period and the martyrdom of Joseph Smith in 1844. By mid-century, over 1500 Latter-day Saints had served full-time missions.[5]

Like other Christian faiths that thrived in, or grew out of, the spiritual hothouse of antebellum America, the church developed its own approach to evangelism, which enabled it to spread beyond its upstate New York origins. Previously, I have labeled this the Euro-American missionary model.[6] Because early Mormon evangelism emerged from a North American and western European historical context, its missionary methods privileged the West over the East. During the church's first century, the Latter-day Saints largely focused their missionary energies on the peoples of the Christian, Western world. They believed that Jesus Christ's original gospel had been lost through apostasy until Joseph Smith restored the primitive church in 1830. As a result, all non-Mormon Christians, perhaps even more than the non-Christian "heathens," were believed to be in dire need of the message of the restoration.

American evangelical Protestants, on the other hand, targeted primarily non-Christians living in non-Western lands. Notable exceptions included Native Americans, Hispanic and Asian immigrants, and the members of domestic religious groups they considered deviant, especially the Mormons in Utah. But these evangelistic endeavors generally fell under the rubric of "home" rather than "foreign" missions. (The dichotomy of "foreign" and "home" missions did not exist in the Mormon worldview. All areas outside of Utah were considered simply the "mission field.") American Protestants enjoyed vast experience proselytizing in the Eastern world, unlike the Latter-day Saints. As a result, they too advanced their own missionary model, one quite distinct from that of their Mormon contemporaries.

Therefore, observers can learn a great deal by comparing six major points of the two groups' missionary models: evangelistic practices, personal backgrounds, roles of women, missionary training, financial arrangements, and human deployment.

To begin with, Latter-day Saints have evangelized differently than their Protestant counterparts, especially when it comes to missionary practices. By the late nineteenth century, the American Protestant foreign missionary enterprise was reeling from internal debate over the propriety of various types of proselytizing initiatives. Conservative Protestants fought to do away with English-language teaching to the natives and other forms of Westernization. They believed that missionaries were sent abroad to teach the Christian gospel, not to transform local cultures into Western enclaves. More liberal American Protestants advocated a reinterpretation of Christian evangelistic practices. They argued that Christianization went hand in hand with civilization and advanced a number of criticisms of mainline missionary work as part of their agenda. During this same era, Latter-day Saints largely focused on preaching Christ, not advancing Western culture, especially not American culture, which they often viewed as the antithesis of their gospel message. Unlike some Protestant missionary organizations, the Latter-day Saints have not typically offered educational or social welfare services in the mission field.[7]

Mormon missionaries spent most of their time tracting, or canvassing neighborhoods and busy streets while handing out printed leaflets or other literature on Latter-day doctrines. They sold or loaned the pamphlets to interested persons and then tried to arrange a teaching meeting to discuss unique Latter-day Saint doctrines. The missionaries also used local newspapers to their advantage, especially since the larger dailies were often the organs of anti-Mormon rhetoric. Church writers penned editorials and explanatory essays to defend their cause and spread their message. They also announced preaching meetings through local broadsides. Mormon elders and sisters held public preaching meetings whenever and wherever they could. They even rented other Christian church buildings to hold large audiences. Some Sundays they showed up at Protestant services and were invited to preach by kind clergymen. But after sharing their message of apostasy and restoration, the Latter-day Saints were rarely invited back. In some cases, the missionaries arranged for spirited debates with other religious leaders to stir up excitement.[8]

Second, the personal backgrounds of Mormon and Protestant missionaries have differed in important ways. American Protestant missionaries were grounded in this world but driven by an otherworldly spiritual cause. Missionary service was an elective exercise for Protestant men and women. Foreign missions were demanding undertakings that required incredible commitment and long-term fortitude. Mission boards carefully screened prospective applicants for deep spirituality and evidence of personal transformation. Candidates shared their powerful moments of conversions in their paper applications to demonstrate that they were qualified for the work. The applicants were also expected to feel a specific sense of evangelistic purpose. They felt compelled to work beyond domestic ecclesiastical opportunities. The Protestant missionary model was traditionally based on self-selection: one felt called by God, not an organization.[9]

In contrast to many American Protestants, most committed Latter-day Saint men have not traditionally viewed evangelism as optional. During the first century of the church, Mormon men were issued unsolicited short-term missionary assignments by church leaders. Those who were "called" to the work were expected to fulfill the assignments regardless of their personal, financial, or physical conditions. They did not participate in the geographic selection or timing of their callings. During the early Utah period, the Mormon missionary system became more routinized and institutionalized. Geographically isolated in Utah from other Americans, church leaders replaced the freelance missionary system with the more organized appointed-missionary system. General authorities began calling missionaries from the pulpit during the church's semiannual General Conferences held in April and October in Salt Lake City. Mormon men were often surprised to hear their names called, but the vast majority responded willingly.

A demographic snapshot helps us better understand the backgrounds of the early Latter-day Saint missionaries. Their ages ranged from twenty to forty-eight, with the average being thirty-five years old. Given their average age, it is no surprise that most of the men were married with children. About a quarter of these men had previously served at least one mission. Although there was no formally set mission length, they served on average for thirty months. Throughout the 1860s, church leaders continued to call missionaries during General Conference, which made the semiannual event a time of great excitement and anxiety for male church members and their families. The average Mormon missionary age increased to thirty-seven during this decade. But most of these men were serving missions for the first time. Male church members increasingly served only one full-time mission during their lifetimes, a change from earlier times when many served multiple assignments.[10]

Elders continued to receive their assignments during General Conference during the 1870s. The length of missionary tenure decreased dramatically to only fourteen months, or less than half the length of the previous decade, easing the burden on family members left at home. The average missionary age increased to forty. During the 1880s, male Latter-day Saints mercifully learned of their missionary assignments by unsolicited letter, rather than the surprise call during General Conference. These calls were issued by apostles assisted by members of a missionary committee. The average age of the missionary dropped to thirty-five. Most were still married men with wives and children. Moreover, the mission length increased to twenty-four months.

By the late nineteenth century, the majority of missionaries came from the ranks of second-generation Latter-day Saints living in Utah. Few had previous evangelizing experience. The length of mission had been unofficially standardized at about twenty-four months. The age had also decreased to an average of thirty years old. Rather than self-selecting as freelance missionaries, or being called to serve during General Conference, or even just receiving an unsolicited letter in the mail like their predecessors, the missionaries of the 1890s were consulted about the possibility of serving a mission by their local ecclesiastical leaders before they were extended formal assignments.

A growing number of single younger men were being called to shoulder the work of the Great Commission.[11]

A related third point of divergence between Mormon and Protestant missionary programs was the role of women. American Protestant boards made space for women evangelists from almost the beginning. The typical female missionary was an unmarried daughter of a large family from the countryside whose chances for marriage were doubtful. Protestant sisters likely had training as a teacher or nurse and desired to use their talents in foreign lands in the service of Christ. By comparison, Mormon sister missionaries have occupied an ambivalent position within Latter-day Saint proselytizing circles, a conundrum they have faced since being allowed to evangelize full-time beginning in 1898. Although unable to officiate in church ordinances like baptism, these female missionaries have nevertheless made remarkable evangelistic contributions.[12]

Not expected to proselytize full-time like their male counterparts, but welcomed into missionary service nonetheless, Mormon women have enjoyed unique experiences, contributions, and challenges that invite thoughtful interpretation. As Tania Rands Lyon and Mary Ann Shumway McFarland point out, there are some important differences that define the female LDS missionary experience: "Women's low numbers relative to men in the mission field are the results of an amazingly effective and self-regulating church policy which discourages women from choosing a mission while simultaneously welcoming those who do and allowing for no desiring missionary to be turned away."[13]

From the earliest days of the church's organization, married women served alongside their husbands in a variety of missionary capacities. Single women likewise shared the good news of the restoration with their families and friends through a variety of means, although the first officially called single sisters were not called as full-time missionaries until 1898, unlike their American Protestant female counterparts who evangelized together with single men throughout the nineteenth century. During the late nineteenth century, it was helpful to have female missionaries in the scattered fields of labor so that non-Mormons could see what Mormon women were actually like, especially during the antipolygamy persecutions. During this same period, a growing number of single sisters desired to serve missions, an opportunity given to their male counterparts.

Beginning in 1898, a small number of sisters were allowed to serve, an innovation that was applauded by many who came to appreciate the value of female missionaries for being able to make inroads where Mormon men were unwelcome. The rhetoric suggested that they were welcome to serve, and were praised in some church periodicals by returning mission presidents who came to appreciate their contributions. At the same time, male church leaders were quick to point out that while sisters were appreciated, missionary work was a priesthood responsibility. Over the years the presence of single sisters became the norm in mission fields, as did their acceptance by those presiding over them. Thus, it remained a "two-track system based on sex" for the missionaries well into the mid-twentieth century. Over the years the church policy regarding age at the time of service and length of service continued to change; but two constants were that women were older than elders when called, and that they served shorter missions than elders. Again, rhetoric from Salt Lake leaders continued to focus on the service of male missionaries and their priesthood responsibilities.[14]

During the Second World War, service in the armed forces depleted the ranks of men available to serve as missionaries; the number of women serving increased accordingly, perhaps to almost 40 percent of the entire missionary workforce. Still, the age of eligibility continued to be older for women than for men. And in the early 1970s, the tenure of sister missionaries dropped from twenty-four months to only eighteen months. The rationale seemed to be that in the late teen years, mission service was the priority for men. As for the women, missionary service was good, but temple marriage and motherhood were better. Unlike all worthy young men who were expected to serve missions, women had to deal with the ambiguity of church policy to make the decision themselves: should they serve missions or not? By the mid-1980s about 20 percent of the Mormon missionary force was made up of single sisters.

Despite the ambivalence and ambiguities surrounding sister missionary service, one thing is clear. Like the men, women who serve missions believe themselves to have been called by revelation and set apart to their missionary responsibilities by priesthood authority. Elders and sisters now begin their missionary service with intensive preparation at one of the seventeen Missionary Training Centers located around the world. When they arrive in their assigned fields of labor, men and women evangelize using the same missionary practices, lesson materials, and designated work schedules, except for the minority of sisters who are assigned to host visitors on Temple Square in Utah, or at other historic sites, or those asked to fulfill humanitarian roles. In short, while single-sister missionaries are slightly older, serve for a shorter period of time, and are not expected to serve full-time missions or perform priesthood ordinances, the daily evangelistic experience of Mormon women and men has become remarkably similar.[15]

In fact, in October 2012, church president Thomas S. Monson made history when he announced in General Conference that the church was lowering the missionary service age for full-time missionaries. Beginning that month, men could now start their missions at age eighteen (one year earlier than before) and women at age nineteen (two years earlier than before). This policy change had an immediate impact on the number of both male and female missionaries. There was an outpouring of interest, causing the church to create a number of new missionary fields of labor. The surge in missionary applications drove up the number of missionaries dramatically, adding tens of thousands of elders and sisters to the missionary ranks of the Latter-day Saints. By 2014, there were more than 80,000 men and women serving full-time missions for the church in more than 400 missions around the world.

Missionary training is a fourth point, which illuminates the difference between the Mormon and Protestant missionary initiatives. Although most of the early luminaries of the Protestant foreign evangelistic enterprise were graduates of prestigious New England divinity schools and universities, the majority of missionaries during the late nineteenth and early twentieth centuries had studied at lesser-known denominational colleges and Bible schools. In contrast, the amateur Latter-day Saint evangelists received informal and narrow preparation. During much of the nineteenth century, church leaders did not provide a training regimen to the thousands of missionaries they assigned around the world. Instead, they expected the elders to learn how to be missionaries as they proselytized. The men learned what they could from more experienced missionaries and asked about evangelism conditions from returning missionaries. Some men prepared informally for their callings by studying the scriptures, practicing preaching, and even learning the basics of their foreign language as they sailed across the oceans to their missions.[16]

Beginning in 1867, church leaders offered more formal theological training through the reestablishment of the School of the Prophets in Salt Lake City. Joseph Smith had arranged this education program in Kirtland, Ohio, and Nauvoo, Illinois, to help train new church leaders and future missionaries. These classes quickly spread throughout Utah, where male members gathered weekly to study Mormon doctrine and discuss church government and administration. Simple preparation for evangelism was also offered, but it never was the main attraction. Brigham Young discontinued the classes in the fall of 1872. Thereafter, missionaries received informal training through the church's auxiliary organizations, including Sunday schools and the Young Men's Mutual Improvement Association. Despite these educational opportunities, the church's mission presidents bemoaned the lack of training their elders received before arriving in the mission field. Few of the evangelists had any higher education, in stark contrast to their coached Protestant colleagues.[17]

Historically, the Mormon elders received most of their training when they reached their mission fields. They learned how to evangelize by watching other missionaries, especially more senior companions and mission leaders. But in some missions, the elders did not always evangelize in pairs, stunting their learning curve. Some studied foreign languages by watching others. There was no formal training at this time. It was all on the job. The elders who lacked language skills were sometimes sent to live with member families who helped them learn the language. Ideally, church leaders paired prospective elders and their language skills, if any, with specific mission fields. For example, during the first century of the church, Danish-speaking missionaries were generally assigned to Denmark, their Swedish-speaking counterparts were usually sent to Sweden, and so on. Due to the massive immigration to Utah of tens of thousands of European converts, the languages of Western Europe did not prove a stumbling block to the Mormon missionary program.[18]

By the late nineteenth century, however, the number of prospective missionaries with native language skills decreased in tandem with the plummeting European immigration. Aware of the problem, church leaders encouraged immigrant converts to teach their children (future missionaries) their native languages. Nevertheless, church leaders did not offer formal missionary training until 1899, when they provided classes at several of the church's educational academies. And these classes focused more on gospel study and the acquisition of social graces and missionary methods than on language training. This limited preparation paled in comparison to the missionary schooling of their Protestant contemporaries at divinity schools and missionary colleges. The church did not offer foreign-language classes to its missionaries until after the Second World War.

A fifth variance between the Mormon and Protestant missionary approaches has been the financial arrangements of their evangelists. The majority of American Protestant missionaries were lifetime salaried professionals. They viewed their calling to the work of proselytizing as both a spiritual avocation and a temporal vocation, and relied on the financial generosity of mission boards and Christian organizations back in America for their support. In contrast, the Mormon elders financed most of their nineteenth-century missions by relying on the New Testament model of traveling without "purse or scrip," meaning evangelizing without cash or personal property (Matthew 10:9–10; Luke 10:4). They relied totally on those they met on a daily basis in their missionary fields. Joseph Smith dictated several revelations encouraging the reestablishment of this practice (D&C 24:18; 84:78). His successor, Brigham Young, was likewise a proponent of this financial arrangement, having served numerous missions to North America and Great Britain, where he relied on the financial generosity of others.[19]

During the movement's early decades, the majority of Mormon missionaries were married, requiring the monetary maintenance of their families left behind. Given the economic circumstances in Utah at the time, this required great sacrifice of wives and children. Although the men were expected to leave their families for several years in the best financial shape possible, many had to rely on the contributions of fellow church members for their survival. Local church leaders were responsible for making sure these missionary families had funds sufficient for their needs. Church leaders created a short-lived Mission Fund in 1860 to help pay for these expenses. Latter-day Saints were encouraged to donate money, food, goods, and clothing for these temporarily fatherless families. In subsequent years, church members cultivated missionary gardens and farms to feed these dependents. By the late nineteenth century, however, unmarried young men were displacing married older men as the church's missionary force, so the need to take care of missionary families diminished.[20]

How Mormons and Protestants have geographically deployed their missionary personnel is a final distinction that needs to be highlighted. American Protestants evangelized almost exclusively in non-Christian, non-Western nations, especially Asia, Africa, and the Near East. The global deployment of Mormon elders and sisters was almost the exact opposite for much of its history. Unlike the Protestants, early Latter-day Saints focused their resources on the Christian, Western world. In theory, the restoration was supposed to be a global religious tradition, a message for all. In reality, its missionary program spread unevenly around the world. During the nineteenth century, Mormon leaders called over 12,000 full-time missionaries. Specifically, they assigned 53 percent of all formally called missionaries to evangelize throughout the United States and Canada and designated 40 percent of laity to missionize in Europe, especially in Great Britain and Scandinavia. Mormon authorities sent the remaining 7 percent of elders and sisters to the peoples of Asia and the Pacific. In short, they allocated an eye-popping 93 percent of their missionaries to the Atlantic world during this era.[21]

The evolution of the Mormon missionary program has been influenced by racial, religious, and logistical concerns. Sociologist Armand Mauss argues that certain LDS theological tenets have focused church missionary efforts toward certain races and peoples, while at the same time diverting resources away from other groups. This worldview evolved in sync with contacts, exchanges, and encounters between Latter-day Saints and other peoples, as well as according to developing scriptural interpretations. Early Mormon evangelists were encouraged to search out the "believing blood" of Israel, the elect, typically those with Anglo-Saxon heritage identified by many Christians as being connected with biblical lineages. During the first century of the restoration, the Mormons enjoyed their greatest successes in the North Atlantic world, where they believed the elect could be readily located and converted. They also felt they had discovered the elect in areas not traditionally connected with biblical lineages, such as Native Americans and Pacific Islanders, whom they linked to Book of Mormon peoples.[22]

It took a major decline in missionary success in the Christian Atlantic world, mixed with a heavy dose of millennialism in Utah, to convince Mormon leaders that it was time to explore evangelism among these other groups. Beginning in the early twentieth century, for instance, Latter-day Saints opened missionary work in East Asia. Although early efforts in Japan saw little success, and the program was ultimately shuttered during the years leading up to and during the Second World War, the church began to experience real growth in Asia during the second half of the twentieth century, especially in Japan, Taiwan, the Philippines, and most recently Mongolia. Although the church sent a handful of missionaries to Latin America, mostly Mexico, during the late nineteenth century, the full-fledged evangelization of Latin America would not begin until the mid-twentieth century, especially as church leaders expanded traditional understandings of "Lehite" blood from that of the Native Americans and Pacific Islanders to those of Latin descent. An explosive number of conversions resulted, convincing the leadership that missionary successes were indeed connected to lineage and spiritual inheritances.

Although Mormon missionaries evangelized white European colonists living in South Africa beginning in the 1850s, they did not do conversion work among the black Africans, who were restricted from holding the priesthood. Church evangelistic priorities changed in 1978, however, when President Spencer W. Kimball announced a change in priesthood policy, which now allowed those of African descent to hold the priesthood and participate in temple rites. Thereafter, Latter-day Saint missionaries enjoyed remarkable success in South Africa and West Africa among blacks, many of whom had waited for the "promised day" to come. In the past three decades, the church in West Africa has become an important growth center. Now a decade into the twenty-first century, Mormon missionaries teach and baptize anyone interested in their mission, regardless of race and perceived scriptural lineage. This shift to a global, color-blind approach to evangelism has had enormous consequences for what was once a primarily white, American church.

In summary, the Mormon missionary model has differed in important ways from the American Protestant evangelistic approach. The Latter-day Saints have historically focused on preaching Christ among Christian peoples, rather than

exporting Christianity and Western culture to non-Western nations. The vast major-
ity of Latter-day Saints labored in the United States, Canada, Great Britain, and
Scandinavia. Conversely, American Protestants served the peoples of the Levant, South
Asia, Africa, and East Asia, who knew little, if anything, of Christ.

Second, unlike the Protestants who operated schools, hospitals, and churches, the
Mormons have tracted, held preaching meetings, engaged in intra-Christian debates,
and contacted prospective converts on the streets. Third, Mormon missionaries, especially by the late nineteenth century, had come from quite homogeneous backgrounds.
The majority were living in Utah when they received their mission calls and most had
no formal schooling beyond secondary education. American Protestants, on the other
hand, hailed from across the Northeast and Midwest, representing numerous denominations. While LDS women did not formally evangelize until 1898, Protestant females
constituted a major force within the foreign missionary enterprise. Fourth, while sister
missionaries are older, serve for a shorter period of time, and are not expected to serve
full-time missions or perform priesthood ordinances like their male counterparts, the
daily evangelistic experience of Mormon women and men have become remarkably
similar.

That Mormon elders have been historically sent on their missions with little if any
missionary training was a fifth major difference. While some attended theological
classes before departing, most learned how to be missionaries once they arrived in
their fields, in intensive on-the-job-training. In contrast, most Protestant men and
women enjoyed the benefits of higher education. Nearly all received formal missionary training through their mission boards before leaving the country. Sixth, Mormon
missionaries were short timers in their fields of labor, usually staying about two
years before returning to their prior vocations. For much of the nineteenth century
they traveled without purse or scrip. These amateurs and their families eventually
had to pay much of the cost of their voluntary missionary service. By contrast, their
Protestant counterparts often committed the balance of their lives to further the
cause of Christ. These professionals were financed through mission board fundraising activities back in America.

Clearly, the Latter-day Saints have developed a unique method of evangelism, which
historically grew out of a Protestant North American and western European historical
context. The Mormons' Anglocentric missionary approach enabled them to enjoy grand
success in the United States and Canada, as well as in Great Britain, Scandinavia, and
parts of continental Europe. Their mode of evangelism and theological claims to be the
heirs of primitive Christianity fired the imagination of prospective converts already sat-
urated in biblical culture. The church that started with six members in 1830 ballooned to
over 271,000 by the beginning of the twentieth century, largely as a result of aggressive
missionary work.

By the opening of the twenty-first century, that number would grow to over ten million members. This entrenched pattern of evangelism, however, has paradoxically
hampered Mormon missionary efforts in non-Christian, non-Western nations. Their
emphasis on converting other Euro-Americans, at the expense of Asians, Africans, and

Latinos, had an unintended consequence: until recently, Mormons have struggled to adapt their approach to non-Christian, non-Western audiences. It would not be until after the Second World War, and the true beginnings of Mormon globalization, that church leaders and missionaries would substantially retool their missionary model for their varied international investigators. As a result, the church accelerated its enormous growth around the world, led by its evangelization efforts. Nevertheless, the Latter-day Saints will continue to learn how to and wrestle over how much to accommodate foreign cultures in places like Africa.

Young Mormon elders and sisters, dressed in white shirts and dark suits or conservative dresses, have become the public face of the church in the twenty-first century. On June 25, 2007, Mormon leaders gathered at the Missionary Training Center in Provo, Utah, to celebrate an evangelistic milestone. Just over 175 years since Joseph Smith's brother, Samuel, first set out to proselytize with a knapsack filled with copies of the Book of Mormon, the *one millionth* Mormon missionary was beginning his two-year service. He joined the other 53,000 full-time young men and young women who were then evangelizing in the church's 350 missions around the world.

Yet the 2007 Latter-day Saint evangelistic landmark and its implications for religions in America and abroad remains one of the most unremarked developments in historical and religious studies. "There is no other religious denomination in the world—Catholic, Protestant, or non-Christian—whose full-time evangelizing force is even close in size to that recruited, trained, and supported by the LDS Church," sociologists Gary Shepherd and Gordon Shepherd point out.[23] As such, the study of Mormon missiology need not—and should not—continue to fall between the cracks of "traditional" Christian mission histories.

Notes

1. Whittaker, "Mormon Missiology," 466.
2. Hutchison, *Errand to the World*, 15–42.
3. Shipps, *Mormonism*, 54–58.
4. Ellsworth, "History of Mormon Missions in the United States and Canada," chap. 5.
5. Hughes, "Profile of the Missionaries," 5–7.
6. Neilson, *Early Mormon Missionary Activities in Japan*.
7. Hutchison, *Errand to the World*, 138–45.
8. Hughes, "Profile of the Missionaries," 88–99.
9. Rabe, "Evangelical Logistics," 70–83.
10. Hughes, "Profile of the Missionaries," 175–80.
11. Ibid., 177–85.
12. Madsen, "Mormon Missionary Wives in Nineteenth Century Polynesia."
13. Lyon and McFarland, "Not Invited, But Welcome," 71–72.
14. Ibid., 72–76.
15. Ibid., 78–99.

16. Rabe, "Evangelical Logistics," 74–75.
17. Hughes, "Profile of the Missionaries," 37–41.
18. Ibid., 41–46.
19. Wierenga, "Financial Support of Foreign Missions," 343–46.
20. Hughes, "Profile of the Missionaries," 49–56.
21. Irving, *Numerical Strength and Geographical Distribution of the LDS Missionary Force*, 9–15.
22. Mauss, "In Search of Ephraim."
23. Shepherd and Shepherd, *Mormon Passage*, 9.

BIBLIOGRAPHY

Carpenter, Joel A., and Wilbert R. Shenk, eds. *Earthen Vessels: American Evangelicals and Foreign Missions, 1880–1980.* Grand Rapids, MI: William B. Eerdmans, 1990.

Ellsworth, S. George. "A History of Mormon Missions in the United States and Canada, 1830–1860." PhD diss., University of California at Berkeley, 1951.

Hughes, William E. "A Profile of the Missionaries of the Church of Jesus Christ of Latter-day Saints, 1849–1900." Master's thesis, Brigham Young University, 1986.

Hutchison, William R. *Errand to the World: American Protestant Thought and Foreign Mission.* Chicago: University of Chicago Press, 1987.

Irving, Gordon. *Numerical Strength and Geographical Distribution of the LDS Missionary Force, 1830–1974.* Salt Lake City: Historical Department of the Church of Jesus Christ of Latter-day Saints, 1975.

Kunz, Calvin S. "A History of Female Missionary Activity in The Church of Jesus Christ of Latter-day Saints, 1830–1898." Master's thesis, Brigham Young University, 1976.

Lyon, Tania Rands, and Mary Ann Shumway McFarland. " 'Not Invited, But Welcome': The History and Impact of Church Policy on Sister Missionaries." *Dialogue: A Journal of Mormon Thought* 36, no. 3 (Fall 2003): 71–101.

Madsen, Carol Cornwall. "Mormon Missionary Wives in Nineteenth Century Polynesia." *Journal of Mormon History* 13 (1986–87): 61–85.

Mauss, Armand L. *All Abraham's Children: Changing Mormon Conceptions of Race and Lineage.* Urbana: University of Illinois Press, 2003.

Mauss, Armand L. "In Search of Ephraim: Traditional Mormon Conceptions of Lineage and Race." *Journal of Mormon History* 25 (Spring 1999): 131–73.

Neilson, Reid L. *Early Mormon Missionary Activities in Japan, 1901–1924.* Salt Lake City: University of Utah Press, 2010.

Price, Rex Thomas, Jr. "The Mormon Missionary of the Nineteenth Century." PhD diss., University of Wisconsin Madison, 1991.

Rabe, Valentin H. "Evangelical Logistics: Mission Support and Resources to 1920." In *The Missionary Enterprise in China and America*, ed. John K. Fairbank, 56–90. Cambridge, MA: Harvard University Press, 1974.

Shenk, Wilbert R., ed. *North American Foreign Mission, 1810–1914: Theology, Theory, and Policy.* Grand Rapids, MI: William B. Eerdmans, 2004.

Shepherd, Gary, and Gordon Shepherd. *Mormon Passage: A Missionary Chronicle.* Urbana: University of Illinois Press, 1998.

Shipps, Jan. *Mormonism: The Story of a New Religious Tradition*. Urbana: University of Illinois Press, 1985.

Wierenga, Richard S. "The Financial Support of Foreign Missions." In *Lengthened Cords: A Book about World Missions in Honor of Henry J. Evenhouse*, ed. Roger S. Greenway, 335–57. Grand Rapids, MI: Baker Book House, 1975.

Whittaker, David J. "Mormon Missiology: An Introduction and Guide to the Sources." In *The Disciple as Witness: Essays on Latter-day Saint History and Doctrine in Honor of Richard Lloyd Anderson*, ed. Stephen D. Ricks, Donald W. Parry, and Andrew H. Hedges, 459–538. Provo, UT: FARMS, 2000.

CHAPTER 14

THE MORMON TEMPLE AND MORMON RITUAL

JAMES E. FAULCONER

As of mid-2015, the Church of Jesus Christ of Latter-day Saints had 144 operating temples, a more than sevenfold increase since 1981, when there were twenty—itself almost double the number in 1961, when there were twelve. The number of temples built is only a rough-and-ready guide to the number of people participating in temple worship, but it appears that though formal, ritualized worship has rapidly declined in the West, it has rapidly increased among Mormons. This increase is especially odd given the extremely informal character of Mormon weekly worship: Mormons attend a set of weekly Sunday services in which there is virtually no formal liturgy apart from the Lord's Supper; yet they also go to the temple, though not necessarily on a weekly basis, where they participate in a highly formalized liturgy.

To provide a basis for reflecting on LDS temple worship I will give an overview of the temple and its ritual. Mormon temples differ from other ecclesiastical buildings in that they are used exclusively for sacred, participatory rituals rather than weekly worship, preaching, and instruction. Mormons who enter temples do so to perform these rituals.

In principle there is only one temple rite, but as it exists now it has been divided into four parts that are performed separately.[1] I assume they have been separated to make it easier for people to take part, since it would take several hours to do all of the ritual at one time. Logically the first part is baptism for the remission of sins and the laying on of hands for the gift of the Holy Ghost. These are done for the living outside the temple, prior to taking part in temple worship, so in the temple these ordinances are done by proxy for the dead (preferably for one's own ancestors). These may be performed by any member of the LDS Church over the age of twelve, but they are usually done by adolescents, who are not allowed to perform the other parts of the temple ritual. (As a rule, one must be eighteen to do so.) The result is that adults infrequently take part in proxy baptisms or laying on of hands for the gift of the Holy Ghost, except as officiators.

The next part of the ritual is the initiatory ordinance, a symbolic washing and anointing, and the gift of the garment. Many things have been said about the sacred garment that Mormons wear under their ordinary clothing, much of it exaggerated. For Mormons, the locus for understanding the meaning of the garment is Genesis 3 and the parallel Mormon scripture, Moses 4 (in the Pearl of Great Price). When Adam and Eve were driven from the Garden, God dressed them in coats of skins to cover their nakedness (Genesis 3:21; Moses 4:27). The garment symbolizes those coats. Thus it symbolizes the promise that God will not leave his children forsaken, that though they wander in the world, they will finally be redeemed. Garments offer spiritual protection, reminders of temple worship and of the covenants Mormons make as part of that worship. Those familiar with other forms of religious clothing, such as the Catholic devotional scapular or the *tzitzit* of some Jews will understand that Mormon garments are similar.

The third part of the ritual is what Mormons refer to as "the endowment," the part of the rite most often associated with temple worship. It is a participatory enactment of the story of Creation, Adam and Eve in the Garden of Eden, the Fall, mortal life, resurrection, and entrance into God's presence. The cosmological significance of this part of temple worship is obvious. Mormons reenact the creation of the world and the origin of humanity, as well as its divine destiny, each time they engage in temple worship, and they look forward to a future made possible by God.

Andrew Ehat has described the endowment as "a staged representation of the step-by-step ascent into the presence of the Eternal,"[2] and many Mormons will talk about it in those terms. But the temple rite is more than a *representation* of that ascent. Like Pentecostals, when Mormons talk reflectively about sacred rites, they tend to describe them as something done merely in remembrance. Yet also like Pentecostals, Mormons expect to encounter the Spirit in their communal worship.[3] David O. McKay, a mid-twentieth-century LDS prophet, recognized that expectation when he said that the endowment "is the step-by-step ascent into the Eternal Presence,"[4] rather than only a representation of that ascent. In principle, in Mormon experience temple worship is an encounter with God. Thus, after completing the endowment, a person enters the celestial room, a bright room with couches and chairs intended for contemplation and meditation. No rituals are performed there and reverent quiet is the expectation.

In the celestial room celebrants assume that they can enter into the presence of God by receiving, as promised in Doctrine and Covenants (D&C) 109:15, "a fulness of the Holy Ghost." But Mormon scripture also suggests another possible experience of God in the temple. The dedicatory prayer for the first Mormon temple, that in Kirtland, Ohio, asks "that thy holy presence may be continually in this house" (D&C 109:12). And in a revelation received by Joseph Smith in that temple, a revelation in which Christ appears to him and to Oliver Cowdery, Christ says "I will manifest myself unto my people in mercy in this house" (D&C 110:7). This promise, made in a direct revelation of Christ himself, can be read as opening the possibility of a similar revelation for those who take part in the temple ceremonies. There are few records of any such encounters, but the son of Lorenzo Snow tells of his father having seen Christ in the Salt Lake City Temple.[5] Mormons are counseled not to discuss such experiences broadly,[6] so the absence of records of them says little about their frequency. Many Mormons believe that a direct revelation of God is possible in the temple, even if uncommon.

Participants in the temple ritual begin dressed all in white, and as they move through the ritual ascent, they don various articles of clothing with ritual meaning. No titles but "brother" and "sister" are used. No distinction is made among those who take part—except for things that distinguish men and women (such as dresses and pants) and, more significantly, except for women sitting on one side of the room and men on the other. As Kathleen Flake notes, "the LDS temple ritual suspends all distinctions except the one which it wishes to ritualize, namely gender."[7] That separation is overcome when celebrants enter into the celestial room, where men and women are not divided and can mingle together in meditation.

The crowning ordinance of the temple, the fourth part, which completes the previous parts, is the "sealing" ceremony, or marriage for eternity. The ritual of the temple is not formally complete until that sealing has been performed. After it has been performed, the distinction between man and woman, denoted by their separation in the earlier parts of the rite, is no longer just overcome, as it is in the celestial room. Rather than remaining a difference merely overcome in a kind of neutrality, with marriage the ritualized male-female difference is made productive, bringing the woman and the man together as an eternal unit. This new Adam and this new Eve are promised the possibility of being sealed to one another eternally as husband and wife, potentially a king and a queen in God's kingdom. In principle they are now one rather than two, but that one is complex rather than atomistic. This new unit is neither male nor female, but eternally male *and* female.

Temple worship is not something one celebrates merely as an individual, nor is its meaning something one can understand merely in individualistic terms. As Edward Casey points out, the commemoration of ritual "has to do with overcoming the separation from which otherwise unaffiliated individuals suffer. Still more radically, commemoration suggests that such separation is a sham. If it is true that 'to be is to participate,' the beings who participate cannot be atomic entities. . . . The commemorators are already deeply conjoined, bonded at the most profound level."[8] At the height of the temple ritual is a rite conjoining and bonding male and female at the most profound level.

The unity of this new conjunction of male and female, in which neither defines the whole by itself, is implicitly described in Doctrine and Covenants 121: "The powers of heaven cannot be controlled nor handled only upon the principles of righteousness. That they may be conferred upon us, it is true; but when we undertake to cover our sins, or to gratify our pride, our vain ambition, or to exercise control or dominion or compulsion upon the souls of the children of men, in any degree of unrighteousness, behold, the heavens withdraw themselves" (D&C 121:36–37). The promise of Mormon scripture is that the relationship established on this principle of nondomination will bring the man-woman into the presence of God, where "The Holy Ghost shall be thy constant companion, and thy scepter an unchanging scepter of righteousness and truth; and thy dominion shall be an everlasting dominion, and without compulsory means it shall flow unto thee forever and ever" (D&C 121:46).

Latter-day Saints believe that children born to those who have been sealed in the temple are also sealed to their parents. They are said to be "born in the covenant."

Those children not born in the covenant can be sealed to their parents in a ceremony very much like the marriage ritual. Sealings, like the other temple rituals, are done for both the living and, by proxy, for deceased ancestors. Theologically the point of sealing, whether of husbands and wives or of children and parents, is to bring all humankind who will into one large and eternal family: the children of Abraham ("in thee shall all the families of the earth be blessed" [Genesis 12:3]); the family of God.

Mormons do these temple rites once for themselves, and then again on behalf of specific dead persons whenever they return to the temple. There is no set expectation for temple attendance, though there is an unwritten expectation that worthy members will participate in temple worship at least once a month if they are near enough to a temple to make that possible. Mormons say that those who have been through this ritual ascent have "received" their endowment, and they speak of participation in temple ritual as "doing temple work."

If asked about the temple ritual, Mormons are likely to say that it is "sacred not secret." Though that way of talking about temple worship is understandable, it is unintentionally inaccurate. LDS scripture says "That which cometh from above is sacred, and must be spoken with care, and by constraint of the Spirit" (D&C 63:64). Mormons understand the temple rite from that perspective, as something that comes from above. So the temple ritual is secret *because* it is sacred: it is sacred in that it is a knowledge set apart from other kinds of knowledge and treated differently; it is secret in that temple and other kinds of knowledge differ at least in that the former is not to be revealed to the uninitiated.[9]

The fact that the temple ritual is an almost exclusively oral ritual marks the difference between the two kinds of knowledge: though the ritual is part of the Mormon canon, it is not available in written form. Those leading the ritual as well as its celebrants must repeat it from memory.[10] In principle, putting something to writing makes it public. Insisting that the temple ritual remain oral contributes to its esoteric character.

Secrecy and orality also change the character of the ritual. As Edward Casey points out, the stability of writing encourages those who take up the written word to do so relatively passively, while "ritual is action-oriented and may even lack [as it does for Mormons] any specific form of notation."[11] Because Mormons are prohibited from speaking of the temple ritual outside the temple, except in general terms, and because even within the temple participants do not rely on the written word, temple ritual does not have the stability of writing. Instead, its stability comes from the repetition of the acts by those taking part. That underscores the participatory character of the rites. We should expect, then, that the experience of the person engaged in temple ritual tends more toward an active, first-person experience than a more passive, third-person one.

Because of the esoteric character of the temple rite and because anyone going into the temple is there either to take an active part in its rites or to officiate in doing so (there are no spectators nor is the temple available for meditation only), those who are not Mormon are not allowed to enter the temple after it has been dedicated. In fact, Latter-day Saints may not enter unless they have obtained a recommendation of worthiness from their ecclesiastical leader. In other words, only those who will be taking part in the ritual are allowed to enter the temple. Given the secrecy enjoined on celebrants and the practice of allowing only certain people to take part in temple worship, Mormons clearly distinguish "between the holy and profane" (Ezekiel 22:26), marking the former with sacred space, exclusion, silence, clothing, and ritual.

With some regularity ordinary members of the LDS Church as well as its leaders (for example, Sylvia H. Allred in a 2008 General Conference of the church[12]) speak of the temple as a place of learning. LDS scripture describes it that way: the temple is "a place of instruction for all those who are called to the work of the ministry" (D&C 97:13). In Doctrine and Covenants 76, God says of those who serve him:

> Great shall be their reward and eternal shall be their glory. And to them will I reveal all mysteries, yea, all the hidden mysteries of my kingdom from days of old, . . . And their wisdom shall be great, and their understanding reach to heaven; . . . For by my Spirit will I enlighten them, and by my power will I make known unto them the secrets of my will—yea, even those things which eye has not seen, nor ear heard, nor yet entered into the heart of man. . . . But great and marvelous are the works of the Lord, and the mysteries of his kingdom which he showed unto us, which surpass all understanding in glory, and in might, and in dominion; which he commanded us we should not write . . . and are not lawful for man to utter; . . . (D&C 76:6–10, 114–15).

Mormons understand that prophecy to include the temple in its fulfillment. And the temple is a place in which to learn "things which have been kept hidden from before the foundation of the world" (D&C 124:41).

What are the things kept hidden that those engaged in temple worship learn? Brigham Young described the endowment as providing "all those ordinances in the House of the Lord, which are necessary . . . to enable you to walk back to the presence of the Father, passing the angels who stand as sentinels, being enabled to give them the key words, the signs and tokens, pertaining to the Holy Priesthood, and gain your eternal exaltation."[13] The ritual performances learned and the covenants made make it possible to return to God. Though many contemporary Mormons may not understand the "key words, the signs, and tokens" as literally as did Young, they continue to understand the temple rite as enabling them "to walk back to the presence of the Father," both now and in the hereafter.

As education in returning to the Father, the LDS temple rite is best understood if one understands that Mormons—to some degree like the Eastern Orthodox and Wesleyan traditions—understand salvation in terms of partaking in the divine nature (2 Peter 1:4) rather than only in terms of the removal of sin, atonement.[14] Of course, there is no participation in divine life without the atonement. Though the difference between the two views often goes unremarked, it is dramatic and affects the way those in each group understand the other. For some Christians salvation means justification, God's judgment that the individual is no longer under condemnation. For Mormons and others, it means coming to live the life made possible by God (which includes no longer being under condemnation). The LDS temple ritual is best understood as ritually making divine life possible.

However, as is true for other sacramental rites, what is taught in the temple is not theoretical or theological knowledge. Nathan Mitchell notes that sacraments "cannot be reduced to a single grand design, pattern, or rubric."[15] This is equally true of the Mormon temple rites. There is no instruction in beliefs. Those taking part are not required "to believe or disbelieve an ideology."[16] There is nothing that most people would immediately recognize as instruction in divine life; the Mormon temple rite is nothing like a classroom. If anything, it is more like a theater. The instruction that occurs in the temple ritual happens through participation in it: temple ritual incarnates religion in bodily practices. As Jennifer Lane says "through the ordinances we participate in a way of being that we are becoming."[17]

That replacement of theoretical and theological knowledge with the knowledge gained in bodily action reflects the Mormon understanding of religion, that it is incarnate in practices more than in beliefs. Of course beliefs are important to Mormons. But beliefs are important as integral to practices rather than as undergirding them.[18] The practices of the temple rite and the practices to which a celebrant covenants herself are the apogee of Mormon worship and religious life.

Recall that the ritual of the endowment centers on a participatory retelling of the story of Creation, the Garden of Eden, the Fall, and life in mortality. Though it is important to recognize that there is no one theory or explanation of ritual,[19] studies in memory, ritual, and narrative offer a way of understanding this retelling.

If we think of memory merely as recollection, as we usually do, then it will seem strange to understand the ritual repetition of the biblical story of Creation and the human Fall as a form of memory. But Casey[20] and others, such as Mitchell,[21] distinguish commemoration, a category under which we can easily include the Mormon temple ritual, from simple recollection, like remembering to buy bread on the way home from work. For such thinkers, in commemoration we remember something specific *with* others, whatever we recollect as individuals. In commemoration we remember by doing something together; memorializing occurs in the acts of the group rather than in the particular psychological states of those taking part.

Barbara DeConcini says that this kind of memory "conveys the re-calling or re-presenting of something not as absent but as presently operative by its effects."[22] Memorializing memory occurs in the effects of the memorial's actions. Further, Casey says "It is almost as if the absence of recollection on my part—and doubtless that of other individuals—was somehow being compensated for by an activity that occurred at the level of the group"[23]—in DeConcini's terms, by the effects wrought in the group. Casey gives the example of his participation in a Memorial Day observance, arguing that he does not remember those being memorialized who died in the wars because he knew none of them. Nevertheless, even in the absence of specific recollections, memorialization—com-memoration, "remembering together"—occurs.[24] Casey's understanding of commemoration, supplemented by DeConcini's reflections, is directly relevant to understanding what Mormons do in their temple ritual.

Casey's observations lead him to conclude that commemorative acts have four formal features: they are acts of reflection, they allude to the event commemorated, they involve bodily action, and they require collective participation. Further, commemorative acts have three structural features: they are solemn, they memorialize, and they perdure.[25] The three structural features are easy to see in Mormon temple worship: the rites are solemn, they memorialize the events that lay the groundwork for the Christian understanding of the need for salvation, and they have continued through time. What remains is to see how they are acts of reflection and what the bodily action and communal participation that we have seen are central to the temple rite look like through the lens of Casey's thought.

Mormons talk about the temple as a place of learning makes clear that Mormons understand what happens there as reflective, and the temple ritual's reenactment of the story of the first several chapters of Genesis makes it clear that the rite alludes to the commemorated event, namely the creation of the world, including human beings. Mormon reflections on the temple ritual can produce any number of possible results. For example, the story of God's creation of the world may cause a participant to reflect on the movement of human existence from chaos to order, perhaps as the movement from sin to justification, through God's intervention in the world. Thinking about the story of Adam and Eve, and the command that they procreate, might bring someone to understand that significance comes to human sexuality, and by inference also other human relations and practices, only through the symbolic, something ultimately given by and related to God.

Or recalling that only as Adam and Eve are cast out of the Garden of Eden are they told that they are like the Gods (see Genesis 3:22), someone taking part in the endowment rite may wonder what it means that only outside the garden, in the world as we know it, are human beings like the Divine. A person reflecting on her temple worship might think about the Fall and come to understand that only if man and woman are brought together in a permanent relationship can human beings be in the presence of God. Marriage sealing and sealings to children are essential to life in His presence. Mere individuals, those unsealed to an eternal family as either parent or child, whether male or female, are cut off from that presence. Relation to God is inescapably social—as is temple worship itself.

However, reflection, as important and fulfilling as it can be for the individual, is not the heart of the temple rite. More important is what happens in the physical, collective reenactment of the journey from the beginnings of creation to mortal existence after the Garden of Eden and then into the presence of the Father. As DeConcini remarks, ritual remembering "is not simply an interior state of mind but is enacted by a community, and . . . this activity involves, among other things, telling stories."[26] Those participating in Mormon temple worship do not merely hear the story told in the ritual or watch someone ritually reenact it. They take part in the reenactment, moving from place to place, performing specified actions as part of the story. Ritual participants memorialize Adam and Eve and the founding events of the Christian human narrative by reenacting the story of Creation, Garden, Fall, and life in the world.

Silvia Pierosara has argued "that the construction of self-relation is narratively organized,"[27] and Casey helps us understand the role that participation and bodily action can play in that narrative organization. We can surmise that participation in the temple narrative gives identity to its participants: by their physical participation in the rite celebrants can be imagined to say "We are the new Adam and the new Eve." As DeConcini says, in ritual "we re-member who we are," and this enacted remembering "requires of the believing community not a denial of the critical perspective out of which our history / fiction distinctions arise, but a recollecting of ourselves beyond critical thinking, an imaginative and faithful remembering which opens us up to a second naiveté."[28] Having ritually become Adam or Eve, each celebrant finds himself or herself identified in a symbolic order given by the Father and mediated by the Son, an ordering of not just individual lives, but of the cosmos and the community, as directed by and toward God.

That symbolic order makes the second naïveté possible for temple ritual celebrants. Participants in the temple rite recognize who they are individually and together, and they recognize the significance of who they are: "We are those who are walking on the path toward God." The result of participation in temple ritual is a being-one-with God and the church. This self- and community- and God-recognition provides material for reflection, but through its effects it also gives new *pre*reflective meaning to the world of celebrants. It gives them a new identity. The temple provides a meaning for the world from which all other meanings can be understood and judged. It changes the way those who take part in it see their lives and the world they live in.

The celebrant acts out the story and, returning to the temple to do proxy work for the dead, acts it out again and again, doing the ritual for others and becoming more and more ingrained in its celebration. In doing so he lives and relives the founding story that makes sense of human life.[29] The celebrant ties the memorialized past of Adam and Eve to his present, making that present into something new through the memorialized link.

It may be tempting to understand this memorializing as the repetition of a merely mythic, nonhistorical event. But consider a similar case. Brevard Childs has argued that it is important to Judaism that there *was* an Exodus, however much its retelling may have been shaped by historical, political, social, and liturgical needs: "For Israel the structure of reality was historical in character and not mythical."[30] Similarly, though Mormon belief will seem naïve in the negative sense to most contemporary intellectuals, it is important to Mormons that there were persons whom we call Adam and Eve who in some sense did what they are portrayed as doing in the temple ritual. The memorialization of a real event in the past is the vehicle for a present encounter with the Divine.

In that encounter Mormon temple worshipers relate the significance of those real events to the reality of their own lives: there was a real original couple who fell and made Jesus's death necessary, and the celebrant finds her life—past, present, and future—defined by that real fall and real atonement and by the real possibility of return to the presence of God as a family.

Again, a comparison of Mormonism with Judaism is helpful. Childs says: "Israel's memory functions to assure the proper celebration of the Sabbath by remembering the nature of the Sabbath in Egypt at the time of the Exodus. Memory has a critical function of properly relating the present with the past."[31] If DeConcini is right that ritual takes us "beyond critical thinking," Childs's argument is that such a beyond does not mean an absence of or disconnect from critical thought. To be sure, ritual celebration connected to a past cannot be simply reduced to the usual categories of history and fiction. Critical thought which tries to force ritual commemoration into one of those possibilities fails because it does not understand the character of ritual thought. But as Casey's analysis of memory shows us, the fact that ritual commemoration remembers a purportedly historical rather than a mythical event does not mean that its only critical options are to choose between history and fiction.

The Mormon commemoration of Adam and Eve serves a critical function similar to the Jewish celebration of the Sabbath or of Passover: it recalls to its participants events in history that define who they are and how they should be in the world, and it does so by putting those events into a narrative of self- and communal-identity that is ordered by God. Remembering the past of the Creation and the Fall serves to assure that celebrants will live in the world in the ways required by the order of Creation and Fall.

Taking part in the temple ritual, the celebrant becomes part of the divine narrative, no longer merely an individual cut off from God. His or her new present is linked to the hoped for and promised future when, as part of a couple and a larger, eternally linked community, they will stand in the presence of God. As is true for most Christians, that future is not simply some cataclysmic end of time and history. It "is rather the fulfillment of what has happened in time"[32] and it opens a new, real future for the Mormon worshiper, both now and in the hereafter.

Mormons seldom envision life in the hereafter as timeless. Instead, it is an unending time in which they will accomplish things. For example, Brigham H. Roberts says: "How very plain it is when we once learn about our future heaven. . . . How inconsistent to look for a heaven beyond space! The heaven of the Saints is something we can look forward to in the confident hope of realizing our inheritances and enjoying them forever, when the earth becomes sanctified and made new."[33] Contemporary Mormons are often less sure than their predecessors about what will be done in the hereafter, but they are no less sure that it is a real and ongoing future rather than a timeless eternity. Worshipping in the temple, the past, present, and future are tied together into a meaningful whole for the celebrant.[34]

There may sometimes be an emotional affect to participation in temple worship, but the affect of temple worship does not appear to be intentionally emotional. Instead, its affect has to do with "its *power to create receptivity in the community that uses it.*"[35] One can easily understand that being together for an hour or so, wearing the same clothing, and doing the same things in a ritual that focuses on the nature of human existence and its purposes is likely to make those who take part more receptive to a feeling of unity. An emotional affect might be expected. But for the Mormon taking part in temple worship, considerably more is going on than that. Central to temple worship is covenant making. The rites of the temple are the medium through which celebrants are made ready to receive the covenants enmeshed in those rites and to accept the complex unity they imply as the central structural feature of reality.

Describing the covenants made in temple worship, James E. Talmage, an early twentieth-century apostle of the LDS Church, said celebrants covenant: "to observe the law of strict virtue and chastity, to be charitable, benevolent, tolerant and pure; to devote both talent and material means to the spread of truth and the uplifting of the [human] race; to maintain devotion to the cause of truth; and to seek in every way to contribute to the great preparation that the earth may be made ready to receive her King,—the Lord Jesus Christ."[36] The covenants made during temple worship's reenactment of individual and communal salvation history are central to its affect. Embedded in the narrative of the rite, the covenants of temple worship give that narrative its fundamental meaning. Childs has said, "Memory serves to link the present commandments as events with the covenant history of the past."[37] That describes well how Mormons understand the covenants they make in the temple: those covenants and commandments link them to the covenant history of the past, from Adam and Eve to the present. In temple ritual the covenants become part of the divine history and define the divine future.

Walter Brueggemann has said that covenant is "an enduring commitment by God and his people based on mutual vows of loyalty and mutual obligation through which both parties have their lives radically affected and empowered."[38] Indeed on a Christian understanding, the teaching of the Old Testament is that the covenant established with Abraham was intended to solve the problem of human mortality and sin: "God has in principle solved that problem with the establishment of this covenant."[39] Throughout the Old Testament the covenants that God's people make with him identify them as his people. Israel is told that its bounds will be set by God and that it should make no covenants with anyone other than God (for example, Exodus 23:31–32). Equally so, those taking part in temple worship are expected to find their lives "radically affected and empowered" by the covenants they make: a new identity for both them and those they are among; new relations to each other; new relations to God; and new, exclusive obligations to the LDS Church and to God.

Like Jews—and without believing that they have taken the place of the Jews in God's covenant—Mormons understand themselves to be God's people, and the covenants of the temple rite give them an understanding of what that requires, an understanding of both the bounds of "modern Israel" (a name by which Mormons, like others, sometimes describe themselves) and the binding of the members of that community.

Throughout the Old Testament, God identifies himself as a covenant maker and covenant keeper by calling himself "the God of Abraham, the God of Isaac, and the God of Jacob" (for example, Exodus 4:5).[40] The covenants God makes identify him as God: he is the Being who has made covenant with Abraham and Abraham's heirs. Equally, the covenants he has made with Israel identify who they are: "I have surely seen the affliction of my people" (Exodus 3:7) and, in contrast, "I was wroth with my people, I have polluted mine inheritance, and given them into thine hand" (Isaiah 47:6): Israel is the nation with whom God has covenanted. In the Book of Mormon, Israel is specifically referred to as the covenant people: "O ye Gentiles, have ye remembered the Jews, mine ancient covenant people?" (2 Nephi 29:5). The covenant making of temple worship brings Latter-day Saints into that covenant people.

Imbibing the symbolic order given by temple worship's commemoration of the Creation, the story of Adam and Eve, and the eschatological end-time, Mormons understand their celebration of temple rites in terms of covenant: participants bind themselves to God, to the Church of Jesus Christ of Latter-day Saints, and to each other through the covenants they make, and they give significance to their own and human history by doing so. They are the people who have made those covenants, as their sacred garment constantly but secretly testifies to them, and he is the God whom they recognize and pledge to hear (see Deuteronomy 6:4). Those engaged in temple worship pledge loyalty to God, the church, and fellow Saints, and in doing so they are empowered in history by being included in Israel. For Mormons the temple is a sacred space in which divine law and covenant are given in the divine Presence.[41] That divine law gives religious identity to those who participate in its rituals. And those rituals give the meaning of a symbolic order to the world outside the temple, bringing Jew and Gentile, bond and free, male and female (compare Galatians 3:28) together into the complex family of God.

NOTES

1. For background on the temple ritual, see Buerger, "Development of the Mormon Temple Endowment Ceremony"; Brown, "Early Mormon Adoption Theology and the Mechanics of Salvation"; and Stapley, "Adoptive Sealing Ritual in Mormonism."
2. Ehat, "Who Shall Ascend into the Hill of the Lord," 54.
3. Archer, "Nourishment for Our Journey," 84–85.
4. Quoted in Ehat, "Who Shall Ascend into the Hill of the Lord," 58.
5. Snow, "An Experience of My Father's," 677.
6. See, for example, D&C 6:12.
7. Flake, "Not to be Riten," 13.
8. Casey, *Remembering*, 250.
9. Flake, "Not to be Riten," 2.
10. See Flake, "Not to be Riten," 5–7, for a more nuanced discussion of the oral character of the temple rite.
11. Casey, *Remembering*, 221.
12. Allred, "Holy Temples, Sacred Covenants."
13. Young, "Necessity of Building Temples," 1853, 2: 31.
14. Cf. Archer, "Nourishment for Our Journey," 23.
15. Mitchell, "Sacrament," 357.
16. Flake, "Not to be Riten," 14.
17. Lane, "Embodied Knowledge of God," 64.
18. See Faulconer, *Faith, Philosophy, Scripture*, 61–64, 95–101.
19. Bell, "Authority of Ritual Experts," 98.
20. Casey, *Remembering*, 216–17.
21. Mitchell, "Sacrament," 355.
22. DeConcini, "Remembering," 91.

23. Casey, *Remembering*, 217.
24. Ibid., 216–17.
25. Ibid., 223.
26. DeConcini, "Remembering," 95.
27. Pierosara, "Asking," 74.
28. DeConcini, "Remembering," 110–11.
29. Ibid., 110.
30. Childs, *Memory and Tradition in Israel*, 82.
31. Ibid., 53.
32. DeConcini, "Remembering," 141.
33. Roberts, *Mormon Doctrine of Deity*, 283–84.
34. Archer, "Nourishment for Our Journey," 95; Casey, *Remembering*, 228–30; and Childs, *Memory and Tradition in Israel*, 51, 55, 58–59.
35. Mitchell, "Sacrament," 363.
36. Talmage, *House of the Lord*, 84.
37. Childs, *Memory and Tradition in Israel*, 51.
38. Brueggemann, *Bible Makes Sense*, 10.
39. Davie, "The Rationale for the Development of an Anglican Covenant."
40. Goddard, "Communion and Covenant," 163.
41. Flake, "Not to be Riten," 6.

BIBLIOGRAPHY

Allred, Sylvia H. "Holy Temples, Sacred Covenants." An address delivered at the General Conference of the Church of Jesus Christ of Latter-day Saints, Salt Lake City, Utah, October 2008. https://www.lds.org/general-conference/2008/10/holy-temples-sacred-covenants?lang=eng.

Archer, Kenneth J. "Nourishment for Our Journey: The Pentecostal *Via Salutis* and Sacramental Ordinances." *Journal of Pentecostal Theology* 13, no. 1 (2004): 84–85.

Bell, Katherine. "The Authority of Ritual Experts." *Studia Liturgica* 23 (1993): 98–120.

Brown, Samuel M. "Early Mormon Adoption Theology and the Mechanics of Salvation." *Journal of Mormon History* 37, no. 3 (Summer 2011): 3–52.

Brueggemann, Walter. *The Bible Makes Sense*. Rev. ed. Cincinnati, OH: St. Anthony Messenger, 2003.

Buerger, David John. "The Development of the Mormon Temple Endowment Ceremony." *Dialogue: A Journal of Mormon Thought* 20, no. 4 (Winter 1987): 33–76.

Casey, Edward S. *Remembering: A Phenomenological Study*. 1987. 2nd ed. Indianapolis: Indiana University Press, 2000.

Childs, Brevard. *Memory and Tradition in Israel*. London: SCM, 1962.

Davie, Martin. "The Rationale for the Development of an Anglican Covenant." Inter Anglican Theological and Doctrinal Commission. http://www.thinkinganglicans.org.uk/uploads/GS1661annex3.html.

DeConcini, Barbara. "Remembering: A Hermeneutic of Narrative Time." PhD diss., Emory University. Ann Arbor, MI: University Microfilms, 1980.

Ehat, Andrew F. "Who Shall Ascend into the Hill of the Lord." In *Temples of the Ancient World: Ritual and Symbolism*, ed. Donald W. Parry, 48–60. Salt Lake City: Deseret, 1994.

Faulconer, James E. *Faith, Philosophy, Scripture*. Provo, UT: Maxwell Institute, 2010.

Flake, Kathleen. "'Not to be Riten': The Mormon Temple Rite as Oral Canon." *Journal of Ritual Studies* 9, no. 2 (Summer 1995): 1–21.

Goddard, Andrew. "Communion and Covenant: A Theological Exploration." *International Journal for the Study of the Christian Church* 8, no. 2 (May 2008): 155–70.

Journal of Discourses. 26 vols. Reported by G. D. Watt et al. Liverpool: F. D. and S. W. Richards et al., 1851–86; reprint, Salt Lake City: n.p., 1974.

Lane, Jennifer. "Embodied Knowledge of God." *Element* 2, no. 1 (2006): 59–69.

Mitchell, Nathan. "Sacrament: More than Meets the Eye," *Worship* 83, no. 4 (2009): 350–65.

Pierosara, Silvia. "Asking for Narratives to be Recognized." *Études Ricœuriennes / Ricœur Studies* 2, no. 1 (2011): 70–83.

Roberts, Brigham H. *The Mormon Doctrine of Deity: The Roberts-Vander Donckt Discussion*. Salt Lake City: Horizon, 1903.

Snow, LeRoi C. "An Experience of My Father's." *Improvement Era* 36, no. 11 (September 1933): 677, 679.

Stapley, Jonathan A. "Adoptive Sealing Ritual in Mormonism." *Journal of Mormon History* 37, no. 3 (Summer 2011): 53–117.

Talmage, James E. *The House of the Lord: A Study of the Holy Sanctuaries Ancient and Modern*. 1968. Rev. ed. Salt Lake City: Deseret, 1971.

Young, Brigham. "Necessity of Building Temples—The Endowment" [April 6, 1853]. *Journal of Discourses* 2: 29–33.

CHAPTER 15

....

LIVED RELIGION
AMONG MORMONS

....

TONA J. HANGEN

LIVED RELIGION

....

WHEN social scientists Robert D. Putnam and David E. Campbell profiled Mormonism for their survey of contemporary religious practice in the United States, *American Grace*, they began by attending the Pioneer Ward in a "nondescript" suburban Salt Lake meetinghouse. They noted its "manicured" appearance, devoid of church-like "architectural cues," and described its interior as "plain," "sparse," and "functional." They noticed the arrival of "large families and young couples," and dutifully documented the content and tenor of the sermons assigned to members of the congregation. Mormons indeed have distinctive Sunday worship practices: their three-hour-long Sunday meetings are highly structured, conducted according to both written and unwritten protocol with a remarkable sameness the world over, and welcoming of small children, outsiders, prospective converts, and visitors. Anyone interested, as Putnam and Campbell were, in the everyday fabric of Mormon life, might do well to begin with Mormons on Sunday: starched, pressed, and on their best behavior.[1] But the texture and inner realities of Mormonism can be fully grasped only by looking at where—and how—Mormons actually live their religion: through embodied ritual; in sacred space and time; in densely interlocked social and kin networks; and in negotiating tensions inherent to Mormonism and its adaptation to diverse cultural settings. A lived-religion approach helps us go beyond stereotypes of cookie-cutter conformity and to recast Mormonism's growing diversity not as fragmentation or declension, but as evidence of the fertility of its soil for the human religious imagination.

Lived religion is the vibrant culture always thrumming below a church's official radar, where improvisation, resistance, blending, and creativity are found in abundance, captured in community studies, symbology, language, bodies, objects, buildings, landscapes, noncanonical texts, and religious narratives, including folklore. Lived religion seeks to understand and reconstruct subjective religious experience (what Bourdieu calls *habitus*) by granting legitimacy to the religious experiences and beliefs of a community's marginalized or deviant elements as well as, or even in preference to, its elite and official ones. In so doing, a lived-religion approach treats religion not as a stable and closed system (despite any religion's strenuous claims to be just so) but as a volatile, tensile, and even playful one. While Mormonism exerts strong pressure on its members to conform within a very narrow range of well-defined behaviors and perspectives, there is unexpected plurality and dynamism in the ways believers practice Mormonism.[2]

Just as folklore's interest lies in vernacular narratives as opposed to official ones, so the interdisciplinary study of "lived religion" privileges laity and their actual religious practices—although, as Eliason notes in chapter 29 in this volume, in Mormonism the distinction blurs considerably. As a practical matter, the absence of paid clergy broadens the number of theological perspectives to which a congregation will be exposed, and provides regular speaking and teaching opportunities to people who are excluded from the priesthood (which is extended only to worthy men). But this model does throw together leaders and followers in a complex tangle. If "the laity" comprises nearly everyone in Mormonism, and leaders learn mainly by doing rather than through formal professional training, then lived Mormonism is, in that sense, the only kind there is.

Let me suggest four dimensions of Mormon lived religion, keeping in mind that these are something of a moving target. The first is the most basic and physical level, grounded in the body. The second is the way Mormons create and inhabit symbolic physical and social spaces. The third is Mormon "sociality," webs of human social and kinship connections. Last is Mormonism's effort to balance contradictory cultural possibilities in dynamic tension. Such tension is intrinsic to all living systems, and the contradictory possibilities are ripe for exploration and negotiation.

Mormon Bodies: Materiality

Mormon lived religion is evident in the body and the ways that religious experience is embodied, inscribed upon, or performed by gendered bodies. Douglas Davies describes Mormon *habitus* as gestural and performative, as when Mormons sustain callings, give testimony, or fold their arms for prayer. Since devout Mormons eschew tattoos or piercings, wear temple garments, and dress conservatively, it is easy to spot one—or to spoof one on stage. Mormon foodways include strong taboos that derive from the Word of Wisdom, but also from regional American food practices that take on iconic status within Mormon culture: potluck suppers, "funeral potatoes," and green jello salad being among the most widely noted. Mormons at work in community service wear bright yellow "Mormon Helping Hands" vests, a reminder that hands are especially important—the right hand raised to the square for priesthood ordinances and to sustain new callings; the "laying on of hands" for healings, bless-ings, and ordinations; the firm handshake as the usual Mormon greeting (it even being advised for the identification of visiting spirits in Doctrine and Covenants 129); bringing someone into the church is "extending the hand of fellowship." As these few examples suggest, Mormonism has intricate bodily practices, many of which are deeply gendered.

Mormons exhibit a high degree of personal discipline, but reject Christian asceticism. In Mormon theology bodies are necessary, good, and indeed eventually eternal. Unlike many other religious traditions, Mormons do not radically oppose flesh and spirit. Heavenly Father and Heavenly Mother are thought to be embodied deities; the righ-teous soul's ultimate state will be an immortal, perfected, human body which can con-tinue to procreate and work. For Mormons, therefore, physical and sexual appetites are not inherently evil but powerful and divine attributes, particularly vulnerable to Satan's temptation. They must therefore be contained and channeled, in a complex understand-ing of the body that regulates modesty in dress (especially for girls and women), but at the same time unhesitatingly celebrates high-calorie potluck feasts. In particular, temple ordinances depend on a mortal body to enact ritual gestures and perform ritual speech, and to be immersed, anointed, blessed, and specially clothed. For temple-going Mormons, repeating these rituals *physically* reinforces spiritual teaching; it engraves those experiences in bodily memory and literally encodes them into the fabric of the Mormon garments.

Jennifer Huss Basquiat noted that the modern Haitian converts she studied related to Joseph Smith as an ancestor figure, strongly identifying with Smith's low social station and visionary answers to religious seeking. Largely nonliterate, Haitian Latter-day Saints told, enacted, and performed the Joseph Smith story in place of reading it. The temple ritual of Mormon baptism for the dead overlaid onto tradi-tional Haitian reverence for ancestors. Collective rituals such as Mormon testimony meetings, General Conference, and family home evenings became "definitional cer-emonies" where members performed, and thereby embodied, Mormonism. Haitian Saints made Mormon history and stories their own, especially through somatic experiences of weeping, joking, memorization, and bodily postures. Similar findings characterized Hildi Mitchell's portrait of late twentieth-century British converts, whose testimonies, prayers, and patterns of textual exegesis elicited certain con-ditioned physical responses: "pounding heart, tingling warmth, weeping, sense of peace"—which could then be reconstituted in other sacred settings from these bodily memories. The "correctly taught" Mormon body finds such experiences spiritually uplifting and interprets them as the influence of the Holy Ghost or the love of God and Jesus Christ. Elsewhere, Mitchell describes how Mormons link bodies and LDS temples as homologous concepts: holy repositories for the divine, subject to strict regulation and to notions of physical purity. Because Mormons enter temples only by recommendation from an ecclesiastical authority, "the Temple serves as a powerful control over bodily behavior and influences what bodies can wear, ingest, and do in a very immediate and intimate manner."[3]

SPACE AND TIME: COSMOLOGY AND RITUAL

Somatic memories and embodied practices point us not only to the body, but to the physical spaces and time through which that body moves. Sacred spaces help constitute Mormon lived religion as they reflect Mormon belief, cosmology, and boundary making. From the earliest years of the faith, Mormons have been builders and makers. They constructed bowers, homes, temples, irrigation systems, meetinghouses, and even entire cities, each imprinted with religious notions of how to divide and use space. Practicing Mormons move among interlocking holy spaces—home, chapel, city, temple, historic sites, and even nature itself—to commune with the divine through enactment, story, ritual practice, and sensory experience.

Home is the locus of family life and pious household devotional practices, including prayer, religious instruction, and the determined exclusion of unsavory influences. While few Mormon homes have shrines or icon corners, many LDS families follow the suggestion of their leaders to prominently display visual images of temples, prophets, or the life of Jesus Christ. Popular LDS Christ-themed art depicts him not suffering and bleeding on the cross, but purposefully performing miracles, affectionately embracing and teaching children, or in gestures that draw attention to his resurrected (but indelibly marked) body. A thriving cottage industry provides many homes with Mormon-themed art, word plaques, stitched samplers, and the like, which telegraph the household's faith to new arrivals and help maintain the religious orientation of family members.

The church's relatively unadorned meetinghouses and chapels serve as both Sunday houses of worship and de facto community centers. Cultural geographer Richard Francaviglia, traveling among communities in rural Utah originally founded by Mormons in the nineteenth century, observed "a peculiar combination of pragmatic and spiritual forms" with chapels of "architectural sobriety." This trend continues with meetinghouses constructed in the twentieth century, which tend to be utilitarian brick or concrete buildings devoid of stained glass and carrying minimalist architectural ornamentation. At the core of most of these buildings is a pair of twinned communal spaces: a chapel, with fixed pews and pulpit, and a "cultural hall," half basketball court and half theater. Flexible spaces like the cultural hall speak to the variety of functions meetinghouses serve in Mormon life. As just one example, my own meetinghouse in suburban Massachusetts is in almost daily use to accommodate weekday morning youth seminary classes, a monthly community blood drive, an ecumenical Christmas concert, a secular homeschool group's Shakespeare troupe, a playgroup for mothers of young children, a genealogical library open to the public, and a weekly round of activities for cohorts from school age to the elderly.

Mormon spatial organization can be traced in community planning as well, seen throughout the West wherever Mormons first gathered and established industrious agricultural colonies. Joseph Smith's 1833 "Plat for the City of Zion" established a replicable pattern for Mormon villages that balanced religious, residential, and public zones with surrounding farm fields and irrigation systems that reflected the communal organization of Latter-day Saint household economies. Mormon zeal transformed the physical landscape of the American West, taking for itself the bee and the beehive as the symbol of the fusion of work, industry, and spirituality. Thomas Carter's study of polygamous Mormon housing in the late nineteenth century revealed families cobbling together new residential architectural forms from familiar forms at hand and gendering the spaces in ways that leave traces of evidence about how Mormons "lived the principle" in everyday life. Scrutinizing the style, size, placement in the community, and definition of family and private spaces in such houses enriches our understanding of early Mormonism's social world. Nineteenth-century Mormon men enjoyed mobility among their properties and households, while Mormon women were constrained or planted in, ideally, individual living spaces—in line with American Victorian ideals that defined (and morally elevated) "home" as centered on an increasingly isolated female domesticity.[4]

Conceptions of time "condition how people see reality and therefore what they choose, who they become, how they interpret worthiness, and what they imagine time to be for." Mormons not only align spaces and landscapes with religious ideas, but also organize both sacred and mundane time according to them. Latter-day Saints orient themselves on a cosmic timeline, anchored in the idea that they live in the "latter days" (which implies former ones, of course). History stretches backwards to draw upon elements of primitive Christianity and from Old Testament patriarchy, and extends even farther back to an imagined preexistence. Their sense of time also stretches forward to anticipate a millennial future and a triumphant family reunion in the eternities. Mormons live inside this sacred continuum, encountering a series of staged commitments requiring progressive, genuine personal sacrifice and profession of sincere faith. These commitments—comprising both community responsibilities and covenantal ordinances—are "staged" both in the sense of being progressive and in the sense of being rituals to be performed in social venues. New fathers hoist their tiny children for the congregation to coo over at the end of a blessing, members raise their hands in support of every ward calling, and couples kneel at the temple's altars to be sealed in marriage. As Saints move through their progression of ordinances and levels of participation, they mark time on a cosmic calendar. But because, for Mormons, religious progression is eternal, one is never in stasis. Few Mormons have a single "born-again" moment; rather, personal transformation is understood as a process that bridges mortality and the afterlife. Whereas born-again Christians enter a state of completion before God—which confers a certain confidence—Latter-day Saints have no such assurance. In Mormon parlance, they've "entered the gate" and are "clinging to the rod," "enduring to the end," receiving "line upon line"—all metaphors of restless striving and momentum but not completion.[5]

"THAT SAME SOCIALITY": KINSHIP
AND BOUNDARY MAKING

Mormons do not primarily live their religion as isolated individuals, striving for perfection in solitary. Rather, the arc of their soul's trajectory traces densely networked communities, centered on the family or the congregational unit or more often, a fusion of the two. In her comparative study of Mormons in upstate New York (where the church began in 1830) and in the Salt Lake City region, Fanella Cannell highlights the importance of Mormon materiality and kin relations in defining a distinctive LDS lived religion. She reminds us that instead of being incidental to, or even a mere laboratory for, living Christian principles, family life is sacred work. Kinship *is* religion. Mormon genealogy is a spiritual practice, an act of rescue and consecration which binds kin both on earth and in the eternities, making "the Celestial Kingdom . . . the realm of 'clans.'" As Davies argues elsewhere, "while it is perfectly possible, in theological terms, to conceive of salvation in almost all Christian churches and denominations quite apart from any formal consideration of the family, this is impossible in the Church of Jesus Christ of Latter-day Saints."

In the ideal of Mormon social organization, every person consecrates effort, resources and talents to build the kingdom and strengthen its constituent parts. Theoretically, no one sits on the sidelines, and as Mormons work alongside one another and resolve conflicts that inevitably arise, they animate the teachings of the church by *living*, not merely professing, gospel tenets. Most church responsibilities ("callings") place Mormons into small problem-solving leadership teams such as auxiliary and quorum presidencies, bishoprics, ward or stake councils, or companionships as missionaries or visiting and home teachers. Since callings rotate frequently, Mormons generally have many chances to feel part of a larger collective and to see the church's operations up close from different perspectives. Missions, especially, channel young Latter-day Saints into intensive service for eighteen months to two years with a significant impact on their identity as Mormons and on their spiritual capacity and leadership ability. Missionaries form their own tight-knit but temporary Mormon subculture with distinctive slang, rituals, and traditions. Davies calls Mormons a "highly achievement-motivated group," reminding us that Max Weber described the movement as "half-way between monastery and factory."[6]

One way actual Mormon "sociality" can be explored is by surveying its boundaries (who is Mormon and who is not?) and network mapping its social topography (how do Mormons relate to one another?). How Mormons identify themselves, and those in and outside the faith, suggests the richness and complication of their social relations. In simplest terms, there are "members" and "nonmembers." But "members" can be "active" or "inactive," like machinery that is either running or idle. The old-fashioned term "Jack Mormon," for someone who had lapsed in certain areas—perhaps even spectacularly lapsed—but who still claims Mormon membership or cultural identity, still persists but is used with less frequency. Gradations of Mormon identity and boundary setting now include a wide spectrum of belief and belonging. An "orthodox" or "true-believing" Mormon or "true-blue Mormon" (TBM) aligns with church teachings and counsel as closely as possible. A "nonliteral" Mormon may selectively reject the veracity of certain LDS beliefs, claiming to hew instead to the spirit or intent of the religion's core. There are "liberal" and "progressive" Mormons, who see the faith's teachings as compatible with an open-minded stance on social-justice issues, gender equality, or sexual identity. "Cultural Mormons" were born and raised in LDS families and are conversant with Mormon language and culture, but no longer practicing; "New Order," "nonliteral," or "uncorrelated" Mormons remain connected while not professing faith in all of the church's doctrines. "Syncretic Mormons" actively borrow and blend from other religious traditions such as Zen Buddhism, New Age spirituality, or paganism. Since many Mormons are in part-member families there may be far more blending than the church generally acknowledges. More comparative work would be beneficial to explore where Mormon self-identities overlap with other communities of belief and practice, such as political groups, feminists, homeschoolers, and home-based business entrepreneurship, where Mormons have been prominent (for example, Amway, Shaklee, NuSkin, Creative Memories, Stampin' Up!, and Pampered Chef).

The degree to which Mormons integrate each other into social, financial, and political relationships suggests that network mapping and community studies may be a useful methodological approach to understanding Mormon sociality. One remarkable, but rare, example of Mormon self-conscious social archiving was the experimental documentation of one year (1984–1985) in the Elkton, Delaware, Ward. The project was carried out by Richard and Claudia Bushman, who mobilized their ward to record and save nearly everything that happened in or was printed for church meetings and to conduct oral histories with as many of the ward members as were willing to participate. The resulting portrait, edited by Susan Taber and published as *Mormon Lives: A Year in the Elkton Ward*, to some degree replicates the form and intent of earlier mission and ward histories issued under the imprimature of the BYU Family History and Community Studies Center, but with greater intention and detail.[7]

The Elkton project was doubly unusual because it sought to capture the kinds of sources least likely to be archived, reprinted, or promoted in official church venues. Mormon folk theology, storytelling, humor, pathos, and speech patterns come through clearly in Sunday talks and lessons, which are almost never archived or printed. General Conference talks preserve some of this linguistic richness, but in them we get very little of women's voices and none from young people with emerging articulations of their religious selves. Testimonies and blessings are even more ephemeral. Mormon amateur theatricals have a long history, including road shows, skits, musicals, and other performances, but scripts or recordings of them are scarce. Something more of the rich lived reality of Mormonism was captured by the pre-1970 church magazines (which were much less concerned with presenting a unified or agreeable public face of the religion to the world), including the *Relief Society Magazine, Young Women's Journal, Improvement Era*, and *Juvenile Instructor*, which included paid advertisements aimed at the LDS market and illustrate the consumer preferences, language, and habits of Mormons both as buyers and sellers in earlier eras.

Increasingly, the virtual realm has become another Mormon social and religious space, and some of the social "mapping" I suggested earlier could take the form of data mining of blogs, online sites, repositories, and discussion boards. Two examples may suffice: Second Life (a three-dimensional "virtual world" website built and populated by users' avatars) and the "Bloggernacle." David Scott toured Mormon virtual spaces in Second Life, including a "virtual island" named Adam-ondi-Ahman created by an enthusiastic Mormon Second Life user (the name references a Missouri community named by Joseph Smith that is said to have significance in the anticipated Millennium). Scott discussed the island's free-floating Mormon signifiers that marked sacred (virtual) space and mimic popular Mormon visual representations, but since the island's creator presented them without an orienting narrative flow or context, visitors' avatars arriving at the virtual location encountered a chaotic pastiche of Mormon objects and ideas. Scott considered it a "cacophony" and "smorgasbord" rather than a cohesive religious virtual reality—yet it proved valuable for unintentionally revealing how Mormon "religious plausibility structures" emerge in cyberspace's discursive practices.[8]

Adapting the term "blogosphere" to the ever-growing solar system of Mormon-themed blogs, the Bloggernacle encompasses hundreds of blogging communities centered on discussing Mormon culture, theology, and social practices. Bloggernacle communities replicate some of the social and discursive aspects of face-to-face Mormonism, but subvert others: age, ethnicity, gender, and activity status are flattened or obscured by the medium, opening possibility for new arrangements that would be impossible in brick and mortar congregations. Bloggernacle users comprise a parallel peoplehood, but one that is unusually open to questioning, discussing, and even criticizing church rhetoric and doctrine. Bloggers in Mormonism have done for the church what online journalists have done for mainstream news outlets—created an alternate universe of amateurs whose web presence profoundly altered the former landscape of discourse. The Bloggernacle receives some tacit recognition with, for example, the "Back Bench" digest column in the church-owned *Deseret News* based in Salt Lake City, and, since 2008, scattered mentions by church leaders have acknowledged LDS blogging and sought to appropriate it as a tool to reinforce Mormon identity.

Cultural Tensions in Mormonism

The simultaneous existence of Mormon virtual communities and face-to-face socialities should alert us to the possibilities for complication and permeability in Mormon lived religion. Robert Orsi has suggested that in addition to somatic experiences and social relations, lived religion also encompasses the "characteristic tensions [which] erupt within these particular structures."[9] In Mormonism, two of these characteristic tensions are between center and periphery (or, to put it another way, between centrifugal pulls of correlation and centripetal forces of the grassroots), and between the supernatural and the rational. Cultural tensions like these provide a spectrum of possibilities for believers and give the religious system living, adaptive strength.

One key tension is the pull between center and periphery, or "Salt Lake" and "the mission field." Despite Mormonism's lay clergy and relatively dispersed leadership structure, there is at the same time a strong hierarchy and centralized authority. Some even speak of "two churches of Mormonism."[10] Salt Lake Mormonism is both real—in that it is the physical and spiritual center of a worldwide faith—and mythical, in that Mormon leaders, prophets, and scriptural exemplars become highly idealized almost to the point of myth. By "mythical," I hardly mean fictional, but rather people of whom powerful nonhistorical stories are told, such as cultural types (mothers in Zion, stripling warriors, pioneers, "Molly Mormons"). Even non-Mormons can be transformed *ex post facto* into mythical Mormons, startlingly roped into the orbit of the faith as if they were "Mormons like us." This includes the American Founding Fathers, for whom the vicarious temple work has been done many times over, Mormonism's "adopted" Christian theologian C. S. Lewis, and Old Testament Jews who are portrayed in Mormon popular visual art as conducting their religious ceremonies precisely like costumed modern Mormons.

Headquarters, Salt Lake, and "Zion" comprise the unattainable center and the self-representation of sanctioned Mormon channels, filtered through an increasingly media-savvy instruction paradigm. True, by deconstructing these and similar idealized portraits, we might derive something of the faith's official creed and priorities, its values and taboos. But such "pedestal" narratives take us only partway to where Mormon life actually happens and where the faith is defined, generated, and regenerated. They conform to standardized tropes of Mormon storytelling and as such represent only a reported—and subsequently highly edited—Mormon experiential reality. In the pews the ideal breaks down quickly. Surely no one lives in Zion all the time, though all strive for it; the lived reality is always in tension with the sanitized ideal. The "I'm a Mormon" media campaign on the church's mormon.org website, launched in 2010, refreshingly allows Mormons to admit this to themselves and to the outside world. More than one observer has noted that these relatively unscripted, user-generated media creations now serve as a digital repository of the lived experience of contemporary Mormonism, since they position themselves in the space between official narratives and the folks in the pews.

Another way to express this tension is to describe the uneasy balance between correlation and folk "embellishment." Mormons celebrate being a "peculiar people" at the same time they place a high premium on conformity and sameness within the faith. The latter tendency was accelerated by the twentieth-century church correlation movement which included the development of a common curriculum and set of guiding principles, manuals, and organizational strategies to render Mormonism replicable across an infinite number of cultural and geographic settings. Mormons may have little liturgy, a sparse sacred calendar and an affinity for personal revelation rather than top-down instruction, but even tiny children are taught to sing "Follow the Prophet" in vigorous chorus, and Latter-day Saints rarely deviate from their established forms of talks, prayers, or meeting structures.

At the same time, though, Mormons exhibit a lot of creative and playful adaptations through a process not unlike "crowdsourcing" of information on the Internet. The hegemony of correlation is only ever partial. Mormonism's radical openness to spiritual gifts and spontaneous emotionalism, as well as its members' own experiences with divine communication, are all aspects of the faith that show no signs of going dormant. In her study of Haitian members, Basquiat used the concept of *bricolage* for how Mormons assemble a meaningful religious self, and the term applies as well in settings where Mormonism is deeply rooted as where it is new and raw. Common Mormon cultural practices involve processes of selection, repurposing, collage, and embellishment. Through scrapbooking, keeping of genealogy records, crafting, and (more recently) blogging, many Mormon women juxtapose disparate elements together with something much more than decorative purpose. While no good Mormon would dream of tagging a wall with spray paint, American Mormons frequently design and purchase elaborate vinyl lettering for the interior walls of their home, to literally inscribe faith-promoting quotes or family mottos on their metaphorical doorposts.

Similarly Mormons can take a plain theology, with very little scriptural basis (say, the War in Heaven or Heavenly Mother), and embellish it with considerable speculative theology. Two scriptural testaments weren't enough, so Mormonism has a third in the Book of Mormon. Mormons seek "further light and knowledge," receive spiritual understanding "line upon line, precept upon precept," and engage in linguistically and visually rich personal annotation of their scriptures. In the author's youth in the 1980s, Mormon teens competed in rowdy multicongregational contests to locate memorized scripture passages at lightning speed, altering the text's very surface with colored pencil, crayon, or even a fine dusting of talcum powder between the pages to help give a winning edge. All of these flourishes enrich LDS culture with layers of creative accretion and oral tradition in ways that correlation cannot easily co-opt.

The kinds of sources which play with this tension between correlation and crowdsourcing are myriad, particularly objects and cultural products which evidence Mormon symbology and language in everyday use. One might point here to an entrepreneurial streak energizing the made-for-Mormons market for books, craftwork, art, music, film, media, and household objects. Similarly, a parallel universe of uncorrelated manuals and supplemental material like lesson helps and clip art coexists, sometimes uneasily, with the church's official instruction manuals—especially for church and Family Home Evening lessons aimed at children and youth. Internet memes that self-satirize Mormon life are now firmly part of the Mormon cultural landscape, replete with insider humor (one recent example is the "BYU Memes" Facebook page at http://www.facebook.com/ BYUMemes, which went online in February 2012).

Correlation and embellishment or crowdsourcing are not always at odds, but they do represent contrasting approaches to religious identity and knowledge. By holding them in creative tension, Mormonism largely succeeds in reining in the enthusiasm of millions of independent thinkers, who may all seek personal revelation and are given license to preach, theologize, and teach in front of children, youth, adults, congregations, and the whole world on the Internet. As Janet Dolgin put it, writing about Mormonism in the early 1970s, "the individual Mormon is his own symbol maker, [a] 'sect in himself'"; "at critical moments the sources of authority (at the relevant level) can be called into play to prevent Mormons from escaping, as it were, to become absolutely independent."[11]

A last richly productive tension is between the supernatural and the rational, inasmuch as they can be separated in Mormon experience. Latter-day Saints conceive of their earthly realm as coexisting alongside and interacting with a supernatural one peopled with unembodied spirits, angels and demons, a resurrected Christ whose love is manifest in a Holy Ghost, and embodied Gods—male and female. The boundary or "veil" between these worlds has elastic qualities: it can thicken, become thinner, be transparent or opaque, lift or fall, be torn or mended, and be "passed through" at death or near-death.

Mormons systematize their theology and practices in highly rational ways—calculating the four steps of repentance, or discussing how to find out the veracity of the Book of Mormon as a kind of sure-fire formula. Nonetheless, supernaturalism, miracles, and inexplicability are ever present in Mormon life. Although few Mormons in the twenty-first century talk openly about visions and angelic visitors, which abounded in early Mormon writings, dreams still remain a vital source of supernatural intervention and communication. Stories of divine assistance with genealogy from eager departed ancestors is a common trope. Mormon anointings and blessings provide healing (usually, in such stories, to the dismay and disbelief of trained medical professionals); fasting, praying, and placing a name on the temple roll to be prayed for during temple sessions, lends strength to the ailing or helps someone cope with a personal trial.

Light often figures prominently in these narratives. In the First Vision Joseph Smith saw a "pillar of light" descending from heaven; someone's face may seem to glow or an apparent directional beam shine on a street sign in answer to a prayer or as part of a spiritual prompting. My own father recalls, while a graduate student, having lost a ring that had great personal value to him. One day he was walking across a lawn at his college and suddenly saw the ring centered in a circle of light on the grass, and picked it up without breaking stride or feeling any sense of surprise. Only later did he pause to analyze and wonder what had just happened. Accounts like this abound, widely shared as stories, in talks, and in oft-forwarded emails. Tom Mould has noted that in Mormon talks and testimonies, this kind of "unsolicited revelation" tends to dominate narrative tradition.[12] In other words, rational responses are largely unexamined in Mormon culture; they go without saying, so to speak, but Mormons revel in miraculous, otherworldly experiences that reinforce their sense of being chosen and guided.

LOCATING "REAL, LIVE" MORMONS

In the conceptual spaces between these binary tensions there is much room for creativity, negotiation, and plurality. Mechanisms of change and adaptation are built in to the Mormon system, and so these tensile tuggings do not threaten the inherent stability of the Mormon worldview and lived experience, even though that lived reality is becoming more diverse and less tethered to a common history. It was still possible in Roman Catholic sociologist Thomas O'Dea's time of the 1950s to write about Mormons as a tight-knit white American minority who had assimilated along with and in the same time period as the new immigrants of the late nineteenth century, albeit along a completely different historical trajectory.[13] As Mormons, somewhat uneasily, reentered the American polity after Utah statehood, they were (like Ellis Island arrivals, to some degree), "newcomers" to the newly multicultural nation. Right in line with the assimilationist Americanization campaigns of the early twentieth century, Mormons came through the forge of the Depression and the Second World War, emerging on the other side as thoroughgoing Americans, trailing clouds of ethnic glory.

However, it is no longer accurate to describe Mormons this way. The majority now live outside the United States, and we need much more understanding of what their lived experience is like and how Latter-day Saints negotiate identity, language, history, and spirituality. The lived religion of Mormonism needs to include not only canonical narratives and practices and the experiences of orthodox practicing Mormons, but also believers whose historical experiences and ethnic backgrounds don't match the experience of Utah pioneer-stock Mormons and those whose affiliation with the church is strained. It is unhelpful to marginalize such people as imperfect or lesser Mormons, or to discredit the authenticity of their religious experience. Instead of perceiving fragmentation of a prior cohesive social order as a negative aspect of the church's transformation into a global religion, we may need to define Mormonism more broadly to acknowledge its new reality.

Even though successful white English-speaking Mormons remain, to a large degree, the public face of the church, its real members are increasingly mixed-race, polyglot, and working class. Hildi Mitchell observes that "underneath Mormonism's apparent unity lies a diversity which most Mormons do not recognise."[14] Programs originally built with geographically compact Utah wards in mind must adapt to urban *barrios*, rural townships, and refugee camps. Even Mormon missionaries serving in Europe and North America increasingly find that they work with diasporic migrant populations from Africa, Asia, and Latin America. These new aspirational Mormons are hardworking, upwardly mobile, and willing to find a spiritual home in a highly systematic religion with a corporate-like structure. Mormonism has yet to invent new narratives, identities, culture heroes, and organizational strategies for this reality—but those will come. The 1978 revelation extending the priesthood to all worthy men in the church, regardless of race, has had profound and rapid consequences. Within a single generation, especially when combined with the post–Cold War opening of the former Eastern bloc to active Mormon proselytizing, Mormon lived religion is no longer singular, but richly plural. Whereas monumental temples used to serve as the cosmological and often geographical centers of majority-Mormon communities in the Rocky Mountain West, more compact versions are now widely dispersed to carefully seed the church into fertile soil in places very unlike Utah, Idaho, and Arizona.

Mormonism probably always will use the nineteenth-century experience as a touch-stone (rendering it more myth-like with each passing year), but the real dynamism of the faith is here and now, in the making. It is sitting in the benches of concrete-block chapels, heard in the corrugated-roofed neighborhoods where home and visiting teach-ers re-create Mormon sociability, and it hallows tropical rivers into latter-day "waters of Mormon" for baptisms. The new grassroots of Mormonism's lived religion will be found not only in its historic culture region and in digital media environments, but in small units around the world where Mormons who may have never been to Utah or seen Nauvoo craft new hybrid identities, practices, and understandings.

NOTES

1. Putnam and Campbell, *American Grace*, 351–35.
2. Bourdieu, *Outline of a Theory of Practice*, 73; Orsi, "Everyday Miracles," 16.
3. Davies, *Mormon Culture of Salvation*; Cannon, "Sacred Clothing"; Cannell, "Christianity of Anthropology"; Basquiat, "Embodied Mormonism"; Mitchell, "Being There," 26–44; Mitchell and Mitchell, "For Belief," 88.
4. Francaviglia, *Believing in Place*, 160–61; Parera, "Mormon Town Planning"; Carter, "Living the Principle."
5. Barlow, "Toward a Mormon Sense of Time."
6. Cannell, "Christianity of Anthropology," 337; Davies, *Mormon Culture of Salvation*, 145. For missionary life, see Shepherd and Shepherd, *Mormon Passage*; Carpenter, *Eighteen Months*; Knowlton, "Go Ye To All the World"; Weber in Davies, *Mormon Culture of Salvation*, 3.
7. Taber, *Mormon Lives*.
8. Scott, "The Discursive Construct of Virtual Angels, Temples, and Religious Worship."
9. Orsi, "Everyday Miracles," 7.
10. Molen, "Two Churches of Mormonism"; Quinn, "LDS 'Headquarters Culture' and the Rest of Mormonism."
11. Dolgin, "Latter-day Sense and Substance," 526, 546.
12. Mould, "Narratives of Personal Revelation among Latter-day Saints," 499. See also Brady, "Transformations of Power"; Introvigne, "Embraced by the Church?"
13. O'Dea, *Mormons*.
14. Mitchell, "Good, Evil and Godhood," 181.

BIBLIOGRAPHY

Barlow, Philip L. "Toward a Mormon Sense of Time." *Journal of Mormon History* 33, no. 1 (Spring 2007): 1–37.
Basquiat, Jennifer Huss. "Embodied Mormonism: Performance, Vodou, and the LDS Faith in Haiti." *Dialogue: A Journal of Mormon Thought* 37, no. 4 (Winter 2004): 1–34.
Bourdieu, Pierre. *Outline of a Theory of Practice*. Trans. Richard Nice. Cambridge Studies in Social Anthropology no. 16. New York: Cambridge University Press, 1977.
Brady, Margaret K. "Transformations of Power: Mormon Women's Visionary Narratives." *Journal of American Folklore* 100, no. 398 (December 1987): 461–68.

Cannell, Fenella. "The Christianity of Anthropology." *Journal of the Royal Anthropological Institute* 11, no. 2 (June 2005): 335–56.

Cannon, Helen Beach. "Sacred Clothing: An Inside-Outside Perspective." *Dialogue: A Journal of Mormon Thought* 25, no. 3 (Fall 1992): 138–48.

Carpenter, Melissa Baird. *Eighteen Months: Sister Missionaries in the Latter Days*. Orem, UT: Millennial, 2007.

Carter, Thomas. "Living the Principle: Mormon Polygamous Housing in Nineteenth-Century Utah." *Winterthur Portfolio* 35, no. 4 (December 1, 2000): 223–51.

Davies, Douglas J. *The Mormon Culture of Salvation: Force, Grace, and Glory*. Aldershot, UK: Ashgate, 2000.

Dolgin, Janet. "Latter-day Sense and Substance." In *Religious Movements in Contemporary America*, ed. Irving I. Zaretsky and Mark P. Leone, 519–46. Princeton, NJ: Princeton University Press, 1974.

Francaviglia, Richard V. *Believing in Place: A Spiritual Geography of the Great Basin*. Reno: University of Nevada Press, 2003.

David D. Hall, ed. *Lived Religion in America: Toward a History of Practice*. Princeton, NJ: Princeton University Press, 1997.

Introvigne, Massimo. "Embraced by the Church? Betty Eadie, Near-Death Experiences, and Mormonism." *Dialogue: A Journal of Mormon Thought* 29, no. 3 (Fall 1996): 99–119.

Knowlton, David Clark. "Go Ye To All the World: The LDS Church and the Organization of International Society." In *Revisiting Thomas O'Dea's The Mormons: A Contemporary Perspective*, ed. Cardell K. Jacobson, John P. Hoffmann, and Tim B. Heaton, 389–412. Salt Lake City: University of Utah Press, 2008.

Mitchell, Hildi J. "'Being There': British Mormons and the History Trail." In *Reframing Pilgrimage: Cultures in Motion*, ed. Simon Coleman and John Eade, 26–44. New York: Routledge, 2004.

Mitchell, Hildi J. "Good, Evil and Godhood: Mormon Morality in the Material World." In *Powers of Good and Evil: Moralities, Commodities and Popular Belief*, ed. Paul Clough and Jon P Mitchell, 161–84. New York: Berghahn, 2001.

Mitchell, Jon P., and Hildi J. Mitchell. "For Belief: Embodiment and Immanence in Catholicism and Mormonism." *Social Analysis* 52, no. 1 (Spring 2008): 79–94.

Molen, Ron. "The Two Churches of Mormonism." In *The Wilderness of Faith: Essays on Contemporary Mormon Thought*, ed. John Sillito, 26–35. Salt Lake City, UT: Signature, 1991.

Mould, Thomas. "Narratives of Personal Revelation among Latter-day Saints." *Western Folklore* 68, no. 4 (Fall 2009): 431–79.

O'Dea, Thomas F. *The Mormons*. Chicago: University of Chicago Press, 1957.

Orsi, Robert A. "Everyday Miracles: The Study of Lived Religion." In *Lived Religion in America: Toward a History of Practice*, ed. David D. Hall, 3–21. Princeton, NJ: Princeton University Press, 1997.

Parera, Cecilia. "Mormon Town Planning: Physical and Social Relevance." *Journal of Planning History* 4, no. 2 (2005): 155–74.

Putnam, Robert D., and David E. Campbell. *American Grace: How Religion Divides and Unites Us*. New York: Simon and Schuster, 2010.

Quinn, D. Michael. "LDS 'Headquarters Culture' and the Rest of Mormonism: Past and Present." *Dialogue: A Journal of Mormon Thought* 34, nos. 3–4 (Fall–Winter 2001): 135–164.

Scott, David W. "The Discursive Construct of Virtual Angels, Temples, and Religious Worship: Mormon Theology and Culture in Second Life." *Dialogue: A Journal of Mormon Thought* 44, no. 1 (Spring 2011): 85–104.

Shepherd, Gary, and Gordon Shepherd. *Mormon Passage: A Missionary Chronicle.* Urbana: University of Illinois Press, 1998.

Taber, Susan. *Mormon Lives: A Year in the Elkton Ward.* Urbana: University of Illinois Press, 1993.

PART IV

MORMON THOUGHT

CHAPTER 16

MIND AND SPIRIT IN MORMON THOUGHT

PHILIP L. BARLOW

WHAT follows explores the distinctive meanings and values Mormons assign to "intellect," "spirit," "revelation," and cognate terms. How did Joseph Smith construe the concepts and their connections? In what ways have his heirs absorbed, adapted, neglected, or tamed his radical ideas? What behaviors and inclinations have his teachings bred among Mormons in the contemporary developed world where rationalism, empiricism, naturalism, technology, and science hold sway? How do Mormons come to trust their worldview, come to know what they think they know?

In his impassioned rebuke of legalistic interpreters of Jewish tradition, Martin Buber balked at notions of the Torah as a closed domain: "O you secure and safe ones who hide yourselves behind the defense-works of the law so that you will not have to look into God's abyss!" he chided. Buber spurned the illusion of finality in God's speech: the false "security and abundance" of his critics whom he saw as deaf to God's unfolding disclosure. "For to you God is one who created once and not again; but to us God is he who 'renews the work of creation every day.' To you God is one who revealed himself once and no more; but to us he speaks out of the burning thorn-bush of the present."[1]

Buber's views developed in a Hasidic-tinged matrix untouched by the buoyant optimism of Mormonism. Yet his passion parallels aspects of Mormon sensibilities, including a regard for God's ongoing speech.

One thing that Mormons do not typically share with Buber is his embrace of a probing "holy insecurity" before the *mysterium tremendum*. Many Latter-day Saints seek or claim certainty: "I *know* [that Jesus is the Christ, that the Book of Mormon is 'true,' that my Heavenly Father loves me]." Believers espouse revelation of the sort recorded in the Bible or proclaimed by Joseph Smith and, more quietly, by his successors. Despite pronounced distinctions, Mormons speak of "the Spirit" in ways that resemble the Quakers' "inward light" or analogous sensibilities among other Christians. Saints call daily on God's spirit to help resolve problems and deepen faith, to inform attitudes and actions, to direct and testify, to sustain, protect, illuminate, and comfort.

In devotion and practice, Mormons incline to be innocently at home with mystery. So at home, that they commonly *de*mystify the Spirit. This they do not by "demythologizing" revelation *à la* Thomas Jefferson or theologian Rudolf Bultmann, culling the "super" and retaining the natural. Rather, the Saints demystify by *familiarity* with the supernatural. Many of them are secure in precise definitions and protocols of the workings of the "Holy Spirit." They may interpret feelings, ideas, instincts, intuitions, and sometimes dreams as "spiritual promptings" from a divine realm that inspire daily lives. These promptings are accessible to all people, but enduringly available to those who have accepted the ordinances of baptism and receipt of "the gift of the Holy Ghost" (Acts 2:38). For such believers, the world has not lost its enchantment, but is charged with divine influence.

Byproducts of this orientation have accrued over time. One, natural and ironic in equal measure, is a species of anti-intellectualism running through the tradition. It is a mistake to think of this as intrinsic to Joseph Smith's teachings. Yet from the movement's launch by Smith's proclamation of new light and authority from the heavens, a coolness toward "intellectualizing" has never been rare. Of what import is human reason before revelation from God?

Even apart from revelatory claims, the LDS version of this aversion to intellectualism is part of a long and diffuse stream in the cultural history of the United States, in which Mormonism first took root.

Friction with intellectuals across the land has a long-established link to religion, grounded in a natural tension between head and heart, between spiritual and intuitional claims versus materialist, philosophical, and empirical ones. The first American colonial intellectuals, as a class, were the Puritan clergy and before the mid-eighteenth century most college graduates planned for the ministry. The initial broad challenge to a learned clergy was also a religious one, which helped from the 1730s to ignite the episodic and migrating revivals we call the Great Awakening, as well as its nineteenth-century successor. To their revivalist critics, and with exceptions, the educated ministers had grown cerebral, genteel, content, unregenerate, and tepid—a lulling hindrance to the salvation of souls.

Persuaded that their Reformation forebears had not gone sufficiently far, a swarm of Seekers, Millenarians, Baptists, Anabaptists, and Quakers confronted the established clergy, engendered lay preachers, proclaimed a religion of the deprived, and championed emotion, intuition, and inspiration while submerging learning and nuanced doctrine. Joined by Independents and Methodists as the nineteenth century approached and emerged, exhorters discarded written sermons, some declaring their education came by "the immediate impression of the Holy Ghost," which provided spontaneous sermons. The awakeners were not the first of the devout to discount education and human intelligence, of course. Tertullian, himself an intellectual, had for 1500 years rhetorically provoked Christians to ponder what Athens had to do with Jerusalem. In Christianity's first decades, Paul had cautioned his converts to distinguish the gospel from worldly wisdom (1 Corinthians 1:18–29). Still, in the American colonies, the revivalists were the first to spark derision of intellect and learning into a burning social movement.

The popular success and perceived insolence of these itinerant upstarts "from miscellaneous occupations" naturally incited resistance in some quarters. "They needed no Books but the Bible," mocked one early opposer.[2] "They pleaded there was no Need of Learning in preaching, and that one of them could by the SPIRIT do better, than the Minister by his Learning; as if the SPIRIT and Learning were Opposites."

But the new American republic declared all men "created equal" and came to believe it in more than one sense. Thus arose the Age of Jackson, of "the common man." By 1830 and especially through the exertions of lay and itinerant exhorters, Baptists and Methodists, rather than Episcopalians, Congregationalists, and Presbyterians, comprised the largest denominations in three-quarters of the nation's territory.

This tradition of democratic anti-intellectualism overlapped the rise of Mormonism, which reaped a disproportionate harvest of converts among Methodists and Seekers. The new faith chaffed at aristocracies, rejected a trained ministry, scoffed at "philosophies of men, mingled with scripture," claimed new authority independent of previously established ecclesiastical channels, ordained all worthy and baptized men, foresaw an imminent millennium, encouraged extemporaneous preaching, and proclaimed direct personal access to God. In this mix, formal learning on religious matters struck many as dispensable. Undergirding all was Mormons' faith in living prophets, deepened over time by an accruing reverence for their stature and authority.

Misgivings toward intellectuals have continued in swaths of Mormonism throughout its history. The attitude in these cultural zones may condescend toward "worldly learning": The revealed doctrines of the church "are either true or not true. Our testimony is that they are true. Under these circumstances we may not permit ourselves to be too much impressed with the reasonings of men, no matter how well-founded they may seem to be."[3] In this spirit, countless Sunday classes, whose texts are restricted to scripture and corseted manuals shaped by committee at church headquarters, incline toward catechism. Lay teachers pose questions designed to elicit socially scripted responses. Joseph Smith is widely cited in support of the notion that God commonly chooses "the foolish and weak things of the world to confound the wise and mighty." Smith did make such proclamations, but a closer look at his teachings on learning, intelligence, spirit, and revelation reveal them to be complex and expansive.

JOSEPH SMITH'S INTELLECTUAL LEGACY

An oft-quoted Book of Mormon passage at once captures and sponsors something of Mormon reservations toward intellectuals: "O the vainness, and the frailties . . . of men! When they are learned they think they are wise, and they hearken not unto the counsel of God" (2 Nephi 9:28).

As in Smith's teachings generally, however, the enemy targeted here is not intelligence or education, but pride. Arrogance is rarely fetching, but Mormon scripture deplores its toxins, which may leave a person or clan inured to the plight of the poor, engulfed in pedantry, blind to talents of the underprivileged, unappreciative of organization and authority, numb to inspiration, oblivious to variant ways of knowing, beguiled by a mirage of monopoly on truth, deluded in self-sufficiency, and deaf to what God offers and requires. Joseph Smith did deride the conceits of worldly learning, just as his revelations warned of undue reliance on wealth, social standing, ostentation, physical or military might, and religious or civil authority infected by "unrighteous dominion." But it was not prosperity, beauty, strength, authority, or intelligence he censured. It was their abuse: virtues and graces transmogrified into idols. To Smith, intelligence was of the essence, literally, of human composition and was equally essential to the means and object of salvation and exaltation.

The first Mormon's dearth of education is sometimes exaggerated, but remains well documented. Raised in an impoverished home, the young Smith did manage to cultivate rudimentary skills. The limits of how far these had developed by age twenty-six, two years after the publication of the Book of Mormon, is thrice captured by the spelling, syntax, and content of an 1832 reminiscence of his boyhood years, penned in his own hand. When he had lived under his parents' roof, he remembered, both parents and children were consigned to hard labor for the survival of the family of eleven. Hence, wrote Joseph, "I was deprived of the bennifit of an education suffice it to say I was mearly instructtid in reading writing and the ground rules of Arithmatic which constuted my whole literary acquirements." Though untrained, the boy had displayed a pronounced curiosity and an astoundingly creative engagement with the world around him. According to his mother, he read less and pondered more than his siblings. He often studied the Bible and was invested in the religious debates of his day.[4]

The mature Smith, as a religious leader, could be sensitive about his unlearned past. He compensated by surrounding himself with men possessed of skills and credentials he lacked. In measuring his own formal knowledge against that of associates such as Oliver Cowdery, a school teacher and later a lawyer; Sidney Rigdon, a polished orator and former Campbellite preacher; and John C. Bennett, a medical apprentice, eventual Methodist preacher, persuasive lobbyist, and would-be founder of universities, Smith signaled a self-consciousness, sometimes a defensiveness, about his own provincialism. He punctuated his sermons betimes with fervent jabs at the theologically "learned doctors" of his time and place, and at those who thought "a man cannot preach unless he has been trained for the ministry."

Despite these elements, Smith came partially but briskly to transcend his beginnings. In something of a theological Big Bang, the Prophet unleashed over several years an extraordinary, complex quest for knowledge, the scope, conception, and end of which became cosmically vast. Before his early death at age thirty-eight, Smith's cumulative revelations and emergent ritual would beckon women and men to a redefined salvation and an extension of salvation: "exaltation" in the highest heaven. Attaining exaltation hinged on a perpetual amplification of knowledge, wisdom, and intelligence as much as on grace, covenant, and righteousness.

Smith's revealed schema posited the existence of free and willing intelligences eternally progressing before, during, and after earth life—progressing in character, cooperation, and capacity under God's tutelage. Such progress constitutes the essence, glory, and destiny of those who would "fulfill the measure of their creation." Intelligence, Smith taught, was core to what made up humans eternally, even before they became enfleshed—indeed, before the world's creation. Infused with potential virtue, spiritual growth, and proper relations with others, intelligence comprised an ontological link between humans and the God they worshipped—the greatest intelligence of all. This heady thrust came to pervade Smith's mature discourse and the ritual he bequeathed to the movement he founded.

Enlarged and made evident by revelation, the path of progress also demanded thought and old-fashioned study. "Intelligence cleaves unto intelligence," which cannot be created or destroyed but only organized and developed. "Whatever principle of intelligence we gain in this life will rise with us in the hereafter" (Doctrine and Covenants [D&C] 88:40; 93:29, 36; 130:18; Abraham 3).

As this cosmology was unfolding, Smith received a revelation in 1833 situating man "in the beginning with God," although the revelation did not expound upon the nature or substance of this existence (D&C 93:29).[5] It further defined intelligence as "light and truth" and the "glory of God." Smith's revelation linked obedience to the acquisition of further light and truth until one is glorified and "knoweth all things" (D&C 93:28, 29, 36). Smith here may have incidentally channeled perfectionist thinking from the contemporary holiness movement within Methodism, but the latter centered on the dissipation of the desire to sin; its moral preoccupation lacked Mormonism's cosmological aspects.

"Enlightenment" in this context clearly was no mere nineteenth-century afterclap of eighteenth-century ethics and rationalism. Mormon perfection was not to be achieved simply by adhering to a biblical or commonsense moral code, but also by attaining more light or intelligence, including a revealed sense of identity as an eternal spirit-intelligence and of God's purposes. Knowledge and intelligence, therefore, became crucial components in Smith's both ontology and soteriology.

A revelation, received in 1832–33, ostensibly clarified the source from which light, truth, and intelligence emanated, but did so by dissolving distinctions among traditional terms—conflating, for example, what others would have distinguished as physical, spiritual, intellectual, and metaphorical light. Christ, as the "light of truth," was "in all and through all things," including the sun, moon, and stars. His light also was the "law by which all things are governed, even the power of God." Smith's revelation placed Christ at the center of the cosmos as the radiant energy that infused life into all of God's creations. In Smith's cosmology, Christ served also as the gatekeeper and distributor of godly knowledge, as the source that "quickeneth your understandings." Smith's revelation, by defining the light of Christ as the source of truth, established a Christology that ascribed both knowledge and matter as a portion of the divine (D&C 88:6–13).[6] Mormon ritual, including the temple endowment, absorbed rhetorical elements pointing to a godly enlightenment. "Light," "truth," and "knowledge" blend as forces that even on earth thin "the veil" to reveal celestial glory.

With his evolving concept of organized intelligences seeking knowledge, Smith reemphasized God as the source of knowledge in an 1842 discourse: "As far as we degenerate from God we descend to the devil & lose knowledge & without knowledge we cannot be saved."[7] Smith also endowed heavenly worlds as facilitators of knowledge. The earth, in Smith's eschatology, would serve in its sanctified state as "a great Urim and Thummim" where "all things" concerning lower kingdoms would be manifested to the earth's inhabitants (D&C 130:7–10).

In a ritual reenactment of humankind's eternal destiny containing instructions on the priesthood, Smith "endowed" practitioners with divine knowledge. When in 1842 he introduced the ritual that would become the temple ceremony, Smith emphasized that the ordinance could "be received only by the Spiritual minded: and there was nothing made known to these men, but what will be made known to all Saints of the last days." Metaphorical "keys" promised endowed persons access to celestial glory if faithful; these included the divine knowledge necessary to gain access to celestial realms. Without the endowment of knowledge and power, Saints would be unable to "abide in the presence of [God] in the Eternal worlds."

By 1842, language about the centrality of acquired godly knowledge suffused Smith's theology and ritual. His panorama envisioned a span of existence from pre-earth intelligences, through embodied human experience, to resurrected, exalted, and eternal persons comprising perfected character and perfected intelligence. Smith's teachings thus connected God's power to the scope of His knowledge, a concept that reprised ideas in Abraham 3 (translated principally in 1835), but also in some ways laid the foundation for Smith's most expansive theological tenet yet: the potential for humans to become, in the eternities, like God.[8]

Three months before his own death, Joseph Smith's discourse at the funeral of his friend King Follett consummated his cosmological vision. Spirits were capable of eternal "enlargement" with the ultimate "privilege" to "advance" like God. The mind or "intelligent part" of man was "coequal [coeternal, consubstantial in potential] with God." The ultimate imperative for humankind was to "learn how to be a god yourself."[9] One aspect of this experiential education, in Smith's reckoning, may have come through his prophetic experience. Abraham Heschel's analysis of the biblical Hebrew prophets led him to conclude: "The fundamental experience of the prophet is a fellowship with the feelings of God, . . . which comes about through the prophet's reflection of, or participation in, the divine pathos."[10] This suggests a distinctive way of "knowing," and an arresting sample of Smith's version is his account of Enoch's horror at the vision of human sin God showed him (Moses 7:27–37).

Smith's distinctive ideas on the human potential for divinization (related to *theosis* in early eastern Christianity) required the perfection of matter as well as the gradual intellectual and moral advancement of spirits until they had achieved wholeness. Smith thus saw a world where, coupled with grace, human striving, learning, cooperation, and obedience could result, in the eternities, in individuals, families, and communities partaking of the divine nature.

A true "Mormon anti-intellectual," then, is a contradiction in terms. To the extent that Joseph Smith's teachings are central to one's religious baseline, a wedge driven between the mind and the spirit would constitute apostasy. It would contravene the eternal essence of self and the self's defining urge: to grow in capacity and quality. It would inflict a type of spiritual damnation: impeding progress toward a central object of human existence.

Still, Mormonism's diverse hierarchy and millions of followers in international settings and across time naturally produce diversity in understanding, interpreting, and applying Joseph Smith's unsystematized teachings. This diversity may be glimpsed by considering the range of ways that Saints receive, shape, and maintain their faith.

MORMONS' WAYS OF KNOWING

Although we restrict our view to Western religious traditions extant when Mormonism arose, all religious groups develop ways of knowing, and authorities and principles for doing so. About the time of Joseph Smith's first vision, American Unitarianism took institutional form, drawing on forces percolating for a century and more by insisting on the application of learning and reason in construing revealed scripture. New England's Transcendentalist brood rejected—and caricatured—"the corpse-cold" rationalism of Unitarianism's founding generation in favor of direct "Intuition" through the lens of nature. Religious humanists responded conversely, going further than early Unitarians by rejecting revelation and miracle altogether and holding that knowledge of reality derives essentially from observation, experimentation, and reasoned analysis. Within the Christian heritage, Quakers (not all of them Christian) came to accent an inner light and communal inspiration, denying the Bible or Christ as the final revelation. Roman Catholics hold scripture's authority to entwine with the tradition bequeathed by the church and the interpreting magisterium vested in each pope and the bishops in communion with him. Where did Christians obtain their divine scriptures in the first place, they ask of Protestants, except by the custody of the early church, delivered to a series of authorized successors? Methodists theologize in four-part harmony, on the basis of John Wesley's "Quadrilateral." The twentieth-century originator of this term came to rue it as a descriptor of Methodist method because it implied to the public that the four "sides" of the formula are equal. For Wesley, however, *scripture* is prime; doctrine, derived from scripture, must comport with orthodox Christian *tradition*; truth and faith come alive through *experience*; and the whole should be defensible through *reason*.

Despite such proclivities, the epistemic wellsprings of any religion, as they are applied in life, are commonly more implicit, complex, syncretic, evolving, and varied than formal statements suggest or than adherents may be aware of. Mormonism presents an illuminating case study.

On the first Sunday of each month, Latter-day Saints hold a "testimony meeting" in which, rather than hearing prepared homilies, members of the congregation rise, often spontaneously, and share their witness (of God's reality and love, perhaps, and of Christ's sacrifice; of the truth and the goodness of the Book of Mormon, the guidance of prophets, and daily life in the church). If one were to query those who had "testified" about the basis of their faith, the predominant response would entail the sense that God through the Holy Spirit and their experience had touched their hearts, given them assurance. Latter-day Saints reason, of course, like anyone else, but their reasoning is largely informal. Traditionally most are wary of overly intellectualizing their faith. Doing so might signal excess trust in human means, produce an aridly abstract belief rather than a heartfelt trust, and render believers vulnerable to the next clever logician to challenge what they hold sacred, what they *feel* more deeply than what they think.

"Anti-intellectualism," to the extent that it thrives in popular Mormon society, is not a hatred of intelligence. It is a preference for practicality over philosophy, action over abstraction, prophetic over intellectual authority, obedience over questioning, faith over doubt, humility over intellectual pride, communal loyalty over independent thought, and intuition and spiritual promptings over unaided reason as the primary form of intelligence.

Like others, Mormons pray daily for spiritual guidance and peace. They may feel the spirit's prompt in their choice of mate or occupation or in financial decisions, in an action to protect or discern the needs of a family member or acquaintance, in preparing a sermon to give in church. Adherents hope or believe that their bishops (unpaid pastors serving each ward or congregation) and stake presidents (who preside over a cluster of wards) were called to their assignments through inspiration received by general church authorities, as were the general authorities in their own stations. Both general and local authorities feel subject to divine guidance in directing their respective spheres. Each congregation, in turn, is staffed by lay members who are "called" through inspiration and practical needs for tasks that help the congregation function. Ideally, each member serves in a "calling": to visit and support specific families each month, to lead young men or women in their activities, to teach a Sunday school class, to direct or accompany or sing in the choir, or to steer the women's organization or a priesthood quorum. These members, in faith, access spiritual guidance for their respective duties in church service and for their private lives.

Inspired guidance is held as available to all believers, but the potential for conflicting inspirations is constrained by the principle of authority over one's proper domain, and no more. One may receive revelation for one's own life, for one's children, for one's assignment in the ward, but only the bishop is thought to have the authority ("keys") to receive inspiration to direct the affairs of his congregation as a whole. Only the apostles as a group and, uniquely, the church's president (presiding apostle) receive revelations authoritative for the general church. Through principles worked out in the church's early decades, Mormon revelation is thus at once democratic and hierarchically ordered.

Beyond revelation, Mormons typically retain faith in other biblical gifts of the spirit. The seventh of the now-canonized thirteen articles of Mormon faith, penned by Joseph Smith in 1842, asserts: "We believe in the gift of tongues, prophecy, revelation, visions, healing, interpretation of tongues, and so forth." This sounds Pentecostal, and earliest

Mormonism did decry the paucity of these gifts in traditional Christianity as a sign of degeneration from the power of the first-century church. Moreover, the Mormons experienced their own Pentecost in March 1836, during an eight-hour dedication service of the first Mormon temple at Kirtland, Ohio. Many of the thousand in attendance reported that God literally granted, in their presence, Joseph Smith's petition in the service's preceding prayer:

> Let it be fulfilled upon them, as upon those on the day of Pentecost; let the gift of tongues be poured out upon thy people, even cloven tongues as of fire, and the interpretation thereof. And let thy house be filled, as with a rushing mighty wind, with thy glory (D&C 109:36–37).

Members in attendance reported experiencing this "rushing mighty wind"; others saw glorious visions and prophesied. People of the neighborhood, it was said, saw light like a pillar of fire resting on the temple and came running in awe; some participants spoke in tongues. As with the first-century Pentecost at Jerusalem (Acts 2:1–13), skeptics present in 1836 Kirtland discounted or mocked the event, noting the presence of wine in the congregation and that many had been fasting in advance of the dedication. Still, cultural memory of the spiritual outpouring retains a place in twenty-first-century Mormonism.

The spirituality of contemporary Latter-day Saints, however, has less in common with Pentecostalism than with, say, evangelicalism and in some respects the inner light of Quakers. Glossolalia is not a noticeable feature of today's LDS Church. Its appearance at a contemporary meeting, especially in the developed world, would disturb those in attendance scarcely less than if it broke out at a Presbyterian service. The untamed phenomenon of 1830s Mormon experience invited regulation, as with Paul and his converts anciently. It has been long since Brigham Young and his generation made glossolalia and other ecstatic states a sporadic feature of worship.

"Speaking in tongues" in today's Mormonism is experienced as a tempered xenoglossia, as in this 2008 reader's comment on a not untypical blog:

> My brother learned Hungarian in 2 months to go on a mission. He speaks like a pro. [In] most college courses or high school language courses you would never be speaking anywhere near that well after years of study. That is the gift of tongues to me.... In my understanding, the gift of tongues is given by the power of the priesthood for a specific purpose, like missionary work, and not just because you think it would be cool.[11]

The drama in the account is more restrained than narratives common in earliest Mormonism, yet the writer perceives divine assistance.

More rare and explicit miracle is not expunged in contemporary Mormon sensibilities. Nor is it wholly confined to uncritical minds. A public example is Dr. T. Edgar Lyon, educated at the Universities of Chicago and Utah, who became a prominent historian, author, and teacher in the middle decades of the twentieth century. As a young man, Lyon had been called to a mission in the Netherlands, was discouraged at the prospect of having to master Dutch, and was startled when Apostle Melvin Ballard blessed him, prior to his departure, with the gift of tongues. The day following his arrival in Holland, Lyon marveled at understanding two sermons spoken in Dutch. Several weeks later, he reported, he was able both to understand and to speak comfortably in Dutch, without an American accent, he was told, to a particular man outside his home, leaving his experienced missionary companion incredulous. "[The ability] came just like that," Lyon recalled, "and left me [just as quickly]. But to me it gave me the feeling, 'I can learn it. I'm going to try.' "[12]

Whether viewed through an emic lens from within the believing community or from an etic, anthropological vantage, such lore contributes to the fabric of Mormon consciousness—how the world is imagined and encountered, how individual and group faith is shaped and sustained. In another context, reports like Lyon's might fruitfully be compared to analogous patterns among other religions. They might also be studied in conjunction with more secular renditions of extraordinary phenomena, such as Carl Jung's attestation of *synchronicity* (temporally coincident occurrences of apparently acausal but meaningful—even protective or redemptive—events), which he linked to his concept of the collective unconscious. It might be compared as well to prominent psychiatrist M. Scott Peck's definition and narration of "miracles" witnessed in his own life and in his practice.[13] At present, we must content ourselves with a glance at how Latter-day Saints acquire and sustain their religious faith.

The Moroni Paradigm and its Limits

The Book of Mormon concludes with an exhortation from a purported ancient leader, Moroni, son of the prophet, military head, historian, and custodian-editor of the annals after whom the Book of Mormon is named. The chronicle portrays Moroni as the last known survivor of his people, whose demise through corruption and warfare he mourns. Before adding his final inscriptions and burying the metallic records that centuries later would, in providential translation, become the Book of Mormon, Moroni proffers an admonition:

> And when ye shall receive these things, I would exhort you that ye would ask God, the Eternal Father, in the name of Christ, if these things are not true; and if ye shall ask with a sincere heart, with real intent, having faith in Christ, he will manifest the truth of it unto you, by the power of the Holy Ghost. And by the power of the Holy Ghost ye may know the truth of all things (Moroni 10:4–5).

If one accepted the Book of Mormon as revelation, it followed, for most, that the gifts of the Spirit continued in modern times and that Joseph Smith was what he claimed to be. A classic example of how many converts experience the promise in Moroni 10 is recounted by early apostle Parley Pratt:

> As I read . . . the Spirit of the Lord came upon me . . . and enlightened my mind, convinced my judgment, and riveted the truth upon my understanding . . . just as well as a man knows the daylight from the dark night. . . . I did not know it by any audible voice from heaven, by any ministration of an angel, by any open vision; but I knew it by the spirit of understanding in my heart—by the light that was in me . . . and I bore testimony of its truth to the neighbors that came in.[14]

Somewhere in the course of Mormon history, perhaps not until the late nineteenth century, the passage in Moroni 10 dethroned all others as the standard understanding of revelation and conversion to the faith through the Book of Mormon. Virtually every Mormon missionary proffers Moroni's exhortation to prospective converts. The hegemony of the passage in Mormon ranks remains.

In the beginning it was not so. During the first decades of the church Moroni 10 sketched but one way among others of coming to conviction. These paths included that of potential converts, like John Corrill, who studiously compared the Book of Mormon to the Bible, reasoning to verify the former by the latter. They included also the persuasion of some through the behavior and testimony of others, such as the eleven first-hand witnesses of Joseph Smith's gold plates, whose testimony they were unable to impeach. Other converts told of personal revelation received independently of the Book of Mormon.[15]

Because revelation was theoretically available to all, claims that rivaled Joseph Smith's arose in the early church, inducing authorities to issue qualifications concerning any revelation's trustworthiness. Leaders grew alarmed about enthusiasm—"some very strange spiritual operations"—and warned that while disciples were not to treat prophecies with contempt, yet they must test or "prove all things" and "hold fast that which is good" (often citing 1 Thessalonians 5:20–21, as did anti-Mormons urging reasoned critique of the Saints). Joseph Smith declared a revelation in May 1831 reinforcing the relevance of judicious discourse: since false and deceiving spirits were abroad in the world, church members were to seek discernment by gathering to "reason together, that ye may understand." Conjuring Isaiah, the revelation continued: "Let us reason even as a man reasoneth one with another face to face" (D&C 50:2–3, 10–13; Isaiah 1:18). The revelation further proclaimed that those who were under the influence of the Holy Spirit and those who witnessed their experience would naturally understand one another. All other spirits were of the devil (D&C 50:17–23). Thus spiritual claims were to be checked by rational assessment as much as the converse.

In short, the understandings that twenty-first-century Saints tether to Moroni 10 did not dominate original Mormonism as the path to conversion in the way it later came to. Indeed, a survey of citations of the Book of Mormon found in LDS literature before the Mormon exodus to the Rocky Mountains discloses that verses cited from *anywhere* in the Book of Moroni were rare.[16] Not until the mid-twentieth century did the church print editions of the Book of Mormon with the excerpt of Moroni 10:4–5 placed at the beginning as the first thing readers saw.

While Moroni's words have inspired hundreds of thousands, the coronation of the passage in Mormon consciousness in recent generations has an underside. More often in private than in public (though the Internet is changing this), one encounters disappointed church members, despondent missionaries, resistant potential converts, or bitter former Mormons who tell of a failed, sometimes wrenching, struggle. They have read the Book of Mormon, they say, and prayed earnestly with all the faith they could find, sometimes for months or years. Those who have not had the anticipated experience have sometimes doubted the Book of Mormon, the church, themselves, or God. The promise in Moroni 10 backfires for some.

Or at least modern cultural presumptions about the passage can miscarry. In the longer span of Mormon history, as we have seen, Moroni 10 did not always dominate epistemologies of faith. And in the wider realm of Mormon scripture an array of elements and paths to faith appear. The Book of Mormon prophet, Alma, for example, proposes an "experiment," with faith sprouting gently as a nurtured seed whose goodness and viability can take experiential, organic root, its components tested as it grows (Alma 32). His father, also Alma, asserts the need to give away one's sins in preparation for conversion, and to yearn to "be called [God's] people," to "bear one another's burdens," "to mourn with those that mourn," "comfort those that stand in need of comfort," and "stand as witnesses of God at all times and in all things and in all places" (Mosiah 18:7–9). In a related vein, the gospel of John casts Christ as saying that preliminary participation in his principles is itself a road to "knowing": "If any man will do his will, he shall know of the doctrine, whether it be of God, or whether I speak of myself" (John 7:17). Matthew's rendition of the Sermon on the Mount asserts that the behavior and experience of those making religious claims serves as a gauge for seekers: "by their fruits ye shall know them," whether good or bad (Matthew 7:15–20). Patterned after Paul's list of spiritual gifts and insistence that not all disciples received the same ones (1 Corinthians 12), Joseph Smith proffered revelation that extended distinctions: "To some it is given by the Holy Ghost to know that Jesus Christ is the Son of God. . . . To others it is given to believe on their words, that they also might have eternal life." (D&C 46:13–14). Strikingly, Mormon scripture even declares that some with faith have been led by the Holy Spirit unawares: "And whoso cometh unto me with a broken heart and a contrite spirit, him will I baptize with fire and with the Holy Ghost, even as the Lamanites, because of their faith in me at the time of their conversion, were baptized with fire and with the Holy Ghost, *and they knew it not*" (3 Nephi 9:20; emphasis added). The image of one being baptized with fire without awareness warrants pondering. But it is clear that the paradigms for receiving faith are not monolithic in Mormon scripture, let alone in the diverse experiences of millions of participants.

The inability to be certain of religious truth may put one at sea in a tight religious community inclined to proclaim its certainty. This dynamic contributes to a struggle besetting a widening circle of Latter-day Saints. The grapple with doubt is frequently painful, lonely, psychological, epistemological, and spiritual. In other instances it takes on a social dimension, spread by word of mouth and the Internet, as people seek places of safety where all questions are allowed, discussed with candor, and faith is not seen as at odds with critical thinking.

Sometimes one's doubts reach critical mass, morphing into frustration, disbelief, even hostility. Sometimes the critical mass becomes social; one may join a proud movement of skeptics: members or former members who feel betrayed by the church that taught them faith without critical thought. These may absorb reinforcement from the like-minded. Private turmoil may combine with a belated exposure to complex issues in Mormon history (polygamy, perhaps; the historicity of the Book of Mormon, Joseph Smith's imperfections) or to controversial church policy on social issues (gay marriage, the role of women in church and society, racial discrimination prior to 1978).

A broader context for this challenge to faith is egalitarian America's eroding trust in banks, Congress, and all manner of institutions, including organized religion, the withdrawal from which affects virtually every contemporary denomination. And Mormonism is nothing if not organized and disciplined—in natural tension with the lure of a do-it-yourself subculture whose creed is become, "I'm spiritual, not religious." A broader context yet may be seen across today's technologized, connected world, where a wedge between generations in *most* religious traditions is apparent.

In opposition to these currents in the Mormon world is the thriving mainstream church, the influential stream of testimony issuing from LDS leaders whom adherents esteem as inspired, as well as the deep bonds of community, experience, service, and whisperings of the spirit as understood in the common Mormon culture.

A Mormon intelligentsia contributes an additional dimension to LDS faith. The religion has always produced intellectuals, a portion of them shedding their faith. Only since the 1960s, however, has a sizable and sustainable *community* of well-educated and committed Latter-day Saints congealed, intent on exploring Mormon faith with critical rigor, independent of church auspices, with their own organizations and publications, while engaging scholars of any or no faith. In the twenty-first century, the church itself, led by but not restricted to its historical department, has signaled increased regard for transparent and rigorous scholarship focused on religion, some of it in response to Internet-fueled challenges to faith. The church has, for example, sponsored exhaustive, candid, and top-tier research on unflattering episodes, such as the infamous massacre of a wagon train at Mountain Meadows in 1857 in the context of the Utah War. The church is also publishing virtually the entire corpus of Joseph Smith's papers in more than twenty volumes, along with hundreds of thousands of other important documents. It has posted on its website conservative but informed and responsible statements addressing the most delicate issues in its history, including polygamy, the translation of the Book of Mormon, and the nature of the Book of Abraham. It is rewriting educational materials, taking pains not to overlook human error in the faith's unfolding. The church website now declares:

[Making] sense of encounters between faith and reason—no matter the religious tradition—is part of the human religious experience. . . . Mormon doctrine stresses the need and responsibility to engage both head and heart in decision making, in learning, in relationships and in worship. . . . All understanding, whether spiritual or rational, is worked out in constant questioning and discovery. The Prophet Joseph Smith said, "By proving contraries, truth is made manifest." . . . Latter-day Saints do not expect God to simply hand down information. He expects us to wrestle with the complications of life through prayerful searching and sound thinking. "You must study it out in your mind," Mormon scripture teaches, and then answers will come. This pattern of inquiry opens Mormons to expanding spiritual possibilities.[17]

Like other believers, LDS scholars and thinkers talk of a spiritual dimension, but their lot is made more complex through engagement with, and responsibility to, the hard thought and evidence of science, social science, the arts, and the humanities. The ways that Mormon thinkers bridge the life of the mind and spirit range widely.[18]

A small army of researchers, clustered in but not exclusively housed at Brigham Young University, takes one tack by defending the historicity of the Book of Mormon through attempted proof or establishment of plausibility. Sometimes their argument is archaeologically based, as with the work of anthropologist John Sorenson, who has articulated the most influential theory for an ancient American historical setting for the events portrayed in the Book of Mormon, namely a restricted Mesoamerican area of only a few hundred square miles. He supports his theories with, among other things, a bibliography of thousands of entries from a dozen languages treating evidence of pre-Columbian voyages to the Americas. Sorenson argues for more than 400 points where the Book of Mormon text corresponds to characteristic Mesoamerican situations, statements, allusions, and history, rendering more complex the standard depiction of the western hemisphere as peopled anciently solely through Asian migrations crossing a former land bridge at the Bering Strait.

Other defenders of historical plausibility marshal literary analysis, such as John Welch's 1967 discovery of elaborate instances of the ancient literary form, chiasmus, in the Book of Mormon. This militates, he contends, toward reading the book as a genuinely ancient text characterized by Hebrew literary patterns not recognized by scholars in the United States until a century after the Book of Mormon was published.

In yet other respects this sort of argument for the plausibility of Mormon claims is grounded on numerous obscure parallels between the ancient world and the Book of Mormon or contemporary LDS theology and ritual, which Joseph Smith was unlikely to be aware of. The import of these parallels is premised on the notion that Mormonism comprises a restoration of truths and authority lost through ancient apostasy. The godfather of such arguments is the late prolific prodigy Hugh Nibley, who elaborated similarities between contemporary Mormonism and ancient elements such as the obscure figure of Enoch, the practice of temple ritual and symbology, the doctrine and practice of baptism for the dead, and early Christian Gnosticism. In pursuing these themes, Nibley called upon a vast reservoir of linguistic skills in Egyptian, Hebrew, Greek, Latin, Arabic, Dutch, French, German, Italian, Old Norse, Russian, and others.

Many thinkers describe spiritual influences in ways not unlike the general church membership, though in ways also conversant with the academy. Harvard-trained philosopher Truman Madsen poses questions to seekers anxious about their sense of the sacred. Three examples (here shortened and paraphrased) suggest the line of inquiry: Have you ever received what [Joseph Smith] calls "pure intelligence flowing into you" or a quickening in your soul that binds you to a truth or a person or a sacred place; a drawing power toward something or away from something that you cannot trace into your ordinary environment? Have you ever been lifted beyond your natural ability when giving a talk or lesson? Have you ever prayed and been lifted beyond yourself, both in manner and in the content of your expression, so that it became more than a dialogue with yourself? If so, Madsen implies, you have experienced the Holy Spirit.

For some intellectuals, a sense of miracle and certainty retain a prominent role. Astronaut and nuclear and space physicist Don Lind tells of receiving a priesthood blessing before flying on the space shuttle Challenger in 1985. Dr. Lind was promised "in the name of the Lord" that he would "go and come in safety." He details the "miracle" that subsequent investigation showed to have spared his mission, by three-tenths of a second, from the historic tragedy that befell the exploding Challenger and its crew nine months later. "Much of [my faith] comes from the inner whisperings of the Holy Spirit," writes Lind, but some of it derives from miraculous events ("and I've had many more similar experiences") that "change a casual beginning testimony into an unshakable certainty that the Lord exists and watches over us individually."[19]

For others, certainty is not part of the recipe and the urge to prove is not strong. Historian Richard Bushman describes himself as a questioner and sympathizer to philosophic quandaries, but remains a Mormon on simpler grounds. "That which is truly good, is true," he has written. And "When I followed my religion I became the kind of man I want to be." Of excess abstraction Goethe famously said, "Theory, dear friend, is gray, but the golden tree of life springs ever green." Veins of Bushman's thought run parallel. For this Mormon intellectual, theories and rational discourse have at times seemed "a little capricious and unreal and, in the end, compared to the experience of life itself, not serious."

Terryl and Fiona Givens stress the importance of a faith freely chosen, proposing that the certainty so widely sought is not only inaccessible to most people, but perhaps counterproductive. Like Voltaire, they find an existential equilibrium in the evidence for and against God and a meaningful universe. Hence how we construe the world—what value and meaning we assign to our joys, pain, lives, and relationships—is not based strictly on the evidence, but on how we respond to that evidence. We judge not merely by our wits, but are pulled also by claims on our values, yearnings, fears, appetites, and egos. "What we choose to embrace, to be responsive to, is the purest reflection of what we are and what we love. That is why faith, the choice to believe is . . . an action . . . laden with moral significance." The call to faith is not

> some test of a coy god, waiting to see if we "get it right." It is the only summons, issued under the only conditions, which can allow us fully to reveal who we are, what we most love, and what we most devoutly desire.

To believe or not to believe: that is the question enabling "the freest possible projection of what resides in our hearts."[20]

Mormon intellectuals typically embrace science, reason, and critical thought *en masse*, but insist that reason and empiricism are not the only channels through which to access reality. "One cannot think too well" about religion or any other matter, writes one, "but one can think too much," as when a violinist, orator, or athlete grows overly deliberate, neglecting their instincts and marring performance. Science is essential to modern knowledge, but is an inadequate tool for the kinds of knowing that come through art, music, instinct, conscience, love, and beauty.[21]

Mormons, then, may speak simply of "a reason for the hope that is in them" (1 Peter 3:15), holding allegiance to scripture, alluding to the words of living prophets, attesting to the Spirit that feeds their faith. Beneath the surface and in practice, however, that faith is grounded in a highly syncretic compost with many variants. Each of these epistemic streams colors and shapes how the others are construed. The Mormon experience of inspiration is mediated, interpreted, and conditioned by reasoned discourse or assumptions, proof-texts from scripture, and the instruction and framework of parents, teachers, leaders, and peers. All these are in turn culled from a much larger tradition forged, accruing, amended, and bequeathed across the generations, then filtered by personal and social experience, individual and group interpretation, application and feedback.

Perhaps there are as many combinations and inflections of such elements, beneath conscious and official principles, as there are believing Mormons. To followers of Joseph Smith, the whole is framed by the workings and wrestlings of the mind and spirit. For mind and spirit, now merged in flesh, is what humans—and their God—eternally are.

NOTES

1. Friedman, *Martin Buber*, chap. 26.
2. Chauncy, *Seasonable Thoughts*, 259.
3. Letter (November 12, 1947) from the church's First Presidency, headed by George Albert Smith, in response to Dr. Lowry Nelson, who had respectfully explained his concerns as a Mormon sociologist about the church's then current position forbidding black men from being ordained to the priesthood.
4. *History of the Church of Jesus Christ of Latter-day Saints*, 4: 78. Wilford Woodruff, in 1875, classified Joseph Smith as an "illiterate youth" who was able to "fulfill the measure of his appointment," Woodruff, "Parable of the Ten Virgins," 1875, 18: 118; Davidson et al., *Joseph Smith Papers: Histories*, 1: 11; Joseph Smith, History, 1838–1856, vol. A-1, 2–3, Joseph Smith Papers; Barlow, *Mormons and the Bible*, chap. 1.
5. Smith's revelation hints at a more materialist interpretation of the word "spirit": "For man is spirit. The elements are eternal" (D&C 93:33), later made more explicit, "All spirit is matter, but it is more fine or pure" (D&C 131:7–8). While Smith's ontology was sharply distinctive in America, Platonic theologians had long ago conceded the divine must be made of a substance, even if that substance was immaterial.
6. The pervasiveness of the light of Christ for Smith paralleled closely the doctrine of emanation associated with the neo-Platonic philosopher Plotinus.

7. Ehat and Cook, *Words of Joseph Smith*, 113–14.

8. Joseph Smith, History, 1838–1856, vol. C-1, 1328, Joseph Smith Papers; Bushman, *Joseph Smith*, 452.

9. Joseph Smith, Discourse, Nauvoo, IL, April 7, 1844, as reported by William Clayton, 14-17, Joseph Smith Papers.

10. Heschel, *Prophets*, 26.

11. "Do Mormons believe in tongues?" *Yahoo Answers*. https://answers.yahoo.com/question/index?qid=20070614080508AA6VoEh.

12. Lyon, Papers, ca. 1935–1989; see also, Arrington and Bitton, *Saints without Halos*, 144.

13. Peck, *Road Less Traveled*, 225–312.

14. Pratt, "Reminiscences and Testimony of Parley P. Pratt," 1856, 5: 194.

15. Patterson, "Divine Revelations/Delusions Revealed," 54–66.

16. Grant Underwood found only eight instances: Underwood, "Book of Mormon Usage in Early LDS Theology," 57.

17. "Mormon and Modern."

18. Several hundred compact statements of faith are available at www.mormonscholarstestify.org. Longer essays are periodically found in Mormon-oriented journals such as *BYU Studies* or *Dialogue: A Journal of Mormon Thought*. More in-depth treatment and collections facilitating comparison are exemplified in the works by Philip Barlow, Richard Bushman, Terryl and Fiona Givens, and Robert Rees in the references. Specialized professional groups of Mormon artists, writers, scientists, counselors and psychotherapists, and scholars in the humanities and social sciences are exploring the realm of faith implicitly and sometimes explicitly. Blogs of varying character, with their inherent strengths and weaknesses and generally not refereed for quality, contribute to this sphere.

19. Lind, "Testimonies."

20. Bushman, "My Belief"; Bushman, "Reasons."; Givens and Givens, *God Who Weeps*, 4-5.

21. Barlow, "Ten Commandments for Balancing the Mind and the Spirit on Campus," 154–55; Givens and Givens, *Crucible of Doubt*, 16–17.

BIBLIOGRAPHY

Arrington, Leonard J., and Davis Bitton. *Saints without Halos: The Human Side of Mormon History*. Salt Lake City: Signature, 1981.

Barlow, Philip L. *Mormons and the Bible: The Place of the Latter-day Saints in American Religion*. Rev. ed. New York: Oxford University Press, 2013.

Barlow, Philip L., ed. *A Thoughtful Faith: Essays on Belief by Mormon Scholars*. Centerville, UT: Canon, 1986.

Barlow, Philip L. "Ten Commandments for Balancing the Mind and the Spirit on Campus." In *A Twenty-Something's Guide to Spirituality*, ed. Jacob Werrett and David Read, 134–71. Salt Lake City: Deseret, 2007.

Bushman, Richard L. *Believing History: Latter-day Saint Essays*. Ed. Reid L. Neilson and Jed Woodworth. New York: Columbia University Press, 2007.

Bushman, Richard L. *Joseph Smith: Rough Stone Rolling*. New York: Alfred A. Knopf, 2005.

Bushman, Richard L. "My Belief." In *A Thoughtful Faith: Essays on Belief by Mormon Scholars*, ed. Philip L. Barlow, 17–27. Centerville, UT: Canon, 1986.

Bushman, Richard L. "Reasons." *Mormon Scholars Testify*. January 2010. http://mormonschol-arstestify.org/396/richard-lyman-bushman.

Chauncy, Charles. *Seasonable Thoughts on the State of Religion in New-England*. Boston: Rogers and Fowle, 1743. http://books.google.com/books?id=N84CAAAAQAAJ&printsec=frontco ver&source=gbs_ge_summary_r&cad=0#v=onepage&q&f=false.

Corrill, John. *A Brief History of the Church of Christ of the Latter Day Saints (Commonly Called Mormons): Including an Account of Their Doctrine and Discipline; With the Reasons of the Author for Leaving the Church*. St. Louis: Author, 1839.

Davidson, Karen Lynn, David J. Whittaker, Richard L. Jensen, and Mark Ashurst-McGee, eds. *The Joseph Smith Papers: Histories*. Vol. 1: *1832–1844*. Salt Lake City: Church Historian's Press, 2012.

Ehat, Andrew F., and Lyndon W. Cook, eds. *The Words of Joseph Smith: The Contemporary Accounts of the Nauvoo Discourses of the Prophet Joseph*. Salt Lake City: Bookcraft, 1980.

Friedman, Maurice S. *Martin Buber: The Life of Dialogue*. Chicago: University of Chicago Press, 1955.

Givens, Terryl L. *People of Paradox: A History of Mormon Culture*. New York: Oxford University Press, 2007.

Givens, Terryl L. *Wrestling the Angel: The Foundations of Mormon Thought: Cosmos, God, Humanity*. New York: Oxford University Press, 2014.

Givens, Terryl L., and Fiona Givens. *The Crucible of Doubt: Reflections on the Quest for Faith*. Salt Lake City: Deseret, 2014.

Givens, Terryl L., and Fiona Givens. *The God Who Weeps: How Mormonism Makes Sense of Life*. Salt Lake City: Ensign Peak, 2012.

Hofstadter, Richard. *Anti-Intellectualism in American Life*. New York: Knopf, 1963.

Heschel, Abraham. *The Prophets*. New York: Harper Perennial Modern Classics, 2001.

History of the Church of Jesus Christ of Latter-day Saints. 7 vols. Salt Lake City: Deseret, 1948–50.

The Joseph Smith Papers. http://josephsmithpapers.org/.

Journal of Discourses. 26 vols. Reported by G. D. Watt et al. Liverpool: F. D. and S. W. Richards et al., 1851–86; reprint., Salt Lake City: n.p., 1974.

Letter, George Albert Smith to Lowry Nelson, 12 November 1947, in Lowry Nelson writings and papers, 1948–1974, MSS 17, box 4, fd. 2. Special Collections and Archives, Utah State University, Logan, UT.

Lind, Don L. "Testimonies." *Mormon Scholars Testify*. January 2010. http://mormonscholarst-estify.org/497/don-l-lind.

Lyon, T. Edgar. Papers, ca. 1935–1989, MS 9468, Church History Library, Church of Jesus Christ of Latter-day Saints, Salt Lake City, Utah.

"Mormon and Modern." *Newsroom*, July 6, 2012. http://www.mormonnewsroom.org/article/mormon-and-modern.

Mould, Tom. *Still, the Small Voice: Narrative, Personal Revelation, and the Mormon Folk Tradition*. Logan: Utah State University Press, 2011.

Nibley, Hugh W. *The Collected Works of Hugh Nibley*. 19 vols. Salt Lake City: Deseret, 1986–2010.

Noll, Mark A. *The Scandal of the Evangelical Mind*. Grand Rapids: William B. Eerdmans, 1994.

Patterson, Sara M. "'Divine Revelations/Delusions Revealed': Historical Understandings of Revelation in Debates over Mormonism." PhD diss., Claremont Graduate University, 2005.

Peck, M. Scott. *The Road Less Traveled: A New Psychology of Love, Traditional Values and Spiritual Growth*. New York: Touchstone, 1978.

Pratt, Parley P. "Reminiscences and Testimony of Parley P. Pratt" [September 7, 1856]. *Journal of Discourses* 5: 193–201.

Rees, Robert, ed. *Why I Stay: The Challenges of Discipleship for Contemporary Mormons*. Vols. 1 (and 2 forthcoming). Salt Lake City: Signature, 2011.

Reeve, W. Paul, and Michael Scott Van Wagenen, eds. *Between Pulpit and Pew: The Supernatural World in Mormon History and Folklore*. Logan: Utah State University Press, 2011.

Smith, Joseph. "Discourse, Nauvoo, IL, April 7, 1844, as Reported by William Clayton, 14–17, Joseph Smith Papers." http://josephsmithpapers.org/paperSummary/discourse-7-april-1844-as-reported-by-william-clayton.

Sorenson, John L. *An Ancient American Setting for the Book of Mormon*. Salt Lake City: Deseret and FARMS, 1985.

Sorenson, John L. *Mormon's Codex: An Ancient American Book*. Salt Lake City: Deseret, 2013.

Underwood, Grant. "Book of Mormon Usage in Early LDS Theology." *Dialogue: A Journal of Mormon Thought* 17, no. 3 (Autumn 1984): 35–74.

Webb, Stephen H. *Jesus Christ, Eternal God: Heavenly Flesh and the Metaphysics of Matter*. New York: Oxford University Press, 2011.

Welch, John W., ed. *Chiasmus in Antiquity: Structures, Analyses, Exegesis*. Provo, UT: Neal A. Maxwell Institute, 1998.

Woodruff, Wilford. "Parable of the Ten Virgins" [September 12, 1875]. *Journal of Discourses* 18: 109–22.

....

CHAPTER 17

THE NATURE OF GOD
IN MORMON THOUGHT

....

DAVID L. PAULSEN AND HAL R. BOYD

In the *New York Times Magazine*, Harvard's Noah Feldman writes matter-of-factly: "a majority of Americans have no idea what Mormons believe."[1] This appears to be particularly true with regard to the Latter-day Saint understanding of God and the Trinity.[2] Consequently we attempt to outline in this chapter the general Latter-day Saint doctrine of deity by briefly identifying the sources on which LDS theology rests, using these sources to set out ten distinctively LDS teachings regarding God the Father and the Trinity, and exploring the theological and philosophical advantages of these doctrines while also briefly addressing some common criticisms leveled against them. Throughout the piece we affirm that the God of Mormonism resembles the God portrayed in biblical scripture.

After experiencing a remarkable theophany, philosopher Blaise Pascal famously drew a distinction between the God of the Bible and the God conceived by theologians. Pascal called the former the God of Abraham, Isaac, and Jacob, and the latter the God of the philosophers. Though variously conceived, the God of the philosophers is usually portrayed as being beyond any possible comparison to earthly entities—an all-supreme, all-controlling, all-determining being that is wholly other, immaterial, immutable, impassible, atemporal, and nonspatial.[3] The God of Abraham, Isaac, and Jacob and the God of Mormonism differ radically from the God of the philosophers.

The God of Mormonism is not all-controlling or all-determining; instead He endows mortals with agency, allowing them an important role in deciding morally significant outcomes. Additionally, the God of Mormonism is not wholly other, immaterial, immutable, or impassible, but is gloriously embodied, presiding over the Godhead (or Trinity) as a profoundly possible Father and loving God. Mormonism's God is not the creator of all things out of nothing, but the organizer of the cosmos out of chaotic matter and other eternal realities. As Harold Bloom observed: "The Yahweh who closes Noah's ark with his own hands, descends to make on-the-ground inspections of Babel and Sodom, and who picnics with two angels under Abram's terebinth trees at Mamre is very close, in personality and dynamic passion, to the God of Joseph Smith, far closer than to the Platonic-Aristotelian divinity of Saint Augustine and Moses Maimonides."[4] *This* God is not the God of logical construct; rather He is the God who revealed himself to Abraham, Isaac, and Jacob—and to various latter-day prophets including Joseph Smith.

1 Sources of the Mormon Understanding of God and the Trinity

The LDS Church has no systematic or official theology as such.[5] Its doctrines regarding God the Father and the Trinity are based not primarily on rational theologizing, but on what it believes to be divine self-disclosures. In modern times, these divine self-disclosures commenced with a personal visit by God the Father and Jesus Christ to the young Joseph Smith. Years later Smith taught: "Could we read and comprehend all that has been written from the days of Adam on the relation of man to God . . . we should know little about it. . . . Could you gaze into heaven five minutes, you would know more than you would by reading all that ever was written on the subject."[6] Smith and other prophets have claimed many such gazes.

Thus the Mormon understanding of God is primarily derived from thoughtful reflection upon these revelations collected in the church's Standard Works, which include the Bible, the Book of Mormon, the Doctrine and Covenants, and the Pearl of Great Price. Together with official declarations of the First Presidency of the church, the Standard Works constitute the principal sources for LDS theology. Additionally, members give significant weight to noncanonized discourses by Joseph Smith and other latter-day prophets and apostles.

2 God the Father and the Trinity: Mormon Understandings

Reflection on the Mormon canon and the wider discourse leads us to ten affirmations about the Latter-day Saint understanding of God the Father and the Trinity. With some exceptions to be noted, these affirmations are shared by the vast majority of reflective Latter-day Saints.

1. Mormons believe that God the Father is a temporally eternal, self-existent divine being. He has always existed and will always exist.[7] He is not dependent on anyone or anything other than His own nature for His existence.

Scriptures in the LDS canon repeatedly declare God to be eternal or everlasting. From the prayerful psalmist we read, "Before the mountains were brought forth, or ever thou hadst formed the earth and the world, even from everlasting to everlasting, thou art God" (Psalm 90:2). Isaiah refers to God as "the high and lofty One that inhabiteth eternity" (Isaiah 57:15), and the Book of Mormon prophet Nephi describes God's course as "one eternal round" (1 Nephi 10:19; see also Alma 37:12).

In 1840, Joseph Smith pronounced his own view: "I believe that God is eternal. That he had no beginning, and can have no end. Eternity means that which is without beginning or end."[8] Also, in his watershed King Follett discourse delivered just two months prior to his death, Smith explicitly affirmed, "We say that God himself is a self-existent being. . . . It is correct enough. God *is* a self-existent being."[9]

Some LDS thinkers have suggested that Heavenly Father may be timeless, having no temporal location or duration. Taken together, however, scripture and datum discourse suggest that God is temporally rather than timelessly eternal. On this point, Latter-day Saints depart from classical Christian theology, but they are hardly alone. Increasingly, influential contemporary Christian thinkers reject the Augustinian, Thomistic, and Calvinistic conceptions of divine timelessness, and they do so on biblical as well as philosophical grounds. These scholars include Nicholas Wolterstorff, Stephen Davis, Richard Swinburne, Clark Pinnock, Nelson Pike, and Anthony Kenny, to name just a few.

Some of them, such as Richard Swinburne, find the doctrine of timelessness logically incoherent; he says,

> The claim that God is timeless . . . seems to contain an inner incoherence and also to be incompatible with most things which theists ever wish to say about God."[10] Similarly, Anthony Kenny states: "the whole concept of a timeless eternity, the whole of which is simultaneous with every part of time, seems to be radically incoherent. For simultaneity as ordinarily understood is a transitive relation. If *A* happens at the same time as *B*, and *B* happens at the same time as *C*, then *A* happens at the same time as *C*. . . . [O]n this view, the great fire of Rome is simultaneous with the whole of eternity. Therefore, while I type these very words, Nero fiddles heartlessly on.[11]

Others reject divine timelessness on biblical grounds. For instance, Nicholas Wolterstorff points out: "The biblical writers do not present God as some passive factor within reality but as an agent in it. Further, they present him as acting within *human* history." Indeed, Wolterstorff says, if we are to accept the biblical witness of God as redeemer, we must conceive of him as everlasting rather than timeless, "This is so because God the Redeemer is a God who *changes*. And any being which changes is a being among whose states there is temporal succession." Nevertheless, he continues, "there is an important sense in which God as presented in the Scriptures is changeless: he is steadfast in his redeeming intent and ever faithful to his children. Yet, *ontologically*, God cannot be a redeeming God without there being changeful variation among his states."[12]

Some proponents of divine timelessness claim that the doctrine is necessary to preserve God's absolute sovereignty and illimitability. But Stephen Davis persuasively argues that temporality in no way diminishes God's status: "He can still be an eternal being, i.e., a being without beginning or end. He can still be the creator of the universe.

He can still be immutable in the sense of remaining ever true to his promises and purposes and eternally retaining his essential nature. He can still be the loving, omnipotent redeemer Christians worship."[13]

2. God the Father is the fount of divinity. Both God the Son and God the Holy Spirit are begotten of Him, yet each is fully God, possessing all of the properties essential to divinity.

While God the Son and God the Holy Spirit are, like the Father, eternal, self-existent persons, Mormons also believe both were spiritually begotten of the Father long before our world's beginning. The New Testament alludes to Christ as the firstborn of the Father in the spirit (see Colossians 1:13–15; Hebrews 1:5–6) and the Only Begotten of the Father in the flesh (see John 1:14; 3:16). Inasmuch as God the Father begot the Son and the Holy Ghost, God the Father is, as Joseph Smith put it, "God the first"[14] in the Godhead.

In a rare doctrinal exposition entitled "The Father and the Son" published in 1916, the First Presidency and the Quorum of the Twelve Apostles of the church declared that "Jesus Christ is the Son of Elohim [God the Eternal Father] both as spiritual and bodily offspring; that is to say, Elohim is literally the Father of the spirit body of Jesus Christ and also of the body in which Jesus Christ performed his mission in the flesh." These church leaders deliberately refrained from making any further claims regarding the process by which the Father sired the Son's spiritual or mortal body, saying that "no extended explanation . . . seems necessary."[15] The Book of Mormon states that Christ would be born of the virgin Mary "who shall . . . conceive by the power of the Holy Ghost and bring forth a son, yea, even the Son of God" (Alma 7:10). While the LDS canon provides considerable detail regarding the Holy Ghost's work and witness, it offers less insight into his intrinsic nature or origin.

Additionally, holy writ does not fully explain how or why Jesus and the Holy Ghost are divine beings—perhaps divinity is intrinsic to their self-existent natures, comes from their begotten enlargements, is somehow acquired developmentally (see Doctrine and Covenants [D&C] 93:14), or some combination of the three (see John 5:26). Yet, scripturally it does appear that they, in some way, derive their divinity from God the Father (see John 5:26).

3. God is also in some literal sense the Father of the human family and the husband of a Heavenly Mother.[16] Men and women are "begotten sons and daughters of God" (see D&C 76:24; Hebrews 12:9). Spirit bodies, though invisible to ordinary human perception, are nonetheless material and in the form of our bodies of flesh and bones (see D&C 131:7–8).

While the *how* of human spiritual generation from the Father has not been revealed, Latter-day Saints understand human beings, qua spirits, to be "offspring" of God the Father in some genetic or quasi-genetic sense. We read in Hebrews: "we have had fathers of our flesh which corrected us, and we gave them reverence: shall we not much rather be in subjection unto the Father of spirits, and live?" (Hebrews 12:9). The 1916

First Presidency statement adds, "God the Eternal Father, whom we designate by the exalted name-title 'Elohim,' is the literal Parent of our Lord and Savior Jesus Christ, and the spirits of the human race."[17] More recently, an official proclamation from the First Presidency of the church and the Quorum of the Twelve Apostles in 1995, affirms that "all human beings—male and female—are created in the image of God. Each is a beloved spirit son or daughter of heavenly parents, and, as such each has a divine nature and destiny."[18]

It must also be noted that the Latter-day Saint conception of "spirit" is nontraditional. In canonized revelations we read, "There is no such thing as immaterial matter. All spirit is matter, but it is more fine or pure, and can only be discerned by purer eyes; we cannot see it; but when our bodies are purified we shall see that it is all matter" (D&C 131:7–8). In other words, spirits are materially embodied persons, humanlike in form, though invisible to ordinary human perception. In the Book of Mormon, the preincarnate Christ appears to the brother of Jared and says, "Behold, this body, which ye now behold, is the body of my spirit; and man have I created after the body of my spirit; and even as I appear unto thee to be in the spirit will I appear unto my people in the flesh" (Ether 3:16).

4. God the Father is the creator from chaos, not from nothing. God the Son was His active agent in this creation process, and it was He who created our world and worlds without number. Their most fundamental purpose in creation is "to bring to pass the immortality and eternal life" of the human family (Moses 1:39, Pearl of Great Price [PGP]).

The LDS canon clearly teaches that God's creations are formed with material from an extant chaos and not *ex nihilo* (see Abraham 4:1, 7, 12, 14, 16, 25, 31, PGP). The First Presidency has said that "the Creator is an Organizer. God created the earth as an organized sphere; but he certainly did not create, in the sense of bringing into primal existence, the ultimate elements of the materials of which the earth consists, for 'the elements are eternal' (D&C 93:33)."[19] Latter-day Saints find themselves in accord with the views of prominent Catholic scientist and philosopher Stanley L. Jaki, who writes:

The caution which is in order about taking the [Hebrew] verb *bara* in the sense of creation out of nothing is no less needed in reference to the [English] word *creation*. Nothing is more natural, and unadvised, at the same time, than to use the word as if it has always denoted creation out of nothing. In its basic etymological origin the word *creation* meant the purely natural process of growing or of making something to grow.[20]

For Mormons, *creatio ex nihilo* is a postbiblical intrusion into Christianity. Nonetheless, they unequivocally affirm that God the Father is the ultimate creator and organizer who provided the possibility and context for our earthly experience. Latter-day Saint discourse also allows for some to believe that God is the author of natural laws (see D&C 88:7, 36–38, 42), while others believe that God understands a priori laws and employs them with perfect mastery (see Alma 42:13, D&C 82:10). No prophetic statements to our knowledge have definitively settled this issue one way or the other, but some have offered the possibility that God creates some laws while obeying and mastering others.

As mentioned earlier, Latter-day Saints do not believe God the Father acted alone in creating the world(s); Mormons believe that Jesus Christ worked under the direction of God the Father as an agent in bringing about the creation of the earth and of worlds without number: "And worlds without number have I created; and I also created them for mine own purpose; and by the Son I created them, which is mine Only Begotten. . . . And there are many that now stand, and innumerable are they unto man; but all things are numbered unto me, for they are mine and I know them" (Moses 1:33–35, PGP).

Beyond such brief descriptions, Latter-day Saints believe God remains taciturn regarding the nature of His work elsewhere in the cosmos. Mormons only speculate that His creative works are similar in nature and purpose to those involved in the creation of our earth.

5. God is a morally perfect person who is unchangingly loving, just, merciful, veracious, and faithful.

With the possible exception of the view that love is necessarily *responsive*, LDS understanding of God's perfect goodness does not differ significantly from more mainline Christian views.

6. Consistent with His perfect love, God is profoundly passible.

Mormons view God as their loving Heavenly Father. As their Father, they believe He is at times moved with compassion and is profoundly affected by mortal actions. For example, Enoch, an antediluvian prophet, became an eyewitness of the Father's sensitive and responsive nature:

> And it came to pass that the God of heaven looked upon the residue of the people, and he wept. . . . And Enoch said unto the Lord: How is it that thou canst weep, seeing thou art holy, and from all eternity to all eternity? . . . The Lord said unto Enoch: Behold these thy brethren; they are the workmanship of mine own hands, and I gave unto them their knowledge, in the day I created them . . . but behold they are without affection, and they hate their own blood. (Moses 7:28–29, 32–33, PGP)

Additionally, both the Book of Mormon narrative and the Bible portray the tender and profound passibility of God the Son, who Mormons believe is the express image of his Father's person (see Hebrews 1:1–3). And, as such, Mormons accept the doctrine that as Christ is, so also is God the Father (see Matthew 11:27). Elder Jeffrey R. Holland, a current member of the Quorum of the Twelve Apostles, suggested, "Jesus did not come to improve God's view of man nearly so much as He came to improve man's view of God and to plead with them to love their Heavenly Father as He has always and will always love them."[21] Therefore, Mormons believe in the tender passibility of God the Father, who loves each of His children profoundly. Additionally, for Latter-day Saints the Father's passibility is directly linked to his embodiment.

7. God the Father is a gloriously embodied person.

Mormons believe God the Father has a body precisely because He has revealed himself as an embodied being—most clearly for Latter-day Saints during Joseph Smith's First Vision. The fourteen-year-old boy met with the Father and Son and saw them as separately embodied beings. Smith later expressed this to his followers, teaching that the Father possesses an exalted body similar to that of the Son's. "If the veil were rent today," he proclaimed, ". . . you would see him like a man in form—like yourselves."[22]

Today, there is considerable evidence that Hebrew prophets and the earliest Christians also believed in an embodied God.[23] For this reason, and on philosophical grounds, an ever-increasing number of mainstream Christian thinkers are open to the idea of divine embodiment.[24]

Of course, for Latter-day Saints, God the Father does not possess a body in the image of "our vile body," but has a "glorious body, according to the working whereby he is able even to subdue all things unto himself" (Philippians 3:21). Some critics have argued that, in affirming God's embodiment, Latter-day Saints must necessarily conclude that God's body is subject to the same limitations as our own "vile" mortal bodies. Holland clarifies,

> If the idea of an embodied God is repugnant, why are the central doctrines and singularly most distinguishing characteristics of all Christianity the Incarnation, the Atonement, and the physical Resurrection of the Lord Jesus Christ? If having a body is not only not needed but not desirable by Deity, why did the Redeemer of mankind redeem *His* body, redeeming it from the grasp of death and the grave, guaranteeing it would never again be separated from his spirit in time or eternity? *Any who dismiss the concept of an embodied God dismiss both the mortal and the resurrected Christ.*[25]

Indeed, as Holland points out, the argument by natural theologians that God must be incorporeal, without body or parts, contradicts the common Christian affirmation of God the Son's birth, death, and subsequent resurrection with a fully glorified body. This contradiction is best expressed in the following inconsistent triad:

(1) Jesus of Nazareth exists everlastingly with a resurrected body.
(2) Jesus of Nazareth is God.
(3) N (if x is God, then x is incorporeal).

8. God the Father is the presiding member of the Godhead or Trinity, which consists of three separate beings who are one in thought, will, action, and love.

LDS doctrine does not fully accept the view of the Trinity outlined in the Nicene, Athanasian, and other classical Christian creeds. Mormons believe strongly "in God, the Eternal Father, and in His Son, Jesus Christ, and in the Holy Ghost" (Articles of Faith 1:1, PGP), but unlike creedal Christianity, Mormons reject the notion that the Godhead comprises a single indivisible substance. Joseph Smith stated: "I have always and in all congregations . . . declared God to be a distinct personage, Jesus Christ a separate and distinct personage from God the Father, and that the Holy Ghost was a distinct personage and a Spirit: and these three constitute three distinct personages and three Gods."[26]

Though the above passage is often cherry-picked by polemicists to accuse Mormons of tritheism, polytheism, or even atheism, Latter-day Saint scholars, including Robert Millet, Blake Ostler, Daniel Peterson, and David Paulsen, argue that on the whole Latter-day Saint doctrine teaches that the Trinity consists of three distinct persons, who form one mutually indwelling divine community—one Godhead. Though not a single substance, the Mormon Godhead is perfectly united in will, action, thought, and love. Therefore, the Mormon conception of the Godhead is more akin to what contemporary Christian theologians call Social Trinitarianism.

A Social Trinitarian might describe the union or indwelling oneness of the members of the divine community as *perichoresis*. Perichoresis seeks to explain how the Father can be "in" the Son and the Son "in" the Father (see John 10:30, 38; 14:10–11; D&C 50:43; 93:3). Cornelius Plantinga described it thus: "Each member is a person, a distinct person, but scarcely an *individual* or *separate* or *independent* person. For in the divine life there is no isolation, no secretiveness, no fear of being transparent to another. Hence there may be penetrating, inside knowledge of the other as other, but as co-other, loved other, fellow. Father, Son, and Spirit are 'members one of another' to a superlative and exemplary degree."[27]

Restoration scriptures further solidify the view that Mormons are Social Trinitarians in the sense outlined above (see 2 Nephi 31:21; Alma 11:44; 3 Nephi 11:36; D&C 20:28; Joseph Smith—History 1:8–20, PGP). The Book of Mormon describes, "the will of the Son being swallowed up in the will of the Father" (Mosiah 15:7). In explaining this passage, LDS philosopher Blake Ostler observes:

> There is only one God because the will of the Son is "swallowed up" in the will of the Father. There are clearly two wills, for the Son has a will that is distinct from the Father's will, but he willingly subordinates his will to the Father's will so that only one will is actually expressed in the divine relationship, i.e., the Father's. In this sense, by completely subordinating his will to the Father's will it follows that the Father's will is always realized and thus the one God is, *in this sense*, both the Father and the Son.[28]

Thus, while the Son and Holy Ghost possess distinct minds and wills, and exhibit distinct actions, the Godhead thinks, wills, and acts *ad extra* as one. This is shown explicitly in Jesus's preincarnate declaration in the Book of Mormon: "Behold, I come unto my own . . . to do the will, both of the Father and of the Son" (3 Nephi 1:14). As explained above, it is the will of the Father that both the Son and the Holy Ghost freely choose to take the Father's will as their own will—this loving and free choice to unite divine wills is expressed in Joseph Smith's revelations that there is only *one* doctrine (see 2 Nephi 31:21), judgment (see Alma 11:44), baptism (see 3 Nephi 11:27), and record (see 3 Nephi 11:36) of the Father, Son, and Holy Ghost. As Elder Holland put it, "I think it is accurate to say we believe [the Godhead is] one in every significant and eternal aspect imaginable except believing Them to be three persons combined in one substance."[29]

9. God the Father is almighty, all-knowing, and omnipresent. His power, knowledge, and presence are sufficient to insure the fulfillment of all his purposes and promises.

Mormon scriptures repeatedly affirm that God is almighty (see Genesis 18:14; Alma 26:35; D&C 19:1–3), all-knowing (see Matthew 6:8; 2 Nephi 2:24), and everywhere present (see Psalm 139:7–12; D&C 88:7–13, 41). Yet, as we read these relevant scriptural passages pertaining to God's power, knowledge, and presence, they appear more as pastoral-like assurances intended to shore up faith that God can and will fulfill all of his purposes and promises. For instance, in the New Testament we find the assertion, "For with God nothing shall be impossible" in conjunction with God's miraculous powers and abilities to fulfill His purposes (Luke 1:37).

While Mormons believe that "For with God nothing shall be impossible," they do not believe, for example, that God can create a rock that is too heavy for Him to lift. Mormon leader and thinker Brigham H. Roberts noted:

The attribute 'Omnipotence' must needs be thought upon also as somewhat limited. Even God, notwithstanding the ascription to him of all-powerfulness in such scripture phrases as 'With God all things are possible,' 'Nothing shall be impossible with God'—notwithstanding all this, I say, not even God may have two mountain ranges without a valley between . . . even he may not act out of harmony with the other eternal existences which condition or limit even him.[30]

Yet, in a series of 1834 lectures on faith, early church leaders taught that if one is to have saving faith in God, she must (among other things) have a correct idea of God's character, perfections, and attributes. She must not only understand that God is unfailingly loving, gracious, forgiving, merciful, just, no respecter of persons, and veracious, but she must also understand that God has power over all things. Similar reasoning may be given for why each person must understand that God is not only almighty, but also all-knowing and omnipresent, in order for each person to trust in God's ability to fulfill His promises unto salvation.[31]

10. With respect to divine perfections that do not admit of a ceiling or upper limit, God the Father is eternally self-surpassing but unsurpassable by others.

This doctrine is known in the church as the doctrine of "eternal progression." Joseph Smith envisaged God as eternally self-surpassing many years before Christian process thinkers began to even glimpse this idea.

Unlike the other declarations on Mormon theism, this one has scant basis in canonized scripture. Joseph Smith, however, taught it as have many of his successors in prophetic and apostolic offices. In Joseph's King Follett discourse, he declared:

> What did Jesus do? Why; I do the things I saw my Father do when worlds came rolling into existence. My Father worked out his kingdom with fear and trembling, and I must do the same; and when I get my kingdom, I shall present it to my Father, so that he may obtain kingdom upon kingdom, and it will exalt him in glory. He will then take a higher exaltation, and I will take his place, and thereby become exalted myself.[32]

Notice that Smith's statement implies that divine persons progress. Obviously, he did not see divine perfection as a state of static completeness, but as a dynamic life—one of unending growth and progress. God, *qua God*, is eternally self-surpassing.

Of course, this prompts the question whether God is eternally self-surpassing in *all* respects. On this point, faithful Latter-day Saints sometimes disagree. Most would no doubt concur with what Smith clearly taught, that God is eternally self-surpassing in glory, dominion, and kingdoms. Likewise most would probably agree that God is eternally self-surpassing in creativity and creative activity. Some influential LDS thinkers, including Presidents Brigham Young (who served from 1847 to 1877) and Wilford Woodruff (who served from 1887 to 1898), even considered God eternally self-surpassing in both knowledge and power.

Brigham Young said, "the God I serve is progressing eternally [in knowledge and power], and so are his children; they will increase to all eternity, if they are faithful."[33] In agreement with Young, Wilford Woodruff stated, "If there was a point where man in his progression could not proceed any further, the very idea would throw a gloom over every intelligent and reflecting mind. God himself is increasing and progressing in knowledge, power, and dominion, and will do so, worlds without end. It is just so with us."[34]

Yet, other church leaders, including President Joseph Fielding Smith and Apostle Bruce R. McConkie, have passionately denied that God can surpass himself in knowledge. Joseph Fielding Smith asserted, "Do we believe that God has all 'wisdom'? If so, in that, he is absolute. If there is something he does not know, then he is not absolute in 'wisdom,' and to think such a thing is absurd."[35] It is enough to point out the nuanced views on this issue and state that we believe the stronger arguments favor the view of God as ever-increasing.

3 CONCLUSION

God's personality and attributes merit deep theological exploration. But, as Pascal understood, His sublimity is often best expressed through a personal testimony.

Elder Holland delivered just such a witness in a 2003 address, capturing the ethos of the God of Abraham, Isaac, and Jacob (and Mormonism):

> I bear personal witness . . . of a personal, living God, who knows our names, hears and answers our prayers, and cherishes us eternally as children of His spirit. I testify that amidst the wondrously complex task inherent in the universe, He seeks our individual happiness and safety above all other godly concerns. We are created in His very image and likeness, and Jesus of Nazareth, His only begotten Son in the flesh, came to earth as the perfect mortal manifestation of His grandeur. In addition to the witness of the ancients, we also have the modern miracle of Palmyra, the appearance of God the Father and His Beloved Son, the Savior of the world, to the boy prophet Joseph Smith. I testify of that appearance, and in the words of that prophet I, too, declare: "Our heavenly Father is more liberal in His views and boundless in His mercy and blessings, than we are ready to believe or receive."[36]

Notes

1. Feldman, "What Is It about Mormonism?" Survey data show that despite extensive coverage of the LDS Church and its beliefs during Governor Mitt Romney's 2012 presidential run, the vast majority of citizens "learned little or nothing about the Mormon religion during the presidential campaign." See Pew Forum on Religion and Public Life, "Americans Learned Little about the Mormon Faith."
2. Pollster Gary Lawrence finds that only 23 percent of those surveyed could correctly identify the Mormon understanding of the Trinity; Lawrence, *How Americans View Mormonism*, 49. See also, Lawrence, *Mormons Believe*.
3. Although Christians added the Trinity to this depiction, they did not alter its fundamental features. Indeed, some might say that the Christian thinkers reinforced this depiction, insisting that God is so absolutely transcendent that he created the world out of nothing.
4. Bloom, *American Religion*, 97.
5. Some LDS thinkers, most prominently James Faulconer, argue that because Mormonism has no official systematic theology, Latter-day Saints are "atheological." While intriguing, and in some respects persuasive, this view inadequately addresses the long-standing and continued influence of reason-based theologizing on LDS Church doctrines and revelations. See Givens, *Wrestling the Angel*. For more discussion on this topic, see also Faulconer, "Rethinking Theology"; Faulconer, "Why a Mormon Won't Drink Coffee But Might Have a Coke"; and Baker, "Shadow of the Cathedral."
6. Smith, *Teachings of the Prophet Joseph Smith*, 324.
7. Some have speculated about whether God always existed as God or became God. Recent church leaders have stressed the scripturally based teaching that God is the one and only true God, who has always been our God and will always be our God.
8. Smith, *History of the Church of Jesus Christ of Latter-day Saints*, 4:78.
9. Smith, *Scriptural Teachings of the Prophet Joseph Smith*, 396. Italics added.
10. Swinburne, *Coherence of Theism*, 220.
11. Kenny, "Divine Foreknowledge and Human Freedom," 264.
12. Wolterstorff, "God Everlasting," 181–82.
13. Davis, *Logic and the Nature of God*, 24.

14. Smith, *Teachings of the Prophet Joseph Smith*, 190.
15. First Presidency and Council of the Twelve Apostles, "Father and the Son."
16. Though we do not explicate the attributes of Heavenly Mother in this chapter, or extensively explore Her relationship to Heavenly Father, these topics are addressed in Paulsen and Pulido "A Mother There."
17. First Presidency and Council of the Twelve Apostles, "Father and the Son."
18. First Presidency and Council of the Twelve Apostles, "The Family," 102.
19. First Presidency and Council of the Twelve Apostles, "Father and the Son."
20. Jaki's analysis of the etymology of creation inclines to the "natural process of growing"; this complements but is not identical to Joseph Smith's interpretation that the Hebrew *creation* meant to organize or fashion. Jaki, *Genesis 1 through the Ages*, 5–6.
21. Holland, "Grandeur of God," 70.
22. See Smith, *Scriptural Teachings of the Prophet Joseph Smith*, 349.
23. Paulsen, "Early Christian Belief in a Corporeal Deity," 105–16.
24. Webb, *Jesus Christ, Eternal God*.
25. Holland, "The Only True God and Jesus Christ Whom He Hath Sent," 40–42.
26. Smith, *Teachings of the Prophet Joseph Smith*, 370.
27. Plantinga, "Social Trinity and Tritheism," 28.
28. Ostler, *Exploring Mormon Thought*, 3: 258–59; emphasis added.
29. Holland, "The Only True God and Jesus Christ Whom He Hath Sent," 40.
30. Roberts, "Seventies Course in Theology," 70.
31. See Doctrine and Covenants of the Church of the Latter Day Saints: Carefully Selected from the Revelations of God, and Compiled by Joseph Smith Junior. Oliver Cowdery, Sidney Rigdon, Frederick G. Williams, -[Presiding Elders of said Church.]-Proprietors.; Kirtland, OH: F. G. Williams & Co., 1835. http://josephsmithpapers.org/paperSummary/doctrine-and-covenants-1835#!/paperSummary/doctrine-and-covenants-1835&p=13.
32. Smith, *Scriptural Teachings of the Prophet Joseph Smith*, 392.
33. Young, "Weakness of the Human Mind," 1867, 11: 286.
34. Woodruff, "Blessings of the Saints," 1857, 6: 120.
35. Smith, *Doctrines of Salvation*, 1: 6–7.
36. Holland, "Grandeur of God," 70.

BIBLIOGRAPHY

Baker, Jacob. "The Shadow of the Cathedral: On a Systematic Exposition of Mormon Theology." *Element* 4, no. 1 (Spring 2008).

Bloom, Harold. *The American Religion*. New York: Chu Hartley, 2006.

Blomberg, Craig L., and Stephen E. Robinson. *How Wide the Divide? A Mormon and an Evangelical in Conversation*. Downers Grove, IL: InterVarsity Press, 1997.

Davis, Stephen T. *Logic and the Nature of God*. Grand Rapids, MI: William B. Eerdmans, 1983.

Faulconer, James E. "Rethinking Theology: The Shadow of the Apocalypse." *FARMS Review of Books* 19, no. 1 (2007): 175–99.

Faulconer, James E. "Why a Mormon Won't Drink Coffee But Might Have a Coke: The Atheological Character of the Church of Jesus Christ of Latter-day Saints," *Element* 2, no. 2 (Fall 2006): 21–37.

Feldman, Noah. "What Is It about Mormonism?" *New York Times Magazine*, January 6, 2008.

First Presidency and Council of the Twelve Apostles. "The Family: A Proclamation to the World." *Ensign* 25, no. 11 (November 1995). http://www.lds.org/ensign/1995/11/the-family-a-proclamation-to-the-world?lang=eng.

First Presidency and Council of the Twelve Apostles. "The Father and the Son: A Doctrinal Exposition by the First Presidency and the Twelve." *Improvement Era* 19, no. 10 (August 1916): 934–42.

Givens, Terryl L. *Wrestling the Angel: The Foundations of Mormon Thought: Cosmos, God, Humanity.* New York: Oxford University Press, 2015.

Griffin, David Ray, and James McLachlan. "A Dialogue on Process Theology." In *Mormonism in Dialogue with Contemporary Christian Theologies,* ed. Donald W. Musser and David L. Paulsen, 161–210. Macon, GA: Mercer University Press, 2007.

Holland, Jeffrey R. "The Grandeur of God." *Ensign* 33, no. 11 (November 2003): 70–73.

Holland, Jeffrey R. "Mormonism 101." A lecture at Harvard Law School, Cambridge, MA. March 20, 2012. http://www.mormonnewsroom.org/article/harvard-elder-holland-mormonism-remarks.

Holland, Jeffrey R. "The Only True God and Jesus Christ Whom He Hath Sent." *Ensign* 37, no. 11 (November 2007): 40–42.

Jaki, Stanley, L. *Genesis 1 through the Ages.* Royal Oak, MI: Real View, 1998.

Journal of Discourses. 26 vols. Reported by G. D. Watt et al. Liverpool: F. D. and S. W. Richards et al., 1851–86; reprint, Salt Lake City, UT: n.p., 1974.

Kenny, Anthony. "Divine Foreknowledge and Human Freedom." In *Aquinas: A Collection of Critical Essays,* ed. Anthony Kenny, 255–70. New York: Doubleday, 1969.

Lawrence, Gary. *How Americans View Mormonism.* Orange, CA: Parameter Foundation, 2008.

Lawrence, Gary. *Mormons Believe . . . What?!* Orange, CA: Parameter Foundation, 2011.

Madsen, Truman G. *Eternal Man.* Salt Lake City, UT: Deseret, 1966.

McMurrin, Sterling. *Philosophical Foundations of Mormonism.* Salt Lake City: University of Utah Press, 1959.

McMurrin, Sterling. *Theological Foundations of the Mormon Religion.* Salt Lake City: University of Utah Press, 1965.

Millet, Robert L. "1 + 1 + 1 =?" In *The Vision of Mormonism: Pressing the Boundaries of Christianity,* 65–73. St. Paul, MN: Paragon House, 2007.

Millet, Robert L. "God and Man." In *No Weapon Shall Prosper: New Light on Sensitive Issues,* ed. Robert L. Millet, 345–78. Provo, UT: BYU Religious Studies Center, 2011.

Oaks, Dallin H. "Fundamental Premises of Our Faith." A lecture at Harvard Law School, Cambridge, MA, February 26, 2010. http://www.mormonnewsroom.org/article/fundamental-premises-of-our-faith-talk-given-by-elder-dallin-h-oaks-at-harvard-law-school.

Ostler, Blake T. *Exploring Mormon Thought.* 3 vols. Salt Lake City: Greg Kofford, 2008.

Ostler, Blake T. "Worshipworthiness and the Mormon Concept of God." *Religious Studies* 33, no. 3 (1997): 315–26.

Paulsen, David L. "Divine Embodiment: The Earliest Christian Understanding of God." In *Early Christians in Disarray: Contemporary LDS Perspectives on the Christian Apostasy,* ed. Noel Reynolds, 239–94. Provo, UT: Brigham Young University Press, 2005.

Paulsen, David L. "The Doctrine of Divine Embodiment: Restoration, Judeo-Christian, and Philosophical Perspectives." *BYU Studies* 35, no. 4 (1995–96): 7–94.

Paulsen, David L. "Early Christian Belief in a Corporeal Deity: Origen and Augustine as Reluctant Witnesses." *Harvard Theological Review* 83, no. 2 (1990): 105–16.

Paulsen, David L. "Must God Be Incorporeal?" *Faith and Philosophy* 6, no. 1 (1989): 76–87.

Paulsen, David, and Brett McDonald. "Joseph Smith and the Trinity: An Analysis and Defense of a Social Model of the Trinity." *Faith and Philosophy* 25, no. 1 (2008): 47–74.

Paulsen, David, and Martin Pulido. " 'A Mother There': A Survey of Historical Teachings about Mother in Heaven." *BYU Studies* 50, no. 1 (2011): 70–126.

Peterson, Daniel C. "Mormonism and the Trinity." *Element* 3, nos. 1–2 (Spring–Fall 2007): 1–43.

Pew Forum on Religion and Public Life. "Americans Learned Little about the Mormon Faith, but Some Attitudes Have Softened." Washington, DC: PEW Research Center, 2012. http://www.pewforum.org/files/2012/12/Knowledge-and-Attitudes-about-Mormons.pdf.

Plantinga, Cornelius. "Social Trinity and Tritheism." In *Trinity, Incarnation, and Atonement: Philosophical and Theological Essays*, ed. Ronald J. Feenstra and Cornelius Plantinga, 21–47. Notre Dame, IN: University of Notre Dame Press, 1989.

Roberts, B. H. *Seventies Course in Theology: Fourth Year*. Salt Lake City, UT: The Deseret News, 1907.

Roberts, B. H., and Rev. C. Van Der Donckt. *The Mormon Doctrine of Deity: The Roberts-Van Der Donckt Discussion*. Salt Lake City, UT: The Deseret News, 1903.

Smith, Joseph, Jr. *History of the Church of Jesus Christ of Latter-day Saints*. Ed. B. H. Roberts. Salt Lake City, UT: Church of Jesus Christ of Latter-day Saints, 1950.

Smith, Joseph, Jr. *Scriptural Teachings of the Prophet Joseph Smith*. Ed. Joseph Fielding Smith and Richard C. Galbraith. Salt Lake City, UT: Deseret, 1993.

Smith, Joseph, Jr. *Teachings of the Prophet Joseph Smith*. Ed. Joseph Fielding Smith. Salt Lake City, UT: Deseret, 1938.

Smith, Joseph Fielding. *Doctrines of Salvation: Sermons and Writings of Joseph Fielding Smith*. 3 vols. Ed. Bruce R. McConkie. Salt Lake City, UT: Bookcraft, 1954–56.

Swinburne, Richard. *The Coherence of Theism*. Oxford: Clarendon Press, 1977.

Webb, Stephen H. "Godbodied: The Matter of the Latter-day Saints." *BYU Studies* 50, no. 3 (2011): 83–100.

Webb, Stephen H. *Jesus Christ, Eternal God: Heavenly Flesh and the Metaphysics of Matter*. New York: Oxford University Press, 2011.

Webb, Stephen H. *Mormon Christianity: What Other Christians Can Learn from the Latter-day Saints*. New York: Oxford University Press, 2013.

Wolterstorff, Nicholas. "God Everlasting." In *God and the Good: Essays in Honor of Henry Stob*, ed. Clifton Orlebeke and Lewis Smedes, 181–203. Grand Rapids, MI: William B. Eerdmans, 1975.

Woodruff, Wilford. "Blessings of the Saints" [December 6, 1857]. *Journal of Discourses* 6: 115–21.

Young, Brigham. "Weakness of the Human Mind" [January 13, 1867]. *Journal of Discourses* 11: 282–91.

CHAPTER 18

CHRIST, ATONEMENT, AND HUMAN POSSIBILITIES IN MORMON THOUGHT

TERRYL L. GIVENS

THE essential outlines of Mormon theology constitute a fairly simple—if unfamiliar—story. God is the supreme intelligence in the universe, but He is not the source of all being, or even the creator of the human soul. Men and women have existed from eternity as uncreated intelligence. A Heavenly Father and Mother fashion that intelligence into spirit form (or in another reading of Joseph Smith's original under-standing, adopt into familial relationship preexisting intelligences or spirits). Through untold aeons of premortal existence these spirits, by the exercise of their moral agency, acquire knowledge and attributes of godliness under the loving tutelage of their Heavenly Father and Mother. God's self-designated purpose is eventually to shepherd these spirits toward His own exalted condition. At a decreed point in humankind's eternal progress, God orchestrated the creation of this world, in preparation for the human family's ascent (not fall) into mortality.

In God's conception of human existence, moral agency is the bedrock value, the capacity for independent virtuous activity the paramount attainment, and consequent relationships of selfless love and eternal duration the supreme reward. This present stage of mortal incarnation is therefore shrouded behind a veil of forgetfulness, that individual choices might be the more freely rendered. A universal human endowment of the Light of Christ, vestigial intimations of eternal realms and values, counterbalances to some extent the prevailing influences of environment and heredity.

Physical incarnation, as a prelude to eventual resurrection with a glorified body, rep-resents a higher, more developed, and more power-laden form of existence than spiri-tual being. Embodiment in corruptible flesh and blood does not entail the inheritance of any Adamic sin, though it does entail the physical inheritance of traits, conditions, and limitations, that tax and enlarge the human soul in its progress toward self-mastery.

Implicit in this scheme is the recognition that, as the mystic Julian of Norwich wrote, "synne is behovely" (sin is needful).[1] Only by choosing the good do individuals learn to savor and embrace the good. Similarly, only by choosing the evil do human individuals learn what evil is and why it deserves to be rejected. (Only Christ, as God before the foundation of the world and of divine parentage in this life, could perfectly resist its allure.) Sin, or choice that contravenes eternal moral laws, is therefore a necessary part of the mortal experience. Two principles thus come into collision in God's plan for human progression. Moral agency is predicated on a causal connection between choice and consequence. Given the freedom to choose, individuals must be granted the fruits of their choices, good or ill, or such freedom would be only a shadow of genuine agency. Given the uneven playing field called earth, where our untempered spirits contend against bodily weakness, myriad pressures and temptations, and the soul's own imperfect desires, sin is inevitable—and so therefore are its consequences. The inevitability of sin means the inevitability of sinful human natures, and consequent alienation from God, and His heaven. But in His infinite love and compassion, God wills the reintegration of every individual into the heavenly family. The human freedom to sin thus collides with God's desire to save. The problem of how to reconcile this tragic collision is the problem of atonement.

Mormons, like Christians generally, can and do understand atonement in different ways. What follows represents only one attempt at a synthesis of atonement theory based on one understanding of biblical passages, LDS scripture, and pronouncements of Mormon theologians. Mormon theology of atonement can be analyzed in terms of its three aspects: the nature of the alienation in need of repair; the mechanism of the suffering Christ that undertakes to repair the breach; and the human response to Christ's expiation, which concludes the actual process of reconciliation.

ALIENATION

The historic doctrine of original sin, conceived as the root cause of human alienation from God, had two traditional dimensions: a universally inherited (or imputed) *reatus*, or guilt, and a similarly inherited *vitium*, or vice. Some tried, unsuccessfully, to separate the two. When in the twelfth century Peter Abelard denied imputed guilt, he was summarily condemned by the Synod of Sens for teaching "that we did not contract guilt from Adam, but only punishment."[2] With time many Christian traditions came to downplay or deny any actual guilt accruing to Adam's descendants for his sin; at the same time, some religious traditions emphasized an inherited tendency to sin amounting to total depravity. Mormonism rejects completely the doctrine of original sin as a guilty condition that is either inherited by the human family, or imputed to them. God does not hold one individual guilty for the actions of another, Mormonism affirms in an article of faith.

That we have a predisposition to sin, on the other hand, is too readily apparent to deny. However, Mormons do not see this as a necessary condition following from a sinful Adamic heritage; the imperfection of our spirits, the inclination of our wills, do not directly accrue as a consequence of Adam's and Eve's decision; our predicament is the consequence of our imperfect spirits, possessed of imperfectly developed wills, confronting a world deliberately constructed as an arena of challenge, opposition, and temptation. When the Book of Mormon proclaims the "natural man" an enemy to God, it does not mean this in a Calvinist sense; "natural man" in Mormon usage is distinct from innate man.[3] Humans are born free of sin and therefore guilt; but they readily succumb to sinful influences. It is after "they begin to grow up [that] sin conceiveth in their hearts." (Moses 6:55, Pearl of Great Price). Only then are people of a morally accountable age capable of consciously choosing what is evil, committing sin, and finding themselves spiritually remote from God's spirit and influence. The separation from God is not a punishment inflicted by God, but an incapacity of the unrighteous to tolerate His glory, "for no unclean thing can dwell . . . in his presence" (Moses 6:57). A deeply felt guilt is a factor in such isolation, but there is an existential reality involved: sinfulness is a condition "contrary to the nature of God," explains a Book of Mormon prophet (Alma 41:11). A subsequent prophet, Samuel, concurs that doing iniquity is "contrary to the nature of that righteousness" which is the root of God's identity and the source of His perfect joy (Helaman 13:38). So the alienation in need of repair is not a product of God's arbitrary decree, of His anger or desire to punish. Neither is it purely a matter of human guilt or shame before the divine presence. It is a product of a freely chosen sinful condition that is incompatible with God's holiness. "For he who is not able to abide the law of a celestial kingdom *cannot abide* a celestial glory" (Doctrine and Covenants [D&C] 88:7; my emphasis).

Humans bear the spiritual traces of every impure thought, unkind word, and hurtful action they have ever committed (Alma 12:14). The very real detritus of lives tainted by selfishness, carnality, and pride constitutes the prison of sin in which humans entomb themselves. But, Mormonism insists, humans are of divine parentage, and as Wordsworth sensed, their souls resonate with the dim intimations of a heavenly past and a more supernal destiny than the one our poor choices foreshadow. As church father Clement wrote, we at some point come to a vague "reminiscence of better things," and desire to "renounc[e] our iniquities" and "speed back to the eternal light, children to the Father."[4] But we cannot ourselves transcend the consequences of our own choices, or suddenly acquire a new human nature unshaped by our own past. The burden of sin that has become habit, the self-perpetuating spiral of choices that further compromise our will and weaken our resolve, a character impaired by the accumulation of soul-damaging decisions, all conspire to make our predicament hopeless without radical intervention by a superior agent.

VICARIOUS ATONEMENT

Historically, the paramount necessity for divine intervention in human fate concerns what some Christian theologies have considered the inexorable decrees of justice. In Dante's calculus of sin and punishment, man's sin against a perfect God was infinitely vile, and so required an infinite payment—which humans cannot provide. "For no obedience, no humility, / he offered later could have been so deep / that it could match the heights he meant to reach / through disobedience."[5] In this view, only the sacrifice of a perfect God can cancel out the incalculable wrong that was committed. Church fathers early taught that sinners were Satan's by right. Christ's death was the ransom Satan demanded for humankind's release. Origen varied this explanation, by holding that Satan was deceived into thinking he could hold onto Christ instead—but Christ's sinlessness—and His veiled divinity—made that impossible for Satan. Augustine agreed, comparing Christ to the bait in a mouse-trap. Under St. Anselm, satisfaction theory developed. An infinite offense against a perfect God and His justice required the satisfaction of an infinite payment. Only Christ, as human, could share in the debt, and only Christ, as God, could pay that infinite penalty. So only Christ as man-God could accomplish atonement. This idea developed further into the penal substitution theory, which emphasized the human affront to moral law, and the debt owed to justice. In all these cases, either an actual entity, Satan, or a reified universal, Justice, demanded a payment be made for sin. The philosopher Friedrich Nietzsche's analysis seems accurate: Christians have largely treated guilt and mathematical indebtedness as interchangeable, and a prescribed quantity of Christ's suffering seems necessary to zero out the sum total of a human offense, resulting in a state of equilibrium.[6] The Governmental Theory emphasized the need to validate the Law of God by requiring a punishment in accordance with a broken law, maintaining the divine order—though such punishment (suffered by Christ) was not mathematically equivalent to the debt owed by humans.

Some contemporary theologies (and some Mormon writers) seek to avoid medieval notions of justice and a calculus of sin and suffering by moving toward a theory of atonement in which Christ's suffering is the suffering of the supremely empathic One, and its efficacy is based on its inspiring or exemplary nature. In other words, Christ's willingness to identify with us to the point of experiencing the agonizing effects we feel of our sinfulness, motivates us to repent and draw near to God. Eugene England espoused a modified version of Abelard's moral theory of atonement, according to which the justice requiring satisfaction is a human sense of justice, and witnessing Christ's agony allows us to forgive ourselves and be reconciled to God.[7]

Mormon scripture on the subject suggests that "justice" is neither some unimpeachable cosmic universal, nor the inflexible standard of a legalistic heavenly monarch. It is, rather, another name for what, from a human perspective, guarantees the integrity of human choice. This was the view of Brigham H. Roberts in his seminal writing on atonement. Roberts saw the key to understanding atonement in the dominion of law—and specifically in what he called the "inexorableness of law":

> what effect is to cause, in the physical world, so penalty or consequence must be to violation of law in the moral and spiritual kingdom. The inexorableness of law is at once both its majesty and glory; without it neither majesty nor glory could exist in combination with law; neither respect, nor sense of security, nor safety, nor rational faith. . . . We must postulate such conception of the attributes of God that regularity will result from his personal government, not capriciousness.[8]

Roberts' substitution of "consequence" for "penalty," combined with a teleology or ultimate purpose behind the atonement that emphasizes "security" and "regularity" rather than satisfaction or "capriciousness" is a seismic shift beyond the medieval categories of atonement theology, and represents a genuinely Mormon theology of atonement. One might call it a "consequential substitution" theology, one oriented toward the preservation and validation of agency rather than toward divine government or justice per se. Genuine moral agency must entail necessary consequences. Choice must be choice *of something*. In John Stuart Mill's classic treatment, human liberty requires the freedom "of doing as we like, *subject to such consequences as may follow*" (my emphasis).[9] If choice is to be more than an empty gesture of the will, more than a mere pantomime of decision making, there must be immutable guarantee that any given choice will eventuate in the natural consequence of that choice. What kind of freedom would it be, if there were no predicable result attached to any deliberate choice? Secondhand smoke of a thousand types complicates the degree of freedom and accountability behind human choice. But even allowing for the volitional white noise, moral agency, clearly, requires a stable framework within which choices are rendered meaningful and purposeful. "The quality of regularity that can only come of inexorableness . . . is necessary to a sense of security," in Roberts's words.[10]

This appears to be the meaning of Book of Mormon prophet Lehi in his sermon on freedom, when he says "the law is given to men," and that as a result they are "free forever, . . . to act for themselves and not to be acted upon, save it be by the punishment of the law" (2 Nephi 2:5, 26). This point is explicated by one of Joseph Smith's theologically richest revelations. In explaining why God does not simply bestow eternal bliss upon all who die, the revelation explains: "They who remain shall also be quickened; nevertheless, they shall return again to their own place, to enjoy that which they are willing to receive, because they were not willing to enjoy that which they might have received" (D&C 88:32). Imposing a heavenly reward on those who did not choose heaven, in other words, is just that: an imposition on the "unwilling," and an abrogation of the moral agency on which all human life and earthly existence are predicated. This is neither a thinly veiled Pelagianism (man is capable of unaided self-transcendence) nor Byronic pride (I made my bed and will lie in it). It is, rather, an existential view of what salvation means and entails. Identity—human as well as divine—is constituted as the product of choices freely made. Hell does not exist because of some inflexible ultimatum decreed by an impersonal Justice. Reward and punishment are entailed not simply because that is the "fair" or "just" thing for God to do. For God is also merciful, and if humans can remit a penalty out of compassion or mercy, why cannot God? That is the question asked by Alma's son Corianton. Because, as Alma replies, such apparent generosity would undermine the essence of that agency on which moral freedom depends. This is the sense in which C. S. Lewis held that hell is "the greatest monument to human freedom."

Consequences are chosen at the time actions are freely committed. To choose to indulge a desire is to choose its fruit—bitter or sweet—assuming, as Lehi did, that "men are instructed sufficiently" to understand what they are choosing (2 Nephi 2:5). Clearly, and this is a crucial caveat, instruction is never perfect, the playing field is never entirely even, and a host of mitigating circumstances complicate and constrain the agency which humans exercise. In fact, utter obliviousness to the nature of what our choices entail precludes moral accountability altogether. Christ's blood, in these cases, "atoneth for the sins of those who have died not knowing the will of God concerning them, or who have ignorantly sinned" (Mosiah 3:11). But to the degree and extent that choices are freely made, "one [must be] raised to happiness according to his desires of happiness, or good according to his desires of good; and the other to evil according to his desires of evil" (Alma 41:5). It is a truth that harks back to Dante's grim vision of hell, in which God is not present as Judge or dispenser of punishments, because choices are allowed, inexorably, to bear their own fruit. In Alma's Inferno, as well, future states are chosen, not assigned: "For behold," says Alma, "they are their own judges" (Alma 41:7). As Mormon apostle Neal Maxwell wrote, "my desires and choices really will be honored! How manifestly just of God! How trembling for me!"[11] Not propitiation of God or Justice is the point, but the preservation in the universe of real opposites, real stakes. The alternative to this scenario would be a universe in which freedom is effectively nonexistent, choices do not matter, opposites collapse, and as Lehi describes, "all things must needs be a compound in one," with "no righteousness" and consequently "no happiness." So consequences are established ("[a] punishment . . . is affixed . . . in opposition to that of the happiness which is affixed" [2 Nephi 2:11, 10]). And the exaction of those consequences maintains the principle and efficacy of human freedom; to be fully developed agents, humans must learn to live out the consequences of their choices. Those consequences, especially negative ones, provide the motivation and catalyst for persistence in making better and wiser choices with experience ("repentance could not come unto men except there were a punishment" [Alma 42:16]).

Christ's intervention, in assuming the burden of human guilt for sin, thus affirms the law of restoration, the cosmic order whereby human agency is guaranteed by the unfolding of consequences in accordance with law. This is the real meaning of that justice of which the scriptures speak. This is why when we choose to sin, "justice claimeth the creature and executeth the law, and the law inflicteth the punishment; if not so, the works of justice would be destroyed, and God would cease to be God" (Alma 42:22). God stands as a surety behind the system which guarantees moral agency, and that agency requires the continuity between choice and consequence.[12] As the Book of Mormon says in confirmation of Isaiah's words, Christ does more than empathically identify with human pain; His rescue entails surrogate suffering: "he shall bear their iniquities" (Mosiah 14:11; Isaiah 53:11); He was offered "to bear the sins of many" (Hebrews 9:28). The Book of Mormon indicates that Christ voluntarily suffers these consequences on our behalf, in order to uphold the integrity of the whole system of cause and effect, choice and consequence, whereon agency rests. That relationship is manifest through laws that Christ Himself articulates: "Wherefore, the ends of the law [are those] the Holy One hath given, unto the inflicting of the punishment which is affixed . . . to answer the ends of the atonement" (2 Nephi 2:10). Simply circumventing those consequences, out of mercy or any other motive, would not only abrogate human agency, but eliminate the very distinctions that make possible a universe of meaningful differences and thus meaningful existence.

In Book of Mormon language, a clear differentiation of alternatives, the ability to choose them, and the stability and expectation of their unfolding in consequence of such choice, undergird the cosmic order over which God presides and serves as guarantor. "God [is] the administrative power in a perfect reign of law," in B. H. Roberts's words.[13] Without a framework of law that reflects these oppositional realities, choice would be uninformed, consequences random, and agency void. As Alma asks, "how could [man] sin if there was no law? How could there be a law save there was a punishment" (Alma 42:17). Clearly differentiated and predictable possibilities that exist in oppositional relationship are the precondition for a universe in which human beings can function as independent moral agents: "For it must needs be, that there is an opposition in all things. If not so, . . . righteousness could not be brought to pass, neither wickedness, neither holiness nor misery, neither good nor bad. Wherefore, all things must needs be a compound in one" (2 Nephi 2:11).

The challenge of atonement theory is to explain how Christ can intervene in the process, to actually suffer the consequences of human choice in humanity's stead. Christ's identification with human suffering originates in His human incarnation. Though a divine "Son, yet learned he obedience by the things which he suffered" (Hebrews 5:8). In His human form, He suffered all the pains and vicissitudes of the mortal condition. "And lo, he shall suffer temptations, and pain of body, hunger, thirst, and fatigue." But His perfect compassion and infinite empathy, suggests the same Book of Mormon prophet, led Him to suffer vicariously the collective pain of the human race; consequently, He endured "even more than man can suffer, except it be unto death; for behold, blood cometh from every pore, so great shall be his anguish for the wickedness and the abominations of his people" (Mosiah 3:7). This is the Book of Mormon's clearest affirmation of the fact that Christ's love, in an infinitely more perfect version of human empathy, displaces onto himself the collective pain we suffer.

Ultimately, the full extent of Christ's sacrifice was accomplished by His willed experience of the most devastating consequence of human sin: absolute alienation from God the Father. Mormon leaders have intimated the Father's withdrawal of His spirit, and Satan's unleashed assaults, were the vehicles through which His final suffering was effected. The agony in Gethsemane—where Mormon theology centers the principal work of Christ's atonement—was attributed to the withdrawal of God's spirit, at least by implication, in an early 1829 revelation, wherein Christ states that the sufferings He experienced have been known to all, if only in minute degree, "at the time I withdrew my Spirit" (D&C 19:20). John Taylor thought such isolation was combined with His full exposure to Satan's enmity. "He had struggled against the powers of darkness that had been let loose upon him there; placed below all things, His mind surcharged with agony and pain, lonely and apparently helpless and forsaken, in his agony the blood oozed from His pores."[14] Apostle Jeffrey Holland reaffirmed this view of atonement, declaring that Christ's abandonment by God on Calvary was the culmination to his suffering, and described his "concluding descent into the paralyzing despair of divine withdrawal, when He cries with ultimate loneliness, My God My God, why hast thou forsaken me."[15] This view is fully consonant with the view of Timothy Keller, that Christ's physical agony on the cross "was nothing compared to the spiritual experience of cosmic abandonment."[16] Mormon scripture indicates that the divine Presence, sometimes called the Light of Christ, is "the light which is in all things, which giveth life to all things." It enlightens the eyes, quickens the understanding, fills the immensity of space and infuses the universe with beauty and light (D&C 88:13). To be deprived of the Light of Christ is to lack the most essential ingredient in human happiness and spiritual nourishment. And yet, our dependence on and love for the Father can be but a feeble shadow of the bonds that unite Him to His only begotten Son. Christ's pain at His Father's abandonment is beyond human reckoning. His very real experience of the collective consequences of human sin do not only bestow upon him perfect understanding of human pain—it gives Him the moral authority to bestow forgiveness upon all who have sinned. In Dostoevsky's famous impeachment of atonement and reconciliation, he said of an innocent child's horrible suffering, "I don't want the mother to embrace the oppressor who threw her son to the dogs! She dare not forgive him! Let her forgive him for herself, if she will, let her forgive the torturer for the immeasurable suffering of her mother's heart. But the sufferings of her tortured child she has no right to forgive."[17] Christ, however, has earned that right.

Though these scriptural bases suggest the suffering of the atoning Christ was a combination of bodily experience, perfect empathy, and God's abandonment, the essential mystery of the atonement remains just that—a mystery. Whether the quantity of his suffering is the result of some cumulative calculus of all human evils or simply the infinite suffering of which an infinite God is capable, is impossible to say. James Talmage, author of the most authoritative Christology in Mormonism, concluded that "Christ's agony in the garden is unfathomable by the finite mind, both as to intensity and cause . . . in some manner, actual and terribly real though to man incomprehensible, the Savior took upon Himself the burden of the sins of mankind from Adam to the end of the world."[18]

RECONCILIATION

So justification has been accomplished. The demands of justice have been met, or in the Mormon vocabulary, the consequences of a broken law have been expiated. Agency does not require that we entirely bear the burden of our own choices, because those choices were always made under circumstances that were less than perfect. Our accountability is thus always partial, incomplete. Only the unpardonable sin, against perfect light, committed with untainted deliberation, in full and utter knowledge of its meaning and repercussions, is the sin against the Holy Ghost. It cannot be forgiven *not* because it is so grievous or offensive, but because it is the only sin a human can make with no mitigating circumstances. All other sins are performed "through a glass darkly," as it were, where to greater or lesser degree the weakness of the flesh, of intellect, or of judgment intrudes. In all such cases, regret and reconsideration are conceivable. Only the choice of evil made in the most absolute and perfect light of understanding admits no imaginable basis for reconsideration or regret—which are of course at the root of the very meaning of repentance.

In all other circumstances, however, subject to our repentance, Christ's merciful gift deflected the full consequences of our sins and cleared the way for our reconciliation to the Father. But Christ's suffering on behalf of humans—however effected—cannot of itself impart to humans the fruits of obedience. Only righteous actions yield righteousness, only merciful conduct engenders a merciful character, only pure thoughts produce purity. Only compliance with eternal principles, in other words, creates the exalted condition Mormons associate with salvation. This, and not some calculus of desert or merit, is what LDS scripture means in stating that "if you will that I give unto you a place in the celestial world, you must prepare yourselves by doing the things which I have commanded you and required of you" (D&C 78:7). Salvation in Mormon doctrine is not a gift that humans can earn as a reward. The very possibility of self-elevation from our alienated and sinful condition is beyond human reach, and no works we perform can make Christ's intervention obligatory or necessary on His part. His intervention is a free gift which is beyond our capacity to deserve or repay. But the salvation it portends is itself equally beyond His capacity to bestow upon us as a gift. Eternal life, the kind and quality of life that God lives, is a natural and inevitable consequence of compliance with eternal principles, just as God's own standing as God is the natural and inevitable consequence of His perfect harmony with eternal law. That God's merciful inclinations are circumscribed and delimited by law is clearly set forth in a revelation of Joseph Smith. "That which is governed by law is also preserved by law and perfected and sanctified by the same. That which breaketh a law, and abideth not by law, but seeketh to become a law unto itself, and willeth to abide in sin, . . . *cannot be sanctified by* law, neither by *mercy*, justice, nor judgment. Therefore they must remain filthy still" (D&C 88:34–35).

Christ's death and resurrection provide the human race with the gift of their own resurrection and immortality, regardless of their earthly beliefs or conduct. But His intervention in preventing our permanent spiritual death, or separation from God, is contingent upon an individual's *decision* to embrace the opportunity thus afforded and comply with its conditions.

Mormons do not believe that God foreordains a select few to be the beneficiaries of His grace. He desires, and will accomplish, the salvation of virtually the entire human family. (Only those few who never, under any circumstances, will to accept His salvation, will remain sons of perdition, outside the shelter of his grace.) Christ's atonement can unfold only within the framework of human agency's inviolability. However, it is in the realm of the personal and subjective that the effects of the atonement take root and unfold. It is the almost irresistible power of His superabundant love manifest in His choice to suffer what He suffered, that transforms the sinner's heart. "For, behold, the Lord your Redeemer suffered death in the flesh; wherefore he suffered the pain of all men, that all men might repent and come unto him" (D&C 18:11). As long as his "sufferings and death, . . . and his mercy and long-suffering, . . . rest in [our] mind[s]," (Moroni 9:25), we will be drawn to him, and to repent. His experience of every human pain ever suffered is an unparalleled gesture of love. But it also provides the basis for His perfect empathy, which makes it possible for humans to exhibit complete trust and confidence in His comprehension of our pain-filled lives. This is why His role as Savior required that He "take upon him their infirmities, that his bowels may be filled with mercy, according to the flesh, that he may know according to the flesh how to succor his people according to their infirmities" (Alma 7:12).

As with contemporary theologies of the "moral influence" type, Roberts agrees that the atonement's efficacy on individuals was attributable to its exemplary power as a "love-manifestation." "Shall this suffering for others have no benefitting effect upon those others for whom the suffering is endured?" he asked. He finds its exemplary purpose was "to demonstrate, first of all, God-love for man, by a sacrifice that tasks God that man might be saved; and second, to inspire man-love for God, by the demonstration that God first loved man, and how deeply God loves him; and third, to teach man-love for man."[19]

Knowledge of Christ's love and empathy are powerful catalysts to personal transformation. The conditions under which consequent repentance takes place are as generous as Christ can make them, without compromising human agency. The mercy thus freely offered, Christ's supernal grace, cannot extend to the point of *choosing* on behalf of individuals. They must choose, and choose again—that is the essential meaning of repentance in Mormon atonement theology. Christ's atonement sets up the conditions for humans to demonstrate through ever better and wiser choices, made in accordance with ever nobler and purer desires, that it is their will to live in a way consistent with the eternal principles Christ modeled throughout His exemplary life. In Maxwell's view, the point of mortality is to educate our desires sufficiently to choose wisely, since "final judgment will reflect our choices," and our choices reflect our desires.[20] Repentance is therefore an ongoing process of repudiating unrighteous choices, acknowledging Christ's role in suffering the consequences of those sins on our behalf, and choosing afresh to better effect in accordance with purified desire. The process continues—perhaps aeons into the future—until in perfect harmony with the laws that underlie the nature of happiness (and thus the nature of God), humans have reached a sanctified condition that permits of perfect at-one-ment with God. God's desire to save is reconciled with the sanctity of human choice. Love and agency, justice and mercy, meet.

In the ancient temple at Jerusalem, certain offenses required priests to perform the *kpr*, which was "the ritual of restoration and healing." In these cases, the priest carried sacrificial blood into the holy of holies and brought it out again. But "for the great atonement" on the holy day so denominated, the Old Testament scholar Margaret Barker notes, "a greater ritual was demanded." The high priest on this occasion sprinkled blood on various parts of the temple, then he conveyed the sins of the people onto a scapegoat, and sent it into the desert. "Translated into temple terms," she explains, "this means: The LORD emerged from heaven carrying life, which was given to all parts of the created order as the effects of sin were absorbed and wounds healed."[21]

The atonement of Jesus Christ thus foreshadowed is the only act by which the wounds of sin and hurt that rend the world can be repaired. The words of Isaiah 61, which characterize the "suffering servant's" mission "to bind up the broken-hearted, . . . to give unto them beauty for ashes, the oil of joy for mourning," reveal the atonement to be the universe's great "healing power."[22] The atonement is centered on the breach in our relationship with our God. That relationship is the most important one in which we participate, but in some measure this is because it is the foundation of all human relationships of which we are a part, and which are impaired and crippled by sin. Mormonism understands salvation as emphatically a communal enterprise and condition. "There is no such thing as a Zion individual," notes Nathaniel Givens. "Only Zion communities."[23] Atonement makes possible the reconciliation of the entire heavenly family.

Mormons believe that it is God's desire to save and exalt the entire human family. The gospel as restored through Joseph Smith represents an account of God's strategy for so doing, assembled from scattered shards that litter history and culture. The priesthood authority Smith claimed entails the authority to perform those ordinances which were foreordained as the mechanisms by which individuals manifest their desire to be full participants in the process. The highest of those ordinances, performed in temples, enact the supreme end and object of salvation: the linkage of the human family to each other and to God. Atonement is therefore not just "the very root of Christian doctrine," it is the tapestry on which is woven the height and breadth of human meaning, human potential, and human happiness.

Exaltation

In Mormonism's primeval drama, in a cosmic setting of unimagined antiquity, God looks upon a vast multitude of unembodied intelligences, has compassion on their weakness and vulnerability, and "agrees to form them tabernacles."[24] In Brigham Young's words, these beings were all "as helpless and dependent as any creature can be," but God deigned to "bring them together and mankind is brought forth for nobler purposes to be exalted to Godhead."[25] It is a commonplace of Christian orthodoxy that "the drama of salvation began when the Father and Son agreed to redeem the creation from the effects of the fall."[26] In the Mormon mythology, it is at a moment far more remote in time, before the earth is formed or the first man created, that grace irrupts into the universe. God invites other eternal but inferior beings into covenant relationship and family association with Himself. The atonement is the central dynamic which makes possible humanity's upward trajectory through sin and sorrow, growth and experience, toward eventual salvation and exaltation.

The end of all Christian striving is heaven. But heaven has meant many things to many people, from the beatific vision, to pearly gates and streets of gold, to eternal rest. For Mormons, the consummation they devoutly wish is eternal life. And that means not merely a life everlasting, but a destiny modeled on the existence, character, and nature of God Himself. This follows from the fact that "endless" or "eternal" is God's name (D&C 19; Moses 7:35); eternal life is therefore the life that God lives. Anything that Mormonism has to say about the nature of salvation, exaltation, or theosis must therefore be grounded and understood in the context of what Mormonism has to say about the divine nature, which they adore and seek to emulate. And one scripture comes closer in Mormon thought than any other to modeling what such a process entails.

Sometime in 1830, Smith reconstituted an Enoch text—missing, he said, from the book of Genesis. One chapter described a fearsome cost of discipleship, what might be considered a Mormon version of the "eternal weight of glory."

> And Enoch said unto the Lord: How is it that thou canst weep, seeing thou art holy, and from all eternity to all eternity? And were it possible that man could number the particles of the earth, yea, millions of earths like this, it would not be a beginning to the number of thy creations; . . . how is it thou canst weep? The Lord said unto Enoch: Behold these thy brethren; they are the workmanship of mine own hands, and I gave unto them their knowledge, in the day I created them; and in the Garden of Eden, gave I unto man his agency; And unto thy brethren have I said, and also given commandment, that they should love one another, and that they should choose me, their Father; but behold, they are without affection, and they hate their own blood; . . . Wherefore, I can stretch forth mine hands and hold all the creations which I have made; and mine eye can pierce them also, and among all the workmanship of mine hands there has not been so great wickedness as among thy brethren . . . wherefore should not the heavens weep, seeing these shall suffer? . . . And it came to pass that the Lord spake unto Enoch, and told Enoch all the doings of the children of men; wherefore Enoch knew, and looked upon their wickedness, and their misery, and wept and stretched forth his arms, and his heart swelled wide as eternity; and his bowels yearned; and all eternity shook. (Moses 7:29–41)

Enoch is drawn into the divine nature—his heart swells wide as eternity—through a shared act of vicarious pain for the spectacle of a suffering humanity. Through this mentoring in the cosmic perspective, the divine potential of man and the divine nature of God are shown to be the same. Godliness turns out to be more about infinite empathy than infinite power, and the divine nature constitutes infinite capacity for pain as well as joy. Humans can become partakers of the divine nature, through adoption into God's heavenly family, but that implies a love that has its wrenching costs as well as supernal blisses. Enoch's vision is not all about pain. The vision ends with a foretaste of a happier destiny in store, in a place called Zion: The Lord tells him, "Then shalt thou and all thy city meet them there, and we will receive them into our bosom, and they shall see us; and we will fall upon their necks, and they shall fall upon our necks, and we will kiss each other; And there shall be mine abode" (Moses 7:63–64).

God is first and foremost a relational being, and the condition toward which all righteous endeavor leads is one of participation in heavenly relationships that are eternal. God's title as Father is universally acknowledged throughout the Judeo-Christian traditions. For Mormons, the relationship is literal; the divine order is one of extended filiation, loving relationships that extend in every direction. Heaven is not merely an abode in God's presence, but a continuation and sacralization of human relationships in an eternal sphere. In Joseph Smith's hereafter, "the same sociality which exists among us here will exist among us there, only it will be coupled with eternal glory, which glory we do not now enjoy."[27]

In addition to being a perfectly loving being, God is perfectly holy. Life in the family, community, and church provide the context and the catalysts for an ongoing sanctification. As Young explained,

> the gospel . . . causes men and women to reveal that which would have slept in their dispositions until they dropped into their graves. The plan by which the Lord leads this people makes them reveal their thoughts and intents, and brings out every trait of disposition lurking in their [beings]. . . . Every fault that a person has will be made manifest, that it may be corrected by the Gospel of salvation, by the laws of the Holy Priesthood.[28]

In this regard, Mormonism is in full agreement with the position of Cardinal John Henry Newman, who said, "Good works . . . are required, not as if they had any merit of their own, nor as if they could . . . purchase heaven for us." But through "our acts of charity, self-denial, and forbearance" we will become "charitable, self-denying, and forbearing. . . . These holy works will be the means of making our hearts holy, and of preparing us for the future presence of God."[29] In LDS thought, only obedience to law can sanctify us, because only obedience to law creates the causal conditions under which our character is transformed in accordance with our choices.

Finally, God is all knowing and all wise. For Smith especially, sanctification was connected with knowledge. "The principle of knowledge is the principle of salvation," he declared.[30] We must know the moral as well as physical laws of the universe, if we are to live in perfect harmony with them. "Man may advance by effort and by obedience to a higher and yet higher laws as he may learn them through the eternities to come."[31] This rationale explains a Mormon emphasis on knowledge acquisition that can at times appear gnostic. "When you climb a ladder," Joseph explained, "you must begin at the bottom rung . . . and go on until you have learned the last principle of the Gospel. It will be a great while *after the grave* before you learn to understand the last, for it is a great thing to learn salvation beyond the grave and it is not all to be comprehended in this world."[32]

Ultimately, however, Mormons understand God's nature, and human salvation, to be the simple extension of that which is most elemental, and most worthwhile, about our life here on earth. However rapturous or imperfect, fulsome or shattered, our knowledge of love has been, we sense it is the very basis and purpose of our existence. For Mormons, heaven holds out the promise of a belonging that is destined to extend and surpass any that we have ever known in this wounded world.

Divine families encircled by his fire and light are the very essence of life and eternal life; without them this earth—indeed this cosmos—will have missed the measure of its creation.[33]

NOTES

1. Julian of Norwich, *Showings*, 39.
2. Synod of Sens, "Condemnation of Peter Abelard," 734.
3. As Paul employs the term, in the King James Version, "natural man" is an intimation of an *acquired* worldliness, not a statement about human ontology, inherited nature, or innate attributes. In his triple parallelism, the apostle contrasts "the spirit of the world" with the spirit that is "of God"; what "man's wisdom teacheth" with what "the Holy Ghost teacheth"; and "the natural man" with "he that is spiritual" (1 Corinthians 2:12–15).
4. Clement of Alexandria, "Instructor," 2:217.
5. Alighieri, *Paradiso*, 97–101.
6. "The German word 'schuld' means both debt and guilt," he points out; Nietzsche, *Genealogy of Morals*, 47.
7. England, "That They Might Not Suffer," 141–55.
8. Roberts, *Truth, the Way, the Life*, 404.
9. Mill, *On Liberty*, 28.
10. Roberts, *Truth, the Way, the Life*, 405.
11. Maxwell, "Free to Choose?"
12. The closest preceding atonement theory may be the governmental theory of Hugo Grotius and later Jonathan Mayhew, who believed, in Brooks Holifield's phrase, that "having promulgated a moral law, God could not permit its subversion without allowing the destruction of the moral order itself"; Holifield, *Theology in America*, 133.
13. Roberts, *Truth, the Way, the Life*, 408.
14. Taylor, *Mediation and Atonement*, 150.
15. Holland, "None Were with Him."
16. Keller, *Reason for God*, 30.
17. Dostoevsky, *Brothers Karamazov*, 227.
18. Talmage, *Jesus the Christ*, 613.

19. Roberts, *Truth, the Way, the Life*, 453–54.
20. Maxwell, "Free to Choose?"
21. Barker, *Great High Priest*, 49–50.
22. Hafen, "Beauty for Ashes," 7–13.
23. Givens, "Zion and the Economies of Heaven."
24. Smith, *Words of Joseph Smith*, 68.
25. Young, *Complete Discourses*, 1: 350.
26. Holifield, *Theology in America*, 36.
27. Smith, *Words of Joseph Smith*, 169.
28. Young, *Complete Discourses*, 2: 1009.
29. Newman, *Parochial and Plain Sermons*, 10.
30. Smith, *Words of Joseph Smith*, 200.
31. Talmage, "Philosophical Basis of Mormonism," 153.
32. Larson, "King Follett Discourse," 202.
33. Madsen, "Are Christians Mormon?," 89.

BIBLIOGRAPHY

Alighieri, Dante. *Paradiso*. Trans. Allen Mandelbaum. New York: Bantam, 1984.

Barker, Margaret Barker. *The Great High Priest: The Temple Roots of Christian Liturgy*. London: Continuum, 2003.

Clement of Alexandria. "Instructor." In *The Ante-Nicene Fathers*, ed. Alexander Roberts and James Donaldson, 2: 209–96. Grand Rapids, MI: William B. Eerdmans, 1977.

Dostoevsky, Fyodor. *The Brothers Karamazov*. Trans. Constance Garnett. New York: Barnes and Noble, 2004.

England, Eugene England. "That They Might Not Suffer: The Gift of Atonement." *Dialogue: A Journal of Mormon Thought* 1, no. 3 (Autumn 1966): 141–55.

Givens, Nathaniel. "Zion and the Economies of Heaven." Unpublished manuscript, 2014.

Hafen, Bruce C. "Beauty for Ashes: The Atonement of Jesus Christ," *Ensign* 20, no. 4 (April 1990): 7–13.

Holifield, E. Brooks. *Theology in America*. New Haven, CT: Yale University Press, 2003.

Holland, Jeffrey R. "None Were with Him." General Conference address, April 2009. http:// www.lds.org/general-conference/2009/04/none-were-with-him?lang=eng.

Julian of Norwich. *Showings*. Ed. Denise Baker. New York: Norton, 2005.

Keller, Timothy. *The Reason for God*. London: Hodder and Stoughon, 2008.

Larson, Stan. "The King Follett Discourse: A Newly Amalgamated Text." *BYU Studies* 18, no. 2 (Winter 1978): 193–208.

Madsen, Truman G. "Are Christians Mormon?" *BYU Studies* 15, no. 1 (Autumn 1974): 73–94.

Maxwell, Neal A. "Free to Choose?" BYU Devotional, March 16, 2004. http://speeches.byu. edu/reader/reader.php?id=5822.

Mill, John Stuart. *On Liberty*. 2nd ed. Boston, MA: Ticknor and Fields, 1863.

Newman, John Henry Newman. *Parochial and Plain Sermons*. San Francisco, CA: Ignatius, 1997.

Nietzsche, Friedrich. *The Genealogy of Morals*. Trans. Horace B. Samuel. Stilwell, KS: Digireads, 2007.

Roberts, Brigham H. *The Truth, the Way, the Life.* Ed. John W. Welch. Provo, UT: BYU Studies, 1994.

Smith, Joseph. *The Words of Joseph Smith: The Contemporary Accounts of the Nauvoo Discourses of the Prophet Joseph Smith.* Ed. Andrew F. Ehat and Lyndon W. Cook. Provo, UT: Religious Studies Center Brigham Young University, 1980.

Synod of Sens. "Condemnation of Peter Abelard." In *Creeds and Confessions of Faith in the Christian Tradition.* Vol. 1: *Early, Eastern, and Medieval,* ed. Jaroslav Pelikan and Valerie Hotchkiss, 734. New Haven, CT: Yale University Press, 2003.

Talmage, James E. *Jesus the Christ.* Salt Lake City: Deseret News, 1915.

Talmage, James E. "The Philosophical Basis of Mormonism." In *The Essential Talmage,* ed. James Harris, 142–62. Salt Lake City: Signature, 1997.

Taylor, John. *The Mediation and Atonement.* Salt Lake City, UT: Deseret, 1882.

Young, Brigham. *Complete Discourses.* Ed. Richard S. Van Wagoner. Salt Lake City, UT: Smith-Petit Foundation, 2009.

CHAPTER 19

··

THE PROBLEM OF EVIL
IN MORMON THOUGHT

··

JAMES M. MCLACHLAN

Strange! that you should not have suspected years ago—centuries, ages,
eons, ago!—for you have existed, companionless, through all the eternities. Strange, indeed, that you should not have suspected that your universe and its contents were only dreams, visions, fiction! Strange, because
they are so frankly and hysterically insane—like all dreams: a God who
could make good children as easily as bad, yet preferred to make bad
ones; who could have made every one of them happy, yet never made a
single happy one; who made them prize their bitter life, yet stingily cut it
short; who gave his angels eternal happiness unearned, yet required his
other children to earn it; who gave his angels painless lives, yet cursed his
other children with biting miseries and maladies of mind and body; who
mouths justice and invented hell—mouths mercy and invented hell—
mouths Golden Rules, and forgiveness multiplied by seventy times seven,
and invented hell; who mouths morals to other people and has none himself; who frowns upon crimes, yet commits them all; who created man
without invitation, then tries to shuffle the responsibility for man's acts
upon man, instead of honorably placing it where it belongs, upon himself;
and finally, with altogether divine obtuseness, invites this poor, abused
slave to worship him![1]

THUS ends Mark Twain's bleak and blistering indictment of theism, *The Mysterious
Stranger*. The question here is not whether one can show—as theistic thinkers from
Augustine to Alvin Plantinga have done—that it is logically consistent to believe that
such a being as an omniscient, omnipotent, and omnipresent being that exists outside space and time and created the world *ex nihilo* could exist; the real question is
why would anyone, except perhaps out of fear and awe for the tremendous power of
such a being, want to worship Him? Many of the most famous literary rebels from
Ivan Karamazov to Dr. Rieux rebelled against such a being, and it was not the simple

logical incoherence of the idea of God and evil that bothered them. It was the notion that an all-powerful, perfect, and self-sufficient deity would create a world full of sinners whose fate would be temporal suffering here and eternal suffering hereafter. That this being was so perfect that He required no world, and no other beside Himself, yet created them anyway, many to suffer here, others to suffer eternally in hell. Twain's nineteenth-century Mormon contemporaries Joseph Smith, Brigham Young, Orson and Parley Pratt, Charles W. Penrose, Brigham H. Roberts, and Wilford Woodruff didn't believe in such a deity—and escape the indictment such a worldview implies.

DIVERGENCES FROM TRADITIONAL THEISM

The Mormon philosopher Sterling McMurrin claimed that Mormonism was "in principle basically non-absolutistic." This did not mean that in their everyday discourse Mormons didn't talk about God using the same absolutist terms as other Christians, only that their idea of God would not let them do so consistently.[2] The absolutism that McMurrin claimed that Mormons should never lust after entails the claim that God is utterly distinct from all realities other than Himself, who possesses all of the following characteristics: causal ultimacy, being the temporal and/or metaphysical source of all realities other than divine nature itself; complete sovereignty, or unrivaled (incontestable) power and dominion over all reality; eternity, being timeless and immutable and thus outside of space and time; simple, not having a composite nature, not being comprised of parts, hence, being literally incorruptible. God participates in no genus or species, thus exists as Pure Being; and, of course, He possesses the famous "omnis": omniscience, having complete, infallible knowledge of everything that can be known; omnipotence, being capable of precipitating (causing) any event or situation the bringing about of which (a) is not logically impossible and (b) is not incompatible with other attributes of the divine nature; omnipresence or immutability (changelessness), existing outside and independently of the stream of temporal events and thus ever present; and finally, omnibenevolence, being absolutely and infallibly good, incapable of moral error, malice, or wrongdoing. God is also unique in that She or He possesses the foregoing attributes in ways that could not conceivably be duplicated or even remotely imitated.

As we shall see, it's hard to imagine how, without radically redefining these characteristics of the transcendent deity of classical theism, any of them would fit the Mormon God. Mormon theologies, even in their most conservative versions, don't see God as completely ontologically distinct from human beings. Joseph Smith's God emerges as an embodied human being. This is important to note at the beginning because the traditional problem of evil doesn't arise for Mormons in the same way it arises for other theists. Or, to be more precise, it arises only to be dismissed once Mormons pass from the language they share about God with other Christians, which Mormons (and one might argue the entire Judeo-Christian scriptural tradition) use hyperbolically as a language of praise, to discussion of the problem in philosophical terms. At this point they fall back on authoritative pronouncements from their unique scriptural traditions and founding authorities, in which terms like omnipotence are defined in ways quite different from most of the theistic traditions. Omnipotence, for example, has been used in Mormon writings to mean almighty, or all the power that a being can possess given they exist alongside other self-existing free beings that logically limit omnipotence. Just as most creedal Christians and traditional theists place limits on omnipotence when they define it as doing what is logically possible, so Mormons and process thinkers argue this means that God is limited by the activity of other free beings. The reasoning seems to be that it is just as inconsistent to say that God could force beings to act against their freedom as to say that God could create a square circle; both violate rule of logic. The first statement is to misunderstand freedom as the second is to misunderstand geometry. Thus God is understood as having all the power any being could have and is thus in religious terms "Almighty."[3] But just as for the process theologian such statements follow from a radically theologically reconceived idea of God, so are Mormon conceptions of God radically different from most creedal Christians and most theists, even process theists. Despite the shared rhetoric in relation to God it is almost as meaningless to apply the standard formulations of the logical and evidential problems of evil to Mormonism as it is Buddhism. The problems confronting Mormons relating to the problem of evil and suffering are, as they are for Buddhists and process theologians, different from those confronting creedal Christians and most traditional theists. I am not saying that Mormon ideas of divinity have eliminated the problem of suffering any more than Buddhists have, but the problem has to be understood quite differently for Mormons than for creedal Christians or traditional theists. The problems that arise for Mormons have more to do with the possible eschatological triumph over evil and suffering than with whether or not God is responsible for it.

A TRADITIONAL STATEMENT OF THE PROBLEM AND A TRADITIONAL DEFENSE

I will illustrate what I mean by allusion to the basic statements of the problem of evil. For example, the famous statement from Epicurus via David Hume lays out the problem of evil for theists:

> Either God would remove evil out of this world, and cannot; or He can, and will not; or, He has not the power nor will; or, lastly He has both the power and will. If He has the will, and not the power, this shows weakness, which is contrary to the

nature of God. If He has the power, and not the will it is malignity, and this is no less contrary to His nature. If He is neither able nor willing, He is both impotent and malignant, and consequently cannot be God. If he is both willing and able (which alone is consonant to the nature of God), whence comes evil, or why does he not prevent it?[4]

The easiest way of framing the argument is in the following terms. If God is

1. omnipotent and omniscient (all-powerful, created everything, and knows everything);
2. omnibenevolent (completely good);
3. why do suffering and evil exist?

This is an old question and one that isn't going away anytime soon and always bears retelling. There have been many able and subtle defenses of God's omnipotence, omniscience, and omnibenevolence from theists, and it's not my purpose to repeat them here.[5] Suffice it to say that since Augustine the majority position of absolute or creedal theists has been some version of the aesthetic defense.[6]

One way to eliminate the problem is to see suffering and evil as "prima facie" or "apparent" evil. It may be that the evils of this world only appear so and if we could see how they work into the totality we would understand they are all for the best. Perhaps they serve some greater purpose. In this respect they would not be genuine evil. In the *Enchiridian* Augustine likens God to a great artist with creation as his canvas. When we complain of the suffering of creatures in the world, "We are like people ignorant of painting who complain that the colours are not beautiful everywhere in the picture: but the Artist has laid on the appropriate tint to every spot."[7] Augustine emphasizes what this means in the *Confessions*: evil does not exist from God's point of view because from the "eternal perspective" it is all good. Its value lies in the great diversity it contributes to existence.[8] In *De Ordine* Augustine holds out the promise of a vision of beauty which will answer all our questions about the injustice and suffering of this world. "I shall say no more, except that to us is promised a vision of beauty. . . . Whosoever will have glimpsed this beauty . . . that in the intelligible world, every part is as beautiful and perfect as the whole."[9] This is certainly the message of a great deal of theistic writing from Augustine to Rumi, to Bunyan and Dante, to C. S. Lewis.

But for the Twains, Ivan Karamazovs, and Rieuxs among us such a position seems to not take the suffering of living beings in time seriously enough, and in its nonuniversalist iterations the position requires the eternal damnation of a significant portion of the human race, for the perfect whole includes hell. But what if there is genuine evil? What if hell, holocausts, and all the horrors of history don't contribute to the overall beauty of the universe?

MORMON REJECTIONS OF CREATION
EX NIHILO

In the 1844 King Follett discourse, Joseph Smith explicitly rejected creation *ex nihilo* and affirmed the notion of creation from chaos, contending that God organized the world from chaotic matter as a human being might "organize and use things to build a ship." "Hence, we infer that God himself had materials to organize the world out of chaos—chaotic matter—which is element, and in which dwells all the glory. Element had an existence from the time he had. The pure principles of element are principles that never can be destroyed. They may be organized and re-organized, but not destroyed. Nothing can be destroyed. They never can have a beginning or an ending." [10] Like process theologians, Mormons reject the notion of a personal creator God as the sole ground of being.[11] In traditional forms of theism, creation *ex nihilo* protects the power, knowledge, and transcendence of God. In giving up creation *ex nihilo* Mormons essentially give up the absolutism of God as it is usually understood. Along with this, Mormons gave up the absolute transcendence of God. God is involved in space and time. But Smith continued his discourse in an even more radical vein. "The first principles of man are self-existent with God. . . . God Himself found Himself in the midst of spirits and glory. Because He was greater He saw proper to institute laws whereby the rest, who were less in intelligence, could have a privilege to advance like Himself."[12] Human beings existed premortally and in some sense eternally, are not ontologically different from God, and can become like God.

Thus Mormons give up God's utter transcendence, placing God within a cosmic struggle in space and time with chaos to bring order to reality. Such a position frees God of Twain's critique that God "could make good children as easily as bad, yet preferred to make bad ones." Placing God with humans within the world struggle and giving God all the power and knowledge that it is possible for a being to have eliminates the critiques that might pertain to an utterly transcendent omnipotent deity. At the same time, however, the move may open God to critiques about the deity's power to save the world from chaos.

THE POSSIBILITY AND ACTUALITY OF
EVIL: OPPOSITION IN ALL THINGS

Perhaps the key passage in LDS scripture that reveals the Mormon understanding of the existence of suffering and evil is found in the Book of Mormon assertion of the "Opposition in All Things." Here the movement from the unity of undifferentiated chaos to the actuality of existence described by later Mormon theologians and teachers finds its scriptural origin.

> For it must needs be, that there is an opposition in all things. If not so, . . . righteousness could not be brought to pass, neither wickedness, neither holiness nor misery, neither good nor bad. Wherefore, all things must needs be a compound in one; wherefore, if it should be one body it must needs remain as dead, having no life neither death, nor corruption nor incorruption, happiness nor misery, neither sense nor insensibility. Wherefore, it must needs have been created for a thing of naught; wherefore there would have been no purpose in the end of its creation. (2 Nephi 2:11–12)

Personal beings emerge with opposition, otherness, in relation to others. Without the creature, without nature, without real others, there is no determination about reality, there is nothing to say about it. It is not will, not body, not space. If one called such a being perfect, it would have to be the perfection of perfect vagueness, perfectly boring, perfectly empty. The centrality of the personality of God, a personality tied to choice and relation to others, is central to Mormonism. This idea appears in the Book of Mormon in Lehi's famous instructions to Jacob in 2 Nephi 2. God creates the world in relation to already-existing, and perhaps eternal, chaos. The eschatology that is described in this passage reflects a movement from an unconscious or dead unity—either in Eden or earlier in the premortal existence in which humans are in the presence of God or in the unity of the primal chaos before God's creative acts—to an alienated conflictual multiplicity that is this world, and then, finally, into a freely chosen, conscious unity in multiplicity or sociality of love in both this world and the world to come, where Jesus's proudest boast will be that the unity came about through the "unfettered choice" of all concerned. In this view, the plurality of the world, with all its conflicts, is clearly superior to the serenity of the One. But this also means that evil is possible. The actuation of freedom entails the whole sweep of human history, with its multifaceted instantiation of the possibility of good *and* evil. With the monolithic identity of mere nature left behind, the actual God, the Word in the form of humanity and creation itself, suffers through all of human history. This movement from the serenity of oneness to the difficulties and richness of the world is superior to eternity thought of as static, unchanging perfection.

But the opposition of all things always had the potential for dynamism. It is the potentiality at the heart of freedom. But it is also the possibility of everything that happens, good as well as evil, happiness as well as suffering. Out of that which precedes the opposition of all things, reason and unreason, good and evil, joy and pain, all the oppositions are born. The fall from Eden produces the possibility of a choice between the opposites of liberty and life on the one side and captivity and death on the other (2 Nephi 2:27). This is a very fortunate fall in which human beings become subjects capable of choice, eventually capable of becoming like God but also capable of the greatest evil. But it is not simply human evil that Lehi describes; the opposition goes all the way down. The potentiality of freedom that is the source of all things also makes possible the joy and suffering. This is the unavoidable structure of reality that has God and humanity working to create love and order from the chaos of potentiality. "Adam fell that men might be; and men are, that they might have joy" (2 Nephi 2:25).

LDS philosopher David Paulsen has interpreted this text as giving a new understanding of divine omnipotence, suggesting that God has the power to "bring about any state of affairs consistent with the nature of eternal existences." This allows us, says Paulsen, to take an " 'instrumentalist' view of evil where pain and suffering become means of spiritual development. God is omnipotent, but he cannot prevent evil without preventing greater goods or ends—soul-making, joy, eternal (or Godlike) life—the value of which more than offsets the disvalue of evil."[13] I think the passage refers to something more radical than simply an instrumentalist view wherein evil becomes the means of moral development. The foundational status of opposition suggests that this struggle is just the nature of reality, to exist is to suffer. God is also involved in the struggle; the opposition goes all the way down. God also is trying to create a world from the chaos of reality; to be is to be involved in the struggle.

The movement from the unity and meaninglessness of the "compound in one" to the struggle of the opposition in all things, that includes the possibility of suffering and evil, is the movement to the creation of the subject, the person. Alma 42:3, 7 discusses the "fall" as a movement from the innocence of the garden to becoming, to subjects or persons capable of following their own will.

> Now, we see that the man had become as God, knowing good and evil; and lest he should put forth his hand, and take also of the tree of life, and eat and live forever, the Lord God placed cherubim and the flaming sword, that he should not partake of the fruit. . . . And now, ye see by this that our first parents were cut off both temporally and spiritually from the presence of the Lord; and thus we see they became *subjects* to follow after their own will. (Alma 42:3, 7; my emphasis)

METAPHYSICAL GUARANTEES OF GOODNESS

Two key elements of Twain's critique are that God didn't need to make the world and that God has no morals. John Hick argues that we need to gain virtue but God didn't; God was eternally virtuous. But the soul-making is all the way down in Mormonism. Here Mormonism, at least as interpreted by some Mormon thinkers, shows itself at odds not only with most traditional theisms but with process theology.

What is it to be holy and what is it to be ethically good? Can one be good who has never been tempted, who really does not know what it is to make a moral choice? Charles Hartshorne is correct in his critique of Anselm's explication of compassion and Aquinas's explication of God's love. In each case, they fail to see that being moved by another is key to these virtues. But some Mormons have carried this critique of impassibility beyond compassion to moral goodness. Being morally good is to feel, or as least to have felt, the temptation to evil and resisted it. This is the power of Christ's prayer in the garden that the cup be taken from him, or of the note of despair on the cross (Matthew 27:45–46). It is in these moments that we perhaps feel the greatest solidarity with Him. This is certainly the case in LDS scripture. In a letter from the Liberty Jail that became section 122 of the Doctrine and Covenants (D&C), Joseph Smith prays for his relief and that of his people. The effectiveness of Christ's response that this experience will be for his good depends on the rhetorical query that "The Son of Man hath descended below them all, Art thou greater than he?" (D&C 122:8). Since LDS doctrine holds that Christ is the Jehovah of the Old Testament, the contrast between the answer given by Christ to Joseph Smith and Jehovah to Job is important. Jehovah seems almost perplexed by Job's complaints, demonstrates his power over the forces of evil and chaos, the Leviathan and Rahab, and Job is silenced (Job 38–40). Jehovah seems not to understand why Job complains and is tempted to despair. One might interpret this passage to say that Jehovah has not yet become the embodied Christ. He is not yet perfect. He must do what Alma says he will do: he must suffer our infirmities to understand us. This is a part of his perfection: "And he will take upon him death, that he may loose the bands of death which bind his people; and he will take upon him their infirmities, that his bowels may be filled with mercy, according to the flesh, that he may know according to the flesh how to succor his people according to their infirmities" (Alma 7:12).

The experience of embodiment, including temptation to do evil, plays an important part of perfection and may be the difference between Matthew 5:48 and 3 Nephi 12:48. Jesus does not claim perfection until after the resurrection. The experience of life, suffering, despair, death, and temptation, and the victory over them is, far more than power, the reason for the worship of Christ. In fact in sections 88 and 121 of the Doctrine and Covenants these are the sources of divine power. What makes Ivan Karamazov's story of the Grand Inquisitor so powerful is that the Grand Inquisitor attacks Christ on the point that traditional Christianity has made so important, his difference from us. Christ as God possesses a freedom and power of will qualitatively different than humans, so he turns down the temptations of bread, power, and security—a moral triumph that, the Grand Inquisitor believes, is beyond human capacity. It is God's "holy will" that Ivan attacks in the story. The Inquisitor asks Christ how can a God, for whom temptation is hardly real because he is so strong, demand the free response from humans who are not powerful enough to resist the temptations of bread, security, and power. If one is naturally good and has only an abstract comprehension of alienation, fear, and the temptation to despair, can we say that He/She really understands the other person and can demand moral goodness of them?[14] We must remain with the suffering creatures in the dark part of God's beautiful painting. If God is to be good in any really human sense of the term God has to have experienced temptation and overcome it. Goodness is a matter of will and not being.

This is the strength of Joseph Smith's teaching in the noncanonical King Follet Discourse that God was once human. God remembers what it was to be tempted. In becoming God, God has overcome temptation but this is a question of will and not being. When Alma says that were God to coerce our repentance, even though acting out of His mercy, mercy would rob justice and God would "cease to be God" (Alma 42:13, 22, 25) it seems that it must be possible for God to do so. It is metaphysically possible that God could *coerce* our response but God *will* not do it. Will is more fundamental than being. This is not to say, like John Hick and the traditional free-will theologians, that God freely limits His power so we might be free. Rather, though it might be possible for God as person to coerce, with that act God would cease to be God; for to be God is to be morally perfect. God cares, in part, because God, while a finite, human, person, developed compassion through the experience of temptation and suffering in human existence. God thus fully realizes how significant temptation and suffering are for human beings because God experienced mortality. Joseph Smith and Brigham H. Roberts describe God as a person, morally perfected in love, who is fully related to other persons. A part of this perfection—at least according to the King Follett discourse in the case of the Father—has been the experience of life as a finite individual with all the temptations.

PROMETHEAN ELEMENTS: BUILDING ZION

An important element of the Mormon response to the problem of evil is human responsibility to remake the world from the unjust to the just. There is a popular Mormon joke that captures this element of Mormonism.

> A man dies and is met by St. Peter, who tells him that he can see heaven, and then hell, and decide where he wants to be. He first sees heaven and it is wonderful, then St. Peter takes him to hell, and leaves the man alone to consider the setting. After a moment, the man finds St. Peter. "Hell is beautiful!" he says. St. Peter runs over and looks. The land is green and beautiful.
> St. Peter looks at the man and says "Damn! The Mormons have been irrigating again!"

The joke seems based on a statement by Joseph Smith that if the Saints were all sent to hell they could, by working together, build heaven. "I see no faults in the Church, and therefore let me be resurrected with the Saints, whether I ascend to heaven or descend to hell, or go to any other place. And if we go to hell, we will turn the devils out of doors and make a heaven of it."[15] The Mormon philosopher William H. Chamberlin, who was a student of Josiah Royce, claimed God requires human cooperation in overcoming the chaos of the world. Zion, he believed, "cannot be built by divine hands alone."[16]

All of this reveals a certain promethean element to the Mormon solution of the problem of suffering and evil. The salvation of the world cannot happen by divine means alone. But building a temporal utopia would not be enough either. A solution to the world's evil will require human action in cooperation with the divine. Ivan Karamazov rebelled against both God and secular Utopias alike because the dead served as the manure for the happiness of future generations. From Joseph Smith's earliest vision of the Angel Moroni, who subtly hints of a way to bind the dead to the living, Smith is preoccupied with the problem of the unredeemed dead (Malachi 4:5–6). When Smith finally develops a theology of vicarious salvation, he cites the Malachi passage by way of explanation (D&C 128:17–18):

> And again, in connection with this quotation I will give you a quotation from one of the prophets, who had his eye fixed on the restoration of the priesthood, the glories to be revealed in the last days, and in an especial manner this most glorious of all subjects belonging to the everlasting gospel, namely, the baptism for the dead; for Malachi says, last chapter, verses 5th and 6th: *Behold, I will send you Elijah the prophet before the coming of the great and dreadful day of the Lord: And he shall turn the heart of the fathers to the children, and the heart of the children to their fathers, lest I come and smite the earth with a curse.*

Turning the hearts of fathers to children and children to fathers included overcoming the injustices of the past, and competition for resources between generations, but most importantly creating a link with the dead. Once again the theme was cooperation and sociality between all of humanity, living and dead. Smith continued:

> I might have rendered a plainer translation to this, but it is sufficiently plain to suit my purpose as it stands. It is sufficient to know, in this case, that the earth will be smitten with a curse unless there is a welding link of some kind or other between the fathers and the children, upon some subject or other—and behold what is that subject? It is the baptism for the dead. For we without them cannot be made perfect; neither can they without us be made perfect.

The idea that there needed to be some kind of welding link between the living and the dead included once again the relational idea that neither could be made perfect without the other. Wilford Woodruff remembered the excitement of baptisms for the dead in the Mississippi River "Because of the feeling of joy we had, to think that we in the flesh could stand and redeem our dead."[17] The joy was being able to do something toward the salvation of the dead, toward making the world right. This goes beyond the usual notion of soul making, to a transgenerational community making. Human beings participate in the redemption of the world, and are in fact necessary to its redemption because it can be redeemed only through the creation of a community, a sociality.

CHRIST AND SUFFERING

The Promethean elements of the Mormon solution to the problem of evil may at first appear incredibly optimistic, utopian, perfectionist, Neo-Pelagian, and humanist, but this would miss their uniqueness. The central figure in overcoming evil and death is

Jesus Christ. It is Christ who shows the way and opens the possibility of any of the seem-ing Promethean characteristics of Mormon perfectionism. Like all humanity Christ is the divine become human, a premortally existent being made flesh. Unlike the rest of humanity Christ bears the whole of human suffering upon him. Christ not only suf-fers for sins, he suffers our pain. "And he cometh into the world that he may save all men if they will hearken unto his voice; for behold, he suffereth the pains of all men, yea, the pains of every living creature, both men, women, and children, who belong to the family of Adam"(2 Nephi 9:21). To "hearken to his voice" is not only to believe in Jesus but to change and become like him. The Book of Mormon prophet King Benjamin says humans must experience a mighty change in their hearts. They must come to see "when ye are in the service of your fellow beings ye are only in the service of your God" (Mosiah 2:17). To do this one must overcome the self-love of our individual natures for "the natural man is an enemy to God" and will be until he yields to the "enticings of the Holy Spirit" (Mosiah 3:19). Later, anticipating Matthew 25: 25–41, Benjamin says the rich man who turns away from the supplication of the poor because he thinks that person deserves his poverty greatly needs to repent, the message being that one follows Christ by doing what he did, living a life for others. Indeed, this is the message of the baptismal prayer in Mosiah 18 that the followers of Christ must mourn with each other and bear one another's burdens. To change from the essentially self-centered being, the natural man of Mosiah 3:19, is to undergo what is called a "mighty change of heart" and like Christ to be more concerned with others than with one's self (Alma 5). This is a type of kenosis (Philippians 2) in which, like Christ, we empty ourselves of our claims on divin-ity to become the servants of others to join them in their suffering. Christ does this per-fectly in ways that the rest of humanity can hope to only approximate. We are not forced into this new life but are drawn to it by Christ's example. In 3 Nephi, Christ says this explicitly that he is "lifted up upon the cross, that [he] might draw all men unto [him]" (3 Nephi 27:14).

Is Such a God Powerful Enough to Defeat Chaos and End Suffering?

Traditional theists and creedal Christians bedeviled by the problem of evil must con-tinually return to it and discover ways to defend the justice of God amid the suffering of the world. In a similar way, Mormons will always confront the problem of whether their understanding of God can provide a being powerful enough to end evil, chaos, and suffering. The basic Mormon response to this question has to be along the lines that the universe is social and relational; evil, born of chaos and egoism, will show itself to be ultimately unworkable and eventually destroy itself. This seems to be the message of the Mormon scriptural tradition. Section 76 of the Doctrine and Covenants, also referred to by Mormons as "The Vision" for the way it lays about the purposes of the Mormon

Plan of Salvation, speaks of a final victory over chaos and death in the deification of humanity.

> They are they who are priests and kings, who have received of his fulness, and of his glory; And are priests of the Most High, after the order of Melchizedek, which was after the order of Enoch, which was after the order of the Only Begotten Son. Wherefore, as it is written, they are gods, even the sons of God—Wherefore, all things are theirs, whether life or death, or things present, or things to come, all are theirs and they are Christ's, and Christ is God's. And they shall overcome all things. (D&C 76: 56–60)

The sources of evil and suffering are in chaos and arise with individuation and life. They are part of the opposition of all things but are also the source of freedom and joy. Natural evil and suffering arise with the creation of the world and are part and parcel of existence. It will take time to overcome them. In this sense one could say that for Mormons the creation of the world is ongoing and will not be completed until the establishment of the kingdom of heaven. Moral evil arises also from the opposition but from the possibility of individuality and freedom. If I am free I can refuse to enter into relation with the other and with God. I can turn my back on the poor man who asks my help; I can turn my back on God and deny the relational character of reality. In this respect, Jesus is the obedient son, the archetype of moral self-sacrifice, and Lucifer is the archetype of self-will. The key observation of Douglas Davies in his *Joseph Smith, Jesus, and Satanic Opposition: Atonement, Evil, and the Mormon Vision* is that in Mormonism, evil is associated with apostasy from the truth, willful rebellion. Satan is the archetype of such rebellion through extreme self-will. Evil is rebellion against the community, the effort to make oneself God over all, including the council of heavenly beings that create the world. He writes about the great council "The Heavenly Council reveals obedience and unanimity cohering: Jesus is obedient in the absence of command. Lucifer pleased only himself through desire for personal glory, revealing profound disobedience. Gethsemane manifests the outworking of that obedience in Christ's direct engagement with evil to make atonement for humanity."[18] Where obedience, and acceptance, answering the call of the other, leads to creation of love, apostasy ends in isolation, the self-centered egoist cuts himself from all others; and since reality is founded in relation to others, they lose their relation to reality. The Mormon apostle John A. Widtsoe saw such beings withering toward, but never achieving, nothingness. "As they are eternal, it is doubtful if they can ever fully destroy themselves. Nevertheless, as they oppose law, they will at last shrivel up and become as if they were not."[19] Brigham Young went further, saying these "Sons of Perdition" would fall into their component parts and cease to exist as individuals. They return to that one that is as "if it were dead." "They will be decomposed, both soul and body, and return to their native element. I do not say that they will be annihilated; but they will be disorganized, and will be as it they had never been; while we live and retain our identity and contend against those principles which tend to death or dissolution."[20]

SOCIALITY: THE FINAL OVERCOMING
OF SUFFERING

"When the Savior shall appear we shall see him as he is. We shall see that he is a man like ourselves. And that same sociality which exists among us here will exist among us there, only it will be coupled with eternal glory, which glory we do not now enjoy" (D&C 130:1–2). This passage contains the most concise statement of the Mormon response to the problem of suffering. The sociality that we experience here is the prefiguring of the perfection of sociality that we will experience finally in the next world. This is not to say that Mormonism is otherworldly; the point is to work to eliminate suffering and injustice so far as is possible here in order to create the Kingdom of God on earth. One has an intimation of eternity in human love and friendship. But even if we were able to create paradise here, there are literally billions who would never get to participate in such an earthly ideal. The final encompassing sociality has to come in immortality. The kingdom of heaven fully appears only at the end of history.

NOTES

1. Twain, "Mysterious Stranger," 743–44.
2. McMurrin, *The Theological Foundations of the Mormon Religion*, 35–40. At the beginning I would like to make it clear that any project like this in relation to Mormonism is fraught with problems, not the least of which is talking about Mormon "theology." In a religion without creeds it's difficult to describe universally accepted approaches to anything. Joseph Smith expressed this antipathy for creeds more than once and the key notion here is his desire to go "further," to enter into the presence of the divine; Smith *Teachings of the Prophet Joseph Smith*, 57.

    Any Mormon theology is always going to be tentative. James Faulconer claims Mormonism is, by its nature, atheological, Mormons can never have adequate theologies only provisional ones; Faulconer, "Why a Mormon Won't Drink Coffee But Might Have a Coke."
3. David Paulsen and Blake Ostler use just such a strategy in their theodicies. See Paulsen, "Joseph Smith and the Problem of Evil"; Paulsen and Ostler, "Sin, Suffering, and Soul-Making."
4. Hume, *Dialogues Concerning Natural Religion* 63.
5. To name just a few: Aquinas, *On Evil*: Adams, *Horrendous Evils and the Goodness of God*; Adams and Adams, *Problem of Evil*; Hick, *Evil and the God of Love*; Plantinga, *God, Freedom, and Evil*; Swinburne, *Providence and the Problem of Evil*.
6. Most versions of the "free will" defense ultimately end up offering an aesthetic justification for creatures being blessed with free wills, thus making a richer world for the glory of God. Even John Hick's soul-making theodicy ends up resting on aesthetic considerations. God has created a more glorious universe because of the development of beings who tend or labor toward perfection. What all of these theodicies still defend is a perfect being theology in which God's perfection is demonstrated but in no way enhanced by the creation of the world; Clayton, *Problem of God in Modern Thought*.

7. Augustine, *Enchiridian on Faith Hope and Love*, 3.2.2.
8. Augustine, *Confessions*, 7:13.
9. The complete quotation reads:

> . . . I shall say no more, except that to us is promised a vision of beauty—the beauty of whose imitation all other things are beautiful, and by comparison with which all other things are unsightly. Whosoever will have glimpsed this beauty—and he will see it, who lives well, prays well, studies well—how will it ever trouble him why one man, desiring to have children, has them not, while another man casts out his own offspring as being unduly numerous; why one man hates children before they are born, and another man loves them after birth; or how it is not absurd that nothing will come to pass which is not with God—and therefore it is inevitable that all things come into being in accordance with order—and nevertheless God is not petitioned in vain?
>
> Finally, how will any burdens, dangers, scorns, or smiles of fortune disturb a just man? In this world of sense, it is indeed necessary to examine carefully what time and place are, so that what delights in a portion of place or time, may be understood to be far less beautiful than the whole of which it is a portion. And furthermore, it is clear to a learned man that what displeases in a portion, displeases for no other reason than because the whole with which that portion harmonizes wonderfully, is not seen; but that in the intelligible world, every part is as beautiful and perfect as the whole. (Augustine, *De Ordine*, 185)

10. Larson, "King Follett Discourse," 203.
11. Whitehead argued that if God were the metaphysical ultimate, the ground of all being, God would also be the source of evil: "If this conception be adhered to, there can be no alternative except to discern in Him the origin of all evil as well as of all good. He is then the supreme author of the play, and to Him must be ascribed its shortcomings as well as its success"; Whitehead, *Science and the Modern World*, 161.
12. Larson, "King Follett Discourse," 204.
13. Paulsen, "Joseph Smith and the Problem of Evil."
14. I realize that for traditional Christians and Dostoevsky himself this was the Divine/Human mystery of Christ. For Mormons divinity and humanity merge; Christ is the most divine because the most perfect human.
15. Smith, *Teachings of the Prophet Joseph Smith*, 316.
16. William H. Chamberlin, "A Christmas Sentiment," *The White and the Blue*, December 12, 1912.
17. Davies, *Joseph Smith, Jesus, and Satanic Opposition*, 180.
18. Ibid., 164.
19. Widtsoe, *Rational Theology*, 79.
20. Young, "Peculiarity of 'Mormons,' " 1858, 7: 57.

BIBLIOGRAPHY

Adams, Marilyn McCord. *Horrendous Evils and the Goodness of God*. Ithaca, NY: Cornell University Press, 1999.

Adams, Marilyn McCord, and Robert Merihew Adams, eds. *The Problem of Evil*. Oxford: Oxford University Press, 1990.

Aquinas, Thomas. *On Evil*. Trans. Jean Oesterle. Notre Dame, IN: University of Notre Dame Press, 1995.

St. Augustine. *De Ordine*, chap. 19, trans. Robert P. Russell. In *Philosophies of Art and Beauty: Selected Reading in Aesthetics from Plato to Heidegger*, ed. Albert Hofstadter and Richard Kuhns, 173–84. Chicago: University of Chicago Press, 1964.

St. Augustine. *The Enchiridian on Faith Hope and Love*. Chicago: Henry Regnery, 1966.

Augustine of Hippo. *Confessions*. Trans. Henry Chadwick. Oxford: Oxford University Press, 1998.

Bushman, Richard L. *Joseph Smith, Rough Stone Rolling*. New York: Vintage, 2005.

Brightman, Edgar S. *The Problem of God*. New York: Abbington, 1930.

Clayton, Phillip. *The Problem of God in Modern Thought*. Grand Rapids, MI: William B. Eerdmans, 2000.

Cobb, John. *A Christian Natural Theology*. Philadelphia, PA: Westminster, 1965.

Davies, Douglas J. *Joseph Smith, Jesus, and Satanic Opposition: Atonement, Evil, and the Mormon Vision*. Farnham, UK: Ashgate, 2010.

Dostoevsky, Fyodor. *The Brothers Karamazov*. Trans. Richard Pevear and Larissa Volokhonsky. New York: Farrar, Strauss and Giroux, 1990.

Faulconer, James E. "Why a Mormon Won't Drink Coffee But Might Have a Coke: The Atheological Character of the Church of Jesus Christ of Latter-Day Saints." *Element* 2, no. 2 (Fall 2006): 21–37.

Flake, Kathleen. "Evil's Origins and Evil's End in the Joseph Smith Translation of Genesis." *Sunstone* 20, no. 3 (August 1998): 24–29.

Givens, Terryl L. *People of Paradox: A History of Mormon Culture*. New York: Oxford University Press, 2007.

Givens, Terryl L. *When Souls Had Wings: Pre-Mortal Existence in Western Thought*. New York: Oxford University Press, 2010.

Hick, John. *Evil and the God of Love*. Rev. ed. San Francisco: Harper & Row, 1978.

Hume, David. *Dialogues Concerning Natural Religion*. Ed. Richard H. Popkin. Indianapolis, IN: Hackett, 1980.

Journal of Discourses. 26 vols. Reported by G. D. Watt et al. Liverpool: F. D. and S. W. Richards et al., 1851–86; reprint., Salt Lake City: n.p., 1974.

Larrimore, Mark Joseph. "Introduction: Responding to Evils." In *The Problem of Evil: A Reader*, ed. Mark Joseph Larrimore, xiv–xxx. Oxford: Blackwell, 2001.

Larson, Stan. "The King Follett Discourse: A Newly Amalgamated Text." *BYU Studies* 18, no. 2 (Winter 1978): 193–208.

McMurrin, Sterling, "Some Distinguishing Characteristics of Mormon Philosophy." *Sunstone* (March 1993).

McMurrin, Sterling. *The Theological Foundations of the Mormon Religion*. Salt Lake City: University of Utah Press, 1964.

Millennial Star, 18, no. 15 (1856): 227.

Ostler, Blake T. *Exploring Mormon Thought: The Attributes of God*. Salt Lake City: Greg Kofford, 2001.

Ostler, Blake T. *Exploring Mormon Thought: The Problems with Theism and the Love of God*. Salt Lake City: Greg Kofford, 2006.

Paulsen, David L. "Joseph Smith and the Problem of Evil." *BYU Studies* 39, no. 1 (2000): 53–65.

Paulsen, David L., and Blake T. Ostler. "Sin, Suffering, and Soul-Making: Joseph Smith on the Problem of Evil." In *Revelation, Reason, and Faith: Essays in Honor of Truman*

G. Madsen, ed. Donald W. Parry, Daniel C. Peterson, and Stephen D. Ricks, 237–84. Provo, UT: FARMS, 2002.

Penrose, Charles W. "The Personality of God—Vagueness of the Common Idea of Deity—Who and What God Is—the Spirits of Men the Offspring of God—Spirit not Immaterial—the Trinity Creed of Christendom—Man May Become Like God in His Glory" [November 16, 1884]. *Journal of Discourses* 26: 25–26.

Plantinga, Alvin. *God, Freedom, and Evil.* New York: Harper & Row, 1974.

Roberts, Brigham H. *Comprehensive History of the Church of Jesus Christ of Latter-day Saints.* Salt Lake City: Deseret, 1930.

Roberts, Brigham H. *Mormon Doctrine of Deity: The Roberts-Vander Donckt Discussion.* Salt Lake City: Horizon, 1903.

Smith, Joseph Fielding, ed. *Teachings of the Prophet Joseph Smith.* Salt Lake City: Deseret, 1938.

Smith, Joseph. *The Words of Joseph Smith: The Contemporary Accounts of the Nauvoo Discourses of the Prophet Joseph Smith.* Ed. Andrew F. Ehat and Lyndon W. Cook. Provo, UT: Religious Studies Center Brigham Young University, 1980.

Swinburne, Richard. *Providence and the Problem of Evil.* Oxford: Clarendon, 1998.

Twain, Mark. "The Mysterious Stranger." In *The Portable Mark Twain.* New York: Random House, 1974.

Underwood, Grant. *The Millenarian World of Early Mormonism.* Urbana: University of Illinois Press, 1999.

Widtsoe, John A. *Rational Theology: As Taught by the Church of Jesus Christ of Latter-day Saints.* Salt Lake City, UT: Signature, 1997. http://www.worldcat.org/title/rational-theology-as-taught-by-the-church-of-jesus-christ-of-latter-day-saints/oclc/37606158?referer=di&ht=edition.

Whitehead, Alfred North. *Science and the Modern World.* New York: Mentor, New American Library, 1948.

Young, Brigham. "Peculiarity of 'Mormons'—Obedience to the Dictates of the Spirit—Knowledge of the Truth etc." [June 27, 1858]. *Journal of Discourses* 7: 54–58.

....

CHAPTER 20

EMBODIMENT AND SEXUALITY IN MORMON THOUGHT

....

SAMUEL MORRIS BROWN AND KATE HOLBROOK

THE 1980 Mormon novel *Charly* tells the story of a young mother facing death from cancer. As Charly tries to make sense of her imminent passage, she explains the afterlife in decidedly physical terms. She assures her husband, the narrator, that in heaven she will prepare a "nice little mansion" with a "racquetball court" for her family. She then begins to ponder her husband's future on earth as a widower: he is young and will surely want to remarry. In a distinctively Mormon turn of phrase, she explains "you're not only looking for a wife for you, but you're looking for a sister for me." The narrator, an unapologetically provincial Latter-day Saint (LDS) boy named Sam, concludes that this concrete discussion tempered their suffering over Charly's departure: "making definite plans about our being together after this life took away some of the terror."[1] In its adolescent sort of way, *Charly* attempts to demonstrate the explanatory power of LDS afterlife beliefs about the persistence of embodiment and human relationships.

But such beliefs do not always provide the anticipated comfort. LDS physician-historian Lester Bush recalled an actual young LDS mother dying from cancer. Facing a situation much like that of the fictional Charly, this woman penned a note to be read at her funeral forbidding family and church members from attempting to console her children by telling them that she had been called on a mission beyond the veil.[2] She felt that this folk explanation for premature death would violate the sanctity of the human bond she shared with her children. No promise of a providential solution to her untimely death would allow her to repeat the rhetoric favored by her friends and neighbors.

These two approaches to the searing horror of the premature death of a young mother, one insipid fiction, the other brutal reality, speak to central questions for Latter-day Saints. These urgent questions have a way of tumbling over each other in practice. Understanding embodiment as "entanglement"—a word we intend in the positive sense of being interconnected, enmeshed, interdependent—orders and illuminates the rush of questions such tragedies motivate. We pursue this metaphor throughout this chapter as a way of bringing storied LDS traditions about embodiment and sexuality into contact with the lived experience of believers. Entanglement, while not a technical theological term, allows us to clarify the stakes and meaning of LDS understandings of life and its aftermaths. What does it mean to have existed before birth as a material spirit? What is the purpose of life if spirit has always been material? How durable in the next life are the vows and entanglements between spouses, whose bodies become one, as the Bible describes, in the act of sexual intercourse? What of the entanglements of children and parents (and other kin) who share blood and genes in physical mortality—how are they connected in heaven?

The concept of embodiment as entanglement is a constant in LDS beliefs and practices relating to the body. We argue that LDS theologies orient thinking about and behavior around bodies toward the facilitation of long-term relationships: between individuals and God, between wives and husbands, among family members, and among members of the human family.

In this chapter, we sort through the various threads of embodiment as entanglement: spirit with matter, spirit with body, body with body, spirit with spirit. We then use these images of entanglement to recontextualize the LDS "Plan of Salvation." In a final section, we trace the ramifications of entangled embodiment into discussions about how to present and dress the body. We consider ways that LDS modesty rhetoric governs bodies to facilitate eternal relationships, both on the local and the global scale.

1 SPIRITS ENTANGLED IN MATTER

Considerable ink has been spilt in debates about the meaning of Mormon materialism, a discussion recently invigorated by an American theologian writing within Catholicism who has situated Mormon materialism—especially the concept of a material Christ—in braided strands of Christian history.[3] While "materialism" has meant different things at different times, philosophical materialism largely represents the claim that there is no nonmaterial soul separate from the material body. In contrast to the often nontheistic account of materialism (in which the "soul" is merely an artifact of consciousness or brain function), Smith proposed a dualistic model of spirit separable from body. He argued that spirit was merely a more pure form of matter, complexly echoing early Christian arguments like Tertullian's disputations with Gnostics.

Smith's philosophical positions on matter need to be understood in the context of his own experience and his strong anti-Calvinism as well as his reconception of Christian history. Smith protected the persistence of human personality, fought against the concept of *creatio ex nihilo*, and assaulted the image of an "immaterial" God. His divine anthropology (the belief that God, angels, and humans are conspecific in some important sense), itself an answer to death and an explanation of resurrection, pushed him toward the view that God was material and if God was material, then so were human beings, including their spirits.[4]

In the hands of Orson Pratt and some other early Mormon thinkers, Smith's claims evolved into a complex panentheism (the belief that the divine pervades every part of nature but cannot be reduced to nature) or even perhaps panpsychism (all of nature participates in mental consciousness).[5] These views—in which the entire universe comprised conscious atomic bits—moved beyond what Smith himself had endorsed. Smith was not a formal philosopher and did not engage in usual philosophical discourse. In point of fact, most philosophical materialists would be surprised to find themselves even nominally in Smith's camp. Smith did not take a philosophical position on atomism or Platonic idealism or Gnosticism; he argued that to be alive was to exist physically, that human life was coeternal with divine life, and that consciousness entangled with physicality was central to life. For Smith, material spirit—spirit entangled in matter—was always a story about the persistence of human relationship. The body would and should evolve and progress, but it would do so entangled with a material spirit that, in turn, became entangled with other bodies and spirits.

LDS ideas about human embodiment have always also been theologies, accounts of God's nature. Some early Mormons, exemplified by Orson and Parley Pratt, seem most taken with LDS embodiment theology as a common-sense solution to the "metaphysical" "opinions" of orthodox clergy (the Pratts argued, in consummate circularity, that Protestants were atheists because they worshiped a God of immaterial substance[6]). They believed that creedal Christian beliefs in a Platonic-sounding God who existed immaterially beyond creation were false; with frontier wisdom they saw the holes in Protestant logic. These folk logicians' glee at besting theologians was only part of the early Mormon acceptance of divine embodiment, though. There were much more personal valences to support the dissemination of LDS teachings on embodiment.

2 SPIRITS ENTANGLED IN BODY

Joseph Smith promulgated a variety of ideas about embodiment through his life, suggesting that embodiment was central to the meaning of life, that it would persist into the afterlife and that embodied life encompassed even God Himself. Smith did not finalize a systematic approach to embodiment during his lifetime, but he did make several points reasonably clear. In heated protest against Protestant ideas about the nature of God, Smith preached that even "spirit" was material, just a more "fine" or "pure" matter than ordinary, physical matter. He also taught that embodiment was central to the conquest of death. The promise of a body forever was the promise of death overcome, especially to the extent that the relationships that arise during mortal embodiment remain intact through the afterlife. Smith also emphasized that temporal embodiment was a mechanism and a metaphor by which human beings matured toward godliness, a state of perfect embodiment in which the capacity to relate and love is utterly unlimited.

Writings about these ideas in Mormonism have leaned toward the theoretical and abstract: God and Christ are eternally embodied, humans are embodied on earth in a way that shapes their embodiment in the afterlife, everything in the universe is material. But what does embodiment mean fundamentally, practically? What does it mean to look at a hand and recognize it as one's own? What does it mean to hold a pen and trace it across paper, to feel its light pressure against knuckles and fingertips? For the early Latter-day Saints, what did it mean to wrestle, to plow, to harvest produce or slaughter livestock? What does it mean to share sexual intimacy with a spouse, to watch subsequently as new life—occasionally, graciously—arises within the womb of a woman? What did it mean that Jesus Christ was embodied, clothed in flesh not entirely different from ours, then resurrected into a new body on earth before ascending in that body back to heaven?

Embodiment, "having" or "partaking" of a body in modern Mormon parlance, represents a nexus for possible answers to these questions, even as it serves at times to motivate the questions themselves. Pain and the possibility of death are never far from the earthly body. A single false step or incautiously closed door can yield a broken hip or a crushed finger. Each voyage on foot or by automobile or bicycle or airplane may end in wreckage of vehicle and body. Bodies are physically fragile—mutable, susceptible to damage and at least partial repair—but in their physical temporality and fragility mortal bodies are important to our eternal identity. Mormons have since the beginning believed that the entanglement of premortal spirit with mortal body is sacred and central to the meaning of life. Our identities and our bodies metamorphose as we progress from fetus (a life largely hoped-for and only tenuously physical) to infancy through childhood and adolescence, then into adulthood, maturity, and finally advanced age (a life largely remembered and only tenuously physical). With each transition, spirit remains entangled with body, and this entanglement for early Mormons was physical rather than only metaphysical.

The entanglement of body and spirit can be difficult for observers to understand, particularly two centuries after Smith's career. Often framed as the mind:body problem in philosophy, it is in essence the question of how to associate what we see as fleeting and corruptible, prone to pain and disability, with what we perceive to be constant and pure and above pain or disability. Traditionally, Christians have seen the body as representing what is fallen and corruptible and unreliable; Mormons have dissented from that view in complex ways.

The historical traditions of Mormonism are multivocal: though they are largely protests against prevalent Christian beliefs, at other times they incorporate such traditional Christian concepts. Sometimes Mormons, while rejecting original sin and the utter depravity of human beings, have seen the body as an "enemy to God." Particularly around the control of sexual behavior, traditional Christian views of the body have led to popular LDS skepticism of physical experience. Although Joseph Smith himself may only have seen blood as contaminated (late in life he preached that blood would be replaced by spirit in the afterlife, a key distinction between mortal and resurrected bodies), some of his heirs have seen the entire body as suspect.

Communication theorist John Durham Peters inverted the usual calculus in a provocative essay suggesting that we have not sufficiently considered ways the body can be corrupted by the spirit.[7] In Peters's analysis the body is a sacred miracle that ought not to be blamed for our petty jealousies and rage. That type of creative inversion of traditional narratives fits well within the LDS tradition, even as it has not been broadly disseminated.

3 BODIES ENTANGLED WITH BODIES

In LDS theology bodies exist in part to allow the creation of relationships between individuals, an entanglement of body with body. Although sexual intimacy is the most obvious way in which humans entangle with each other, interhuman entanglement is much broader than physical sexuality. To bear or nurse a child, hold a loved one in celebration or consolation, to wipe away tears, wash away vomit, or change soiled clothing, to guard the failing body of one who can no longer care for himself—all these intimate encounters represent body-with-body entanglement.

For many thinkers, embodiment is central to the social atomism that dominates modern Western political philosophy. The body is a natural border, a way to aggregate and segregate rights, obligations, privacy, and other important legal notions. The individual, meaning (roughly) the conscious person and her own body, is the center of Western meaning and jurisprudence. We are individuals, on this view, as solitary as the bodies into which we are born.

Mormon theology tends to reject this isolating view on many fronts. The Mormon body is a locus for entanglement rather than primarily a marker of separation from others. Sexuality, including specifically Mormon concepts of sexuality, threatens social atomism by entangling people with each other. So do religious and cultural beliefs and practices surrounding embodiment. Smith, particularly in his Nauvoo theology and liturgy, made the strong claim that (a) spousal relationships sealed in his temple had the capacity to heal the rift in humanity and make the partners "one flesh," to entangle them in more than merely symbolic terms, and (b) the relationships that arise from human intimacy constitute a union more powerful than death, heaven, or hell. Smith's descriptions of embodiment were intensely relational. Humans acquired mortal bodies as part of God's plan for their ultimate happiness. The central responsibility during that period of temporal embodiment was to create relationships with other embodied individuals (for example, to marry, raise children, and be incorporated into a church or civic community).

The Mormon vision of embodiment and sexuality contains the possibility of a robust communalism. It is more than just the physical entanglement of sexual intimacy. The fact that a physical body survives death, and does so within human relationships, emphasizes the close association between resurrection and interconnection in early Mormon theology. Smith's resurrection was intensely communal and highly physical.

Resurrected humans clasped hands and embraced, as family members drew each other from their graves.

Sexual intimacy represents perhaps the most dramatic mode by which humans are entangled with one other. Sex represents a mediation and transgression of personal borders and boundaries. Sexual connections and the family relationships they generate and support play complex but generally central roles in most societies and indeed most individual lives. Sex gets at human identity, at the structure and durability of human attachments and the interface between appetites/passions and aspirations/ideals. All lives have been created through sexuality; many lives have been disrupted or ruined by it.

LDS views about sexuality and its persistence occur within the context of Christian tradition. Early Christian philosophies tended to see the body as a temporary burden from which believers would be liberated in the afterlife. There was no sex in such an anticipated afterlife; indeed death was an escape from sexuality, perhaps even from gender itself.[8] Luke 20 contains a famous response by Christ to a Saducean thought experiment which supported the general Christian view of the persistence of sexuality; no one would "marry" or be "given in marriage" in the afterlife. Whether humans will be sexless angels or whole-souled worshipers of God or actually merged into the body of God through theosis, the types of relationships humans create with each other on earth generally end with it.

For American Protestants in the early nineteenth century, a domestic model of heaven gained ground, a sort of continuation of life on earth, albeit an eternal life free from suffering and the fear of death, where people would continue to love each other. Most American Protestant believers shied away from the question of whether sexual relationships would persist into eternity; most assumed sexuality would no longer exist after resurrection, even if their family ties did. The Swedish mystic Emanuel Swedenborg, an intellectual influence on the domestic heaven, taught that affection between people after death would blossom into "conjugial love," a relationship that could include physical intimacy. Swedenborg's scandalous claim found little traction among American Protestants, no matter how strong their attachment to the domestic heaven.[9] (Even Swedenborg did not seem to believe that couplings would lead to new progeny, however.) While Swedenborg is a relevant antecedent, we should be careful to avoid facile comparisons between Swedenborg and Joseph Smith—Smith's view was more sacerdotal than sensual, more parental than companionate.

Joseph Smith entered preexisting debates about sexuality and left a complex legacy. He rejected, both practically and theologically, the proto-Victorian sentimentalization and atomization of marriage. The Victorian model emphasized more a nucleus of family than an extended kinship system and focused more on the sentimental love associated with marriage. Marriage became more private, less public. In response to Victorianism, Smith emphasized more the power of "friendship" and mutual commitment, incorporating intimate relationships between the sexes into his much broader "Chain of Belonging," a kinship network of human relationships sealed by a power he called priesthood.[10] Though he steadfastly proclaimed the persistence of human relationships through eternity, Smith does not appear to have intended the domestic heaven of his Protestant peers.

With his Chain of Belonging, Smith seemed to anticipate that humans would learn to love the way God loves. Yet for most Christians, Mormons among them, God loves universally. God balances particularity—the specifics of each human life—with the generality of the entire human family. He loves the one even as he loves all. Divine love encompasses everyone and is augmented rather than diminished when it discovers new objects of love. Mormon polygamy suggested that humans could possess a spousal love that did not lessen as it expanded to multiple spouses.[11] While a love like God's—at once fully particular and fully general—was treacherously hard to achieve in practice, through polygamy Smith pointed toward the future possibility that humans could be interconnected without jealousy or strife. Smith believed that the human family was larger than the traditional nuclear family of parents and children. But Smith and his followers also loved spouses and children with incredible specificity and believed that God loved in the same way.

4 SPIRIT ENTANGLED IN SPIRIT

Mormons famously believe that spousal relationships, perhaps even in their sexual dimensions, will persist through mortal life and into the afterlife. Belief in eternal sexuality and procreation seems to raise two important questions. First, what does it mean for humans to belong to each other? Second, by what mechanism do humans come to belong to each other? The two topics are distinct, though participants and observers have not always appreciated the distinction. One answer to the first question is that the entanglement of human beings with each other in family relationships constitutes the fabric of the universe.

In many respects the parental is the relationship of eternal relevance within Mormon theology. Parenthood is the relationship between God and Christ and between both of them and humans; parenthood is the relationship created through both procreation and sacred adoption, it is the relationship that—according to Joseph Smith—held the potential to vouchsafe salvation even if a child should fall away from the church.[12] While the spousal is the archetype of a chosen relationship, parental entanglements can happen by both choice and biology. The biological exemplar of the parental relationship feels spontaneous, irresistible, constitutional. The child feels like a part of the self, both physically and metaphysically. The Mormon belief in durable family relationships seems to emphasize a love that is both chosen and irresistible—both types of entanglement are sacred. That shared sanctity portends a certain fluidity of association in the Mormon afterlife.

The persistence of marital and parental relationships into the afterlife raised the possibility of what early Mormons called "eternal increase." Because God's godhood was parenthood within early Mormon theology, parental relationships would continue to expand in the afterlife. The realities of eternal increase became scandalously concrete in a doctrine called "spirit birth" that arose in the aftermath of Smith's death. On this reading, postmortal humans become pregnant and give birth in an endless cycle of fertility. Sexual intimacy, the entanglement of two bodies that creates another physical body, has been a common way for Mormons to understand the creation of new relationships in the afterlife. That a sexual metaphor should come so readily to hand to account for human cosmic origins is not surprising given Mormon assumptions about parallels between human life and the life of the cosmos. Whether it should remain normative for Latter-day Saints is less clear, as an adoptive model probably better reflects Smith's thought.

Joseph Smith identified sacerdotal adoption (by which humans could create sacred relationships with each other based on the relationship between Christ and other humans) as a model for the durable entanglement of humans with each other, suggesting the possibility that durable human entanglements patterned on parenthood could be based in chosen relationships.[13]

The essential characteristics of Joseph Smith's generative afterlife are a sacerdotal power known by various names (most durably "priesthood") that enables the creation of relationships among ultimately eternal beings. The earthly facsimile of this grand process is the saving rituals of the temple, inflected by the sacred experience of parenthood. Neither requires strictly biological exemplars of relating.

5 THE PLAN OF SALVATION

When Mormons use the term "Plan of Salvation," they generally have in mind the foundational narrative in which humans begin (to the extent that verb means anything in eternity) with Christ in a "premortal" world before earth life, then become mortal (much as Christ did through the Incarnation) as spirit enters body, then achieve salvation with the still-embodied Christ in heaven. These general contours gesture toward the internal complexity of the Mormon theology of entangled embodiment, but they represent a useful template for further discussion.

Joseph Smith did reveal a reasonably specific outline for the temporal process by which (material) spirits become entangled in (mortal) bodies. Alongside traditional Christian narratives about the Incarnation of Christ, early Latter-day Saints described a Plan of Salvation for humanity, a plan that encompassed even Christ. Over time the plan came to mean that humans preexisted their mortal birth, that they experience mortality as a kind of training phase for celestial afterlife, and that a special kind of embodiment will persist in the kingdoms of heavenly glory. What precisely Smith taught about the Plan of Salvation is probably open for some discussion. Other early leaders and thinkers—William Phelps, Parley and Orson Pratt, Brigham Young, John Taylor, Eliza Snow, and others—coalesced around a model most forcefully elaborated in the Pratt brothers' writings. They taught that the human experiences of kinship and reproduction are central to the natural history of the cosmos. They saw a spiritual existence before mortal birth, a probationary period during mortality in which the grade of blessedness in the afterlife is determined. These early Mormons taught that this cycle will repeat forever, "worlds without end." There is the possibility, Orson Pratt and Lorenzo Snow particularly taught, that God is such a parent himself, one who progressed through his own mortal adolescence. One simple summary of the Plan employed in late twentieth-century proselytizing materials, notes that "When we are born into this life, each of us receive[s] a physical body. These earthly bodies are mortal and imperfect. Receiving a physical, mortal body is a step to obtaining a glorified, immortal body like our Father has."

Modern Latter-day Saints often refer to mortality as the time to "receive a body," but at some level this phrase is misleading since humans are materially embodied before their mortal embodiment and are still materially embodied after mortal death. According to LDS belief, humans become entangled during mortality with a body that seems to have two chief characteristics. The mortal body is made from "coarse" matter, and it is prone to pain and decomposition—according to Smith this resulted from the presence of blood (the same fluid that Christ spilled to effect atonement), which would be replaced with pure spirit (Smith never clarified how this celestial blood differed from the person's own spirit, though Orson Pratt apparently believed the two did not differ).

The Mormon theology of embodiment as entanglement—spirit entangled with matter forever, entangled with a mortal and corruptible then an immortal and incorruptible body, the purpose of the entire cycle to entangle human beings with each other eternally—suggests the need to frame mortality as maturation rather than embodiment per se. Embodiment represents on this view a grand cycle of progressive entanglement. Mormons attend particularly to the story of Adam and Eve, extended and contextualized in Nauvoo Temple liturgy, as a representation of the correspondence between the human life cycle and the arc of cosmic history. Adam and Eve, deriving in the Genesis account from one fleshly body, serve as a powerful reminder of the centrality of human–human entanglement to the plan.

In some respects, the Mormon Plan of Salvation is a retelling of the Sphinx's famous riddle of antiquity patterned on the progression of human beings through the mortal life cycle. The mythic lion-human Sphinx asked seekers one of history's most famous riddles: what animal walks on four legs in the morning, two legs in the afternoon, and three legs in the evening? The answer, pregnant with insight about human life, maturation, and death, was humans—they crawl on all fours in infancy, walk upright as adults, and use a cane (the third leg) in advanced age.[14] Within a maturational model, preexistence with spirit bodies represents a kind of childhood (part of the storied transition from "intelligence" to "spirit" in Mormon preexistence would on this analogy perhaps represent a cosmic infancy), while mortality represents adolescence, and postmortal life represents adulthood. In each phase, as in life, humans are embodied, risk the pain of separation, struggle for progress, and entangle themselves with other human beings. The mortal phase of the life cycle is rather like human adolescence. It is a time of making choices, of exercising agency. Mortals assess and define, reassess and redefine their identity, struggle to define their relationships with their parents and each other. Mortals are prone to make bad decisions, sometimes obtusely, sometimes dangerously.

As with adolescence, mortality is not just a probationary period meant to test the mettle of individual wills but a time to learn to relate to other human beings. In the postmortal phase of embodiment, human entanglement will persist. Indeed, on the Mormon reading, the entanglement of intelligent beings with one another will never cease but expand forever. Given the future trajectory, the mortal sojourn should be spent entangling our lives with others' lives. Such an approach to mortality draws on deep roots in earliest Mormon theology.

This maturation model provides a context for understanding the purpose of mortal life. If humans have existed materially before their mortal births, what then is the significance of mortality? What happens in mortal life that is essential? One could protest that the focus on mortal life is artificial. Humans will entangle themselves with other humans, before, during, and after mortality. To ask the purpose of mortality is at some level to forget that entanglement affects all stages of humanity's cycle of eternal growth. Still this dismissal is not entirely satisfactory. Why do our mortal bodies die? Why do they break, feel pain? Why are we sometimes so base in our dealings with each other? The reasons for mortality presumably should speak to those questions even if a final answer is never entirely clear. We suspect that the answers to these questions will be personal to some degree, specific to life experience. But in general terms, we see a Mormon theology of embodiment as a story about acquiring the capacity to create new parental or parentally inflected relationships. On this view, part of the power of our mortal entanglements is their temporality. We are living in a sea of partial, transient impressions, of moments dimly remembered. By entangling with mortal bodies, we entangle with time. There is something about creating relationships in the face of imperfection, inside the vagaries of time, that represents the meaning of mortal life. There seems to be a capacity, a mode of being that we can best encounter in the midst of the temporal storm of mortality. That capacity, and the relationships created as it matures, is what persists with us in the afterlife.

6 Entanglement in Practice: Dressing the Body

Within the theology of embodiment as entanglement, Mormons have seen the ways they present their bodies to others as important to the creation and maintenance of communities. "Modesty," as a set of notions about how the body should be presented, facilitates committed, long-term relationships for individual couples and strengthens individual commitment to the broader community. The surface of the body, particularly in its visual presentation, affects the processes of entanglement on several levels. Latter-day Saints have especially enjoined "modest" dress and deportment on their young women and men since the origins of the movement. Modesty rhetoric has changed over time, depending on the particular contexts and challenges Mormons faced. In the nineteenth century, modesty rhetoric emphasized much more the role of community—women were to dress modestly to avoid importing expensive clothing from outside Mormon society and to decrease envy among the Saints. As Mormons became less separate economically and as the mores of the broader society became more permissive, rhetoric about modesty focused much more sharply on the sexual elements of dress.[15] This transition from broader community to individual sexual relationships seems to have mirrored a rhetorical transition toward less emphasis on communalist utopianism and a greater emphasis on the sanctity of the Victorian family nucleus.

As protest against constraints on sexual expression became more prominent within American society in the middle to late twentieth century, LDS rhetoric attained an even more urgent tone. As in many cultures, women have been the focus of Mormon modesty rhetoric. Women have been cautioned that their virtue (by which is meant their virginity at the time of marriage) is their greatest possession. They have also at times been warned that failure to dress modestly will inflame the passions of male observers and peers. In the latter twentieth century, modesty has come to mean that legs should be covered above the knees, chests and shoulders should be covered entirely; clothing should not disclose a woman's curves in detail. While conservative, upper-middle-class attire is enjoined on both boys and girls, the intensity of rhetoric seems greater when applied to young women. Critics of this approach have emphasized that such an approach can lead to blame of victims of sexual assault and exoneration of men for cruelty to women in negotiations over sexual intimacy. Whatever their effects, strategies for dressing the female body have been an important part of community efforts to regulate entanglements. Recognizing the power of sexual entanglement and the many options for nondurable sexual entanglements, prescriptions of modesty emphasize the need to protect people and their bodies from intrinsically ephemeral relationships of casual sexuality.

The cultural interchange around virtue and modesty remains a problem of empirical observations and ideological aspirations. Empirically it seems true to many observers that women who wear more sexualized clothing are more likely to have sexual encounters outside conservative norms. That this connection probably represents association rather than causation is rarely discussed—women less committed to conservative sexual norms or more drawn to peer-group identities outside the Mormon fold may be more likely to wear more sexualized clothing. The two phenomena may well result from the same underlying cultural difference. Even such an account is not wholly adequate, though, as cultural identities are constructed with input from both individual and society; the two elements can influence each other. By dressing in ways that signal membership in competing communities, adolescents and young adults may influence the future course of their cultural affiliation and behavior. Church leader Kathleen Hughes argued that modesty means dressing in a way that shows "we are children of God." Where a community like the Latter-day Saints defines itself in terms of family structure and community obligations, it seems likely that language about sexuality and continence would attach to strong markers of group membership like dress, speech, and modes or objects of entertainment. Because identity is so commonly tied to the body as expressed through modes of dress, patterns of sexualized dressing can become a locus for contests over control and autonomy in ways that can become self-fulfilling prophecies. In colloquial terms, a particularly self-aware young person might think: *I dress differently because I choose to (demonstrate affiliation with more secular cultural sensibilities), and my LDS community responds negatively, drawing its boundaries more tightly, so I feel less positive about my membership in the LDS community, while I feel a closer bond with people who represent these more secular sensibilities.*

In our current age of technological sophistication, bodies are dressed from both the outside and the inside. Much to the chagrin of some church leaders, LDS women have turned to plastic surgery in similar numbers to non-Mormon women of the same socioeconomic aspirations. There are even reports of LDS surgeons providing priesthood blessings to patients at the beginning of a breast augmentation procedure.[16]

Church leaders' criticism of plastic surgery represents those leaders' endorsement of a self-presentation that facilitates long-term and salutary entanglement over a self-presentation intended only to improve social location. One late twentieth-century apostle decried the apparent ubiquity of plastic surgery in terms that invoked modesty and the dignity of women. He hoped to provide women a space free from the threats to self-esteem that widespread cosmetic surgery posed.[17] Some critics of Mormonism have suggested that plastic surgery is a response to the powerlessness women experience in a patriarchal society that values them primarily as associates or subordinates to males. LDS women almost certainly undergo plastic surgery for a variety of reasons, though. Some are drawn by low self-esteem or driven by the demands of indecent spouses. Others may see plastic surgery as a legitimate extension of the power of clothing to establish a physical presence or maximize beauty. Given the relative safety of plastic surgery in the modern era, they may see it as difficult to distinguish qualitatively from ear piercings or treatments for acne and other well-accepted methods for changing the body's appearance. Mormon use of plastic surgery probably is also another chapter in an old story, the desire for upward mobility within American society. Just as immodest dress risks entangling a believer with outside culture, so can cosmetic surgery. Plastic surgery is a marker of wealth and glamorousness. Like the brick homes, advanced education, silver utensils, and fine furniture of late colonial America, "tummy tucks," facial manipulations, and silicon bags inserted into the soft tissues of the chest wall represent in part an aspiration to belong to the peer group of modern America's nobility, now the celebrity class. That Mormonism should fail to deter such behavior is ideologically frustrating for many committed Latter-day Saints.

The entangled embodiment of LDS theology represents a complex and vibrant collection of interconnected traditions that speak to the fundamental meanings of life and community. Entanglement holds within itself a central tension. Navigating that tension provides important strength to the Mormon tradition, but such navigation can be fraught with peril. The difficult question, on careful consideration, is how best to achieve the state of divine love so fundamentally associated with God. What experiences in mortality will best train a person to love with divine love, to be entangled as God is entangled? The two extreme strategies are to love very well a small number of people or love less well a larger number of people. Many modern Mormons would endorse the former, while many in the nineteenth century, particularly the leadership, supported the latter. We suspect a complex and paradoxical dance approaches the best answer, in which the quality of relationships predominates, but in which those relationships should be outwardly focused. Families, nuclear and extended, church congregations and neighborhoods can and should know each other well, but those secure relationships should form the foundation for blessing the lives of others beyond those relationships. The intense feelings of passion and loyalty that accompany sexual intimacy suggest that it should not be included in such an outward focus. We believe that the legacy of polygamy can be best sublimated through an expanding sense of (non-sexual) community and belonging that incorporates monogamous families into an infrastructure of entanglement. Foster children, adoption, community involvement, and other mechanisms of expanding community are central to fulfilling early Mormon aspirations for entangled embodiment.

NOTES

1. Weyland, *Charly*, 91–94.
2. Bush, *Health and Medicine among the Latter-day Saints*, 27.
3. Webb, *Jesus Christ, Eternal God.* McMurrin, *Theological Foundations of the Mormon Religion*, provides a somewhat dated treatment of these debates. See also Paulsen, "Doctrine of Divine Embodiment."
4. On divine anthropology, see Brown, *In Heaven as It Is on Earth*, chap. 9. Webb argues for the importance of Christology in what Brown has called early Mormonism's ontological *imitatio Christi*.
5. Hazen, *Village Enlightenment in America*, 44–47, 57–58.
6. In other words, if God were immaterial, then he did not exist; since Protestants believed in an immaterial God, they did not believe that God existed. On this logic see especially Hazen, *Village Enlightenment in America*, 40–41.
7. Peters, "Reflections on Mormon Materialism."
8. Brown, *Body and Society*, is the standard treatment of sexuality in early Christianity.
9. McDannell and Lang, *Heaven*, 126, 140, 183, 233–36.
10. On the Chain, see Brown, "Early Mormon Chain of Belonging."
11. Brown, *In Heaven as It Is on Earth*, 236–46.
12. On parents securing salvation for their offspring, see Brown, "Early Mormon Adoption Theology and the Mechanics of Salvation," 42–44.
13. On early Mormon adoption theology, see Stapley, "Adoptive Sealing Ritual in Mormonism," and Brown, "Early Mormon Adoption Theology and the Mechanics of Salvation."
14. On the riddle of the Sphinx, see Regier, *Book of the Sphinx*.
15. Blakesley, "A Style of Our Own."
16. Jones, "I Had a Girl!," 14–16, 31.
17. Holland, "To Young Women."

BIBLIOGRAPHY

Blakesley, Katie Clark. "'A Style of Our Own': Modesty and Mormon Women, 1951–2008." *Dialogue: A Journal of Mormon Thought* 42, no. 2 (Summer 2009): 20–53.

Brown, Peter. *The Body and Society: Men, Women, and Sexual Renunciation in Early Christianity*. New York: Columbia University Press, 1988.

Brown, Samuel Morris. "Early Mormon Adoption Theology and the Mechanics of Salvation." *Journal of Mormon History* 37, no. 3 (Summer 2011): 3–52.

Brown, Samuel Morris. "The Early Mormon Chain of Belonging." *Dialogue: A Journal of Mormon Thought* 44, no. 1 (Spring 2011): 1–52.

Brown, Samuel Morris. *In Heaven as It Is on Earth: Joseph Smith and the Early Mormon Conquest of Death*. New York: Oxford University Press, 2012.

Brown, Samuel Morris., and Jonathan A. Stapley. "Mormonism's Adoption Theology: An Introductory Statement." *Journal of Mormon History* 37, no. 3 (Summer 2011): 1–2.

Bush, Lester E. Jr. *Health and Medicine among the Latter-day Saints*. New York: Crossroads, 1993.

Hazen, Craig James. *The Village Enlightenment in America: Popular Religion and Science in the Nineteenth Century*. Urbana: University of Illinois Press, 2000.

Holland, Jeffrey R. "To Young Women." *Ensign* 35, no. 11 (November 2005): 28–30.

Jones, Lillith. "I Had a Girl!" *Exponent II* 28, no. 2 (2006): 14–16, 31.

McDannell, Colleen, and Bernhard Lang. *Heaven: A History*. 2nd ed. New Haven, CT: Yale University Press, 2001.

McMurrin, Sterling M. *The Theological Foundations of the Mormon Religion*. Salt Lake City: University of Utah Press, 1965.

Paulsen, David L. "The Doctrine of Divine Embodiment: Restoration, Judeo-Christian, and Philosophical Perspectives." *BYU Studies* 35, no. 4 (1995–96): 7–94.

Peters, John Durham. "Reflections on Mormon Materialism." *Sunstone* 16, no. 4 (March 1993): 47–52.

Regier, Willis Goth. *Book of the Sphinx*. Omaha: University of Nebraska Press, 2004.

Stapley, Jonathan A. "Adoptive Sealing Ritual in Mormonism." *Journal of Mormon History* 37, no. 3 (Summer 2011): 53–117.

Webb, Stephen H. *Jesus Christ, Eternal God: Heavenly Flesh and the Metaphysics of Matter*. New York: Oxford University Press, 2011.

Weyland, Jack. *Charly*. Salt Lake City, UT: Deseret, 1980.

PART V

MORMON SOCIETY

CHAPTER 21

....

THE SOCIAL COMPOSITION
OF MORMONISM

....

TIM B. HEATON AND CARDELL K. JACOBSON

Two important events in the first decade of the twenty-first century brought great attention to the Church of Jesus Christ of Latter-day Saints commonly referred to as the Mormon Church or the LDS Church. The first was the 2002 Winter Olympics, which were staged in Utah, headquarters of the LDS Church. The second was the candidacy of two members of the LDS Church, Mitt Romney and Jon Huntsman, Jr., for the Republican presidential nomination. Despite the publicity, many people continue to have misperceptions about the LDS Church. In this chapter we present some demographic, social, and religious characteristics of LDS Church members in the hope that the additional information will clarify misunderstandings.

Several studies have demonstrated that members of the LDS Church have interesting distinctive social characteristics.[1] Most of this research is based on United States samples, and our analysis refers to the US unless otherwise noted. But religious group characteristics are not static, due to internal dynamics, the changing characteristics of the US population, and shifting membership created by conversion and disaffiliation. Our goal is to update and advance understandings of social characteristics in three important ways. First, we examine evidence from recent national surveys to assess current distinctiveness. We also provide comparative data of LDS characteristics in four countries where the national censuses include religion and where the LDS Church has a significant number of members. Second, we use the General Social Survey (GSS) to examine trends in the characteristics of members of the LDS Church in the United States. The GSS allows us to consider trends in the Mormon differences from 1972 to 2010. We categorize social life into socioeconomic status, religiosity, family life, health and happiness, and social and political attitudes. Third, we assess the salience of key differences. We define salience as the degree to which differences are greater among those who play a central role in the religious community as indexed by frequency of religious participation and educational attainment based on the assumption that those with higher education and more frequent participation have more influence in the organization.

DESCRIPTION OF DATA SOURCES

We use the data from several sources to examine the social and demographic characteristics of members of the church. Much of our analysis relies on the General Social Surveys conducted by the National Opinion Research Organization at the University of Chicago from 1972 to 2010.[2] This survey is a nationally representative sample of approximately 1400 individuals, which was conducted yearly until 1978 and biannually, with a doubled sample size, since then. It includes a variety of questions about religion. Though the number of LDS in any one survey is small, we report data for each decade (1972–79, 1980–89, 1990–99, and 2000–10) to examine trends in the LDS community.

We augment this analysis with two recent national surveys that focus on religion. The first of these is the American Religious Identification Survey (ARIS) conducted by City University of New York in 2007.[3] Second, we include data from two surveys done by the Pew Research Center. The first Pew study was conducted only among members of the LDS Church from October 25 to November 16 of 2011.[4] It was a telephone survey of 1019 adult LDS respondents. The survey oversampled regions of the country where "Mormons are most numerous" and the sampling process involved "re-contacting Mormons identified in prior Pew surveys" to better represent LDS populations in other areas of the country. Thus, the survey may not be as representative of all LDS members as it would be if they had used a completely random sample. Nevertheless, the Pew sample is a reasonably representative sample of LDS in the United States, and it has the most recent data available nationwide. The other Pew study was a nationally representative survey of 35,556 people. This second survey, published in 2008, included 576 individuals who self-identified as members of the Church of Jesus Christ of Latter-day Saints. Finally, we use census data from four countries besides the United States: Mexico, Brazil, Chile, and the Philippines.[5] These countries are relevant because they have large LDS populations and because the country censuses ask people to identify their religion.

1 DEMOGRAPHICS

The LDS Church claimed a total membership of 13.2 million members in 2007 and 13.8 million as of January 2010. These are members of record, all those alive and who have been baptized at age eight or later and children of record (those under eight who have been blessed, but not yet baptized). The Church Almanac lists 5.9 million in the United States in 2007 and 6.1 million in 2010; the other members live outside the United States in countries throughout the world. The LDS Church counts all who have ever been baptized as LDS unless their names have been removed from the records by excommunication, or by their own request. Others may no longer self-identify as LDS even though the official records of the church still list them as members. The surveys

Table 21.1 United States General Social Survey: sample sizes by decade

| Decade | Religion | | Total |
	Not LDS	LDS	
1970s	10,583	69	10,652
1980s	13,992	249	14,241
1990s	13,077	146	13,223
2000s	16,769	202	16,971
Total	54,421	666	55,087

we rely on estimate the number of members differently; they rely on self-identification of religious affiliation. The 2007 ARIS survey extrapolated from their surveys to estimate that 3.158 million people in the United States were LDS in 2007 (1.4 percent of the population). Mexico, Brazil, Chile, and the Philippines are the only countries outside the United States with at least 500,000 members of the LDS Church. The ARIS survey also reports that 1.4 percent of the adult population in 2008 self-identified as LDS. The Pew survey found that 1.8 percent of the people in the United States say they were LDS in their childhood, but only 1.7 percent currently identified as LDS.

The numbers (LDS and the national samples) from the GSS are presented in Table 21.1. Although the numbers change by decade, largely due to changes in sampling frames used, the 1.2 percent of the total sample who identify as LDS is consistent with other surveys.

Most of the members of the LDS Church living in the United States live in a corridor from Idaho (381,000 members), south through Utah (1.88 million) and Nevada (174,000) to Arizona (381,000). This distribution represents the historical settlement patterns established early the history of the church in the West. California has 757,395 members (all numbers from *Church Almanac*, 2009–10). These states contain 59.6 percent of the members in the United States and 26 percent of all 13.8 million members in the world.[6] The Pew study reports that 76 percent of their LDS sample live in the "West." According to the ARIS survey, just over half of the people living in the intermountain states are LDS (53 percent).

Race

The LDS Church does not keep records by race or ethnicity, nor has it throughout its history. Researchers have made some estimates of race and ethnicity from the surveys. For example, 86 percent of the LDS respondents in the Pew survey were White; three percent self-identified as Black, 7 percent as Hispanic, and 7 percent were listed as "other" in the survey. The "other" category would include Asian and Polynesian. These categories

Table 21.2 Race and ethnicity of LDS members in the four countries, estimated by percentage that speak other languages

	Mexico		Brazil		Chile		Philippines	
	LDS	Country	LDS	Country	LDS	Country	LDS	Country
% who speak an indigenous language or member of Indigenous group								
	4.4	10.3			4.2	4.5		
% who speak								
English							79.4	72.3
Philippino							93.4	91.1
Race (Brazil)								
White			61.2	55.0				
Black			6.3	6.7				
Indigenous			.5	.4				
Asian			.3	.5				
Brown			31.1	36.8				
Unknown			.5	.6				

add to more than 100 percent because Hispanic identity is asked separately from the race question. Thus, respondents could be both Hispanic and Black or White and Hispanic. The ARIS data show an even higher proportion of Whites among Mormons, 91 percent. Only 3 percent of the ARIS LDS sample report their race as Black and 3 percent were listed as Hispanic. In other countries, LDS members are also not likely to belong to ethnic or racial minority groups (see Table 21.2).

2 SOCIOECONOMIC STATUS

Education

Mormons have an educational advantage compared with the national population. This difference has persisted in recent surveys. Figure 21.1 shows the trend. The graph shows that Mormons have somewhat higher educational levels than the population as a whole, and the trends in educational attainment between the LDS and others in the GSS data are parallel. The dip in the 2000s, however, is greater for Mormons. Moreover, the gap between LDS men and women appears to be growing, while the national gender gap is narrowing. Some of these recent changes may reflect variations in the sampling frames used. Overall, a multiple regression analyses of the GSS data indicates that LDS have nearly one more year of schooling than the rest of the nation. But the increase in education is less dramatic for Mormons even after controlling for Mountain Region. Statistical tests for interaction terms indicate that the gender difference in education is no greater

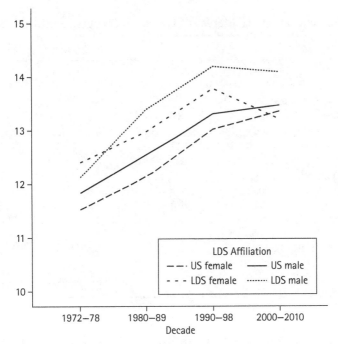

FIGURE 21.1 Trends in educational attainment (education measured on a scale from 0 to 20 years completed)

for Mormons than for the national population of females and that the trend in educa-tion is similar for LDS males and females. The failure of these statistical tests to confirm the widening gap apparent in the graph highlights the need for larger samples to detect this trend.

The two surveys (ARIS and Pew) have slightly different numbers on the education of the LDS sample, but all are within the margin of error for surveys. Those with a high school education or less in the ARIS and Pew survey are 37 percent and 39 percent. Those who attended some college in the two surveys are (34 percent vs. 32 percent), and those who have graduated from college are (20 percent and 18 percent). Similar num-bers have professional or graduate degrees (8 percent and 10 percent). In other words, about 30 percent of the LDS in the two US samples had graduated from college or had advanced degrees. This figure is roughly the same as the general population in the United States. In 2010, 87 percent of the total American population had graduated from high school and 30 percent had graduated from college or had an advanced degree.[7]

For the LDS women the story is somewhat different. The LDS women in Utah have less education that the non-LDS women in Utah. They are slightly more likely to be only a high school graduate (24.1 vs. 18.8 percent) and less likely to have completed a gradu-ate education (8.3 vs. 17.5 percent). For LDS women living outside of Utah, the pattern is reversed (25.6 vs. 30) for non-LDS completed high school only. But the pattern is simi-lar at the graduate level (7.0 vs. 12.9). Phillips and Cragun also note that, overall, the

Table 21.3 Education and literacy of LDS members outside the US (aged 18+)

	Mexico		Brazil		Chile		Philippines	
	LDS	Country	LDS	Country	LDS	Country	LDS	Country
Educational attainment (percent)								
No schooling	4.0	11.6	3.6	13.2	2.5	4.7	2.1	3.3
Some primary	11.5	24.3	9.0	19.2	8.1	12.9	13.0	16.0
Primary completed	18.7	24.4	40.7	41.2	33.1	35.1	29.8	33.6
Lower secondary completed	27.6	20.4	8.5	4.0	8.3	6.2	–	–
Secondary completed	19.0	9.3	26.9	14.8	24.5	19.4	17.4	18.6
Some college	7.3	3.2	6.1	3.1	8.9	8.4	22.2	16.9
Post-secondary technical	.6	.3	–	–	11.3	8.3	5.0	4.0
University completed	11.3	6.5	5.3	4.6	3.2	4.9	10.5	7.6
Literacy								
% literate	96.3	86.0	96.7	84.7	98.0	95.5	95.1	92.3

educational differences between LDS and non-LDS women outside of Utah are not statistically significant (note: the total sample size of LDS women living outside of Utah in the Pew study is only 285).

In sum, both the ARIS data and the Pew data show few large differences between the LDS and the national averages on educational attainment. The GSS data show some difference, but it is modest. LDS in the United States have about the same education as others in the United States. Where there are differences, the LDS tend to have slightly higher educational attainment.

In other countries, the educational attainment of Mormons is somewhat higher than the national average. In each country, LDS members are more likely to go beyond primary schooling. They are also more likely to have college experience in each country except Chile (see Table 21.3). One explanation for these outcomes is that the LDS missionaries in each of these countries are often assigned to urban areas where the population is more likely to have higher education, occupational, and employment levels. And the members may be heeding the church's emphasis on obtaining higher levels of education.

Employment Status, Occupation, and Income

The LDS Church has long placed an emphasis on the family, and leaders have often encouraged women to stay home with their children. Thus, it is not surprising that the number of LDS women in the workforce is somewhat lower than the nation as a whole. The ARIS data show that only 25 percent of LDS women in the United States work full-time, compared to 39 percent of all US women. The percent of the LDS women who work part-time, on the other hand, is higher than women nationally (23 percent compared to 14 percent). LDS women in the ARIS sample are also more likely to describe themselves as housewives (26 percent compared to 13 percent in the nation).

Comparable data from the GSS by decade are illustrated in Figure 21.2. The data show that LDS women are less likely than other women to work full-time. Multivariate analysis adjusting for age and region indicates that LDS women are only 60 percent as likely to work full-time as women nationally.

Lower full-time employment by LDS women is also observed in the last ten years of the GSS, and the gap between LDS women and women nationally appears to have widened in the most recent decade. This difference in the rate of decline is not statistically significant, however. We find that the association between frequency of church attendance and full-time employment is more negative for LDS women than is the case nationally. Full-time employment is especially low among the LDS women who regularly attend church. LDS men are less likely than other men to be employed full-time in recent decades. This could be a function of age, as LDS men are somewhat more likely to report working part-time or being in school. The LDS also tend to be slightly younger. The difference in full-time work is also not statistically significant.

The data from the four other countries tell a somewhat different story. Compared to their national populations, LDS members are a little more likely to be in the labor

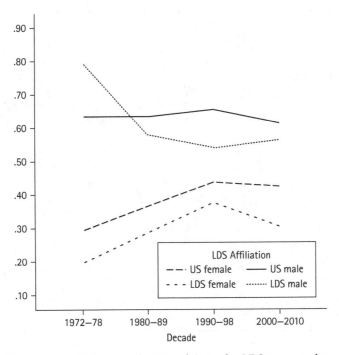

FIGURE 21.2 Full-time employment in the United States by LDS status and gender

force in Mexico and Brazil, but not in Chile. Corresponding to higher levels of educational attainment and urban residence, LDS members are more likely to be in white collar occupations, and less likely to be farmers (see Table 21.4). These results likely reflect where LDS missionary efforts are directed—in the more urban areas. The emphasis on education in the LDS Church also may attract those who have higher educational levels.

Since LDS members in the four countries (where data are available) are more likely to be employed, more likely to be in white-collar occupations, and less likely to be farmers, their average income and wealth are somewhat higher in Mexico and Brazil. Measures of income and wealth indicate that Mormons are better off than the average person in Mexico and Brazil, but comparable to the national average person in Chile and the Philippines (see Table 21.5). The census data in these countries also present a wealth index based on household possessions.

The income of the LDS members in the United States, however, is roughly comparable to other Americans. The Pew study showed that roughly a quarter (26 percent) of the LDS members in the United States has incomes less than $30,000. Just over a fifth has incomes between $30,000 and $50,000, and between $50,000 and $75,000 (21 percent and 22 percent respectively). Finally, a sixth (16 percent) has incomes from $75,000 to $100,000, and over $100,000. The sample of all Americans has slightly more people at

Table 21.4 Employment and occupational data on LDS members in four selected countries

	Mexico		Brazil		Chile		Philippines	
	LDS	Country	LDS	Country	LDS	Country	LDS	Country
Employment status (percent)								
Employed	58.7	54.8	57.7	56.9	45.2	48.1	–	–
Unemployed	.8	.6	14.1	8.5	9.6	7.4	–	–
Inactive	40.5	44.6	28.1	34.7	45.2	44.5	–	–
Occupation (percent)								
Senior officials	2.9	1.9	4.7	4.3	4.4	5.8	2.9	2.4
Professional	13.0	7.6	8.6	5.5	6.7	9.5	10.3	6.8
Technicians	5.4	2.7	12.4	7.8	15.4	13.9	4.7	3.1
Clerks	13.0	7.5	12.4	7.5	9.9	8.5	4.8	4.3
Service/sales	20.2	14.9	26.5	21.5	18.0	12.6	7.4	6.5
Skilled agriculture	6.0	24.5	1.6	21.5	2.2	5.2	25.8	35.3
Crafts	18.6	17.3	14.9	15.0	14.4	12.8	12.1	10.6
Operators	7.6	8.7	9.0	8.9	7.8	8.7	8.9	8.8
Elementary occupations	11.7	12.8	8.2	7.3	20.2	21.9	22.4	21.6
Armed forces	.2	.2	1.6	.8	1.0	1.0	.8	.7
Other	1.4	1.8	–	–	–	–	–	–

Table 21.5 Income and wealth of LDS members in Mexico, Brazil, Chile, and the Philippines

	Mexico		Brazil		Chile		Philippines	
	LDS	Country	LDS	Country	LDS	Country	LDS	Country
Average wealth index	3.36	2.99	3.62	2.98	3.93	3.98	1.84	1.85
Average earnings	3970	3343	694	633	–	–	–	–
Average total income	3815	2968	466	425	–	–	–	–

the top income levels, over $150,000, whereas the LDS sample has more in the middle income groups.

3 Religious Beliefs and Practices

Beliefs

Mormons are a believing people. The Pew data show that 100 percent of their LDS sample believe in "God or a universal spirit." This compares to 92 percent in their national sample. Further, 90 percent of the LDS say they are absolutely certain that God exists, and an additional 8 percent say they are fairly certain (compared to 71 percent and 17 percent nationally). Evangelicals' beliefs in God are comparable to the LDS respondents. Ninety-one percent of the LDS view God as a "personal God," compared to 60 percent of the United States and 79 percent of those who identify as Evangelical. Almost all (98 percent) LDS believe in a life after death and 88 percent of them are "absolutely certain" of a life after death (compared to 50 percent of the total sample). Ninety-five percent of the LDS profess a belief in a heaven, compared to 74 percent of the full sample.

A high percentage of LDS members express strong beliefs in basic Christian doctrines. For example, 80 percent completely agree that "miracles still occur today," compared to 47 percent of the national sample. Nearly 6 in 10 (59 percent) say they believe "angels and demons are active in the world" compared to 40 percent of the total sample (and 61 percent of Evangelicals) who say this. Mormons do not take the Bible as literally as Evangelicals, however. When asked if the "Bible is the Word of God taken literally word for word," only 35 percent of the LDS respond in the affirmative; most (50 percent) say it is not taken literally.

The LDS are more likely than all other groups to describe their religion as the one, true faith leading to eternal life (80 percent compared to 24 percent of the national population and 36 percent of the Evangelicals). Finally, they are far more likely (69 percent) to say they have "witnessed or experienced a divine healing" than the 36 percent of the Pew national sample.

Religious Practices

Mormons are also more active in religious practices than their national counterparts. Ninety-two percent of the LDS in the Pew sample say they are an official member of a local church compared to 61 percent of the national sample. Further, 75 percent say they attend religious services once a week or more (compared to 39 percent of the national sample and 58 percent of the Evangelicals). Mormons say they pray several times a day (66 percent compared to 38 percent of the national sample), participate in prayer groups (64 percent compared to 23 percent), read scriptures outside of religious services (76 percent compared to 35 percent), and work more with children or youth (45 percent compared to 17 percent of the national sample). At least part of the explantion for these results is that LDS congregations have no professional ministry, and so most positions are filled by lay members.

The LDS also say they participate regularly in social activities of the church (25 percent say at least once a week), and they say they do community volunteer work through their place of worship (21 percent say at least once a week). The respondent's positive response to this question likely includes working with youth and young children.

The trends in religious attendance of the LDS vary from the national trends as well. Whereas the national trend is toward less frequent church attendance, the Mormon trend is relatively flat. Additionally, whereas the national data show that females, more than males, report frequent church attendance, the difference between male and female attendance of the LDS members is not large and appears to be quite stable for the past three decades (Figure 21.3).

Religious Identification

Mormons also report greater strength of religious identification (on a scale from 1 to 4) than other Americans, and the trend in strength of identification is positive for Mormons, but negative for the country as a whole (Figure 21.4). The Pew surveys found that 83 percent of the LDS said religion was "very important" to them. Nationally, only 56 percent said it was very important to them. Considering both frequency of attendance and identification with religion, religion in the United States appears to be declining. The LDS, on the other hand, appear to have slightly stronger religious attendance and identification over the past forty years. The trend for the LDS from the 1970s to the 1980s increased, then remained strong.

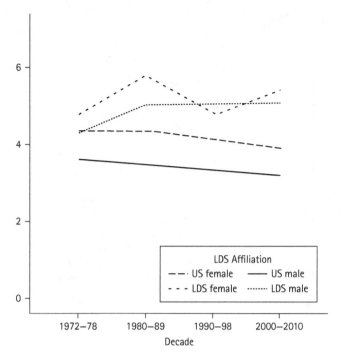

FIGURE 21.3 Frequency of attendance at religious services (scale is from 0 for never to 8 for more than once a week)

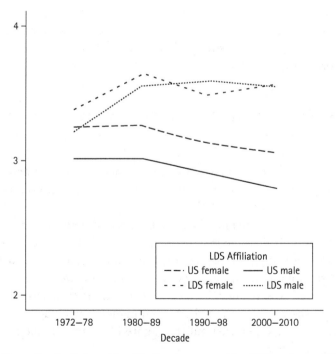

FIGURE 21.4 Strength of religious identifcation by sex and by LDS and non-LDS affiliation

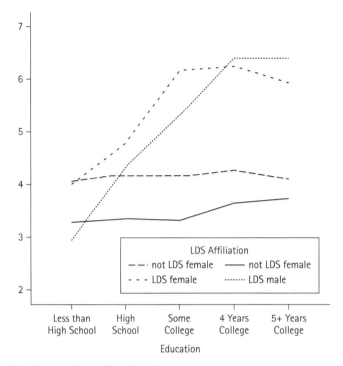

FIGURE 21.5 Church attendance by education

Whereas church attendance is essentially unrelated to education for the United States as a whole, education is strongly and positivey related to church attendance for Mormons (Figure 21.5). This is a strong relationship for Mormons and this relationship plays an important role.

4 MARRIAGE, FAMILY, AND GENDER

LDS doctrine and culture emphasize the importance of marriage and the marriage practices of the LDS reflect these beliefs and values. Figure 21.6 shows the proportion of adults currently married. Although marriage is declining in the United States and for LDS as well, men are more likely to be married than women, and Mormons are 1.77 times more likely to be married than other Americans. These comparisons occur even after adjusting for age, region, and time period. The Pew study shows similar results; it found that 71 percent of the LDS sample were married; only 9 percent were divorced or separated. Twelve percent had never married and 5 percent were widowed. The 71 percent was the second highest percentage of all the groups. Hindus were higher (78 percent) but that figure likely reflects the immigration of Hindu families together.

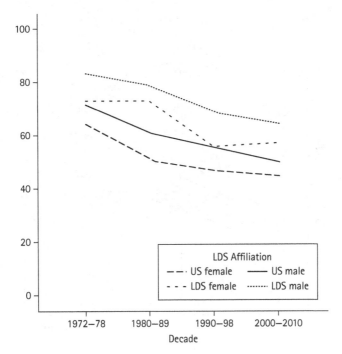

FIGURE 21.6 Percentage of LDS and Americans married by decade

The Pew study also shows that LDS members are highly likely to be married to some-one of the same faith (83 percent). The next highest endogamy rates are for Catholics (78 percent), Jews (69 percent), and Historically Black Churches (69 percent). The endogamy rates for other groups such as most Protestant groups are much lower. Members of those faiths are likely to be married to other Protestants, however. Marriage is particularly salient among more educated Mormons: the relationship between educa-tion and being married is positive in the United States, and even more positive among Mormons.

The proportions of the ever married population currently divorced, separated, or ever divorced are increasing (Figure 21.7). The proportions of both the nation and the LDS who have been divorced have increased quite dramatically over the four decades cov-ered by the GSS. The proportion of the LDS who have ever been married and divorced has remained lower than the national average, particularly for LDS males. If there is good news here, it is that the rate of divorce appears to have leveled off for the LDS in the last decade. Divorce is less likely among the more educated and among frequent church attenders, and these two patterns are accentuated among Mormons. This figure does not distinguish between "active" LDS and those who do not attend. Other studies have shown large differences in divorce between active and inactive LDS.

The LDS cultural and religious emphasis on marriage and families is also reflected in reported ideal family size (Figure 21.8). Mormons report having a larger ideal family size (the number of children they would like to have) than the US average. The average

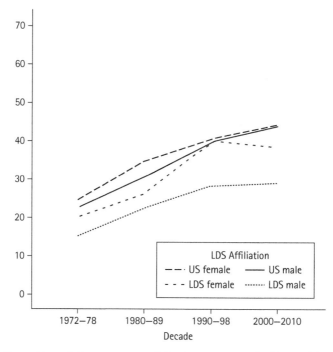

FIGURE 21.7 Proportion of those ever married who are currently divorced by decade

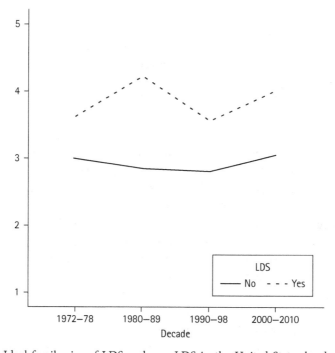

FIGURE 21.8 Ideal family size of LDS and non-LDS in the United States by decade

difference is one child more for Mormons. The trend line is not statistically different for Mormons than for the national population, but the positive relationship between church attendance and ideal family size is larger for Mormons than for the national population. The general tendency in the United States is for more educated people to report having a somewhat smaller ideal family size. The reverse is the case for Mormons, however (Figure 21.9). For the LDS, the ideal family size increases with education. The Pew study also found that the LDS tend to have more children than the national sample. Twenty percent of the LDS families reported having three or more children compared to only 9 percent of the national sample, and 9 percent report having four or more children. These percentages of the LDS subsample are the highest of any of the groups examined in the Pew data.

The family characteristics of the LDS in the four other countries are reported in Table 21.6. Members of the LDS faith are slightly more likely to have never married compared to national averages in these other countries. They are also less likely to be in consensual unions; the LDS Church emphasizes the importance of marriage and discourages living together. Lower rates of widowhood among the LDS are likely due to the smaller size of the elderly population among the LDS. LDS members are less likely than others to report having only a religious marriage (in Mexico and Brazil). Rates of separation and divorce are higher among LDS members in each country except the Philippines. It is not clear whether this is because the divorced and separated are

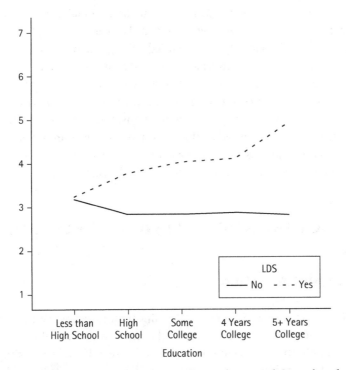

FIGURE 21.9 Ideal family size of LDS and non-LDS in the United States by education

Table 21.6 Family characteristics of LDS members (aged 18 and over)

	Mexico		Brazil		Chile		Philippines	
	LDS	Country	LDS	Country	LDS	Country	LDS	Country
Marital status (percent)								
Never married	25.1	22.6	32.7	27.7	31.6	30.0	27.7	27.1
Civil marriage	25.0	14.9	15.7	11.6	49.0	49.5	61.3	60.7
Religious marriage	.7	3.6	.4	3.0				
Civil and religious marriage	33.0	36.6	36.4	32.7				
Consensual union	5.6	12.7	5.6	15.0	8.2	9.4	4.4	5.3
Separated	4.0	3.0	2.2	2.3	6.1	5.1	1.4	1.4
Divorced	2.2	1.0	2.8	2.0	.7	.5		
Widowed	4.4	5.7	4.2	5.6	4.5	5.6	5.2	5.5
Average number of children ever born (females)								
	2.39	2.78	2.17	2.75	2.43	2.38	–	–

more inclined to join or because conversion to the LDS faith may be disruptive in some households. The LDS women in these countries have noticeably fewer children (15 to 20 percent) in Mexico and Brazil. Their family sizes are comparable to the national average in Chile. The apparent low fertility of Mormons in Mexico, Brazil, and Chile occurs because these Mormons are more educated that the national averages and are more likely to be in mixed-faith marriages where fertility is lower.

In sum, the emphasis on family life is marked among Mormons in the United States, as evidenced by higher rates of marriage, lower rates of divorce, and larger ideal family sizes. These family characteristics are particularly salient for the most educated Mormons and those who attend church regularly. Emphasis on marriage is also seen in some other countries with large LDS populations, but it is less clear in the cases of divorce and family size. When education and marriage type are taken into account, Mormons have larger families, and the association between education and family size is less negative for Mormons than for the national populations.

5 SOCIAL AND POLITICAL ATTITUDES

Attitudes about Abortion

In this section we examine the social and political attitudes of the LDS samples. We begin with attitudes about abortion, one of the most controversial topics both in the United States and in the LDS community. The Pew research study asks simply whether abortion should be legal in all cases, most cases, illegal in most cases, and illegal in all cases. Only 8 percent of the LDS in the Pew Survey say that abortion should be legal in all cases (compared to 18 percent of the national sample). Conversely, 70 percent of the LDS in the Pew survey say that abortion should be illegal in most or all cases (compared to 43 percent of the national sample and 61 percent of the Evangelicals).

The GSS also asks more specific questions about when abortion should be available. LDS attitudes toward abortion depend on motivations for the abortion, as is the case nationally. In the case of the mother's health being seriously endangered there is wide acceptance of abortion, and Mormons are similar to the national population (Figure 21.10). In cases of serious health defects for the baby or rape, somewhat fewer people think abortion is acceptable and Mormons have lower approval than the national population. In cases of unwanted pregnancies, poverty, or single motherhood, there is even less acceptance of abortion, and Mormons are even less accepting than the nation at large. The trend has been a gradual decline in the acceptance of abortion and this can be observed among the LDS population as well, but the test for the difference in trends between Mormons and the nation is not statistically significant. Moreover, church attendance is negatively associated with acceptance of abortion, and this association is similar for Mormons and the national population. However, the relationship between education and acceptability of abortion is positive in the nation, but negative for Mormons and the difference is statistically significant.

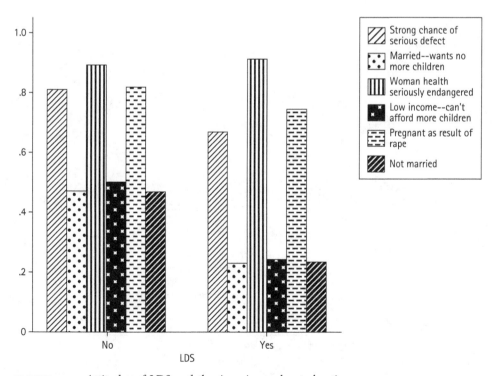

FIGURE 21.10 Attitudes of LDS and the Americans about abortion

Attitudes about Family Roles

Mormon men, compared to other men in the United States, express stronger preferences for mothers to be in the home with children. GSS respondents were asked three questions on this issue: whether children suffer if the mother works, whether preschoolers suffer if the mother works, and whether it's better for the man to work and the wife to take care of the home. Responses were combined and coded on a scale from 1 (strongly disagree) with these statements to 4 (strongly agreed). The results are shown in Figure 21.11. Men are higher on this scale than women and Mormons are higher than the nation as a whole. Statistical analysis suggests that the trend is downward (less traditional) for all groups and that people who attend church more frequently are more likely to say mother's roles should be at home. Tests for interactions between religion and gender and religion and trend, are not statistically significant, however. In other words, Mormon men and women tend to favor more traditional familial roles for women, but they follow the national trend over time and their religious participation has a similar influence to that observed among other Americans. On the other hand, the relationship between education and favoring familial roles for women is negative in the national population, but nearly flat for Mormons.

Mormons also tend to be more conservative on other family-related issues. Specifically they are less likely to favor sex education in public schools, relaxing divorce

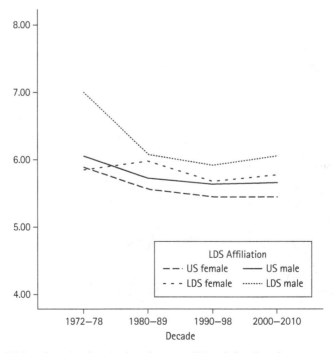

FIGURE 21.11 LDS and national attitudes about traditional family roles

laws, sex before marriage, extramarital sex, or homosexual relations (Figure 21.12). If these items are combined into a scale, there is an indication that the national trend is to become more favorable toward these issues, but the LDS trend is to become less favorable. This is an area where the gap between LDS and national attitudes is increasing. Not surprisingly, people who attend church more frequently are more conservative on family values, and Mormons are no different in this regard. However, higher educational attainment is associated with more liberal family values in the nation, but the reverse is the case among Mormons.

Analysis not reported here indicates that Mormons are not very different from the national population with regard to attitudes regarding race. The GSS also includes a few measures of wellbeing and Mormons have somewhat higher averages on these measures, but the differences are not great.

Political Identification

Mormons tend to be Republican and conservative. On a seven-point scale ranging from 0 for strong Democrat to 6 for strong Republican, with independents scoring in the middle Mormons are 4.5 above the national average of about 4 (Figure 21.13). The results from the Pew study are somewhat stronger; 65 percent of Mormons say they are

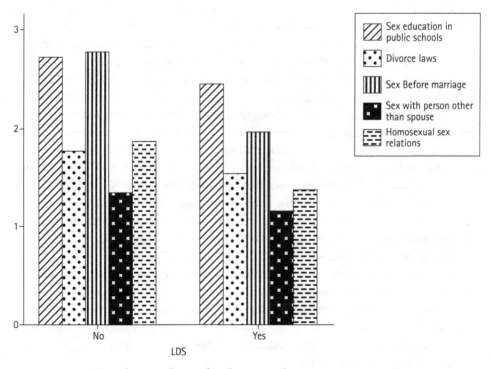

FIGURE 21.12 LDS and national attitudes about sexual issues

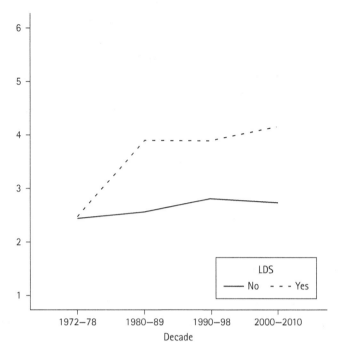

FIGURE 21.13 Political party identification (higher is Republican on scale 0–6)

Republicans. Only 22 percent identified themselves as Democrats. The LDS in the ARIS data also show a strong identification with the Republican Party. Only 14 percent say they are Democrats, 59 percent say they are Republicans, and 27 percent are independents. In Utah two-thirds (66 percent) of the LDS identify with the Republican Party, whereas 56 percent of those outside the state of Utah identify as Republicans. The differences are not as great when considering political orientation. When the LDS respondents in the GSS were asked to rate themselves on a scale ranging from 1 for extremely liberal to 7 for extremely conservative, Mormons are above 4 compared to a national average below 3. There was also a noticeable shift to the right among Mormons in the 1980s (Figure 21.14). This was the decade in which the LDS Church took a strong stance against the Equal Rights Amendment for women. Since that time the LDS Church has also been active on conservative issues such as the Defense of Marriage Act and Proposition 8 in California, which overturned the California Supreme Court's ruling on same-sex marriage. The church has justified its positions on these issues saying that they are theological or moral issues.

In general, those who attend church tend more often to be more Republican and conservative, and this tendency is even greater for Mormons. Sixty percent of the LDS in the Pew survey identified themselves as conservative; only 10 percent said they were liberal.

Nationally, education tends to be associated with slightly more liberal political views. With the exception of postgraduate education, however, Mormons with higher education tend to be more conservative.

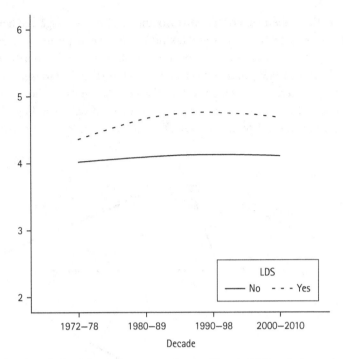

FIGURE 21.14 Political identification conservative vs. liberal, LDS and the nation

The Pew surveys show that the LDS members generally have strong views about a variety of political issues. They are more likely than the population to say the government should do more to protect morality in society (54 percent compared to 40 percent), but less likely to say that "the government should do more to help needy Americans, even if it means going deeper into debt" (49 percent compared to 62 percent). The LDS also opt for smaller government with fewer services (56 percent compared to 43 percent for the national sample).

Mormons are somewhat more likely than the national population to support the military. When asked, "What is the best way to ensure peace?," the LDS are more likely than the national sample to say through military strength (37 percent compared to 28 percent). Conversely the national sample is more likely to say good diplomacy is the best way to ensure peace (59 percent compared to 49 percent). At the same time, the LDS are more likely to want the country to be "active in world affairs" (51 percent compared to 36 percent).

CONCLUSION

We present Figure 21.15 as a way to summarize the key results of numerous comparisons. It shows the factors that best distinguish Mormons from the national GSS samples. The important factors include educational attainment, frequency of church attendance, political orientation (liberal or conservative), being in a first marriage and having an ideal family size of three or more children, and taking a conservative position on family-related issues, including the role of mothers, opposition to abortion, and opposition to sex education, liberal divorce laws, and sex outside of heterosexual marriage. Mormons are higher on each of these characteristics than the population as a whole. In some areas the gaps between Mormons and the nation are increasing, (including church attendance and attitudes toward sexual behavior); none of the differences between the LDS

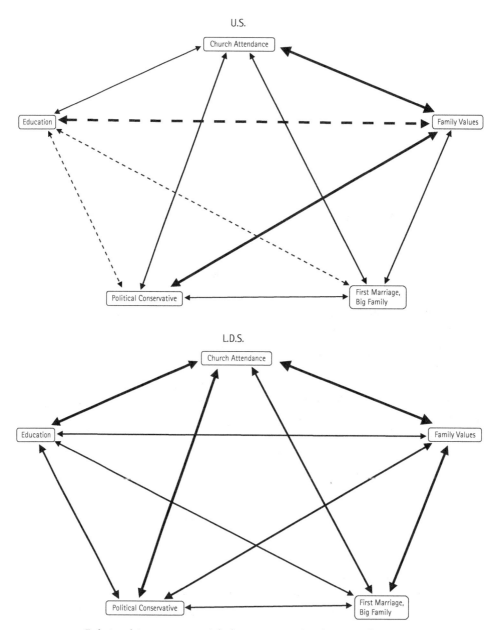

FIGURE 21.15 Relationships among social characteristics for the United States and Mormons

and the nation appear to be converging. Arrows in the graph show the strength of the relationships—thicker lines show stronger relationships. Solid lines show positive relationships and dashed lines show negative relationships. Not surprisingly, the correlations among church attendance, family values, political conservatism, and being in a first marriage with a large ideal family size are positive for Mormons and the nation as a whole. The connection between church attendance and these other characteristics is somewhat more pronounced in the LDS population. The most striking difference in the two graphs is the role of education. In the nation, education has a negative or weak relationship with each of the other factors, and the negative relationship between education and conservative family values is particularly strong. By contrast, for Mormons, education has a positive relationship with each other factor, and the relationship between education and church attendance is quite strong. So the national pattern is for the more educated and the most religious (as measured by attendance) to tend to disagree on family and political issues. Among Mormons, education and church attendance reinforce each other and promote political and familial conservatism. Education and regular religious participation increase a person's potential influence in the LDS Church. The LDS Church has a religiously active, educated core that tends to be conservative in both the political and family spheres.

The two other recent national surveys (ARIS and PEW) generally confirm the tendencies in the LDS membership to be religiously involved and to take a more conservative position on political and social issues. Once these data become available to researchers in analyzable form, we expect to see the correlations with education and church attendance replicated.

Data from four other countries show the LDS to have some socioeconomic advantage that is associated with urban residence and a greater tendency to be married. Unfortunately, these data do not include any information on other social and political attitudes. They do show surprisingly small family sizes, given the LDS emphasis on marriage and family. This may be a function of higher socioeconomic status, urban residence, and a high portion of mixed-faith marriages.

In 2012 the Republican candidate for the presidency of the United States was a devout Mormon with substantial education, who espouses conservative political and family values. In many ways, Mitt Romney is the prototypical Mormon according to our analysis. We end with the caveat that overgeneralization from average tendencies can be misleading, however. The majority leader of the Senate also happens to be a Mormon Democrat. In statistical terms, our standard deviations are large and correlations are closer to zero than to one. This means that despite the correlations we report, there is substantial diversity within the LDS samples; not all are prototypical LDS members.

NOTES

1. Cornwall, Heaton, and Young, *Contemporary Mormonism*. Heaton, Bahr, and Jacobson, *Statistical Profile of Mormons*.
2. Smith et al., *General Social Surveys*.
3. Phillips and Cragun. "Mormons in the United States, 1990–2008."

4. Pew Forum on Religion and Public Life, "Mormons in America"; Pew Forum, "US Religious Landscape Survey."
5. IPUMS International.
6. *Church Almanac* 2009 and 2010. Salt Lake City, UT: Deseret News.
7. US Census "2012 Statistical Abstract, Table 229."

BIBLIOGRAPHY

The 2012 Statistical Abstract, Table 229, titled "Educational Attainment by Race and Hispanic Origin: 1970 to 2010" has the URL http://www.census.gov/compendia/statab/2012/tables/12s0229.pdf.

Bahr, Stephen J. "Social Characteristics." *The Encyclopedia of Mormonism*, ed. Daniel H. Ludlow. New York: Macmillan, 1992.

Cornwall, Marie, Tim B. Heaton, and Lawrence A. Young, eds. *Contemporary Mormonism: Social Science Perspectives.* Urbana: University of Illinois Press, 2001.

Duke, James T., ed. *Latter-day Saint Social Life.* Provo, UT: Religious Studies Center, Brigham Young University, 1998.

Heaton, Tim B. "Demographics of the Contemporary Mormon Family." *Dialogue: A Journal of Mormon Thought* 25, no. 3 (Fall 1992): 19–34.

Heaton, Tim B. "Four Characteristics of the Mormon Family: Contemporary Research on Chastity, Conjugality, Children, and Chauvinism." *Dialogue: A Journal of Mormon Thought* 20, no. 2 (Summer 1987): 101–14.

Heaton, Tim B. "How Does Religion Influence Fertility?: The Case of Mormons." *Journal for the Scientific Study of Religion* 25, no. 2 (1986): 248–58.

Heaton, Tim B. "Vital Statistics." *The Encyclopedia of Mormonism*, ed. Daniel H. Ludlow. New York: Macmillan 1992.

Heaton, Tim B., Stephen J. Bahr, and Cardell K. Jacobson. *A Statistical Profile of Mormons: Health, Wealth, and Social Life.* New York: Edward Mellen, 2004.

Heaton, Tim B., and Sandra Calkins. "Contraceptive Use among Mormons, 1965–75." *Dialogue: A Journal of Mormon Thought* 16, no. 3 (Autumn 1983): 106–09.

Heaton, Tim B., and Kristen Goodman. "Religion and Family Formation." *Review of Religious Research* 26, no. 4 (1985): 343–59.

IPUMS International. http://international.ipums.org/international/. Accessed February 26, 2015.

Jacobson, Cardell K, John P. Hoffmann, and Tim B. Heaton, eds. *Revisiting Thomas F. O'Dea's "The Mormons": Contemporary Perspectives.* Salt Lake City: University of Utah Press, 2008.

Pew Forum on Religion and Public Life. "Mormons in America: Certain in Their Beliefs, Uncertain of their Place in Society." January 12, 2012. Washington, DC: PEW Research Center. http://www.pewforum.org/2012/01/12/mormons-in-america-executive-summary/.

Pew Forum on Religion and Public Life. "US Religious Landscape Survey: Religious Affiliation: Diverse and Dynamic." February 2008. Washington, DC: PEW Research Center. http://religions.pewforum.org/pdf/report-religious-landscape-study-full.pdf.

Phillips, Rick, and Ryan T. Cragun. "Mormons in the United States 1990–2008: Socio-demographic Trends and Regional Differences." Program on Public Values, Trinity

College, Hartford, CT. August 12, 2012. http://commons.trincoll.edu/aris/files/2011/12/Mormons2008.pdf.

Smith, Tom W, Peter Marsden, Michael Hout, and Jibum Kim. *General Social Surveys, 1972–2010*. Chicago: National Opinion Research Center; Storrs: Roper Center for Public Opinion Research, University of Connecticut, 2011. http://www.sagepub.com/wagner4e/study/materials/GSS_Codebook.pdf.

CHAPTER 22

....

CELESTIAL MARRIAGE
(ETERNAL AND PLURAL)

....

KATHRYN M. DAYNES

CONCEPTIONS of heaven have been many and varied over the centuries. For Mormons, heaven comprises three degrees of glory; the highest of these, the celestial kingdom, encompasses three heavens, the highest of which is exaltation. While all others will be single, those who are exalted will live with their families, while husbands and wives continue to increase their posterity. The reward of living in an eternal family is not simply a hope but rather is embedded in Mormon theology and temple ordinances Mormons believe are essential for exaltation. But only those who live worthily and whose marriages are sealed for eternity by the proper priesthood authority will enjoy celestial marriages. Nineteenth-century members of the Church of Jesus Christ of Latter-day Saints believed that plural marriages were the highest form of marriage, meriting the greatest glory among those exalted. Plural marriage was so honored that ending it took time and two manifestos (1890 and 1904), but the sealing of all eternal marriages, not only plural ones, and the prevalence of monogamous marriages paved the transition to a strictly monogamous system in the early twentieth century.

Initial development of this family-centered theology is shrouded by the lack of historical documents, the shaded testimony of those recalling events long after their occurrence, and the distortions of opponents. An early intimation that Mormons believed marriages transcended earthly life is found in the marriage ceremony adopted in 1835. The presiding official was to ask God's blessing to help the couple fulfill their covenants "from henceforth and *forever*" (Doctrine and Covenants [D&C], 1835 ed., 101:2; emphasis added). Four years later, prophet and founder of the church, Joseph Smith, was more explicit in teaching the doctrine of eternal family organization to Parley P. Pratt. "I learned that the wife of my bosom might be secured to me for time and all eternity; and that the refined sympathies and affections which endeared us to each other emanated from the fountain of divine eternal love." Pratt rhapsodized, "Now I loved—with a pureness—an intensity of elevated, exalted feeling."[1] Taught this way, Saints accepted marriage for eternity with unalloyed joy.

Such was not the case with plural marriage, a doctrine intertwined with eternal family relationships but whose early development is, if anything, more obscure. The beginnings of this doctrine probably were prompted by questions about the multiple wives of Abraham, Jacob, David, and others when Joseph Smith was engaged in a translation of the Old Testament in 1831. Sealing, a concept that later became an integral part of plural marriage, also had its origins in 1831. Ordinances were sealed so that their validity was eternal. This practice was rooted in the power given to Jesus's disciples: "Whatsoever thou shalt bind on earth shall be bound in heaven: and whatsoever thou shalt loose on earth shall be loosed in heaven" (Matthew 16:19). The sealing of ordinances was then applied to marriage, creating a relationship extending beyond death.

The authority to seal marriage ordinances was restricted to one person at a time, initially Joseph Smith, in the only revelation canonized about the eternal nature of marriages. Although internal evidence indicates part of this revelation dated from 1831, it was not committed to paper until summer of 1843. Its purpose was to persuade Emma Smith to accept her husband's other wives, although the practice was never publicly taught in Nauvoo. Church leader Joseph F. Smith stated in 1878 that the revelation as it stood "was not designed to go forth to the church or to the world. It is most probable that had it been then written with a view to its going out as a doctrine of the church, it would have been presented in a somewhat different form."[2]

The major part of the revelation briefly provides the theological foundations of celestial or eternal marriage. Earthly contracts and vows are not valid in heaven; thus, for a man and wife to be married for eternity they must be married on earth by one who has the authority to bind in heaven what is bound on earth. Those without such marriages will live "separately and singly, without exaltation, in their saved condition, to all eternity" (Doctrine and Covenants [D&C] 132:17). A man and his wife married for eternity by proper authority will be rewarded by receiving "their exaltation" (D&C 132:19), which is "a far more, and an exceeding, and an eternal weight of glory" (D&C 132:16) than received by others. This first section uses the singular construction "a man marry a wife" four times (verses 15, 18, 19, 26), clearly indicating that marriages sealed for eternity leading to exaltation include monogamous ones. The theological *raison d'être* for plural marriage, given in the latter part of the revelation, was rooted in the promise given to Abraham that "both in the world and out of the world should [his seed] continue as innumerable as the stars" (D&C 132:30), a promise encompassing Joseph Smith and others who were righteous. Despite the promise that more would be revealed and the revelation's relative brevity for so momentous a change in marital practice, Joseph Smith wrote nothing further on the topic in the subsequent eleven months before his death.

The outlines of the theological foundations of eternal marriages, both monogamous and polygamous, are clear in the revelation, but several points remained ambiguous. Among these is the verse "Prepare thy heart to receive and obey the instructions which I am about to give unto you; for all those who have this law revealed unto them must obey the same" (D&C 132:3). "This law" most plausibly refers to the section immediately following, which predicates exaltation upon obeying the commandment to enter into eternal marriage covenants, including monogamous marriages. Nevertheless, some have thought "this law" refers to plural marriage. Even if this were the case, those to whom "this law" was revealed were severely restricted. The revelation was committed to paper specifically for Emma Smith's eyes, certainly not for the church in general. But the revelation did not succeed in its original purpose. Although Emma Smith accepted her husband's plural wives and was sealed to him for eternity in May 1843, by July she had returned to her original opposition to plural marriage.

Others, however, did comply—reluctantly, to be sure—when Smith privately introduced this new theology to them and told them they must take additional wives. By June 1844, when Smith was killed, about thirty other men, including most of the twelve apostles, had married plural wives. Not all marriage sealings were plural ones, however. During Joseph Smith's lifetime, apostles Wilford Woodruff and George A. Smith were each sealed for time and eternity to his first and only wife, demonstrating that the blessings of eternal marriages extended to monogamous sealings. Moreover, Parley P. Pratt was sealed to his deceased spouse, as were a number of other Saints. In short, in theology and practice, marriage was transformed during Smith's lifetime from a relationship between a man and a woman until death parted them to an eternal relationship between a man and a woman, a man and several women, and/or a person to a deceased spouse.

Following Joseph Smith's death, which intensified many Saints' loyalty to their martyred prophet, the numbers in polygamous marriages expanded greatly, especially after the temple was dedicated in late 1845. Perhaps as many as 10 percent of those in Nauvoo lived in polygamous families as they began their trek west.

On the other hand, Nauvoo polygamous marriages did not bear all the elements associated with marriage: plural wives did not take their husbands' surnames, they did not openly cohabit, and plural marriages were not openly acknowledged beyond a small circle of people. The Nauvoo period is best understood as protopolygamy, since the secret nature of these marriages precluded developing practices and traditions for everyday living in plural families. Even after arrival in Utah, however, these developed slowly because polygamous families were left to work out living patterns that fit their own situations.

Leaving Nauvoo in 1846, LDS society was under stress because the entire core community was on the move. Unlike most other colonizing efforts, in which the metropole sends out settlers and remains a source of support for them, the twelve thousand Mormons left whatever they could not pack into covered wagons as they crossed the Mississippi River and headed to the frontier. This massive enterprise strained the Mormons' meager resources, especially because few Saints were wealthy and the poorest members, evicted from Nauvoo in September by surrounding settlers, required aid from the already struggling body of Saints. To be sure, crucial cash was provided by pay received for Mormon men enlisting to fight in the Mexican War, wages paid to men for labor in the Iowa villages through which they passed, small amounts of cash raised from "begging missions" to succor desperately poor Mormons, and later in Utah the trade generated by the forty-niners needing supplies on their way to California. But by and large the community was dependent on its own resources to transport thousands of people to Utah—not only those abandoning Nauvoo but thousands of converts who came later—as well as to transform the frontier into towns and farms.

While living in plural marriages was a trial for many—a refiner's fire—polygamy served social purposes that aided cohesion of the community. Plural marriages incorporated most single women and widows with their children into family units. It not only increased the number of a man's wives but also multiplied the kinship networks of everyone in that plural family. At the end of the nineteenth century, lineal families with ties between generations would become emphasized, but during the frontier period, when settlers were heavily dependent upon each other for economic survival and protection, horizontal familial relationships were extended by adding wives to the family. This overlapping web of familial relationships was further strengthened by adopting a person, male or female, to "parents," generally church leaders. Creating a sacerdotal family based on Joseph Smith's teachings, adoptions were initiated in the Nauvoo Temple, but since this rite could be performed only in temples, these were not resumed until the first temple in Utah was dedicated in 1877. The most morally binding obligations are to one's family, and religious rites created eternal horizontal relationships and generated large kinship groups on whom one could call for aid. To be sure, unrelated church members assisted each other, and kin were not all equally helpful, but people who personally rely on others often emphasize horizontal relationships or common descent from a recent ancestor. The Latter-day Saint community—moving, changing, expanding, and constantly incorporating new converts—was thus enabled to quickly form a cohesive society based not only on common church membership but also on familial relationships.

Incorporating new converts was a necessity, given the thousands who arrived after initial settlement in Utah. Many of these were foreign born and by 1870 accounted for 67.9 percent of Utah residents twenty-five years or older. Plural marriage helped to break down barriers quickly between the various nationalities. The example of Manti is illustrative. First settled in 1849 by former Nauvoo residents, Manti began receiving Scandinavian converts in 1853. Unlike most immigrant communities in nineteenth-century America, in which marital exogamy usually does not take place until the second or third generation, plural marriage permitted first-generation immigrants to intermarry with spouses of other nationalities. Sophia Klauen Petersen, a widow with five children who emigrated from Denmark in 1856, was destitute when she arrived in Utah. She and her family were asked to go to Manti, where they moved into cramped quarters in the fort with the American-born Smith family. Three months later she became Albert Smith's second wife.

The majority of polygamists married spouses born in the same country, but by 1880 in Manti, 45 percent of polygamous husbands and 22 percent of plural wives were married to a spouse whose country of birth differed from their own. The greater part of these spouses came from countries sharing the same or similar languages. Like Sophia Petersen and Albert Smith, however, 9 percent of plural wives and 19 percent of polygamous husbands married a spouse born in a country with a different language. Plural marriage was thus an important factor in building a common Mormon culture out of the disparate converts arriving in Utah before 1890.

Plural marriage was also a means for taking care of women without male breadwinners in an impoverished frontier society. Women's occupations—teaching, sewing, and domestic service—paid poorly, and few other options were open to women during early settlement, except becoming a plural wife. With opportunities so constrained, economically disadvantaged women were more likely to marry into plurality than other women. In Manti, about a third of plural wives had previously been widowed or divorced, and about another third had fathers who were dead or not in Utah, types of women solely or largely dependent on their own meager resources and underpaid skills. It is not astonishing that a church believing marriage was necessary for exaltation but with limited financial resources would foster the marriage of the fatherless and widows, nor is it surprising that economically disadvantaged women who shared those beliefs would choose the honored role of mother and wife, even plural wife, over impecunious spinsterhood.

Polygamous husbands needed both religious and economic attributes to attract wives. Most church leaders married plural wives, but so also did many other men considered worthy. Though few husbands were wealthy by the standard in the "States," polygamists were in general among the wealthiest in their own communities. By marrying additional wives, a polygamist not only gave those wives some right to his resources, but also distributing those resources among their large families mitigated the growing per capita economic inequality among the Saints. One goal of the early church was to eliminate large economic divisions among its members, and it instituted several programs to achieve that end. Plural marriage undoubtedly promoted economic equality at least as well as those other programs. Certainly it proved more long-lasting than any church economic program except tithing, and it was sufficiently widespread to have a significant impact.

Polygamy was also sufficiently widespread, especially in the early decades of settlement, to have a demographic impact. The revelation on plural marriage indicated that increasing one's posterity—"doing the works of Abraham"—was central to its practice. At first blush, it appears that polygamy suppressed the birth rate. While first wives had the highest number of births, subsequent wives had on average fewer children than monogamous women. The stated purpose of plural marriage, however, was not to increase the overall birth rate but rather to increase the number of children born to and raised in righteous homes. Because only men deemed worthy received approval of church leaders to enter plural marriage, the number of children for some worthy men was greater than had they remained monogamous.

Nevertheless, plural marriage affected the entire Mormon community, not simply those who practiced it. In the first decades of settlement, demand for wives impacted all women, increasing the proportion of women who ever married to almost 100 percent, suppressing the average marriage age for women when the percentage of new polygamous marriages was at its peak, and providing widows and divorced women of child-bearing age opportunities to soon remarry. Hence, more women were married for more of their fertile years, thus having more opportunities to conceive children than otherwise would have prevailed. Overall, Mormon pronatalist beliefs resulted in large families, especially for women who married before age twenty. First wives bore about ten children, subsequent plural wives bore about 8.5 children, and once-married wives had about 9.5 children. The high birth rate and continued convert immigration into Utah created a strong central core of Saints, either by descent or consent, in the Mormon culture region—Utah and portions of surrounding states—by the end of the nineteenth century.

Contributing to that strong central core was the deep-seated sense of identity most Latter-day Saints had with their church and Mormon culture. That sense of identity preceded settlement in Utah and widespread knowledge of polygamy, forged in the fires of persecution and a sense of themselves as the latter-day House of Israel. But plural marriage strengthened that Mormon identity in the face of pressure by Protestants and the federal government to stamp out the practice. While the majority of Mormons did not practice plural marriage, all could believe in it and in fact were enjoined to do so. As laws became more punitive toward polygamy and the church, members had to choose whether they stood with the church, reinforcing the sociological boundaries between Mormons and others.

In 1852, when Orson Pratt first publicly announced in a special conference that the Latter-day Saints were practicing plural marriage, he did not wish to build barriers but rather to demand that Mormons be enfolded in the rights the Constitution granted for the free exercise of religion. "If it can be proven to a demonstration," he claimed, "that the Latter-day Saints have actually embraced, as a part and portion of their religion, the doctrine of a plurality of wives, it is constitutional." Pratt thus sought to prove that plural marriage was integral to Mormon theology. He told the assembled congregation that they must receive the law and not reject it, implying that the revelation of 1843 was now the law of the church. While accepting plural marriage—believing in it—would lead to members' marrying additional wives, the necessity of actually doing so to be exalted remained ambiguous. Pratt discussed having one's marriage sealed as crucial, and sealings were performed for monogamous as well as polygamous marriages.[3] No vote was taken to accept the revelation, although such votes were not general practice at the time. It was not included in the Doctrine and Covenants until a new edition was published in 1876, approved by a church vote in 1880.

The number of plural marriages increased in 1852 but hardly as much as one would expect had Saints believed their exaltation depended on it. The Mormon Reformation of 1856–57 had a much greater impact on the practice of polygamy than did Pratt's public announcement. In 1855, Brigham Young acknowledged, "Some say, 'I would do so [enter plural marriage], but brother Joseph and brother Brigham have never told me to do it.'" The perception remained that plural marriage was a commandment to certain individuals, not to every Mormon. Apparently most did not believe taking additional wives was essential for exaltation, although Young in a private discussion in 1856 opined that it was. Answering the question whether to avoid damnation one needed to take more wives than one, he answered, "I think it includes the whole law with its covenants."[4] The "whole law" meant marrying multiple wives, but the qualifier "I think" indicates he referred to his own views and was not making a doctrinal pronouncement.

Utah was then experiencing a severe economic crisis. Grasshoppers had eaten much of the crop in 1855, and the following hard winter killed a high proportion of their livestock. Many resorted to gathering weeds to survive. The famine was exacerbated by a record number of immigrants arriving in the Valley. In these desperate circumstances church leaders initiated a Reformation to eliminate sin. Among these was the sin of omission—not obeying the command to enter plural marriage. Bishops and home missionaries visited families with the message that the command to live plural marriage must be obeyed.

Infused with millennial fervor, Latter-day Saints responded overwhelmingly. "Nearly all are trying to get wives," wrote Wilford Woodruff on April 1, 1857, "until there is hardly a girl fourteen years old in Utah, but what is married, or just going to be." Some believed exaltation was restricted to those who entered plural marriage, as shown by these lines from the "Reformation Song": "Now, this advice I freely give, / If exalted you would be, / Remember that your husband must / Be blessed with more than thee."[5] According to Stanley Ivins's figures, 65 percent more plural marriages occurred in 1856 and 1857 than any other two years of Mormon polygamy. Similarly, a study of Manti polygamists shows that new plural marriages spiked in 1857, with almost twice as many marriages as the two next highest years, 1846 in Nauvoo and 1869, when the railroad arrived in Utah. Moreover, the 1860 Manti census shows that only two women over sixteen years old had never been to the marriage altar; they were both eighteen. Demographically, the Mormon population had reached what Davis Bitton and Val Lambson call "unsustainably high polygyny prevalence"—the saturation point.

Soon, however, some newlyweds found that it was easier to get married than to remain married. The spike in plural marriages in 1856 and 1857 was followed by a peak in the next two years in the number of cancellations of sealings. Studies of Manti and Payson show that the percentage of plural marriages ending in divorce during the nineteenth century was around one in six, about one-third of the divorce rate in the United States today.

After the Reformation church leaders never made such an effort to adjure the general membership to enter plural marriage. While the revelation's ambiguity remained about whom the law of plurality applied to, the church made no statements over the signature of the First Presidency, an important means of clarifying church doctrine and policy. Although sermons by leaders were not in complete concurrence, most agreed on two issues: that members' belief in plural marriage was essential and that its practice was rewarded in the hereafter with a greater degree of glory among those exalted than would result from a monogamous sealing.

Reluctance of many members to enter plural marriage is evident in the warnings from the pulpit not to reject or deny the principle. Orson Pratt cautioned in 1874, "Those who *reject* this principle reject their salvation, they shall be damned, saith the Lord." The sin is finding fault with plural marriage or a determination not to enter into it. In this context of warning members about not "obeying or *submitting to it in our faith or believing this order*," Brigham Young declared, "The only men who become Gods, even the Sons of God, are those who enter into polygamy. Others . . . may even be permitted to come into the presence of the Father and the Son; but they cannot reign as kings in glory, because they had blessings offered unto them, and they *refused* to accept them." Tellingly, in the same passage, he stated, "If you desire with all your hearts to obtain the blessings which Abraham obtained [exaltation], you will be polygamists *at least in your faith*." On another occasion, Young similarly stated, "A Man may Embrace the Law of Celestial Marriage in his heart & not take the Second Wife and be justified before the Lord."[6] The admonitions are not that every member must enter plural marriage but that every member should believe in it.

While a couple whose marriage was sealed merited exaltation on condition that they lived a righteous life, sermons emphasized that those in plural marriage would achieve an even greater eternal reward. Exaltation meant living in the presence of the Father and His Son, but among those earning such an eternal award, pluralists would merit "the *fullness* of the Lord's glory in the eternal world," "attain to the *fullness* of exaltation in the celestial glory," or be "more advanced." Joseph F. Smith made this point explicit: "Man may receive great reward, exaltation and glory by entering into the bond of the new and everlasting covenant [eternal marriage], if he continue faithful according to his knowledge, but he cannot receive the *fullness of the blessings* unless he fulfills the law." Nevertheless, he stressed, "This law [of plurality] is in force upon the inhabitants of Zion," which he said meant that every man who had the ability to practice plural marriage "in righteousness" should do so.[7] Among members, however, views differed. Annie Clark Tanner thought that "if one wanted to attain the very pinnacle of glory in the next world there must be, at least, three wives." Others accepted the principle, but only for women who would not otherwise have married. When Martha Cragun Cox became a plural wife, a friend told her: "It is all very well for those girls who cannot very well get good young men for husbands to take married men, but she [Martha] had no need to lower herself, for there were young men she could have gotten." A Manti maiden, unsure what to believe, wrote Brigham Young asking whether she should accept her polygamous or her bachelor suitor. When Young recommended she marry the bachelor if he "reciprocate[d] your feelings and wishes in this matter," she did so and never entered polygamy.[8]

Despite the greater eternal reward merited by plural marriage, not all could become pluralists, as George Q. Cannon acknowledged: "Take our own Territory: the males outnumber the females; it cannot therefore be a practice without limit among us." Disabilities and poverty were additional constraints. In general, Latter-day Saints tried to be faithful in living plural marriage, but most were monogamous. The proportion living in plural families reached its height in the late 1850s, declining thereafter, although the absolute numbers had grown by 1880. In Manti, for example, the population living in plural families was 43 percent in 1860 and declined to 36 percent and 25 percent in 1870 and 1880, respectively. But the number in plural families increased from 1860 to 1870 and then remained fairly stable over the next decade. The prevalence of polygamy varied considerably over time and among communities, and the relatively large percentages identified as living in polygamous homes exclude monogamous parents, siblings, and children of pluralists living in households separate from their polygamous relatives. A remarkable number of Mormons lived some years of their lives in plural households.

Characterizing the nature of plural marriages is difficult because every polygamous marriage, like every monogamous one, is unique. Generalizing about plural marriages is even more problematic because there are not just two personalities interacting in the relationship, but three or more. Beyond the personalities of the individuals within a marriage, however, are other, more general factors influencing the nature of these plural marriages. Some of these factors are the ages at which husbands and wives married, the family's wealth in relation to its size, the number of wives a husband had at one time, the number of children and their distribution among the wives, the living arrangements of the wives, and the area where the family lived, whether long settled or just being colonized. Another crucial factor that affected every plural family was the time in which they lived. Men and women in Nauvoo and early Utah had to overcome their strong prejudices against nonmonogamous marriages and pioneer methods of living in plural families; those marrying from about 1860 to 1880 had become accustomed to polygamy but often lived long enough to experience hiding from federal deputies and endure prison sentences; those marrying in the 1880s began their relationships under the cloud of possible prosecution; and some marrying after 1890 found even fellow Mormons treated them as embarrassing remnants of the past.

Religious conviction was the foundation of plural marriage, the more necessary because living it could be difficult for both men and women. Besides increased financial responsibilities, men needed to meet the emotional needs of multiple wives, not always successfully. Returning from a mission, Franklin D. Richards brought shawls and other presents for his wives and told them to choose. His tearful first wife had to inform her hapless husband that each wife would rather have a gift chosen especially for her. Though many wives expressed love and respect for their husbands, those who developed strong relationships with the other wives or with their own children often coped better than those who desired close emotional ties with husbands. Lamenting in her journals her loneliness even when her husband traveled, John Hindley's second wife, Jane, became distraught when he married another wife: "I have suffered in my feelings More than I can tell." The birth of that wife's first child brought more grief: "What I have just passed through God only knows my feelings cannot be expressed." Through it all, however, her love for her husband never wavered and it even grew for the first wife. Plural marriage had been a trial for her but also a blessing, she wrote.

Other polygamous wives agreed. In her autobiography, Elizabeth Macdonald also called it a trial but added that "the self control I have attained is of more value to me than all I could possibly have obtained by avoiding it." Martha Cragun Cox in her reminiscences was positive about her relationship with the other wives: "To me it is a joy to know that we laid the foundation of a life to come while we lived in that plural marriage, that we three who loved each other more than sisters . . . will go hand in hand together down all eternity. That knowledge is worth more to me than gold and more than compensates for the sorrow I have ever known." Finding plural marriage a trial at times, Martha Hughes Cannon, the first female state senator in the United States, nevertheless quipped to a reporter of the *San Francisco Examiner*: "If her husband has four wives, she has three weeks of freedom every month." Polygamous wives generally found positive aspects of plural marriage more than compensated for its difficulties; truly unhappy wives received divorces.

Most church leaders, including local leaders, entered plural marriage soon after their calling, if they were not already pluralists. Admonitions to church leaders increased in the 1880s. Seymour B. Young was commanded to take a plural wife when he was called to the Council of Seventy in 1882, and two years later George Q. Cannon averred, "He did not feel like holding up his hand to sustain anyone as a presiding officer over any portion of the people who had not entered into the Patriarchial [*sic*] order of Marriage."[9]

Such admonitions were given in the face of federal authorities beginning to arrest and imprison increasing numbers of polygamists. The Edmunds Act, passed in 1882, made unlawful cohabitation a crime and opened the way for successful prosecutions. In Utah alone, over two hundred men had been indicted by the end of 1886. While some polygamists agreed to obey the law in the future, most who pled guilty or were found to be so by juries, served prison sentences, and were released to praise as martyrs by the Mormon community. In 1887, Congress augmented its strategy of punishing individuals in order to abolish polygamy and passed the Edmunds-Tucker Act, striking at the church itself by making provision for the escheat of its property.

The number of men going to prison reached its peak in 1888 but escheating of church property relentlessly continued. As the pressure on the church mounted, leaders were cautioned against saying anything about plural marriage from the pulpit, couples wanting to enter plural marriages were advised to go to Mexico, the 1887 constitutional convention in Utah included a provision making bigamy and polygamy a misdemeanor, and in 1888 the church's attorney argued on the basis of the 1843 revelation that "plural marriages were permissive."[10] Despite these attempts at conciliation, the escheatment of church property continued, and in May 1890 the US Supreme Court upheld the disincorporation of the church and forfeiture of its assets. But only when federal officials began proceedings to confiscate the temples—crucial for the performance of saving ordinances for both the living and the dead—did the church act definitively.

On September 25, 1890, Wilford Woodruff, president of the church, published an Official Declaration, commonly called the Manifesto. Denying that the church had been encouraging polygamy or permitting new plural marriages in the past year, Woodruff declared "my intention to submit to those laws [forbidding plural marriages], and to use my influence with the members of the Church over which I preside to have them do likewise. . . . I now publicly declare that my *advice* to the Latter-day Saints is to refrain from contracting any marriage forbidden by the law of the land" [emphasis added] (D&C Official Declaration 1). Under inspiration, as he later explained, and to save temples from confiscation, Woodruff suspended the law of the church to practice plural marriage. Henceforth, the law regarding plural marriage referred to in the 1843 revelation would apply to no member of the church, a momentous change. On the other hand, the Manifesto avoided mentioning continuing cohabitation of those already living in plural marriages, who continued to be subject to the laws of the land. In short, the desired result was a return to ante-Edmunds-Tucker, when individuals were answerable for practicing plural marriage, but the church itself was not held responsible.

The Manifesto's meaning became clearer only through later decisions and adjudications. In 1891, when Woodruff testified before the Master in Chancery about the disposition of escheated church property, he indicated the Manifesto applied throughout the world and included continuing cohabitation. Those entering plural marriage after the Manifesto "would be liable to excommunication." In 1900, Lorenzo Snow, then president of the church, issued a statement that the church had "positively abandoned the practice of polygamy, or the solemnization of plural marriages, in this or any other State" (Mexico was not mentioned), and that the church did not "advise or encourage unlawful cohabitation." The distinction follows the Edmunds Act, which provided for different punishments for polygamy—entering plural marriage within the statute of limitations—and continuing cohabitation. The Snow statement declared any member disobeying the law "must bear his own burden" and be answerable to the laws of the land, articulating the church's policy that individuals, not the church, would be responsible for infringements of laws against plural marriage.[11]

Because plural marriage was so ingrained in Mormon beliefs, over two hundred plural marriages were contacted between the Manifesto of 1890 and 1904, most of which took place in Mexico. Far more prevalent were those polygamists who continued cohabiting with their wives. According to church statistics, the number of plural families in the United States was reduced from 2,451 in 1890, to 1,543 in 1899, and still further to 897 in 1902. Divorce accounted for only 4 percent of the decrease between 1890 and 1899, revealing dedication to their spouses, but 31 percent were broken by death, the advanced age of many polygamists inevitably reducing the number of cohabiting plural families. One polygamist continuing to cohabit with his wives was Joseph F. Smith, who became president of the church in 1901. To avoid what the US Supreme Court had called "flaunting in the face of the world the ostentation and opportunities of a bigamous household," he resided with his first wife, his other wives living a short distance away in houses they owned. Confessing his wives had borne eleven children since the Manifesto, he nevertheless averred that he was not "openly and obnoxiously practicing unlawful cohabitation."[12]

This confession was delivered before the Senate Committee on Privileges and Elections investigating whether Reed Smoot, senator from Utah and apostle in the church, should be allowed to hold his seat. Although Smith declared he was willing to answer to the law, Smoot claimed that Smith's admission shocked national leaders more than reports of new polygamous marriages. In the wake of his testimony, Smith presented a Second Manifesto to a church conference in April 1904. It ignored continuing cohabitation but was stringent about new marriages: "All such [plural] marriages are prohibited, and if any officer or member of the Church shall assume to solemnize or enter into such marriage he will be . . . liable to be . . . excommunicated therefrom." Although a few marriages were subsequently contracted without incurring church discipline, by 1910 two apostles had been dropped from the Quorum and a committee established to investigate new marriages and discipline those responsible. Francis

M. Lyman, president of the Twelve who headed the committee to enforce the Second Manifesto, was essentially correct about the relationship between the two manifestos: "When [the Woodruff Manifesto] was given it simply gave notice to the Saints that they need not enter plural marriage any longer, but [the Manifesto of 1904] made that manifesto prohibitory."[13]

These two manifestos revealed what was fundamental to the church. The 1890 Manifesto saved the temples from forfeiture, while the 1904 Manifesto paved the way for increased missionary work. In 1894, Woodruff announced that henceforth members would be sealed to their biological parents rather than church leaders, and that members' responsibility was to research their ancestry and seal the generations to each other. The emphasis was thus changed from the horizontal bonds of plural families to the lineal relationships to one's progenitors. Because the ordinance to seal parents and children could be performed only in temples, retaining the temples was even more essential in the late nineteenth century than it would have been before this change. Moreover, the Smoot hearings and the 1904 Manifesto helped over time to improve the church's image, and Smoot as a national leader negotiated the admittance of missionaries into some European countries.

Plural marriages performed secretly in the fourteen years after the 1890 Manifesto, however, inadvertently lent scope to those who refused to accept change after 1904. After their excommunications, they began to meet together, claiming a religious authority higher than that of the church they had left and developing a priesthood organization after the mainstream church's "Final Manifesto" in 1933 iterated that plural marriages could no longer be performed. While agreeing on the necessity of polygamy, the group later fractured, the Fundamentalist Church of Jesus Christ of Latter Day Saints (whose leader assigns spouses for its members) and the Apostolic United Brethren (which permits husbands to choose additional wives) being among the largest of the divisions. In addition, other groups arose with competing claims of authority to continue plural marriages, and some polygamists are "independents," or unaffiliated with any specific group. These groups collectively denominate themselves Fundamentalist Mormons. An estimated 38,000 people, primarily in the Rocky Mountain region, consider themselves Fundamentalists, although not all belong to families headed by practicing polygamists. Not surprisingly, the mainstream church is not only completely separate from these groups but also disputes the umbrella term of Fundamentalist Mormons because it disagrees about what beliefs and practices are fundamental to Mormon doctrine.

Polygamous societies differ from each other, just as polygamous marriages do. Polygamy is not a marriage system; it is a category encompassing many different marriage systems. Rules, traditions, and practices vary between groups and change over time. Living in plural marriage among the Apostolic United Brethren is a considerably different experience from living among the Fundamentalist Latter-day Saints, and both differ from the Mormon experience in the nineteenth century. Each is shaped not only by ideas and practices within the group but also by the groups' relationship to the surrounding society. Generalizations and assumptions of similarity between various groups practicing polygamy are thus often misleading. Moreover, mainstream

Mormons have retained the original revelation on celestial marriage but tied it to its strictly monogamous marriage system. Today, Mormons are still adjured to prepare to live as families in the hereafter, but they are also counseled to focus on the present by making their homes a little heaven on earth—celestial families in this terrestrial realm.

NOTES

1. Pratt, *Autobiography of Parley P. Pratt*, 297–98.
2. Smith, "Plural Marriage," 1878, 20: 29.
3. *Deseret News Extra*, Salt Lake City, September 14, 1852, 14–22.
4. Young, "Plurality of Wives," 1855, 3: 265; Woodruff, *Journal*, April 15, 1856, 4: 411.
5. Young, "Plurality of Wives," 1855, 3: 265; Woodruff, *Journal*, April 15, 1856, 4: 411; *Deseret News*, November 26, 1856, 302.
6. Pratt, "God's Ancient People," 1874, 17: 224 (emphasis added); Young, "Beneficial Effects," 1866, 11: 268–69 (emphasis added); Woodruff, *Journal*, October 24, 1871, 7:31.
7. Pratt, *Deseret News Extra*, Salt Lake City, September 14, 1852, 14–22; "William Clayton's Testimony" (emphasis added); Cannon, "Blessings Enjoyed by the Saints," 1883, 24: 146; Smith, "Plural Marriage," 1878, 20: 30–31 (emphasis added).
8. Tanner, *Mormon Mother*, 73; Cox, *Face Toward Zion*, 111; Arrington, *Brigham Young*, 315.
9. Cannon, "Hostile Feeling towards the Saints," 1882, 24: 47; Larson and Larson, *Diary of Charles Lowell Walker*, 2: 629.
10. "Utah's Cause," *Deseret News,* February 22, 1888.
11. "The Church Cases," *Deseret Weekly News*, October 24, 1891, 583; "Polygamy and Unlawful Cohabitation," *Deseret News*, January 8, 1900, 4.
12. *Cannon v. United States*, 116 U.S. 55 (1885); *Proceedings before the Committee*, 1:324.
13. "Official Statement by President Joseph F. Smith," *Deseret Evening News*, April 6, 1904, 1; "President Lyman Very Emphatic," *Deseret Evening News*, October 31, 1910, 1.

BIBLIOGRAPHY

Alexander, Thomas G. *Mormonism in Transition: A History of the Latter-day Saints, 1890–1930*. Urbana: University of Illinois Press, 1986.

Alexander, Thomas G. "The Odyssey of a Latter-day Prophet: Wilford Woodruff and the Manifesto of 1890." In *In the Whirlpool: The Pre-Manifesto Letters of President Wilford Woodruff to the William Atkin Family, 1885–1890*, ed. Reid L. Neilson, 57–96. Norman: Arthur H. Clark, 2011.

Arrington, Leonard J. *Brigham Young: American Moses*. New York: Alfred A. Knopf, 1985.

Bean, Lee L., Geraldine P. Mineau, and Douglas L. Anderton. *Fertility Change on the American Frontier: Adaptation and Innovation*. Berkeley: University of California Press, 1990.

Bennion, Lowell C. "Plural Marriage." In *Mapping Mormonism: An Atlas of Latter-day Saint History*, ed. Brandon S. Plewe, 122–25. Provo, UT: Brigham Young University Press, 2012.

Bennion, Lowell C. "Ben," Thomas Carter, and Alan L. Morrell. *Polygamy in Lorenzo's Snow's Brigham City: An Architectural Tour*. Salt Lake City: University of Utah, 2005.

Bitton, Davis, and Val Lambson. "Demographic Limits of Nineteenth-Century Mormon Polygyny." *BYU Studies* 51, no. 4 (2012): 7–26.

Brown, Samuel M. "Early Mormon Adoption Theology and the Mechanics of Salvation." *Journal of Mormon History* 37, no. 3 (Summer 2011): 3–52.

Cannon, George Q. "Hostile Feeling towards the Saints" [June 25, 1882]. *Journal of Discourses* 24: 38–50.

Cannon, George Q. "Blessings Enjoyed by the Saints" [May 6, 1883]. *Journal of Discourses* 24: 141–49.

Cannon v. United States, 116 US 55 (1885).

Cox, Martha Cragun. *Face Toward Zion: Pioneer Reminiscences and Journal of Martha Cragun Cox.* N.p.: Francis N. Bunker Family Organization, Isaiah Cox Family Organization, Martha Cragun Branch, 1985.

Daynes, Kathryn M. *More Wives than One: Transformation of the Mormon Marriage System, 1840–1910.* Urbana: University of Illinois Press, 2001.

Doctrine and Covenants of the Church of the Latter Day Saints. Kirtland, OH: F. G. Williams, 1835.

Embry, Jessie L. *Mormon Polygamous Families: Life in the Principle.* Salt Lake City: University of Utah, 1987.

Flake, Kathleen. *The Politics of American Religious Identity: The Seating of Senator Reed Smoot, Mormon Apostle.* Chapel Hill: University of North Carolina Press, 2004.

Foster, Lawrence. *Religion and Sexuality: Three American Communal Experiments of the Nineteenth Century.* New York: Oxford University Press, 1981.

Gordon, Sarah Barringer. *The Mormon Question: Polygamy and Constitutional Conflict in Nineteenth-Century America.* Chapel Hill: University of North Carolina Press, 2002.

Hales, Brian C. *Joseph Smith's Polygamy.* 3 vols. Salt Lake City, UT: Greg Kofford, 2013.

Hales, Brian C. *Modern Polygamy and Mormon Fundamentalism: The Generations after the Manifesto.* Salt Lake City, UT: Greg Kofford, 2006.

Hardy, B. Carmon. *Solemn Covenant: The Mormon Polygamous Passage.* Urbana: University of Illinois Press, 1992.

Hardy, B. Carmon. *Doing the Works of Abraham: Mormon Polygamy, Its Origin, Practice, and Demise.* Vol. 9 of *Kingdom in the West: The Mormons and the American Frontier.* Edited by Will Bagley. Norman, OK: Arthur H. Clark, 2007.

Ivins, Stanley S. "Notes on Mormon Polygamy." *Western Humanities Review* 10, no. 3 (Summer 1956): 229–39.

Journal of Discourses. 26 vols. London: LDS Booksellers Depot, 1854–86.

Larson, Karl A., and Katharine Miles Larson, eds. *Diary of Charles Lowell Walker.* 2 vols. Logan: Utah State University Press, 1980.

Mineau, Geraldine P., Lee L. Bean, and Douglas L. Anderton. "Migration and Fertility: Behavioral Change on the American Frontier." *Journal of Family History* 14, no. 1 (1989): 43–61.

Peterson, Paul H. "The Mormon Reformation." PhD diss., Brigham Young University, 1981.

Pratt, Orson. "God's Ancient People" [October 7, 1874]. *Journal of Discourses* 17: 214–29.

Pratt, Parley P. *Autobiography of Parley P. Pratt.* Salt Lake City, UT: Deseret, 1979.

Prince, Gregory A. *Power from on High: The Development of Mormon Priesthood.* Salt Lake City, UT: Signature, 1995.

Quinn, D. Michael. "LDS Church Authority and New Plural Marriages, 1890–1904." *Dialogue: A Journal of Mormon Thought* 18, no. 1 (Spring 1985): 9–105.

Shipps, Jan. *Sojourner in the Promised Land: Forty Years among the Mormons.* Urbana: University of Illinois Press, 2000.

Smith, George D. *Nauvoo Polygamy: ". . . But We Called It Celestial Marriage."* Salt Lake City, UT: Signature, 2008.

Smith, Joseph F. "Plural Marriage" (July 7, 1878). *Journal of Discourses* 20: 24–31.

Stapley, Jonathan A. "Adoptive Sealing Ritual in Mormonism." *Journal of Mormon History* 37, no. 3 (Summer 2011): 53–117.

Tanner, Annie Clark. *A Mormon Mother.* Salt Lake City: Tanner Trust Fund, University of Utah Library, 1991.

U.S. Senate. Committee on Privileges and Elections. *Proceedings before the Committee on Privileges and Elections of the United States Senate in the Matter of the Protests against the Right of Hon. Reed Smoot,* a Senator from the State of Utah, to Hold His Seat. 59th Cong., 1st sess., S. Rept. No. 486. Washington, D. C.: Government Printing Office, 1904-6. 4 vols.

Van Wagoner, Richard S. *Mormon Polygamy: A History.* 3rd ed. Salt Lake City, UT: Signature, 1992.

Woodruff, Wilford. *Wilford Woodruff's Journal.* Ed. Scott G. Kenny. 9 vols. Midvale, UT: Signature, 1983.

"William Clayton's Testimony," *Historical Record* 3 (6 May 1887): 225–26.

Young, Brigham. "Beneficial Effects" [August 19, 1866]. *Journal of Discourses* 11: 266–72.

Young, Brigham. "Plurality of Wives" [July 14, 1855]. *Journal of Discourses* 3: 264–68.

CHAPTER 23

MORMON DOCTRINE ON GENDER

VALERIE M. HUDSON

THE Church of Jesus Christ of Latter-day Saints professes doctrine on issues of sex and gender that is simultaneously quite traditional and profoundly radical. In other work, I have asserted that the LDS faith is the most feminist of the Christianities. Through an explication of church doctrine on these issues, that claim may be more rigorously assessed.[1]

CHURCH DOCTRINE AND CHAPEL PRACTICE

Before embarking on our doctrinal discussion, it is important when discussing issues of sex and gender in the LDS Church to be alert to the distinction between church doctrine and what might be termed "chapel practice." While I will argue that church doctrine is remarkable in its teachings on women and male-female relations, the full instantiation of that doctrine in how members live and conduct church activities at the local level, and even higher levels, has not always been uniformly implemented. For example, there have been practices one might point to even within recent decades where obvious slippage has occurred: for example, at one point, women would not be asked to pray in sacrament meeting in certain locales. Then that practice was superseded in these same locales by women not being called upon to open a sacrament meeting with prayer, though they might be asked to offer the closing prayer. Today, women may be asked to offer either the opening or closing prayer in sacrament meetings throughout the church, and it is considered completely unremarkable that they do. In other words, while we could engage the issue of discrepancy between doctrine and practice in the LDS Church, it is always more fruitful to examine doctrine: practice is simply too dynamic, and is too often struggling to catch up to doctrine, to be a central focus of this entry. We will simply say that where chapel practice is found to be at odds with church doctrine on issues of sex and gender, we have seen tangible and substantial movement in a positive direction, prodded by the church's general leadership, to bring the former in line with the latter, and that we expect such movement to persist in the future.

ETERNALITY OF SEX: WOMEN ARE CREATED IN THE IMAGE OF GOD

Speaking as a woman who was a member of another Christian faith before converting to the LDS religion, the phrase in Genesis 1:27 where we are told that "male and female" are created "in the image of God" had always presented a bit of a mystery. With God addressed as Father, with Christ clearly gendered male, how is it that a female is in the image of God? We know that some within the Abrahamic tradition have interpreted this mystery to mean that woman is a step further away from God than man because man shares the same gender as God and woman does not. Indeed, some in early Christianity were even doubtful that women possessed souls as a result of this sexual discrepancy.

LDS doctrine removes the mystery entirely. Men and women are created in the image of God, because the term "God" means "an exalted man and an exalted woman united in the new and everlasting covenant of marriage" (Doctrine and Covenants [D&C] 132:19–20). We believe that women are of divine heritage, because all the children of God have a Heavenly Mother, who stands as an equal to our Heavenly Father in the family organization of the heavens.[2] Indeed, without this joining of male and female, we are told that divinity cannot be (D&C 132:20). As Elder Bruce D. Porter has put it, "The differences between men and women are not simply biological. They are woven into the fabric of the universe, a vital, foundational element of eternal life and divine nature."[3]

As a result of this belief, it comes as no surprise that the LDS hold as doctrine that human souls are eternally sexed. The LDS "Proclamation on the Family" states that gender is "an essential characteristic of individual premortal, mortal, and eternal identity and purpose."[4] Sex is not, then, a secondary characteristic of our souls that we will move beyond in the hereafter, but a primary characteristic of our souls, that marked us before mortality, marks us during mortality, and will persist into the eternities.

Furthermore, this doctrine means that a woman's body is no curse, as has often been erroneously inferred given the assumed male gender of God, but rather a great reward to God's daughters for faithfulness in the premortal existence. Female biology is not a shackling constraint placed upon women, but is rather the highest physical expression possible of their divine heritage as created in the image of our Heavenly Mother. Breasts, womb, and ovaries are not some burden to be borne for the time of mortality, which burden God does not place on men, but rather a liberation of our spirits to act in the material world as females. To gain a body of flesh and bone would be to gain what our Father and Mother in Heaven possess, for they, too, are embodied, according to LDS doctrine.

Even to this day, as I attempt to write the above paragraphs in as dispassionate a fashion as is warranted for the *Oxford Handbook*, tears of joy spring to my eyes unbidden.[5] Woman is not a derivative or deformed incarnation of the divine that is more properly gendered male. She is not more constrained or cursed by her sexual physiology. To be a woman is to be inherently of divine potential, for we have a Mother there.

GOD IS NOT AND CANNOT BE A BACHELOR

If human souls are eternally sexed, the question of what the relationship between male and female is meant to be naturally arises. For that answer, we look to the relationship between our Heavenly Mother and Heavenly Father as the template to realize our divine potential. We believe that our Heavenly Parents are married in the new and everlasting covenant (D&C 132:19–20), and we believe that as soon as a male soul and a female soul were first on the earth in the persons of Adam and Eve, our Heavenly Parents ensured that they also entered into the new and everlasting covenant of marriage, and that this occurred even before the Fall.[6]

What is the new and everlasting covenant of marriage? As explained in Doctrine and Covenants section 132, it is a specific earthly ordinance that must be administered by those possessing the authority of God to do so. It is a relationship of eternal love, equality in the context of eternal difference, perfect fidelity, and commitment to offspring. Marriage is the pact of peace between the sexes, and between parents and children—the peace that makes divinity possible. As such, not only do the LDS believe that God is not a bachelor, they believe he *cannot* be a bachelor and be God. Only marriage between a man and a woman can create the state of being that we term godhood.

This means that the sons and daughters of God are the offspring of an eternally committed, heterosexual marriage relationship between their Parents—and that there would be no sons and daughters without that marriage relationship. While we do not believe God created our spirits *ex nihilo*, the LDS do believe that the current organization of our spirits that allows us to claim a divine destiny was the product of the loving relationship between our Heavenly Parents. That also means that our destiny as God's children is to follow in their footsteps, and enter into the new and everlasting covenant of marriage ourselves, and bring forth our own offspring. While the children we bring forth in mortality are more properly seen as God's children, over whom we have a custodial relationship, in the eternities we believe we will bring forth our own offspring with our eternal companion.[7] As the Parents do, so will the children one day, if they have proven themselves worthy.

Here we see an element of LDS Church doctrine that may be perceived as quite traditional, perhaps even anachronistic, in today's world. The LDS believe that men and women are to marry each other; that marriage has been defined by God as inherently heterosexual. Furthermore, men and women are not to have sexual relations before marriage, and they should not have sexual relations with any besides their spouse once they are married. Importantly, children should be conceived only within marriage: according to the Proclamation on the Family, "Children are entitled to birth within the bonds of matrimony, and to be reared by a father and mother who honor marital vows with complete fidelity." In addition, "Husband and wife have a solemn responsibility to love and care for each other and their children."

To enter into marriage then, is to walk the path of divinity.[8]

Equality Is a Defining Characteristic of Marriage: The Garden of Eden and Beyond

In many religious traditions, marriage is not conceived as a relationship of equality, but rather a relationship of a leader (the man) to a subordinate (the woman). In the Abrahamic tradition, this type of construct of inequality within marriage derives from a particular interpretation of several scriptures in Genesis, perhaps the most prominent involving: (1) the secondary creation of Eve from Adam; (2) Eve being termed a "help-meet" for Adam by God, interpreted to mean that Eve's purpose was to act as some type of junior assistant to Adam; and (3) Eve's original transgression which precipitated the Fall and marked her as presumably less faithful and true than Adam, and thus properly placed in a subordinate position under his presumed more faithful leadership.

But inequality is not the mark of marriage in the new and everlasting covenant. To see this, we must look again at the story of the Garden of Eden and the Fall. When interpreted according to LDS doctrine, the same three circumstances that have led others to see inequality as God-mandated in marriage lead the LDS to see equality as God-mandated in marriage. To see this, we must consider the grand work of God, which is to "bring to pass the immortality and eternal life of man" (Moses 1:39, Pearl of Great Price). Since the work of God is the work of men and women together as marriage partners, there is a deep resonance between the marriage relationship and the Great Plan of Happiness. Marriage between men and women produces, if you will, the Great Plan of Happiness, and fulfills the purpose of godhood. Nowhere is this made more clear than in the story of the Garden of Eden and the Fall.

To begin our discussion, LDS doctrine concerning the Fall is an essential precursor. The LDS do not believe that the Fall was a great tragedy, but rather a foreordained blessing and progression for the children of God. The LDS also do not believe that Eve sinned in partaking of the fruit of the First Tree. And because the LDS do not believe Eve sinned, we also do not believe that Eve was punished for her role in taking the fruit, but rather rewarded.

In order to "bring to pass the immortality and eternal life" of God's children, at a certain stage in their spiritual development, it would be necessary for them to enter into full agency and to exercise that agency so that God might see whether each soul would choose to use their agency for good or for evil. This plan for their further development was presented to the children of God, and some rejected it and refused to progress. For the remainder, the necessity of a Savior, who would be able to overcome the inevitable sin and death that would result, was understood, and Christ stood forth as the one worthy, willing, and ordained to effect this role. A time and a place for the children to make this great leap were also ordained.

The plan would be, as it were, a great round. We would journey forth from our heavenly home, losing our memories of that place, and be brought forth, embodied in flesh, as actors in the material world with full agency to choose either good or evil. Within the heart of each soul born would be placed the Light of Christ, which would lead us toward good and away from evil if we followed its counsel. Some have called this our conscience. If we chose well, we would be empowered to return home, this time not as little children, but as those who had earned the right to progress toward godhood. If we did not choose well, we might never return home.

A garden was planted; the Garden of Eden. No doubt there were many different types of flora and fauna therein, but the narrative hinges on two trees. The first tree is called the Tree of the Knowledge of Good and Evil, and the second tree is called the Tree of Life. Into this garden were placed two beings: a man, and then a woman. Already it is interesting to note that our story centers on two trees and two people. The identical number, we shall see, is no coincidence.

As noted previously, some have suggested that Adam was created first to show that Eve was but a derivative or less perfect manifestation of God's image, or to show that man is the primary face of humanity, and woman the secondary face. However, LDS Church leaders have stated very plainly that this interpretation is wrong. For example, Elder Earl C. Tingey has said, "You must not misunderstand what the Lord meant when Adam was told he was to have a helpmeet. A helpmeet is a companion suited to or equal to us. We walk side by side with a helpmeet, not one before or behind the other. A helpmeet results in an absolute equal partnership between a husband and a wife. Eve was to be equal to Adam as a husband and wife are to be equal to each other."[9]

If the sequence of creation does not signify any lessening of the equality between men and women, what does it signify? When we remember LDS doctrine that the Fall is not a tragedy, but a great blessing foreordained by God, and when we remember that the number of persons in the garden (two) matches precisely the number of important trees in the garden (two), we begin to sense that there are two stewardships in bringing to pass the Great Plan of Happiness. The two stewardships are represented by the two trees, and these two stewardships are apportioned between the two persons in the garden, Adam and Eve—and the stewardships are not apportioned randomly.

To investigate which stewardship is given to which person, we must ask what the stewardships of the two trees represent. The Second Tree, the Tree of Life, represents in LDS doctrine the partaking of those ordinances which will enable us, if we prove ourselves worthy through the quality of our choices, to qualify to return to our heavenly home, and there progress in our divine destiny to become like our Heavenly Parents. In LDS theology, these ordinances signifying our path home include the ordinances of baptism, the laying on of hands for the gift of the Holy Ghost, the temple rites of washing, anointing, and endowment, ordinances of sealing in marriage and parenthood. In LDS doctrine, the assignment of providing these ordinances to those who are worthy to receive them has been given, from the beginning, to the sons of Adam. The right to give the fruit of the Second Tree, the Tree of Life, to others, is the male role in the Great Plan of Happiness, and the authority to do so is given by ordination and office in the priesthood of God.

However, the Tree of Life is not the only tree in the Garden of Eden, and Adam is not the only child of God there. There is another tree, another child of God, another stewardship in the Great Plan. What does partaking of the fruit of the Tree of Knowledge of Good and Evil represent? Just as the Tree of Life is, in a sense, the doorway back to our heavenly home, so the Tree of the Knowledge of Good and Evil represents the doorway from our heavenly home into this mortal realm of embodiment and full agency.[10]

Partaking of the fruit of this First Tree means to enter into mortality with a mortal body that may suffer and die, to enter into full agency in a material world, and to have awakened within us the Light of Christ that will serve as our guide home. In pondering the meaning here, we are led to ask: Is it not through women that souls journey to mortality and gain their agency, and through their nurturing love that the Light of Christ is awakened in each soul? Women escort every soul through the veil to mortal life and full agency. Even the Savior was escorted into his mortal ministry by a daughter of God. In this sense, even Adam was "born" of Eve, as he hearkened unto her and accepted the gift of the fruit of the First Tree from her hand.

In this light, the fruit of the First Tree symbolizes the gift of women to all humanity, and the role and godly power and authority of women in the Great Plan of Happiness. It was not Adam's role to lead out with regard to the First Tree; it was not his stewardship to give of the fruit of the First Tree to others. Eve was created second to show us this, to show that Adam was not foreordained to open the door to mortality. It was Eve's stewardship to open the door to the great journey of the children of God.

With this LDS reading of the Garden of Eden story, it is clear that LDS doctrine cannot assert that Eve sinned by partaking of the fruit of the First Tree. And, indeed, that is the case: it is LDS doctrine that Eve did not sin in partaking. Elder Dallin H. Oaks has said: "Some Christians condemn Eve for her act, concluding that she and her daughters are somehow flawed by it. Not the Latter-day Saints! Informed by revelation, we celebrate Eve's act and honor her wisdom and courage in the great episode called the Fall."[11] Notice the words used—words so infrequently used in most Christianities when referring to Mother Eve—celebrate, honor, wisdom, courage. Oaks goes on to say that partaking of the fruit was the minimum transgression necessary to effect the Fall, but that Eve did not sin, for she was still in a state of innocence when she partook.

If Eve did not sin, if her partaking of the fruit was her foreordained stewardship representing women's stewardship and power in the Great Plan, if it took great wisdom and courage to lead out as she did, then not only must there have been celebration in heaven when she partook, but it is also inconceivable that God punished Eve for her act. And that, too, is LDS doctrine: the LDS do not believe that Eve was punished for her role in the Fall, but rather rewarded.

Let us look again at what many Christianities believe to be punishment for the Fall. First the ground is cursed, so that hard work will be necessary to keep oneself alive in mortality. However, the LDS puts an emphasis on the phrase, "cursed *for thy sake*" (Moses 4:23; emphasis added). While the ground was cursed, the effect was a blessing for the human family. This set in motion the law of opposites, as explained by Father Lehi in his great sermon in the Book of Mormon (see 2 Nephi 2). In this sermon, Lehi points out that agency is nothing without there being "opposition in all things" (2 Nephi 2:11). There could be no distinction between truth and lies, virtue and vice, pleasure and pain, good and evil, if there was no such opposition; everything would be "a compound in one" (2 Nephi 2:11) and choice would have no meaning for it would have no effect (2 Nephi 2:12). The cursing of the ground was an acknowledgement that for the Great Plan to unfold, agency must confront opposition.

Second, Eve is told that she will labor to bring forth children, and this will require effort and sacrifice on her part. Speaking as a mother on behalf of Mother Eve, we can only surmise that she greeted this news with joy: she would become a mother at last! In LDS theology, children are one of the greatest blessings God can bestow. It is inconceivable that Eve received this news of her new power to bear children with sorrow, though she was told motherhood would entail that emotion. Indeed, Eve had waited the untold expanses of premortality to finally obtain this power, and now the time had finally arrived. We surmise her heart leapt with joy, and she did not view this turn of events as a curse. She would become the Mother of All Living.

Last, some point to the wording of the King James Version of Genesis 3:16 as a testament that God was upset that Eve has partaken of the fruit, and thus decreed that Adam should rule over her, because obviously she was incapable of ruling herself wisely. Given that the LDS believe Eve acted with wisdom and courage in fulfilling her stewardship in the Great Plan, this interpretation makes no sense. Indeed, since Eve had led out in righteousness, and at this point Adam has not yet fulfilled his role in the Great Plan because the stewardships are sequenced (that is, one cannot partake of the fruit of the Second Tree without having first partaken of the fruit of the First Tree), it would make more sense for God to decree that Eve rule over Adam! But God has a better vision in mind than hierarchy between his son and his daughter: as recounted by Elder Bruce C. Hafen and his wife, Marie: "Genesis 3:16 states that Adam is to 'rule over' Eve, but . . . *over* in 'rule over' uses the Hebrew *bet*, which means ruling *with*, not ruling *over*. . . . The concept of interdependent equal partners is well-grounded in the doctrine of the restored gospel. Eve was Adam's 'help meet' (Genesis 2:18). The original Hebrew for *meet* means that Eve was adequate for, or equal to, Adam. She wasn't his servant or his subordinate."[12]

From this LDS interpretation, we now see in Genesis 3:16 that God was reassuring Eve that Adam would in fact fulfill his role in the Great Plan, making them truly equal in power to save, truly equal partners and helpmeets to each other. Hierarchy was not to exist between them; though different in sex, they were to treat each other as equals. As President James E. Faust put it, "Every father is to his family a patriarch and every mother a matriarch as coequals in their distinctive parental roles."[13] But perhaps Elder L. Tom Perry put it best: "There is not a president and vice president in a family. We have co-presidents working together eternally for the good of their family. . . . They are on equal footing. They plan and organize the affairs of the family jointly and unanimously as they move forward."[14]

When we step back and look at the entire plan, it is a plan of joyous equal partnership between men and women, who work together to enable God's purpose to bring about the immortality and eternal life of man to come to pass. It is a plan of mutual hearkening; Adam hearkens to Eve and accepts her gift of the fruit of the First Tree, and Eve hearkens to Adam and accepts his gift of the fruit of the Second Tree. It is, indeed, a Plan of Happiness for both men and women.

EQUALITY AND LOVE

We pause to contemplate the integral relationship between equality in the context of difference and love. For love to exist between man and woman, for their relationship to be all that their Heavenly Parents would hope for them, they must regard each other as equals: there is simply no other way. Indeed, in Latter-day Saint theology, there is a crucial relationship between equality and love, which we must not overlook. Think about the love of God and of our Savior: we readily acknowledge that we are not their equals. But, heretical as it is to many other faiths, we believe that God ultimately hopes, plans, and acts to create a path for his children to become as God is. In the end, what God hopes we will become are God's friends, not God's servants or perpetual inferiors (D&C 84:77). The truest, most noble love is the love of a superior for an inferior where the superior makes every sacrifice so that the inferior might, if willing, rise to become an equal. And that is the wonder of the Savior's Atonement: He, a superior, suffered and died so that all who will, male and female, will become equal heirs with Christ (D&C 88:107), will receive "all power" and the "fullness" of God (D&C 76: 54–56, 94–95; 132:20). And in this highest realm, "he makes them equal in power, and in might, and in dominion" (D&C 76:95).

Parental love in mortality emulates godly love. Healthy parental love sacrifices so that our children may one day stand as our equals, and be not only our children, but our friends.

But there are also relationships in which people come together not as superiors and inferiors with the hope that the inferiors might be made equal; there are relationships in which people are to come together as presumed equals, and this presumption of equality becomes a spiritual mandate. The terms used in the scriptures help us understand this is a commandment: "[It] must needs be . . . an organization of my people . . . that you may be equal in the bonds of heavenly things, yea, and earthly things also . . . you must prepare yourselves by doing the things which I have commanded you" (D&C 78:2–7; see also 38:24–27). And why the presumption of equality? That we may truly love our neighbors, for if we cannot envision them as our equal, as ourselves, we cannot really love them. A Zion community lives the fullness of this commandment. Zion, for Mormons, is a place where the saints are equal in both heavenly and temporal things, as noted above (D&C 70:14; 78:5–7). Zion must come together presuming the equality of each person and then acting on it to remove any discordance between the ideal and the lived situation.

Thus it is in the units of Zion—the marriages of that community. Spouses are to enter their marriage relationship convinced of each other's equality. They cannot form a relationship that will be blessed by God if they come to the marriage altar unsure of each other's equality or doubting it, or not even thinking about how it should order their relations. The first utterance after God, according to LDS doctrine, married Adam and Eve in the Garden of Eden, was Adam's bold declaration of Eve's equality with him—that they would be "one flesh" (Genesis 2:23–24). (Adam even put in an injunction against patrilocal marriage, where wives live with their husband's family, because of its inherent ability to turn a marriage into an unequal one favoring the husband [Genesis 2:24].)

Gender equality is thus not some gratuitous element of God's vision of marriage: rather, we are commanded to presume the equality of our spouse as we approach the marriage altar, for otherwise we cannot truly love them. As Mormon apostle Richard G. Scott has stated, "In some cultures, tradition places a man in a role to dominate, control, and regulate all family affairs. This is not the way of the Lord. In some places the wife is almost owned by her husband, as if she were another of his personal possessions. That is a cruel, mistaken vision of marriage encouraged by Lucifer that every priesthood holder must reject. It is founded on the false premise that a man is somehow superior to a woman. Nothing could be farther from the truth."[15]

We hopefully deepen that vision of our spouse's equality through the divine work that is procreation and parenthood. Indeed, given that we believe Adam and Eve lived this law, a marriage reflecting the equality of the spouses is *the ultimate traditional marriage*.

Men, Women, and the Future of Their Societies

The restoration of the priesthood by the LDS Church takes on added significance above and beyond placing the fruit of the Tree of Life within our grasp once more. The restored priesthood not only restores right relations between man and God; it restores right relations between men and women. The men of the LDS Church are a covenant brotherhood of men whose duty to God includes treating the daughters of God the way God wants them treated. Where else in the world can be found a brotherhood of men who believe that God wants them to adhere to a single standard of sexual fidelity? To seek to become married and to stay married? To uphold the equality and safety and flourishing of women? To have children and actively taking part in raising them? To value their daughters as much as they value their sons? To abhor abuse, pornography, neglect? To commit to parity in burden-sharing, including housework and decision making, within marriage? This is what LDS men pledge, as part of their duty to their God.

From the perspective given here, priesthood is not something extra given to men. Priesthood is a man's apprenticeship to become a Heavenly Father, and women have their own apprenticeship to become a Heavenly Mother. The earthly ordinances of the body and of agency, such as pregnancy, childbirth, and lactation—that is, the ordinances of the First Tree—are not less powerful or less spiritual than the ordinances of the Second Tree. Women have their own godly power and authority. Noteworthy in this respect is that every body bears the mark of his or her mother—the navel mark—in their very flesh.[16]

Even more importantly, what this tells us is that the central drama in all societies from God's perspective is male-female relations, and not treaties and wars and the price of oil, or how the stock market is doing. We learn this most poignantly from the sermon preserved as Jacob chapters 2 and 3. Jacob is speaking to his people, the Nephites. The Nephites have the scriptures, the temple and its priesthood ordinances, and prophets to guide them, whereas their enemies, the Lamanites, have none of these things. Nevertheless, Jacob is constrained to tell the Nephites that God will destroy them as a people, while preserving the Lamanites. This must have been a shocking, perhaps unbelievable, assertion to the minds of the Nephites. Jacob explains to them the reason: the Nephites have broken the hearts of their wives and children by their whoredoms and adulteries, whereas among the Lamanites, "their husbands love their wives, and their wives love their husbands; and their husbands and their wives love their children" (Jacob 3:7).

This offers a remarkable insight into the mind of our Heavenly Parents. Apparently, a society where love and equality between men and women have died *cannot live the gospel*. God might as well start over and not let any further souls be born into it. A true and loving partnership between men and women is the bedrock of the Great Plan of Happiness. In this way, the situation of women is a barometer of how near spiritual death a civilization has become. But a society where the husbands love their wives, the wives love the husbands, the parents love the children, and the children love the parents is "gospel sod." God can always send to such a society angels to minister, prophets to prophesy, golden plates to provide scripture, and so forth. But the bedrock must be there first. That means that gender equality is not some politically correct ideal or a maraschino cherry placed last atop the Zion sundae . . . gender equality is at the very heart of Zion, for that is how our Heavenly Father and Heavenly Mother live.

EDUCATION, TALENTS, COUNSEL, CONSENT

Given this vision of equality between men and women in the sight of our Heavenly Parents, it should come as no surprise that LDS doctrine encourages all, both male and female, to fulfill the measure of their creation and magnify the talents that God has given them. After his wife Marjorie's death, President Gordon B. Hinckley shared some tender moments from their marriage. One of the most poignant of those was, "In our old age my beloved companion said to me quietly one evening, 'You have always given me wings to fly, and I have loved you for it.'"[17] There must be room enough in a marriage for the dreams of both the husband and the wife, and sweet encouragement from each to the other to follow those dreams.

LDS doctrine implies that women should seek education in the same measure as men do. When he was president of Brigham Young University, Dallin H. Oaks stated, "[W]e make no distinction between young men and young women in our conviction about the importance of an education and in our commitment to providing that education."[18]

And as President Hinckley memorably said:

> The whole gamut of human endeavor is now open to women. There is not anything that you cannot do if you will set your mind to it. I am grateful that women today are afforded the same opportunity to study for science, for the professions, and for every other facet of human knowledge. You are as entitled as are men to the Spirit of Christ, which enlightens every man and woman who comes into the world. . . . You can include in the dream of the woman you would like to be a picture of one qualified to serve society and make a significant contribution to the world of which she will be a part.[19]

LDS doctrine states that spiritual gifts and talents come in equal measure to women as well as men (D&C 42). God has given both their sons and their daughters these talents in order that all the human family might benefit from their development and use. From the earliest days of the church to the present, LDS women have become physicians and dentists, business owners and academics, politicians and philanthropists, in addition to nurses and teachers.[20] As Elder M. Russell Ballard has said, "Is a woman's value dependent exclusively upon her role as a wife and mother? The answer is simple and obvious: No. . . . Every righteous man and woman has a significant role to play in the onward march of the kingdom of God."[21]

Indeed, a hallmark of a Zion society is that all are equal in giving counsel and in giving consent to the affairs of the society (D&C 104). This injunction applies to men and women as well. Men and women should be equally involved in the shaping of the world in which they and their families live. Indeed, it is arguable that the world is not in as good shape as it might be because of the dearth of female involvement in community and national decisionmaking, which lack is contrary to the wishes of God. As President Gordon B. Hinckley put it, "I have often thought that if great numbers of the women of all nations were to unite and lift their voices in the cause of peace, there would develop a worldwide will for peace which could save our civilization and avoid untold suffering, misery, plague, starvation, and the death of millions."[22] The greater involvement of women in the world around them can only be to the good, according to LDS beliefs, and it is noteworthy in this regard that the territory of Utah was one of the very first locations in the world to extend suffrage to women.

Last, but by no means least, the church champions the cause of women worldwide. As we have seen in this chapter, LDS General Authorities have spoken out boldly against the subordination of women, and have actively encouraged—even demanded—that women be treated as equals within the membership of the church. As Elder Richard G. Scott has stated, "I encourage any man who is reluctant to develop an equal partnership with his wife to obey the counsel inspired by the Lord and *do it*."[23] This emphasis on sincerely equal partnership between men and women is a hallmark of the LDS Church. As Elder Alexander B. Morrison so bluntly put it, "The Church cannot bow down before any traditions that demean or devalue the daughters of God."[24] And the reason the church cannot bow down is that it would forfeit the blessings of our Heavenly Father and Heavenly Mother were it to do so. Inequality between men and women cannot lead a soul, or a church membership, to heaven.

In sum, then, LDS doctrine concerning women is simultaneously profoundly revolutionary and profoundly traditional. Of all the Christianities, only the LDS believe that we have a Heavenly Mother in addition to a Heavenly Father, and that without marriage between the sexes, divinity could not exist. Of all the Christianities, only the LDS believe that Eve was the heroine of the story of the Garden of Eden, and that God did not subordinate her to Adam either before or after she partook of the fruit of the first tree. Only the LDS Church preaches that the Great Plan of Happiness is contingent on the truly equal partnership between man and woman. At the same time, the LDS believe that to fully participate in women's role and power in that plan, marriage and family should be sought by women (and men), children should be conceived within the bonds of marriage, and that marriage must be defined in heterosexual terms, all of which are quite traditional views. With this interesting mix of the traditional and the revolutionary, and with the church's insistent calls for greater equality between men and women among its own membership and in the world, and in its encouragement of LDS women to develop their talents and gifts and contribute those to their societies, LDS beliefs on sex and gender constitute a powerful alternative to established religious views, Christian or non-Christian, on the foundational issues of who men and women are, and how they are to relate in the sight of God. In a sense, then, the most feminist act one might contemplate would be to preach the Restored Gospel of Jesus Christ.

NOTES

1. In this chapter, we will confine ourselves to a discussion of LDS doctrine concerning women and concerning male-female relations. "Gender" is a broad construct, which might include an examination of such issues as same-sex attraction, intersexed individuals, and so forth, but we will delimit this discussion to the male-female dyad. Furthermore, it might seem pertinent to this chapter's theme to treat issues such as doctrine concerning polygamy, but that Abrahamic sacrifice deserves a fuller discussion, which we have provided elsewhere; see Cassler, "Polygamy."
2. A comprehensive examination of the LDS doctrine of Heavenly Mother can be found in Paulsen and Pulido, "A Mother There."

3. Porter, "Defending the Family in a Troubled World."

4. It should be noted that since "gender" is a social construct, we cannot say that any particular gender construct of the mortal world is eternal. We do know that "sex" is eternal, and we hope that our notions of gender will move closer to those lived in heaven as we live the truths of the restored gospel.

5. Indeed, emboldened by the understanding that my place as a daughter of God is as a full equal to the sons of God, I question whether the requirement of dispassion in academic endeavor is not in fact a gendered construct meant to marginalize female voice.

6. President Joseph Fielding Smith: "The first marriage performed on earth was the marriage of Eve to Adam, and this was before there was any death, therefore it was intended to be forever"; Smith, *Answers to Gospel Questions*, 3:23. Spencer W. Kimball taught: "Adam and Eve were married for eternity by the Lord"; Kimball, *Teachings*, 292.

7. President Gordon B. Hinckley taught, "Never forget that these little ones are the sons and daughters of God and that yours is a custodial relationship to them, that he was a parent before you were parents and that he has not relinquished his parental rights or interest in these little ones"; Hinckley, "Remarks at the Salt Lake University Third Stake Conference".

8. And this is how we understand why the LDS Church in 2008 was willing to endure great hardship by working on behalf of Proposition 8 in California, which would maintain the heterosexual definition of marriage in that state.

9. Tingey, "Simple Truths from Heaven."

10. We know there was at least a partial agency in heaven, or there could have been no dispute over the Plan of Happiness, and no defection of a third of the host of heaven. But it is also clear that full agency comes with embodiment and with the veil drawn over our minds that permits us to forget what we knew premortally of the reality of God.

11. Oaks, "Great Plan of Happiness," 72–75.

12. Hafen and Hafen, "Crossing Thresholds and Becoming Equal Partners," 24–29.

13. Faust, "Prophetic Voice," 4.

14. Perry, "Fatherhood, an Eternal Calling."

15. Scott, "Honor the Priesthood and Use It Well," 44–47. Moreover, contrary to scripture and the teachings of latter-day prophets, some men and women have interpreted *presiding* to mean that after equal counsel, equal consent is not necessary because the presider (or husband) has the right of final say. But President Boyd K. Packer explained: "In the Church there is a distinct line of authority. We serve where called by those who preside over us. In the home it is a partnership with husband and wife equally yoked together, sharing in decisions, always working together"; Packer, "Relief Society," 73.

16. Indeed, it can be readily observed that those religions that despise the body tend to be those religions that also devalue women—for the body is one of the great gifts given to the human family by women.

17. Hinckley, "Women in Our Lives," 84.

18. Oaks, "Women and Education."

19. Hinckley, "Words of the Prophet," 2–5.

20. See Hudson et al., forthcoming.

21. Ballard, "Women of Righteousness."

22. Hinckley, "Ten Gifts from the Lord."

23. Scott, "Honor the Priesthood and Use It Well," 46.

24. Morrison, International Society meeting.

BIBLIOGRAPHY

Ballard, M. Russell. "Women of Righteousness." *Liahona* 26, no. 12 (December 2002): 34–43.

Cassler, Valerie Hudson. "Polygamy." *Square Two* 3, no. 1 (Spring 2010). http://squaretwo.org/Sq2ArticleCasslerPolygamy.html.

Faust, James E. "The Prophetic Voice." *Ensign* 26, no. 5 (May 1996). http://www.lds.org/ensign/1996/05/the-prophetic-voice?lang=eng.

Hafen, Bruce C., and Marie K. Hafen. "Crossing Thresholds and Becoming Equal Partners." *Ensign* 27, no. 8 (August 2007): 25–29.

Hinckley, Gordon B. "Remarks at the Salt Lake University Third Stake Conference" [November 3, 1996]. *Church News*, March 1, 1997.

Hinckley, Gordon B. "Ten Gifts from the Lord." *Ensign* 15, no. 11 (November 1985). http://www.lds.org/ensign/1985/11/ten-gifts-from-the-lord?lang=eng.

Hinckley, Gordon B. "The Women in Our Lives." *Ensign* 34, no. 11 (November 2004): 82–85.

Hinckley, Gordon B. "Words of the Prophet: Seek Learning." *New Era* 37, no. 9 (September 2007): 2–5.

Hudson, Valerie M., S. Matthew Stearmer, Kaylie Clark, and Alixandra Lewis Adams. *Men and Women Working towards Zion*. Forthcoming.

Kimball, Spencer W. *The Teachings of Spencer W. Kimball*. Comp. Edward L. Kimball. Salt Lake City, UT: Bookcraft, 1982.

Morrison, Alexander B. International Society meeting, Provo, Utah, August 1994. Comment in Q&A period.

Oaks, Dallin H. "The Great Plan of Happiness." *Ensign* 23, no. 11 (November 1993). http://www.lds.org/ensign/1993/11/the-great-plan-of-happiness?lang=eng.

Oaks, Dallin H. "Women and Education" [Excerpt from a BYU Devotional Assembly, Provo, Utah, February 12, 1974]. *Ensign* 5, no. 3 (March 1975). http://www.lds.org/ensign/1975/03/insights/women-and-education?lang=eng&query=women+and+education.

Packer, Boyd K. "The Relief Society." *Ensign* 28, no. 5 (May 1998). http://www.lds.org/ensign/1998/05/the-relief-society?lang=eng.

Paulsen, David, and Martin Pulido. "'A Mother There': A Survey of Historical Teachings about Mother in Heaven." *BYU Studies* 50, no. 1 (2011): 70–126.

Perry, L. Tom. "Fatherhood, an Eternal Calling." General Conference, April 2004. http://www.lds.org/general-conference/2004/04/fatherhood-an-eternal-calling?lang=eng.

Porter, Bruce D. "Defending the Family in a Troubled World." *Ensign* 41, no. 6 (June 2011): 12–18.

Scott, Richard G. "Honor the Priesthood and Use It Well." *Ensign* 38, no. 11 (November 2008): 44–47.

Smith, Joseph Fielding. *Answers to Gospel Questions*. Vol. 3. Salt Lake City: Deseret, 1957–63.

Tingey, Earl C. "The Simple Truths from Heaven." CES fireside, Brigham Young University, Provo, Utah, January 13, 2008. http://lds.org/library/display/0,4945,538-1-4399-1,00.html.

CHAPTER 24

....

MORMONS AND RACE

....

MARGARET BLAIR YOUNG
AND DARIUS AIDAN GRAY

THE consequences of our actions become possible and often inevitable with our first accommodations of guiding principles—for either good or ill. Just as there is a biological genealogy, so there are philosophical roots to historical trajectories. Surely the American founding fathers knew that slavery could not endure in a nation with the ideals articulated in the Declaration of Independence, and yet it was allowed as part of "the great compromise." With that accommodation, the Civil War became not only possible but inevitable. For us in the twenty-first century, the fall-out of all that followed that war—Jim Crow laws, segregation, inequality in all forms and places, and the stubborn endurance of racialist policies and beliefs in many churches, including the Church of Jesus Christ of Latter-day Saints—also appeared on the historical trajectory, modified only by bold leaders and (as perceived by many) divine intervention.

The philosophical progenitors of the slave trade were justified by selections and interpretations of biblical verses. The idea of a lineage curse from the supposed ancestors of all Africans—Cain and Canaan—would ultimately result in ships crowded with newly enslaved people. Started by various rabbis in the fourth century, and repeated by Europeans in the fifteenth century to justify the slave trade, interpretations of Genesis 9:20–27 (Noah cursing his grandson, Canaan, for Ham's sin—which curse, through hopscotch genealogy,[1] included the curse of Cain) became a justification for the unthinkable. If the early slave traders could find some scriptural rationale for their actions, if they could find evidence that God saw black Africans as ordained to servitude rather than endowed with inalienable human rights, the crimes of the trade could be shrugged off as God's will, and uneasy consciences salved. By the nineteenth century, when the LDS religion was established, the idea that blacks of African descent carried a curse to be "servants of servants" (Genesis 9:25) was fully embedded in American society, and naturally imported into this new religion. What was sometimes referred to as "The Negro Doctrine" comprised the LDS Church's priesthood restriction, denying any man of African lineage ordination in the priesthood, which all other Mormon men could receive. The restriction also affected black women. They could not participate in LDS temple rituals—the most significant ordinances of the faith.

In the generation of Mormons born after the priesthood restriction was lifted, we still find some acceptance of the folklore which undergirded it, but generally we see a resistance to any racialist teachings. The "Bloggernacle" (the worldwide archipelago of Mormon-themed blogs) has featured numerous young scholars addressing the race issue with historical knowledge that their grandparents did not have. The effect of the Internet and its ability to publicize opinions and news globally cannot be overestimated. This was demonstrated profoundly during the week of February 28 to March 3, 2012. A *Washington Post* article dated February 28 quoted Brigham Young University Religion professor Randy Bott explaining that the LDS priesthood restriction was necessary not only because the curse of Cain/Canaan affected all of African lineage, but because blacks hadn't been ready for the onerous power of that priesthood. Jason Horowitz's article quotes Bott saying, "God has always been discriminatory" concerning to whom he grants the authority of the priesthood. The professor, according to Horowitz, compared blacks to a young child prematurely asking for the keys to her father's car. "Until 1978," he quotes Bott, "the Lord determined that blacks were not yet ready for the priesthood."

The Bloggernacle reacted instantly. Within hours of Horowitz's article being published, it was being actively discussed online. The reaction from LDS Public Affairs was equally swift. Within a day, the Church released two statements. The first named Bott and distanced itself from his comments. This official statement went further than any heretofore made on the race issue:

> The positions attributed to BYU professor Randy Bott in a recent *Washington Post* article absolutely do not represent the teachings and doctrines of The Church of Jesus Christ of Latter-day Saints. . . . For a time in the Church there was a restriction on the priesthood for male members of African descent. It is not known precisely why, how, or when this restriction began in the Church. . . . The Church is not bound by speculation or opinions given with limited understanding. We condemn racism, including any and all past racism by individuals both inside and outside the Church.

This statement not only acknowledges the priesthood restriction, but admits ignorance about when, how, and why it came into being in the first place. There is a strong implication that human error could well be responsible for the ban.

The second Church statement, issued the same day, continued the strong rhetoric of the first:

> The origins of priesthood availability are not entirely clear. Some explanations with respect to this matter were made in the absence of direct revelation and references to these explanations are sometimes cited in publications. These previous personal statements do not represent Church doctrine.

Nearly as important was the reaction of a group of BYU students, who independently distributed over a thousand flyers on BYU's campus, declaring:

As the rising generation of LDS youth . . . we believe the passages of our holy scripture that declare us all equal before God regardless of gender, race or economic and social status. We recognize the need to be forthright about the history of our faith which . . . is blemished in the way all human narratives are.[2]

These statements stand in stark contrast to the attitudes and official proclamations given just sixty-three years earlier, when the First Presidency of the LDS Church released an official statement on August 17, 1949:

The attitude of the Church with reference to Negroes remains as it has always stood. It is . . . [a] direct commandment from the Lord, on which is founded the doctrine of the Church from the days of its organization, to the effect that Negroes . . . are not entitled to the priesthood at the present time.[3]

This statement referenced both the curse of Cain and "the conduct of spirits in the pre-mortal existence" as justifications for the restriction, validating LDS Apostle Orson Hyde's 1845 speculation that those who were neutral in the pre-earth War in Heaven were forced to accept black bodies in mortality.

For Latter-day Saints, fidelity to Church leaders, who are considered prophets, seers, and revelators, has usually been a litmus test for discipleship. It is assumed by many Mormons that the First Presidency and Quorum of the Twelve meet periodically with Jesus Christ himself. Furthermore, a statement made by Wilford Woodruff to prevent widespread apostasy when he issued a manifesto against polygamy was used outside the Manifesto's context and suggested prophetic infallibility. Woodruff said, "[T]he Lord will never permit me or any other man who stands as President of this Church to lead you astray. . . . If I were to attempt that, the Lord would remove me out of my place, and so He will any other man who attempts to lead the children of men astray from the oracles of God and from their duty."[4] These words, in variation, were repeated by successive Church presidents and other leaders, implying that any utterances by the president of the Church had God's stamp of approval. A common quip among Mormons of the twenty-first century claimed that Catholics said the Pope was infallible, but didn't really believe it, whereas Mormons said their leaders were fallible, but didn't really believe it.

Mormons' loyalty to their Church leaders and their perception that the Quorum of the Twelve Apostles and the First Presidency were unified in their views gave the 1949 statement binding power. In that period, before *Brown v. the Board of Education* or Dr. King's march on Washington, the nation was still racially divided, and the old ideas of black inferiority had not given way to the movement which was just around the corner. The arc of history had not yet confronted Mormonism's "Negro doctrine," and few if any faithful Mormons questioned the statement that the priesthood restriction had "always stood." In fact, however, there is no reliable evidence that it started with Church founder Joseph Smith and much to suggest that he would not have approved of it. It is true that Smith believed in the curse of Cain/Canaan, but he would have been an anomaly in the nineteenth century had he not.

There were several important years which could have changed the historical trajectory of Mormonism and its associated race issues and could have created an image of the LDS Church as one leading the way to egalitarianism, not one following the headlights of other faiths. In fact, though there were some concessions to blacks, the restrictive policy remained for 126 years. Had the Church followed the direction set by Joseph Smith, the Mormon religion might have been even more progressive than the Quakers, who maintained segregation even as they famously manned posts on the Underground Railroad. Black history in early Mormonism indicates that segregation might not have been a Mormon practice. Elijah Abel, identified by census records either as mulatto or as black, was ordained to the Melchizedek priesthood by Joseph Smith himself in 1836, and received initiatory ordinances in the Kirtland Temple—the only temple rituals given at that time. Smith was possibly alluding to Abel when he said, "Go to Cincinnati or any city, and find an educated Negro, who rides in his carriage, and you will see a man who has risen by his own mind to his exalted state of respectability."[5] Elijah Abel was in Cincinnati at the time Smith said these words. Had he not left Nauvoo before the expanded temple ordinance—the endowment—was given, he likely would also have received it.

During Joseph Smith's lifetime, it was anticipated that people from all nations would gather with the Latter-day Saints, as indicated by this prediction in 1840.

> [W]e may soon expect to see flocking to this place, people from every land and from every nation; the polished European, the degraded Hottentot and the shivering Laplander; persons . . . of every tongue, and of every color; who shall with us worship the Lord of Hosts in His holy temple.[6]

Joseph Smith's evolving view of blacks and his progressive abolitionism were still developing when he was killed in 1844. At the time of his death, he was running for the presidency of the United States. His platform called for the emancipation of all slaves, with compensation for their former owners raised by the sale of public lands. It proclaimed, "Break off the shackles from the poor black man, for an hour of virtuous liberty is worth an eternity of bondage!" This sentiment echoed the revelation Smith recorded in 1833, when two black men had already been baptized into the Church: "[I]t is not right that any man should be in bondage one to another" (Doctrine and Covenants [D&C] 101:79), though the presidential platform went further in calling for the emancipation of all slaves by 1850. Even when Smith was assassinated, Mormon missionaries—including Brigham Young—were carrying his platform across the nation as part of their missionary endeavors.

With the Church founder dead, many assumed that the Latter-day Saints would leave Nauvoo and return to their previous homes. Such was not the case. With renewed fervor, the Saints completed the Nauvoo Temple and prepared for their journey west, to a more isolated locale. Though the black participants on that trek included slaves and freeborn blacks, the pioneers were all a group, and cooperated as required by the rigors of the trip. The LDS perception of races was still influenced by the times, but there was much remarkable about the unified efforts of black and white.

Their first camp was called Winter Quarters. Here, William McCary, a mixed-race, self-styled prophet who persisted in bedding white woman under the pretext of authorized polygamy, was cast out. After McCary's expulsion, the prominent Parley P. Pratt described him as ineligible for the priesthood because he carried the blood of Ham in him, paraphrasing the Pearl of Great Price, which had not yet been canonized as Mormon scripture. Brigham Young, however, assured McCary that his treatment had nothing to do with his race, and told him that skin color was not an issue to Mormons.[7] Young then alluded to the distinguished black convert in Lowell, Massachusetts, Quacko Walker Lewis, as an example of equality in Mormonism: "It has nothing to do with the blood for [of] one blood has God made all flesh," said Young. "We have one of the best Elders, an African, in Lowell."[8] This statement was made in 1847, as the pioneers prepared for the long trek, arriving in Utah later that same year. With the vanguard company were three "colored servants": Oscar Crosby, Hark Lay, and Green Flake. Their presence, and the subsequent presence of approximately sixty slaves, may have been a motivating factor in the first turning point setting the restriction. The slaves were the most valuable "property" of the Southern pioneers, and were sometimes used as tithing.

Brigham Young knew freeborn black converts Jane Manning and Isaac James, who had been married in his Nauvoo home and who were well acquainted with Joseph Smith. (Jane even claimed that Emma Smith had asked her if she would like to be adopted into the Smith family as their child, a proposition she declined—much to her later regret.) Young likely knew several African American priesthood holders as well: Elijah Abel, Quacko Walker Lewis, Joseph T. Ball, and Isaac Van Meter. None of these men was a slave, however, and none came west with the first pioneer companies. All but Elijah Abel and Q. Walker Lewis had left the Church prior to the Mormon exodus. Still, it seems odd that only two years after declaring Lewis to be "one of the best Elders," Young stated, "Because Cain cut off the lives [sic] of Abel . . . the Lord cursed Cain's seed and prohibited them from the Priesthood."[9]

The next year, 1850, brought another turning point away from Joseph Smith's antislavery direction: The California Compromise emancipated slaves in California and let New Mexico and Utah choose to be either free or slaveholding according to popular sovereignty. Utah became a slaveholding territory—though with semantic distinctions. LDS lobbyist Dr. John Bernheisel suggested that the presence of slaves in Utah would cause the federal government to deny territorial status. Brigham Young then substituted the word "service" for "slavery." His 1852 speech declaring Utah's slaveholding status was called "An Act in Relation to Service." The first Utah territorial legislature, all Mormon men and one a slaveholder, legalized "servitude." [10] (This included indentured servitude for Native Americans, whom the Mormons sometimes purchased and educated.) With passage of the act, the way was prepared for the next curve in the course, steering the trajectory directly into the priesthood restriction. Brigham Young as governor of the state made his famous speech to the territorial legislature declaring the restriction, as written verbatim by his scribe, George Watt: "If there never was a prophet or apostle of Jesus Christ [that] spoke it before, I tell you, this people that are commonly called Negroes are the children of old Cain. I know they are; I know that they cannot bear rule in the Priesthood."[11] When Wilford Woodruff summarized Young's speech, however, he added a phrase, which has survived in many if not most historical accounts: "Any man having one drop of the seed of Cain in him cannot hold the Priesthood, and if no other prophet ever spake it before, I will say it now, in the name of Jesus Christ, I know it is true, and others know it!" This version of Young's words, including the "one drop" rule may be the reason anyone with the slightest indication of African features or ancestry was denied the priesthood until President David O. McKay started making exceptions to the rule.[12]

Though Young's speech apparently set the restrictive policy, it was not canonized as a revelation from God or voted on by the body of Mormons. The fact that it came in a political speech, not in dictated scripture as Joseph Smith's words often did, made it questionable, though the questions would not be raised for another twenty-seven years. Even when Elijah Abel—whose priesthood had not been challenged—arrived in Utah and petitioned for the rest of his temple blessings, Young denied him. This denial represents the solidifying of the restriction, especially given the fact that Joseph Smith himself had ordained Abel.

Nonetheless, Mormon missionaries were called to Africa in August of that same year. Officially, the South Africa mission opened in 1853. Missionaries happily reported that there were African tribes already practicing polygamy—then a "doctrine" of the Latter-day Saints, revealed openly in 1852. (One of the first missionaries to the African continent, Jesse Haven, had self-published and distributed a tract called "The Plurality of Wives and Celestial Marriage." Haven had been declared the president of the Church [mission president] at the Cape of Good Hope.[13]) Though the missionaries met black tribes, their proselytizing was generally limited to the white population. Several white families were converted and made the long journey to Utah—at least one family bringing a black South African child (Gobo Fango) with them.

These first missionaries to South Africa were apparently aware of the Church's racial restrictions. Jesse Haven described the Malay tribe in a way that distinguished them from those of African lineage, believing the Malays to be descendants of Abraham by Hagar. He noted that their hair was straight and that they had "none of the Negro features in them."[14]

While Utah was making decisions on slavery and on the limitations for blacks in the LDS religion, the rest of the nation was moving inexorably toward the Civil War, which would also put a temporary halt to missionary labors in South Africa.

Segregation in America was not only commonly accepted but generally considered a divine order. Mormons, however, did not segregate their congregations, but there were so few blacks in Utah territory after the California Compromise (many blacks—slave and freeborn—went to California after the gold rush) that segregation would have left no religious support for black Latter-day Saints. Racial separation, therefore, came in the form of the priesthood restriction, barring all blacks from any activity requiring the priesthood, including temple worship. This was, of course, contradictory to the 1840 prophecy that even the "Hottentot" would worship with the Saints in the temple.

Many Mormons seemed unaware of global implications the restriction included, however. After the American Civil War had ended and all slaves were emancipated, the *Deseret News* published a hopeful account of Africa's future as a distant branch of Mormonism, focusing on the Congo, and suggesting that Africa was ripe for missionary work:

> Stanley the traveler has furnished the world with a complete map of the course of that mighty river, the Congo, down in Africa. A fresh field is opened to missionary labor. The benighted tribes of the wilds of Africa will not long be left without the knowledge of the world's Redeemer. . . . The emancipation of the colored race in the United States and opening up of the long hidden regions of interior Africa are indications of the workings of the Almighty towards the lifting up and final redemption of this branch of the human family.[15]

Despite this generous vision of Africa's Mormon future, the restriction was recognized by Church leaders—though it was not a fully settled issue. After Brigham Young's death in 1877, Elijah Abel petitioned new president John Taylor for his endowment. Abel's wife was dying, and he wanted to be sealed to her—married for eternity, which could happen only in LDS temples.

In retrospect, the meeting to consider his petition was one of most important about the priesthood restriction in Church history. Held in 1879, it made the possibility of reversing the priesthood restriction at least conceivable. Present were President John Taylor, his secretary John Nuttall, Abraham O. Smoot, and Zebedee Coltrin. This meeting was not to ascertain what Brigham Young had said about blacks and the priesthood (that was in the public record), but about what Joseph Smith had said.

Abraham Smoot, who had been a slaveholder himself and had served a mission in the Southern States, was sure of the instructions he had received. Smoot claimed that all missionaries in the South were forbidden to baptize slaves without the master's consent, or to ordain any slave to the priesthood. This was not surprising, since the Church position of noninterference with slavery was well known—largely because there had been a consequential misunderstanding between the Mormons and Missouri's frontiersmen when the Saints had lived there. LDS leader William Phelps had published a newspaper article called "Free People of Color," which was immediately interpreted as a call for slaves to join the Latter-day Saints. Phelps quickly recanted it, but the Mormons were nonetheless seen as a threat to Missouri's strict rules regarding blacks.

Coltrin claimed to have first-hand knowledge of Smith's position, and made more specific claims, as President Taylor's secretary recorded:

> Saturday, May 31st, 1879.
>   Coltrin recounted his argument with Brother Green [about blacks' right to the priesthood] and said that the two drove directly to the Mansion House to ask the

prophet in person. According to Coltrin, "Brother Joseph kind of dropped his head and rested it on his hand for a minute, and then said, 'Brother Zebedee is right, for the spirit of the Lord saith the Negro has no right nor cannot hold the Priesthood.'" Coltrin went on to say: "Brother [Elijah] Abel was ordained a Seventy because he had labored on the Temple, and when the Prophet Joseph learned of his lineage he was dropped from the Quorum, and another was put in his place."

Coltrin added, "I washed and anointed Elijah Abel myself in the Kirtland temple. But in doing so, while I had my hands upon his head, I never had such unpleasant feelings in my life."

There was a problem with Coltrin's claims, though. The year he purportedly had the conversation with Smith was 1834, but Coltrin himself ordained Abel a Seventy in the priesthood in 1836.[16]

Future Church president Joseph F. Smith had even stronger evidence that Coltrin's memory of the events—forty-five years in the past—was flawed. He was certain that Abel's priesthood had never been withdrawn, since he had personally seen two certificates verifying Abel's status—one issued in 1841 and another after Abel's arrival in the Salt Lake Valley. These certificates were provided by Abel himself, and the suggestion that he had been dropped from the quorum was tabled—for a time. Coltrin's memory that he had washed and anointed Abel in the Kirtland Temple was also challenged. Elijah Abel said that Coltrin had not performed the ordinance, though he had ordained Abel to the office of a Seventy—which was verified by certificate.[17]

The 1879 meeting, however, did not change the Church's racialist policy. Elijah Abel, though assured that he still held the Melchizedek priesthood, was not permitted to receive the endowment. He served his third mission for the Church in 1884, returning ill and dying two weeks later. His obituary, published in the *Deseret News*, emphasized the fact that he had been ordained to the priesthood and specified the certificates of ordination by date.

On the day of Elijah Abel's death, Jane Manning James walked to President John Taylor's house. Though the conversation she had hoped to have did not happen, she dictated a letter to the president two days later—on the day of Abel's funeral:

> Dear Brother, I cauled [sic] at your house last Thursday to have conversation with you concerning my future salvation. . . . I realize my race and color and cant expect my Endowments as others who are white. . . . God promised Abraham that in his seed all the nations of the earth should be blest & as this is the fullness of all dispensations is there no blessing for me[?][18]

This was the first of many visits Jane James would make to Church leaders. To some, she reported that Emma Smith had invited her to be sealed as a child to the Smiths and that she now wanted that sealing. Her desire was not granted; instead, she was given a peculiar alternative: She could be sealed to Joseph Smith as a servant, but not as his child. Apparently, she did not object, and the sealing ritual was carried out in the Salt Lake

Temple in 1902. Jane did not enter the temple, however; Bathsheba Smith (one of Joseph Smith's plural wives) served as her proxy. Nevertheless, Jane did not cease petitioning for what other Saints enjoyed—the complete endowment.

Yet one more possibility to revise the priesthood restriction presented itself in 1895, eleven years after Elijah Abel's death. Once more, Abel was discussed by the Quorum of Twelve. Joseph F. Smith not only disputed claims that Abel had been dropped from the quorum but added that Joseph Smith Jr. had personally ordained him, and that Abel was made a High Priest after serving as a Seventy. The information seemed to have no effect, however. Nothing changed.

Few blacks with memories including the Church's Nauvoo days were still living as the twentieth century began. Fewer than one hundred blacks were in Utah at the turn of the century, but only three had lived long enough to remember Joseph Smith and Nauvoo: Green Flake, Jane Manning James, and her brother, Isaac Lewis Manning. Flake died in 1903; Jane James died in April, 1908; Isaac Manning died three years later. Jane's death, given her long residence with the Saints, arguably had a huge impact on the Church's direction. There were editorials published around the time she died suggesting that the ancient apostles likely went to China and Africa, and stating that "No one is so black that he is not one of God's creatures."[19] But such rhetoric was not the most enduring consequence of her death. Only four months afterwards, there was another turn of the trajectory—this one favoring the restriction and further entrenching it. Joseph F. Smith, who had spoken at her funeral and who now served as president of the Church, reversed his previous, documented disagreements with Zebedee Coltrin's account. Now he stated that Joseph Smith Jr. had indeed declared Elijah Abel's ordination null and void. Smith's reversal happened in August 1908. Few if any still alive recalled the events of 1879 or had the historical knowledge to contradict Smith's new stance.

In South Africa during that same month, a native convert and a Zulu chief both expressed a desire to preach to their own people. The Quorum responded that, as the First Presidency had ruled, there should be no proselytizing among native tribes of Africa.

Thus the restriction continued, and there was at least the appearance of unity among the LDS hierarchy.

We might consider the period from 1908 forward a new era in black LDS history, one which included virtually no influential blacks from the Nauvoo era, and in which the Church's institutional memory began to revise its past according to Joseph F. Smith's own revision—that the priesthood restriction had existed from the Church's beginnings. For several decades, it was a nonissue in LDS theology. When young apostle David O. McKay made a worldwide tour in 1921, he was unaware of the policy, confronting it only when an African man in Hawaii desired temple blessings. Likewise, when LDS sociologist Lowry Nelson was asked in 1947 how difficult it would be to recognize African features in Cubans, so that missionaries could avoid ordaining them, he was stunned that the restriction existed and publicly expressed his dismay. This was also the year when the first correspondence from Nigeria arrived at Church headquarters, requesting tracts and other teaching materials. It would be over a decade (1959) before the request was granted.

Facing the nation's growing awareness of the Mormons' racialist exclusions and the global challenges to missionary work, Church president George Albert Smith's administration released the carefully worded 1949 statement, previously quoted: "It is . . . [a] direct commandment from the Lord . . . that Negroes . . . are not entitled to the priesthood at the present time."

Despite the strong words of the statement, there were quiet modifications to the policy. Under George Albert Smith's guidance, skin color or distinguishing racial characteristics were no longer disqualifiers for priesthood in the Philippines. Only verifiable descent from black Africa prevented ordination.

David Oman McKay became president of the Church of Jesus Christ of Latter-day Saints in 1951—just as the civil rights movement was gaining momentum. In that same year, Linda Brown's father sued the school board of Topeka for excluding his daughter from a nearby "white" school and forcing her to bus for an hour to her inferior "black" school. The case, *Brown v. the Board of Education*, would involve a few other black students, and would ultimately be heard by the US Supreme Court, resolved in favor of the black students—a major step in civil rights.

By the time of David O. McKay's administration, his cousin, Monroe Gunn McKay, was serving a mission in South Africa, following in his own father's footsteps. Monroe McKay's father, James Gunn McKay, had been a missionary in South Africa from 1906 to 1910, when only eight missionaries—without a mission president—served there. James McKay reported giving a blessing to a "colored" man promising that his descendants would receive the priesthood. When Monroe McKay served his mission (1950–53), there were 150 missionaries, serving under mission president Evan P. Wright. Candidates for baptism had to trace their genealogy out of Africa before they could be ordained to the priesthood—something many were loath to do, because most would encounter evidence of black ancestry. The social consequences of acknowledging such lineage were severe. A total of seventy-five people of European descent joined the Church during the span of Monroe McKay's mission, receiving baptism in the crocodile-infested lower Zambezi River. Missionaries were discouraged from preaching to blacks, and would commonly refer to neighborhoods they avoided as having been "touched with the tar brush."

By this time, missionaries had also gone into Rhodesia (1950). Monroe McKay, with companions Theron Bigler, Gale Wegglend, and DeMar Hogan, decided to dedicate Southern Rhodesia, later named Zimbabwe, to the preaching of the gospel. They dismounted their bicycles and pronounced a blessing on the country. DeMar Hogan "prophesied extensively, that shortly the Church would not only spread around Zimbabwe, but go into Northern Rhodesia, and that they would thank us for being there." Mission president Evan Wright expressed concern about the dedication because it was unauthorized. Monroe answered, "If they want to undo it, they can." Apostle James E. Faust officially dedicated Uganda, Kenya, and Zimbabwe in October

1991, and Monroe sent him a copy of the earlier dedication, with the playful note: "I see you've re-done my work." Elder Faust was not amused.

Upon his return from his mission, Monroe McKay spoke in stake conference. Spencer W. Kimball, then a young apostle, was present to hear the newly returned missionary speak about Abraham prevailing upon the Lord to change his mind. "Surely we can prevail upon the Lord to have the Church leaders change their minds and have the Prophet visit South Africa," Monroe said. Kimball met him after the meeting and confided, "I've been after him for years. You go see him and tell him what you told us. Meanwhile, I'll work on him in Salt Lake City."

Monroe went to visit his cousin, President McKay, who told him, "Monroe, I'll tell something not even my counselors know. I'm planning on going to South Africa."[20]

True to his word, President McKay flew from London to Johannesburg in 1954, where Latter-day Saints were waiting, singing "We Thank Thee O God for a Prophet." During this visit, President McKay saw the race situation first hand, and spontaneously instructed the mission president, "If they look white, give them the priesthood." These words would characterize his position until the end of his presidency:

> Why should every man be required to prove that his lineage is free from Negro strain especially when there is no evidence of his having Negro blood in his veins? I should rather, much rather, make a mistake in one case and if it be found out afterwards suspend his activity in the Priesthood than to deprive 10 worthy men of the Priesthood.[21]

President McKay came back from Africa to a nation moving relentlessly toward the full force of the civil rights movement. The priesthood restriction had taken on global significance. Within months of his return, McKay appointed a special committee of the Twelve to study the race issue. They concluded that the priesthood ban had no clear basis in scripture but that Church members were not prepared for change—a concern similar to one raised by Apostle Mark E. Petersen as to whether the government of South Africa might be offended if missionaries proselytized the Nigerian people. The debate over the restriction involved not simply facts but fears.

Fear seemed a national plague at this time, as forces for and against civil rights confronted each other. The year after President McKay's visit to South Africa, Emmett Till was murdered in Mississippi and Rosa Parks refused to surrender her seat to a white passenger in Alabama, thus initiating the Montgomery bus boycott (1955). Attention was soon to focus on the LDS Church and its past statements and current practices regarding race. The consequences of the Church's position extended beyond America. In Nigeria, where 5,000 people had independently organized themselves into ninety-seven unauthorized church units and were awaiting more material and official leadership, a Nigerian student in the United States, Ambrose Chukwu, read John Stewart's *Mormonism and the Negro*, a book replete with racist folklore. Chukwu falsely characterized it as one of the most important works in LDS theology and wrote an editorial for the March 1963 *Nigerian Outlook*, revealing the racism he had encountered.

Filling a church assignment, LaMar Williams had spent several years looking into the unofficial Mormon churches in Nigeria, and had made suggestions as to how church branches might be organized and function without their own priesthood leadership. With Chukwu's report, however, and new antidiscrimination laws in Nigeria, the Nigerian government concluded that the LDS faith was based in white superiority. No visas were granted to missionaries. There were still plans to open a mission there, but the Biafran war (1967–70) prevented further action. At the same time, potential converts in Ghana were also requesting materials and missionaries.

The immediate concerns for the LDS Church, however, were more local. In Salt Lake City, the NAACP planned to protest LDS General Conference in October 1963. University of Utah professor Sterling McMurrin was asked to meet with the group to negotiate a plan and prevent the protest. He asked the NAACP to delay its protest until the end of the Sunday morning conference session, so that the Church could make a strong, pro–civil rights statement during that session. If the statement were not made, the protest would go on as planned.

On Sunday morning, President Hugh B. Brown (counselor to David O. McKay) read the following—actually written by McMurrin:

> During recent months both in Salt Lake City and across the nation considerable interest has been expressed in the position of the Church of Jesus Christ of Latter-day Saints in the matter of civil rights. We would like it to be known that there is in this Church no doctrine, belief, or practice that is intended to deny the enjoyment of full civil rights by any person regardless of race, color, or creed.[22]

There was no protest that day by the NAACP. This did not mean, however, that there would be no protests in succeeding years against the LDS Church and its associated entities, particularly Brigham Young University. As it happened, the most effective protests would not come from political organizations but athletic ones, and even individual athletes.

On October 17, 1969, fourteen football players at the University of Wyoming went to their athletic complex wearing black armbands. They were planning on protesting Brigham Young University in the upcoming game, the armbands their symbol. Coach Lloyd Eaton summarily revoked their scholarships and dismissed them from the team. Though other teams throughout the United States had already protested BYU, the firing of the "Black Fourteen" unleashed a national fury against BYU as a symbol of the Mormon Church and its "Negro doctrine." Throughout the nation, black athletes and their supporters wore black armbands to show solidarity.

Those protestors were joined in their concern over the restriction by President Hugh B. Brown, who in that same year wrote:

> Personally I doubt if we can maintain or sustain ourselves in the position which we seem to have adopted but which has no justification as far as the scriptures are concerned so far as I know. I think we are going to have to change our decision on that. . . .

I think it is one of the most serious problems confronting us because of course it affects the millions of colored people.[23]

In Brazil, the issue was particularly troubling. The country was so racially mixed that African ancestry was not always easy to identify. Until 1965, Mormon missionaries would often look at family pictures and ask about them. If a picture showed someone with African features, the missionaries might ask, "Is that your maid?" Should the answer indicate that the person was a blood relative, the missionaries would give an extra "discussion"—which was used for the rest of the decade and into the 1970s for potential converts with obvious African features. The words were scripted:

> Anciently, it was revealed who could receive the priesthood. . . . It was also revealed who could not receive the priesthood. . . . Are you acquainted with the story of Abel and Cain? God revealed anciently that the lineage of Cain could not receive the priesthood. . . . Since the beginning of this dispensation, Joseph Smith and all of the successive presidents of the Church have taught that the Negroes . . . cannot receive the Priesthood. Now, do you know if any of your ancestors were Negro or descendants of Negroes?

In the 1960s, despite President McKay's significant modifications (eliminating restrictions for Melanesians, Fijians, and any who did not themselves manifest African features), missionaries were often still tracing family histories to identify converts who should be denied the priesthood. This likely was founded in Wilford Woodruff's addition of "one drop" to his summary of Brigham Young's words pronouncing the restriction.

President McKay, faced with contradictory mandates to take the gospel into all the world and (as he perceived it) to also restrict priesthood from those of African lineage, was praying about the issue continually, but reported not getting an answer. His cousin, Monroe McKay, who believed the restriction to be wrong, felt that the president was not asking the right question. He believed the question should involve action: "Lord, we're going to be giving them the priesthood. If you don't want it, look us up," instead of, "Lord, should we give them the priesthood?"

President McKay was hardly passive, though. He famously supported Professor Sterling McMurrin in referring to the restriction as a "policy" rather than a "doctrine"— a semantic distinction which likely emboldened Apostle Hugh B. Brown to propose a reversal of the ban. Most of the Quorum of the Twelve, those uniquely empowered to change such things, sided with President Brown and agreed to pursue a change. President McKay was incapacitated and near death at the time, giving Brown room to act. The president of the Quorum of the Twelve, Joseph Fielding Smith, was also infirm due to age, and the next most senior apostle, Harold B. Lee, was out of the country when Brown made his proposal. When Lee returned, he addressed President Brown's attempt and insisted that it not move forward. Moreover, he had all members of the Twelve sign a statement he had already drafted sustaining the status quo. Even Hugh B. Brown, though in tears when he reported his acquiescence, signed it. The statement reaffirming the restriction, released to the public on December 15, 1969, restated the Church's support for civil rights, but did not back down from banning those of African descent from all rights and privileges associated with the priesthood. It also contained language implying that the restriction was divinely mandated and had always been the Church's policy:

> [W]e believe the Negro, as well as those of other races, should have his full Constitutional privileges as a member of society. . . . However, matters of faith, conscience, and theology are not within the purview of the civil law. . . . From the beginning of this dispensation, Joseph Smith and all succeeding presidents of the Church have taught that Negroes, while spirit children of a common Father, and the progeny of our earthly parents Adam and Eve, were not yet to receive the priesthood, for reasons which we believe are known to God, but which He has not made fully known to man.[24]

The year 1969 was the final year prior to 1978 when the potential for change in the LDS Church's restriction was a real possibility. A convergence of events afterwards began momentum for the policy's reversal nine years later.

Upon David O. McKay's death in 1970, Joseph Fielding Smith, who had written prolifically in support of the "curse of Cain" premise and the long-standing speculation that those born into "Negro" bodies had earned an inferior status because of events before their births, became Church president. Despite his writings, it was under his administration that the Genesis Branch, a support group for black Mormons, was started and made an official church unit. The branch was supplementary to other LDS Church meetings. Its members gathered only monthly, but the organization included a Relief Society, a Primary, and a youth group. Genesis members were expected to receive the sacrament at their individual wards.

After Smith's death, Harold B. Lee—who had not wanted any blacks admitted to Brigham Young University—became the Church president. He died only eighteen months into his administration. Next in line was Spencer W. Kimball, a man who had spoken boldly against prejudice directed toward Native Americans. Despite his boldness in calling prejudice a "monster," he nonetheless believed that righteousness would lighten black skin, an idea founded in the Book of Mormon (2 Nephi 5:21). Kimball was a firm defender of Native Americans' dignity and rights. He was not so strongly attached to blacks. He lived with the biases of his day, but showed compassion for the few blacks he knew. He and his wife attended Genesis Group picnics, and he freely kissed the children before departing. Soon after the group was organized in 1971, he personally delivered Christmas baskets to the Genesis presidency yearly.

The Church's trajectory was finally beginning to curve toward equality. The most decisive turns, though not recognized at the time, began in 1973, when Spencer Woolley Kimball became president of the Church and *Dialogue: A Journal of Mormon Thought* published Lester Bush's seminal article "Mormonism's Negro Doctrine: An Historical Overview," which gave solid documentation for Elijah Abel's priesthood and drew the whole institutional memory into question. Was there actually a scriptural basis for the restriction? Had it been in place from the Church's beginnings? The article detailed Coltrin's claims that Elijah Abel had been "dropped from the quorum" once his race was discovered, and that Joseph Smith had personally said blacks could not hold the priesthood, and then showed the obvious gaps between these statements and actual history. More importantly, Bush documented the fact that Joseph F. Smith had provided records proving Abel's recertification to his priesthood office.

On May 25, Elder Mark E. Petersen called President Kimball's attention to "an article that proposed the priesthood policy had begun with Brigham Young, not Joseph Smith, and he suggested that the President might wish to consider this factor." The article, according to Kimball's son Edward, was almost certainly Bush's.[25] In addition (or perhaps because of the Bush article), lay Church members were resisting the policy. One (Douglas Wallace) ordained a black man to the priesthood, in defiance of policy, and was summarily excommunicated. Others, less defiant but equally troubled, wrote to President Kimball. Of particular significance was Chase Peterson, an LDS branch president in Cambridge, Massachusetts, as well as dean of admissions at Harvard, and later president of the University of Utah. Peterson and some of his counselors and branch leaders wrote to President Kimball, expressing their concern and offering possible remedies to the situation. Peterson received a direct reply from President Kimball, which thanked him for the "delightful letter" and for the suggestions.[26]

Along with spending many hours in study and prayer, Kimball asked others in the hierarchy to investigate the restriction and its history. Finally, on June 1, 1978, President Kimball assembled the First Presidency and all members of the Twelve who were able to come to the temple. On this day, President Kimball offered the prayer, asking if the Church might extend all priesthood privileges, including those pertaining to the temple, to men and women of African lineage. All in the room felt that they received revelation guiding them to reverse the 126-year-long restriction.

The change of policy was announced on June 8, 1978. The announcement, eventually voted on by the Church membership (according to accepted procedure), was canonized and placed in the Doctrine and Covenants as Official Declaration 2 (the first declaration being Wilford Woodruff's manifesto stopping polygamy). It opened the doors for black Latter-day Saints throughout the world, and lifted barriers to missionary work in Africa. Eventually, there were missions throughout the African continent, and temples built or planned not only in Johannesburg and Durban, South Africa, but in Kinshasa, Democratic Republic of Congo; Aba, Nigeria; Accra, Ghana; and Abidjan, Ivory Coast. A Missionary Training Center was soon built in Ghana. In Brazil, the São Paulo temple, which was dedicated the year of the priesthood revelation and likely influenced the timeline for the events of June 1, 1978, became the first of many in that country.

Official Declaration 2 announced that the priesthood was now available to "all worthy [LDS] males," and called it "the long-promised day," echoing statements by Brigham Young that eventually blacks would receive every blessing whites had, and President McKay's reiteration that "at some time in God's eternal plan" blacks would receive the priesthood. However, it did not address the two pillars of pseudodoctrine which had upheld the policy: the curse premise and the assumption that blacks had misbehaved in some way before their lives on Earth. Therefore, though blacks were ordained to the priesthood from 1978 forward, the philosophical progenitors which had originated the restriction were not repudiated.

Two months after the priesthood revelation was made public, Elder Bruce R. McConkie gave an important speech to all Church Education System employees. Though it was not officially endorsed, it was frequently quoted to deal with the lingering folklore surrounding the race issue. McConkie stated, "Forget everything that I have said, or what President Brigham Young or President George Q. Cannon or whomsoever has said in days past that is contrary to the present revelation. We spoke with a limited understanding."

In the first Church statement after the 2012 *Washington Post* article, McConkie's words were channeled: "The Church is not bound by speculation or opinions given with limited understanding."

Despite such bold statements, McConkie's own book *Mormon Doctrine*, which included egregious misstatements about race, was only superficially revised for its 1979 reprinting. The revision retained statements suggesting that God had a "caste system" designating blacks as a "caste apart" from whites. It remained one of the best-selling books at Church-owned Deseret Bookstore until it was allowed to go out of print in 2010. Even after its disappearance from the shelves, however, other books rife with racist assumptions remained—largely because they were written by earlier Church leaders.

At last, in 1998, it appeared that there would finally be a Church statement disavowing the philosophical underpinnings of the priesthood restriction. Larry Stammer of the *Los Angeles Times* reported on May 18 that within a month a statement could come from Church headquarters repudiating teachings linking skin color to curses from God. In fact, such a statement was being constructed, but had undergone only preliminary review. When Stammer's article came out, senior Church officials said they knew nothing of a coming disavowal. The planned statement was summarily tabled. Once again, when the trajectory toward equality in the LDS Church could have finished its arc, Official Declaration 2 was said to "speak for itself," with no further clarification. The folklore about blacks continued to be taught—to the displeasure of many—in seminaries, Sunday school classes, and BYU religion courses.

Later, Church president Gordon B. Hinckley became aware of personal consequences black Latter-day Saints were suffering because of the persistent folklore, and crafted an important speech about the race issue, delivered in April 2006 in the priesthood session of General Conference. "How can any man holding the Melchizedek priesthood arrogantly assume that he is eligible for that priesthood whereas another, who lives a righteous life but whose skin is of a different color, is ineligible?" he asked. For many, that rhetorical question, without a time frame such as "since 1978," was the closest thing to a repudiation they dared hope for.

There was more to come, however. Just over a month after the February 2012 *Washington Post* article quoted Professor Bott and then two Church statements followed,

Elder D. Todd Christofferson addressed the issue in April's General Conference. His approach was careful and subtle, but the message was unmistakable.

The talk admitted that "there had been and still persists some confusion about our doctrine and how it is established." It went on to address the LDS belief in continuing revelation, referencing Peter's experience of learning that God is no respecter of persons through a vision commanding him to eat food which had heretofore been forbidden. Peter (considered by many Mormons to be the president of the ancient Christian Church) was told, "What God hath cleansed, that call not thou common" (Acts 10:15). Elder Christofferson referred to this as an example of revelation, but said that doctrine can also be established in a council. Citing Acts 15, he told about the discussion of the law of circumcision—an issue which was not resolved among the council until after "much disputing." After Peter spoke declaring that God "put no difference between us and them," other apostles began offering support, and the council finally united in its pronouncement of doctrine.

Elder Christofferson spoke openly about the patterns of determining doctrine. In the most significant passage of his talk, he said:

> The president of the Church may announce or interpret doctrines based on revelation to him. Doctrinal exposition may also come through the combined council of the First presidency and Quorum of the Twelve Apostles. Council deliberations will often include a weighing of canonized scriptures, the teachings of Church leaders, and past practice. But in the end, just as in the New Testament church, the objective is not simply consensus among council members, but revelation from God. It is a process involving both reason and faith. . . . It should be remembered that not every statement made by a church leader, past or present, necessarily constitutes doctrine.

His emphasis on the process, which includes weighing scriptural mandates against teachings of the modern church and past practice, presented a new paradigm for some Mormons. Unity is the final result of councils, not the precondition, he explained. If it appears that past practice or past teachings are out of harmony with the scriptures (such as those Elder Christofferson chose for his examples), then there must be a change in the doctrinal exposition, involving both reason and faith. His emphasis on the fact that a Church leader's words are not necessarily doctrine further reminded his listeners that the LDS Church is dynamic and ideally self-correcting.

In a revealing story, Christofferson described Brigham Young railing against the federal government in a morning session of General Conference, then returning for the afternoon session and saying, "You heard Brigham speak this morning. Now the Lord will speak through Brigham." By acknowledging that not all words a prophet utters are divinely inspired, Christofferson provided a way to contextualize the idea that God will not allow His prophet to lead the people astray. He channeled the language of the two February 29, 2012, Church statements, reinforcing both, and paving the way for future declarations.

Progress was quick. A new preface to Official Declaration 2 (the 1978 announcement) was added and thus canonized in the Doctrine and Covenants:

> The Book of Mormon teaches that "all are alike unto God," including "black and white, bond and free, male and female" (2 Nephi 26:33). Throughout the history of the Church, people of every race and ethnicity in many countries have been baptized and have lived as faithful members of the Church. During Joseph Smith's lifetime, a few black male members of the Church were ordained to the priesthood. Early in its history, Church leaders stopped conferring the priesthood on black males of African descent. Church records offer no clear insights into the origins of this practice. Church leaders believed that a revelation from God was needed to alter this practice and prayerfully sought guidance. The revelation came to Church President Spencer W. Kimball and was affirmed to other Church leaders in the Salt Lake Temple on June 1, 1978. The revelation removed all restrictions with regard to race that once applied to the priesthood.

Though this new header was a welcome addition, it did not name the parts of the racism it condemned—including the belief in a lineage curse or in premortal performance as justification for the ban. Conceivably, a Mormon could read the header and count him/herself as not being a racist while still believing in the old folklore.

In the Church's October 2013 General Conference, Elder Dieter Uchtdorf went a step beyond where Elder Christofferson had gone in April 2012. "There have been times," he said, "when members or leaders in the Church have simply made mistakes. There may have been things said or done that were not in harmony with our values, principles or doctrine."

Many interpreted these words as alluding specifically to racist teachings of the past. Viewed in retrospect, Elder Uchtdorf's sermon likely prepared the Church for the most significant advancement in acknowledging and repudiating the untenable supports for past racialist policies.

On December 6, 2013, the "parts" of racism which some Mormons might cling to were specifically addressed. On its website (www.LDS.org), the LDS Church officially renounced the philosophical foundations of its former priesthood restriction, and contextualized the restriction within the cultural norms of the nineteenth century. Contrary to the 1949 statement declaring that the restriction had always been Church doctrine, the new statement acknowledged that it did not exist under Joseph Smith, but started under Brigham Young. It named Elijah Abel and Jane Manning James as early black members, and most important, disavowed previous justifications for the ban:

> Today, the Church disavows the theories advanced in the past that black skin is a sign of divine disfavor or curse, or that it reflects actions in a premortal life; that mixed-race marriages are a sin; or that blacks or people of any other race or ethnicity are inferior in any way to anyone else. Church leaders today unequivocally condemn all racism, past and present, in any form.

Because of Mormon growth, and events such as the 2002 Winter Olympics held in Salt Lake City, publicity over Mormon efforts to preserve traditional marriage during California's fiercely contested Proposition 8 referendum, and Mitt Romney's successive presidential campaigns in 2008 and 2012, the media have spoken of a "Mormon Moment" in American culture. To the extent that this "Moment" endures, public focus will remain on the race issue in the Church of Jesus Christ of Latter-day Saints. This focus will surface, for example, every time the curtain opens on Broadway's *The Book of Mormon*. As Elder Price sings, "I believe that in 1978 God changed his mind about black people!" the priesthood restriction is recalled. As Elder Cummings opens the Book of Mormon in Uganda, while preaching to Africans, he comes upon the passage in 2 Nephi 5: "the Lord God did cause a skin of blackness to come upon them." He quickly turns the page and talks about the cursed color being yellow. The Mormon past is easy fodder for a Broadway satire, and prominent Mormons will continue to be confronted by the race issue—often framed within some version of the question, "How can you be a member of a racist church?"

That question reduces the LDS Church to its unfortunate historical turns and assumes that the totality of the Mormon religion can be summed up and contained in the time-bound words of some past leaders.

The most important question is how Mormons will heal as a people and a community. Even after the Church's renunciation of prior support for the priesthood ban, the wounds of the restriction will likely affect Mormons for decades. Anglican Archbishop Desmond Tutu stated, "I believe we have underestimated what Apartheid did to all of us." Likewise, Mormons rarely understand the price of the restriction for all members who let their hearts be trained to accept intolerance and racial division; in the loss of all black pioneers' descendants from Church membership; in the mistreatment of many black Latter-day Saints, resulting in a "revolving door" of membership; in the disastrous self-deceptions of any who justified their prejudices by suggesting that God had approved them; even in the message of white privilege that the hierarchy presents simply by the obvious predominance of Europeans and especially Americans in its ranks.

It is sad and ironic that a church that could have had the strongest reputation in America for egalitarianism, given the hopeful signs in its beginnings, followed trajectories which led to its being perceived as racially intolerant. Though there is a growing black membership, the Mormon Church retains fewer African American converts than those of any other ethnicity. Latter-day Saint meetings in the United States are sometimes dotted with black members, though many congregations have few or none. In inner-city Atlanta, Washington, DC, Cincinnati, and St. Louis, there are many faces of color, and the leadership is predominantly black.

Obviously, all congregations in African countries, Haiti, Belize, and elsewhere are filled with black Mormons, though retention of converts varies from country to country. Worldwide, converts of African descent number approximately 700,000—332,900 in sub-Saharan Africa alone. Missionaries in the Democratic Republic of Congo (DRC) report an 80 percent retention rate of their converts, but acknowledge that cultural traditions such as a belief in sorcery and especially the exorbitant bride price (dowry) required by the government present huge stumbling blocks to Church growth. When the groom can't afford the dowry, the couple generally live together, a condition which disqualifies them for baptism. Other African countries retain fewer members than the DRC, for various reasons. Vusumzi Mpi, a branch president in Nigeria interviewed in 2011, stated that many members in his country dissociate themselves from the Church when they learn of LDS leaders' past statements on race and of the full implications the priesthood restriction entailed. Nonetheless, considering that in the 1960s there were only 300–400 Latter-day Saints of African descent worldwide, the growth of Church membership among those who were largely ignored prior to 1978 is monumental.[27]

There are other promising signs. There is more diversity in the hierarchy than there was twenty years ago—including Elder Joseph Sitati, from Kenya, and Elder Edward Dube, from Zimbabwe, in the First Quorum of the Seventy, and area authorities from other African countries and from Atlanta, Georgia. We must assume that these men represent a growing trend. Nonetheless, the future trajectory of Mormonism must include Latter-day Saints recognizing their own images in the history of racial bias, acknowledging that truth, and then moving communally and individually toward reconciliation—black with white, past with present, restriction and exclusion with the most generous horizons of hope.

Notes

1. Generally, only Mormons conflated the curse of Cain with the curse of Canaan. Other religions, however, commonly held that the "mark" which God put on Cain was black skin. In fact, the mark is never specified in scripture.
2. Provo Peace Forum, untitled flyer, February 29, 2012. Over a thousand fliers were distributed by many students at BYU, including members of the Black Student Union.
3. First Presidency Statement on the Question of Blacks within the Church, August 17, 1949, quoted in Bringhurst, *Saints, Slaves, and Blacks*, 230.
4. Woodruff, October 6, 1890. Besides being added to Official Declaration 1 in the 1981 edition of the Doctrine and Covenants, Woodford's words have been used in all LDS Church auxiliary organizations, and were repeated by Ezra Taft Benson as the fourth "fundamental" in following the Prophet ("Fourteen Fundamentals") and repeated again in two talks in General Conference, October 2010 (Costa, "Obedience to the Prophets," and Duncan, "Our Very Survival"). According to Edward Kimball (son of Spencer W. Kimball), his father was concerned about Elder Benson's talk, nervous that it might be misunderstood as something fostering a mentality of surrendering individual thought to authoritarian pronouncements (see Kimball, *Lengthen Your Stride*, 160–61).
5. Roberts, *History of the Church*, 4: 217 (January 2, 1843).
6. *Times and Seasons* 1, no. 12 (October 1840), cited in Roberts, *History of the Church*, 4: 213.
7. At Winter Quarters, Brigham Young told McCary, "We dont care about the color," and then asked those around him to voice their agreement, saying, "[D]o I hear that from all?" The question was met with a resounding, "Aye!" (see Church Historian's Office, General Church Minutes, 1839–1877, CR 100 318, Box 1, Folder 52, 26 March 1847, Church History Library, Salt Lake City, Utah).
8. Ibid.

9. Brigham Young papers, February 1849.

10. Semantics were slippery in reference to slavery or servitude. Brigham Young told Horace Greeley that there were indeed slaves in the territory and continued, "If slaves are brought here by their owners in the states, we do not favor their escape from the service of their owners" (see Greeley, *Overland Journey*, 211–12).

11. Young, "Speach by Gov. Young in Joint Session of the Legeslature. Feby. 5th 1852 giving his veiws on slavery" [*sic*].

12. Professor W. Paul Reeve (personal communication with Margaret Young, February 2, 2012) has expounded on the distinctions between Young's original speech and its summation in Wilford Woodruff's writings, concluding that the Woodruff version inserts "key words" not in the original, resulting in serious consequences, since the Woodruff version was more frequently quoted. It should be noted that there were exceptions to the rule, notably Elijah Abel's son and grandson, who were both ordained to the priesthood.

13. Wright, "History of the South African Mission," 71.

14. Ibid., 81.

15. *Deseret Weekly News*, December 5, 1877.

16. L. John Nuttall, journal; quoted in Stephens, "Life and Contributions of Zebedee Coltrin," 54–56.

17. Bush, "Mormonism's Negro Doctrine," 17, 31, 52n29.

18. Wolfinger, "Test of Faith," 148.

19. "The Colored Races," *Deseret Evening News*, March 14, 1908.

20. Monroe McKay, interview with Darius Gray and Margaret Young, June 7, 2012.

21. Minutes to a special meeting with President McKay, Jan. 17, 1954; quoted in Prince and Wright, *David O. McKay and the Rise of Modern Mormonism*, 421n77.

22. See McMurrin, "Note on the 1963 Civil Rights Statement."

23. Hugh B. Brown, quoted in Quinn, *Mormon Hierarchy*, 13–14. Brown's concern is also documented in Edwin Firmage's afterword to the memoirs of his grandfather (see Brown, *Abundant Life*, 142).

24. First Presidency Circular Letter, December 15, 1969.

25. Kimball, "Spencer W. Kimball and the Revelation on Priesthood," 54n148.

26. Peterson, *Guardian Poplar*, 150–51.

27. Stewart and Martinich, *Unfinished Task*.

BIBLIOGRAPHY

Benson, Ezra Taft. "Fourteen Fundamentals in Following the Prophet." In *1980 Devotional Speeches of the Year*, 26–30. Provo, UT: Brigham Young University Press, 1981.

Bringhurst, Newell G. *Saints, Slaves, and Blacks: The Changing Place of Black People within Mormonism*. Westport, CT: Greenwood, 1981.

Brown, Hugh B. *An Abundant Life: The Memoirs of Hugh B. Brown*. Ed. Edwin B. Firmage. 2nd ed. Midvale, UT: Signature, 1999.

Bush, Lester E., Jr. "Mormonism's Negro Doctrine: An Historical Overview." *Dialogue: A Journal of Mormon Thought* 8, no. 1 (Spring 1973): 11–68.

Chukwu, Ambrose. "They're Importing Ungodliness." *Nigerian Outlook*, March 5, 1963, 3.

"Church Statement Regarding 'Washington Post' Article on Race and the Church." *Newsroom*, February 29, 2012. http://www.mormonnewsroom.org/article/racial-remarks-in-washington-post-article.

Christofferson, D. Todd. "The Doctrine of Christ." *Ensign*, 42, no. 5 (May 2012): 86–90.

Costa, Claudio R. M. "Obedience to the Prophets." *Ensign* 40, no. 11 (November 2010): 11–13.

Duncan, Kevin R. "Our Very Survival." *Ensign* 40, no. 11 (November 2010): 34–36.

Greeley, Horace. *An Overland Journey, from New York to San Francisco, in the Summer of 1859*. New York: 1860.

Hinckley, Gordon B. "The Need for Greater Kindness." *Ensign* 36, no. 5 (May 2006): 58–61.

Horowitz, Jason. "The Genesis of a Church's Stand on Race." *Washington Post*, February 28, 2012. http://www.washingtonpost.com/politics/the-genesis-of-a-churchs-stand-on-race/2012/02/22/gIQAQZXyfR_story.html.

Kimball, Edward L. *Lengthen Your Stride: The Presidency of Spencer W. Kimball*. Salt Lake City, UT: Deseret, 2005.

Kimball, Edward L. "Spencer W. Kimball and the Revelation on Priesthood." *BYU Studies* 47, no. 2 (2008): 5–78.

McConkie, Bruce R. "All Are Alike unto God." CES Religious Educators Symposium address, August 18, 1978. http://speeches.byu.edu/index.php?act=viewitem&id=1570.

McConkie, Bruce R. *Mormon Doctrine*. 2nd ed. Salt Lake City: Bookcraft, 1966, 1979.

McMurrin, Sterling. "A Note on the 1963 Civil Rights Statement." *Dialogue: A Journal of Mormon Thought* 12, no. 2 (Summer 1979): 60–63.

Official Declaration 2 [September 30, 1978]. Doctrine and Covenants. Salt Lake City: Church of Jesus Christ of Latter-day Saints, 2013. http://www.lds.org/scriptures/dc-testament/od/2?lang=eng.

Peterson, Chase. *The Guardian Poplar: A Memoir of Deep Roots, Journey, and Rediscovery*. Salt Lake City: University of Utah Press, 2010.

Prince, Gregory A., and Willam Robert Wright. *David O. McKay and the Rise of Modern Mormonism*. Salt Lake City: University of Utah Press, 2005.

Quinn, D. Michael. *The Mormon Hierarchy: Extensions of Power*. Salt Lake City, UT: Signature, 1997.

"Race and the Church: All Are Alike Unto God." Official Statement. *Newsroom*, February 29, 2012. http://www.mormonnewsroom.org/article/race-church.

"Race and the Priesthood." December 6, 2013. https://www.lds.org/topics/race-and-the-priesthood?lang=eng.

Roberts, Brigham H. *Comprehensive History of the Church of Jesus Christ of Latter-day Saints*. Salt Lake City, UT: Church of Jesus Christ of Latter-day Saints, 1930.

Stammer, Larry B. "Mormons May Disavow Old View on Blacks." *Los Angeles Times*, May 18, 1998, A-1, 20–21.

Stephens, Calvin R. "The Life and Contributions of Zebedee Coltrin." Master's thesis, Brigham Young University, 1974.

Stewart, David G., Jr., and Matthew Martinich. *The Unfinished Task: Taking the Gospel to the Nations, International LDS Church Growth Almanac*. Henderson, NV: Cumorah Foundation, 2012.

Stewart, John J. *Mormonism and the Negro*. Orem, UT: Bookmark, 1960.

Uchtdorf, Dieter F. "Come, Join with Us." *Ensign* 43, no. 11 (November 2013): 21–24.

Wolfinger, Henry. "A Test of Faith: Jane Elizabeth James and the Origins of the Utah Black Community." In *Social Accommodation in Utah*. Ed. Clark S. Knowlton, 126–72. Salt Lake City: American West Occasional Papers, 1975.

Woodruff, Wilford. October 6, 1890. Official Declaration 1. Doctrine and Covenants. Salt Lake City: Church of Jesus Christ of Latter-day Saints, 1981.

Wright, Evan P. "A History of the South African Mission, Period I, 1852–1903." Typewritten manuscript, self-published.

Young, Brigham. Church Historian's Office, General Church Minutes, 1839–1877, CR 100 318, Box 1, Folder 52, 26 March 1847. Church History Library, Salt Lake City, Utah.

Young, Brigham. Brigham Young Papers. February 1849. Church History Library, Salt Lake City, Utah.

Young, Brigham. "Speach by Gov. Young in Joint Session of the Legeslature. Feby. 5th 1852 giving his veiws on slavery" [*sic*]. MS d 1234, Box 48, folder 3, dated February 5, 1852. LDS Church Historical Department, Salt Lake City, Utah.

CHAPTER 25

AUTHORITY AND DISSENT IN MORMONISM

ARMAND L. MAUSS

ONE of the stereotypes sometimes encountered about Mormons is their supposed sheep-like obedience to authority, or their lock-step compliance with whatever their leaders demand, whether in religion, politics, or any other realm of life. Some might therefore be surprised to learn that there is any such thing as dissent in the Church of Jesus Christ of Latter-day Saints. Actually, dissenters and potential dissenters can draw for support upon significant theological resources in the LDS heritage itself, as well as upon the Christian and American traditions more generally.[1] One of the many paradoxes in the Mormon heritage is that intellectual freedom is as fundamental a principle of the gospel as obedience, and the recurring tension between the two has been recognized by scholars and commentators both inside and outside the church. Catholic sociologist Thomas F. O'Dea, in a generally sympathetic treatment, found many dilemmas remaining in the Mormon heritage by 1950, including the "dilemma of authority and obedience versus democracy and individualism," or, at the operational level, "consent versus coercion," especially for intellectuals. More recently, LDS scholar Terryl Givens identified several historic "paradoxes" in Mormonism, including that between "authority and radical freedom," which he also saw as especially acute for intellectuals. What were "dilemmas" for O'Dea, and "paradoxes" for Givens, were called "contraries" by LDS essayist Eugene England.[2] Of course, it's all well and good for scholars to analyze dilemmas, paradoxes, and tensions as intellectual abstractions in a given religious culture, but the real significance of these becomes apparent only as we see how religious people actually assign priorities when they have to make choices between the two sides of a paradox. Historical cases can shed some light on how the Mormon Church and people have struggled with these tensions.

In the fall of 1993, six high-profile Mormon scholars and intellectuals were excommunicated or otherwise disciplined by the Church of Jesus Christ of Latter-day Saints, a fate visited as well upon several more of their colleagues during the rest of that decade. Because the six cases all occurred about the same time, they came to be called "the

September Six," but in truth they were but an especially conspicuous segment of a much larger network of young, well-educated Mormons who had been publishing and lecturing on Mormon history and culture since the 1960s—but outside the auspices or control of the church itself. Some of the topics they addressed were considered controversial and sensitive by Mormon authorities, and properly discussed only under their purview. As the intellectuals gained audiences both inside and outside the church, many leaders apparently feared a loss of control over how the religion was being understood and presented. Since the September Six episode was actually the culmination of a long process and period of tension between church leaders and intellectuals, it presents a convenient opportunity to explore the issue of authority vs. dissent in the modern Mormon Church.[3]

In the mass media, and in the minds of sympathizers of the six, this episode epitomized a church hierarchy that had become anti-intellectual, repressive, and theologically retrograde. Among the Mormon rank-and-file, there was little awareness of what issues or events had led up to the church discipline of the six, but there was a general assumption that the parties had been guilty of apostasy in some form—if not, indeed, serious sin. Mormons have always understood excommunication to be reserved only for the most egregious offenses and incorrigible offenders. Of course, there had been many cases of church discipline, including excommunications, throughout Mormon history. Also, private disagreements with the leadership have always occurred from time to time, and plenty of disaffected members simply drop out for greater or lesser periods.[4] What made these cases remarkable, however, was that the offenders were mostly intellectuals, and their offenses appeared to be some variety of heresy, an uncommon cause for disciplinary action in the Mormon tradition. The term "heresy" was not used in these cases and is, in fact, rarely found in the Mormon lexicon. The offenses were instead described by authorities in alternative terms, such as apostasy, or teaching false doctrine, or even the ambiguous "conduct unbecoming a church member." Such terms, rarely well defined, are found in the *Church Handbook of Instructions* (or simply the *Handbook*)[5] among its provisions for church discipline. This manual, in its various iterations and under various titles, has provided official guidance and policies for church leaders and members for a century. As might be expected in a burgeoning bureaucracy, the manual has become increasingly large and complex. The 2010 version consists of Book 1, which contains (among other matters) instructions on church discipline and is available only to priesthood leaders; but Book 2, on more routine matters, is available online to the general public.

Public dissent on intellectual grounds is not common in Mormon church life, and there is no special provision for it in church governance. Dissenters must thus find their own social space. They must also find their own boundaries in many respects, for the church has neither a formal theological system nor professional theologians. Its leaders are all lay persons recruited from secular occupations, and they teach "doctrines," rather than theology as generally understood. Those doctrines have undergone certain changes since the church began and are, furthermore, intertwined with a certain official historical narrative, so that doctrine is often difficult to distinguish from history.

Actually, the September Six and others could be called "dissenters" only in the sense that they had resisted admonitions from the LDS hierarchy to stop discussing publicly and in print certain doctrines and historical events that the hierarchy considered especially sensitive, embarrassing, or not open to discussion. Alternatively, they could also be considered "whistle-blowers," if only inadvertently.[6] The topics to be avoided apparently included (but were not limited to) the practice of polygamy by Mormon leaders well into the twentieth century; origins of early church racial discrimination; feminist critiques of church governance; aspects of the temple ritual; the authenticity of the official narrative of the church's beginnings; and the historicity of the foundational church scripture, the Book of Mormon. Such topics might hold endless fascination for intellectuals, but not for most members, who usually content themselves with faith-promoting stories, pastoral instruction, and apologetic discourse.

Whether or not the sheer number of disciplinary cases climaxed by the September Six was unprecedented is questionable, given the mass apostasies and excommunications during several earlier periods of Mormon history. Yet one compilation indicates that the volume of excommunications during the final decades of the twentieth century was perhaps ten times what it had been for any earlier comparable period, and "apostasy" was the charge in the great majority of those cases.[7] Since that number could well have included many who had joined schismatic groups, it's hard to know how many would have been considered dissenting intellectuals. During this same period, the church also revised its policy toward disaffected members by permitting them to formally renounce their membership by mail, rather than putting them through the excommunication process as "apostates." As official pressure from the hierarchy continued during the late twentieth century, many disillusioned intellectuals opted for that quieter exit lest they should become objects of disciplinary action later.

So what happened in the second half of the twentieth century to produce such an outbreak of dissent and disciplinary reactions to it? Such developments cannot be understood in an organizational vacuum, as though we were looking at a modern morality play and trying to distinguish the good actors from the bad ones. Each side in the confrontation can be expected to have its own narrative, with its own construction of events and its own invocation of lofty ideals. Episodes of this kind, rather, must be understood in the context of a specific organization—in this case, the LDS Church—and with a recognition of the historical forces at work within that organization. Not that individual motives and actions are irrelevant, but only that they are insufficient if we are to understand confrontations between authority and dissent as part of typical organizational experience.

The Organizational Matrix

The LDS Church is a modern, complex, bureaucratic organization with a membership as large as that of many a nation in the world. If, as Shakespeare said, "all the world's a stage," then so is each of the world's social organizations. Church leadership, from general to local, contains numerous formal roles, whose occupants might personalize or stylize them to some extent, based on their respective personalities, training, talents, and experiences—just as no two actors will play a Shakespearean role in exactly the same way—though the above-mentioned *Handbook* does impose certain constraints on the "script." Yet the players can be expected, both individually and collectively, to have motivations similar to those of other leaders in hierarchies and bureaucratic roles. There is little reason to doubt that "the Brethren" take seriously their fiduciary responsibility for the church and its members. Accordingly, when they feel that they have been publicly criticized or that there has been a public challenge to their authority or teachings, they are likely to respond with public and private reproofs, or in aggravated cases, with some sort of discipline or reprisal.[8] Such responses might sometimes seem excessive, especially to outside observers, and they often have unintended consequences. But they are responses structured, if not always required, by the roles which the priesthood leaders and bureaucrats occupy, sometimes moderated and sometimes exaggerated by the family ties, social networks, and alliances that individual apostles and other leaders bring to their callings, as well as by their personal styles, preferences, and prejudices—yet all essentially understandable.[9] Less predictable are cases in which individual apostles have asserted themselves aggressively in matters of personal importance to them, or in their own vested organizational interests, sometimes to the dismay of their more reserved colleagues.

Most organizations—and especially religions—seem to have trouble with their intellectuals, and dissenters of any kind always carry the potential for schism. The intellectuals disciplined by the church during the closing decades of the twentieth century were not schismatic by intention, nor did they represent any organized movement. Yet they were part of an informal "constituency" with a special interest in the production and consumption of sophisticated literature and commentary on LDS theology, history, or culture. That constituency has certain component networks, each with a special focus, though these networks also overlap somewhat. Some intellectuals focus mainly on apologetics; others prefer detached and critical analysis; and still others are comfortable with either mode.[10] In the specific case of the intellectuals involved in the September Six episode and the precursory unrest, most had been active and devout church members with a preference for independent and analytic studies of the Mormon experience. They had formed a network based largely in the new organizations and publications that had arisen outside church control since the mid-1960s: *Dialogue: A Journal of Mormon Thought*; the Mormon History Association (and its journal); and *Sunstone* (both the symposia and the magazine).

THE HISTORICAL BACKGROUND

Such, then, was the organizational context in which the September Six episode developed and played itself out. Yet that whole process was also contingent upon a certain history of authority and dissent in Mormonism. Although the struggle between the two had occurred frequently in the nineteenth century, especially during its founding years, the issues that were most contentious in that century have not remained very relevant to the modern Mormon experience. This chapter, therefore, focuses on the twentieth century as providing the most meaningful background for understanding the evolving relationship between authority and dissent in the contemporary LDS Church. The first question is, why did so many intellectuals of the 1960s–1990s feel entitled to continue in their controversial public lectures and writings, even as the disapproval of some leaders became apparent? Perhaps it was because they had grown to maturity in a church with an appreciation for intellectuals and their pursuits, a church that often encouraged as much education as possible, advocating "free agency," freedom of thought, and to "seek learning . . . by study and also by faith" in *all* fields of study (Doctrine and Covenants [D&C] 88:78–79, 118). The church had, in fact, produced a number of accomplished intellectuals throughout its history and had made good use of them as articulate apologists. During the nineteenth century, most of these had been talented autodidacts, but during the first half of the twentieth century, many young Mormons went outside Utah—and even abroad—for advanced education, and some of these were later enlisted in church service. Indeed, by midcentury, several of the apostles themselves had earned doctorates from respectable universities.

The LDS president at midcentury, David O. McKay, seemed to personify such broad intellectual ideals in his own career as an educator, and in his General Conference addresses that so often quoted classical literature. His counselor in the First Presidency, Hugh B. Brown, had urged students, in a 1969 devotional address at BYU, to "preserve, then, the freedom of your mind in education and in religion, and be unafraid to express your thoughts and to insist upon your right to examine every proposition. We are not so much concerned with whether your thoughts are orthodox or heterodox as we are that you shall have thoughts."[11] Even the church's own religious education system had sent some of its promising young faculty east during the 1930s for advanced academic studies in religion at (for example) the University of Chicago. Some of these, notably Lowell L. Bennion and T. Edgar Lyon, had been mentors during the 1940s and 1950s to thousands of devout and inquisitive young Mormons in the LDS Institute of Religion at the University of Utah, including many who were later to become worrisome intellectuals to certain church leaders.

Throughout the first half of the century, the church had rarely moved against its internal critics and dissenters in any formal or explicit way—unless, of course, they were involved in organizing schismatic movements (especially the various polygamous sects). Many Mormon authors writing before midcentury, either in fiction or in nonfiction, exposed some of the darker aspects of the Mormon experience, but they were not disciplined. Some felt shunned by their fellow Mormons and decided to leave Utah, and perhaps the church as well, becoming a "lost generation" of writers and intellectuals. Juanita Brooks, despite strong disapproval from both members and leaders for her candid 1950 study of the Mountain Meadows Massacre, stayed on to distinguish herself with later works. The only serious public case of the discipline of an intellectual during this period was the excommunication of Fawn McKay Brodie for a sympathetic but essentially debunking biography of Joseph Smith. A midcentury study group of faculty at the University of Utah engaged in sharply critical discussions of church doctrines, policies, and even leaders for several years, with no disciplinary action, despite the definite misgivings of some apostles. The prominent philosophy professor Sterling M. McMurrin was targeted by his stake president for excommunication in 1954 until church president David O. McKay himself offered to be a witness for the defense! Lowry Nelson, a well-known Mormon sociologist wrote letters to the First Presidency criticizing its policies toward black people and eventually attacked the church publicly in a 1952 national magazine article, all with no apparent church discipline.

By midcentury, furthermore, new and larger sociodemographic realities were also emerging in the Mormon world with eventual consequences for the intellectual environment. During the 1940s and 1950s, a large contingent of youthful Mormon military veterans, mostly male, returned from two major wars entitled to financial support for higher education through the so-called GI Bill. Encouraged also by a Mormon culture that valued education and upward mobility, this age cohort was the first to achieve college and graduate education in large numbers. Often the education was obtained outside the traditional Mormon homeland, which contributed to the dispersion of this youthful population to other parts of the country. All of this education and travel produced a generation of young Mormons that was, on the whole, more comfortable in the outside world, and more sophisticated intellectually, than earlier generations had been. From their numbers also came a new scholarly interest in Mormonism—and much of the later dissent, as well.[12]

It was against this background, then, that a group of young Mormon intellectuals felt free in 1965 to establish *Dialogue: A Journal of Mormon Thought*, "an independent quarterly . . . to express Mormon culture and to examine the relevance of religion to secular life." A journal with a similar purpose, *BYU Studies*, had been publishing since late 1959, but its scope and content seemed limited by its church auspices, so *Dialogue* was considered the first truly independent journal of its kind. During the same year, the Mormon History Association held its inaugural meeting in San Francisco under the leadership of Leonard J. Arrington and several colleagues in the history department at Utah State University. And why not? Mormon scripture had always urged that the Saints should "be anxiously engaged in a good cause, and do many things of their own free will, and bring to pass much righteousness" (D&C 58:27–28).[13] A few years later, in 1972, Arrington became the first professional academic to be made the official Church Historian, with the backing of some prominent apostles. This development seemed to signal a degree of appreciation in high places for endeavors of a more critical and intellectual kind in Mormon religious life, rather than only the traditional apologetic and devotional kind.[14]

Not surprisingly, independent publications and forums then began to proliferate outside church control, including *Sunstone* magazine in 1974, the annual Sunstone Symposium in 1979, and eventually other venues devoted to academic and intellectual studies of the Mormon experience—all included in what Arrington once called "the unsponsored sector" of Mormon discourse and publication. True to their independent auspices, these journals began to air issues that were of deep concern to Mormons (like others) of the 1960s and 1970s, including racism in church policy; women's roles, especially outside the home; the church and war; and the origin and historicity of the Mormon scriptural canon. These were also, of course, issues considered very sensitive by Mormon leaders, especially the more conservative ones, who became alarmed at their apparent loss of control over the discussion of such issues among church members. A few leaders voiced support for these new publications and forums, and for the good intentions of their authors, but it was soon apparent that they did not represent the leadership consensus. The strongly conservative reaction of the leadership more generally cannot be understood without reference to a fundamental reorientation of the church that occurred during the second half of the century.

DISSENT IN A PERIOD
OF ECCLESIASTICAL RETRENCHMENT

Quite independently of relationships between church leaders and intellectuals, and certainly unbeknownst to the latter, the LDS Church during the 1960s was entering a period of organizational and ideological tightening that might be called a "retrenchment." This process, which continued and intensified until the end of the century, has been analyzed in some detail elsewhere.[15] It began as a new generation of leaders came to power with growing concerns that Mormonism might have paid too high a price for the national assimilation and respectability that it had achieved during the first half of the century. No such rationale was explicitly offered for the retrenchment process, but it seems in retrospect to have been launched in reaction to threats perceived from both external and internal sources. Externally, the church had been watching with alarm the rising national influence of a youth-driven culture that normalized, and increasingly legitimized, a liberated and hedonistic lifestyle and threatened to undermine the family. Internally, the rapid growth and dispersion of the church membership was straining the minimal bureaucratic structure developed in an earlier age to manage the organization.

As if in response to all these developments, a retrenchment program was inaugurated during the 1960s, starting with "correlation," a reorganization and coordination of the bureaucracy, which became the vehicle for giving the hierarchy a fuller and more centralized control over all other aspects of the retrenchment. There were three chief features of "correlation." (1) All the operations of the church, including its major auxiliary organizations and their teaching materials and curricula, were brought directly under the control of the apostles and the presidency. (2) The second echelon of top church leadership, the Seventy, was expanded from an obsolescent group of seven presidents (but no members) to several quorums of Seventy. The first two quorums of Seventy, in particular, were charged with assisting the apostles in the administrative reach of the priesthood worldwide into all aspects of ecclesiastical life, even down to the local level. (3) A large professional bureaucracy, a civil service, as it were, was created and interposed between the general membership and these "general authorities" of the priesthood.

Besides this organizational proliferation, and greatly facilitated by it, came an ideological retrenchment that sought to recover some of the unique aspects of the LDS religion and way of life that the apostles felt had been lost, or had fallen into disuse, during the assimilation of Mormonism earlier in the century. A political aspect of the retrenchment was a turn to the right in national politics and a willingness to intervene more strenuously in certain political campaigns over issues that the leaders regarded as fundamentally moral in nature. Political involvements of the church were nothing new in Mormon history, but during most of the twentieth century those involvements had taken the form mostly of pronouncements over the pulpit and tactical interventions through elected Mormon politicians, rather than expensive, wholesale campaigns. Furthermore, the Saints had not shown a strong penchant for following their leaders in political matters. The first flexing of this new political muscle was a successful campaign against ratification of the Equal Rights Amendment (ERA) passed by Congress in 1972, which the church leaders regarded as a threat to the traditional family. A minority of LDS women, especially outside Utah, were openly critical of the church's heavy-handed and somewhat surreptitious opposition to the ERA. A few either left the church or were excommunicated, including Sonia Johnson, a national figure among the critics.

The LDS campaign against the ERA provoked the first important outbreak of dissent to that point in the century. Some of it was organized (e.g., Mormons for ERA), but much of it was expressed in *Sunstone* (both the magazine and the symposia), in *Dialogue*, and in the newly created *Exponent II*, a moderately feminist tabloid started by Mormon women in the Boston area. Increasingly the church leaders kept a wary eye on any members, especially intellectuals, who advocated feminist theology or ideals contrary to the traditional Mormon patriarchal prescriptions for women's roles. Increasingly in pulpit discourse, especially in General Conferences, church members began to hear appeals for obedience, supported by scriptures and slogans from the nineteenth century—such as "obedience is the first law of heaven"—and calls to "follow the Prophet," who will "never lead the church astray;" and "whatever [the prophets] speak shall be the word of the Lord [and] the voice of the Lord."[16]

Intellectuals were especially distressed in witnessing what happened to Leonard J. Arrington, the new Church Historian, as he and his "new Mormon history" project came under fire from conservative apostles. Although Arrington had been installed by the First Presidency in 1972, a turnover in the leadership of the church by 1974 had created a new and more conservative political constellation among the leaders. The new president of the church, Spencer W. Kimball, remained a supporter and ally of Arrington, but he was often in poor health during his term, and the new president of the Quorum of the Twelve, Ezra Taft Benson, was well known for his especially vigorous and conservative religious and political apologetics.[17] Benson, backed by a group of like-minded apostles, became a consistent critic of the scholarly (as contrasted with devotional) historical publications produced by Arrington and his colleagues and led a successful campaign to oust them from the Church Historical Department.[18]

Throughout the 1980s, the apostolic campaign became much more vigorous and public against authors of unauthorized publications on controversial and sensitive issues. Examples of this campaign, at least from the viewpoints of the targeted individuals, are provided at some length elsewhere.[19] As the decade began, two of the more conservative apostles, Elders Benson and McConkie, each delivered a long, no-nonsense address at BYU obviously intended for the benefit of intellectuals (including BYU faculty) inclined to comment on religious doctrines and policies. Benson's included injunctions to follow the *living* prophet (as contrasted with deceased predecessors) in all things (religious *and* secular); McConkie's listed "seven deadly heresies" to avoid, including the theory of organic evolution. The next year, Elder Packer delivered an address to the church education faculty insisting that LDS history must be taught with due recognition of the hand of deity in all matters, in contrast to a strictly academic or "objective" narrative.

At BYU, history professor D. Michael Quinn, in a lecture to a student group, critiqued Packer's views, much to the detriment of his own future career. Indeed, all BYU faculty were soon reminded that as employees of the church they were expected to use special discretion in their public speaking and writing, and were put on notice that they should not resort to unsponsored venues such as *Dialogue* and *Sunstone* for their publications and lectures. Several BYU professors, who had been active in speaking and writing publicly about church history and policies, began to encounter difficulties with their continued employment, which was eventually terminated or they were pressured to leave for other academic positions.

Other episodes receiving considerable publicity included a rather dramatic personal campaign by Elder Mark E. Petersen, one of the most conservative apostles, to single out more than a dozen intellectuals in different states during 1983 and require their local leaders (usually stake presidents) to summon them for interviews about their attitudes toward the church. Most were active members of the church, including one or two bishops! Then, in 1984, a new and candid biography of Emma Smith (one not very flattering to her husband, the Prophet) resulted in an apostolic order to all the bishops and stake presidents in the Salt Lake City area that the two female authors of this biography were not to be allowed to speak publicly in any church meeting. In the same year, Quinn's stake president was ordered to revoke his temple privileges over a long article he had published in *Dialogue* demonstrating that polygamy had persisted, with the approval of church leaders, well into the twentieth century. Finally, in 1990, several intellectuals and others, including the then editor of *Dialogue* and former bishop F. Ross Peterson, were called in by church authorities and threatened with a revocation of temple privileges for having made comments (all favorable) to inquiring news reporters about recent changes in Mormon temple rituals (Peterson succeeded in getting his discipline reversed through intervention by influential church friends and leaders).

Relationships between authorities and intellectuals were further exacerbated by three challenges to the hierarchy that did not come from any pesky intellectuals. The first was the discovery in 1985 of the nefarious and murderous career of forger Mark Hofmann, who had sold the church archives a number of fraudulent documents supposedly casting doubt on certain key aspects of the official Mormon historical narrative. In the process, he had deceived not only the president of the church and several other leaders, but more tellingly, the entire Mormon scholarly establishment, including most independent intellectuals. Gloating media commentators wondered what kind of "prophets, seers, and revelators" could be so easily deceived by a clever forger. The second challenge was the 1989 apostasy and excommunication of George P. Lee of the Seventy, a Navajo protégé of the late President Spencer W. Kimball. Lee protested the dismantling of the special educational programs in the church for Native Americans (considered "Lamanites") and rejected the right of the apostles to do so. The third was from an organized, fundamentalist schismatic group calling itself the True and Living Church (TLC), which accused the LDS Church of having fallen away from its original purity. The TLC had a strongly millennial survivalist feature and proved very disruptive to the LDS communities in central Utah, necessitating the issuance by Mormon leaders of a series of "danger signs" to warn the faithful against such superconservative schisms. Ultimately, dozens of TLC dissidents were excommunicated.

As the 1990s arrived, several talks by church leaders, in General Conferences and elsewhere, were warning members about turning to "alternate voices" or unspecified "symposia" for information about the church, which many in the intellectual constituency took to be a warning against participating in the very venues and publications in which their network had always been based. It became clear also that disciplinary action of various kinds, which supposedly originated at the local stake or ward level, was now being instigated on orders from the hierarchy itself. The apostolic reach into local disciplinary proceedings was greatly enhanced by the formation, in 1992, of the Committee to Strengthen Church Members (a wonderfully Orwellian name!). This committee of staff, operating under the supervision of two apostles, was charged with browsing the publications and forums in which intellectuals frequently appeared and identifying statements about church leaders, policies, or doctrines that might provide grounds for mandatory interviews with stake presidents.[20] The stage was thus well set for the 1993 drama of what came to be known as the September Six. Clearly it was not a sudden ambush but the climax of at least two decades of increasing efforts by the LDS hierarchy to constrain a restive network of critical intellectuals.

FROM RETRENCHMENT TO RAPPROCHEMENT AND CO-OPTATION

As the century ended, the confrontations between dissent and authority in the church seemed to have largely run their course.[21] Almost no incidents occurred during the first decade of the twenty-first century, and there were no indications that others might be on the horizon. Several reasons help to explain this new calm after the storm. No doubt the excommunications of the 1990s made clearer the boundaries of acceptable dissent for any who wanted to retain church membership, and gave many other intellectuals an incentive simply to resign their membership preemptively. On the leadership side, probably the most important reason was the ascendancy of a new series of church presidents with somewhat more tolerance for dissent, and with a more inclusive disposition toward intellectuals and others not fitting the conventional LDS mold. By 1994, the conservative senior apostles who had led the church into retrenchment had nearly all passed from the scene, and the new First Presidency was led by Howard W. Hunter (1994–95).

The first president to have been born in the twentieth century, Hunter had been an early proponent of Arrington's abortive 1972 project to professionalize the writing of Mormon history. In ill health even as he took the helm, he was soon succeeded by Gordon B. Hinckley (1995–2008) and then by Thomas S. Monson. All of these presidents seem to have shared a more conciliatory posture toward inside dissenters as well as toward outside critics. President Hinckley, in particular, also had a keen understanding of the benefits of engaging the mass media in an effort to influence the Mormon public image, and he greatly increased both the professional strength of LDS Public Affairs and its role in representing the interests of the church to the outside world. A new and more proactive public relations effort was directed at taking greater control of the public portrayal of Mormons and their religion, both by staying ahead of the news cycle and by seeking access to interviews and columns in the media—an effort, it would seem, to co-opt the image-making process to some degree.

Not that the church was abandoning its political interventions on issues it regarded as crucial. By the turn of the new century, the church was already intervening overtly in political contests in various states, especially California, over same-sex marriage, a practice it regarded as potentially destructive to the entire institution of marriage throughout society, but especially to that institution as understood in Mormon doctrine. The most controversial examples of intervention occurred in the California campaigns over Proposition 22 (2000) and Proposition 8 (2008), in which LDS members were importuned by their leaders to contribute substantially both in time and in money. Little effort was made to hide the church's political efforts, which were eventually successful, but at the cost of great hostility, and some retaliation, on the parts of gay rights advocates and sympathizers.

The LDS membership seems generally to have supported both church campaigns, but there was a conspicuous minority of dissenters, some of whom went very public with their misgivings about church involvement in these cases (especially Proposition 8). Some even resigned their church membership over the matter. Yet the contrast with the LDS political campaign against the ERA in the 1970s was clear: in the 2000 and 2008 campaigns, the church insisted that all forms of support were entirely voluntary, and dissenters were to be left alone. One group of dissenters even set up a website (www.mormonsformarriage.org) opposing Proposition 8 (but *not* the church's political intervention). There were reports of various kinds of pressures and sanctions against such dissent in some wards and stakes, usually of an informal kind, but not as general church policy, and no reports of church discipline (if there was any) came to public attention. Certain other political issues (including immigration policies) also arose early in the new century, in which some prominent Mormons found themselves at odds with the political positions of the church, but with no particular consequences.

If the new century has brought seemingly greater tolerance for internal reluctance to join in some of the church's political campaigns, members are still expected to refrain from public lobbying and political campaigns of their own aimed at changing church policies or teachings. This was made clear from two cases in 2014 that attracted considerable public attention. Both involved members who had publicly cultivated organizations and followers in opposition to certain church restrictions based on gender or sexual preference. Both were strenuously admonished, and one was very publicly excommunicated in June of that year, apparently for crossing the line from personal advocacy to political organizing and pressuring.[22] All such efforts by the LDS Church in maintaining discipline and the boundaries of orthodoxy have costs of their own, of course, a reality not lost on church leaders. At the end of 2011, the Church Historian himself remarked on an almost unprecedented exodus from the church of members who had been disaffected in recent years. This disaffection has apparently been driven not only by recent conflicts over political differences (internal and external), but also by growing doubts, even among the most faithful, about some of the fundamental truth claims of the religion itself. Such doubts are perhaps an inevitable consequence of discoveries, both on the Internet and in newly available church documents themselves, of episodes, practices, and doctrines in early Mormon history that some members find discrediting.[23]

As though in response to some of the doubts and political controversies among potential dissenters, the church has begun to show a new appreciation for the work of scholars and intellectuals, including many who are independent of church control and occasionally critical. Rather than publicly sanctioning or complaining about the latter, the church attempts to respond in scholarly terms, or even to co-opt the subject, as it did, for example, when it commissioned three of its best scholars to write a two-volume work, the first of them published by Oxford University Press, in response to earlier controversial accounts of the tragic Mountain Meadows Massacre. Meanwhile, books and articles that had brought church discipline for their authors in the 1980s are now recognized with equanimity by many of today's leaders as part of a fuller and more accurate account of the Mormon story, rather than as a threat to the integrity of that story. New studies of polygamy (including polyandry) in early Mormonism, of race relations in the LDS experience, controversial new biographies of church presidents, and many other books and articles independently published by LDS intellectuals, which might once have resulted in church discipline, were published in the new century with complete impunity. Indeed, the opening of a new church library and archives, which itself symbolized a new outreach to the world's scholars, was the occasion for the following remarkable statement on the LDS *Newsroom* site:

> The Church cannot undertake [the writing of its history] on its own. It requires a groundswell of countless individuals—from within and without the

Church—operating on their own personal inspiration. The story of the Church will inevitably be told as historians of good faith are given access to the library's records and archives. . . . It is in the interests of the Church to play a constructive role in advancing the cathartic powers of honest and accurate history. In doing so, the Church strives to be relevant to contemporary audiences that operate under changing cultural assumptions and expectations. A careful, yet bold presentation of Church history, which delves into the contextual subtleties and nuances characteristic of serious historical writing, has become increasingly important. If a religion cannot explain its history, it cannot explain itself.[24]

This is clearly an invitation to all comers acting "in good faith" to participate in the study of the Mormon past—no more warnings about "alternate voices." Looking even at the present, indeed, the church has also enlisted all willing members, including independent intellectuals, to join in a new conversation about the Mormon world. In effect, all willing church members have been urged to act individually in penetrating the new world of electronic media on both church-sponsored sites and numerous independent websites and blog sites which the church cannot hope to control or even monitor through the Committee to Strengthen Church Members, or by any other practical means.[25] It is as though the church leaders have recognized a certain inevitability about their loss of control over how the church is discussed on these sites and has decided that its interests are better served by maintaining a constructive relationship with them than by trying to curtail them.

This means that unfriendly websites must be tolerated, of course, but it has also opened the way for a plethora of sites (sometimes called the "Mormon Bloggernacle") where independent intellectuals and others can express themselves, in either devotional or critical terms—anonymously if necessary—with little concern about reprisals from church authorities.[26] Since a large number of informed and thoughtful Mormons have established these sites, and/or have been more or less regular contributors, they have constituted a new dimension of the "unsponsored sector" in Mormon studies. This development, in effect, has co-opted and contained much of the motivation that internal critics and dissenters once had for controversial public commentary on Mormon history and culture. As the new century opened, the church welcomed the appearance of new courses in Mormon Studies taught by regular faculty at various colleges and universities, and actually lent moral support to the establishment of academic chairs in Mormon Studies at Utah State University, the Claremont Graduate University in southern California, and the University of Virginia. All of these academic developments have occurred outside church control and without any church initiative. A new era in the relationship between the church's authorities and its intellectuals seems to have arrived with the new century. Dissenters, whether intellectuals or others, now have a great variety of venues in which to offer critiques about all matters Mormon, but the church response has become more tolerant and more sophisticated.

CONCLUDING REFLECTIONS: AUTHORITY AND DISSENT IN MODERN MORMONISM

Any effort at a succinct statement of the relation between authority and dissent in contemporary Mormonism would perforce be an oversimplification. However, the brief historical overview offered here suggests some important inferences, very few of which derive from the *Handbook* or from any other formal documents or provisions. As in most complex organizations, *informal* traditions and expectations can loom at least as large as the formal provisions in an actual operative sense. In any case, historical developments in Mormon history during recent decades suggest the following *inferences*:

(1) The LDS Church has a highly centralized and bureaucratized structure led by a priesthood hierarchy. One need not gainsay its claims to divine guidance, or the conscientious fiduciary intentions of its office-holders, in order to recognize that it operates in the classical pattern of other large bureaucracies, including:

    (a) a preference for predictability through the use of rationalistic and legalistic procedures allowing for as few exceptions to routine as possible;

    (b) individual and collective behavior predicated upon well-established roles and responsibilities, stylized and customized only somewhat by personal traits, preferences, and external influences;

    (c) the maintenance of "social distance" between leaders and members (the more so the higher the leaders' ranks) in order to mitigate the influence of personal, emotional considerations in decision making (including disciplinary proceedings);

    (d) the greater the rank and power of individuals in the leadership, the greater their social and political "capital," and thus the greater their freedom to assert personal prerogatives outside of the leadership consensus and the collective decision-making process (as a few apostles did during the 1980s).

(2) The confrontations between dissenting intellectuals and church leaders after the midcentury, and the church's continuing involvement in certain controversial political issues, have left certain unresolved questions surrounding the future of dissent and dissenters in the Mormon world. To the extent that the *Handbook* provides the formal and official operating procedures in the church, there are no provisions for any of the traditional democratic procedures such as lobbying, protesting, or elections of leaders, as there are in the American Protestant bodies—and even in the Community of Christ (formerly the Reorganized Church of Jesus Christ of Latter Day Saints), which has drawn on a much earlier Mormon tradition of "common consent" to move, both in doctrine and in polity, closer to the conventional Protestant model. In the mainstream Mormon model, however, there remains no provision for "dissent" or

"dissenters." There are provisions only for offenses such as apostasy, teaching false doctrine, acting contrary to the order of the church, behavior unbecoming church members, and the like. There is much ambiguity in such provisions, but it is a *functional* ambiguity, since it gives priesthood leaders, local and general, the flexibility to deal with individual cases in ways that seem the most appropriate under the prevailing circumstances. It might also, however, leave dissenters and potential dissenters in jeopardy of discovering the boundaries only in the breach thereof, for in operational terms, those boundaries turn out to be wherever the general authorities say that they are at any given point in time.

(3) Members of the church who are inclined to question, dissent from, or even criticize church doctrines, policies, or leaders are unlikely to experience any formal discipline or other sanctions as long as they express themselves privately or among small groups of friends. However, once they take their concerns to public forums, publications, or the mass media, their jeopardy of church discipline greatly increases, the more so under the following conditions:

(a) Leaders believe the church to be under significant threat from internal or external influences subversive to the central teachings and mission of the church.

(b) Church policies respond to such threats in reactive ways (e.g., retrenchment) more than in proactive ways (e.g., engagement with critics in the mass media and in academia, as in the new century).

(c) General authorities of the church decide to reach into local stakes to initiate discipline or admonitions to specific dissenters.

(d) An individual general authority with high rank, political capital, and an especially assertive disposition takes a personal interest in a situation or in an individual case of dissent.

(e) Dissenters or critics use imperative or prescriptive language advocating change, rather than detached and analytical observations about certain church teachings or policies and their likely empirical consequences (i.e., "counseling the Brethren").

(f) Dissenters or critics persist in publicly airing their concerns after having been admonished by leaders, especially if they attempt to mobilize followings for lobbying and public pressure on leaders to change policies or doctrines.

(g) Dissenters or critics express themselves in arrogant, angry, or disrespectful terms.

(4) Whenever a public confrontation develops between a dissenter or critic and church leaders, a cost-benefit calculation can be expected to occur on both sides.

(a) The leaders will have to consider the likely outcomes (favorable or unfavorable), for the individual and for the church, of proceeding with discipline or other sanctions. In a large and impersonal bureaucracy, considerations are not likely to include the feelings of individuals or their families and friends, but they might include the social and political capital of powerful intercessors (as in the midcentury case of Sterling McMurrin and the 1990 case of Ross Peterson).[27]

(b) The dissenters in question, especially after having been admonished to desist, will have to assess what kinds and how much social and political capital they have available in the form of protective friends in high places, and/or what they have earned through their own records of faithful service. They will also have to consider how to prioritize their personal values in the given situation: To what will they give first place? Their personal intellectual autonomy? Their fundamental spiritual commitments ("personal testimonies" in the Mormon argot)? Their loyalty to the church as an institution? Family ties and tranquility?

Ever since midcentury, many Mormon intellectuals have felt strongly about questions of race, gender, and politics in the LDS Church, as well as about the authenticity of official church accounts of key historic events. Each such person has faced a difficult cost-benefit calculation based on his or her own constellation of basic values. During the period of "retrenchment," many of these quietly left the church, formally or informally, and still others stayed on, continuing their often edgy writing and lecturing in the face of official frowns, and perhaps discipline. In some cases, they were excommunicated, often at great personal cost socially and emotionally, or even in lost careers if they were church employees. Even though probably most intellectuals, whatever their feelings on the pressing issues, stayed on with faith and hope in the eventual resolution of their misgivings, it is those who departed that will be remembered as another "lost generation" of Mormon scholars and intellectuals.

NOTES

1. For example, the Book of Mormon teaches that God's children are "free forever, knowing good from evil; to act for themselves and not to be acted upon" (2 Nephi 2:26); and the LDS scripture Doctrine and Covenants 58:28 declares that "the power is in [mortals], wherein they are agents unto themselves. And inasmuch as (they) do good, they shall in nowise lose their reward." Doctrine and Covenants 121:37 also warns leaders against the use of the priesthood for gratifying pride or vain ambition, "or to exercise control or dominion or compulsion upon the souls of [people] in any degree of unrighteousness." To the extent that any leader attempts to misuse the priesthood in that way, "the Spirit of the Lord is grieved; and when it is withdrawn, Amen to the priesthood or the authority of that man."

2. O'Dea, *Mormons*, 222–23, 242–45; Givens, *People of Paradox*, 3–19; and England, *Why the Church Is as True as the Gospel*, 4, 14.

3. Experiences of some of the dissenters disciplined during this period are discussed from their own perspectives in Lindholm, *Latter-day Dissent*. See accounts also in Anderson, "LDS Intellectual Community and Church Leadership"; and in Givens, *People of Paradox*, 213–27.

In this chapter, I have not included any discussion of dissent at the church's Brigham Young University, which has been periodic throughout its history. While often related to issues elsewhere in the LDS Church, dissent at BYU (as at other universities) has also occurred within the context of issues specific to the campus and to academic culture. Student dissent, furthermore, especially at BYU, has always faced the special constraints of an administrative environment *in loco parentis*. See Bergera and Priddis, *Brigham Young University,* for references to dissent at BYU in the early and middle twentieth century; and Waterman and Kagel, *Lord's University*, for a study of dissent later in the century (including the years surrounding the September Six).

4. Levi S. Peterson has offered some charitable and constructive (if unorthodox) advice to LDS members who find themselves in various forms and degrees of dissent from official church strictures. See his "The Art of Dissent among the Mormons," *Sunstone*, February 1994, 33–39.

5. From 1968 the title was *General Handbook of Instructions*. Since 1998, it has been called the *Church Handbook of Instructions*, or simply *Handbook*.

6. On the roles and importance of the disaffected members of religious communities, including dissenters and whistle-blowers, see Bromley, *Politics of Religious Apostasy*.

7. Bergera, "Transgressions in the LDS Community," 123–25.

8. Social scientists have been studying the typical characteristics of bureaucracies for at least a century, and among their recurrent findings is the tendency for governing elites to use their decision-making power at times in the interest of protecting their own positions and careers. See, e.g., Gerth and Mills, *From Max Weber*; and Michels, *Political Parties*.

9. The reasoning and terminology here come from the study of organizations in mainstream sociology and social psychology. See, e. g., Peter M. Blau, *Exchange of Power in Social Life*; and Cialdini and Trost, "Social Influence, Social Norms, Conformity, and Compliance."

10. Robert M. Emerson, "Exchange Theory, Part 2"; and Cook, "Network Structures from an Exchange Perspective."

11. Brown, "Eternal Quest—Freedom of the Mind."

12. This cohort and its significance in Mormon intellectual life is discussed in Walker, Whittaker, and Allen, *Mormon History*, chap. 3; Arrington, *Adventures of a Church Historian*, chap. 4; and in Mauss, *Shifting Borders and a Tattered Passport*, various chapters.

13. Doctrine and Covenants 58:27–28.

14. Arrington, *Adventures of a Church Historian*, chapter 5.

15. Mauss, *Angel and the Beehive*.

16. This process is akin to what Walter van Beek calls "creeping infallibility" in his "Infallibility Trap."

17. For two decades from the early 1970s to the early 1990s, Elder Benson was either president of the Quorum of the Twelve Apostles or president of the church itself, and he led an apostolic movement that greatly intensified the retrenchment program already underway, especially where scholars and intellectuals were concerned. Even as he became feeble toward the end of his administration, the efforts to control LDS intellectuals and their products were continued under his aegis by other conservative apostles.

18. Arrington, *Adventures of a Church Historian*, chap. 10; and Bitton, "Ten Years in Camelot."

19. Anderson, "The LDS Intellectual Community and Church Leadership"; and Givens, *People of Paradox*, 213–27.

20. Givens, *People of Paradox*, 226; and "First Presidency Cites Scriptural Mandate for Church Committee," *Church News*, August 22, 1992, 7.

21. This section is taken from a much more thorough treatment of the retrenchment reversal in Mauss, "Rethinking Retrenchment."

22. Peggy Fletcher Stack, "Founder of Mormon Women's Group Threatened with Excommunication," *Salt Lake Tribune*, June 11, 2014, http://www.sltrib.com/sltrib/news/58056757-78/church-women-mormon-lds.html; Stack, "The Mormon Question Now: Who Might Be Next?" *Salt Lake Tribune*, June 12, 2014, http://www.sltrib.com/sltrib/news/58062791-78/church-lds-kelly-women.html.csp; and Stack, "Dehlin's Mormon Leader Delays Meeting to Await 'De-escalation,'" *Salt Lake Tribune*, June 16, 2014, http://www.sltrib.com/sltrib/news/58068437-78/dehlin-kelly-disciplinary-lds.html.

23. For a more recent recognition, even by church leaders, of large-scale defections in the modern Mormon ranks, see Peter Henderson and Kristina Cook, "Special report: Mormonism Besieged by the Modern Age," *Reuters*, January 30, 2012, http://uk.reuters.com/article/2012/01/30/uk-mormonchurch-idUKTRE80T1CP20120130; and Peggy Fletcher Stack, "Mormons Tackling Tough Questions in Their History," *Salt Lake Tribune*, February 3, 2012, http://www.sltrib.com/sltrib/news/53408134-78/church-lds-mormon-faith.html.csp.

24. "'A Record Kept': Constructing Collective Memory," *Newsroom*, June 11, 2009, http://newsroom.lds.org/article/a-record-kept-constructing-collective-memory. As though implementing the principles laid down in this policy statement, the church began, in late 2013, to publish, on its official website (http://www.lds.org/topics), a series of essays on difficult and sensitive historical issues. These treatments were both more transparent and better informed by scholarship than the superficial versions that had appeared there earlier. New topics included Book of Mormon and DNA Studies; Book of Mormon Translation; First Vision Accounts; Plural Marriage and Families in Early Utah; and Race and Religion. More were scheduled to follow. A note at the bottom of each new essay acknowledges the contributions of scholars in its preparation. See Peggy Fletcher Stack, "Abraham to Blacks to Brigham: Mormon Essays Confront Tough Questions," *Salt Lake Tribune*, August 8, 2014, http://www.sltrib.com/sltrib/blogsfaithblog/58183736-180/church-essay-lds-tribune.html.csp.

25. The official LDS website for outreach to non-Mormons is www.mormon.org; but Mormons are now encouraged to enter into conversations about their religion on any websites available, lest they abdicate to others the right to define Mormonism and its public image. See, e.g., Ballard, "Sharing the Gospel Using the Internet."

26. To see just how extensive this Bloggernacle is, go to the Mormon Archipelago at http://www.ldsblogs.org.

27. By the turn of the new century, heightened official concern over unnecessary and unwanted public criticism of the church's treatment of intellectuals might have brought some unsolicited and unexpected "political capital" also in support of Elbert E. Peck (1996–99) and Thomas W. Murphy (2002), both of whom were threatened repeatedly by their stake presidents with church discipline, but which ultimately was called off seemingly by the intervention of higher church authorities. See Gary James Bergera, "'Only Our Hearts Know'—Part 2: Sunstone During the Elbert Peck Years, 1993–2001," *Sunstone*, July 1993, 27–28; Elbert Eugene Peck, "Thinking Is a Social Act," *Sunstone*, June 2014, 33; and John W. Kennedy, "Mormon Scholar Under Fire," *Christianity Today*, March 1, 2003, http://www.christianitytoday.com/ct/2003/march/14.24.html?start=1.

BIBLIOGRAPHY

Anderson, Lavina Fielding. "The LDS Intellectual Community and Church Leadership: A Contemporary Chronology." *Dialogue: A Journal of Mormon Thought* 26, no. 1 (Spring 1993): 7–64.

Arrington, Leonard J. *Adventures of a Church Historian*. Urbana: University of Illinois Press, 1998.

Ballard, M. Russell. "Sharing the Gospel Using the Internet." *Ensign* 38, no. 7 (July 2008): 58–63. http://lds.org/ensign/2008/07/sharing-the-gospel-using-the-internet?lang=eng.

Benson, Ezra Taft. "Fourteen Fundamentals in Following the Prophet." *Liahona*, June 1981. BYU address, February 26, 1980.

Bergera, Gary James. "Transgressions in the LDS Community: The Cases of Albert Carrington, Richard R. Lyman, and Joseph F. Smith, Part 1." *Journal of Mormon History* 37, no. 3 (Summer 2011): 119–61.

Bergera, Gary James, and Ronald Priddis. *Brigham Young University: A House of Faith*. Salt Lake City: Signature, 1985.

Bitton, Davis. "Ten Years in Camelot: A Personal Memoir." *Dialogue: A Journal of Mormon Thought* 16, no. 3 (Autumn 1983): 9–33.

Blakely, Thomas A. "The Swearing Elders: The First Generation of Mormon Intellectuals." *Sunstone* (December 1985).

Blau, Peter M. *Exchange and Power in Social Life*. New Brunswick, NJ: Transaction, 1986.

Bradford, Mary L. "The Odyssey of Sonia Johnson." *Dialogue: A Journal of Mormon Thought* 14, no. 2 (Summer 1981): 14–47.

Bradley, Martha Sonntag. *Pedestals and Podiums: Utah Women, Religious Authority, and Equal Rights*. Salt Lake City: Signature, 2005.

Bringhurst, Newell G. *Fawn McKay Brodie: A Biographer's Life*. Norman: University of Oklahoma Press, 2003.

Bromley, David G., ed. *The Politics of Religious Apostasy: The Role of Apostates in the Transformation of Religious Movements*. Westport, CT: Praeger, 1998.

Brown, Hugh B. "Eternal Quest—Freedom of the Mind." *Dialogue: A Journal of Mormon Thought* 17, no. 1 (Spring 1984): 77–83.

Bush, Lester E., Jr. "Excommunication and Church Courts: A Note from the *General Handbook of Instructions*." *Dialogue: A Journal of Mormon Thought* 14, no. 2 (Summer 1981): 74–98.

Bush, Lester E., Jr. "Excommunication: Church Courts in Mormon History." *Sunstone* (July–August 1983).

Church of Jesus Christ of Latter-day Saints. *Church Handbook of Instructions*. Books 1 and 2. Salt Lake City: Intellectual Reserve, 2010.

Cialdini, Robert B., and Melanie R. Trost. "Social Influence, Social Norms, Conformity, and Compliance." In *The Handbook of Social Psychology*. 4th ed., ed. D. T. Gilbert, S. T. Fiske, and G. Lindzey, 2:151–92. New York: McGraw-Hill, 1998.

Cook, Karen S. "Network Structures from an Exchange Perspective." In *Social Structure and Network Analysis*, ed. Peter V. Marsden and Nan Lin, 177–99. Beverly Hills, CA: Sage, 1982.

Emerson, Robert M. "Exchange Theory, Part 2: Exchange Relations and Networks." In *Sociological Theories in Progress*, ed. J. Berger, M. Zeldich, and B. Anderson, 2:61–83. Boston: Houghton-Mifflin, 1972.

England, Eugene. *Why the Church Is as True as the Gospel*. Salt Lake City: Bookcraft, 1986.

Geary, Edward A. "Mormondom's Lost Generation: The Novelists of the 1940s." *BYU Studies* 18, no. 1 (Fall 1977): 89–98.

Gerth, Hans, and C. Wright Mills, eds. *From Max Weber*. New York: Oxford University Press, 1947.

Givens, Terryl L. *People of Paradox: A History of Mormon Culture*. New York: Oxford University Press, 2007.

Johns, Becky. "The Manti Mormons: The Rise of the Latest Mormon Church." *Sunstone* (June 1996).

Johnson, Sonia. *From Housewife to Heretic*. Garden City, NY: Doubleday, 1981.

"The Lee Letters." *Sunstone* (August 1989).

Lindholm, Philip. *Latter-day Dissent: At the Crossroads of Intellectual Inquiry and Ecclesiastical Authority*. Salt Lake City: Greg Kofford, 2010.

Mauss, Armand L. "Alternate Voices: The Calling and Its Implications." *Sunstone* (April, 1990).

Mauss, Armand L. *The Angel and the Beehive: The Mormon Struggle with Assimilation*. Urbana: University of Illinois Press, 1994.

Mauss, Armand L. "Authority, Agency, and Ambiguity: The Elusive Boundaries of Required Obedience to Priesthood Leaders." *Sunstone*, March 1996.

Mauss, Armand L. "Rethinking Retrenchment: Course Corrections in the Ongoing Campaign for Respectability." *Dialogue: A Journal of Mormon Thought* 44, no. 4 (Winter 2011): 1–42.

Mauss, Armand L. *Shifting Borders and a Tattered Passport: Intellectual Journeys of a Mormon Academic*. Salt Lake City: University of Utah Press, 2012.

McConkie, Bruce R. "The Seven Deadly Heresies." BYU Address, June 1, 1980. http://speeches.byu.edu/reader/reader.php?id=6770&x=50&y=6.

McMurrin, Sterling M., and L. Jackson Newell. *Matters of Conscience: Conversations with Sterling M. McMurrin*. Salt Lake City: Signature, 1996.

Michels, Robert. *Political Parties*. Chicago: Dover, 1962. (Originally published 1911.)

Nelson, Lowry. "Mormons and the Negro." *The Nation*, May 24, 1952.

Newsroom. "'A Record Kept': Constructing Collective Memory." *Newsroom*, June 11, 2009. http://newsroom.lds.org/article/a-record-kept-constructing-collective-memory.

Peterson, Levi S. *Juanita Brooks, Mormon Woman Historian*. Salt Lake City: University of Utah Press, 1996.

Peterson, Levi S. *Juanita Brooks as a Mormon Dissenter*. Salt Lake City: Signature, 2002.

Oaks, Dallin H. "Alternate Voices." *Ensign* 29, no. 5 (May 1989). http://www.lds.org/ensign/1989/05/alternate-voices?lang=eng.

O'Dea, Thomas F. *The Mormons*. Chicago: University of Chicago Press, 1957.

Packer, Boyd K. "The Mantle is Far, Far Greater than the Intellect." *BYU Studies* 21, no. 3 (Summer 1981): 259–78.

Quinn, D. Michael. "On Being a Mormon Historian (and Its Aftermath)." In *Faithful History*, ed. George D. Smith, 69–111. Salt Lake City: Signature, 1992.

Quinn, D. Michael. "Plural Marriage and Mormon Fundamentalism." *Dialogue: A Journal of Mormon Thought* 31, no.2 (1998): 1–68.

Sillitoe, Linda, and Allen D. Roberts. *Salamander: The Story of the Mormon Forgery Murders*. Salt Lake City: Signature, 1990.

Turley, Richard E. *Victims: The LDS Church and the Mark Hofmann Case*. Urbana: University of Illinois Press, 1992.

Van Wagoner, Richard S. *Mormon Polygamy: A History*. Salt Lake City: Signature, 1986, especially chapters 17–19.

Van Beek, Walter E. A. "The Infallibility Trap: The Sacralisation of Religious Authority." *International Journal of Mormon Studies* 4 (2011): 14–44.

Walker, Ronald W., David J. Whittaker, and James B. Allen, eds. *Mormon History*. Urbana: University of Illinois Press, 2001.

Waterman, Bryan, and Brian Kagel. *The Lord's University: Freedom and Authority at BYU*. Salt Lake City: Signature, 1998.

CHAPTER 26

....

MORMONISM AND MEDIA

....

JOHN DURHAM PETERS

Mormonism as a Media Religion

....

MEDIA should be understood not only as the channels and institutions that propagate messages and symbols, but also as elemental techniques that organize time, space, and power. This view of media, developed by Canadian scholars such as Harold Adams Innis (1894–1952) and Marshall McLuhan (1911–1980) and more recently by German-speaking media theorists and historians, has proven enormously fruitful for understanding the constitutive role media play in religious traditions. All religions feature media of various sorts and the "book religions" of Judaism, Christianity, and Islam make attitudes toward media into central items of religious vision and practice. Many of the Ten Commandments concern media, for instance, in setting out the proper naming of deity, a ban on pictures of the divine, the calendar of worship (including the Sabbath), and the proper bearing of testimony. All three of the ethical monotheisms hallow certain writings (through canons of scripture), places (through pilgrimage in space), and events (through pilgrimage in time or remembrance), and make abundant metaphoric use of notions of communication in portraying the work of angels and preaching. The Jewish notion of the Torah as a universe complete unto itself, the Christian notion of the Gospel as the good news of the Word made flesh, and the Muslim notion of the Qur'an as a divine dictation renewed in every oral recitation have all stimulated a vast wealth of practice and reflection within each tradition on the question of how meanings are made from media.

Mormonism's history is rich with media in both the traditional and expanded sense of the term. Thanks to their mission to preach the gospel to all the world, Latter-day Saints have long been active and creative builders of media institutions such as publishing, broadcasting, film, visitor's centers, and now the Internet. But Mormonism is hardly unique in having well-developed theories and practices for getting the word out. Visions of a technically enabled utopian religious and political community have shaped the religious imagination throughout the entire new world. Many American Protestants couched their mission in the language of an expanding kingdom of God whose mystic chords of communication would knit everyone together into a beloved community. Evangelicals were central players in the development of new forms of oral and print communication in nineteenth-century America, and the Bible has a fascinating publishing history in the same era, including Mormon experiments.[1] Nonetheless, there are special factors in Mormon media history that deserve attention, especially its striking rebound from nineteenth-century vilification to a prominent presence in politics, sports, popular culture, and journalism in the United States and elsewhere today. The stunning shift in media images of Mormons from Victorian villains to viable presidential candidates is the result of concerted and informal public-relations campaigns, of a long history of communication aimed at reaching and shaping the public mind.

Mormons, then, have always used media to send and shape their message. But media have also played a deeper, less practical, more transcendental role in Mormon history, doctrine, and culture. Mormonism, as a religion whose culture was forged in the westward expansion of the North American continent and whose media-friendly theology spans heaven and earth, has always treated the symbolic management of space, time, and human relationships as absolutely central to its experience. Mormons have used media not only as channels for outreach, but also as things to think with. Both will be treated in what follows.

Publishing and Privacy

Like the three great monotheisms of Judaism, Christianity, and Islam, Mormonism is a book religion, and takes its name from its central book. The Church of Jesus Christ of Latter-day Saints began with an act of publishing, and continued ever since to be actively involved in print media both for internal and external constituencies. The Book of Mormon was even quickly circulated in pirated excerpts, an honor that has befallen most major texts in the past several centuries. Without the diverse media of printing press, oratory, word of mouth, evangelizing travel on foot, horseback, or boat, early Mormonism is entirely unthinkable. The early history of the church is in large part its publishing history—not simply because newspapers such as the *Millennial Star* or *Times and Seasons* are such precious sources for historians, but because they themselves were chief actors in the drama of evangelization, coordination between scattered members and headquarters, and creation of a distinctive culture. The church has always been an active media proprietor to this day.

In all media history, imagination and concrete practice always go together, and it is no different in the Mormon case. Mormonism began as a revelation, with the heavens reopened by divine messengers to church founder Joseph Smith in 1820, and the movement's language about its mission has always mixed, in a way impossible to distinguish, the two registers of religious revelation and print publication. The Book of Mormon is exceedingly self-conscious about its quality as a book, constantly and self-consciously signposting the intricacies of its textual construction and authorship. Its narrative of the "marvelous work and a wonder" that the book enables is completely recursive, the book's publication itself being a significant part of its message. The Book of Mormon offers a theology of scripture—the words that God gives to peoples are definitive of their identity as groups, and the flowing together of people in the gathering of Israel is simultaneously the flowing together of scriptures into a super canon (2 Nephi 29). But the Book of Mormon is also constantly on edge about the dangers of publication. A significant portion of the text is "sealed," that is, held back from the eyes of the world. In chiaroscuro language about the light and darkness of open and hidden books (for example, Alma 37, Ether 4) that recalls the rhetoric of the Enlightenment, the Book of Mormon makes it clear that both concealment and revelation can have dire consequences. The Urim and Thummim, seer stones used by Joseph Smith to translate and see into the heavens (which uncannily resemble some of today's smart phones), are dangerous media if they fall into unauthorized hands.

Put more broadly, Mormon media history is marked by a fundamental tension between publication and exposure. From the beginning, Mormonism was a new revelation and a new concealment. The Book of Mormon was a publication to all the world, but its source, the golden plates, was hidden from public inspection. Even as Joseph Smith called his followers to canvass the earth and bring the news of the restored gospel to "every creature," he also developed strong esoteric practices and cultures of secrecy, culminating in the systematic obscuring of the practice of polygamy in Nauvoo. (Once settled in the Rockies the church was completely open about the practice, sending Orson Pratt in 1852 to Washington, DC, to represent the church, where he characteristically published a newspaper, *The Seer*, which has since proved to be a goldmine for critics seeking the more extravagant ideas of nineteenth-century Mormonism).

Mormonism has always been marked by the tension—expressed in different ways in different eras and contexts—between its double face of aggressive publicity (about its message) and aggressive privacy (about the temple, finances, historical archives, even demographic data). Confidentiality and guarded circulation of information are even part of the everyday functioning of Mormon congregations; those who have accepted callings (assignments to serve) are not supposed to tell anyone until they are properly presented for "sustaining" before the entire congregation. The attitude that some things are sacred and off-limits to discussion is a key part of Mormon culture, and its appreciation for the powers of secrecy has sometimes brought it into conflict with the self-image of America as the land where liberty is measured by a willingness to speak freely about any subject. The sanctioned destruction in 1844 of the printing press of the *Nauvoo Expositor*, a newspaper that had criticized Joseph Smith, is the most poignant symbol of this conflict, and sparked the chain of events that led to his assassination. Some of Smith's enemies saw themselves as defenders of openness against tyranny and secrecy; he saw himself as a guardian of divine treasures.

Some of Mormonism's central documents self-consciously stage a drama of counteracting negative press. The first sentence of Joseph Smith's canonical life narrative is a rectification of bad publicity: "Owing to the many reports which have been put into circulation by evil-disposed and designing persons . . . I have been induced to write this history, to disabuse the public mind, and put all inquirers after truth in possession of the facts." In the rough-and-tumble culture of frontier journalism, Smith suffered from a lot of black ink, the *Warsaw Signal* being a particular thorn in his side during his final years. Not that he couldn't dish it out: his complaint about "the whole concatenation of diabolical rascality and nefarious and murderous impositions that have been practiced upon this people" in his 1838 letter from Liberty Jail shows that he could sling purple prose with the best of them. This passage comes in a call for church leaders to document the abuses they suffered, so that it can be published "to all the world," which will then stand "without excuse." For Smith, such publication would do nothing less than call forth the Lord from his hiding place. Publishing was never simply a matter of ink, paper, and press: it played a central role in God's plan for the world in the latter days.

The theme of responding, sometimes preemptively, to criticism or persecution runs throughout Mormonism's history. The Manifesto or Official Declaration 1 that officially ended polygamy in 1890 (though the practice was not decisively proscribed until 1904) begins with a crisis of media management. "Press dispatches having been sent for political purposes, from Salt Lake City, which have been widely published. . . ." The Manifesto is explicit about its status as a media message intervening in the public sphere, and of course it marks the point at which Mormons began to take over the institutions that had once given them so much grief—the Victorian family, American nationalism, entrepreneurial capitalism, and the Republican Party.

The mentality of being in a fish-bowl watched by an approving or critical world has been a structuring element in Mormon media and culture since it embarked on a program of assimilation instead of isolation around the turn of the twentieth century. As in many minority cultures, Mormons treasure and remember commentary, especially laudatory, from prominent outsiders, and carry around a reflexive awareness of the gaze of friends or foes. The doctrinal centrality of Jesus Christ has never been in doubt, for instance, but the conspicuous Christocentrism of Mormon self-presentation since the 1970s, even down to its revised logo in 1995, seems a response to evangelical criticism, and has shifted ordinary language and worship among Latter-day Saints themselves. A sense of the gaze of outsiders continues to shape everyday Mormon discourse in church settings, where teaching and discussion in Sunday school, for instance, will often slant toward the orthodox middle lest tender minds be shaken. (This reflex goes very deep. Recently I attended church in Beijing, China, where government policy bans proselytizing and the mixing of non-Chinese and Chinese members. Nonetheless, the man conducting the meeting dutifully explained the meaning of fast Sunday "to those who might not be familiar with it.") As a rule, media cannot be used to shape the perceptions of outsiders without also altering the perceptions of insiders.

The key figure for leading the church into audiovisual media production for purposes of missionary work and image building was surely Gordon B. Hinckley, apostle since 1960 and church president from 1995 to his death in 2008, though some of the impetus can be traced to his mission president and mentor, John A. Widtsoe, who, as an apostle overseeing Europe in the late 1920s and 1930s, longed for more effective outreach materials. There are volumes to be written on Mormon media production and reception—mainstream, alternative, and oppositional, from early muckrakers such as Obadiah Dogberry up through the church's entry into the digital world of what Benjamin Peters calls "open-source Mormonism." A history of post-Manifesto public relations, from the Tabernacle Choir's coming-out performance at the Columbia World Exposition in Chicago in 1893 to the recent "I'm a Mormon" campaign, would show that media messages are never only symbolic flotsam designed to change attitudes or build good will; they are among the key means of building cultures and identities.

THE LOGISTICAL IMAGINATION

Joseph Smith was unquestionably one of American history's great creators of symbols, visions, and practices. He has often been seen as the impractical visionary to Brigham Young's practical organizer, but he clearly was intensely interested in experimenting with and inventing new modes of familial, ecclesiastical, governmental, and social organization, as Richard Bushman has demonstrated.[2] Both Smith and Young can be seen as communications innovators. The entire religion turned on a reestablishment of communication between heaven and earth, God and angels again in touch with men and women. It restored possibilities of communion long lost from the earth. And, in its central historical narrative of the trek and settlement of the Mountain West up though the culture's still remarkable organizational discipline, Mormonism has heavily invested in media as modes of social organization. Social and political forms are themselves key media of communication.

Smith and Young possessed considerable managerial skill at coordinating far-flung global enterprises. From the beginning, Mormonism was figured as a global communications and transportation network; it has always existed as a web uniting distant points. It was born global. When the witnesses to the Book of Mormon directed their testimony to "all nations, kindreds, tongues, and people," they were not only invoking an old biblical formula; they were announcing a program. The longest continuously existing congregation in the church is not found in Utah, but in Preston, England (since 1836); the population (and publishing) center of the church around 1850 was Liverpool, England; Mormons have been in New York City continuously since 1831; there were Mormons in Hawaii and San Francisco before there were in Salt Lake City; and by the late 1830s, missionaries were spanning the globe, especially but not only Europe, as marked by apostle Orson Hyde's famous dedication of the land of Palestine for the return of the Jews in 1841 (a memorial park marks this event today on the hillside of the Mount of Olives). Today, there are more members outside the United States than inside, and Spanish may soon become the majority language of the church's members. Mormon centers have always been connected to distant outposts, and an interesting history could be written of the flows of people, goods, and practices between distant points. Even in its moment of later nineteenth-century mountain retreat, Mormon organization maintained a network character. This "wealth of networks" persists today in the relatively rich "social capital" possessed by Latter-day Saints.

Print media, organizational innovation, and a culture that produced burning devotion were all essential for the establishment of the "kingdom of God in the latter days." The settlement of the Rockies involved elements that Harold Innis emphasized in media history, such as organizational will, "monopolies of knowledge," and the fur trade. Indeed, Canadian fur traders Étienne Provost and Peter Skene Ogden, the first Europeans to explore the Wasatch Front around 1824–25 and whose names adorn two of its main cities, brought Utah into the continental network that Innis studied in his history of the fur trade. Utah's early European history linked it with the Hudson Bay and with the Pacific Northwest, networks spanning the continent.

William Cronon has wonderfully shown the role that Chicago played as an Innis-like control point for a vast territory of staples and goods, the "Great West" as he calls it, but one might see Nauvoo, Chicago's erstwhile rival in the 1840s, as an alternative point of remote control for the Mormon settlement of the American West.[3] As Nauvoo was emptied of its majority Mormon population by 1846, this influence remained spectral, a bit in the way that a traffic accident, even when cleared, will continue to alter traffic patterns for hours afterwards; St. Louis, Missouri, and Iowa City, Iowa (in the 1850s), were also important points of embarkation for the trek west. Salt Lake City itself was the hub of a city-based empire that directed the traffic in the kingdom of Deseret, as Brigham Young sent colonizers to remote spots of Utah, Idaho, Nevada, California, and Colorado. As "the crossroads of the west," Salt Lake City has always seen itself as—and always has been—a transnational spot, the central point of the international gathering prophesied by Isaiah, whose words are immortalized on the "This is the Place Monument," a key memorial medium marking space and time in the Salt Lake Valley: "all nations shall flow unto it" (Isaiah 2:2). Demographically, that prediction is quite correct. There is a Zionism of sacred and secular space in Mormondom, and an increasing culture of memory and pilgrimage connected with sites important to its history.

Fred Turner has noted that the western frontier historically has fostered innovations in time, space, and social organization. The frontier takes novelty as self-legitimation; as the famous line goes, Utah's sky was so vast that even God could be reinvented there. Brigham Young built and rebuilt networks, both global and within Deseret, designed infrastructures of all sorts, and with his social, economic, and familial experimentation, fostered "collaboratories" for the invention of new practices and visions. Polygamy and communal economic production were clear modes of community invention. Joseph Smith had a bureaucratically baroque imagination (for example, in his vision of priesthood quorums consisting of 12, 24, 48, and 96 members), and Brigham Young had a logistical genius for motivating and building a political-economic empire. The church's culture continues to be bureaucratically baroque, abounding in meetings, committees, councils, quorums, societies, wards, branches, stakes, districts, areas, regions, and so forth, although the most recent trend is toward simplification and streamlining. "Organizational creativity" has long been a mark of the church's culture and hierarchy.[4] The core of its organizational life is the productive but sometimes painful tension between hierarchy and *Gemeinschaft*, a top-down ecclesiastical structure coexisting with local bonds of kin and kind.

The center of Young's infrastructure was the temple, the symbolic center and basis of the grid on which the valley was laid out. "The grid is the geometry of empire"[5] and most addresses in the Salt Lake valley continue to pay homage to the temple's location. Not simply the binding point of heaven and earth, the temple was also the point from which power emanated to the surrounding territory, a space-binding and time-binding medium for both earth and heaven. Deseret was what Mormon scholar Hugh Nibley calls a hierocentric state.

On the temple block was the Tabernacle (preceded by the Bowery), the central site of oratory and indoctrination. A team of secretaries recorded the sermons there in shorthand, published (first in Liverpool in the early 1850s) as the *Journal of Discourses* (whose more recent digitization is a great boon for critics of the church who seek nuggets of doctrinal weirdness that long had lain dormant in the printed edition). The *Journal of Discourses* thus depended on an oral-textual transmission link. There is a Mormon history of secretaries and dictations. There are very few documents in Joseph Smith's own hand, and his use of secretaries started with the translation of the Book of Mormon. Today there is a reliable text for very few of Joseph Smith's sermons, and one of his most important, the King Follett address, exists in four variants. The difficulty of taking dictation encouraged experimentation with an entirely new script, the Deseret alphabet, Mormonism's contribution to many quirky exhibits in the annals of English spelling reform. This effort to provide a purely phonetic English was also motivated by the Babel of tongues among the international influx of immigrants in the kingdom of Deseret who were trying to learn English. Everything could be made over again—the family, the polity, the economy, even the system of writing.

Though it might not seem like an obvious medium of communication, Brigham Young's control of water was also a key part of his centralized management of infrastructure. Without irrigation, no Salt Lake City. So-called "hydraulic societies" are not found only in ancient China and Egypt, but also throughout the American West, where water remains the single most politicized commodity. Water control and social power go together, and Brigham Young had his finger on the key flows that governed the kingdom of Deseret—whether economic, hydraulic, sexual, or spiritual. As the prophet and secular leader, he possessed a "monopoly of knowledge" in the most classic sense, but he encouraged his people to find spiritual truth for themselves. The blend of centralized prophetic command and individualist study-it-out-in-your-own-mind autonomy continues to shape Mormon infrastructures of association and belief.

THE AMPLIFIED AND MUTED VOICE

The voice has always been a fascinating topic for religious thinkers, and the field of acoustics itself has a long history as an effort to hear and amplify the word of God. Mormonism has its own dramas of the voice, as the Deseret alphabet already suggests.

Joseph Smith's First Vision in 1820 started with an episode in which he found his tongue bound "so that I could not speak." Throughout Joseph Smith's career as an orator, a tension of proclamation and muteness prevailed. Early on, Smith appointed Sidney Rigdon to speak for him, like Aaron for Moses. The classic ordeal of prophetic stammering, the voice seeking to outshout the wind, to be heard amid the competition of nature and culture, is a central theme of his King Follett sermon, his last significant speech before his death in 1844. The theological daring of the sermon is nicely complemented by the physical drama of its delivery to a large crowd in a grove of trees by the Mississippi River in Nauvoo, the wind threatening to carry away his voice from his people, as his assassination was soon to do with his presence. The King Follett discourse can be read as the founding drama of Mormon broadcasting, with Smith's voice and the wind engaging in a contest of amplification, physical speech and eternal truth trying briefly to come together.

The Tabernacle on Temple Square in Salt Lake City was designed with an acoustic precision—still proudly demonstrated by tour guides today—to carry the voice and sound of prophetic utterance.[6] It would be interesting to know how much the work of a distinguished string of LDS acoustic scientists was inspired by the project of designing an architectural space for the gospel's voice to go forth: Harvey Fletcher, Vern O. Knudsen, Carl Eyring, and S. S. Stevens. (Philo Farnsworth, one of several inventors of television, was another Mormon media engineer.) The Tabernacle, like the more recent Conference Center, was a place for the voice to emanate into all nations. Since the 1920s, the Tabernacle was retrofitted as a broadcast studio, and the Conference Center was designed from the beginning as a major production facility. Weekly broadcasts of the Tabernacle Choir, ongoing since 1929, are a hallmark of Mormon vocal investments, and the semiannual General Conferences are carried on an infrastructure of satellites installed in the 1980s and via Internet and cable television. There is a subtle theology of voice and assembly that undergirds General Conference, not to mention a distinctive and minimalist audiovisual rhetoric, such as the glacially slow zoom on speakers and the lush sonic warmth of the Tabernacle Choir. As a rough generalization, the level of Mormon musical culture is higher than of Mormon visual culture. Despite "a goodly portion of painters and artists," image and illustration in church publications are often quite mediocre.[7] Sound certainly has a much more resonant religious backing than image in Mormon theology.

MORMON MEDIA THEOLOGY

Technologies, even the most practical of things, exist within a vaster set of assumptions and expectations. Each new technology offers a new journey into an imagined future or past. In American social and religious thought, technologies and particularly telecommunications have been central to speculations about human nature and the social order, and Mormon thought is rife with commentary on media and visions of possible forms of life. Space-spanning media have inspired theological speculations that reveal many characteristic themes of Mormon thought: building the kingdom of God, empire, continuing revelation, the perfection of the future state, and the family relationship between God and human beings. Telecommunications were a semidivine means of propagating the kingdom of God in space and time. Again, the theology of media is rarely separate from on-the-ground media practice in Mormonism, which was always a practical religion and rarely given to systematic theology.

In *On Liberty* (1859), John Stuart Mill made a passing comment on Mormonism: "Much might be said on the unexpected and instructive fact that an alleged new revelation, and a religion founded on it, the product of palpable imposture, not even supported by the *prestige* of the extraordinary qualities in its founder, is believed by hundreds of thousands, and has been made the foundation of a society, in the age of newspapers, railways, and the electric telegraph."[8] For Mill the time was out of joint: Mormonism was an anachronism "in the age of newspapers, railways, and the electric telegraph." From their inception, such media have been hailed as signs of modernity, the peculiar mark of an irrevocable difference from the past. But Mormonism, like many other religious movements, saw itself not as opposed to the spirit of the age, but as working with it, and more emphatically, it believed that newspapers and telegraphs were quite amenable to religious uses. (The railroad cut a scarier figure in Utah history, breaking apart its mountain isolation in 1869 and bringing into Zion "outside" influences, a geographical notion of vague cultural threat that persists to this day on the Wasatch Front.) The telegraph did not oppose revelation: many religious Americans saw it as a form of revelation, a particularly novel kind.[9] And new mass media in their day were often popularly received in cultural categories of ancient pedigree. Mormonism is not unique among conservative religions in quickly adapting modern communication devices to its own purposes. Its exceptional, utopian, geographically remote status made railroads, telegraphs and satellites, and other forms of action at a distance of particular interest; and its distinctive theological and cosmological imagination, of a materialist vintage, makes such issues especially salient.

Two key strains in Mormon media theology deserve note: the idea that the holy spirit is a material substance, and the belief in divine records. The first will be treated at greater length here, but the second is perhaps more profound.

A long line of Mormon thinkers has been excited by physical metaphors for the workings of the holy spirit, which Joseph Smith taught is material. Two key figures are the apostles brothers Parley Parker Pratt and Orson Pratt, who speculated on universal spiritual communications, accelerated bodiless travel, and expedited acquisition of knowledge. Their thinking about communication deserves a fuller treatment and, indeed, Mormon cosmology in general is full of interesting material for historians of communication thought.

Parley Pratt's 1853 sermon "Spiritual Communication" takes stock of the recent explosion of spiritualism.[10] The principle that the dead can speak to the living is a true one that is compatible with Mormon philosophy, he argues, noting several key revelations to Joseph Smith from figures once dead (such as John the Baptist, Peter, James, and John, or Jesus himself). But as there are many spirits of the dead, and some are idle or mischievous, wicked or adulterous, many spiritualist manifestations are not to be trusted. Communication with the dead should be governed through proper channels for proper purposes: belief in Jesus is one check, priesthood is another. Very much in the tradition of Doctrine and Covenants (D&C) 50 and 1 Corinthians 14, Pratt makes reason and common sense the criteria for judging the worth of spiritual phenomena and disciplining them to fit in overall rational patterns. Here is the characteristic Mormon mix of charismatic and bureaucratic authority. (Max Weber has been all but irresistible to Mormon intellectuals at least since the 1930s, when Mormon sociologist, thinker, and humanitarian Lowell L. Bennion was the first American to write on Weber.)

Orson Pratt's speculations on the "Medium of Communication in the Future State" (1854) draw on Mormon sources, such as D&C 88 and Moses 1, and on gnostic traditions of postbody cognitive improvements. Like Moses gazing on the vast workmanship of God's hands, Pratt feels overwhelmed by "the immensity of knowledge" that lies beyond our grasp. Learning truth is always a joy, and so would not resurrected beings and angels be capable of quicker methods? Our current modes of communicating knowledge by speaking and writing are imperfect and slow. What if we had a perfect language revealed to us, such as the language of Adam? Pratt anticipates something like parallel rather than serial processing, minds being able to communicate and receive "vast numbers of ideas, all at the same time, on a great variety of subjects." The Holy Ghost could "unfold that knowledge to another spirit, all in an instant, without this long tedious process of artificial and arbitrary sounds, and written words." If Moses could see all the particles of creation and count them at once, there must be ways that the mind can speed up in its scope and understanding, so as to "unfold a world of knowledge in a moment." In one minute in the spirit world we could learn more than an entire lifetime. The same quickening of our minds will apply to our bodies in the future state. "We look forward to the joyful time, when we shall burst" our mortal bodies and travel at the speed of light, the speed at which he says the spirit moves (in a long tradition of physicalized idealism). Our memories will be improved and "will come out, like the daguerreotype likeness."[11]

Perhaps the most important early twentieth-century figure in spiritual materialism is the Norwegian-born biochemist and apostle John A. Widtsoe. In his short and key doctrinal book with the characteristic title of *A Rational Theology* (1915, followed by multiple editions), he built on his scientific training to explain the workings of divine communication in terms of ethereal vibrations. "By proper preparation and exertion [men and women] may intercept messages from out of the directly unknown, as completely as this may be done by man-made instruments." He likens revelation to radio: "by the well tuned coil of wire the wireless message is taken out of space." Like Parley Pratt, Widtsoe distinguishes between the Holy Ghost ("the third member of the Godhead") and the holy spirit, a sort of substance.

> The holy spirit permeates all things of the universe, material and spiritual. By the holy spirit the will of God is radio-transmitted, broadcasted as it were. It forms what may be called the great system of communication among the intelligent beings of

the universe. The holy spirit vibrates with intelligence; it takes up the word and will of God as given by him or by his personal agents, and transmits the message to the remotest parts of space. By the intelligent operation and infinite extent of the holy spirit, the whole universe is held together and made as one unit. By its means there is no remoteness into which intelligent beings may escape the dominating will of God.[12]

This sort of thinking is not unique to Mormonism; it was central to late Victorian ether physics. But Mormonism was a particularly hospitable habitat for ideas about communication as spiritual transmission.

Widtsoe was not only interested in celestial transmission but in recording, and here he found the real moral stakes. He imagined a kind of proto-Google:

So thoroughly permeated with the holy spirit is the immensity of space that every act and word and thought are recorded and transmitted everywhere, so that all who know how to read may read. Thus we make an imperishable record of our lives. To those whose lives are ordered well this is a blessed conception; but to those of wicked lives, it is most terrible. He who has the receiving apparatus, in whose hands the key is held, may read from the record of the holy spirit, an imperishable history of all that has occurred during the ages that have passed in the world's history. This solemn thought, that in the bosom of the holy spirit is recorded the whole history of the universe—our most secret thought and our faintest hope—helps man to walk steadily in the midst of the contending appeals of life. We cannot hide from the master.[13]

Though religious rhetorics based on wireless communication were pervasive in American life, they do seem to have been well favored by Mormon thinkers. There are some key mid-twentieth-century visions of broadcasting as a miracle by apostles Matthew Cowley and Alvin R. Dyer,[14] but the key late twentieth-century figure is probably Spencer W. Kimball—apostle from 1943 and church president from 1973 to his death in 1985—a charismatic figure who launched a genuinely global missionary effort. He had both an imaginative vision of divine communications and an aggressive program of interpersonal and media outreach.

Kimball's 1972 speech "Voices from Other Worlds" shows his cosmic imagination. "In a short period man has so improved his communication techniques as to hear voices around the world. A few years ago, even with earphones, we could decode only part of the static over the newborn radio. Our first television pictures were very local and very amateurish. Today, we see in our homes a fight in Madison Square Garden, a football game in the Cotton Bowl, the Tabernacle Choir in Chicago, an astronaut on his way to the moon." So far, we are in the familiar realm of broadcasting as metaphor for divine communication. He counters an unnamed scientist's claim that humanity's best chance for survival in the nuclear age is to listen to radioed advice from deep in space from other older and wiser civilizations:

"for thousands of years our omniscient Heavenly Father from his 'wise old world' has been trying to get his children to listen hard for such radioed advice and televised wisdom, but they were blind of eyes and dull of ears. They were not connected to the power line.

. . .

Will radioed messages ever come between planets across limitless space? Indubitably, for there have already been coming for thousands of years, properly sent, interpreted and publicized messages of utmost importance to the inhabitants of the earth. Dreams and open vision, like perfected television programs, have come repeatedly. . . . [T]hese interstellar messages—call them what you will, visions, revelations, television, radio—from the abode of God to man on this earth continue now to come to the living prophet of God among us."

Note the juxtapositions: "visions, revelations, television, radio." His materialism blurs human and divine machines.[15]

This was the same man who launched an effort to convert the whole world in a landmark address in April 1974:

the gospel must be preached to every creature. . . . I believe that the Lord is anxious to put into our hands inventions of which we laymen have hardly had a glimpse . . . I am confident that the only way we can reach most of these millions of our Father's children is through the spoken word over the airwaves, since so many are illiterate. . . . Our Father in heaven has now provided us mighty towers—radio and television towers with possibilities beyond comprehension—to help fulfill the words of the Lord that 'the sound must go forth from this place unto all the world.[16]

Much of his vision, based on the multiplying power of transistor radios rather like the *Voice of America* model of serving as a lifeline to those behind the Iron Curtain, was never fulfilled. The missionary program remained largely face-to-face in its preferred channel, but the church's experiments today with online missionary work continue to embrace technical possibilities of spread and effect, and this address marks a major transition in the church's outreach.

Perhaps even more fundamental to Mormon theology is the idea of a divine record. No term is more resonant than "record" in Mormon theology. The movement begins with a record brought back from the ancient past. In this record, the risen Christ tells the Nephites: "all things are written by the Father" (3 Nephi 27:26). This stunning theological proposal has hardly been pondered. For the three monotheisms, texts can be divine if recorded or dictated by a prophet or angels, but there is no notion that Deity engages in writing. God sees, talks, loves, rages, but only writes once, on the Mosaic stone tablets. In Mormonism, He writes often. (In traditional notions of angels as secretaries one could say, "all things are written for the Father," but that is something very different.) Writing is arguably the most fundamental of all media and this insight is bolstered in the fundamental text of Mormon media theology, Doctrine and Covenants (D&C), section 128.

This 1842 letter by Joseph Smith unveils a power of documentation that is also a power of securing matters for the eternities. Earthly and heavenly records run parallel. The section is clearly in tradition of the Jewish *sefer hayyim* (book of the living) or Christian *liber vitae* (book of life) that would contain everything. Joseph Smith explains a kind of writing that would record not only in earth but in heaven, a fundamental communication practice that would stretch not only across distances, but also between time and eternity. Smith imagines a book of life that holds the keys to salvation. (And section 128 erupts in a veritable glossolalia of divine and natural voices tumbling forth to declare the gladness of the restored gospel.) As in 2 Nephi 29, the keeping of records goes together with the joining of peoples. Gathering records into one is the same thing as linking people into familial relationships; Smith uses the term "sealing" for both. A canon of records is at the same time a community of souls.

D&C section 128 authorizes the vast genealogical efforts of the church, which aim at nothing less than a complete archive of every human being who has ever lived since Adam and Eve. The church has already amassed a vast database about pedigrees and kin, now available online for public use. This investment in computer hardware and mountain vaults for storing records is just one expression of the Mormon commitment to a vision of a divine database that is at once archive and assembly, a means of tracking ordinances and a mode of securing salvation.

Despite its lofty media theology, Mormon culture does not always embrace media in their ordinary operation. Like much of American culture, Mormonism is self-divided about the meaning of technology. Mormon rhetoric loves the possibilities of satellites, broadcasting, and the Internet with an at times almost nineteenth-century excitement about media as agents of evangelization. But there is also widespread alarm about how media spread evil influences in our homes and hearts. There has been a steady stream of sermons against poisonous media of various sorts from jazz in the 1920s to television in the 1970s to pornography today. The media are a ready scapegoat for moral ills and a target for those who are unhappy with the shape of modern life; in criticizing media forms and content, Mormons are part of a long conversation that stretches over the past century that includes many voices, secular and religious, highbrow and populist, left-wing and right-wing, feminist and traditional. Any institution concerned about maintaining its logistical hold on time, space, matter, hearts, and minds will have to deal with media as agents of entertainment, ideology, and indoctrination. Media are always bids for spiritual dominion. As far as technology is concerned, the question is always control. When the church sees itself as in charge, enlightenment beckons; when others are, then despair. Thus we end up back with Innis and his constant question about technology and power, and Mormonism's deep dialectic of exposure and concealment.

NOTES

1. Nord, *Faith in Reading*; Gutjahr, *American Bible*.
2. Bushman, *Joseph Smith*, 2005.
3. Cronon, *Nature's Metropolis*; Bushman, "Making Space for the Mormons."
4. Durham, "Political Interpretation of Mormon History."
5. Carey, *Communication as Culture*, 225.

6. Case, "Sounds from the Center."
7. Givens, *People of Paradox*, chap. 10.
8. Mill, *On Liberty*, 85.
9. Carey, *Communication as Culture*, 206–9.
10. P. Pratt, "Spiritual Communication," 1853.
11. O. Pratt, "Language, or the Medium of Communication in the Future State," 1854, 3: 101, 103–5.
12. Widtsoe, *Rational Theology*, 5, 6, 72–73.
13. Ibid., 74.
14. Cowley, "Miracles"; Dyer, *Refiner's Fire*.
15. Kimball, "Other Worlds," 55, 58.
16. Kimball, "When the World Will Be Converted," 10.

BIBLIOGRAPHY

Bushman, Richard L. *Joseph Smith: Rough Stone Rolling*. New York: Alfred A. Knopf, 2005.
Bushman, Richard. "Making Space for the Mormons." In *Believing History: Latter-day Saint Essays*, ed. Reid L. Neilson and Jed Woodworth, 173–98. New York: Columbia University Press, 2004.
Carey, James W. *Communication as Culture*. Boston, MA: Unwin Hyman, 1989.
Case, Judd. "Sounds from the Center: Liriel's Performance and Ritual Pilgrimage." *Journal of Media and Religion* 8 (2009): 209–24.
Cowley, Elder Matthew. "Classic Discourses from the General Authorities: Miracles." *New Era* (June 1975). https://www.lds.org/new-era/1975/06/classic-discourses-from-the-general-authorities-miracles?lang=eng.
Cronon, William. *Nature's Metropolis: Chicago and the Great West*. New York: Norton, 1992.
Durham, G. Homer. "A Political Interpretation of Mormon History." *Pacific Historical Review* 13, no. 2 (1944): 136–50.
Dyer, Alvin R. *The Refiner's Fire: The Significance of Events Transpiring in Missouri*. Salt Lake City, UT: Deseret, 1968. (Originally published 1960.)
Givens, Terryl L. *People of Paradox: A History of Mormon Culture*. New York: Oxford University Press, 2007.
Gutjahr, Paul C. *An American Bible: A History of the Good Book in the United States, 1777–1880*. Stanford, CA: Stanford University Press, 1999.
Innis, Harold. *History of Communications*. Ed. William Buxton, Michael R. Cheney, and Paul Heyer. Lanham, MD: Rowman and Littlefield, 2015.
Journal of Discourses. 26 vols. Reported by G. D. Watt et al. Liverpool: F. D. and S. W. Richards et al., 1851–86; reprint, Salt Lake City, UT: n.p., 1974.
Kimball, Spencer W. "Other Worlds: Voices from Space." In *Faith Precedes the Miracle*, 47–59. Salt Lake City, UT: Deseret, 1972.
Kimball, Spencer W. "When the World Will Be Converted." *Ensign* 4, no. 10 (October 1974). https://www.lds.org/ensign/1974/10/when-the-world-will-be-converted?lang=eng.
Mill, John Stuart. *On Liberty*. Ed. David Spitz. New York: Norton, 1975. (Originally published 1859.)
Nord, David Paul. *Faith in Reading: Religious Publishing and the Birth of the Mass Media in America*. New York: Oxford University Press, 2004.

Pratt, Orson. "Language, or the Medium of Communication in the Future State, and the Increased Powers of Locomotion" [October 22, 1854]. *Journal of Discourses* 3: 97–105.
Pratt, Parley Parker. "Spiritual Communication" [April 6, 1853]. *Journal of Discourses* 2: 43–47.
Widtsoe, John A. *A Rational Theology: As Taught by the Church of Jesus Christ of Latter-day Saints*. 5th ed. Salt Lake City, UT: Deseret, 1946.

PART VI

MORMON CULTURE

CHAPTER 27

....

GEOGRAPHY AND
MORMON IDENTITY

....

RICHARD V. FRANCAVIGLIA

INTRODUCTION: TIME AND PLACE

....

THE Mormons are widely known for their emphasis on—some might say obsession with—history. The reason for this, perhaps, is that the faith is based on a progression of developments in time (as evident in the Book of Mormon) but also because the church as an institution was required by Joseph Smith to keep its history. That having been said, a related subject—geography—is also a major factor in the belief system and development of the Church of Jesus Christ of Latter-day Saints. Although the word geography is not mentioned per se in the scriptures, nor mandated for study by the church, geography is important in Mormon identity. To use an analogy, if the Mormon experience is like a river, history flows along it like water, but that current is guided by the riverbed over which it runs. In a sense, that riverbed cradles and directs the flow of water in this metaphorical river, even though it remains seemingly invisible to most observers. Intimately linked to Mormon history, geography thus became—and remains—an essential element in both defining the Mormon faith and spreading it worldwide.

In both secular education and religious instruction, the disciplines of geography and history are often considered, and usually taught, as separate subjects. As suggested above, though, the separation is artificial. As early as 1612, British explorer-colonizer John Smith argued that geography and history are inseparable, for space and time are interrelated. As Smith colorfully put it, "geography without history seems a carcass without motion, so history without geography wandereth as a vagrant without a certain habitation." In John Smith's time, England had just begun to embark on a bold expansion program that would ultimately witness the establishment of colonies worldwide. Smith, in fact, was well aware that England was—geographically speaking—making history. Fast-forwarding two centuries from John Smith's time to the early 1800s, we can witness another young man who happened to be named Smith also about to make history with geography in mind. In the 1810s, Joseph Smith was poised to play a role in the rich tradition of geographical empire building that was based, in part, on increasingly accurate geographic information and increasingly sophisticated mapmaking. In his secular education, which was admittedly brief, the young Joseph Smith may have encountered early nineteenth-century school geographies that were common in classrooms. These geographies combined both maps and texts, and their goal was to teach students in the relatively new nation of the United States about the world and their place in it. Smith would also be familiar with geography from discussions about the Bible and its cradle of development—the Holy Land—information that was commonly learned from both maps and vivid narrative descriptions and passages. From his revelations and writings, Joseph Smith appears to have been—like the earlier John Smith—keenly aware of the connection between history and geography. Given the proliferation of geographical information and maps on the American frontier during Joseph Smith's youth, we can imagine him developing this connection at a fairly early age.

It is easy to imagine that Joseph Smith found geography and history to be interconnected because two types of documents—historical records and maps—were readily available to him and others who lived in upstate New York at the time of the church's founding. These materials were part of a growing public record available to an increasingly literate population. This literacy included not only reading and writing, but also learning how to read maps such as cadastral surveys. This was also a time in which the pocket map was about to burst onto the scene, and such maps revolutionized geographic thinking. Because they could be carried anywhere and kept close to the chest, so to speak, pocket maps could serve as a metaphor for geographic opportunism. Maps, as we shall see, formed a critical tool in communicating LDS beliefs and values at several levels, from the most spiritual to the most mundane.

By the time that Joseph Smith founded what would subsequently be called the Church of Jesus Christ of Latter-day Saints, he and his family were participants in a westward-moving national enterprise. Smith's American empire, though, had already settled the Eastern seaboard, and was now gazing toward the Pacific shore of the continent as its ultimate goal for colonization. As history would soon confirm, the Mormons would not only be part of this terrestrial geographic push westward that, by 1848, would lay open for colonization the entire area from coast to coast. Broader horizons beckoned, and Smith's church, like the entire United States itself, would soon become an international force, as both set their sights worldwide. To achieve this global vision, the Mormons needed to master geography, and by so doing would rewrite history.

ORIGINS: ROOTS AND BRANCHES

The Mormon Church, therefore, was not only positioned in time but also rooted in place. In this regard, consider more deeply the term "Latter-day" in the church's title. On one level, the term is chronological in that it refers to the great transformation that would occur when Christ returned. It is, in a word, millennial, but that carries with it the notion of the end of time itself as we know it. When this occurs, the Mormons would find themselves literally—physically—in heaven. The things that they had built in this world would be the framework in which they would live eternally. Small wonder, then, that the Mormons placed so much effort on building things in this world correctly; the things they built would, in essence, be their heavenly inheritance. The term "latter days" also means the postbiblical time or era in which revelations could be received by prophets. Paradoxically, then, these latter days were not only deeply spiritual times in which revelations could occur; they were also what Mormons and others recognized as the modern times, with their increasing separation of men from God as technology and rapidly increasing social change began to threaten the traditional social order. Not so coincidentally, these latter days were also metaphorical for the modern times in which geography had become an element in worldwide exploration, discovery, and colonization. In naming the church, Smith and his co-religionists used a metaphor for time (modernity) that was subliminally coupled to geography. At this time, the nation was being surveyed and carefully partitioned using the modern Jeffersonian system of rectangular land survey. Unlike the established religions, then, the young Mormon faith was sired in an age of modern continental expansion and increasingly scientific measurement. To astute observers, it was a time when geography and society worked hand in hand to foster both personal and collective fortunes. Joseph Smith, though, could make it do far more. In his hands, geography would play a role in two seemingly separate spheres of activity—religion and geopolitics—that Smith believed to be inseparable. In Smith's times, on a seemingly secular level, information constantly filtered back from the western frontier about the unique peoples and places (and hence opportunities) that awaited expansion. Poised on the frontier and looking westward for inspiration, Smith needed geographical information to make that faith prosper. On yet another level, though, the Latter-day Saints were restless souls who realized that building the church was more than simply an American endeavor. For the church to reach its full potential, it would have to seek converts worldwide.

GEOGRAPHY AND CHURCH BUILDING

As is now becoming obvious, this chapter will demonstrate that a connection between Mormons and geography played out in several ways and had long-term consequences for the church. The thesis here is deceptively simple: as in the case of Mormon history, which is to say narratives about the faith, geography was a factor in Mormon identity from the very beginnings of the faith's founding in the early 1820s. It remains so to the present. As hinted at above, geography also played a role in several aspects of church history and ideology that lie at the core of the religion. These are properly the field of theology, but for the Mormons geography is inseparable from them. In fact, I will argue that identity in Mormon faith is more bound up in geography than is the case in most other faiths. An understanding of geography was, for example, essential to comprehending the migrations of early peoples associated with the Book of Mormon and was thus an element in Mormon scripture. Those migrations described in the Book of Mormon were not only interhemispheric, but also played out in the Americas as lands that had witnessed considerable prehistory. Similarly, geography is embodied in the early church's guidance on how to build the ideal holy city in modern times (the present and future). On a more mundane level, geography played a major role in the early spatial expansion of the church. It continues to play a major role in the Mormon experience today, as suggested by the impressive world maps cast into the north and south facades of the Church Office Building in Salt Lake City. Those maps are yet another reminder that cartography (the art and science of mapmaking) is an integral element in geography. Given the Mormons' intense interest in geography for both ideological and practical reasons, it will come as no surprise that they would also become skilled mapmakers.

Some Definitions

Before demonstrating the impact of the Mormons' propensity to think, believe, and act geographically, I would like to define the term geography to include (but not be limited to) three major components: (1) *location*—that is, the point in space in which something is situated, for example, the geographic location of events described in Mormon scripture, such as Hill Cumorah; (2) *place*—which is to say the character of a particular geographic locale, for example, the creation of Mormon communities, including a distinctively Mormon landscape based on the arrangement of property parcels, and the design and placement of buildings; and (3) *spatial relationships*—such as the ancient human migrations described in the Book of Mormon, and the development of an effective mission system to accomplish the Mormons' proselytizing efforts. Other aspects of geography include the relationship between people and environment, development of regions, and the like, but the three elements identified above—location, place, and spatial relationships—will be emphasized herein. These aspects of what geographers call the "themes of geography" are fundamental to understanding both church history and the Mormon mindset. As will become clear in this chapter, Mormonism involves a nearly constant functioning, one might even say struggle, between two fundamentally different aspects of geography, namely, those place-creating forces that are *centripetal* (that is, drawing things toward a center) and those that are *centrifugal* (that is, pushing outward from a center to multiple, scattered, points). For nearly two centuries, the church has dealt in various ways with keeping both of these forces working harmoniously to create a core identity and yet permit the faith to expand.

LOCATION AS A POINT IN TIME

This all hinges on the concept of geographic location, which is usually depicted today using objective points identified by a grid system of latitude and longitude. Abstractly, geographic location has long been a part of all religious identity. In the Bible, for example, Jerusalem is not considered to be a random point that might be placed anywhere, but rather one having strategic significance in the development of faiths such as Judaism and Christianity. In later times that city assumed importance for Muslims, based also on its geographical position in Islam's interpretation of the life and afterlife. In early nineteenth-century North America, Joseph Smith reaffirmed the significance of geographic location to faith when Hill Cumorah emerged as a pivotal location in the creation of Mormon belief. Quite aside from its topographic character, then, the geographical position of this soon-to-be-sacred location was noteworthy, for it would be part of a larger drama of human migrations. I am suggesting that Hill Cumorah assumed a role not only because it was a rise or prominence in the landscape, but because it had a particular position in abstract space—in this case, the American frontier. To Mormons, then, Hill Cumorah was a location that could in effect pinpoint—and thus substantiate—Mormon chronology in both time and space.

THE CREATION OF MORMON PLACE(S)

In a seminal article on the subject of Mormon geography, historian Philip Barlow noted that "*place* is not merely occupied ground, but space conceived as one thing rather than another."[1] Barlow's statement is a reminder that place is far more than simple geographical location (the position of something with regard to predetermined coordinates), but rather a construct attributing *meaning* to a geographic locale. To do this, a place has to have some identifying characteristic, such as a particular shape. Moreover, however, something significant has to have happened in order for us to transform a location into a place. It might be the scene—and hence site—of something miraculous, such as the communication between a human being and supernatural forces; Moses and Mt. Sinai come to mind and form a prototype for the spiritual encounter that Joseph Smith had on Hill Cumorah.

If locations, in fact, become places only when we name and describe them, thus infusing them with narratives about origin and events, then that process ultimately has to transcend one particular individual and be embraced by culture. In other words, the creation of place usually involves a consensus, though it may (and usually does) originate in the mind of one original observer. As is now apparent, in the case of Mormon geography that original source is the inspired individual Joseph Smith. However, Smith was always a part of broader American frontier culture, and as such he inherited places that were already named using a wealth of place names from the Bible. Tellingly, Smith's birthplace of Sharon, Vermont, bears a biblical name, as does Palmyra, New York, and these may serve to reaffirm the connection with the Holy Land. Smith also imparted a set of new (yet seemingly ancient) place names that would resonate from this new religion: Nauvoo, Illinois, was an early example of this, but even after Smith's death and the Mormons' move westward, place names he brought to light—such as Nephi and Manti (Utah) are examples of his influence. Smith, in other words, not only oversaw the creation of a new religion but also played a role in creating new places.

This is not surprising, for religion has a long history of shaping and sustaining places. What is remarkable, though, is how quickly this process occurred in Mormon and American history. The Mormons, in fact, provide one of the classic case studies of how religious homelands are created. Understanding geographic space and place in light of religion underscores the fact that considerable human emotion is invested in the process. This reminds us that whereas the concept of geographic location might be considered to be scientifically neutral, places are always cultural artifacts and they are always—in the case of religion especially so—regarded subjectively. For our purposes here, it should also be noted that as religions ascribe deep meaning to certain places, they may become rather oblivious to others that have little or no spiritual significance. That helps them root or anchor their narratives and, incidentally, often lays the groundwork for their claiming such places as their own despite the fact that others may have been there first. Holy places worldwide have developed in this manner. The fact that more than one religion can claim a particular location—that is, create a "place" in the same place as another religion—can lead to considerable conflict, as is evident to even the casual observer in Jerusalem.

GEOGRAPHY AND COSMOLOGY:
THE CITY OF ZION

The Mormons have constantly engaged in geographic discourses since the inception of the church in the early nineteenth century. One of the earliest examples of geographically oriented scripture to link cosmology and geography involves the creation of Mormon communities on earth according to the rectangular geometry emphasized in the Book of Revelation and other biblical sources. This materialized in Joseph Smith's plan for the City of Zion (1833), which had several permutations in the Middle West and later in the West. Smith envisioned a perfect city based on rectangular design, which, as some Mormons say in the folk vernacular, would be "right with the compass and right with God." The Bible was the ultimate source of such cities. According to scripture, the perfect city will appear at the time of the Apocalypse. One can envision looking down from a position over Jerusalem, with its narrow crooked streets, being transformed into an orderly place—that is, one whose perimeter and core show a type of rectangular geometric order—by the hand of God. Mormons used the grid extensively in their creation of towns, but it appears that Nauvoo, Illinois, represented the first place the Mormons created and hoped to sustain a place using the City of Zion as a plan. Said to be divinely inspired, the City of Zion was both an abstract and a practical model for town development. It is noteworthy that one of the first Mormon documents was a map of the City of Zion by Joseph Smith (who provided the vision and wording) and his multitalented scribe Frederick G. Williams (who gave it visual form by drawing the lines, so to speak).

As a geographical and cartographic vision, the City of Zion plan was enduring. As historians of urban planning have long noted, the City of Zion plan, or derivations thereof, helped the Mormons found settlements in varied places. In fact, numerous aspects of the ideal city found their way into the Interior West as Mormons migrated there to escape persecution. Salt Lake City and hundreds of Mormon villages in the would-be state of Deseret (which the Mormons carefully described for federal authorities largely using watershed boundaries) are part of this legacy. When such communities were touted by church authorities as places in which the angels would visit, the Mormons used the visual quality of their settlements—what geographers commonly call the cultural landscape—to brand places in the American West as their own. This, to my knowledge, is a trait largely confined to the Mormons. As opposed to almost every other American cultural or religious group, whose settlement landscape tends to reflect economic and broader cultural systems, the Mormons deliberately created a religious landscape based in part on the division of land (street layout and property parcels) and architecture (religious buildings). It was, after all, the Mormons whose leaders urged the laying out of communities based on a religious model of centralized church squares, wide streets, and both domestic and religious buildings in brick and stone—in the process creating one of the most distinctive landscapes in nineteenth- and early twentieth-century America.

It should be noted that the creation of the City of Zion, while seemingly endorsing as sacred ground the one place where it would be located, would ideally be repeated—that is, diffused elsewhere in space to become additional sacred places. That was Joseph Smith's intention. After the establishment of the prototype, other cities would be built in its image elsewhere, until the globe was covered by such cities; through this process, the entire world would become, in a word, Mormon. One legacy of Smith's emphasis of cardinal directions in the City of Zion plan is evident in the phenomenal sense of direction that Mormons in the intermountain West developed. The visible topography of mountains flanking valleys in the "Basin and Range" region may also help impart a sense of direction, but Mormon street naming is also a factor. In navigating a city or town using street names like 600 North and 500 East, residents are constantly aware of their position in a geographic grid. This, however, can also extend to personal space: for example, a Mormon is likely to say, as he or she helps arrange the furniture in a room, that the piano should be moved a few feet to the west, or a picture should be straightened so that it doesn't dip to the east—a reminder that Mormons are subconsciously aware of things in a geographic grid. The closest analogy that might be made here is the Muslim ability to at all times be aware of the *Qibla*, or direction in which Mecca lies, and toward which devout Muslims pray five times a day. However, the Mormons' sense of all four cardinal directions is linked to something even broader (the entire landscape surrounding them) though it, too, is similarly cosmological in nature. And yet, even for Mormons, one direction—east—seems paramount. East is, in fact, the direction that most Mormon temples face, which is especially evident in the statues of the angel Moroni, whose trumpet points toward the rising sun, likely in deference to the New Testament passage that says Christ will come from the east upon his millennial return. As a geographical metaphor, this means that both the sun, and the son, will rise from that cardinal direction.

Geography and Diaspora:
The Lamanite Experience

Consider next a core Mormon belief that is also rooted in geography, namely, that migrations of displaced peoples linked the New World and the Old World in ancient times. This may seem more like history than geography, for a time period is stated and journeys are recounted in considerable detail. However, it depends on a geographical knowledge of both the Old World and the New World. No other religion has such a geographically based narrative that connects the two hemispheres, but then again those other faiths were created before the existence of the New World was known to believers, for example, of the Judeo-Christian tradition. To summarize this experience of the Jaredites and Nephites in two migrations, peoples of the ancient Near East left that part of the world we now call the Middle East on a journey to the Americas. Given the early (pre-Columbian) time frame here, these migrations are controversial indeed. Since the founding of the church, in fact, Mormons have attempted to delineate—that is, map—the actual routes taken by these early travelers. And just as early, nonbelievers tried to debunk these migrations as so much Oriental fantasy, which they frequently equated with Persian tales. The veracity or falsehood of these migrations is not of concern here. Suffice it to say that people of both persuasions have combed the Book of Mormon for geographic clues that might prove or disprove the Lamanite journeys. Clues such as the position of bodies of water and peninsulas, for example, form the crux of determining where (in addition to when) these voyages occurred. Some Saints—both scholars and lay people—are studying this controversial field called "Book of Mormon geography." They have produced an especially interesting, albeit controversial, body of literature that sheds light on the power of belief to shape geographic perceptions.

The concept of Lamanite migration brings into clearer perspective an important aspect of Mormon geography, namely, that it can be viewed as both event(s) in time and as metaphor(s) in space. In essence, the Lamanite journeys reposition biblical history in a New World setting. By so doing, they simultaneously redefine Native American ethnicity and globally empower North America by placing it center stage, rather than at the periphery, of Judeo-Christian religion. Far from meaning that America was a cast-off of the Old World, then, the Mormon theological claim geographically places America front and center in a spiritual debate that had been operative since early modern times. That debate hinges on a fundamental question: how could the Bible be true if in it the indigenous peoples of the New World are not accounted for? The Bible, after all, is supposed to be the definitive statement about the origins of mankind. The Mormon belief that ancient peoples had migrated to the Americas involved considerable geographical revisionism. In Mormon thought, America was, or rather became, the real Promised Land. God's intention was for America to become a land "choice above all other lands." With this wording, the Mormons did nothing less than reposition the Judeo-Christian tradition; tellingly, they used geographical metaphors to do so. Joseph Smith's statement that the Garden of Eden was to be found in Missouri could be taken literally if one looked at a map of North America. Like the Garden of Eden in Mesopotamia, that fertile area in the new continent's midsection also lay between two impressive rivers—the Mississippi and the Missouri. We do not know whether Smith really believed this claim about the Garden of Eden being in America, or if he employed it to make a point. However, his claim is understandable in light of two common systems of describing places at the time, namely, biblical literalism and literary embellishment. In that sense, as Scott Trafton has shown, the Mississippi River functioned in the role of "the American Nile" and would similarly separate a free people from an enslaved one in the mid-nineteenth-century American frontier. Given the passionate political speeches Smith made about freedom in the western lands at the time, that American river served its purpose well. Ultimately, the result of the Mormon tendency to reimagine geography was to dignify their North American homeland as the locale where genuine religious events had not only taken place in the past, but would also take place in the future. Nevertheless, the Mormons are also always aware of a geographic touchstone far to the east, namely, the lands of the Bible. The perennial association of the Mormon experience in America with that enduring and alluring distant geographic locale—which was once called the Near East and is now known as the Middle East—can best be understood as part of a broader phenomenon called American Orientalism.[2]

MORMON EXODUS: THE GATHERING AS A GEOGRAPHIC PHENOMENON

Fortuitously, not only Lamanites but also the more modern Mormons themselves are associated with an epic migration bound to religious faith. That migration, however, began in the New World rather than the Old World, and it took place in the nineteenth century rather than in ancient times. Mormon history in the nineteenth century was, in a word, restless. If that term suggests that the Mormons were voluntarily pulled toward new opportunities and places, it should be remembered that they were also pushed there by their opponents. Still, the Saints characteristically viewed challenges as opportunities. Intent on spreading the good news about their new faith, Mormons mirrored the westward thrust of settlement into the American frontier. In their case, the migration began in the New England cultural hearth. In a series of successive moves, the church expanded from its inception in upstate New York, thence westward into Ohio, Missouri, and Illinois by about 1840. Mobility was a fact of life for early Mormons. Although several periods in early church history found the leadership of the Latter-day Saints encouraging the devout to settle in varied locales (for example, Kirtland at first and later Nauvoo), there was also embedded in this new faith the idea that a central place lured. As history and geography would conspire, that place was ultimately located in the interior portion of the Interior West, namely the valley of the Great Salt Lake. Significantly, some maps of the period candidly call this place "New Jerusalem"—a reminder that the prototype was essentially ancient Judaic; in other words, geography reaffirmed the Mormon claim that the Latter-day Saints were, in essence, the modern equivalent of the ancient Jews. The geographic metaphor that enabled Salt Lake City to thrive as the hive of Mormon activity was, with good reason, called "the Gathering." This term suggests that the ultimate goal of Mormon diaspora (as in the Jewish flight from Egypt) was centripetal, namely, the founding of a religious homeland based on a central place. In other words, in Mormon geography, centrifugal forces of dispersal are countered by centripetal forces that lead (back) to home. Geographically speaking, then, the modern Mormon migration is also literally, and often quite consciously, connected to ancient biblical history. Like the Jews' gathering after an epic migration, the Mormon creation of a homeland in the desert involved the geographic concept of a chosen people finding and claiming a chosen land.[3] Few religions can so clearly claim of their territories what Brigham Young proclaimed in July of 1847 as he and his followers neared Salt Lake City: "This is the Place." Tellingly, that place soon had a Jordan River, and its other prominent features, Great Salt Lake and Utah Lake, were also conflated with their Holy Land counterparts, the Dead Sea and Sea of Galilee, respectively.

The dynamic settling of an ostensibly undersettled frontier by chosen people is, of course, the dominant theme of Utah history. In reality, though, the place they selected was not empty at all, but rather populated by others (namely, Native Americans). In addition to converting these native peoples, the Mormons also envisioned European Americans and others migrating here in large numbers as they were converted abroad. At several times in its nineteenth-century history, then, the church positioned—note that pivotal term here for relegating something in space—its followers to come together as part of a collective experience. To achieve this "Gathering," it used a highly centripetal model, seeking to convert people in distant locations and bring them into a vital center where Mormonism would dominate, ideally with little or no interference from, or distraction by, the outside world. From there they would normally be called to settle other communities elsewhere in the region. Ideally, that region would be under the sole control of the Mormons. Ideally, however, is the operative word here because in every place the Saints settled they had to coexist with non-Mormons (whom they call "Gentiles"). Even Great Salt Lake City as the heart of the far-flung Mormon state of Deseret was contested; although originally nominally part of Mexico, and home to indigenous people when the Mormons arrived in 1847, Great Salt Lake City would soon (1848) become part of the United States. Nevertheless, as adapters, the Mormons made the best of their new land—in part by amassing a tremendous amount of geographic information about it. They knew that knowledge is power, and that geographic information is essential to success. In this endeavor to collect information and map the region, the Mormons worked independently as well as in concert with the federal authorities. Consider, for example, scientist-explorer Howard Stansbury's mid-nineteenth-century expedition, which reconnoitered the region in search of geographical and geological information. Among the members of this scientific expedition were Mormons such as the talented Albert Carrington. When the tension between federal authorities and Mormons mounted in the late 1850s, the Saints conducted their own expedition into the White Mountains (in today's Nevada) to determine where they might find solitude and live unmolested. On this expedition was the Mormon mapmaker James H. Martineau, who mapped portions of the region, and went on to become one of the West's important cartographers. Still, we tend to hear little about Martineau in most accounts of the mapping of the West, primarily because the Mormon role in this process has been so neglected by scholars who instead emphasize the non-Mormon mapmakers associated with federal projects such as railroad surveying. This is regrettable, for it was Martineau who played a major role in surveying the transcontinental railroad through Utah in 1868–69 and who was widely praised at the time by those who knew his work, including Gentiles.

THE SPREAD OF A WORLD CHURCH: MORMON EXPANSION

As the Saints struggled to keep control of their hard-won homeland in the American West, they also continued to expand outward as a global institution. This began in the nineteenth century, but became possible by the mid-twentieth century, by which time Mormon temples had been built on most continents, and the church membership had become increasingly foreign born. It has been said that migration to the United States is still a goal of many from abroad who convert to this faith, but in reality the church had begun to discourage migration to Utah by about 1900. By the mid to late twentieth century, in fact, Mormonism had become undeniably international in nature: ideally, the faithful would now stay in their original homes on other continents to fulfill the goal of a universal presence. The ramifications of this on the character of the church are enormous, for in shedding its American character it also found simplifying its message necessary, as evident in the correlation movement of the 1960s, which, some claim, came at the expense of theological substance.

But this type of tension has long typified Mormonism: from its inception, in fact, both centrifugal and centripetal forces have characterized the geography of the Mormon experience. Every impulse to gather followers in a central place meant first gathering additional members, many of them new converts, from distant locales. In spreading outward to the far reaches of the earth, the church is closely linked to the Christian proselytizing that claims that an individual true believer can prove his or her true belief only by spreading the gospel of Jesus Christ to other prospective believers. With good reason, then, social scientists branded such expansive faiths (including Islam) *universalizing* religions. Missionary activities occur both at home (that is, in the United States) and abroad. Given the fact that less is known about distant places, the overseas expansion of Mormon faith into places like the South Pacific required considerable geographic knowledge and, ultimately, cartographic skills. Therefore, although the process by which Mormons missionize the world is often justly regarded as a spiritual activity, it also requires worldly geographic abilities to succeed. Looked at geopolitically, the Mormons had to develop an understanding of the world's geography in order to become a world power, so to speak. The record shows that they did so with considerable skill. A look at the journals of Mormon missionaries in the field reveals how effectively they used both the written word and maps to chart the way. Although these records are ostensibly kept as a way of recording the church's history, they reveal the Mormons' skill in geography that accompanies all successful world exploration, colonization, and commerce. A reminder of how seamlessly history and geography combine in the Mormon experience is evident in the career of Assistant Church Historian Andrew Jenson, who was both a historian and a geographer at heart. Jenson not only traveled worldwide on behalf of the church, but also had a huge map painted on his wall to demonstrate, and confirm, the global presence of church activity. This underscores the premise that Mormons used maps as both cosmological and practical tools. In their use of maps and other geographical information, the Mormons are both akin to, and yet transcended, other Americans. One area on this map of the world—a huge area stretching longitudinally about 7000 miles from North Africa to Southeast Asia—is largely controlled by Muslims who resist missionaries from other faiths. Given the widespread prohibition against proselytizing by non-Muslims in majority-population Muslim countries, about a third of the world remains off limits for the present. Even the Holy Land—which had been visited by Orson Hyde, who held a ceremony consecrating the area for Mormons in 1841 (about six years *before* the Mormons reached their own desert Zion in Utah), and where Brigham Young University has a center in Jerusalem—is now regarded as a somewhat hazardous area due to concerns about terrorism. This, though, only confirms that global expansion has always had its risks. As virtually every Mormon would agree, in the optimistic tradition of this faith, the worldwide geographic stage is not only fraught with obstacles, but also rich in opportunity.

NOTES

1. Barlow, "Space Matters," 25.
2. See Francaviglia, "Like the Hajis of Meccah and Jerusalem."

3. See Francaviglia, "Chosen People, Chosen Land: Utah as the Holy Land," in *Go East, Young Man*, chap. 3.

BIBLIOGRAPHY

Barlow, Philip L. "Space Matters: A Geographical Context for the Reorganization's Great Transformation." *John Whitmer Historical Association Journal* 24 (2004): 21–39.

Bushman, Richard. "Making Space for the Mormons." In *Believing History: Latter-day Saint Essays*, ed. Reid L. Neilson and Jed Woodworth, 173–98. New York: Columbia University Press, 2004.

Carmack, Noel. "Running the Line: James H. Martineau's Surveys in Northern Utah, 1860–1882." *Utah Historical Quarterly* 68, no. 4 (2000): 292–312.

Farmer, Jared. *On Zion's Mount: Mormons, Indians, and the American Landscape*. Cambridge, MA: Harvard University Press, 2008.

Francaviglia, Richard V. *Believing in Place: A Spiritual Geography of the Great Basin*. Reno: University of Nevada Press, 2003.

Francaviglia, Richard V. *Go East, Young Man: Imagining the American West as the Orient*. Logan: Utah State University Press, 2011.

Francaviglia, Richard V. "'Like the Hajis of Meccah and Jerusalem': Orientalism and the Mormon Experience." Annual Arrington Lecture. Paper 18. Logan: Utah State University Press, 2012. http://digitalcommons.usu.edu/arrington_lecture/18/.

Francaviglia, Richard V. *Mapping and Imagination in the Great Basin: A Cartographic History*. Reno: University of Nevada Press, 2005.

Francaviglia, Richard V. *The Mapmakers of New Zion: A Cartographic History of Mormonism*. Salt Lake City, UT: University of Utah Press, 2015.

Francaviglia, Richard V. *The Mormon Landscape: Existence, Creation, and Perception of a Unique Image in the American West*. New York: AMS Press, 1978.

Gaustad, Edwin Scott, and Philip L. Barlow. *The New Historical Atlas of Religion in America*. New York: Oxford University Press, 2001.

Jackson, Richard H. "Mormon Perception and Settlement." *Annals, Association of American Geographers* 68 (September 1978): 317–34.

Jackson, Richard H. "The Mormon Experience: The Plains as Sinai, the Great Salt Lake as the Dead Sea, and the Great Basin as the Desert-cum-Promised Land." *Journal of Historical Geography* 18, no. 1 (1992): 41–58.

Meinig, D. W. "The Mormon Culture Region: Strategies and Patterns in the Geography of the American West, 1847–1964." *Annals, Association of American Geographers* 55 (June 1965): 191–220.

Olive, Phyllis Carol. *The Lost Lands of the Book of Mormon: A Geographical and Historical Study of the Book of Mormon Using the New York Setting at a Time when Primeval Forests and Ancient Waters Filled the Land*. Springville, UT: Bonneville, 2000.

Priddis, Venice. *The Book and the Map: New Insights into Book of Mormon Geography*. Salt Lake City, UT: Bookcraft, 1975.

Reps, John. *Town Planning in Frontier America*. Princeton, NJ: Princeton University Press, 1969.

Stump, Roger. *The Geography of Religion*. Lanham, MD: Rowman & Littlefield, 2008.

Trafton, Scott. *Egypt Land: Race and Nineteenth-Century American Egyptomania.* Durham, NC: Duke University Press, 2004.

Washburn, J. A., and J. N. Washburn. *From Babel to Cumorah.* Salt Lake City, UT: Deseret, 1937.

Yorgason, Ethan R. *Transformation of the Mormon Culture Region.* Urbana: University of Illinois Press, 2003.

CHAPTER 28

....

MORMON POPULAR CULTURE

....

JANA RIESS

In the opening scene of the *South Park* episode "All about Mormons" (air date November 19, 2003), a new student named Gary is introduced to his class at South Park Elementary. "Gary was a state champion in wrestling *and* in tennis," the teacher boasts. "He also maintained a 4.0 grade point average at his old school, *and* has been on two national commercials for toothpaste!" With this opening salvo, *South Park* simultaneously mocks and admires Mormonism's squeaky-clean image and reputation for producing superstars. The episode goes on to showcase the religion's close-knit family structures and loving domestic piety. The Mormons' very teeth are brighter. However, the episode counterbalances this disarming appraisal of the Mormon lifestyle with incisive critiques of Mormon beliefs, which are upheld as ludicrous: angels with white skin who claim to be resurrected Native Americans, golden plates that conveniently disappear when the prophet Joseph Smith is asked to produce them for inspection, and a Genesis creation myth that takes place in prosaic Jackson County, Missouri.

The *South Park* portrayal of Mormonism reflects American popular culture's long-standing suspicion of LDS theology, and in that sense the episode fits into a predictable trajectory of cartoons, novels, films, and television shows that have shown distrust for the religion and its beliefs. What has changed, however, is popular culture's increasing willingness to love the sinner and hate the sin, as it were. In the nineteenth century, both the LDS Church and its members were routinely vilified, but more recent popular culture examples uphold Mormons as not only tolerable but often as "model minority" figures. The *South Park* episode encapsulates the new admiration of Mormons as people ("Why do you have to be so freakin' nice all the time?" Kenny demands. "It isn't *normal!*"), while also standing in a long tradition of popular culture's scorn for Mormon theology.

South Park is not alone in its lauding of Mormons as individuals; in fact, it stands in a tradition of what historian Jan Shipps has called an evolution "from satyr to saint." In other words, Mormonism has gone from being perceived as a religion of vile debauchers to one filled with upright—and even uptight—knights of a vanishing moral code. This chapter explores three perennial themes that pertain to issues of Mormonism and popular culture: a fascination with Mormon sexuality; a suspicion of the LDS Church as a powerful and therefore dangerous institution; and uncertainties relating to Mormon assimilation into the American cultural mainstream. While the focus of those three themes is on mainstream culture's subjective "gaze" on Mormonism as a shifting object of scrutiny, each section also surveys recent attempts by Mormons to utilize various forms of popular culture, particularly film and television, to represent themselves. Mormons since the 1990s have turned to popular culture as a means of self-expression—and even self-definition.

From Harem to Homespun: Mormon Sexuality through American Eyes

Since its inception in 1830, Mormonism has been a source of continued fascination in American popular culture, particularly its unusual sexual practice of polygamy. First introduced in the 1830s in Kirtland, Ohio, but not revealed to the general public until 1852, plural marriage appealed to the darker strains of the American imagination. Some political cartoons in the 1850s depicted its potential comic side—to wit, a caricature of LDS prophet Brigham Young being victimized by "too much mother-in-law"—but the major thrust was of the dangers of such an atypical marital practice being permitted to survive within the borders of the United States. Political cartoons in popular publications lambasted Mormon polygamy as a "harem" or "zenana" and compared it to another religion perceived as dangerous, Islam. So powerful was the harem imagery that when Richard Burton visited Utah from England in 1860, he expressed surprise at the absence of minarets and domes.

Not just cartoons but also songs, plays, and novels condemned and sensationalized the practice of polygamy. Much of the anti-Mormon literature of the period was written by women. In 1881, the short-lived women's periodical *Anti-Polygamy Standard* accused polygamy of "beating down the innate and holy instincts of womanhood, outraging her affections, blunting her perceptions and sensibilities, and making her, as near [as] possible, an animal, raised to be at first man's plaything, and later his slave." A cottage industry of antipolygamy fiction arose, stories that often depicted an upright Victorian family whose patriarch was lured into Mormonism, dragging his loving wife and children with him. Once in the clutches of this false religion, the husband typically broke any promises he had made to the first wife about never taking another. The first wife would have to stand by helplessly as the family's fortunes evaporated in the pursuit of ever-younger brides who attempted to lord it over the first wife and usurp her rightful position. Many of the novels ended with the first wife being forced to take in laundry or run a boarding house to support her children, who remained her only comfort in a dreary and friendless Mormon society.

Antipolygamy novelists' vociferous objections to Mormon polygamy often revealed more about the objectors' own fears than they did about Mormonism per se. Terrified of divorce—which in non-Mormon America was generally initiated by husbands and left their ex-wives with little—anti-Mormon writers decried the ease and prevalence of divorce in Utah, never seeming to realize that divorce regulations were lax precisely to empower women with the freedom to seek divorce if they so chose. Mormon women were oppressed in these novels not just by polygamy but by the scandalous specter of having to take a job outside the home—an opportunity that, incidentally, some Mormon women apologists for polygamy argued actually demonstrated how forward-thinking and enlightened their society was in comparison with the rest of Victorian America, in which the rise of a new leisure class had encouraged an ideal of female decorum that bordered on uselessness.

In other words, anti-Mormon novels such as *Elder Northfield's Home, Or, Sacrificed on the Mormon Altar* and *The Fate of Madame La Tour* conjectured what would happen if the novelists themselves suddenly found that their own husbands had taken additional wives, without also importing the entire Mormon context of communitarianism and religious commitment that undergirded polygamy. Such fiction sold well, with *The Fate of Madame La Tour* allegedly boasting 100,000 copies in print after the publication of its second edition in 1882.[1]

It wasn't just Mormonism's alleged penchant for appealing to the basest desires of male libido that was a concern. Popular culture products of the time reflected America's tensions about not only male sexuality, but women's as well. One famous pre–Civil War cartoon showed Mormon women marching into battle with their babes lifted up high and their husbands literally crouching behind their skirts. In the foreground is an outrageously buxom Mormon woman, her breasts jutting forward as she presents a squalling infant, her commodious hips and protruding bustle overemphasizing female sexuality. That sexuality is depicted as aggressively dominant: the uniformed soldiers shown in the background are fleeing not the armed yet cowering Mormon men, but the specter of strong, hypersexualized Mormon women.

With this background, it's astonishing to reflect on the complete change that more than a century has wrought in American perceptions of Mormon sexuality, both male and female. Mormons in popular culture today are depicted at best as sexless or at worst as entirely repressed. As Terryl Givens has aptly observed, "It is now because Mormons occupy what used to be the center that they fall into contempt. The embrace of ultraconservative values, not their flagrant rejection, is now construed as the source of Mormon perfidy."[2] The shift in popular culture from depicting Mormons as libidinous to portraying them as prudish is not due to internal shifts within Mormonism so much as a sea change in the wider culture. The sexual revolution of the 1960s and 1970s, the widespread availability of birth control, the rise of age at first marriage, and the growth of cohabitation have made celibacy a far rarer value than it once was. Between 1969 and 1973, the percentage of all Americans who said that premarital sex was "not wrong" nearly doubled, from 24 to 47 percent, then continued inching upward. Among younger Americans, the percentage is much higher: roughly four out of five in the 18–29 age group have said they don't disapprove of premarital sex.[3] Mormon views, by contrast, are far more conservative: a 2011 Pew study showed that 79 percent of Mormons classified premarital sex as morally wrong.[4] A Mormon lifestyle of sexual abstinence outside of marriage is now a profoundly countercultural choice.

On a popular culture front, we see this represented in films like *Latter Days* (2003), in which a Mormon missionary's sexual awakening is dramatic precisely because its juxtaposition with his straight-laced lifestyle is so striking. It's highly visible in the HBO series *Big Love* (2006–11), in which the nonpolygamist LDS characters, including Barb's mom, are narrow-minded and judgmental of any family arrangement that is not heterosexual monogamy.

But an emphasis on Mormon virginity—minus the stereotype of the intolerant judgment of others—is also readily apparent in Mormon-generated cultural products, such as the low-budget, web-only programs *The Mormon Bachelor* and *The Mormon Bachelorette*. These reality shows are explicitly modeled after ABC's hit series *The Bachelor* and its spinoffs in all ways but one: there is no sex. Instead, the Mormon dates consist of "clean" fun like a trip to the arcade or an ice cream parlor, followed by giggly discussions of missionary experiences and life goals—which often include getting married in the temple. Such dates end not in a hot tub or in bed but with a friendly hug and perhaps a peck on the cheek. With such cultural efforts Mormons themselves play into the rhetoric of LDS sexual propriety and earn a certain prestige for doing so. Just as a wider host culture seeks to define itself in contrast to a minority, so too a minority discovers and re-creates its identity by emphasizing disparities between its own values and those of the host culture.

In fashion, this has become evident in the popular "modest is hottest" campaigns of the early twenty-first century. In print ads broadly circulated by conservative religionists, including Mormons, various actresses such as Emma Watson extol the value of not showing too much skin. While modesty has been a virtue long commended by Mormons—particularly for young women—the "modest is hottest" campaigns reveal an interesting tension with the host culture. With this national trend, Mormons are able to align with something stylish while distinguishing themselves in a tangible way from a larger culture they perceive as promiscuous. Unfortunately, the values Mormons choose to affirm here promote the ongoing sexual objectification of women. The "modest is hottest" ads adhere to the primacy of the male gaze in which women are judged primarily by their appearance. The only thing that has changed is that what is valued is the esteemed attractiveness of covered shoulders, thighs, and midriffs. The adoption of the adjective "hot" reflects a desire to negotiate some participation in the sexual mores of the surrounding culture; Mormon young women want to be perceived as sexy and tempting while remaining within the acceptable boundaries of their religion.

There have been several attempts to test exactly what those boundaries might be. In 2008, a Brigham Young University (BYU) graduate was excommunicated for creating and selling a calendar of shirtless returned LDS missionaries. (Undaunted by his excommunication, he followed up the next year with the "Hot Mormon Muffins" calendar of sexy LDS moms and their muffin recipes.) The barely-there costumes worn by Mormon professional ballroom dancer Julianne Hough in the first few seasons of *Dancing with the Stars* solicited some comments from Mormon and non-Mormon viewers, prompting her to confess in an interview that she had a modesty problem.[5] But a prominent Mormon woman on the other side of the spectrum, Stephenie Meyer, seemed to bend over backwards in the other direction with her chaste vampire series *Twilight*, with mixed results. While the secular media repeatedly drew attention to the books' "erotics of abstinence" and debated whether it was realistic in this day and age that Edward and Bella not have sex until their wedding night, the official Mormon bookstore chain, Deseret Book, stopped carrying the *Twilight* novels in their stores because of complaints from LDS customers that they were too steamy.[6]

It's possible that non-Mormons are likewise uncomfortable with the idea of LDS female sexuality. For example, in Michael Chabon's novel *The Wonder Boys*, the character of Hannah is explicitly identified as a Mormon; she is a talented young writer from Provo, Utah, who rents a room in the house of the main character, a novelist-cum-professor who had one bestseller many years earlier and has been afraid of publishing ever since. In the film version, however, references to Hannah's religious affiliation have been cut, despite the fact that the original screenplay had, like the novel, made her Mormonism overt. Moreover, the film has sexualized the character of Hannah, who tells Grady she's not quite a "downy innocent." She is highly provocative with him, giving him feedback on his manuscript while wearing only her underwear.[7] It may be that the filmmakers felt that they had altered the character of Hannah too far from her squeaky-clean image in the novel to continue calling her a Mormon, and that Mormon viewers would object to such a depiction. It may also be, however, that they were themselves uncomfortable with the notion of a young female Mormon who could be simultaneously alluring and moral, sexual and sensible.

Although Latter-day Saints may have become recognized and perhaps stereotyped for sexual repression, America has not lost its appetite for the titillating details of life in polygamy, still practiced by some fundamentalist breakaway groups. Michael Austin notes the strangeness of the persistent fascination with polygamy in popular culture, given that such a tiny fraction of the American population practices it today. Yet for many Americans more than a century after the practice was officially disavowed by the LDS Church, polygamy remains their number-one association with Mormonism. In the months leading up to the 2008 presidential election, 22 percent of newspaper articles about Mitt Romney discussed polygamy, despite the fact that Romney had never been a polygamist and in fact had garnered criticism for claiming that the very idea was distasteful to him. In that same period, 22 percent of articles about Mormonism more generally also discussed plural marriage.[8] As the book *LDS in the USA* puts it, "the persistence of non-LDS polygamous communities continues to be one of the major obstacles to the LDS Church becoming fully accepted in America."[9]

Meanwhile, polygamists themselves have begun utilizing the popular culture forums available to them to endorse and explain plural marriage to an American audience that is simultaneously skeptical and enthralled. After the government's controversial 2008 raid on a compound of the Fundamentalist Church of Jesus Christ of Latter-day Saints (FLDS) in Texas, polygamous wives went on CNN's *Larry King Live* to defend their lifestyle, saying that they were tired of the media simply assuming they were duped polygamous puppets who could not think for themselves. And in 2010, TLC debuted an unusual new reality show called *Sister Wives* that promised to go behind the scenes of a modern polygamous family. Speaking on *The Oprah Winfrey Show* as the series debuted, a member of the Brown family explained the motivation for going public with their story: "We figured that by showing our lives, we'd actually help the society be more transparent, have other people in the . . . lifestyle feel safer about being transparent," explained family patriarch Kody Brown. *Sister Wives* seemed to self-consciously chip away at some of the stereotypes viewers held about polygamy; this family adopted contemporary dress, sent its children to public schools, worked at regular jobs in the community, and used cell phone text messages to court their newest wife.

Sister Wives effectively desensationalized and desexualized polygamy. This was not a reality show depicting sexual deviation or degeneracy; compared to other series, it was positively wholesome. The most dramatic moment may have occurred when one of the wives claimed that things were going along swimmingly for the family and another slapped her hand on her own knee and declared, "Bull*crap*." In short, viewers' expectations for dramatic catfights were routinely denied by the quotidian routines of life in the supersized household. But what made the Brown family most distinctive—the religious beliefs that gave rise to polygamy in the first place—was all kept strictly off-camera. Religious practice was decidedly privatized in the series, as was sexual intimacy.

If contemporary media attention to Mormonism has focused unduly on the tiny minority of fundamentalists who still practice polygamy, it's clear that popular culture's depiction of mainstream Latter-day Saints has made a 180-degree turnaround since the late nineteenth century. At that time, Victorian depictions of Mormonism relied heavily on tropes of its sexual promiscuity, with lascivious males using polygamy as a cloak to cover their sexual appetites. By contrast, representations of Mormon sexuality in the twenty-first century have affirmed the sexual liberation of the host culture by emphasizing an alleged deep repression in the Mormon sexual ethic.

SUSPICION OF INSTITUTIONS

As we have seen, Mormon sexuality, especially as expressed in polygamy, has been a perpetual focus of popular culture treatments of Mormonism, reflecting many of the fears and fantasies of the host culture. Another persistent theme has been an abiding suspicion of the power of the LDS Church as an institution: Is it legitimately American? Can Mormons ever be good, patriotic US citizens? Isn't the church's growing economic power a concern to the entire nation? Although popular culture has evolved in depicting individual Mormons "from satyrs to saints," the same cannot be said for the LDS Church as an institution, which sometimes still comes across as anything but saintly.

Such icy distance is palpable in Tony Kushner's 1991 play *Angels in America*, to which scholar Cristine Hutchison-Jones has pointed as representing an important moment in Mormonism's cultural history. For the first time, Mormonism provided the backdrop for a major literary work of the American theater (a fact that most secular reviewers did not mention but many Mormons dissected with passion). Kushner was clearly fascinated by Mormonism's origin stories, filling the play with stories of visiting angels, buried sacred texts, and visions as well as three central Mormon characters. But as intrigued as Kushner clearly was by Mormonism's communitarian outlier past, he was repulsed by the "conservative institutions" (Republicanism, American exceptionalism, and "trickle down" economics) that he associated with Mormonism's present. "Now they're right wing and horrible," one character says in summary.[10] For Kushner, Mormons symbolized a cautionary tale of a once-radical and creative movement that had degenerated into an institution, a part of the Establishment.

Fear of Mormon theocracy was not new; this had been a persistent trope since Sir Arthur Conan Doyle's 1887 mystery *A Study in Scarlet* had first introduced the character of Sherlock Holmes as the detective who solved a case exposing a dangerous Mormon cabal. As well, political cartoons and media representations had long depicted Mormonism as a social menace that threatened to devour everything decent in its path—a fear that heightened in frenzy each time a Latter-day Saint was positioned for a high national office, whether it be Reed Smoot's election to the Senate in 1902 or Mitt Romney's campaigns for president more than a century later. But what was different about Kushner's portrayal was the play's assumption that Mormonism was *already* a part of the Establishment, a throne of power in itself. Though once an acknowledged pariah, Mormonism had ascended to cultural acceptance, even control—and thus was to be dreaded all the more.

This tension is seen most clearly in the deep cultural backlash that followed the LDS Church's 2008 mobilization of volunteer labor and donations to support California's Proposition 8, an anti-gay-marriage ballot measure that would define marriage as exclusively between a man and a woman. After the motion had passed and it became clear that Mormons had been among its staunchest supporters, several astute commentators noted the irony that while Latter-day Saints had in the nineteenth century gone all the way to the Supreme Court to expand the nation's definition of marriage, they were now the most visible soldiers in a war to restrict it.

The LDS Church's institutional leadership in passing Proposition 8 became a rallying point for public outcry, and its subsequent attempts to make light of its own participation did not help its public image. Shortly after the election, the church released an official statement claiming that its in-kind donations totaled around $2,000, a tiny portion of the full amount raised for the Yes on 8 campaign. In February of 2009, however, the church clarified that the in-kind donations had actually totaled $190,000, but stressed that this represented only one-half of one percent of the campaign. However, many felt it was disingenuous for the church to minimize its involvement by only reporting on "in-kind" institutional participation (that is, paid employee time and travel) rather than the much larger amount donated by individual Mormons who had been prompted to do so by the church. The Family Research Council claimed that Mormons were responsible for raising $22 million; PBS and the *New York Times* both cited a figure of around $19 million of the total generated. Whatever the actual amount, it was clear that the LDS Church's attempts to distance its official institutional involvement by claiming that rank-and-file members were donating of their own free will was a distinction lost on most people who followed the story.

One of the popular culture artifacts to emerge from the controversy was the documentary *8: A Mormon Proposition* (2010). Although the independent film received limited distribution compared to the large-scale media stories and YouTube videos about Proposition 8 in broad circulation, it clearly had an impact. Some reviewers noted the heavy-handedness of the documentary's dramatized scenes, even while celebrating its muckraking as a necessary counterbalance to "institutions that . . . are undermining our democracy." One cited problems with the documentary's facts, but also called it an example of "an intrepid David taking on an evil, cruel-hearted Goliath." Whatever its flaws, the documentary expressed the fury of many people whose suspicion of the LDS Church as an institution was at an all-time high. And the fact that it was subtitled *A Mormon Proposition*—obscuring the Roman Catholic bishops, Orthodox Jews, and African American Protestants who also supported the measure—indicates that the Mormons' unique skill for mobilization and fundraising had made the LDS Church the movement's most visible institution.

At the same time that the post–Proposition 8 controversy was in full swing in early 2009, the third season of the HBO series *Big Love* was addressing the legality of same-sex marriage through the ongoing metaphor of the Henricksons, a fictionalized modern-day polygamist family in the Salt Lake City suburb of Sandy. The Henricksons are the ultimate mavericks, rejecting the broader institutions of government and church in favor of a privatized family faith. Season three's most controversial episode, "Outer Darkness," shows the character of Barb, the family's first wife, "taking out her endowments," participating in Mormonism's most sacred temple ritual on a borrowed temple recommend. Barb is trying to experience one last sacred connection with the LDS Church of her youth before the formal excommunication she knows is coming because her current polygamous status has been discovered. Many Mormons were outraged that the series would depict the religion's holiest and most secret rite, which is open only to members in good standing who hold a current temple recommend. However, *Big Love*'s anti-institutional bent was more openly demonstrated in a season four story arc when Bill, the family's prosperous patriarch, attempts to make public a historical document that the LDS Church is trying its best to sweep under the rug because it would be a public embarrassment. The LDS Church hierarchy here is depicted as duplicitous and scheming, going to extreme lengths to protect a carefully manufactured public image.

On the flip side of such intense drama is the 2011 Broadway musical *The Book of Mormon*, which one scholarly journal has called a "noisy, heartfelt, touching, gaudy, and weirdly illuminating patchwork of tenderness and blasphemy."[11] Even the title of the production is a gentle slap in the face of the LDS Church as an institution: by calling it *The Book of Mormon*, the writers expropriate the literary work that is most associated with the LDS Church, and then turn it to entirely comic ends.

In the show, written by *South Park* creators Trey Parker and Matt Stone, two missionaries who are sent to northern Uganda represent the tension between America's respect for individual Mormons and its misgivings about their church's hierarchy. Elder Price represents the latter well: he is the elder who is going places, the Eagle Scout who is certain he will win converts and glory to the LDS Church. He is also, as Jesus himself tells him in one of the show's funniest sequences, "a dick"—self-centered and shallow. Elder Price's companion, Elder Cunningham, does not at first glance seem like a promising Mormon. He is a follower, socially inept and painfully eager to have Elder Price as a friend who will take charge. But it's Elder Cunningham who stays the course when the going gets rough, wholly reinventing the stories of the Book of Mormon in his enthusiasm to give the Ugandans comfort in the face of widespread AIDS and dangerous warlords. Elder Cunningham's creative approach to doctrine sparks a flurry of baptisms, but when the mission president descends in his white-shirted rigidity to congratulate the elders, the new converts shock him with a musical number about what they have learned. Its bungled Mormon history and theology deeply offend the church's official representative, who pulls the plug on the mission. But Elder Price, now persuaded that Elder Cunningham's approach of loving people is the core truth of Mormonism, stays alongside his companion to continue teaching the new converts. One message here is that the LDS Church as an institution does not have a monopoly on Mormon truth. It's the institution that Elder Price has to jettison in this rite-of-passage tale, not the core values of Mormonism, which are identified as working together, helping each other, and building a better future for all. In the end, tweaking Mormonism's millennialist origins, the show's finale asserts, "the only latter day that matters is tomorrow."

The Book of Mormon musical suggests that in American popular culture today, it's permissible to be spiritual but not religious. In the film *Latter Days* discussed above, for example, the protagonist's awakening requires leaving institutional Mormonism behind while retaining many of the strong character values that the religion imparted—and being a beacon of hope to others who need to learn lessons of love and commitment. Such anti-institutionalism is not unique to American culture's treatment of Mormonism, but mirrors broader trends. One of the most striking features of recent sociological research about religion in America is what some analysts call the rise of "the nones." These are people who claim no religious affiliation on national surveys—not just self-described atheists, who are actually a tiny percentage of the population, but people who are not affiliated with a particular religious institution, even if they share that institution's general beliefs. A 2007 Pew survey of the American religious landscape found that 16 percent of the total adult population self-identified as having no religious affiliation, which was more than double what it was in the 1970s.[12] What's more, the percentage of young adults who reported they were unaffiliated was around a quarter of that demographic's population, showing that a trend toward disaffiliation and anti-institutionalism was very likely to continue. And continue it did: in 2012 Pew conducted a major follow-up study called " 'Nones' on the Rise," which showed a sharp uptick over the earlier statistics. "In the last five years alone, the unaffiliated have increased from just over 15 percent to just under 20 percent of all U.S. adults," the study summarized. Moreover, 32 percent of adults under age 30 said they had no religious affiliation, compared with just one in ten in the age group of Americans age 65 and older. Clearly, disaffection with religious institutions was not unique to Mormonism, but marked a major demographic trend in America more generally.[13]

MORMON ASSIMILATION
AND THE MODEL MINORITY

Although anti-institutional examples continue to proliferate and perhaps even increase in popular culture's notions about Mormonism, a growing countertrend is to show individual Mormons not just as acceptable Americans who are to be tolerated in a religiously diverse culture, but as moral exemplars for others. The first striking public example of this occurred in Donny and Marie Osmond's televised variety show in the late 1970s, in which almost all of the members of their large Mormon family were showcased at one point or another. Squeaky-clean comedy sketches, dance numbers, and G-rated musical performances cemented the Osmond family's image as close-knit and committed to old-fashioned values. Donny may have been "a little bit rock and roll," but compared to the rock and roll that was being performed at the time by KISS, AC/DC, and Pink Floyd, his version seemed quaint and nonthreatening to many Americans.

Beginning in the 1980s, as the larger culture turned its attention to issues of financial prosperity and business success, Mormon figures like Stephen Covey and J. W. Marriott rose to prominence. Covey's *The Seven Habits of Highly Effective People* (1989) did not wear its Mormonism on its sleeve, but its emphasis on character and integrity as the keys to professional leadership derived in part from Mormon values. Magazines such as *Business Week* have periodically wondered aloud about the Mormon propensity to produce so many top executives in comparison to the religion's small presence in the general population, with much of the rationale being laid at the door of the Mormon missionary experience. The discipline imparted, languages learned, and confidence gained in missionary service—as well as the almost military obedience required toward authority figures—are lauded as valuable steps in leadership training.

Indeed, in popular culture, the Mormon missionary experience is a source of continued fascination. One of the most surprising trends might be the use of the Mormon missionary image as a kind of coded symbol for Christian evangelists more generally. John-Charles Duffy has analyzed seven independent films in which LDS missionary characters appear, and discovered that in most of them, the missionary figures are not intended to be specifically LDS but more generically Christian, indicating "a measure of success for LDS efforts to persuade outsiders that they are Christian."[14] The badge-wearing Mormon missionary has become such an assimilated and instantly rec-ognizable figure that it can easily be expropriated for other uses.

That's not to say that popular culture has eroded the distinctions between Mormons and members of other religions. Such differences and stereotypes, if anything, have been reified and even celebrated in the odd medium of reality television. The Mormon presence on reality shows in the early twenty-first century is far out of proportion with Mormons' actual numbers in the population. One explanation is that they only *seem* to be disproportionately represented because their religion is almost never permitted to recede into the background—members of a minority must expect that their minor-ity status will be commented upon, particularly in the artificial constructs of "reality" shows such as *The Biggest Loser* or *Survivor*, which emphasize conflicts between people of different backgrounds. But does that explain why there were two Mormon finalists among the top five contestants in the seventh season of *American Idol*, or four Mormon professional dancers competing on *Dancing with the Stars*?

Additional explanations are possible. One casting director for *Survivor* (won by Mormon Todd Herzog in 2007) mused that Mormon competitors came to the game better prepared than others because in their missions they had already experienced what it was like to be dropped off in the middle of nowhere and forced to survive with people they had never met. That may be, but what is especially interesting about the success of Mormons on such shows as *Survivor, American Idol, So You Think You Can Dance*, and *Dancing with the Stars* is that all of those shows are, at least in part, popular-ity contests: viewers' votes count alongside the professional judges' scores in determin-ing the outcome. It is likely that many Mormons are thrilled enough with the prospect of some among their number competing for major prizes on national television that they call in to vote, then call again. But it is also now likely that non-Mormon view-ers have been impressed enough by these competitors' self-perpetuating stereotype of Mormons as friendly, helpful, and devoted to their faith that there has been some thaw-ing of the ice.

It's not only in the arena of reality television that individual Mormons have been upheld as "model minority" ideals. For example, in 2007 the medical drama *House* introduced a Mormon character who was a morally upstanding person but also flex-ible and broad-minded, challenging the stereotype of Mormons as narrow thinkers. (The character was also African American, which challenged another stereotype that many people have about Latter-day Saints.) And other series have shown one-off Mormon characters who would be ideal neighbors. On *Frasier*, Frasier Crane fires an agent he knows to be unethical in negotiations, but then worries that the Mormon replacement agent—who is unfailingly ethical and professional, and literally wears a Boy Scout uniform—will not be able to play hardball. But in both cases, the writ-ers revealed an ignorance about Mormon belief. Cole on *House* does not pray in the manner or language of a Mormon, for example, and the writers manage to insert digs about "magic underwear" (temple garments), Joseph Smith, and polygamy. In fact, House calls Cole by the nickname "Big Love," even though Cole's character is a single dad and not a polygamist.

MORMON SELF-DEFINITION
THROUGH POPULAR CULTURE

While some Mormons have taken to mainstream America's reality airwaves as visible exponents of their religious faith, others have sought to create their own popular culture predominantly for a Mormon audience. As with *The Mormon Bachelor* and *The Mormon Bachelorette*, these are sometimes knockoffs of trends in the host culture, but increasingly they are meaningful cultural products in their own right.

In 2000, a young filmmaker named Richard Dutcher made headlines with the surprising release of *God's Army*, a drama about the LDS missionary experience as told through the eyes of a "greenie" (new missionary). *God's Army* offered something that Mormon moviegoers had not before seen: a mostly positive (but not propagandistic) portrayal of their faith that had high production values. Dutcher called the success of *God's Army* the "birth of Mormon cinema," noting the emerging market for independent films that were by Latter-day Saints about the Mormon experience. The Association of Mormon Letters awarded *God's Army* its first-ever AML Award for film, the new category a reflection of the LDS literati's hope that Dutcher would prove correct about a new flowering of Mormon cinema.

However, this was not quite the case. A flurry of knockoff missionary films and screwball comedies followed in the wake of *God's Army*, some enjoying modest commercial success (for example, 2002's *The Singles Ward*, which garnered $1.25 million at the box office) but others dead on arrival (for example, *The Home Teachers*, 2004, which earned just $196,000, less than half of what it cost to produce). Even more discouraging than box office receipts, however, was the reality that apart from Dutcher himself, no Mormon filmmakers managed to offer strong scripts and thoughtful commentary while still remaining commercially viable to more than just the art-house crowd. Even Dutcher had difficulty repeating his early success; 2001's *Brigham City*, a dark and compelling murder mystery set in a small Mormon town, did not have breakout box office appeal. Whereas *God's Army* had cost around $300,000 to make and produced more than an eightfold return on investment from theater showings alone, not counting an additional $2 million in sales of its DVD in the first month of its release, *Brigham City* had a budget of $900,000 and barely broke even, bringing in approximately $905,000 at the box office.

Dutcher's independent films demonstrated Mormons' desire and growing ability to depict their own people rather than be at the mercy of Hollywood. Other small indy films have looked at aspects of the LDS experience, such as the 2012 documentary *Duck Beach to Eternity*, which chronicles single Mormons' annual trek to a North Carolina beach for spring break. But it's not just in film and television that we see Mormons' new emphasis on defining themselves; it's also in the Church's own "I'm a Mormon" ad campaign, begun in 2010. In the video ads, people tell their personal stories, which are often emotionally powerful, and end with the simple phrase, "I'm a Mormon." The campaign aims to challenge people's stereotypes about Mormons, and eschews weighty doctrinal teachings in favor of human interest stories. If viewers want to know more about what Mormons believe, they can find out at www.mormon.org; otherwise, the ads choose to emphasize common inspirational themes of family, overcoming difficult circumstances, and developing unique talents. The individuals whose stories are selected by the church fly in the face of what people might expect from orthodox Mormonism—a competitive motorcyclist, a female drummer in a rock band, or a Haitian-American woman who is the mayor of a Utah town. Although it can be argued that focusing on these exceptions actually proves the rule (Mormon Americans are statistically white and conservative, in contrast to the rainbow effect of the ads), they represent a new Mormon emphasis on self-labeling.

CONCLUSION

Whether through public relations, film, or other media, it is clear that Mormons not only wish to take matters into their own hands to tell their stories but have the means to do so. This stands in contrast to the historic trajectory of the intersections of Mormonism and popular culture, in which Mormonism serves as foil for larger trends in America. In the nineteenth century, the sexualization of polygamy through novels and cartoons effectively reified Victorian ideals about monogamous superiority. In the twenty-first century, pop culture examples articulate a Mormonism that is stuck in an old-fashioned and ultimately deleterious sexual ethic that does not accommodate sexual diversity or difference. Both extremes reveal less about Mormonism than they do about what American culture *needs and wants* from Mormonism; a minority religion is tapped to perform cultural work to bolster the mainstream.

However, as Mormons continue to enter that mainstream (to wit, the "Mormon Moment" of 2012, with its unprecedented media coverage), popular culture simultaneously expresses an unease with the institutional LDS Church and a cautious lauding of individual Mormons as members of a model minority. Mormons are depicted as successful (whether in the boardroom or on the ballroom dance floor), hardworking, and honest even while the LDS Church is viewed as overly secretive, wealthy, and powerful.

NOTES

1. Marquis, "Diamond Cut Diamond," 177.
2. Givens, *Viper on the Hearth*, 164.
3. Putnam and Campbell, *American Grace*, 92, 128.
4. Pew Forum on Religion and Public Life, "Mormons in America."
5. Finan, "Julianne Hough Singing & Dancing Queen."
6. Erzen, *Fanpire*.

7. For a helpful discussion of the evolution of Hannah's character from book to film, see "Major Latter-day Saint (Mormon) Character in the movie *Wonder Boys* (2000)."

8. Austin, "Four Consenting Adults in the Privacy of Their Own Suburb," 38.

9. Trepanier and Newswander, *LDS in the USA*, 41.

10. Hutchison-Jones, "Center and Periphery," 11, 26.

11. Hicks, "Elder Price Superstar," 227.

12. See Pew Forum on Religion and Public Life, "US Religious Landscape Survey Report."

13. Putnam and Campbell, *American Grace*, 126, 123. See also "'Nones' on the Rise," Pew Research Center for Religion and Public Life, October 9, 2012, http://www.pewforum.org/2012/10/09/nones-on-the-rise/.

14. Duffy, "Elders on the Big Screen," 124.

BIBLIOGRAPHY

Astle, Randy, and Gideon O. Burton. "A History of Mormon Cinema." *BYU Studies* 46, no. 2 (2007): 12–163.

Austin, Michael. "Four Consenting Adults in the Privacy of Their Own Suburb: *Big Love* and the Cultural Significance of Mormon Polygamy." In Decker and Austin, *Peculiar Portrayals*, 37–61.

Bowman, Matthew. *The Mormon People: The Making of an American Faith*. New York: Random House, 2012.

Decker, Mark T., and Michael Austin. *Peculiar Portrayals: Mormons on the Page, Stage, and Screen*. Logan: Utah State University Press, 2010.

Duffy, John-Charles. "Elders on the Big Screen: Film and the Globalized Circulation of Mormon Missionary Images." In Decker and Austin, *Peculiar Portrayals*, 113–43.

Erzen, Tanya. *Fanpire: The Twilight Saga and the Women Who Love It*. Boston, MA: Beacon Press, 2012.

Finan, Eleen. "Julianne Hough Singing & Dancing Queen." *People*, May 26, 2008. http://www.people.com/people/archive/article/0,,20203998,00.html.

Givens, Terryl L. *The Viper on the Hearth: Mormons, Myths, and the Construction of Heresy*. New York: Oxford University Press, 1997.

Gordon, Sarah Barringer. *The Mormon Question: Polygamy and Constitutional Conflict in Nineteenth-Century America*. Chapel Hill: University of North Carolina Press, 2002.

Hicks, Michael. "Elder Price Superstar." *Dialogue: A Journal of Mormon Thought* 44, no. 4 (Winter 2011): 226–36.

Hutchison-Jones, Cristine. "Center and Periphery: Mormons and American Culture in Tony Kushner's *Angels in America*." In Decker and Austin, *Peculiar Portrayals*, 5–36.

Iversen, Joan Smyth. *The Antipolygamy Controversy in U.S. Women's Movements, 1880–1925: A Debate on the American Home*. New York: Routledge, 1997.

"Major Latter-day Saint (Mormon) Character in the movie *Wonder Boys* (2000)." Last modified March 21, 2005. http://www.ldsfilm.com/movies/WonderBoys.html.

Marquis, Kathy. "Diamond Cut Diamond: The Mormon Wife vs. the True Woman, 1840–1890." In *Women in Spiritual and Communitarian Societies in the United States*, ed. Wendy E. Chmielewski, Louis J. Kern, and Marlyn Klee-Hartzell, 169–81. Syracuse, NY: Syracuse University Press, 1993.

Mason, Patrick Q. *The Mormon Menace: Violence and Anti-Mormonism in the Postbellum South*. New York: Oxford University Press, 2011.

Mauss, Armand L. *The Angel and the Beehive: The Mormon Struggle with Assimilation*. Urbana: University of Illinois Press, 1994.

Pew Forum on Religion and Public Life. "Mormons in America: Certain in Their Beliefs, Uncertain of Their Place in Society." January 12, 2012. http://www.pewforum.org/2012/01/12/mormons-in-america-executive-summary/.

Pew Forum on Religion and Public Life. "US Religious Landscape Survey Report: Summary of Key Findings." June 23, 2008. http://www.pewforum.org/2008/06/23/us-religious-landscape-survey-resources/.

Putnam, Robert D., and David E. Campbell. *American Grace: How Religion Divides and Unites Us*. New York: Simon and Schuster, 2010.

Shipps, Jan. "From Satyr to Saint: American Perceptions of the Mormons, 1860–1960." In *Sojourner in the Promised Land: Forty Years among the Mormons*, 51–97. Urbana: University of Illinois Press, 2000.

Trepanier, Lee, and Lynita K. Newswander. *LDS in the USA: Mormonism and the Making of American Culture*. Waco, TX: Baylor University Press, 2012.

CHAPTER 29

···

MORMON FOLK CULTURE

···

ERIC A. ELIASON

To a devout insider, "Mormon folklore" might seem an oxymoron. To a skeptical outsider, it might seem a redundancy.[1] Both reactions assume definitions of "Mormon"
and "folklore" that differ from how academic folklorists use these terms. "Mormon"
refers not only to official LDS doctrines; it includes all varieties of Mormon people and
their experiences. "Folklore" does not merely mean the bogus, quaint, or pioneer-era
vestigial aspects of Latter-day Saint life. Rather, folklore is the living traditions, stories, and beliefs that are passed on in face-to-face situations outside of official channels. Examples include legends of folk heroes such as the "cussing apostle" J. Golden
Kimball and frontier lawman Porter Rockwell, encounters with the angelic Three
Nephites, Relief Society quilting bees, BYU coed jokes, creative dating traditions, and
the homemade wall charts used to rotate Family Home Evening assignments. Folklore
also encompasses testimonies, conversion stories, and traditional healings by priesthood blessings.

Veracity is not what distinguishes folklore from other forms of cultural expression. Rather, it is the mode of transmission—informal vs. formal, intimate vs. remote,
small group vs. mass media, and oral vs. written. Folklorists distinguish between the
dogmas and practices that disseminate top down through denominational authority structures, and the customs, beliefs, and stories that bubble up from the pews. This
institutional–vernacular cultural divide is often blurred—especially with Mormons,
who have no clergy–laity distinction, often align with the hierarchy's teachings, and
commonly implement top-down directives with personalized folkways. Rather than
merely revealing oddities, folklore transmits Mormons' most cherished experiences.
Folklore provides a window into *actual* beliefs and practices—or "lived religion,"
to use religious studies' new term for the venerable folkloristics concept of "religious
folklife"—rather than the ideal types sometimes proffered by normative proclaimers.
Mormons, as subject matter and as scholars, figure more prominently in folklore than
any other discipline.

Prebirth Experiences, Joseph Smith's Visions, and Experience-Centered Folklore

Rushing to the hospital in April 1947, Jenalyn Wing Woffinden fell unconscious from premature labor pains. The receiving physician doubted she would survive. But after waking she related the following:

> I found myself in the Celestial Room of the Salt Lake Temple. As I walked across the back of the room . . . a man dressed in white robes . . . came up to me and introduced himself as Peter, a disciple of Jesus Christ. He told me I would have great difficulty rearing this child. . . .
>
> Peter then introduced me to the child's spiritual mother who was dressed in white. . . . She told me of the difficulty she had had raising the child in the spiritual world and [said] the only way I would be able to successfully raise [him] would be with unbounded love.

Peter foretold many hardships for the boy, and repeated the charge to love him unceasingly. As of 1964—when Brigham Young University student Russell Bice collected this story from Sister Woffinden's daughter for folklore professor Tom Cheney—the boy's sickly and rebellious nature was validating his mother's vision.

Though dramatic, this story is not doctrinally foundational like Joseph Smith's First Vision. Sister Woffinden is an ordinary Mormon. Her vision, though doubtless important to her family, remains largely unknown to other Mormons. What is remarkable—besides encouraging unrestrained love in an era of ostensible emotional distance—is that thousands of Mormon parents today continue to tell similar stories.

While Sister Woffinden had a sleeping near death experience (NDE), most LDS preborn children narratives describe a wakeful encounter. In 2010, a young Arizona couple began hearing noises in their house and sensed a watcher on their roof: "Joe was outside bringing in the groceries and our bishop drove by. He said to Joe, 'I have a strange question to ask you.' Joe responded, 'I have a strange answer!' Our bishop proceeded to ask if we have ever seen a little girl at our home. Joe just got chills. The bishop explained how the young neighbor girl had been seeing 'Angel girls' on our roof and outside of our home. The Bishop believed these spirits were our own children in spirit waiting to come to our home."

In another instance, a couple agreed to stop talking about having children since this caused too much marital tension. Almost immediately, a blue-eyed little girl with blond pigtails began to visit the wife repeatedly asking to be born. Wearied and deprived of sleep, the wife warily told her husband about these encounters. He replied, "So, she's been bothering you too, has she?"

Folklorists call personal narratives of supernatural encounters "memorates." Memorates featuring spirit children not yet born are prebirth experiences (PBEs). Few have had a PBE, but most Mormons know someone who has. Parents pass them on as etiological narratives of how their children came to be. PBEs often form the most cherished spiritual experience in one's life. Notably, official church publications rarely mention, and neither discourage nor encourage, them. Yet this vibrant folk tradition is deeply dependent on official LDS doctrines, such as people's prebirth spiritual life; spirits' human shape; entitlement to personal revelation; and parenting's centrality to our purpose on Earth. These are not abstract notions only for those few interested in theological esoterica. They are living concepts dramatically emergent in the lives of Latter-day Saints through PBEs.

PBEs suggest a possible correlation between LDS beliefs and scientific findings about the human mind. Folklorists have shown how traditional cultures can pass on sophisticated knowledge that science embraces only later. Ethnobotanists have developed hundreds of modern medicines from traditional remedies around the world. Ethnohistorians have shown that preliterate societies' rigorous oral traditions can perpetuate genealogical information unrecorded by documents but corroborated by genetic testing. However, scholars have less actively plumbed memorates for scientific insights. Folklorist David Hufford is one of the few working to develop ethnopsychology and ethnotheology as disciplines.[2] He regards encounters with spirit children, deceased relatives, and human-shaped beings, both glorious and ominous, as akin to other kinds of first-hand empirical evidence. In his "experience-centered approach," memorates are not anomalies to be ignored or delusions to be cured. They are instead data points—means to uncover the nature of common psychological and spiritual realities.

Bolstered by popular PBE authors Elizabeth and Neil Carman and Sarah Hinze's anecdotal evidence,[3] Hufford's quantitative data show that memorates like PBEs and sleep paralysis (malevolent spirits seizing people in bed at night) happen to about 20 percent of people. This rate does not correlate with psychiatric diagnoses or cultural, educational, or religious background, but seems to occur evenly across populations. Spirit-encounter memorates happen more frequently than the more academically respectable mystic or transcendent states of notable people in various religious traditions. In fact, rather than sensationalizing a mystic experience by presenting as it as tangible, Hufford has found people more likely to obfuscate or "mystify" what were originally straightforward meetings with person-like beings.

According to Hufford, some cultural and religious traditions are better equipped than others to make sense of memorates. Baptists and atheists might not find understanding cobelievers to listen to their PBE, since neither worldview brooks a pre-earth life. Mental health professionals typically offer little help or deem them delusional. Many who've had a PBE understandably remain reticent.

Hufford suggests psychiatry follow ethnobotany and ethnohistory in learning to draw on traditional knowledge—especially if doing so can help patients. Hufford, a Catholic, finds LDS theology particularly well suited to making sense of the full spectrum of spiritual visitations as they actually happen to people across cultures. Hence Mormons tend to be less anxious about sharing them. However, PBE-relating traditions have also developed among Hindus and Buddhists, who understand them quite comfortably in terms of reincarnation. Despite Hufford's contention that robust, cross-culturally similar experiences constitute evidence for a knowable external spiritual reality, his findings may alternately merely demonstrate common powerful subjective psychological experiences.

In either case, the experience-centered approach has potential implications for understanding foundational Mormon memorates—Joseph Smith's First Vision and the Angel Moroni's appearance. The Prophet presented these as literal meetings, not mystic dreams or transcendent impressions. Terryl Givens contends that the great uniqueness of Mormon theology is its nondivision of the spiritual from the material, its foundational episodes' resistance to metaphoric interpretations, and its understanding of humans, angels, and gods as the same class of being at different stages of progression.[4] The experience-centered approach suggests that such understandings are not merely LDS notions, but part of the world's underlying reality—or at least the human mind part of it.

Some scholars see differences between the earliest First Vision accounts and more concrete later ones as evidence that Joseph Smith elaborated a standard mystical experience for his day into one where he met glorified persons face to face. Experience-centered findings make it reasonable to suppose just the opposite—that he remembered human-like beings from the first, but only revealed fuller details later as he felt more comfortable doing so. Even the canonized First Vision account shows signs of reticence. Without later interpretive glosses, a reader might not catch that "personages" refers to God the Father and Jesus Christ. But the echo in the Sacred Grove of the voice that spoke "this is my beloved son in whom I am well pleased" at Jesus' Baptism and at the Mount of Transfiguration suggests as much (Matthew 3:17, 17:5).

Some claim a fabulist Joseph Smith inflated his story from seeing one angel, to just Jesus, to both God the Father and Jesus. But if Smith was inconsistent about the numbers and identities of beings he encountered, he places himself squarely in Old Testament prophetic company. Abraham's and Lot's hospitality toward two or three travelers whom the Bible variously calls "The Lord," "men," and "angels"; Jacob wrestling with what is traditionally glossed as an angel but what the text actually calls "a man" or "God face to face"; Joshua meeting "a man," the captain of God's angelic army, or the Lord himself before the Battle of Jericho; the annunciation of Samson's birth by what his parents are unsure is a man, an angel, or perhaps the Lord himself, are all examples (Genesis 18:1, 2, and 19:1; Genesis 32:24, 30; Joshua 5:13–15, 6:1–2; Judges 13:2–23). Resonant with both experience-centered folklore and Mormon theology, Bible authors present ambiguity as to visitor identity as common in memorates, and that this happened because, men, angels, and gods come in similar form.

James Kugel, Orthodox Jew and Harvard professor of Hebrew literature, explains that the Bible's earliest authors saw humans, angels, and "the God of Old" as all having physical bodies that allowed them to walk and talk together.[5] Only later did Bible authors abandon anthropomorphic gods for the incomparable formless God of Isaiah and Daniel.

For generations, Bible readers have understood early memorate accounts through later authors' and interpreters' metaphorizing eyes. Others, like Joseph Smith, who believed the Bible world was being restored, and experience-centered folklorists who have found such memorates to be a universal norm might say, "Amen" to Kugel's proposed face-to-face encounters and continuity of form among heavenly beings and earthly persons.

But seeing PBEs as emergent from ancient psychic universals helps explain only their content. It does little to explain the particular contexts in which they might occur. Feminist folklorist Margaret Brady suggests PBEs provide wives a revelatory "trump card" forcing foot-dragging husbands to father children.[6] According to Brady, motherhood is women's primary means of validation in LDS patriarchal culture. However, actual LDS households are typically much more egalitarian, even matriarchal, and very few recorded PBEs suggest gender power struggles. When they do, PBEs tend to bring unity, as in the blonde pigtail girl story.

PBEs could also be a response to tensions Mormons feel between church teachings and modern lifestyles. Church leaders have traditionally encouraged large families and discouraged birth control. Such admonitions abated in the 1980s and virtually disappeared in the mid-1990s. But pronatalism remains strong and Mormons still tend to have slightly more children on average than other Americans. With worldly voices calling children a burden, quality better than quantity, and "breeders" threats to the environment, prophetic calls not to limit family size stand in stark contrast. In the struggle to know which path to follow, PBEs can provide clear resolutions to difficult dilemmas. However, even granting these interpretations, just because PBEs can serve certain functions does not mean these functions cause the experiences.

FAITH-PROMOTING RUMORS AND MORMON IDENTITY

Managing the opposing pulls of church and world is a common theme in Mormon folklore. Latter-day Saints are acutely aware of how a different lifestyle and beliefs set them apart from the secular and orthodox Christian worlds. Even as some Mormon-watchers proclaim Mormonism a respectable "new world religion," others still dismiss it as a weird faux-Christian cult. Mormons know of both perceptions. Both highlight otherness rather than inclusion. A dual desire to be special and normal is central to many Mormons' consciousness. Terryl Givens calls this "exile vs. integration" paradox one of the central "fields of tension" that define Mormon identity.[7]

The Christian folk saying, "To be in the world but not of it,"—very loosely paraphrased from the Bible (Romans 12:1–2; John 15:17–19, 17:11–18) and oft repeated in Mormon circles—can produce considerable anxiety as to its meaning, especially in adolescence when both fitting in and finding one's unique identity are so important. The church offers guidance on chaste, sober living and media consumption. The official booklet *For the*

Strength of Youth warns young Mormons "Choose carefully the music you listen to . . . some music carries evil and destructive messages."[8] However, it avoids naming particular popular musicians to embrace or eschew. Mormons are left to determine this for themselves. Mormon youth folklore has expanded into this vacuum of specific guidance in some well-developed ways.

In the 1980s, Latter-day Saint teenagers circulated interconnected rumors about the Irish rock band U2. According to these stories, U2 laced their 1987 album *The Joshua Tree*, with cryptic references to their collective spiritual journey, such as the track "I Still Haven't Found What I'm Looking For." The album's title itself suggested that this seemingly decent band might be joining the church. The clinching proof that U2 would soon resolve the dilemma of "not finding what they are looking for" by converting appeared in the track "Where the Streets Have No Name."

Understanding how this clearly indicated immanent conversions requires delving deep into Mormon esoterica. The possible correlation between the album's title and the Utah locale of the limited-range Joshua tree plant seemed provocative, especially to those who knew that Mormon pioneers crossing the Mojave Desert had given the upward-branched plant its name, in reference to the biblical Joshua lifting his arms in prayer. "Where the Streets have No Name" surely referred to Salt Lake City since Brigham Young's implementation of Joseph Smith's design for the city of Zion, Mormon-settled towns traditionally forgo street names for a numbered grid system.

Mormons' hopeful *Joshua Tree* interpretations are variants of a larger tradition of finding cryptic meanings in popular music albums. (Such as the supposed "Paul is dead" clues to be found in the lyrics and album art of the Beatles' 1968 *White Album* and 1969 *Abbey Road*.) Seeing U2 legends as one facet of a larger tradition of faith promoting rumors about famous soon-to-be Mormons is also important. Soon after the church lifted the priesthood ban on blacks, stories circulated of famous African Americans joining the church—such as pious football star Herschel Walker and popular crooner Lionel Ritchie. Undoubtedly, such tales helped young Mormons feel like their church was quickly getting beyond this uncomfortable policy. With such stories, LDS youth attempt to reconcile their attraction to mainstream popular culture with loyalty to their church.[9] If Bono and The Edge are about the join the church, then listening to their music must be okay. Right? However, by the turn of the twenty-first century, the U2 rumor complex had lost its luster. While millions have converted since 1987, no Irish rock superstars are among them. However, Motown icon Gladys Knight and her family actually are.

WHAT MORMON FOLKLORE IS SIGNIFICANT?

Positive valuation of "faith-promoting rumors" such "famous people joining the church stories" and second-hand PBEs coexists with caution toward them. Sharing such stories may make one seem kooky, even to other Mormons. Merciless Internet debunkings can reveal one as a dupe; but being too skeptical of a friend's personal belief can brand one an unbeliever. Perhaps in a community open to visions, miracles, and prophecies, it is especially important to guard against fakery. But Salt Lake City has no office like the Vatican's that investigates miracles and pronounces them genuine or fraudulent; Mormons are generally on their own in such matters. Many Mormons avoid giving too much credence to such tales the further away they get from first-hand experience. Some first-hand experiences are accompanied by an impression not to share them except in sacred moments.

Focusing on PBEs and sensational urban legends may perpetuate a problem pointed out by William A. Wilson—the most important folklorist to study Mormons. Near the end of a long and fruitful career, Wilson began chastising folklorists, including himself, for focusing on extraordinary—to the exclusion of more common but quieter—varieties of lore. According to Wilson, folklorists, "shape our data not to reveal the essence of the material we have collected, but to please and meet the expectations of those who will read our publications and view our presentations."[10] Wilson's point is akin to arguing for emic (cultural descriptions using insiders' own understandings) over etic (cultural descriptions using scholarly cross-cultural analytical vocabularies) ethnographic writing. Indeed, if PBEs and faith promoting rumors ceased forever tomorrow, it might make little difference to most faithful Mormons.

However, the cessation of Latter-day Saints' more common, but less dramatic, "promptings" would be a devastating existential threat. As Tom Mould's *Still, the Small Voice* examines, promptings are how personal revelation most often works in Mormons' lives. Promptings can come as a strong impression to do something, or to avoid doing something. They are not usually accompanied by an audible voice or visual image. Mormons believe promptings can come unbidden to those who have learned to listen for them. However, they tend to quit coming when they are not followed or the effects of sin cloud the mind. Promptings can warn against physical danger, spiritual danger, or encourage acts of compassion and service. Promptings can be both pivotal moments in one's life and, for some, a steady stream of gentle guidance. To Mormons unfamiliar with folklore studies, calling promptings folklore might seem trivializing. But just because something is folklore does not mean it is not true. In fact, people are more likely to experience and share their most meaningful moments through traditional face-to-face encounters in small group settings than by any other means.

While Wilson's emic argument is worth considering, it is somewhat of a straw man. Serious folklorists don't really want sensationalia that hypes superstitious backwardness. They want persuasive analysis richly illuminating folk groups' distinctive ways and central concerns. Some folklore allows this better than others; it is not always lore the folk regard as most important. Folklorists can glean cultural insight from *both* the most significant sacred aspects of religious traditions as well as trivial fringe phenomena. Consider, the following joke from the 1970s:

Q: Why are crows black?

A: Because they refused to eat crickets in the preexistence.[11]

This joke was in no way central to Mormon experience. But its analysis reveals a trove of references to Mormon ideas and anxieties in a small package. To make sense of it, one must not only know that "crow" is an ethnic slur, but also of the pre-earth spiritual creation of life; premortal spirits making choices that influence the circumstances of their birth; the War in Heaven, where spirits chose the Lord's or Satan's side; the notion that that those less valiant in this struggle were born to people of African ancestry, cursed with dark skin, and blocked from ordination to the priesthood; the decreasing popularity of this explanation at the time; the negative media attention on the church for not ordaining blacks; the discomfort many Mormons felt about the policy; the desire many had to nevertheless support it as the will of God; the folk history of seagulls saving Utah pioneers' crops by eating swarming crickets; historians' questioning the more dramatic versions of the seagull story; the idea that animals had a premortal existence and have souls; and the understanding that animals do not have moral agency like humans.

By cheekily inverting this last idea and venting numerous anxieties of the time, this joke burned quite bright until the church rescinded the priesthood ban in 1978. Folklore's importance is not just in how typical it is, but also in how revealing it is. Unlike many Three Nephite stories, which are variants of more widespread American vanishing hitchhiker urban legends, this joke has no non-Mormon variants. This joke, and cryptic decodings of U2's album, are densely and irreducibly Mormon. They demonstrate how compact language can be in referencing a host of shared knowledge and the often complex and conflicted, nature of peoples' sentiments.

American and Biblical "Folk Magic" and the Foundations of Mormonism

To many academics, the connection between Mormonism and folklore has little to do with jokes, faith promoting rumors, PBEs, or promptings. Instead historians in the 1980s and 1990s focused on the relationship between "frontier folk magic" and the origins of Mormonism. This issue became so charged that it factored in two murders in the most tragic episode in the history of Mormon studies.

Joseph Smith and his associates' involvement in practices such as dowsing for water with divining rods, and searching for buried treasure with seer stones had long been known to historians, as was the common, but not uncontroversial, nature of such practices in Joseph Smith's time. Later in life, Smith reported giving up treasure seeking as youthful folly unworthy of his religious calling. However, in the 1980s, new research suggested a more in-depth and ongoing involvement with "magical" practices than was previously understood—as evidenced by the Smith family's possession of a talisman, an astrological dagger, and magical parchments.

Some scholars suggested that Mormonism's foundation lay more in the world of "frontier folk magic" than in the prophetic biblical world he claimed. This contention was bolstered by the emergence of the infamous "Salamander Letter" purportedly written by Joseph Smith's associate Martin Harris to William W. Phelps describing the results of a treasure hunting trip. This document provided a different account than the canonized version of the Angel Moroni giving Joseph Smith the Golden Plates: "I take Joseph aside & he says it is true . . . the next morning the spirit transfigured himself from a white salamander in the bottom of the hole & struck me 3 times & held the treasure & would not let me have it . . . the spirit says I tricked you again . . ."

When newspaper cartoons depicted the salamander as a small newt-like amphibian, Mormons understandably found the letter unsettling. But if the salamander had been understood as one of the quite distinct beings of the same name in European lore that, like angels, dwell unburnt amid elemental fire, the letter might have seemed a little less troubling.

However, the Salamander Letter and several other newfound documents difficult to square with traditional historical understandings proved to be forgeries. (In retrospect, perhaps the fact the letter had a salamander, or fire elemental—rather than the traditional gnomes, or earth elementals—guarding a buried treasure should have raised some eyebrows.) As the forger's promises to deliver buyers' documents outpaced his ability to create them, he began trying to murder people he feared would expose him. One of his package bombs killed a document collector, and another diversionary bomb intended for a collector's business partner instead killed the partner's wife. In a third explosion, the forger injured only himself and thereby drew enough suspicion for authorities to arrest him.

The bomber was Mark Hofmann, a document dealer legendary for his uncanny "discoveries" of provocative historical documents. In his plea-bargained testimony, he described himself as a practicing Mormon but long-time closet atheist who set out to profit personally by undermining traditional LDS historical understandings. Hofmann is internationally regarded as one of the most masterful forgers of all time and is serving a life sentence in the Utah State Prison. Thanks to him, many historical documents without a verifiable pre-1970's provenance are still suspect. And thanks to sensationalistic reporting, the idea that folk magic is in some scandalous way related to Mormon origins, and the notion that the LDS Church tried cover up its true history, still persist in popular imagination despite Hofmann's exposure and the church's invitations to the press to examine their newly acquired documents.

At the time, most scholars writing about early Mormon folk magic were historians of the American West or American religious history. None were folklore scholars in the field most obviously suited to the topic. The only exception was William A. Wilson's two reviews of historian D. Michael Quinn's *Early Mormonism and the Magic World View*—the overreaching yet still seminal work on the topic.[12]

The lack of folklore-informed engagement on this issue continues to leave misconceptions uncorrected and serious issues unaddressed. Folklorist David Allred, whose work informs this chapter, has sought to remedy this.[13] He reminds scholars how folklorists helped de-exoticize the common magic/religion distinction by showing them to be functionally and structurally very similar concepts whose differences have more to do with culturally constructed notions emerging from relationships of group identity, prestige, and power than they do from any intrinsic qualities of magic or religion. For example, one of the contemporaneous critics of Smith's involvement in scandalous superstitious doings was Doctor Philastus Hurlbut. Ironically, Hurlbut's given name, "Doctor," had nothing to do with professional training. Rather, he got it from being a seventh son and therefore thought to have special healing powers. When Hurlbut opposed Joseph Smith, the belief in seventh-son powers was in a different category than seer-stone–aided treasure digging—at least in Hurlbut's parents' minds when they named him. Today however, many might see both practices as two of a kind.

The presumption that the difference between magic and proper belief is something intrinsic rather than relational to the definer is still very much alive. But on close analysis, complex definitions distinguishing "magical" from "modern" thinking rarely amount to more than, "what *you* do is superstition while what *I* do is science or true religion." One of the biggest surprises rural students have in American university folklore courses, including at BYU, is discovering their suburban peers need to be taught what divining rods are and how to use them. Regardless of class, race, education, wealth, region, or religion, rural students know of holding a forked stick gently in one's hand to feel for the downward tug that points to underground water and a good spot for a well. Dowsing seems not only understandable, but also necessary, in rural areas where families are on their own to secure water, and where hired well-drillers make no guarantees and charge by the foot. City kids are shocked that their country classmates could be such shameless occult dabblers in a modern age where you don't have to think about where water comes from. You just turn on the tap and out it comes—like magic.

Even Joseph Smith himself, as he moved from being a canny country boy to a cultured urbanite, seemed influenced by his new context's negative valuation of divining practices, and made efforts to distance himself from them even as he continued other practices that might seem suspect to cosmopolitan twenty-first-century Americans. But it is simply wrong to assume that divining practices are some long-abandoned exotic aspect of America's frontier past, rather than a continuing worldwide phenomenon used not only by rural Americans, but by soldiers in Vietnam to find enemy tunnels, by oil and precious-metal prospecting companies, and even by contemporary salvage professionals to recover lost treasure. But none of this means that there are not also bogus scams, such as the well-developed industry of luring American investors to fund "sure-fire" efforts to recover caches of loot hidden by Japanese soldiers retreating from the Philippines at the end of the Second World War. These always seem to need a little more financing and never seem to produce for investors.

Some twentieth-century Mormons have persisted in using "magical" means to find precious things underground. Former bishop John Hyrum Koyle was excommunicated in 1948 for repeated claims—against church admonition—that he would save the church from financial ruin with his "Dream mine" near Spanish Fork, Utah. Conversely, Jesse Knight used a divining rod to find a gold mine, making him a wealthy man. Considering his find a gift from God, Knight scrupulously treated his workers well, kept his mine closed on Sundays, and really did help save the church from near financial ruin brought about by its struggle with the federal government over polygamy. While memories of Koyle's audacious claims stir mostly in his local region, Knight has a building named after him at BYU—though his method for getting donation money is mostly forgotten. The main difference between Koyle and Knight has little to do with how they decided where to dig, which was similar. Rather, the difference is that Knight's mine actually produced gold, while Koyle's few remaining stockholders still await that day.[14]

Folklore studies can help dispel naïve notions like the existence of one transcultural and transhistorical "magic worldview" that *other* people have that is distinct from the supposed "nonmagic worldview" of sophisticated moderns. Moderns likely to put on jackets to prevent catching a cold, or wait an hour after eating to go swimming to prevent drowning from cramps, or trust eyewitness testimony to identify criminals in police lineups despite the thorough scientific debunking of each of these contemporary superstitions. Unfortunately, when historians talk about early Mormon folkways, their analysis is often clouded by understanding "folklore" to mean "incorrect notions that uninformed people believe" and "folk magic" to mean "superstition or paganism." Such definitions prevent scholars from seeing value in, or making proper sense of, traditional practices Joseph Smith may have participated in.

Scholars without experience in Mormon studies or folklore venturing into the Mormon magic question, can engage in imaginative "selective reinterpretation" of Mormon intellectual history such as John L. Brooke's Bancroft Prize-winning *Refiners Fire: The Making of Mormon Cosmology, 1644–1844*. Brooke's book takes seeming similarity, rather than clear causal connection, as evidence that LDS doctrinal concepts had their origins in seventeenth-century European occult practices by way of the radical reformation's clandestine undercurrent in colonial New England. Brooke magnifies beyond recognition the significance of what is at best a thin trickle of influence while overlooking much clearer and closer probable inspirations for LDS concepts, such as the Campbell or Stone movement. These Christian primitivists, with whom Sidney Rigdon affiliated before his conversion, used terms such as "restoration," "age of accountability," "baptism as a saving ordinance," and "first four principles and ordinances of the gospel" before Mormons did. Brooke also short shrifts the deeper connections Mormons point to in the biblical near East and early Christianity.

Brooke does point out, however, that those pointing to folk magic as evidence of Mormon credulity overlook past scientific heroes like Isaac Newton's deep delving into magical alchemy. (Newton wrote over a million words on the subject and understood his magical work as indistinct from his scientific pursuits.) Evangelical anti-Mormons do this as well—seeing folk magic as evidence of Joseph Smith's, non-Christian, paganism. However, celebrating Jesus' birth with decorative greenery drawn from pre-Christian Germanic practices, in late December, in an unbroken continuation of Roman festivities in honor of Saturn, god of the harvest, is apparently okay, as is celebrating Jesus's resurrection by painting eggs and fetishizing newborn animals after the manner of worship once direct toward Ostara—the proto-Indo-European goddess of the dawn who gave Easter its name.

Bias in magic identification shows up in the Bible as well. The same Bible that proclaims "thou shalt not suffer a witch to live" and condemns Saul's necromantic visit to the witch of Endor, portrays favorably or without criticism Jacob's using sympathetic magic in showing pregnant sheep bark-stripped rods to make them bear more of the striped lambs Laban agreed to give him; Joseph of Egypt owning a silver divining cup; prophets and apostles using physical objects to discover the will of God, such as casting lots to determine a guilty party or a new apostle; and consulting the bejeweled ephod or Urim and Thummim priestly adornments to determine a course of action or the mind of God (Exodus 22:18; 1 Samuel 28; Genesis 44: 1–5; Jonah 1:7–8; Acts 1: 24–26; Exodus 28: 4, 29:5, 39:2; Leviticus 8:7; Judges 8:26–27, 17:5; 1 Samuel 21:9; 2 Samuel 6:14; Exodus 28: 30; Leviticus 8:8; Deuteronomy 33:8; 1 Samuel 28:6; Hosea 3:4; Ezra 2:63; Nehemiah 7:65.). Such practices seem little different in essence than Joseph Smith using a divining rod, seer stone, or for that matter, a Urim and Thummim to find lost objects or translate ancient records.

Such practices characterize Jesus' ministry as well. It took place in the religious milieu of several other non-Christian religions from which it emerged, including Judaism and what Morton Smith has called "native Palestinian Semitic paganism."[15] Bible scholars generally understand that Jesus's contemporaries interpreted his miracles as magical and that the Gospels depict Christ's actions as akin to magical practice. For example, Christ's removal to the wilderness for forty days parallels shamanistic training. The words Christ used to raise Jairus's daughter, "Talitha cumi," were similar to a magical formula of the day, and Jesus's spitting in dirt to make a paste to anoint a blind man's eyes and then telling him to ritually wash in an enchanted pool would be recognizable to virtually any traditional healer or magician of any time or place.[16]

While some contemporary Bible-believers may be myopic in their criticisms of Joseph Smith, they are correct to see the Bible as a key to understanding Joseph Smith's "magical" practices. According to Bible scholar Shawna Dolansky, a magic–religion distinction "is not represented in ... ancient Near Eastern literatures" and ancient Hebrews did not make a distinction between licit and illicit magico-religious practices based on form or content.[17] In the cultural context of ancient Israel, the prohibitions found in Deuteronomy 18 and Leviticus 19–20 do not categorically condemn magic. "Magic as a category was not illegal. The mediation of divine power in the hands of priests or prophets ... was perfectly legal." According to Bible authors, Moses's turning his staff into a snake was not the same as Pharaoh's magicians doing so, since Moses was a prophet of God and Jannes and Jambres were not. From a biblical perspective, determining whether Joseph Smith's treasure seeking, seer-stone gazing, blessing of "magic" handkerchiefs, and the like, were proper or not, should not be based on whether moderns see them as weird or similar to pagan practices, but whether or not Joseph Smith was an authorized prophet of God. Presumably, since Joseph Smith claimed to be God's instrument for restoring biblical priesthood authority, he would have welcomed this basis for determination.

In both Christendom and Mormondom, the seeming disappearance of "folk magic" either by abandonment or normalization into official practice is partly the result of Max

Weber's routinization of charisma process and partly the result of developing methods of exercising divine authority. What today might be regarded as mixing folk and official practices was seen in the past as an unproblematic unified whole. In nineteenth-century Mormonism, Latter-day Saints, including women, known to have individual healing gifts were as likely to be sought out for laying on of hands and traditional remedies as a chain of command priesthood authority. The now long-forgotten ordinance of rebaptism served not only to signal recommitment to the faith, but also as a cleansing remedy for illness. The consecrated oil today dabbed on one's crown for priesthood blessings was then poured liberally or mixed into ointments and poultices for topical application to wounds, or was drunk straight from the bottle for stomach and bowel ailments.[18] For contemporary Mormons who believe in both medicine and priesthood blessings, but keep them separate, time can divide as well as religion or culture, making ancestral practices seem as unusual as those of exotic foreigners.

To folklorists, magic-seeming practices are not counterevidence to prophetic claims. In light of Joseph Smith's statement that "One of the grand fundamental principles of Mormonism is to receive truth, let it come from whence it may," the idea that the restoration of all truth might draw from folk-magic traditions should be no more shocking than the fact that many Protestant hymns have found their way into LDS hymnbooks. The fact that this issue continues to trouble some perhaps reveals more about modern attitudes toward earlier and unfamiliar practices—and the work Mormon folklorists have yet to do in de-exoticizing them—than it does any problems in Mormon origins.

David Allred suggests:

> Applied to early Mormonism, using the phrase *folk magic* (or "*the magical world view*" [or occult, or hermetic]) presents a debate in which the well is poisoned against understanding and context even before it begins. Joseph Smith did not have a category "folk magic." On the other hand, when scholars use emic terms like *money-digging, seer stone, glass looking*, and *rod* they are on the right track since this insider terminology reveals more about how the practices were viewed by the practitioners. Of course, these terms have the drawback of being unfamiliar to modern readers. However, when the denotation of a term is unclear, the researcher can introduce the term while constructing a context that is consistent with the time and that sidesteps the politicized connotations that are prevalent today.[19]

Richard Bushman and Terryl Givens have suggested that Mormonism is history more than theology. The faithful's defining touchstones are beliefs about what happened in the Sacred Grove and during the translation of the Book of Mormon perhaps even more so than the doctrines that emerged from them. By abandoning negative, politicized understandings of folklore as Allred asks, scholars can begin to recognize that more than even theology or history, folklore forms the essence of Mormonism. This has nothing to do with the validity of its truth claims, or how much "folk magic" may have influenced its beginnings. Folklore goes much deeper to the bedrock of Mormon origins and identity than even sharing PBEs or faith-promoting rumors. LDS missionaries explain to their investigators that the literate culture practice of reading the Bible never gave anybody authority to do anything. Rather, authority comes only through the practice favored in oral culture of an unbroken tradition of laying on of hands that extends back to memorate angelic appearances in the typical folklore setting of personal encounters in small groups. Not just authority, but identity and doctrine pass on most significantly not by literate means, as important as these are, but by folkloric means, such as parents relating episodes of ancestral pioneer history as a Family Home Evening lesson, or as missionaries in an investigator's living room telling in their own words the story of a "personage" God visiting a New York farm boy face to face.

NOTES

1. The author wishes to thank Philip Barlow, David Allred, and Mark Ashurst-McGee for their particularly helpful readings of, and contributions to, this chapter. I could not have written the section on folk magic without the invaluable assistance of David Allred. I have benefitted immensely not only from his excellent work on the topic, but also from his gracious help in the writing of this chapter.
2. Hufford, *Terror that Comes in the Night* and "Beings without Bodies."
3. Carman and Carman, *Cosmic Cradle*; Hinze, *We Lived in Heaven*.
4. Givens, *People of Paradox*, 37–38.
5. Kugel, *God of Old*.
6. Brady, "Transformations of Power."
7. Givens, *People of Paradox*, xv.
8. *For the Strength of Youth*, 22.
9. Tingey, "Famous People and Mormonism."
10. Wilson, "Folklore, a Mirror for What?," 13–21.
11. Van Leeuwen, "Crows."
12. Wilson, reviews of Quinn, *Early Mormonism*, 1987, 1989.
13. Allred, "Early Mormon 'Magic.'"
14. Cantera, "Currency of Faith"; Stegner, *Mormon Country*, 171–81.
15. Smith, *Jesus the Magician*, 68.
16. Mark 5:41; Smith, *Jesus the Magician*, 95. John 9:6–7.
17. Dolansky, *Now You See It*, 20–27, 54.
18. Bush, *Health and Medicine among the Latter-day Saints*.
19. Allred, "Early Mormon 'Magic,'" 184–97.

BIBLIOGRAPHY

Allred, David A. "Early Mormon 'Magic': Insights from Folklore and from Literature." In Eliason and Mould, *Latter-day Lore*, 184–197.
Bice, Russell. "A Child Called Peter." William A. Wilson Folklore Archive, Special Collections, Harold B. Lee Library, Brigham Young University, individual collection assignment FA 02 1.1.1.5.1, (1964).
Brady, Margaret K. "Transformations of Power: Mormon Women's Visionary Narratives." *Journal of American Folklore* 100, no. 398 (December 1987): 461–68.

Brooke, John L. *The Refiners Fire: The Making of Mormon Cosmology, 1644–1844*. New York: Cambridge University Press, 1994.

Bush, Lester E., Jr. *Health and Medicine among the Latter-day Saints: Science, Sense, and Scripture*. New York: Crossroad, 1993.

Cantera, Kevin. "A Currency of Faith: Taking Stock in Utah County's Dream Mine." In *Between Pulpit and Pew: The Supernatural World in Mormon History and Folklore*, ed. Paul W. Reeve and Scott Van Wagenen, 125–58. Logan: Utah State University Press, 2011.

Carman, Elizabeth M., and Neil J. Carman. *Cosmic Cradle: Souls Waiting in the Wings for Birth*. Fairfield, IA: Sunstar, 2000.

Dolansky, Shauna. *Now You See It, Now You Don't: Biblical Perspectives on the Relationship between Magic and Religion*. Winona Lake, IN: Eisenbrauns, 2008.

Eliason, Eric A. *The J. Golden Kimball Stories*. Urbana: Illinois University Press, 2007.

Eliason, Eric A., and Tom Mould, eds. *Latter-day Lore: Mormon Folklore Studies*. Salt Lake City: University of Utah Press, 2013.

Fife, Austin, and Alta Fife. *Saints of Sage and Saddle*. Bloomington: Indiana University Press, 1956.

For the Strength of Youth. Salt Lake City, UT: Church of Jesus Christ of Latter-day Saints, 2011.

Givens, Terryl L. *People of Paradox: A History of Mormon Culture*. New York: Oxford University Press, 2007.

Hinze, Sarah. *We Lived in Heaven: Spiritual Accounts of Souls Coming to Earth*. Provo, UT: Spring Creek, 2006.

Hufford, David J. *The Terror that Comes in the Night: An Experience-Centered Study of Supernatural Assault Traditions*. Philadelphia: University of Pennsylvania Press, 1982.

Hufford, David J. "Beings without Bodies: An Experience-Centered Theory of Belief in Spirits." In *Out of the Ordinary: Folklore & the Supernatural*, ed. Barbara Walker, 11–45. Logan: Utah State University Press, 1995.

Kugel, James L. *The God of Old: Inside the Lost World of the Bible*. New York: Free Press, 2004.

Mould, Tom. *Still, the Small Voice: Narrative, Personal Revelation, and the Mormon Folk Tradition*. Logan: Utah State University Press, 2011.

Quinn, D. Michael. *Early Mormonism and the Magic World View*. Rev. ed. Salt Lake City: Signature, 1998.

Smith, Morton. *Jesus the Magician*. New York: Harper and Row, 1978.

Stegner, Wallace. *Mormon Country*. New York: Duell, 1942.

Tingey, Brent. "Famous People and Mormonism." William A. Wilson Folklore Archive, Special Collections, Harold B. Lee Library, Brigham Young University, Salt Lake City. Folklore Archive Focused Field Project #1163 (1994).

Turley, Richard E. *Victims: The LDS Church and the Mark Hofmann Case*. Urbana: University of Illinois Press, 1992.

van Leeuwen, Barbara. "Crows." William A. Wilson Folklore Archive, Special Collections, Harold B. Lee Library, Brigham Young University, Salt Lake City. Individual collection assignment F 3.10.3.5.1.1 (1978).

Welch, John W., ed. *Opening the Heavens: Accounts of Divine Manifestations, 1820–1844*. Provo, UT: Brigham Young University Press, 2011.

Wilson, William A. "Folklore, a Mirror for What? Reflections of a Mormon Folklorist." *Western Folklore* 54, no. 1 (1995): 13–21.

Wilson, William A. *The Marrow of Human Experience: Essays on Folklore*. Ed. Jill Terry Rudy. Logan: Utah State University Press, 2006.

Wilson, William A. Review of *Early Mormonism and the Magic World View*, by D. Michael Quinn. *Western Historical Quarterly* 20, no. 3 (1989): 342–43.

Wilson, William A. Review of *Early Mormonism and the Magic World View*, by D. Michael Quinn. *BYU Studies* 27, no. 4 (1987): 96–104.

CHAPTER 30

MORMON ARCHITECTURE AND VISUAL ARTS

PAUL L. ANDERSON

In 1947, Minerva Teichert, one of the best-trained and most highly motivated Mormon artists of her generation, wrote that the art of the Latter-day Saints should be "rich in story and backed by a great faith."[1] Her words might serve as both a historical summary of Mormon architecture and art and as an idealistic mission statement for the years to come. Mormon art has given physical expression to a richly varied story, blending unique religious ideals and historical experiences with many outside influences. And considering the thousands of meetinghouses and temples, and also the vast quantity of LDS artistic images often created in difficult times through great sacrifice, it is also clear that Mormon art and architecture have given evidence of "a great faith."

This chapter defines Mormon architecture and art as works that are directly related to the religious life and distinctive cultural identity of the Latter-day Saints. In architecture it focuses on ecclesiastical buildings—meetinghouses, tabernacles, temples, and administrative facilities—but does not discuss domestic, civic, educational, or commercial architecture in Mormon communities. In painting and sculpture, it emphasizes works that deal directly with LDS religious and historical themes, whether created by Mormons or outsiders, with or without Church sponsorship. However, it does not include art by Mormons on more secular subjects. Although encyclopedic completeness is not possible, this chapter will identify some significant patterns, themes, and policies and describe a few of the most outstanding, influential, or widely recognized works that have contributed to an LDS artistic consciousness and heritage—for better or for worse.

The LDS religious tradition has deeply ambivalent attitudes toward the arts. While the thirteenth Article of Faith (Pearl of Great Price [PGP] 1:13; first published in 1842) asserted that the new Church embraced "anything virtuous, lovely, or of good report or praiseworthy," the Protestant cultural traditions most familiar to the Church's founders disapproved of excessive display. Their Methodist, Baptist, Quaker, and

Congregationalist neighbors, while often creating beautifully proportioned and richly crafted places of worship, generally banned religious figurative painting and sculpture from churches and homes. While sharing these austere attitudes, Mormons also harbored somewhat incompatible aspirations to create the glories of a new Kingdom of God on earth.

The artistic expressions of the LDS Church were also complicated by its desire to create a distinctive image, separate from other traditions, but still respectably Christian. The result has been a cultural balancing act. Tolerance for varying degrees of artistic decoration in LDS places of worship has waxed and waned over the years as some Church leaders have insisted on removing "inappropriate" art from meetinghouses and temples that earlier Church leaders had authorized.[2] Artwork has also been reinstalled in places from which it had been temporarily banned. Latter-day Saints have cautiously accepted architectural and artistic influences from many religious sources, seesawing between traditional and progressive elements. The Church has also alternated between actively nurturing the talents of its own artists and commissioning some of its most important projects from well-established outsiders.

BUILDING THE KINGDOM: NINETEENTH-CENTURY MORMON ARCHITECTURE

One of the most striking aspects of early Mormonism is the absolute literalism it brought to the familiar Christian metaphor of building the City of God. The Church's energy and resources throughout the nineteenth century were largely focused on building a vast network of orderly cooperative agricultural villages that would protect the Saints from a hostile and corrupt world. Nearly all Mormon architecture in this period was an integral part of such Mormon communities.

Mormon architecture began with a sacred multipurpose building. In 1833, Church leaders sent a rough sketch of a temple and a plan for the City of Zion to the early Church members in Independence, Missouri. Persecution drove the Mormons out almost immediately, so a similar temple in Kirtland, Ohio (1833–36), became the first significant LDS building. Like so much Mormon architecture to follow, the Kirtland Temple was a mixture of conventional American architectural forms and distinctly unconventional elements. A simple rectangular structure with its gable end facing the street and a bell tower on its roof, it was larger than most Ohio churches and constructed more substantially of stucco-covered stone rather than wood. While large Protestant churches often had one tall worship space with a balcony, the temple was divided into two assembly rooms, one over the other. The lower room served for public worship and the upper room for secular and religious instruction. These assembly rooms had beautiful woodwork with distinctive three-tiered triple pulpits at both ends for the officers of the Aaronic and Melchizedek priesthoods—life-sized organizational charts of the Church's elaborate hierarchy—with handsome windows behind them framing the leaders in halos of light. The attic contained smaller offices and meeting rooms for Church leaders. These different spaces allowed the temple to function as meetinghouse, school, and administrative headquarters.

The Nauvoo Temple (1841–45) was a larger version of the Kirtland Temple, with several significant additions. In its basement was an elaborate baptismal font supported by twelve stone oxen providing for the new practice of proxy baptisms for deceased ancestors. Rows of offices for Church leaders were crowded into mezzanines above the side aisles of the two large meeting rooms. The attic was divided by curtains into rooms for presenting the "endowment," dramatized instructions about eternal salvation, and for performing marriages "for time and all eternity." Symbolic folk-art carvings on the exterior stone walls and colored-glass windows depicted the sun, moon, and stars—symbols of the evolving Mormon doctrines of eternal glory. Both temples were left behind as the Saints moved westward.[3]

When the first pioneers arrived in Utah in 1847, Brigham Young immediately chose a temple site and divided the future city into wards of nine blocks each. With a bishop assigned to each ward, these divisions became the fundamental units of the Church. Mormon architecture developed in new directions as the multiple functions of the early temples were parceled out among other buildings. The tabernacle on Temple Square became the community's central meeting hall. Every ward soon built its own meetinghouse and school (often a single structure at first). The temple assumed more exclusively spiritual functions. The Council House and President's Office housed Church and community administration. Tabernacle, meetinghouse, temple, and office building thus became the characteristic building types of Mormonism.

Plans for the Salt Lake Temple, begun in 1853 by architect Truman O. Angell (1810–87) under Brigham Young's close supervision, aspired to monumental grandeur. Although based on the Nauvoo Temple plan, its exterior had a totally new image. Reflecting Church leaders' missionary travels among England's Gothic cathedrals, as well as American enthusiasm for Gothic and Romanesque Revival styles, the temple included buttresses between deep-set windows, castellations along the parapet, and multiple spires and pinnacles. The three-tiered triple towers at both ends externalized the symbolism of priesthood authority of Kirtland's three-tiered triple pulpits. As in Nauvoo, emblems of the sun, moon, stars, and other heavenly bodies ornamented the buttresses and towers. With its thick stone walls and its upward-pointing spires, the temple was both a fortress and a cathedral connecting the center of the new City of Zion to the heavens. This grand design would require forty years to complete.

The LDS religious buildings actually realized in the 1850s were far less monumental structures, mostly gabled meetinghouses built of adobe. The largest of these, the "Old Tabernacle" (1851–52), was a giant dugout seating 2,500 worshippers, with its floor below ground level and its squat adobe walls supporting large roof trusses. Over the years, ward meetinghouses became larger and more elaborate in design, mostly built in brick or stone—and incorporating towers and arched windows. Only a few early meetinghouses remain, including adobe structures in Grantsville and Toquerville, the brick Salt Lake Tenth Ward chapel, rock churches in Farmington and Parowan, and a handsome wood-frame building in Pine Valley. Many communities also built Relief Society halls and granaries, amusement halls, cooperative stores, dance pavilions, stake offices, academies, and seminaries. Larger settlements constructed impressive tabernacles for regional meetings (stake conferences) and other community events. The first Provo Tabernacle (1856–61) was a well-proportioned adobe structure with a bell tower and fine woodwork that seated 1,100 worshippers. Built a decade later, the St. George Tabernacle (1863–76) looked much like a red-rock version of an eighteenth-century New England church with a tall white spire and a beautifully finished interior including a three-sided balcony.

The second tabernacle built on Temple Square (1863–67) was a truly unique architectural and engineering achievement. Architect William Folsom (1815–1901) planned a hall 150 feet wide and 250 feet long to seat 10,000 people, an enormous challenge without railroad access to manufactured building products. Bridge-builder Henry Grow (1817–91) figured out how to span the space with huge curved lattice trusses similar to those used for New England's covered bridges. The trusses were pegged together with wooden dowels and a very limited supply of metal fasteners. The remarkable structure served as the venue for semiannual Church conferences for over 130 years and continues to be used for Tabernacle Choir broadcasts as well as many other religious and cultural events.

The neighboring Assembly Hall (1876–85) introduced the more elaborate Victorian architecture of the prosperous post–Civil War years to Utah. Architect Obed Taylor (1824–81), a convert from San Francisco, designed the meeting hall with rough gray granite walls, a host of pinnacles, and a central tower temporarily graced with an angel weathervane. Its lively silhouette and elaborate interior inspired exuberant tabernacles in Provo, Brigham City, Heber City, Coalville, Manti, Moroni, Richfield, Cedar City, and Paris (Idaho), all major landmarks of Mormon country.

In the last decade of his life, President Brigham Young directed the erection of three smaller Utah temples that are the jewels of Mormon pioneer architecture. The St. George Temple (1871–77) was a medievalized version of the Nauvoo Temple, with Gothic buttresses, Romanesque windows, and a single tower. Its white plaster walls gleamed against the vermilion cliffs nearby. The temples in Logan (1876–84) and Manti (1875–88) had towers at both ends, like the Salt Lake Temple. President John Taylor approved their new interior arrangement, subdividing the basement and lower meeting room into four impressive lecture halls for the endowment with appropriate murals. The ceremonial procession through these rooms culminated in a palatial Celestial Room. This new arrangement was also adopted for the Salt Lake Temple's interior. Both the Logan and Manti buildings occupied dramatic hillside sites and were beautifully constructed of local stone. The Manti Temple has particularly elegant woodwork and two spectacular spiral staircases.

Integration and Accommodation: Mormon Architecture in the Early Twentieth Century

The completion of the Salt Lake Temple in 1893 was the culmination of pioneer architecture, occurring at a cultural turning point midway between the official abandonment of polygamy in 1890 and Utah's statehood in 1896. The Latter-day Saints rapidly transformed themselves from a dissident minority into loyal citizens seeking a place in the mainstream, and this fundamental change was reflected in the Church's architecture. Aspirations for respectability were embodied in buildings that included many aspects of traditional American and Christian architecture.

The Salt Lake Temple itself exemplified some of these changes. The Church's first college-educated architect, Joseph Don Carlos Young (1855–1938), completely redesigned its interiors in the opulent classical style then popular for mansions and public buildings. He included Tiffany stained-glass windows as well as an annex structure in the modified Byzantine style then briefly popular. These fashionable late-Victorian elements in the Church's most important building implied a new openness to outside influences.

The Church built more than a thousand buildings during the first half of the twentieth century in a wide variety of styles, including Gothic stained-glass windows, Renaissance domes, Romanesque arches, scalloped Spanish Baroque gables, American Colonial steeples, and various modernistic elements. In general, a preference for traditional styles alternated with modern tendencies, with 1900–10, 1920–30, and 1945–55 being mostly traditional, and 1910–20, 1930–40, and 1955–65 showing more modern influences.

The twentieth century began with a Mormon building boom as the Church experienced a degree of peace and prosperity. President Joseph F. Smith reorganized and reinvigorated the Church's administrative structure, creating nineteen new stakes in 1902. Many stake tabernacles and more than 200 new meetinghouses were constructed during the decade. Most meetinghouses included facilities for activities that had previously been accommodated in separate buildings: chapels for worship; amusement halls for social, dramatic, and sports activities; offices for the bishop and clerks; classrooms for Sunday School and Primary (children's programs); and a slightly more elaborate room for the women's Relief Society. As LDS congregations sprang up across the nation, meetinghouses with these comprehensive facilities provided homes for LDS community life.

The most popular style for the new meetinghouses was a Protestant variation of Gothic architecture with a corner tower, a steep gabled roof, and a pointed-arched window. A few of these buildings included handsome stained-glass windows of Joseph Smith's First Vision, expressions of Mormon identity in a traditional Christian format. Other meetinghouses were classical in style, with columned porticos and, in two cases, impressive domes. A few were more exotic, with Spanish Baroque (Mission-style) gables or Italianate towers. Local Church leaders and their architects were free to choose from a rather extensive menu of acceptable styles.

At Church headquarters, an impressive new Administration Building (1912–18) contained the offices of the president and other top leaders. With granite walls and monumental Ionic columns all around, it projected a conservative image—as dignified as a government bureau and solid as a bank. Inside, its marble foyers and wood-paneled meeting rooms exuded stability and permanence. By contrast, the first twentieth-century temple built at the same time was one of the great surprises in Mormon architectural history. The winner in the 1912–13 anonymous competition for the new temple in Alberta, Canada, was a boldly modern design with no spire or pinnacles, a composition of strong horizontal and vertical elements reflecting the influence of Frank Lloyd Wright and other avant-garde architects. Its young architects, Hyrum C. Pope (1880–1939) and Harold W. Burton (1887–1969), also invented a completely original floor plan, with the principal ordinance rooms in four wings surrounding the central Celestial Room. The large assembly room that had been a main feature of earlier temples was now completely absent. The temple interiors were finished with splendid hardwood paneling, harmonious murals, and custom-made furnishings in a modern style.[4] This progressive design opened the way for more than two dozen modern LDS meetinghouses, as well as the smaller modern temple in Hawaii (1915–19), also by Pope and Burton. Some of the best remaining LDS buildings in this style are the Parowan Third Ward, the Ogden Branch for the Deaf, the Garland Tabernacle, and the Montpelier (Idaho) Tabernacle.

The prosperous 1920s were a conservative decade in America architecturally, and the Latter-day Saints followed national trends. Don Carlos Young (1882–1960, son of Joseph Don Carlos Young) and Ramm Hansen (1879–1972) won a 1920 competition for the Arizona Temple with a restrained classical design, its interior centered on a monumental staircase like many great public buildings of the time. In 1923, a new Church Architectural Department began furnishing standard plans for meetinghouses at no cost to local wards and stakes. About 350 red-brick buildings with no towers and Colonial-style details were built, varying in size and decoration. Most included chapels and amusement halls on the main floor and classrooms in the basement. Congregations were free to hire their own architects if they preferred, however, and some chose the equally respectable Tudor style, with steep roofs and half-timbered gables. In California, the first area with substantial membership beyond the Great Basin, congregations generally chose the regionally popular Spanish Colonial style, with stucco walls, arched doors and windows, and tile roofs. The Spanish-modern Hollywood Stake Tabernacle and Wilshire Ward (1927–29), the Romanesque-revival Salt Lake Granite Stake Tabernacle (1928), and the towering Washington, DC, Chapel (1928–33) were outstanding buildings of the period.

The Great Depression greatly reduced construction projects and ended the Church Architectural Department. When building began again slowly in the mid-1930s, many LDS meetinghouses adopted an austere, streamlined modernism, with flat roofs, horizontal bands of windows, and some geometric details. This unusually progressive image was influenced more by commercial and civic Art Deco buildings than by churches of other denominations. Its ultimate example was the Idaho Falls Temple (1937–45) by Salt Lake architects John and Henry Fetzer (1882–1965 and 1906–91) with a modern tower much like the top of a Wall Street skyscraper.

BUILDING FOR AN INTERNATIONAL CHURCH

The post–Second World War years were another major turning point in Latter-day Saint history. Membership had more than quadrupled since 1900 and congregations were growing far beyond Utah due to out-migration and missionary success. By the late 1960s, in response to this unprecedented expansion, the Church had reinvented its meetinghouses and temples, had evolved a new system for design and construction, and was producing new buildings with unprecedented speed.

From 1945 to 1955, the Church outsourced most of its meetinghouse planning to a few Salt Lake architects who designed traditional red-brick Colonial buildings with white-columned porticos and spires. Hundreds of these all-American emblems of Mormonism were reproduced in the United States and Canada. In California and Arizona, local LDS architects designed more modern-looking meetinghouses with occasional use of Spanish decorative elements. As the need for new buildings outstripped the ability to construct and finance them, the use of one building by two (and later three or more) congregations became common.

The most impressive Mormon monument of the period was the huge Los Angeles Temple (1951–56), the first to be built in a major city. Designed by Church architect Edward O. Anderson (1891–1977) in a restrained modern style, its 257-foot tower (twenty-five stories tall) claimed a place on the city's skyline as a powerful symbol of the Church's emergence into a wider world.

Beginning in 1955, a new Church Building Committee under the energetic leadership of California businessman Wendell J. Mendenhall (1907–78) greatly accelerated construction, centralization, and standardization. Its first standard plans were for small meetinghouses in Polynesia, often constructed by young local "building missionaries" trained by experienced American contractors. This program spread to Australia, the Far East, Europe, and the United States, producing more than 2,000 buildings in a decade. Meanwhile, many meetinghouses in western America were commissioned from local architects with some aesthetic freedom. The result was a brief blossoming of modern designs, some with tall, light-filled chapels and handsome exteriors. One of the best, the 1960 Alderwood Ward in suburban Seattle, won design awards from the American Institute of Architects. However, the breakneck speed of the building program overextended Church finances, bringing a new regime of austerity and universal standardization in 1965. The twenty-eight-story Church Office Building (1962–72) in Salt Lake City provided an appropriate corporate image for the increasingly centralized organization.

Architects and designers at Church headquarters have since continued to prepare detailed plans for nearly all meetinghouses. In the 1960s and '70s, the buildings reflected a suburban modernism with low-pitched gable roofs, simple towers, and classroom wings spreading out from the chapel and recreation hall. More compact plans without projecting wings dominated the 1980s, providing more energy efficiency but less ecclesiastical character—their large spreading roofs looked like branch banks, and their windowless chapels were not universally loved. Most of these buildings were later retrofitted with traditional steeples. In the 1990s, the Church, for the third time in the twentieth century, adopted American Colonial details—spires, porticos, and pediments—to give its meetinghouses a familiar religiosity.

Temples were also transformed and standardized. To provide a temple in Switzerland in the 1950s for a multilingual Mormon population, live dramatic performances of the endowment were replaced with a film presentation. Films have been used for all subsequent temples. The new temple exteriors, almost always faced in light-colored masonry, evolved into three basic dignified and solid-looking forms: the rectangular box with a tower over the entrance (e.g., Berne, Tokyo, and Boston), the stack of boxes with a central spire (Oakland, Bountiful, and Panama City), and the box with towers at both ends (Washington, DC, Stockholm, and San Diego). The Angel Moroni statue atop the tower, previously used only on the three largest temples, became a universal feature, beginning with the Jordan River Temple (1978–81). The most distinctive architectural symbols of Mormon spirituality, temples proliferated to serve Mormon communities throughout the world, increasing from eight working temples in 1950 to 144 by 2014.

The most impressive architectural monument of the Church's late twentieth-century growth opened in 2000 across the street from Temple Square: the 21,200-seat Conference Center, reportedly one of the world's largest theater-style auditoriums. Designed by Portland-based architects Zimmer-Gunsul-Frasca, this Mormon megachurch was sheathed in granite to match the temple and half-buried in the hillside to avoid overwhelming the nearby historic buildings. The round assembly room with its embracing balconies celebrates the unity and solidarity of the members who fill its seats for semiannual conferences and seasonal programs.

Nineteenth-Century Painting and Sculpture

Although ecclesiastical leaders commissioned most Mormon architecture, this was not the case with much Mormon painting and sculpture. Some works of art recognized today as the defining artistic achievements of Latter-day Saint cultural history were created by individual artists out of their own personal sense of mission, generally without Church sponsorship, and often without official recognition or appreciation at the time.

Nevertheless, LDS artists have defined and reinforced significant aspects of Mormon identity. In portraits they have provided dignified likenesses of its revered founders and leaders. In history paintings they have created vivid images of the foundational stories of the movement. In landscapes they have celebrated the divinely appointed homeland and sites of Restoration events. In scriptural illustrations, they have brought plausible reality to Book of Mormon and Bible stories. And in temple murals, they have enriched the settings for the religion's most sacred rituals.

Nearly all of the paintings that remain from the movement's beginnings in the American Midwest and the early years in Utah are individual and group portraits of the Church's founders. A pair of portraits of Joseph and his wife Emma may be regarded as the first masterpieces of Mormon art. Now owned and displayed by Community of Christ in its Independence, Missouri, headquarters, these handsome frontal views of the formally dressed couple are the work of an accomplished painter. Joseph recorded sitting for a portrait by "Brother Rogers" in September of 1842—possibly David W. Rogers, a New York City artist.[5] If so, this would be the beginning of a long tradition of employing outside professionals for some of the Church's most important artistic commissions.

A Nauvoo insider, British convert Sutcliffe Maudsley (1809–1881) produced dozens of profile portraits in ink and tempera of the city's elite residents. Another English artist-convert, William W. Major (1804–1854), arrived in Nauvoo in 1844 and continued his artistic career in pioneer Utah. His grand group portrait, *Brigham and Mary Ann Angell Young and Their Children*, gives dignity to the Church's rough-edged leader and his family by showing them as English aristocrats in a palatial country house. Frederick Piercy (1830–1891) illustrated an 1855 Church-published guidebook, *Route from Liverpool to Great Salt Lake Valley*, with accurate and beautiful drawings of the landmarks of the trail beginning with the Nauvoo Temple ruins and ending with a panorama of Great Salt Lake City.

The cultural life of pioneer Utah was enriched by the immigration of talented artists from the eastern United States, Scandinavia, and Britain in the 1850s and '60s. The three most prolific and influential LDS painters of the period were Carl Christian Anton Christensen (1831–1912), who arrived from Denmark in 1857; George Martin Ottinger (1833–1917), who came from New York and other eastern cities in 1861; and Danquart A. Weggeland (1827–1918), who immigrated from Norway in 1862. All three arrived with some artistic training—Christensen and Weggeland had both studied at the Royal Academy of Art in Copenhagen. All subsisted for a time making scenery for local theaters, and Weggeland worked his first Utah winter on a black-and-white mural of Joseph Smith for the Bountiful Tabernacle.[6] Weggeland and Ottinger struggled to eke out a living as painters of portraits and local scenes, and also as art teachers. Their struggle was complicated by outside competition—Ottinger was dismayed when Enoch Wood Perry, a European-trained artist living in San Francisco, passed through Salt Lake City in 1865 and sold $11,000 in portraits to LDS Church leaders and other prominent citizens in four months.[7] Some of these fine paintings formed the beginning of the Church's portrait collection that has continued to the present.

Between 1869 and 1890, C. C. A. Christensen produced the masterwork of LDS history painting. His *Mormon Panorama*, a series of twenty-three monumental images—each was six and a half by ten feet—depicted Mormonism's founding events, from Joseph Smith's visions to the pioneers' arrival in Utah, with unmatched narrative power. The paintings were stitched together in a large roll so Christensen could scroll through them while lecturing to audiences throughout Utah and neighboring states. Mostly forgotten in the early twentieth century, their "rediscovery" resulted in a 1970 cover story in *Art in America* and an exhibition at New York's Whitney Museum of American Art, the most national attention ever given to a work of Mormon art.[8]

Weggeland and Christensen painted temple murals in Logan and Manti. The colorful Manti Creation Room paintings, the only surviving temple mural from pioneer times, are imaginative portrayals of the biblical story with quasi-scientific additions of an ancient sea creature and several early mammals.

A half-dozen British-born converts inaugurated Utah's landscape painting tradition with sublime images of mountains, canyons, and lakes. Henry Lavender Adolphus Culmer (1854–1914) created some of the largest and most impressive of these works. Alfred Lambourne (1850–1926) produced highly romanticized religious landscapes for the new Salt Lake Temple, *Adam-ondi-Ahman* and *Hill Cumorah* (1893). In the latter painting, the sun—a symbol of the restored gospel—breaks through a dark storm at the hilltop like a latter-day Mount Sinai aglow with the divine presence.

GROWING ARTISTIC SOPHISTICATION

The completion of the Salt Lake Temple helped to launch the careers of a new generation of Mormon artists. In 1890, John Hafen (1856–1910) and Lorus Pratt (1855–1923) proposed to the First Presidency that the Church sponsor their studies in Paris in return for applying their newly acquired skills to the temple murals. Their plea was granted, and the two men, with their friend John B. Fairbanks (1855–1940), were on their way to Paris as official "art missionaries" in just three months. They were later joined by Edwin Evans (1860–1946) and Herman Haag (1871–95). Utah painters John Willard Clawson (1858–1936) and James T. Harwood (1860–1940) and sculptor Cyrus Dallin (1861–1944) had preceded them to Paris independently.

All benefitted tremendously from their European studies, learning precise figure drawing and painting in the academies and absorbing the progressive influences of tonalist and impressionist landscape painting outside of the classroom. With Weggeland, four of the art missionaries completed the shimmering Garden and World Room murals in time for the temple's 1893 dedication.[9] Cyrus Dallin, although a non-Mormon, applied his Paris training to the classical Angel Moroni statue for the temple tower—an "*Apollo Belvedere*" with a trumpet.

Younger Utah artists, including Alma B. Wright (1875–1952), Lee Greene Richards (1875–1950), Mahonri M. Young (1877–1957), Lewis Ramsey (1875–1941), and brothers

J. Leo and Avard Fairbanks (1878–1946 and 1897–1987), also studied in France. Clawson, Hafen, and Richards contributed dozens of superb portraits. Many of the best of Hafen's luminous Utah landscapes enriched the offices of Church leaders. Wright, Richards, Evans, and the Fairbanks brothers produced murals and sculpture for later temples. Young, Dallin, and Avard Fairbanks produced dignified sculptural monuments that celebrated the Church's founders and history.

Talented LDS artists who began their careers in the 1910s and '20s worked with these Paris-trained artists before studying under America's best art teachers in eastern schools. Some brought a new vitality to LDS art by applying post-Impressionism and other early twentieth-century movements to Mormon subjects.

LeConte Stewart (1891–1990) studied with Edwin Evans and A. B. Wright in Salt Lake City, then took classes at the New York Art Students' League with the great landscape teacher John Carlson before serving a Church mission to Hawaii. When the murals in Laie's nearly completed temple were damaged by moisture and mold, young Elder Stewart was assigned to paint new ones. He later painted murals in the Alberta and Arizona temples. In his atmospheric Cardston Creation Room, he used a modern pointillistic technique of unblended daubs of color for the early creative periods, with later scenes becoming more realistic. His bold Arizona World Room was a more hard-edged desert landscape inspired by the great Southwestern painter Maynard Dixon, with mesas and low-flying buzzards. In a long career, Stewart painted the Mormon landscape—small towns, pioneer homes, and LDS meetinghouses at the foot of the Wasatch Mountains—with unequalled richness.

Minerva Teichert (1888–1976) learned bold draftsmanship and broad brushwork from George Bridgeman at the Art Institute of Chicago and Robert Henri at the New York Art Students' League. Her mural-sized paintings of dramatic stories from the scriptures and Mormon history ornamented dozens of LDS meetinghouses and public schools in Utah and Idaho. In the 1940s and '50s, she produced more than forty vivid paintings from the Book of Mormon. When Church leaders declined to publish or display them, she eventually donated them to Brigham Young University. Perhaps her greatest masterpiece was her 1947 World Room mural for the Manti Temple—a parade of kings and soldiers, merchants and adventurers passing by the poor of the world. Although her paintings were largely unappreciated for a few decades, by the 1980s and '90s they were frequently published in Church magazines and manuals, displayed in museum exhibitions, and enthusiastically sought by collectors.

Other artists also found new ways to tell Mormon stories. Mabel Frazer (1887 1981) showed pioneers plowing their fields with expressionist energy reminiscent of Van Gogh in her 1929 painting *The Furrow*. The modern-style Idaho Falls Temple provided opportunities to reinterpret traditional decorations in a variety of contemporary idioms including a sleek baptismal font with almost cubist oxen by Torlief Knaphus (1881–1965), a colorful and fanciful Art Deco Garden Room by Robert Shepherd (1909–92), and an "American Scene" World Room by Joseph A. F. Everett (1883–1945) with a humble pioneer farmer and his wife standing in for Adam and Eve in the lone and dreary world.

ART AND ILLUSTRATION
AFTER THE SECOND WORLD WAR

In the last half of the twentieth century, the Church ignored the fashionable abstractions of the art world to embrace the style of popular culture's colorful magazine illustrations and spectacular images from the cinema.

The huge Los Angeles Temple seemed to demand murals with unprecedented scale and drama. In Harris Weberg's (1898–1979) Creation Room, brilliant globes emerge from banks of swirling clouds, filling the room's curved walls like Cinerama special effects. The dazzling Garden Room by non-Mormon illustrator Edward Grigware (1889–1960) created a semitropical Southern California vision of Eden. But because of the Church's shift to filmed presentations of the endowment, these would be the last temple murals for nearly half a century.

Confident theatricality also imbued the best-known LDS artworks of the period: twelve magnificent tableaus from the Book of Mormon by Arnold Friberg (1913–2010). Commissioned by the Primary Association in 1950 for serialization in *The Children's Friend*, these beautifully executed realistic paintings presented the book as a series of exciting adventure stories populated with muscular superheroes. Some editions of the Book of Mormon included them and were distributed by the millions.

In the early 1960s, the Church's plans for a visitors' center on Temple Square and a pavilion at the 1964 New York World's Fair created the need for religious illustrations. For both of these facilities, the Church relied on non-Mormon artists. Stressing that Mormons are Christians, the centerpiece of each exhibit was a heroic-sized marble reproduction of *Christus* by Danish artist Berthold Thorvaldsen (1770–1844). Although originally created for the Lutheran cathedral of Copenhagen and influenced by the artist's studies of antiquities and Catholic sculpture in Rome, this solemn neoclassical portrayal of the resurrected Savior with outstretched arms provided an acceptably realistic, dignified and powerful image for Latter-day Saints. More than a dozen additional copies were later acquired for subsequent exhibitions and missionary centers, and in the early twenty-first century it reappeared as the signature image on the Church's website. Although earlier generations of Mormons generally regarded religious statuary as outside their tradition, small reproductions of *Christus* have become common emblems of devotion in contemporary LDS homes.

Paintings by non-Mormon artists for these two exhibitions also became widely recognized works of LDS art. The best were New Testament scenes by noted illustrator Harry Anderson (1906–1996), a Seventh-day Adventist. Frequently reproduced in Church publications, teaching aids, and prints, these paintings came to define the appearance of Jesus for many Latter-day Saints, including Mormon artists of the next two generations. The Church also commissioned outside illustrators Tom Lovell (1909–97), John Scott (1907–87), and Kenneth Riley (1919–) to produce additional didactic paintings of scriptural and historical subjects.[10] Beginning in 1955, Church publications also featured

New Testament scenes by nineteenth-century Danish artist Carl Bloch (1834–1900) and German painter Heinrich Hofmann (1824–1911).

In 1965, while much official art was being outsourced, LDS artists were giving serious thought to new expressions of their religion. At Brigham Young University, visual arts professor Dale T. Fletcher (1929–90) and his students, as well as writers, musicians, and others, joined in "Art and Belief" discussions that evolved into the 1968 BYU Festival of Mormon Art. The festival continued annually for twenty years. Many artists involved in this movement went on to successful careers, creating some major works of LDS art—Dennis Smith's widely reproduced 1978 Nauvoo women sculptures, Gary Smith's powerful paintings of Joseph Smith, and Trevor Southey's ethereal 1980 priesthood restoration sculpture, to mention three examples.

The following decades saw greatly increased opportunities for LDS artists to display their work to large audiences in exhibitions at the Springville Museum of Art, the Museum of Church History and Art (opened in 1984, now Church History Museum), and the Brigham Young University Museum of Art (opened in 1993). All of these institutions have displayed works representing a variety of traditional, folk, and modern approaches and have mounted exhibitions that encourage viewers to appreciate the spiritual possibilities of more symbolic works, in addition to the Church's realistic illustrations.

As the Church grew in the late twentieth century, so did the number of talented and highly skilled artists. A brief list of a few of the best-known contemporary LDS artists reflects the diversity of their approaches to religious subjects. Wulf Barsch (b. 1943) has produced many stunning symbolic paintings using pure forms of "sacred geometry." James C. Christensen (b. 1942) developed a national audience for his highly detailed fantasies that often express poignant spiritual themes. William Whitaker Jr. (b. 1943), a classical-realist, has produced many fine portraits of Church officials and historical studies. Ron Richmond (b. 1963) has explored LDS spiritual themes in highly realistic but mysterious compositions of chairs, vessels, and textiles. J. Kirk Richards (b. 1976) has painted scriptural stories in richly abstracted compositions. Brian Kershisnik (b. 1962) has used a whimsical approach to serious subjects in sketchy, almost cartoon-like paintings that deal with the relationship of eternal principles with everyday life. And this list is far from complete.

By the end of the twentieth century, several dozen LDS artists and illustrators were successfully marketing paintings, sculptures, and prints for a large commercial audience, including Evangelical Christians and Catholics. Their work ranged from realistic and sometimes sentimental scriptural and historical scenes to more challenging explorations of spiritual themes.[11] Officially approved religious prints by these and other artists, available from Church distribution centers, decorate many homes as well as meetinghouse classrooms and corridors (but not chapels).

In the late twentieth century it also became clear that the definition of Mormon art needed to expand to embrace a wider variety of expressions of an increasingly international membership. Triennial Church-wide art competitions sponsored by the Museum of Church History and Art began in 1987, attracting thousands of artists from around the world with recognition, cash prizes, and purchase awards. These exhibitions, together with the museum's active collecting program, have brought attention to artists and artisans from diverse cultures reflecting their Mormon identity through their own traditions of textile arts, ceramics, woodcarving, and metalwork in addition to painting and sculpture. Many of these works have reached a wider audience through Church magazines and museum publications.[12]

Beginning with the construction of the Columbia River Temple in Richland, Washington (2000–2001), temple murals also reappeared after a half-century's absence. Fine historic murals had been removed from three temples in the early 1970s, when they were converted for the film presentation of the endowment, sparking some public controversy. As other historic temples began using the film presentation, however, murals were preserved, and portions of some banned paintings were eventually restored to their original sites. In Nauvoo and most twenty-first-century temples, new realistic landscape murals have been commissioned for the principal ordinance rooms, generally evoking the buildings' local settings or historical connections.

At the end of the first decade of the twenty-first century, Mormon art was more extensive and varied than ever. Although the institutional Church continued to sponsor conservative and realistic illustrations, an unprecedented number of independent LDS artists pursued their own visions, using increasingly diverse approaches. Religious exhibitions have been among the most popular art events in Utah. BYU's 2011 exhibition of Danish artist Carl Bloch's religious works attracted over 300,000 visitors, making it one of the most visited museum exhibitions in America that year. The growing hunger for spiritually powerful religious art among the Latter-day Saints bodes well for the future of Mormon art.

The Latter-day Saints are a socially conservative people whose strength and success have been founded on their remarkable solidarity and cooperation. Their most widely recognized architecture and art are affirmations of group identity based on a shared historical tradition and firmly held beliefs and values more than individual expressions or social protest. As Minerva Teichert proposed in 1947, Mormon art continues to be "rich in story and backed by a great faith."

NOTES

1. Teichert, handwritten manuscript, 1947, research files, Church History Museum, Salt Lake City, quoted in Oman and Davis, *Images of Faith*, 72.
2. Some Church leaders have felt duty-bound to enforce recent policies discouraging the placement of new art in chapels by removing artworks placed there by earlier generations of Church leaders, including General Authorities. Some Church leaders have objected to representations of Joseph Smith and other prominent leaders in chapels as implying excessive veneration. Some temple murals were deemed to be incompatible with the newer film presentation of the endowment.
3. The Kirtland Temple is owned and beautifully maintained by the Community of Christ. The Nauvoo Temple was completely destroyed by fire and tornado after the Mormons'

departure. A replica of its exterior—with modern temple facilities inside—was constructed by the LDS Church from 1999 to 2002.

4. The building was declared a Canadian National Historic Site in 1992.
5. Oman and Davis, *Images of Faith*, 6.
6. Although personally commissioned by Brigham Young as a tribute to Joseph Smith, this mural was deemed inappropriate by local Church leaders and removed to the LDS Church History Museum in 1980.
7. Olpin, Seifrit, and Swanson, *Artists of Utah*, 186.
8. Carmer, "Panorama of Mormon Life."
9. Herman Haag, the fifth art missionary, was too ill to work on the project.
10. Barrett and Black, "Setting a Standard in LDS Art."
11. Some of the best known of these artists are Walter Rane, Joseph Brickey, Jeff Hein, Greg Olsen, Simon Dewey, Del Parson, Al Rounds, Clark Kelly Price, and Liz Lemon Swindle.
12. An extensive review of international LDS art appears in Oman and Davis, *Images of Faith*, 164–96.

BIBLIOGRAPHY

Barrett, Robert T., and Susan Easton Black. "Setting a Standard in LDS Art: Four Illustrators of the Mid-Twentieth Century." *BYU Studies* 44, no. 2 (2005): 24–95.

Carmer, Carl. "A Panorama of Mormon Life." *Art in America* 58, no. 3 (May–June 1970): 52–71.

Givens, Terryl L. *People of Paradox: A History of Mormon Culture*. New York: Oxford University Press, 2007.

Hamilton, C. Mark. *Nineteenth-Century Mormon Architecture and City Planning*. Oxford University Press: New York, 1995.

Jackson, Richard W. *Places of Worship: 150 years of Latter-day Saint Architecture*. Salt Lake City: Religious Studies Center, Brigham Young University, 2003.

Olpin, Robert S., William C. Seifrit, and Vern Swanson. *Artists of Utah*. Salt Lake City: Gibbs Smith, 1999.

Oman, Richard G., and Robert O. Davis. *Images of Faith: Art of the Latter-day Saints*. Salt Lake City: Deseret, 1995.

CHAPTER 31

....

MORMON LETTERS

....

MICHAEL AUSTIN

> We will yet have Miltons and Shakespeares of our own. God's ammunition is not exhausted. His brightest spirits are held in reserve for the latter times. In God's name and by his help we will build up a literature whose top shall touch heaven.
>
> Orson F. Whitney, "Home Literature," 1888

> God, the best storyteller, has made a better story out of Joseph and the Mormon wandering than fiction will ever equal.
>
> Bernard DeVoto, "Vacation," 1938

ORSON F. Whitney—a nineteenth-century writer, editor, and Mormon apostle—believed that the truth of Mormonism would someday produce the world's greatest literature. Whitney could not help but see Mormonism as a potential wellspring of classic books; literature was humanity's greatest aspiration, and the Church of Jesus Christ of Latter-day Saints was the purest expression of eternal truth, he reasoned. And great truth has ever produced great literature. To a literary mind like Whitney's, literary greatness was a logical part of the overall triumphalism of the nineteenth-century Mormon worldview:

> In God's name and by his help we will build up a literature whose top shall touch heaven, though its foundations may now be low in earth. Let the smile of derision wreathe the face of scorn; let the frown of hatred darken the brow of bigotry. Small things are the seeds of great things, and, like the acorn that brings forth the oak, or the snowflake that forms the avalanche, God's kingdom will grow, and on wings of light and power soar to the summit of its destiny.[1]

Whitney's considerable influence was largely responsible for what scholars of Mormon literature have called—using the title of his essay—the "Home Literature Movement" of the late nineteenth and early twentieth centuries. "Home Literature" in this context refers to literature written by Mormons to Mormons, often with the official or tacit approval of the Church of Jesus Christ of Latter-day Saints. Whitney's own ten-book poem *Elias, an Epic of the Ages* (1904) fits into this category, as does Nephi Anderson's perennially popular novel *Added Upon*, which was published by the church-owned Deseret News Press in 1898 and has been continually in print ever since.

Bernard DeVoto wrote from a very different perspective. Though not a Mormon himself, he was born and raised among Mormons in Ogden, Utah, near the turn of the twentieth century. While DeVoto's writings about the Latter-day Saints were often barbed and critical, he had a better understanding of Mormonism than any other major writer of his day. When he left Utah to become one of America's most respected novelists and literary scholars, he was in an ideal position to tell the story of the Latter-day Saints. In his essay "Vacation," an installment of his monthly "Easy Chair" column for *Harper's Weekly*, he writes that the story of the Mormons:

> was a story which I had known all my life, which I knew better than any other in American history. It held as much as any novelist could ask of farce and tragedy, melodrama, aspiration, violence, ecstasy—the strongest passions of mankind at white heat; the Kingdom of God and mob cruelty and martyrdom; bigotry and superstition and delusion; mystical exaltation and the purity of faith; ambition and its overthrow, persecution and social revolt—all bound up . . . with the sweep of a full century of American life.

However, DeVoto concludes, the novel of the Mormon past must remain "the best book I am never going to write." He judged the subjects of Joseph Smith, Brigham Young, the Mormon migration, and the settlement of the Salt Lake Valley to be too big for fiction. Recalling the argument in Plato's *Republic*, he concludes that "fiction is the reflection of a shadow cast at secondhand on a dull mirror. . . . What drama could any merely mortal story-teller construct that would not be an idle nursery play for children, compared to the one that is written in our own annals, whose first chapter opens on the Hill Cumorah with a new Bible engraved on sheets of gold?"[2] DeVoto did indeed write the story of the Mormons, but he wrote it as a history rather than a novel. His Mormon masterpiece was to be *The Year of Decision: 1846* (1943)—a historical narrative that weaves the powerful story of the Mormon migration into the overall narrative of America's westward movement during the nation's most crucial year of colonization. DeVoto's biographer and fellow Utahan Wallace Stegner, though an even more gifted novelist, was similarly unable to craft fiction out of the Mormon story. Stegner wrote two books about Mormonism—*Mormon Country* (1942) and *The Gathering of Zion* (1964)—both of them histories rather than novels. This pattern continued throughout DeVoto's lifetime and well beyond. The best-known works about Mormonism in the twentieth century—works such as Fawn Brodie's *No Man Knows My History* (1945), Juanita Brooks's *The Mountain Meadows Massacre* (1950), Leonard Arrington's *Great Basin Kingdom* (1958), and Samuel W. Taylor's *Nightfall at Nauvoo* (1971)—have been historical rather than literary accounts of the Mormon story.

But literary canons must eventually be constructed, lest literary critics be left with nothing to do. Since the mid-1970s—which saw the publication of the first Mormon literature anthology (1974) and the founding of the Association for Mormon Letters (1976)—scholars and critics have devoted significant attention to the question, "What is Mormon literature?" Those who have tried to define a workable canon of such literature have often found themselves floundering between Whitney's optimism, which proclaims that there must eventually be great Mormon literature, and DeVoto's resignation, which declares such a thing impossible. We see this clearly in the first attempt at a Mormon literature anthology, *A Believing People* by Brigham Young University professors Richard Cracroft and Neal Lambert. The original textbook for BYU's popular Mormon Literature course, *A Believing People*, had a significant influence on the first group of scholars professionally attracted to the study of Mormon letters. But the canon that Cracroft and Lambert construct in this book consists overwhelmingly of: (1) writings of by LDS leaders or works that appeared in official church publications; and (2) journals, letters, biographies, and other sources that could best be described as "historical." Of the thirty-six works in the anthology that are not classified as poetry, eight are written by LDS general authorities, twenty-three are from sources published by the LDS Church, and twenty are historical texts or primary historical documents such as letters or journals. Only eight of the thirty-six works do not fit into at least one of these categories. Among the works that are classified as poetry, the most frequently cited source is the LDS Hymnal, from which sixteen of the thirty-six entries for the nineteenth century have been drawn.

Most of the literary scholars who emerged around the time of *A Believing People*, however, recognized that a meaningful canon of "Mormon literature" must ultimately be located somewhere between Whitney's "Home Literature," which drives inexorably toward sponsored propaganda, and DeVoto's conviction that the Mormon story could be told only as history. *A Believing People* does indeed gesture—albeit tentatively—toward just such a middle ground. It does so in two ways. First, the editors include works by three midcentury Mormon authors who published to a national audience: Vardis Fisher, Virginia Sorensen, and Maurine Whipple. Just as important, Cracroft and Lambert anthologized several poems and short stories from the new journal, *Dialogue*—which, along with the less scholarly magazine *Sunstone*, would soon provide a crucial platform for the development of literature by and for Mormons that neither requested nor received the imprimatur of the LDS Church.

THE MORMON DIASPORA AT MIDCENTURY

In the second meeting of the Association for Mormon Letters in 1977, BYU professor Edward Geary presented a paper entitled "Mormondom's Lost Generation: The Novelists of the 1940s"—a paper, that has since been published several times and has become a standard starting point for the construction of a Mormon literary canon. Geary uses the term "Lost Generation"—originally applied to American expatriate writers in France in the 1920s—to describe a group of novelists with Mormon backgrounds who started writing in the 1940s and continued through the 1970s. Though these writers were sometimes at odds with their more orthodox coreligionists, their novels were a far cry from almost every fictional portrayal of Mormonism in the first hundred years of its existence. During the nineteenth and early twentieth centuries, books such Robert Louis Stevenson's *The Dynamiter* (1885), Arthur Conan Doyle's *A Study in Scarlet* (1887), and Zane Gray's *Riders of the Purple Sage* (1912) had portrayed Mormon men as violent fanatics and Mormon women as their deluded, brainwashed captives. This new generation of Mormon novelists worked much more diligently to create complex, three-dimensional portrayals of both the Mormons and their history.

However, nearly all of the Mormon novelists of this period were, to some degree, estranged from their home culture. "Most of the writers who emerged during the 1940s were born in the first two decades of [the twentieth] century," Geary writes, "a traditional time in Mormon country, and most grew up in small towns where the transition was perhaps most strongly felt." Most of them ended up leaving the region around the time of the Great Depression, and "for many, leaving the region meant leaving the Church, for they could not clearly separate their Mormon-ness from their Utah-ness." For Geary, then, these novelists were "lost" both geographically and culturally, and nearly all of their novels "have their roots in the author's effort to come to terms with his or her Mormon heritage." The one uniting theme that Geary sees in all of these works is "the central conflict between individualism and authority." In virtually all of these novels,

> The founding of the Church and its growth, migrations, and settlement in the West are "great events," the more so because of the Church's authoritarian structure. The settlement of Mormon country was communal rather than individualistic. . . . Communal values took place over individual tastes; obedience to authority was more important than individual judgment; and the achieving of communal goals mattered more than personal fulfillment—or rather, personal fulfillment was to be attained through the achieving of communal goals.
>   The sympathetic characters in these novels are the ones who experience a tension between the demands of the community and their desires to think and act for themselves.[3]

Among these Lost Generation writers, Geary includes a number of figures who were never well known outside of Mormon circles, such as Maurine Whipple, Paul D. Bailey, Blanche Cannon, and Jean Woodman. He also includes two writers who became much better known for things other than their contributions to Mormon literature. The first of these, Samuel W. Taylor, was the son of excommunicated apostle John W. Taylor and the grandson of the Mormon prophet John Taylor. Though he wrote a number of serious histories, novels, and Hollywood screenplays, his greatest fame rests on the short story "A Situation of Gravity," which became the basis for the successful Disney films *The Absent-Minded Professor* (1961) and *Son of Flubber* (1963). The second, Richard Scowcroft, succeeded Wallace Stegner as the director of the Creative Writing Program at

Stanford University, where he also became chair of the English Department. But outside of Stanford and academic creative writing circles, Scowcroft is generally known, if he is known at all, as the brother of Brent Scowcroft, who served as the National Security Advisor for Presidents Gerald Ford and George H. W. Bush and played a major role in the first Persian Gulf War.

The two most important writers that Geary places in the Lost Generation tradition are Vardis Fisher and Virginia Sorensen, both of whom did achieve substantial literary reputations during their lifetimes. They both ultimately rejected Mormonism as a religion—Fisher became an outspoken atheist, and Sorensen converted to Anglicanism—leading to some debate (especially in Fisher's case) about whether or not they should be classified as "Mormon writers." But scholars are used to making distinctions between religious belief and the culture that it supports, and, from this perspective, there can be no doubt that Fisher, Sorensen, and the rest of the Lost Generation writers, qualify as "Mormon" in their culture if not in their belief.

Vardis Fisher grew up in rural Idaho at the turn of the twentieth century. Though both of his parents came from Mormon backgrounds, and his mother remained fiercely devout, the Fishers did not live near enough to a church to make it part of their lives. Temperance Fisher provided both the spiritual and the secular education for her three children until they were old enough to attend high school in the nearby town of Rigby. While in Rigby, Vardis experienced renewed spiritual interest and was baptized into the Church of Jesus Christ of Latter-day Saints at the age of twenty. Soon afterwards, however, he rejected the Mormon faith and, for the rest of his life, identified himself as an atheist. Fisher earned a degree in English from the University of Utah and went on to receive MA and PhD degrees from the University of Chicago. After holding teaching positions at the University of Utah and New York University, he left academia to pursue a full-time writing career, eventually writing twenty-six novels and several other critical and historical works and becoming one of the Mountain West's best-known writers.

Mormonism features prominently in Fisher's early work. His four autobiographical novels—collectively called *The Tetralogy* (1932–36)—delve deeply into his Mormon upbringing, his mother's ambiguous influence, and his relationship with his first wife, a devout Mormon woman whose 1924 suicide became the transformative event of his life.[4] The *Tetralogy* novels were critically acclaimed but commercially unsuccessful, which caused the young writer to try his hand at the more lucrative fields of regional and historical fiction. After writing several such novels that garnered respectable sales, Fisher decided to tell one of the stories he knew best, and he took up the challenge to write a novel about the founding years of Mormonism. In 1939, only one year after Bernard DeVoto had declared such a thing impossible, he published *Children of God*, a nearly 800-page epic that featured both Joseph Smith and Brigham Young as major characters. *Children of God* stirred passions across the country. In Utah, Mormons denounced the book as an attack on their faith. Many of Fisher's free-thinking friends, however, considered it overly friendly toward the Latter-day Saints, and some even accused him of proselytizing through his fiction. In general, critics praised *Children of God* for its fairness in neither idolizing nor demonizing the Latter-day Saints. Fisher does not take the official LDS view that the church was restored through divine revelation, and he provides naturalistic origins for the events of the church's founding, but he does depict both Joseph Smith and Brigham Young as intelligent, charismatic individuals who were sincere in their efforts to build the Kingdom of God. And unlike nearly every novelist who wrote about Mormons before 1939, Fisher does not sensationalize or denounce polygamy. His most forceful criticisms, in fact, occur in the third section of the book when the Mormons renounce polygamy and began to assimilate into mainstream American culture.

Children of God became a best-seller and received one of the most important literary prizes in America, the Harper Prize, given biannually for excellence in fiction, which carried a monetary award of $7,500 (about $125,000 in 2015 dollars). Fisher became a literary celebrity, spoken of in the same terms as Ernest Hemingway and John Steinbeck (whose *Grapes of Wrath* was also published in 1939). With Harper and Brothers, he had a strong publisher, a good sales record, and a solid reputation as a regional writer at a time when regional writing was hot. But Fisher increasingly came to resent being known only for a novel about a religion that he had rejected. He did not want to be a "Mormon writer," or even a "Western writer." He wanted to write the history of humanity, and soon after the publication of *Children of God*, Fisher conceived of the project that was to consume the remainder of his life: *The Testament of Man*, an epic series of twelve novels that would trace the development of community, sexuality, and religion from prehuman primates through the Jewish and Christian worlds and into the present day. Though some of the individual novels in the series sold well, the series as a whole was neither commercially nor critically successful—and Fisher had trouble finding publishers for some of the later novels. Critics now generally agree that Fisher's obsession with this project drained away the most productive years of one of the twentieth century's most talented and promising writers.

Three years after Fisher published *Children of God*, a thirty-year old writer named Virginia Sorensen (1912–91) published her first novel, *A Little Lower than the Angels* (1942), with the prestigious New York publishing house Alfred A. Knopf. Set primarily in Nauvoo before the Mormon migration, *A Little Lower than the Angels* uses Mormon history as the backdrop for the story of Mercy Baker, the reluctant wife of a Mormon convert, who becomes a witness to many of the events leading up to the great exodus. Sorensen's first novel was well received by both Mormon and non-Mormon audiences, and she followed it up with the similarly well-received Mormon-themed novels *On This Star* (1946), *The Evening and the Morning* (1949), *Many Heavens* (1954), and *Kingdom Come* (1960).

Sorensen, who was born in Provo, Utah, and attended Brigham Young University, always viewed the LDS Church more positively than Vardis Fisher did. She married her first husband, fellow BYU graduate Fred Sorensen, in the Salt Lake City Temple in 1933. Even after she married British writer Alec Waugh in 1967 and converted to Anglicanism, she remained interested in Mormonism and was gratified by the recognition she received from Mormon critics toward the end of her life. However, though Mormon themes and images accounted for the bulk of Sorensen's writings for adults, her major success as a writer came from her award-winning young-adult fiction, including *Curious Missie* (1953), *The House Next Door* (1954), *Plain Girl* (1956), and the 1957 Newbery Award–winning novel and perennial classic *Miracles on Maple Hill*.

Vardis Fisher, Virginia Sorensen, and Mormondom's other "Lost Generation" novelists did not quite become Miltons and Shakespeares, but their accomplishments were not negligible. They wrote modestly successful regional fiction that went a long way toward humanizing a culture that had been demonized for a century in the popular literature of both America and England. In the process, they produced a rich and varied body of work that includes, along with works by Fisher and Sorensen, such well-regarded, nationally distributed novels as Maurine Whipple's *The Giant Joshua* (1941), Ardyth Kennelly's _Peaceable Kingdom_, Richard Scowcroft's *Children of the Covenant* (1945), Samuel W. Taylor's *Heaven Knows Why* (1948), and Paul D. Bailey's *For Time and All Eternity* (1964). It is in these novels, and the other works of the midcentury Mormon diaspora, that scholars of Mormondom have found the beginnings of a Mormon literary canon.

MORMONS AT THE MARGINS

Throughout the 1960s, Mormon-themed literature continued to appear regularly from national presses. By the end of the decade, however, the steady stream had slowed to a very occasional drip. The most likely reason for this decline is that the LDS market—which had supported the sales of most nationally published Mormon books—became large enough to attract niche publishers of its own. By far, the most lucrative segment of the Mormon media market has always consisted of orthodox Latter-day Saints who want books that promote—or at least that decline to challenge—their faith. The vast majority of these books are nonfiction; however, since the 1970s, a more contemporary kind of home literature, found in plays such as *Saturday's Warrior* (1973) and *My Turn on Earth* (1977) and novels such as Jack Weyland's *Charly* (1980), has emerged to meet the demand for literature by the nation's six million members of the Church of Jesus Christ of Latter-day Saints. For a time, such works were published and released by nonofficial or semiofficial outlets, such as Bookcraft Books, which was the largest publisher of LDS fiction in the 1970s and 1980s, and Covenant Communications, which produced books, tapes, and videos for the Mormon market. Both companies, however, were purchased by the church-owned Deseret Book—Bookcraft in 1999 and Covenant in 2006—giving the LDS Church, through its in-house publishing enterprise, a virtual monopoly on literature aimed at a mainstream Mormon audience.

By many measures, this contemporary home literature of Mormonism has been remarkably successful. Novels published by Deseret Book can sell tens of thousands of copies, and one series—Gerald Lund's nine-volume epic *The Work and the Glory* (1990–98)—had combined sales of over one million books. By other measures, however, the editorial dominance of the institutional LDS Church does not bode well for the future of a Mormon literature. Deseret Book now keeps hundreds of fiction titles in print and distributes them through its own bookstores. Official Deseret offerings include murder mysteries, thrillers, romance novels, young adult fiction, historical fiction, speculative fiction, and contemporary Mormon realism. And though the overall quality of literature produced for a broad Mormon audience has increased dramatically since the days of Orson F. Whitney, the production and distribution of such literature remains tightly controlled by the institutional church.

The growth of the Mormon world, however, has created a substantial "niche-within-a-niche" market for a different kind of literature—one that accepts and even seeks out the difficult issues that the more official venues ignore. The first major independent source for Mormon fiction was *Dialogue: A Journal of Mormon Thought*, which was founded in 1966 by LDS scholars studying at Stanford University. *Dialogue* published, and continues to publish, scholarly articles about the Mormon experience from a wide variety of academic fields. But it also publishes short fiction and poetry in almost every issue. In 1974, the somewhat less academically oriented *Sunstone* magazine joined *Dialogue* as a venue for independent Mormon writing, including dramatic works by Mormon playwrights. And in 1980 a group of Utah writers, scholars, and investors founded Signature Books, which has since published both fiction and nonfiction books by writers affiliated with *Dialogue* and *Sunstone*. These independent publishers have not shied away from controversy and, as a result, often find themselves at odds with the LDS Church. But they have provided crucial spaces for the creation and dissemination of Mormon literature that would simply not be accepted by the church's own publishing house.

These independent publication venues have helped to create a cohort of writers who have become well known to a small group of Mormon literati, writers such as Douglas H. Thayer, John Bennion, Linda Sillitoe, Michael Fillerup, Jack Harrell, and Robert Hodgson Van Wagoner. They have also, however, helped several writers—two in particular—gain a larger regional and even a national audience. By most accounts, the two most important figures in this group are Levi Peterson and Phyllis Barber, both of whom have written works that make good candidates for inclusion in the canon of Mormon masterpieces.

Levi Peterson was born and raised in the Mormon settlement of Snowflake, Arizona. He attended Brigham Young University and the University of California at Berkeley, before receiving a PhD in English from the University of Utah in 1965 and beginning his thirty-four-year career as a professor at Weber State University. During this time, he began writing short stories for *Sunstone*, *Dialogue*, and other regional journals—six of which were collected in his first book, *The Canyons of Grace* (1982). Peterson has written that his early stories, like his later ones, deal with two primary themes: "conflicts between belief and disbelief and between sexual impulse and conscience."[5]

Both of these themes reach their fullest expression in Peterson's first and most widely read novel, *The Backslider* (1986). After trying, and failing, to secure a national publisher for *The Backslider*, Peterson published it with Signature Books, where it went on to become a regional best-seller and one of the most important works of contemporary Mormon literature. *The Backslider* tells the story of Frank Windham, a Mormon cowboy growing up in the 1950s and struggling with both his sexual impulses and his wavering faith in Mormonism. Frank continually tries to overcome his doubts and desires, but is unable to do so, sending him further and further into depression. The novel concludes with one of the most famous scenes in all of Mormon fiction. While alone in a bathroom, right after baptizing his pregnant wife, Frank sees a vision of Jesus Christ, dressed as a cowboy and standing in the place of the urinal smoking a cigarette. When Frank announces that he wants to emasculate himself (as his brother has already done) to remove his sexual temptation, Jesus asks him, "why can't you believe my blood was enough. . . . Why do you have to shed yours too?"[6] After experiencing this moment of grace—a crucial part of Protestant Christianity that is rarely discussed in Mormon circles—Frank is able to make small steps toward enjoying the terrestrial life that he has instead of torturing himself constantly for his failure to live up to a celestial standard.

Phyllis Barber grew up in Boulder City, Nevada, in the 1940s and '50s—a community that had grown up a generation earlier as the base of operations for the construction of the Hoover Dam—the massive engineering project that forms the backdrop of her best-known work, *And the Desert Shall Blossom*. This novel revolves around the spiritual struggles of Esther Jensen, a Mormon woman whose husband is one of the thousands employed working on the dam. Through Esther, Barber explores the limited roles available for women in mainstream Mormon culture and the spiritual frustrations produced when orthodoxy collides with patriarchy. As the novel progresses, Esther comes to identify the heroine's own vital nature with the flow of the Colorado River—and, therefore, the stifling role of her male-dominated religion with the Hoover Dam. The novel ends with the completion of the dam and the metaphorical apotheosis of Esther—who realizes that, like the river, she can be frustrated for a time but will eventually triumph over the obstacles in her path. "Nothing can stop me now. I am water," she muses in the book's final paragraph. "Fingers of water splitting into channels finding new paths. There's always a way through."[7]

Both Peterson and Barber have continued to write stories in *Sunstone* and *Dialogue*, and to publish books with Signature—with Peterson serving as the editor of *Dialogue* from 2004 to 2008. They, along with the other writers in their circle, pioneered a new space in Mormon letters that was neither fully inside nor fully outside of the larger Mormon community. Unlike most of the Lost Generation writers, they have stayed close to both the LDS Church and the Wasatch Front—with many of them remaining practicing Latter-day Saints throughout their careers. But they have also accepted the disapproval of their community, and the possibility of official censure, in order to raise issues and create characters that have not been welcome in the official story. In his autobiography, Peterson gives a clear description of the space that he hoped to occupy within the Mormon community when he was writing his major works of fiction: "If, while completing . . . [*Canyons of Grace*] only a year earlier, I had sensed my distance from Mormonism acutely, I by now admitted to an impulse to intensify my involvement with it. I had long recognized that I was no anti-Mormon, having no wish to see Mormonism dwindle and die away. But I did wish to see it liberalize itself, becoming more humane, more adaptable to change, and less at odds with science and learning, and I saw therein an active role for people like me."[8]

MORMONS IN THE MAINSTREAM

In recent years, Mormon writers have made major inroads into the national and international literary markets, beginning in the 1980s, when Orson Scott Card won unprecedented back-to-back Hugo and Nebula Awards for the science-fiction novels *Ender's Game* (1985) and *Speaker for the Dead* (1986). In his public lectures and nonfiction writings, Card has been very outspoken about his Mormon beliefs and has published several fictional works—notably *A Woman of Destiny* (1984) and *Folk of the Fringe* (1989)—that deal with Mormonism directly. He has also used allegorized versions of both the Book of Mormon and LDS history as the basis for his successful series, *The Homecoming Saga* (1992–95) and *The Tales of Alvin Maker* (1987–2003). Other well-known Mormons writing genre fiction include Anne Perry, the best-selling British mystery novelist; Stephanie Meyer, the author of the phenomenally popular *Twilight* saga (2005–8); and Brandon Mull, whose young adult fantasy series *Fablehaven* topped best-seller lists between 2006 and 2010. Unlike Card, these writers do not deal with Mormonism explicitly in their work, but they regularly acknowledge that their religious beliefs have shaped their fiction.

In the somewhat more nebulous category of "literary fiction," writers from Mormon backgrounds have had some success incorporating Mormon culture into serious—or at least frequently praised—works of contemporary literature. For example, in Brady Udall's debut novel *The Miracle Life of Edgar Mint* (2001), the title character, a Native American boy who suffers a near-fatal accident on his reservation, passes through the home of a Mormon family as part of the LDS Indian Placement Program. Similarly, the protagonist of Walter Kirn's *Thumbsucker* (1999) goes through multiple obsessions—including Mormonism—after he is hypnotized at fourteen to cure his thumb-sucking habit. Both authors invoke Mormonism with the authority of personal experience: Udall was raised in a traditional (and politically powerful) Mormon family in Arizona, and Kirn's family converted to the LDS Church when he was twelve, though he did not remain affiliated with the church as an adult. And the Mormon characters in both novels, while often quirky, are generally sympathetic. Judith Freeman, another well-regarded contemporary novelist with Mormon roots, deals with contemporary Mormonism briefly in her novel *The Chinchilla Farm* (1989) and with historical Mormonism extensively in her novel *Red Water* (2002), which centers on the Mountain Meadows Massacre.

Mormon writers have been somewhat more represented in literary nonfiction than in literary fiction—and especially, in memoirs by Mormon women, of which, in academic circles, Terry Tempest Williams's *Refuge: An Unnatural History of Family and Place* (1991) is by far the most influential. *Refuge* blends together two compelling narratives: the public narrative of the 1983 flooding of the Bear River Migratory Bird Refuge, where Williams worked as a naturalist, and the private narrative of her mother's death from ovarian cancer, which occurred at the same time. The Mormon religion that Williams shares with her mother plays an important role in both narratives as the author learns to accept, and even find beauty within, nature's destruction of her places of refuge. *Refuge* has been frequently anthologized in college textbooks and has been the subject of a number of scholarly works and dissertations during the past twenty years. Other recent best-selling memoirs by Mormon women include Deborah Laake's *Secret Ceremonies* (1993), Carol Lynn Pearson's *Goodbye, I Love You* (1995), Martha Beck's *Expecting Adam* (1999), Carolyn Jessop's *Escape* (2007), and Elna Baker's *The New York Regional Mormon Singles Halloween Dance* (2009). These memoirs are often critical of Mormonism, but, collectively, they have had the effect of making the Mormon women's experience part of the general consciousness of the American reading public.

As impressive as these works of Mormon literature are, however, they do not quite fulfill Orson F. Whitney's hopes for Mormon Literature. Mormon culture has not produced Miltons and Shakespeares—world-historical figures who annihilate everything that precedes them and remake literature in their own image. But Bernard DeVoto's dire predictions have also proved groundless. After nearly a century of fighting the good fight, writers who have drawn on Mormon themes and experiences have not experienced "the crash that any man must make who tries to compose fiction out of Joseph Smith and the Mormon people."[9] Like other religious traditions and subcultures, Mormonism has produced its fair share of bad literature, kitsch, sentimental drivel, and overt propaganda. But, in or out of the Mormon world, 95 percent of everything is garbage. It is to the other 5 percent that we must look to construct canons, be they of Mormon literature or of anything else.

No official canon of Mormon literature has ever been proposed or agreed upon, of course. But the same can be said for Catholic literature, Jewish literature, American literature, and indeed "literature" in general. Canons are not the sorts of things that anybody ever agrees about completely—they depend too much on individual preferences, identity politics, and historical contingencies to produce anything like unanimity. But in the forty or so years that scholars have been grappling with the question of what Mormon literature might be, they have discovered, unearthed, and advanced an impressive body of literary work that we should at least consider in any attempt at an answer.

Though bereft of Miltons and Shakespeares, Mormonism has managed to produce a reasonable number of Saul Bellows and Graham Greenes—writers who understand their culture but don't always approve of it, who understand the narrative potential of their history and traditions, and who walk the fine line between "insider" and "outsider" to produce sympathetic yet challenging portrayals of Mormonism's history, culture, and worldview. Occasionally, these authors transcend the boundaries of their culture and use elements of the Mormon story as the background for bigger stories that capture yet unexplored aspects of the universal human experience. And when such a thing happens, we must allow that Mormon literature does indeed have its share of "classics."

NOTES

1. Whitney, "Home Literature," 132.
2. DeVoto, "Vacation," 559–60.
3. Geary, "Mormondom's Lost Generation," 24–25, 27.
4. The four novels in Fisher's *Tetralogy* are *In Tragic Life* (1932), *Passions Spin the Plot* (1934), *We Are Betrayed* (1935), and *No Villain Need Be* (1936).
5. Peterson, *Rascal by Nature, a Christian by Yearning*, 270–71.
6. Peterson, *Backslider*, 355.
7. Barber, *And the Desert Shall Blossom*, 281.
8. Peterson, *Rascal by Nature, a Christian by Yearning*, 279.
9. DeVoto, "Vacation," 560.

BIBLIOGRAPHY

Anderson, Lavina Fielding, and Eugene England. *Tending the Garden: Essays on Mormon Literature*. Salt Lake City: Signature, 1996.

Anderson, Nephi. *Added Upon*. Salt Lake City: Deseret News, 1989.

Bailey, Paul. *For Time and All Eternity*. Garden City, NY: Doubleday, 1964.

Baker, Elna. *The New York Regional Mormon Singles Halloween Dance*. New York: Dutton, 2009.

Barber, Phyllis. *And the Desert Shall Blossom*. Salt Lake City: University of Utah Press, 1991.

Barber, Phyllis. *How I Got Cultured: A Nevada Memoir*. Athens: University of Georgia Press, 1992.

Beck, Martha. *Expecting Adam*. New York : Times, 1999.

Card, Orson Scott. *Folk of the Fringe*. West Bloomfield, MI: Phantasia, 1989.

Card, Orson Scott. *A Woman of Destiny*. New York: Berkley, 1984.

Cracroft, Richard H., and Neal E. Lambert. *A Believing People: Literature of the Latter-day Saints*. 2nd ed. Salt Lake City: Bookcraft, 1979.

DeVoto, Bernard. "Vacation." *Harpers* 177 (October 1938): 559–60.

DeVoto, Bernard . *The Year of Decision, 1846*. Boston, MA: Houghton Mifflin, 1943.

Fisher, Vardis. *Children of God: An American Epic*. New York: Harper and Brothers, 1939.

Fisher, Vardis. *In Tragic Life*. Caldwell, ID: Caxton, 1932.

Fisher, Vardis. *No Villain Need Be*. Garden City, NY: Doubleday, 1936.

Fisher, Vardis. *Passions Spin the Plot*. Caldwell, ID: Caxton, 1934.

Fisher, Vardis. *We Are Betrayed*. Caldwell, ID: Caxton, 1935.

Flora, Joseph. *Vardis Fisher*. New York: Twayne, 1965.

Freeman, Judith. *Red Water*. New York: Pantheon, 2002.

Geary, Edward. "Mormondom's Lost Generation: The Novelists of the 1940s." *BYU Studies* 18, no. 1 (Fall 1977): 89–98.

Jessop, Carolyn. *Escape*. New York: Broadway, 2007.

Kirn, Walter. *Thumbsucker: A Novel*. New York: Broadway, 1999.

Laake, Deborah. *Secret Ceremonies*. New York: William Morrow, 1993.

Pearson, Carol Lynn. *Good-bye, I Love You*. Carson City, NV: Gold Leaf, 1995.

Peterson, Levi S. *The Backslider*. Salt Lake City: Signature, 1986.

Peterson, Levi S. *The Canyons of Grace: Stories*. Urbana: University of Illinois Press, 1982.

Peterson, Levi S. *A Rascal by Nature, a Christian by Yearning: A Mormon Autobiography.* Salt Lake City: University of Utah Press, 2006.

Pryor, Elinor. *And Never Yield.* New York: Macmillan, 1942.

Scowcroft, Richard. *Children of the Covenant.* Boston: Houghton Mifflin Company, 1945.

Sorensen, Virginia. *The Evening and the Morning.* New York: Harcourt, 1949.

Sorensen, Virginia. *Kingdom Come.* New York: Harcourt, 1960.

Sorensen, Virginia. *A Little Lower than the Angels.* New York: Alfred A. Knopf, 1942.

Sorensen, Virginia. *Many Heavens: A New Mormon Novel.* New York: Harcourt, Brace, 1954.

Sorensen, Virginia. *Miracles on Maple Hill.* New York: Harcourt, 1956.

Sorensen, Virginia. *The Neighbors.* New York: Reynal & Hitchcock, 1947.

Sorensen, Virginia. *On This Star.* Reynal & Hitchcock, 1946.

Stegner, Wallace. *The Gathering of Zion.* New York: McGraw Hill, 1964.

Stegner, Wallace. *Mormon Country.* New York: Duell, Sloan & Pearce, 1942.

Taylor, Samuel Woolley. *Heaven Knows Why.* New York: A. A. Wyn, 1948.

Taylor, Samuel Woolley. *Nightfall at Nauvoo.* New York: Macmillan, 1971.

Udall, Brady. *The Miracle Life of Edgar Mint.* New York: Norton, 2001.

Whipple, Maurine. *The Giant Joshua.* Boston: Houghton Mifflin, 1941.

Whitney, Orson F. *Elias: An Epic of the Ages.* New York: Knickerbocker, 1904.

Whitney, Orson F. "Home Literature." In *A Believing People: Literature of the Latter-Day Saints.*, ed. Richard H. Cracroft and Neal E. Lambert, 129–33. 2nd ed. Salt Lake City: Bookcraft, 1979.

Williams, Terry Tempest. *Refuge: An Unnatural History of Family and Place.* New York: Pantheon, 1991.

CHAPTER 32

··

MUSIC AND HEAVEN
IN MORMON THOUGHT

··

MICHAEL D. HICKS

EARLY Mormon apostle Parley Pratt wrote some of the church's hardiest and most persuasive tracts. Some have called him "the father of Mormon pamphleteering" and even
"the Apostle Paul of Mormonism."[1] But Pratt also busied himself with the music of the
church. In 1836, his hymn "Ere Long the Veil Will Rend in Twain" opened the dedication of the church's first temple. Four years later he coedited the church's most popular
hymnbook, which contained at least thirty-six new hymn texts by Pratt. He sang hymns
in public as part of his proselytizing. And he wrote one of the church's most striking
statements about music. To excavate that statement leads one into the foundations of
Mormon thought about music's origins.

In 1855, Pratt published a treatise detailing Mormon belief, a small handbook with the
weighty title *Key to the Science of Theology*. In its twelfth chapter, "Angels and Spirits,"
Pratt explains the many reasons that angels visit people. Among the reasons, he says,
is "to sing them a good song."[2] We have no accounts of Pratt himself experiencing such
singing. But clearly he knew of the idea, which had descended through centuries of religious history into the San Francisco room where he began writing the book. And he
might even have heard tales of other Latter-day Saints who, in dreams or visions, had
heard the music of heaven.

By January 1915, with the church about to plunge into the mainstream of American
culture, Mormon apostle Charles Penrose completed an edition of Pratt's book. Without
credit or notice of Penrose's changes in its pages, this edition formed the basis of all
subsequent editions of the *Key* published by the church's book company for the rest of
the twentieth century. Penrose added a few contemporary doctrines to Pratt's text, but
mostly removed passages large and small—a few words denouncing the Shakers and
Swedenborg, for example, several sentences in Pratt's discussion of the universal "spiritual fluid" by which spirits communicate, and, not surprisingly, large paragraphs of
Pratt's defense of polygamy. Although Penrose kept all of Pratt's other language about
the mission of angels, he deleted the phrase "to sing them a good song." The reason is

unclear. He might have thought the remark a little trivial, possibly even demeaning for divine messengers, or the deletion may have been a mere slip of the pen. But the history of heavenly singing in the church—founded by an angel's delivery of a book to western New York—actually suggests that "to sing them a good song" is one of the few angelic missions that should not be dismissed. Mormon narratives, right up to the present, give evidence that angels persist in the very thing Penrose blotted out.

The world's literature and traditions about angelic singing are so vast as to be impossible to do more than hint at. Musicologist Joscelyn Godwin offers perhaps the most knowing and elegant overview of it. As he observes, "All religious traditions that acknowledge the existence of angels concur in giving them musical attributes."[3] One finds musical angels in Islamic manuscripts, Hindu sculptures, and in every faith system from Buddhism to Kabbalism. Judeo-Christian sacred texts occasionally mention them, especially in apocryphal and pseudepigraphic books. We find many biblical references to angels "praising God" and since praise tends to include singing, we assume that is what the phrase means. Thus, even though the Luke 3 account of angels heralding Jesus's birth mentions only that they were "praising God," Christian tradition generally construes this as *musical* praise. Christmas carols reinforce the idea and probably are the main sources for contemporary Christian beliefs about angels singing: "Oh, Come All Ye Faithful" ("sing, choirs of angels"), "It Came upon the Midnight Clear" ("to hear the angels sing"), "Silent Night" ("heavenly hosts sing 'Alleluia'"), "Angels We Have Heard on High" ("sweetly singing o'er the plain"), and, of course, "Hark! The Herald Angels Sing."

But beyond the generic scriptural account of angelic praise in Luke 3, Judeo-Christian scholars typically point to two other, more specific passages in scripture. The first is in Isaiah 6, where the prophet experiences a vision of God in his temple and hears six-winged seraphs: "one cried unto another, and said, Holy, holy, holy, is the Lord of hosts: the whole earth is full of his glory" (the basis of the *Sanctus* in Roman Catholic liturgy). But that passage, while it does speak of angels crying out, does not mention singing as such. The second is the Book of Revelation, which contains the clearest biblical accounts of heavenly singing. In chapter 5, verses 8–9, the Apostle John sees four beasts and twenty-four elders, all holding harps and singing a "new song." In Revelation 14:3 the 144,000 redeemed souls in heaven also sing a new song, one that "no man could learn" but they. Revelation 15:3 describes the victorious saints who have died singing "the song of Moses" and "the song of the Lamb."

The word "choir" as such never appears in the King James Bible (or indeed almost all major English translations). But the term has its own esoteric place in Christian history. Since the Middle Ages, theologians have outlined various categories of angels, usually nine of them, using "choir" to denote each category. In this usage "choir" need not refer to singing. As the *Catechism of the Summa Theologica of St. Thomas of Aquinas* explains: "Why is the name 'choirs' given to the angelic orders? Because each order in fulfilling its duties in the divine government constitutes a class replete with harmony which makes manifest in a wonderful way the glory of God in this work." Thus the term, with or without explicitly musical meaning, has gotten inextricably tangled with angelic demographics. It reflects "harmony" in its cooperative sense, working together with a single purpose. Music symbolizes that harmony. Still, for centuries Christian iconography—paintings, engravings, stained-glass windows, sculptures, carvings, and the like—have depicted these choirs in the more familiar sense: angels singing.

If they sing, how do they do it? The issue is not so simple. Indeed, one eighteenth-century author rejected the notion of angelic singing, since singing requires physicality and, indeed, air. "One must first declare that there is air in eternal life," wrote Lorenz Christoph Mizler. "One must have investigated the powers and peculiarities of this same air. One must prove that the nature of the ear will not have changed along with the transfiguration of the body. Simply because this is impossible, one also cannot say that there will be music in heaven."[4] But some abstruse interpretations of heavenly singing could transcend that problem. Consider two examples. The first comes from the Nag Hammadi text "The Discourse on the Eighth and Ninth," a Gnostic dialogue concerning conditions in the eighth and ninth spheres that surround the earth, that is, those that make up the divine realm. "For the entire eighth," God instructs his disciple, "the souls that are in it, and the angels, sing a hymn in silence. And I, Mind, understand." The disciple replies, "I am silent, O my father. I want to sing a hymn to you while I am silent." "Then sing it, for I am Mind." Thus God instructs the disciple that, even in the ninth realm, singing silently in the heart works as the truest form of praise and the form that a God who surpasses mere words understands best.[5]

The second and more complex interpretation comes from Emanuel Swedenborg, whose visions and writings about heaven permeated western spiritual culture of the eighteenth and nineteenth centuries. In his visions he sometimes "heard" (that is, perceived) angelic choirs for hours at a time. As was typical for Swedenborg, he described a complex variety of such choirs and what sounds—if any—they made. There were celestial choirs and spiritual choirs, the two distinguishable by their tone colors. There were choirs of little children, detectable because they were not mature enough to act as one. There were strictly "gentile" choirs, noted for their coarser sound. There were also choirs associated with voluntary breathing, others with involuntary; the former became active in waking hours, the latter in dreams. The timbre of angel choirs sometimes seemed indistinguishable from violins and, apparently most often, was merely a feeling, conveyed without sound, of a large group all thinking the same thing at once. Even the "pillar of cloud" described in the book of Exodus, he wrote, was actually an angelic choir. Some choirs, he said acted only by "representations," others by representations and voices, still others by voices alone, and so on—a ponderous taxonomy indeed.[6]

If angels sing, do they play instruments? Early Christian Fathers downplayed instrumental music in favor of vocal music: because songs (a) are sung directly from man's body (no "lifeless" intermediaries), and (b) have words, which like "The Word" itself, sanctify mere sound. Some of the patrists thought God allowed instruments in the Old Testament as concessions to the Jews, but now proscribed them among his New Testament people.[7] Still, in depicting singing among the angels, Christian iconography often shows the angels holding instruments. This probably symbolizes the general idea of music, since depicting singing without instruments is far harder. Nevertheless, some of the Christian visionaries mentioned below did see and hear instruments as well as voices.

If angels sing, why are they sometimes heard on earth? The usual reasons seem to be either to comfort the hearer before dying or to testify to others of a dying person's holy life. In 397 AD Martin of Tours died and the proximate sound of angels confirmed to witnesses his righteousness. Near the end of the tenth century, the English abbot Dunstan fell into a trance in which angels appeared and bid him to sing with them eternally. Three days later, he died. For six months before his death in 1306, St. Nicholas of Tolentino heard a choir of angels each night, which he took as a sign he would soon pass to the other side. The idea of angels singing at death was so ingrained in the Christian psyche that in *Hamlet* (act 5, scene 2) Horatio utters his classic line, "Good-night, sweet prince; / And flights of angels sing thee to thy rest." In 1842, the Irish author Aubrey de Vere explained the process in his lyrical drama, *The Waldenses: Or, The Fate of Rora*, in which angels sing these words to the character of Agnes:

> When a Christian lies expiring
> Angel choirs with plumes outspread,
> Bend above his death-bed singing,
> That when death's mild sleep is fled,
> There may be no harsh transition,
> When he greets the heavenly vision.[8]

Beyond sanctifying the death bed, sometimes angel singing sanctifies a vision, attesting to the divinity of some divine direction being given. Such was the case with the friar Julian Garcia, who dreamed of a beautiful landscape with abundant rivers and springs. Angels appeared and began marking off streets and squares. "Then appeared a flight of angels singing a song of praise to the accompaniment of heavenly music." He sought and eventually found the actual spot on earth and there founded what he at first called "Puebla de los Angeles" (later, Puebla, Mexico).

If angels sing, what words do they sing? In most cases the words seem irrelevant. It is merely the fact that angels make their voices heard that brings cheer. In one tale about St. Francis of Assisi, Christ opened Francis's ears to hear "celestial music." That term sufficed to make the case that he had experienced a miracle. Sometimes, though, the words consist of scriptural or liturgical texts known on earth. In the seventh century, St. Fursy and St. Frodlibert had visions in which they heard angels singing the words of the *Sanctus* (that is, from the words in Isaiah's vision). In the seventeenth century, Athanasius Kircher and Johannes Matheson would both teach that the *Sanctus* was the *only* text angels would sing—forever. By contrast, St. Columbia of Rieti (1477–1501) heard angels singing the *Gloria in Excelsis*. At other times, as in the Book of Revelation, we know only that they sang a "new song," connoting something the hearer did not recognize. Occasionally, the angels dictated such a "new song" for use on earth—as some felt they had done in giving St. Thomas Aquinas his classic *Lauda Sion*.[9]

Although we sometimes read of the "harmony" of angelic singing, before the fourteenth century this probably meant a good vocal blend or a unity of purpose, since "harmony" as we generally think of it was not, so far as we know, a musical idea understood or practiced in the Middle Ages. By the seventeenth century, though, some music theorists taught that angels sing in strict counterpoint. Why would God's music not have the complex order that even earthly artists had mastered? Heavenly music must be rich beyond anything audible on earth and well ordered, of course, because God is "a taskmaster of order, the guiding principle of everything."[10]

The Book of Mormon contains three passages specifically mentioning heavenly choirs. King Benjamin predicts that his death will come soon and his "immortal spirit may join the choirs above in singing the praises of a just God" (Mosiah 2:28). Mormon promises that "he that is found guiltless" will "dwell in the presence of God in his kingdom, to sing ceaseless praises with the choirs above" (Mormon 7:7). The most interesting statement, though, comes in 1 Nephi 1:8 (repeated in Alma 36:22), which records that Lehi, in vision, sees "God sitting upon his throne, surrounded with numberless concourses of angels in the attitude of singing and praising their God." Note the language: he *sees* them in "the attitude of singing," a phrase usually meaning head erect, mouth open, but construes the singing from that visual "attitude." No sound is mentioned.

Joseph Smith did not refer to angelic singing in accounts of his visions. Indeed he said almost nothing concrete about music generally or angelic singing in particular. He did acknowledge, though, that angels of at least one type, seraphs, do sing: at the dedication of the first Mormon temple he prayed that the saints there would "mingle [their] voices" with the seraphs "singing Hosanna to God and the Lamb!" (Doctrine and Covenants [D&C] 109:79). He also warned against being deceived during supernatural experiences, noting—somewhat cryptically—that: "Not every spirit, or vision, or *singing*, is of God" (emphasis added).[11] In other words, though you may hear angelic singing, the singer(s) may be from the wrong side of the spiritual divide.

Smith's successor, Brigham Young, spoke the foundational statements for music and heaven in Mormon thought. On April 9, 1852, Young gave what he called a "short sermon" on the subject of music and "over-righteous" Christian suspicion about its earthly pleasures—particularly those of the violin, that is, the fiddle. God put a love of music in the human heart, Young explained, and that love should not be spurned. Music had "magic power" to tame animals and soothe human anger.[12] Less than two years later, he continued his critique of certain "preachers [who] say that fiddling and music come from hell." His doctrine: "I say there is no fiddling, there is no music in hell. Music belongs to heaven, to cheer God, angels and men." Here at last was a Mormon statement that not only placed music in heaven but gave it a purpose: to cheer, and cheer not only mortals, but heavenly beings as well—even God. The scriptures, particularly the Old Testament, often portray a melancholy God. Music, in Young's statement, provides an antidote.

In 1862, he went even further: "Tight-laced religious professors of the present generation have a horror at the sound of a fiddle," he declared, recalling his repressive upbringing. And then he presented this bold principle: "There is no music in hell, for all good music belongs to heaven. . . . Every sweet musical sound that can be made belongs to the Saints and is for the Saints." In that same year—according to a reminiscent account—Young told George Careless that "he had himself heard the soft and beautiful singing of the angels."

In the maxim "there is no music in hell," though, Young may have resorted to hyperbole. Young sometimes used the term "sweet music" in referring to the music in which he and God delight. In the nineteenth century "sweet music" typically meant music that was harmonious, simple, easily understood, and soothing. Young said he preferred such music, though he would not want to be fed on "a straight diet of [musical] honey" all the time. Yet he objected to composers of his day who would "introduce as much discord as possible into their compositions, without actually destroying the rules of music." One can hardly imagine that he considered such music fit for heaven. God, though no doubt an eternalist, was not a modernist. Young might well have sympathized with the twentieth-century Mormon prophet Spencer Kimball's gloss on Young's original language: "As I listen to the lovely melodies of the Tabernacle Choir and organ, I am comforted by the assurance that there will be beautiful music in heaven, and for that I am most grateful. Some say there will be no music in that other place—but then some sounds that pass for music probably belong to that other place."[13] In other words, heaven would have the sweet music, hell the sour.

As we have seen, Young drew no lines between vocal and instrumental music. Neither seems to have presided over the other. While the steeples of Mormon temples routinely carry statues of the angel Moroni blowing a heraldic bugle-like instrument, Young gave special attention to violins. One often saw handheld string instruments of various kinds in the Christian iconography of angels. But among many early nineteenth-century American Christians, violins symbolized the vernacular music (especially dance music) known as fiddling, which most considered sinful. Brigham Young, however, embraced fiddling as something for which God had given mankind affection, as we have seen. He once explained that those who go to hell will be "unable to raise a decent fiddler there." Rather, "every decent fiddler will go into a decent kingdom: we will have them."

Parley Pratt's brother Orson, probably the leading theologian among nineteenth-century Mormons, gave the most erudite explanation of musical sound in heaven. He began with this hypothetical question about sound itself: "If the God of the Mormonites be like a man in figure, we must suppose the organs of the senses to have the same uses, and to be dependent on the same sources for information; his ears, in consequence, for hearing must be dependent on the transmission of sound. How, then, can he hear his people praying to him in Europe when he is in America?"

In his lengthy answer, Pratt argues that, "Because the *figure* of two substances are [*sic*] alike, that is no evidence that the *qualities* of the two substances are alike" (emphasis in original). The substance of God's flesh and man's differ. "The ear of the fleshly body may be affected by the vibrations of our atmosphere; the ear of a spiritual body may be affected in an entirely different manner. . . . The ear of the fleshly body may be affected by the vibrations of many elastic substances besides the atmosphere. Sound is conveyed through various mediums with different degrees of velocity." And so on, premise upon premise, Pratt shows why God does not need ears to hear and answer prayers. But, "because God knows the nature of music, that is no reason why he may not rejoice in hearing music. One use, then, of the ears of his spiritual body is, no doubt, to hear and rejoice in delightful music, not that it increases the mind. The ear of the Lord may be delighted with sounds, though he receive no additional knowledge by those sounds."[14]

To fully appreciate Pratt's statement, note its two underlying breaks from Christian orthodoxy. First, Pratt relies on the fundamental Mormon philosophy that holds "all spirit is matter"—finer and purer than earthly matter, "but when our bodies are purified we shall see that it is all matter" (D&C 131:7–8). Angels have substance; the world in which they dwell is tangible in some sense. So they sing with "physical" spiritual bodies and their sound vibrates in some palpable medium, even if mortals can hear it only in dreams and visions.

The second point of departure concerns this fundamental question: Who are the angels? Christian theology tended to see angelic beings as distinct from human beings—that is, angels are a higher creature than man, though some Christian scholars occasionally debated whether departed human beings then become "angels" of some sort, as opposed to, say, "ghosts." Joseph Smith, however, had a theology that made even God an exalted man. Regarding angels, he said: "There are no angels who minister to this earth but those who do belong or have belonged to it" (D&C 130:5). He and later LDS prophets explained that the categories of "angels" consisted entirely of not-yet-embodied humans, disembodied humans, and resurrected (or "translated") humans. In that sense, all angelic singing occurred across family lines, one generation of human beings to another, not one species to another.

Because of that genealogical transworld network, it seems natural that Mormon heavenly music is most frequently mentioned at the dedication of LDS temples, most of whose ordinances consist of rituals performed on behalf of the dead. At the Kirtland Temple dedication, some observers saw angels and heard heavenly choirs joining in with the earthly choir, as Smith had prayed would happen. Some people claimed to hear angelic music at the dedication of the Manti Temple. Others heard angels singing at the Salt Lake Temple dedication. Still others claimed to hear an angelic choir after the Tabernacle Choir sang at the dedication of the Swiss Temple.[15]

We should note that not only angelic choirs sing at or near Mormon temples. Sometimes smaller groups or even soloists do so. In 1838, for example, Zerah Pulsipher had a vision in which a steamboat slowly sailed through the air toward the Kirtland Temple and the recently deceased Alvah Beaman stood in the bow of the boat, swinging his hat and singing. And in 1894, Jesse Cannon reported that in the temple he heard "the most beautiful [heavenly] singing, sounding . . . like the tenor voice of Geo. D. Pyper [who was still alive], but none [other] of those present heard it."

Angelic singing at temples, Mormons felt, showed that God had sanctified the buildings, confirming them as his dwelling places. In other instances, people claimed to have heard heavenly singing in order to legitimize their claims to divine callings. A notorious nineteenth-century example is that of Lorin Woolley, who claimed that church president John Taylor had ordained certain men to perpetuate polygamy through the priesthood, even after the church had abandoned it. Woolley said that on that occasion, many in attendance heard an angelic quartet and then double quartet. President Taylor allegedly said, "That is the first time I have heard a heavenly choir." Decades later a heavenly choir confirmed to a religious seeker that the church was true and would soon be introduced into his native land, Ghana. J. W. B. Johnson records that in 1964 he had a vision of "angels with trumpets singing songs of praise unto God and I suddenly joined in." A voice then told him to "take up my work," which led him on a path to the LDS faith and the church's establishment in his country.

The question then, as in earlier Christian history, becomes: what do these Mormon angels sing? There are at least four answers:

1. They sing hymns. In one instance, an angel choir sang "God Moves in a Mysterious Way." In another, a choir of young angels sang the Primary song "Gladly Meeting, Kindly Greeting." In 1927, an angel came to Medford, Oregon, to help missionaries sing the hymns "O My Father," "Love at Home," and "Glorious Things of Thee Are Spoken." At the John Taylor ordination described by Lorin Woolley, the quartet of angels sang "The Birth of Christ," then a double quartet sang "The Birth of Joseph Smith" and "The Seer," followed by "two or three other songs." (Only "The Seer," however—written by John Taylor—is a hymn known by that name in Mormon hymnody.)

2. They sing a personal message for the hearer. The most extreme example may have come in 1881, when David Patten Kimball had an open vision in which he "heard the most beautiful singing I ever listened to in all my life. These were the words, repeated three times by a choir: "God bless Brother David Kimball.""

3. They sing a larger, more public message. Parley Pratt described a heavenly vision in his fictional narrative *The Angel of the Prairies*, written sometime in the mid-1840s and presumably based on experiences about which Pratt had read or heard. Taken by an angel to the "Grand Presiding Council" that rules over the earth, the narrator says that "bands of instrumental music filled the temple with melody indescribable, accompanied with human voices, both male and female, all chiming in perfect harmony in a hymn of triumph, the words of which I could only understand in part. But the concluding lines were repeated in swelling strains of joy." Pratt then gives eight dactylic lines in rhyming couplets, foretelling that, even though mortal things would gradually decay, God and his chosen people would "eternally reign."

4. They sing in the language of heaven itself, not comprehensible to people on earth. Hiram Page, for example, wrote in 1847 that angels personally confirmed to him the validity of Mormonism. "Three of [them] came to me afterwards and sang an hymn in their own pure language."[16]

Still, as with their Christian predecessors, Mormons emphasized the beauty of the heavenly music and the mere fact that people could hear it, whether or not they could discern the words. One of the best of this type is the detailed nineteenth-century account from Harriet Lee, who had what we now call a "near-death" experience (that is, she briefly seemed to die and was resuscitated). In her retelling of it, an angel guides her through various buildings, halls, and rooms, in the last of which she sees many women and children playing and "millions" of men working. "They seemed to have all kinds of music which sounded as coming from the distance as well as close by. I have since heard some of the same tunes here; but I could not distinguish the words. While I was listening to this music, my chaperon said, 'When you return to this place you will join in singing the new song.' "[17]

Two points in this vision stand out. First, the appeal of the tunes yet indecipherability of the words. This dichotomy dovetails nicely with other Mormon visionary descriptions. Mormon pioneer James Abbott, for example, wrote of a feverish dream in which he heard "sweet singing" and string playing on "a new song the words of which I could not understand but the music was the sweetest I had ever heard." Note too that when the fever broke and he woke up, he tried to sing the music for his cousin, but "strangely, it left me the moment I tried to sing it for her." Second, the angel's promise that Lee would one day sing the "new song" continues a Christian theme from the Book of Revelation, as well as the "new song" mentioned and quoted in Doctrine and Covenants 84:98–102: "even from the least unto the greatest, [all] shall be filled with the knowledge of the Lord, and shall see eye to eye, and shall lift up their voice, and with the voice together sing this new song . . ." followed by the words (in English, of course).

Arguably, the most important example of Mormon angel music consists of a Native American appearing to a composer in a dream to give him a tune that would be repeatedly printed and written about in church publications. In 1853, Cyrus Wheelock pronounced a blessing on the head of twenty-four-year-old Thomas Durham, saying that Durham would be beloved in Zion "because of the heavenly strains that thou wilt bring forth, and angels shall reveal and sing unto thee while laid upon thy pillow, the songs that are sung in the heavens above."[18] The grandest fulfillment of this promise, according to Durham, was a dream in which he saw a large group of Navajos form a circle by a river. One of them held a horn, walked to the river, and played a tune. "He missed the two high notes in the latter part of the tune, but I seemed to know what he was trying to get. . . . I awoke and lay thinking whether I should get out of bed and go to the organ and play it, for I knew then that I should not forget it, but as I lay I fell asleep again and I heard the same tune repeated on a horn and I again awoke." At daybreak, Durham went to the organ to play, then wrote the tune down—a simple F-major folk tune in 9/8 time. He soon published a four-part arrangement of the tune—as a new setting of the text "O My Father." Under the name "Nephite Lamentation," he had it printed on a single sheet, the backside of which contained the story behind the song. Under that name it appeared again in the *Juvenile Instructor* in 1902 (without words), in the *Relief Society Magazine* in 1919 (with words), and even as the last instrumental piece in the *Primary Song Book* (1947 edition).

While only a relic today, this tune's resonance should not be underestimated. It represents the giving of a tune by a dead Indian to a Latter-day Saint in a dream, then written down and shared with the musically literate. It follows a well-worn path of Mormon fascination with Indians—Nephites and Lamanites, as they called them—from the Book of Mormon tribes of Hebrew migrants. One of the church's earliest hymns began

> O stop and tell me, Red Man,
> Who are ye? why you roam?
> And how you get your living?
>
> Have you no God;—no home?
> With stature straight and portly,
> And decked in native pride,
> With feathers, paints and broaches,
> He willingly replied:—
>
> "I once was pleasant Ephraim,
> "When Jacob for me prayed,
> "But oh! how blessings vanish,
> "When man from God has strayed!"

Five more verses followed, reviewing Native Americans' Semitic history and millennial destiny. In those same early years, Lucy Mack Smith (Smith's mother) sang a song in tongues, musical glossolalia interpreted and versified as "Moroni's Lamentation." It spoke in the first person the travails of the Nephite prophet who angelically appeared to her son Joseph to deliver the Book of Mormon. W. W. Phelps published a song about Joseph Smith that he called "Go with Me," whose text likened the voice of Smith to the Native American narrator of the then well-known song "The Indian Hunter." After Joseph Smith's assassination, Apostle John Taylor rewrote the popular American song "The Indian's Lament" (which began "O give me back my bended bow") into a paean to the departed prophet, "O Give Me Back My Prophet Dear." The "Angel of the Prairies," about which Parley Pratt wrote, was a dead Lamanite warrior who had come to Pratt to show him the exalted destiny of the Lamanite people—though only after the angel had made heavenly music audible.

The "Nephite Lamentation" continued the Mormon fascination with dead Indians. More important, though, it shifted the Christian tradition of angelic singing into the Native American tradition of the dead bequeathing songs from the spirit world. As Nym Cooke succinctly puts it, "for centuries most Native Americans have viewed musical composition, or transmission, as a 'super-natural act.' "[19] Melodies are not so much composed as *transposed* from one world to the other. A guardian spirit, often an ancestor, gives a song to the receiver in a dream. The receiver then perpetuates the tune by singing it. The literature regarding this quasi-angelic singing continues to grow in the ethnomusicological community. Such giving of tunes by departed spirits suits basic Mormon sensibilities. But for Mormons sacred memory must pass into tangible, preservable form: record-keeping—from quarterly activity reports to books of remembrance—is almost a sacrament. Thus, a tune, like any heavenly communication, must be written down. An angel—a dead Nephite—gave Joseph Smith a book, which he translated via some divine mechanism, dictating it to scribes who wrote it down for others to publish, admire, and use. When an angel—another dead Nephite—came to Thomas Durham to play him "a good song," he "translated" it into musical notation and published it for others to admire and use.

In recent decades, as the church has pursued North American respectability, it has tempered, if not eradicated, its once fundamental belief that Native Americans are blood-lineage Israelites. Correspondingly, music from departed Nephites seems too old-fashioned for modern dreamers. Yet the Mormon impulse to write down heavenly transmissions of music persists. Consider three scraps of anecdotal evidence from my life as a music professor at Brigham Young University.

1. A Mormon woman contacts me with the story that her departed husband has been mediating songs from the other side—dozens of them. She can play them at the piano, sing and record them. But could I find someone to write them down so they could be published as a blessing to the world?[20]

2. A well-schooled, award-winning LDS composer begins in the mid-1980s to have visions of deceased classical composers. They appear to him and dictate new works they have composed in heaven. Since he is musically literate, he writes down these fragments, fresh music from dead composers, and publishes them in booklets he gives away at Mormon symposia and other venues.

3. An elderly white-bearded gentleman arrives at my office one day with a stack of photocopies in his hand. He had prayed for years for the Lord to give him the tune of the "new song" to be sung at the end of the world, as described in Doctrine and Covenants 84. His prayers worked, he says. The tune has been given him from the spirit world. But he knows he had to go further: he has taught himself how to write down the tune he was given. Now, in my office, choking back tears, he presents me with a stapled photocopy of the tune he notated above the sacred text. He asks me to preserve and share it as I choose. The angels' "new song" is now available to learn, note for note.

If these seem mere case studies in applied psychology, what then should we say about the centuries of tales from all cultures, accounts of songs sung by throngs of spirit beings with new music to be learned and sung on earth as it is in heaven?

The fruits of literary or musical creation always hold seeds of mystery: Where do the words come from? Where do the notes come from? We usually think of words bubbling up from our own minds. We think in words, they form part of our identity. Not so with tunes. They seem more a spectral presence in the phenomenal world. So in the end, the supernatural delivery of music directly from heavenly realms seems somehow less strange than the supernatural dictation of prose. In that light Charles Penrose's redaction of Parley Pratt turns a blind eye to this perpetual theme in Mormonism—a theme with, as we have seen, many variations. Even in an enlightened, humanistic age, at least some Mormons continue to believe that angels still come "to sing them a good song," especially one that can be written down for others to read. In a famous critique of Mormon origins, the philosopher Sterling McMurrin bluntly said, "You don't get books from angels."[21] But, all told, where else would you go to get songs?

Notes

1. These quotations are from Crawley, "Parley P. Pratt," 13–26; Givens and Grow, *Parley P. Pratt*.
2. Pratt, *Key to the Science of Theology*, 112.
3. For the Godwin quotation, see Godwin, *Harmonies of Heaven and Earth*, 73. For more on relevant noncanonized Christian texts, see Tvedtnes, *Most Correct Book*, 159–60.
4. Quoted in Yearsley, *Bach and the Meanings of Counterpoint*, 32.
5. Robinson, *Nag Hammadi Library in English*, 295–96.
6. I have assembled these ideas not from a thoroughgoing understanding of Swedenborg's visionary system—if that is indeed possible—but from a study of all the citations in the massive four-volume work of Potts, *Swedenborg Concordance*, 614–15. All of the ideas mentioned in this paragraph may be found on those pages.
7. This is a complicated topic, about which one should consider McKinnon, "The Meaning of the Patristic Polemic against Musical Instruments," 69–82. See also the writings of the patristic fathers excerpted in Strunk, *Source Readings in Music History*, 59–75. See also the quotation by St. John Chrysostom in Miller, *Heaven*, 225.
8. Quoted and discussed in "Poems of the De Veres," 203. For earlier citations in this paragraph, see Adams, *Visions in Late Medieval England*, 97n16; Waller, "Christian Iconography and Legendary Art," 31. The source for the paragraph that follows is Carson, *Mexico*, 235.
9. Sources for this paragraph are Yearsley, *Bach and the Meanings of Counterpoint*, 31; Brewer, *Dictionary of Miracles*, 310; and *Hymns Adapted to the Church Services throughout the Christian Year*, A3.

    The quotation in the paragraph that follows appears in Athanasius Kircher, cited in Yearsley, *Bach and the Meanings of Counterpoint*, 21.
10. Yearsley, *Bach and the Meanings of Counterpoint*, 21.
11. Smith, *Teachings of the Prophet Joseph Smith*, 162. The original manuscript of this discourse reads, "Every spirit, or vision, or singing is not of God." But in the context of Smith's life and oratory at the time, the reordering of words in *Teachings* seems to reflect the intended meaning.
12. Young, "Self-Government," 1852, 1: 48. The quotations by Young in the following three paragraphs are from "Propriety of Theatrical Amusements," 1862, 9: 244 and "Light of the Spirit," 1860, 8: 178; Gates and Widtsoe, *Life Story of Brigham Young*, 81–82 (Susa Young Gates was his daughter); and Brigham Young Office Journal, June 3, 1860.
13. From Kimball's address in the 2 October 1982 General Conference of the church.
14. Pratt, *Absurdities of Immaterialism*, 31–32. For some rumination on the creative implications of this, see Hicks, "All-Hearing Ear."
15. For Kirtland, see Tullidge, *Women of Mormondom*, 208; Hales, "Autobiography of Charles Henry Hales," excerpted on http://www.boap.org/LDS/Early-Saints/HalesF.html. For Manti, see Cannon, Journal; and Sjodahl, *Introduction to the Study of the Book of Mormon*, 233. For Salt Lake, see Manscill, Freeman, and Wright, *Presidents of the Church*, 107. For Switzerland, see the document "Honors," box 2, J. Spencer Cornwall Papers (minimally processed as yet). A complete inventory of temple dedications would doubtless yield more examples.

    The information and quotations in the two paragraphs that follow are from Pulsipher, "History of Zera[h] Pulsipher as Written by Himself"; Cannon, Journal, October 15, 1894; Anderson, *Polygamy Story*, 57–58; Johnson to First Presidency, September 9, 1978.

16. The sources for examples and quotations in these four "answers" are found in Kraut, *Spirit World Experiences*, 8, 22; Hogan, "Singing of a Translated Being," 31–33; Whitney, "Terrible Ordeal," 10–11; Pratt, *Angel of the Prairies*, 14–15; and Anderson, "Personal Writings of the Book of Mormon Witnesses: Hiram Page." A "translated" being in Mormon doctrine is a human who has not died but has been made immortal; later, he or she will be "changed" to a resurrected state.

17. Her entire account appears in Heinerman, *Guardian Angels*, 147–54. The quotations in the paragraph that follows come from "Life Sketch of James Smith Abbott," 12–13.

18. Durham, Journal, January 19, 1853. There are several published accounts of the dream that follows. I took the language here from "Some of Our Composers: Thomas Durham."

19. The latter words are quoting Bruno Nettl. See Cooke, "Sacred Music to 1900," 79.

20. In this, as in the following anecdotes, I will not give the names, out of respect for the living, if not the dead.

21. In Ostler, "Interview with Sterling M. McMurrin," 25.

BIBLIOGRAPHY

Adams, Gwenfair Walters. *Visions in Late Medieval England: Lay Spirituality and Sacred Glimpses of the Hidden Worlds of Faith.* Leiden: Brill, 2007.

Anderson, Max J. *The Polygamy Story: Fiction and Fact.* Salt Lake City, UT: Publishers Press, 1979.

Anderson, Richard L. "Personal Writings of the Book of Mormon Witnesses: Hiram Page." http://maxwellinstitute.byu.edu/publications/books/?bookid=41&chapid=181. Accessed February 24, 2015.

Brewer, E. Cobham, *A Dictionary of Miracles: Imitative, Realistic, and Dogmatic.* Philadelphia, PA: J. B. Lippincott, 1894.

Cannon, Abraham H. Journal, May 25, 1888. Photocopy of holograph in L. Tom Perry Special Collections, Harold B. Lee Library, Brigham Young University, Salt Lake City.

Carson, W. E. *Mexico: The Wonderland of the South.* Rev. ed. New York: Macmillan, 1914.

Collier, Fred C., ed., *The Office Journal of President Brigham Young: 1858–1863 Book D.* Hanna, UT: Collier's Publishing, 2006, 98.

Cooke, Nym. "Sacred Music to 1900." In *The Cambridge History of American Music*, ed. David Nicholls, 78–102. Cambridge: Cambridge University Press, 1998.

Crawley, Peter. "Parley P. Pratt: Father of Mormon Pamphleteering." *Dialogue: A Journal of Mormon Thought* 15, no. 3 (Autumn 1982): 13–26.

Durham, Thomas. Journal, 19 January 1853. Typescript in Church History Library, Salt Lake City, Utah.

Gates, Susa Young, and Leah D. Widtsoe. *The Life Story of Brigham Young.* New York: Macmillan, 1930.

Givens, Terryl L. *People of Paradox: A History of Mormon Culture.* New York: Oxford University Press, 2007.

Givens, Terryl L., and Matthew J. Grow. *Parley P. Pratt: The Apostle Paul of Mormonism.* New York: Oxford University Press, 2011.

Godwin, Joscelyn. *Harmonies of Heaven and Earth: The Spiritual Dimension of Music from Antiquity to the Avant-Garde.* London: Thames and Hudson, 1987.

Hales, Charles Henry. "Autobiography of Charles Henry Hales." In *Windows: A Mormon Family*, ed. Kenneth Glyn Hales. Tucson, AZ: Skyline, 1986.

Heinerman, Joseph. *Guardian Angels*. Salt Lake City, UT: Joseph Lyon, 1985.

Hicks, Michael. "The All-Hearing Ear." *Sunstone* (February 1985).

Hicks, Michael. *Mormonism and Music: A History*. Urbana: University of Illinois Press, 1989.

Hogan, Melvin John. "The Singing of a Translated Being." In *Assorted Gems of Priceless Value*, ed. N. B. Lundwall, 31–33. Salt Lake City, UT: Bookcraft, 1947.

"Honors." Box 2 of the J. Spencer Cornwall Papers. L. Tom Perry Special Collections, Harold B. Lee Library, Brigham Young University, Salt Lake City.

Hymns Adapted to the Church Services throughout the Christian Year. 2nd ed. London: Simpkin, Marhsall, 1860.

Johnson, J. W. B., to First Presidency, September 9, 1978. Edwin Q. Cannon, Papers, Church History Library, Salt Lake City, Utah.

Journal of Discourses. 26 vols. Reported by G. D. Watt et al. Liverpool: F. D. and S. W. Richards et al., 1851–86; reprint., Salt Lake City, UT: n.p., 1974.

Kimball, Spencer. Address to the General Conference of the Church of Jesus Christ of Latter-day Saints, October 2, 1982. https://www.lds.org/ensign/1982/11/the-lord-expects-righteousness?lang=eng.

Kraut, Ogden. *Spirit World Experiences*. Dugway, UT: Pioneer, 1972.

"Life Sketch of James Smith Abbott." Typescript in *Mormon Diaries* series, vol. 14. Harold B. Lee Library, Brigham Young University, Salt Lake City.

Manscill, Craig K., Robert Freeman, and Dennis A. Wright. *Presidents of the Church: The Lives and Teachings of the Modern Prophets*. Springville, UT: Cedar Fort, 2008.

McKinnon, James. "The Meaning of the Patristic Polemic against Musical Instruments." *Current Musicology* 1 (Spring 1965): 69–82.

Miller, Lisa. *Heaven: Our Enduring Fascination with the Afterlife*. New York: Harper, 2010.

Ostler, Blake. "An Interview with Sterling M. McMurrin." *Dialogue: A Journal of Mormon Thought* 17, no. 1 (Spring 1984): 18–43.

Potts, John Faulkner. *The Swedenborg Concordance: A Complete Work of Reference to the Theological Writings of Emmanuel Swedenborg Based on the Original Latin Writings of the Author*. London: Swedenborg Society, 1888.

Pratt, Orson. *Absurdities of Immaterialism*. Liverpool: R. James, 1849.

Pratt, Parley P. *The Angel of the Prairies: A Dream of the Future*. Salt Lake City, UT: A. Pratt, 1880.

Pratt, Parley P. *Key to the Science of Theology, designed as an Introduction to the First Principles of Spiritual Philosophy, Religion, Law and Government, as Delivered by the Ancients, and as Restored in this Age, for the Final Development of Universal Peace, Truth and Knowledge*. Liverpool: F. D. Richards, 1855.

Pulsipher, Zerah. "History of Zera[h] Pulsipher as Written by Himself." Typescript in Harold B. Lee Library, Brigham Young University, Salt Lake City. http://www.johnpratt.com/gen/7/z_pulsipher.html.

Robinson, James M. ed. *The Nag Hammadi Library in English*. San Francisco, CA: Harper & Row, 1977.

Sjodahl, Janne M. *An Introduction to the Study of the Book of Mormon*. Salt Lake City, UT: Deseret News, 1927.

Smith, Joseph. *Teachings of the Prophet Joseph Smith*. Ed. Joseph Fielding Smith. Salt Lake City, UT: Deseret, 1938.

"Some of Our Composers: Thomas Durham." *Juvenile Instructor*, July 15, 1902.

Strunk, Oliver, ed. *Source Readings in Music History: From Classical Antiquity through the Romantic Era*. New York: Norton, 1965.

"The Poems of the De Veres." *Dublin University Magazine*, February 21, 1843.

Tullidge, Edward W. *The Women of Mormondom*. New York: Tuillidge and Crandall, 1877.

Tvedtnes, John A. *The Most Correct Book: Insights from a Book of Mormon Scholar*. Salt Lake City, UT: Cornerstone, 1999.

Waller, J. G. "Christian Iconography and Legendary Art." *Gentleman's Magazine and Historical Review* 37 (January 1852): 30–33.

Whitney, Orson F. "A Terrible Ordeal." In *Helpful Visions: The Fourteenth Book of the Faith-Promoting Series*, 9–22. Salt Lake City, UT: Juvenile Instructor Office, 1887.

Yearsley, David. *Bach and the Meanings of Counterpoint*. Cambridge: Cambridge University Press, 2002.

Young, Brigham. "Light of the Spirit—Course of Missionaries" [September 9, 1860]. *Journal of Discourses* 8: 176–82.

Young, Brigham. "Propriety of Theatrical Amusements—Instructions Relative to Conducting Them" [March 6, 1862]. *Journal of Discourses* 9: 239–41.

Young, Brigham. "Self-Government—Mysteries—Recreation and Amusements, Not in Themselves Sinful—Tithing—Adam, Our Father and Our God" [April 9, 1852]. *Journal of Discourses* 1: 46–53.

PART VII

···

THE INTERNATIONAL CHURCH

···

CHAPTER 33

MORMONS IN LATIN AMERICA

MARK L. GROVER

INTRODUCTION

Moses Thatcher of the Quorum of the Twelve Apostles was pleased with the baptisms. It was November 23, 1879, and he was beginning missionary work in Mexico City. He encountered a prepared congregation excited about becoming Mormons. Within a week of his arrival, eight had joined the church and Plotino Rhodakanaty was named as president of the first branch of the church organized in Latin America. Elder Thatcher had hopes it would be a second England for the church. Forty years earlier, in 1837, two apostles, Heber C. Kimball and Orson Hyde had arrived from the United States and between July 1837 and April 1838 had baptized close to 1500 British converts to the recently organized Church of Jesus Christ of Latter-day Saints. That mission was followed with a second mission to England between 1839 and 1841, during which seven of the church's Quorum of the Twelve Apostles proselytized. An additional 4000 converts joined the church. The immigration of these new British converts to the United States significantly strengthened this new religious movement and provided the numbers for the church to establish itself in the western part of the United States. A steady stream of converts immigrated from England and northern Europe for several years, helping it become a legitimate religious movement that would continue to grow and expand into a twentieth-century world religious movement.

Unfortunately, Elder Thatcher's hope for the rapid establishment of a strong LDS presence in Latin America did not occur. The congregation in Mexico City was soon beset with dissension. The branch president, Plotino Rhodakanaty, a political extremist, was more interested in the socialist aspects of Mormonism than its religious doctrines. He soon left the church, followed by most of his supporters. Political conflicts and the Mexican Revolution between 1910 and 1917 further hampered the church, creating a chaotic environment for members. The American missionaries had to leave the county. Growth and expansion were not the byproducts of this challenging period. The church in Mexico for the first eighty years of its existence was little more than a weak outpost of Mormonism.

Though the beginning was not promising, missionary work in Latin America would eventually have an impact on the church similar to the early British and European missions. But it was to occur in the last half of the twentieth century. The economic and social environment of nineteenth-century Latin America was very different from that of Europe, particularly England. The industrial revolution had had a disruptive effect on society, to the point that missionaries from a new American church could take advantage of the disruption and convince many in Europe not only to change religions but emigrate to the deserts of the western United States.

Nineteenth-century Latin America was a tightly controlled political and social environment in which any social alteration—especially religious change—was unlikely. The nineteenth-century Catholic Church was so dominant in most areas of Latin America that any activity by Protestant or Mormon missionaries was unlikely to prove successful. For religious divergence to occur, the basic social systems had to change. Those changes began in the 1950s, when economic growth and development expanded in the large cities and new political conditions began to emerge. By the 1970s, a pool of potential converts in Latin America had emerged. It was young nineteen-year-old Mormon missionaries, not apostles, who reaped the harvest. The consequence transformed Mormon demographics. By 2010, the baptized members in Latin America represented 39 percent of the church. In terms of convert baptisms, two countries, Brazil and Mexico, represent almost 17 percent of the church.

Just as in the nineteenth century, when Mormonism experienced a Europeanization, as converts from Europe streamed to the Salt Lake Valley, the church is now undergoing a Latinization. There are significant differences, however, from the European experience. Nineteenth-century converts became Mormons by becoming Americans through immigration to the western United States. Latin American Mormons are asked to stay in their countries and create Mormon enclaves within their cities and countries. The creation of Mormonism within a culture that is Latin, Catholic, and often tropical is the struggle that confronts the new Mormon converts. This undertaking is monumental and may be the most different challenge the church has encountered.

THE BEGINNING OF THE CHURCH IN LATIN AMERICA

The first LDS apostle who sought to establish the church in Latin America left perplexed. Apostle Parley P. Pratt was one of the most successful early missionaries of the church. He converted investigators with relative ease. His phenomenal ability to preach and write evolved into a persuasive proselytizing style unequaled by most missionaries of the church. He had success everywhere he went. Consequently, it was frustrating for Pratt to accept the fact that on his four-month mission to Chile in 1851 no one was converted and few actual teaching experiences occurred. He struggled to learn Spanish, but acquired too little to employ his hallmark rhetoric. That personal challenge was actually secondary to the political obstacles in Chile at the time, which made proselytizing by non-Catholics punishable by imprisonment. Frustrated, Pratt returned to the United States suggesting that Latin America was not yet ready for the church. "The constitution establishes the Roman Catholic religion, supports it out of the treasury, and prohibits all others."[1]

Apostle Moses Thatcher, who started missionary work in Mexico, did not have the oratory skills of Parley P. Pratt, but he was an effective administrator. He was an exceptionally bright businessman and became an apostle at the young age of thirty-seven. His business skills were not enough to keep the church in Mexico together and when his first congregation melted away he shifted missionary efforts toward the indigenous population surrounding Mexico City. The church in Mexico struggled in part as a result of an unstable political climate that characterized Mexico for many years. Issues of church governance in Mexico eventually lead to a schism in the church that had its foundation in ideological disputes over American versus Mexican leadership. It was only after the calming of the political waters and the resolution of institutional conflicts in the 1940s that the church was able to grow.

Apostle Melvin J. Ballard was legendary in the church because of his missionary successes—at least, until 1925, when he went to Argentina to open missionary work in South America. He and his two companions baptized six the week they arrived and then only one more over the next six months of their mission. Ballard, like Thatcher and Pratt, did not speak Spanish—an obvious impediment to missionary success. Ballard's two missionary companions, including Rey L. Pratt of the First Council of the Seventy, became ill, and Ballard had to work alone for some of the time, unable to communicate in Spanish. Buenos Aires in the 1920s was a vibrant and evolving city with great opportunity for expansion and growth. But the missionaries found few who were interested in the new American religion. The church struggled in South America much as it did in Mexico, not because of political instability but due to simple lack of interest.

REFORMATION IN LATIN AMERICA

Missionary success in Latin America would require political and social transformations in the region. When growth came to the Mormon Church in Latin America, it was a byproduct of momentous religious change that had striking similarities to the religious reformation of Europe in the sixteenth century. The religious environment in Latin America at the beginning of the twenty-first century was very different from what it had been fifty years earlier.

Latin America is historically the most Catholic region of the world. That identification was established by its Spanish and Portuguese colonizers, who were politically, theologically, and culturally anchored in the Catholic Church. That religious influence remained in Latin America after nineteenth-century independence, reinforced by constitutions that protected Catholicism as the state religion. Other religions were allowed to function but primarily only among the immigrant populations. By the twentieth century liberal reforms supporting religious freedom had been adopted in most Latin America countries, allowing for but not encouraging non-Catholic activity.

Cultural controls had to be relaxed before realistic religious freedom could become a reality. Those changes occurred primarily because of economic transformations. The economic consequences of the Second World War contributed to an acceleration from a traditional agrarian economy to an industrialized one, particularly in the larger countries. These economic changes encouraged a migration of workers to the large cities such as Lima, Peru; Mexico City, Mexico; Buenos Aires, Argentina; and São Paulo, Brazil. These migrants were eager to take advantage of jobs and educational opportunities afforded them in the cities. Separated from the customs and habits of tradition, these new immigrants were psychologically open to new non-Catholic religious groups who were rapidly establishing themselves in the expanding neighborhoods of the cities. Most of these religious groups were evangelical Protestants, who offered to the migrants new and appealing explanations of life, along with secular assistance such as job procurement and social fellowship. Rates of conversion to new religions gained steam after the 1960s.

The Catholic Church was slow to respond to its fading religious dominance and when it did, its answer came primarily from the left in the form of liberation theology. This approach supplemented the religious experience with political and economic rhetoric and activity. Though effective in some areas of Latin America, liberation theology over time lost out to the evangelical Protestants whose religious activities gave greater emphasis to spiritual experiences. Most of these evangelical groups had their origin in Europe and America but before long the movement was dominated by local Latin American organizations and personalities who were able to incorporate Latin American cultural values into their religious approach. In recent years the Catholic charismatics have become a significant competitor in the religious arena.

An additional shift that facilitated proselytizing was Latin America's movement away from traditional patrimonial controls toward more democratic values and systems. This was particularly important in South America during the 1980s, with the elimination of harsh military dictatorships. The consequent atmosphere of political freedom permeated every aspect of society. In religious terms it meant religious affiliation could be as much a matter of choice as other aspects of one's private life. The number of Latin Americans who experimented with other religions became significant.

Growth and Expansion

Mormon interest in Latin America went beyond simple questions of growth and expansion. A strong tenet of the church came from its new volume of scripture, the Book of Mormon. The premise of the book is that a small group of refugees from Jerusalem left the Middle East in 600 BC and migrated to the Americas, bringing with them the promises and blessings of the peoples of Israel. Mormons developed a strong belief that the indigenous population of Latin America was heir to the covenant with Israel, and would eventually accept the gospel in great numbers. Though the focus of LDS missionary efforts was initially with the native populations of the United States, as the leaders recognized that large number of native Americans lived in Latin America they shifted attention to Latin America.

At the end of the Second World War the church was in three countries, Mexico, Argentina, and Brazil. The church chose areas for expansion that were closest to those countries and had a significant presence of American members. The first expansion was into Central America, when John O'Donnal began working for the US government in Guatemala in 1943 and several times requested that the church send missionaries to Central America. In 1946, Arwell Pierce, president of the Mexican Mission, visited with O'Donnal and agreed it was time to dispatch missionaries to Guatemala, who were assigned to the country in September of 1947. Expansion into the rest of Central America occurred within the next few years: Costa Rica and El Salvador in 1949, Honduras in 1952, and Nicaragua in 1953, followed by Panama in 1965 and Belize in 1980. Though it took half a century, there is now a strong presence of the church in all the countries of Central America, with the largest number of baptized members in Guatemala.

In South America, the first expansion after the war was the result of efforts by Frederick Williams, an early missionary in Argentina. He worked for the US State Department and lived in Uruguay during the war. In 1946 he and a few other ex-missionaries from Argentina visited with the church president, George Albert Smith, suggesting expansion of missionary work throughout South America, starting in Uruguay. The First Presidency responded in 1947 by calling Williams to preside over a new mission there. A proportionally high number of missionaries were sent to Uruguay and it has experienced significant growth for many years. Missionaries were subsequently sent to Paraguay in 1950.

THE PRESIDENCY OF DAVID O. MCKAY

For the LDS Church to become firmly established in Latin America, church culture itself had to change. The defensive stance taken by the church during its late nineteenth-century conflicts with the US government and American culture meant that church efforts were focused more on protecting itself in the United States than expansion outward. Missionary work continued during this period though without substantial resources or energy. Many believed that the church had already derived its principal convert strength from early success in Europe, and consequently the purpose of missionary work in the late nineteenth and early twentieth centuries was to glean the few chosen who were still scattered throughout the world. The church appeared to be in a wait-and-see mode rather than a phase of significant expansion.

Dramatic change occurred with the presidency of David O. McKay who became prophet in 1951. The two world wars were over and Western society was in a period of economic recovery and growth. McKay's vision for the church was significantly influenced by his own international experience and a strong belief in the value of missionary work. He moved the Latter-day Saints away from a Zion- (Utah-) centered church to an expansive, truly worldwide organization. He suggested that the leadership not see the international church as mere outposts of Mormonism and pushed the idea of regional and indigenous development. He believed that the nature and structure of the church in the United States could and should be duplicated worldwide. This approach signaled a significant philosophical change, particularly among the leadership, because it suggested that resources were to be more evenly dispersed internationally. The most significant visual indication of that change was the impressive international building program started at this time, which resulted in the construction of hundreds of chapels throughout the world.

The centers of the church became Mexico and South America, initially Uruguay. Mexico in the early years was a challenge. For many years there was a conflict with the American church primarily over the role of native leaders. Schism resulted, with the formation of a parallel Mexican church in 1936, completely staffed by Mexicans and separate from Salt Lake City. The group reunified with the Utah church in 1946 and growth, under the watchful eye of American leaders (many born and raised in the Mormon colonies in northern Mexico), was slow but continual. The first stake (comparable to a diocese) in Latin America was organized in Mexico in 1961. Mormon membership in Mexico passed one million in 2004; the country also has more temples (thirteen) than any other country outside of the United States.

President McKay visited South America in 1954 and felt there was significant potential for growth and expansion. After his visit he delegated members of the Twelve Apostles to visit the small and struggling congregations. The expansion to western South America occurred in 1956, when missionaries were sent to Chile and Peru. The Andes Mission which included Peru and Chile was organized in November of 1959 and then split in 1961 when a separate Chilean Mission was established. President McKay sent a young and energetic general authority, Elder A. Theodore Tuttle of the First Council of the Seventy, to live in South America between 1961 and 1965. Elder Tuttle at first unified and strengthened the church and then pushed to have it established in all the countries of South America which did not have a large Afro-Latin population (because a priesthood ban on members of African descent was still in effect). Between 1964 and 1966, missionaries went to Bolivia, Ecuador, Panama, Colombia, and Venezuela. Missionaries were also sent to Puerto Rico from the Florida Mission in 1964.

The evolution of the LDS Church in Brazil followed a different trajectory, distorted by the racial restrictions that were particularly applicable among the Brazilian population. Resultant conversion patterns included a strong middle class component in urban centers, particularly in the industrial city of São Paulo. A strong core of leadership there led to the organization of the second stake in Latin America in 1966.

THE PRIESTHOOD REVELATION

The final phase of Latin American expansion began after June 1978 with the historic revelation by President Spencer W. Kimball, which extended priesthood participation and temple access to all worthy men regardless of race. Kimball's experience in Latin America made him vividly aware of the effect the restrictive policy had on missionary work, particularly in Brazil and Puerto Rico. With Kimball's announcement of the construction of the São Paulo temple in Brazil in March of 1975, the restriction in such a racially mixed country provoked a reevaluation of the policy. The 1978 lifting of the ban occurred four months before the new temple opened. This change was a decisive event in the evolution of the church in Brazil and other parts of Latin America and the Caribbean, where subsequent Mormon growth exploded.

This change also allowed for the final expansion of the church in the Caribbean. Missionaries were immediately sent to the Dominican Republic and Jamaica in 1978, into Haiti in 1980, and Trinidad and Tobago in 1983. The church has since gone to most of the smaller islands of the Caribbean. The obvious exception is Cuba, which has a few members but limited organizational activity. The church has experienced success particularly in the Dominican Republic and Haiti, however, the English-speaking islands have been less receptive to Mormonism in part due to strong opposition by Evangelical ministers.

A second significant change that spurred church growth during this period occurred on June 24, 1984. With the goal of decentralizing the administration of church government, Area Presidencies were organized throughout the world. The significance of this change was that each area included three general authorities who moved to the regions they administered and were able to facilitate procedures because of decentralized decision making. Three of the thirteen initial areas were in Latin America: Mexico, Brazil, and Argentina. One of the byproducts of the presence of nine general authorities in Latin America was an increased focus on missionary work, due largely to greater contact with mission presidents and missionaries. As a result, the number of missionaries sent to Latin America increased significantly. Simultaneously, the church increased regional budgets. All these developments transformed the LDS Church from a primarily American church into an organization whose population base was shifting to Latin America. In 1960, there were 34,114 baptized members in Latin America representing 2.06 percent of the entire church. By 2010 the numbers had increased to 5,358,433, constituting 38.76 percent of the entire church membership. By 2010, of the twenty countries with the largest number of members, twelve were in Latin America.

The expansion of the church in Latin America was accompanied by a changing demography of the LDS population in the United States. The economic challenges in Latin America in the late twentieth century and the beginning of the twenty-first resulted in a significant increase in immigration from Latin America to the United States. The church did not have a consistent policy regarding immigrant groups, sometimes organizing separate language-based congregations and sometimes integrating immigrant populations into English-speaking wards (parishes). At the beginning of the twenty-first century numerous Spanish-speaking congregations were organized throughout Utah and other parts of the United States and missionary activities focused on this population. In 2011, the church spoke out forcefully in favor of humane immigration policies and attitudes, reflecting no doubt an increased sensitivity to this growing part of their membership.

CHALLENGES OF GROWTH

This period of growth was an exhilarating time for the church, as so many Latin Americans were baptized. Most Mormon families had missionaries who went to Latin America. The expansion of the church was so significant in some areas that in a few years the church went from a small branch of 100 people to numerous congregations with membership numbers in the thousands. Baptisms were held every week in some congregations. The entire church marveled and reveled in the stories of growth and expansion.

Most religious organizations would relish the challenges of rapid growth. The primary difficulty for the church was integrating so many new members into the church, most of whom had little knowledge or understanding of Mormon culture and practices. Since the LDS Church does not have a paid clergy, all activities of the units were led by the members. Occasionally newly baptized members were put in charge of congregation within months of their baptism. Training and supervision of leaders became imperative as the church struggled to maintain cultural and religious continuity.

RETENTION

The efficient and detailed record-keeping practice of the LDS Church has always been successful in registering growth and expansion but much less effective in determining retention and movement out of the church. The reality of religious change for any faith group is that conversion of new members is countered to some extent by defections of old members; retention then becomes a paramount concern. With the nineteenth-century European converts to Mormonism, the effectiveness of retention was measured in large part by the extent of their immigration to the United States. Attendance at meetings or activities connected to the church was not considered the crucial metric it has become. The new twentieth-century converts in Latin America were discouraged from immigrating and were encouraged to remain in their countries of conversion. Religious and cultural changes necessitated by baptism in the church were often accompanied by cultural pressure from family, friends, and society to reverse the decision. This challenge was exacerbated by organizational weaknesses of congregations with minimally trained local leaders and the occasional disagreement between missionaries and local leaders; growth goals often conflicted with the need for stability in the church. Retention became critical for leaders of the LDS Church in the later part of the twentieth century. Though a challenge for the church throughout the world, retention was of greatest concern regarding the surging Latin American membership. The high number of convert baptisms suggested significant growth, but the actual numbers who regularly attended meetings, paid tithing, and claimed membership was significantly lower that the official membership records indicated. The difference between the number of baptized members and those who were participating in the Church was seldom advertised to the outside world but mentioned several times to members and leaders at the semiannual worldwide conferences.

That problem was underscored by an unusual administrative move by the church. In 2002, two apostles were sent to live and preside in areas that had seen some of the most significant levels of growth, Chile and the Philippines. Apostle Jeffrey R. Holland lived in Chile for two years and presided over a significant retrenchment program, meant to slow growth to manageable levels, strengthen the local units, and increase the percentage of active members. Missionaries were encouraged to locate and visit baptized but inactive members with the intent of encouraging them to return to the church. Units at all levels were combined to provide stronger congregations with better leadership. Measures were put in place to ensure that baptisms were better integrated into the local units of the church. (Similar changes were made in the Philippines.) The result for Chile was a significant drop from 10.27 percent yearly growth in 2002 to .52 percent in 2003. The number of stakes went from 112 to 87. Similar forms of retrenchment were introduced throughout Latin America and the percentage of growth for the entire area dropped to between 2 and 3 percent, close to the average for the church in general. Programs of integrations were emphasized throughout Latin America.

CULTURE AND LEADERSHIP

The cultural and political connection of the LDS Church with the United States has always been an issue in Latin America. In the early years, when most missionaries were exclusively Americans, the connection with the United States was obvious and often exploited as a proselytizing tool. Missionaries taught free English classes in the chapels and occasionally preached in English on street corners to attract attention. With the growth of the church and the calling of native Latin Americans as missionaries, those practices were eliminated and the US connection downplayed. Even with these changes the perception of Mormonism as an American church persists globally, due in part to the visual image of the missionary wearing suits, white shirts, and ties. More recently, stories in Latin American newspapers of the sensational activities of US polygamous religious groups were almost always erroneously reported as LDS.

The negative consequences of the connection has impaired the church's public image in Latin America and even led to violence. The Left in Latin America is suspicious of Americans and often connects any activity of American-based organizations as an attempt to augment US influence in the countries. These activities are often seen as being directed by the United States Central Intelligence Agency (CIA). The Left has long attached suspicion to the Mormon missionary program. Charges range from the entire missionary program being part of the CIA to the belief that the missionaries are attempting to change Latin American culture to be more favorable to US political and military hegemony. Even with a decrease of American LDS missionaries, such perceptions persist.

Hostility has occasionally turned violent with the bombing of LDS chapels and occasional murder of LDS missionaries by leftist revolutionary groups. The best-known case was the murder of two LDS missionaries in Bolivia in May of 1989. The most significant governmental action against the church was in Nicaragua when, after the Sandinista revolution of 1979, church property was confiscated and missionaries evacuated. Less dramatic conflicts have resulted in the evacuation of missionaries from Honduras and the departure of American missionaries from Venezuela. These events did not seriously hamper the church's proselytizing because it used missionaries from other Latin American countries.

With the efforts to make the church less conspicuously American there was a parallel effort by the church to delegate more control over the expansion to local leadership. The establishment of the Area Presidency system in 1984 was equally a push to decentralize decision making and to establish controls to prevent deviation from church-wide policies. Those in the Area Presidencies were either Americans or Latin Americans who had been trained within the administrative system of the church. The result is that Mormon worship and practice in Latin America is similar to that found in the United States and significantly different and distinctive from traditional Latin American religious worship.

DEMOGRAPHICS, ECONOMICS, RACE, AND POVERTY

The reality of religious conversion is that it is generally those on the lower economic and social levels of society who are most likely to change religious affiliation. That was the case in nineteenth-century Europe, as the new converts to Mormonism came mostly from the marginal classes. A high percentage were single mothers and young adults. Newspaper reports of the time perpetuated the perception of Mormon converts as society's dregs, although some observers noted the quality of those becoming Mormons and migrating to the United States. Charles Dickens, for example, famously described a Mormon emigrant ship as full of "the pick and flower of England."

The demographic makeup of the LDS Church in Latin America has varied according to time period and geography. The most important factor in the expansion of the church into Latin America was that missionaries went first to large urban centers, generally the capital or the largest city. Consequently, missionary work unfolded among a population connected to the modernization of the country. There were initial attempts to go into small villages and towns but this strategy did not yield success. In the 1880s, for example, missionaries in Mexico City, after the breakup of the first branch, did go to the indigenous villages surrounding the city, but their focus soon returned to the urban areas. The 1928 opening of the mission in Brazil in the small southern German colonies was successful, but in 1935 the Brazilian Mission headquarters was established in the city of São Paulo, even though the city had few members. It was apparent that missionary success would occur in large population centers and not small villages and towns.

Because of the church's doctrinal belief that members of the indigenous population of the Americas were descendants of Israel, activities to expand into the native population centers in small villages were periodically started. Those attempts have had limited success, with the exception of a few places such as the Nivaclé community at Mistolar in Paraguay, or Quiriza, Bolivia. The church launched significant efforts in the Altiplano in the Andes mountains in the 1970 and '80s, where some units of the church were established. The most successful activities were among the Otavalo in Quito, Ecuador, where stakes have been organized among speakers of Kichwa. This area is urban and the Otavalo Indians have been successful in maintaining their historical traditions within the church. There has also been some missionary success in the highlands of Guatemala among indigenous groups. But these activities were the exception and not the rule; missionary work in Latin American has been mostly focused on the European-descent populations. Even in countries with a large indigenous population the racial makeup of the church tends toward Mestizo (mixed), with most coming from European rather than native cultural backgrounds.

As we saw above, Brazil provides an example of a different pattern of growth. The direction of missionary efforts was significantly affected by a church policy restricting the activities of those with African ancestry. The early focus on German immigrants (1928–40) was a pattern that expanded to include other European-descent populations in the immigrant south. When expansion did occur into the historical slave-owning areas of the Brazilian northeast, missionaries worked only with the European populations. Consequently the demographic makeup of the membership of the church prior to 1978 was somewhat distorted in comparison to the population in general, being almost exclusively of European descent and white. Missionaries seldom went to the poor areas because these neighborhoods included a larger percentage of descendants of the Brazilian slave population. The church in Brazil had a membership with higher than average economic means and educational background.

The revelation on the priesthood in 1978 significantly changed the demographics of the church in Brazil. With the opening of all the country to missionary work, the makeup of the church soon reflected the population in general. Missionaries also began to proselytize in poorer neighborhoods that had been avoided due to racial restrictions.

With the push for growth in the 1980s and 1990s, the demographics of the church changed significantly from white to mixed. The congregations in the southern regions of the country remained predominately white, but in the northeast the congregations were primarily persons of African descent. Unlike in the United States, where missionary success has not occurred among the African American population, in Latin America, the church has had success with all races.

PERPETUAL EDUCATION FUND

Under the leadership of Spencer W. Kimball (1973–85), the focus of the church was on missionary work and expansion. One of his goals was to decrease the number of American missionaries serving throughout Latin America in favor of native Latin Americans. This emphasis was successful in that the numbers of Latin Americans who became missionaries increased significantly. Financial support for many of these young missionaries came from a special missionary fund supported by church membership generally in the United States.

The missionary program highlighted the economic challenges of the members. The changing economic level of the converts joining the church was reflected in the young men and women called on missions. Coming from difficult home environments, many of these young missionaries were not educationally prepared to get adequate paying jobs, so that when they returned home from their missions they encountered significant economic hurdles. Church leaders soon recognized that a sizeable percentage of the returned missionaries who had serious economic challenges also struggled to maintain activity in the church. Education and technological training were clearly the solution, but many of these young men and women did not have the economic means to go to school. By the end of the twentieth century a small loan program had been established, administered by the Seminary and Institute program of the church, but the funds were limited. A few private foundations were established by former American missionaries to provide scholarships and loans to young returning missionaries. But what was established was limited in comparison to what was needed.

The church officially responded to the need with a program to help young members of the church with their educational challenges. In the spring of 2001, President Gordon B. Hinckley announced a fund that had similarities to an important church institution of the nineteenth century. New European converts of that era were encouraged to immigrate to the United States but often lacked the financial means to make the expensive journey. In 1849 Brigham Young established the Perpetual Emigrating Fund (PEF) to help new converts finance the trip across the Atlantic. The twenty-first-century version established by Gordon B. Hinckley was a church-administered fund supported by donations that provided loans to (mostly) returned missionaries, so they could receive technical training to make them competitive in the job market. The expectation was that with financial help not only would these young members be able to obtain better employment but there would be a higher retention in the church. The program represents an adaptation of a successful nineteenth-century program to a church confronting twenty-first-century challenges resulting from growth and expansion in the third world.

CONCLUSION

Scholars who study religion in the twenty-first century suggest that Christianity is undergoing a significant change related to doctrine and demography. Many suggest that the center of Christianity has shifted from Europe and the United States to the southern hemisphere, principally Latin America and Africa. Similarly, the type of Christianity that is now prominent has shifted from a liberal Protestant approach to an evangelical conservative view of the world. That shift has had profound repercussions for the Catholic Church as the traditional structure and philosophy of the European church is losing out to the evangelically influenced charismatic form of worship and belief. The twenty-first-century Christian church is different from its predecessor.

Mormonism has experienced similar changes in demography as the population center of the church reflects not only growth in Latin America but expansion among the Latino population of the United States. The highly centralized nature of the Mormon Church has meant that it has avoided many of the philosophical and theological changes that other churches have experienced, but some adjustments have occurred. Just as the growth of the church in the United Kingdom strongly determined the course of nineteenth-century Mormonism, so the expansion of the church in Latin America has made Mormonism a different church than it was fifty years ago. Mormonism's future will continue to be reshaped, as the church in Latin America continues to mature and change.

NOTE

1. Pratt, *Autobiography of Parley P. Pratt*, 502.

BIBLIOGRAPHY

Acevedo, A., Rodolfo. *Los Mormones en Chile*. Santiago: Impresos y Publicaciones Cumora, 1990.

Curbelo, Néstor. *Historia SUD: Relatos de pioneros*. Buenos Aires: author, 2000–. A series of one volume histories of the LDS Church in South America.

Grover, Mark L. *A Land of Promise and Prophecy: Elder A. Theodore Tuttle in South America, 1960–1965*. Provo, UT: Religious Studies Center, Brigham Young University, 2008.

Iber, Jorge. *Hispanics in the Mormon Zion: 1912–1999*. College Station: Texas A&M University Press, 2000.

Pratt, Parley P. *Autobiography of Parley P. Pratt*. Ed. Scot Facer Proctor and Maurine Jensen Proctor. Rev. ed. Salt Lake City, UT: Deseret, 2000.

Romney, Thomas Cottam. *The Mormon Colonies in Mexico*. Salt Lake City: University of Utah Press, 2005. (Originally published: Salt Lake City, UT: Deseret, 1938.)

Tullis, F. LaMond. *Mormonism in Mexico: The Dynamics of Faith and Culture*. Logan: Utah State University Press, 1987.

Williams, Frederick S., and Frederick G. Williams. *From Acorn to Oak Tree: A Personal History of the Establishment and First Quarter Development of the South American Missions*. Fullerton, CA: Etcetera, 1987.

CHAPTER 34

....

MORMONS IN THE PACIFIC

....

R. LANIER BRITSCH

CONSIDERING the difficult circumstances of the church in the 1840s and 1850s, the Mormon venture into Polynesia was amazing. Why, one might ask, did Joseph Smith send missionaries to the South Pacific when the church was only thirteen years old and relatively weak? The answer appears to be twofold. First, Joseph Smith strongly believed that the restored gospel, the true gospel of Jesus Christ, had to be preached to every nation and people. Second, the opportunity presented itself when Addison Pratt, a convert who had sailed the Pacific on whaling ships and spent time in Hawaii as a young man, expressed interest in teaching the gospel to the Hawaiians. Pratt and three companions left Nauvoo, Illinois, in May 1843. Their travels took them to New Bedford, Massachusetts, where they embarked on a whaling ship named the *Timoleon*. It sailed around South Africa, through the India Ocean, and finally into the South Pacific. One elder died of consumption at sea, but the remaining three arrived at the little island of Tubuai in April 1844. Tubuai is around 350 miles south of Tahiti and approximately 3000 miles south of Hawaii. Their intent had been to go on to Hawaii, but Pratt felt strongly that he should commence his proselytizing efforts at that distant spot. His two companions went on with the whaling ship to Tahiti and then on to other parts of what later became French Polynesia.

Over the next several years they had success on Tubuai and in the Tuamotu Archipelago to the east of Tahiti. Several thousand islanders and a number of foreigners accepted the Mormon message and were baptized into the faith. In 1850, other elders and their wives came to the islands as missionaries and teachers. They too learned the Tahitian language and taught the people not only Mormonism, but also the arts of Western civilization. Serious political difficulties with the new French government ultimately forced the closing of the mission in 1852. The mission in French Polynesia was not reopened until forty years later in 1892.

On December 12, 1850, ten Mormon elders arrived in Honolulu from the gold fields of northern California. Before long their numbers were bolstered by additional missionaries. Their success throughout the Hawaiian Islands exceeded that in French Polynesia. By 1854, over four thousand Hawaiians had joined the church.

These two missions—French Polynesia and Hawaii—were the founding missions of the Latter-day Saints in the Pacific. For one hundred years the principle missionary focus of the church in the Pacific was on Polynesia. Other missions were founded in Polynesia as follows: New Zealand, 1854; Samoa, 1888; Tonga, 1891; Cook Islands (Roratonga), 1899 (but it failed and was reopened in 1947). (Because it is not part of Polynesia, Australia is not considered in this article.) In 1951, the church began its steady expansion into other parts of the Pacific, including Micronesia, Melanesia, and several Polynesian "outliers," including Vanuatu and Nauru. The order in which the islands were opened to LDS missionary work was: Guam, 1951; Niue, 1952; Fiji, 1954; New Caledonia, 1961; Vanuatu, 1973; Kiribati, 1975; Northern Mariana Islands, 1975; Federated States of Micronesia, 1976; Marshall Islands, 1977; Belau, 1978; Papua New Guinea, 1980; Solomon Islands, 1995; Nauru, 1995; and Christmas Island, 1999. It is well to know, however, that Mormons lived in most of these islands and island groups prior to the opening of formal missionary work.

The early missions to French Polynesia and Hawaii were meaningful for the Latter-day Saints for several reasons. They were the first foreign-language missions and the first missions of the church in truly foreign cultures. Not only that, they helped to establish in the minds of church leaders and general membership that these people of alien languages, of darker skin, and a more primitive way of life were also God's children and worthy of all of his blessings. The simple efforts of these early missionaries to provide education for their beloved converts set a pattern that was emulated throughout Polynesia in coming generations. Some of the earliest LDS missionaries noted the number of worthy Polynesian values and even some similarities among various Polynesian spiritual beliefs and those of Christianity. Beginning at this early time in French Polynesia and Hawaii the Mormons recognized that many Polynesians had great faith in God's healing power. Further, it was from these first Polynesian missions that many Latter-day Saints—then and now—became convinced that the peoples of Polynesia were descendants of Israel through the lineage of Lehi, a prophetic leader in the Book of Mormon. In short, the belief is that the Polynesians descended from explorers who sailed from some point in Central America not many years before the time of Christ.

Through the Lineage of Lehi

A man named Hagoth, according to the Book of Alma in the Book of Mormon (Alma 63:5–8) was a shipbuilder who gathered a large number of people together and sailed north along the west coast of America. According to the account, he and his ships never returned. This has opened the way for a Mormon tradition that he not only sailed north but also caught major ocean currents that carried his party as far as Hawaii. Descendants of those pioneers moved on from there to the other islands of Polynesia.

In support, some Mormons point to the voyage of the *Kon Tiki* and two plants, the sweet potato, the *kumara* (the Polynesian name for the Peruvian *cumara*) and the bottle gourd, as the main evidences that Polynesians may have come from the Americas. It is clear from the voyage of Thor Heyerdahl's *Kon Tiki* and many other raft voyages that drift voyage from east to west to the Polynesian islands is possible. And John L. Sorenson and Carl L. Johannessen have clearly documented the existence of not only two, but over eighty plants and a dozen microorganisms that definitely traveled from one hemisphere to the other with human carriers. To the botanical evidences advocates add costume and statuary similarities, and the belief that the skin color and physical features of Polynesians and Indians of Meso-America and South America are similar. They also point to Polynesian oral traditions and genealogies. These records are numerous and cover many generations.[1]

On the other hand, scholarly evidence to support a Southwest Pacific origin for the Polynesians is of several kinds: among them are linguistics, archaeological remains (pots and chicken, dog, and pig bones), botanical history, and genetic studies. The languages of Polynesia are part of the vast Austronesia family of languages that extends from Polynesia and Melanesia into Taiwan, through Southeast Asia and to points further west. Despite some evidence of language ties connecting Polynesian tongues to Native American languages, the two groups are still considered by most linguistic historians to be unrelated. The best archaeological evidence for the Southwest Pacific origin of the Polynesians is the widespread use of an ancient pottery type called La Pita. The distribution of varied La Pita patterns suggests a point of origin in New Caledonia.[2] In addition, basic Polynesian canoe-building styles had their origins in the western Pacific. There is evidence that the use of outriggers, double hulls, and sails were innovated one or two millennia before the birth of Christ. Some botanical evidence also points to the Southwest Pacific origins of the Polynesians. The major food crops (taro, breadfruit, bananas, yams, arrowroot, turmeric, paper mulberry [for making bark cloth], sugarcane, and kava), it is argued, had their origins in the islands and mainland areas farther west than the islands called Polynesia.

Finally, while genetic origins are by no means definitely established, it seems clear that prior to the coming of Western man into the Pacific, the Polynesians were one people. Jo Anne Van Tilberg reports that Polynesians are genetically quite uniform and "definitely related to east Asian" people. "Recent genetic research," she writes, based on an inherited condition known as alpha thalassemia, suggests that the major strain of the Polynesian bloodline came from Western Polynesia.[3]

In sum, the preponderance of evidence supports the "orthodox" academic position that the major portion of what we call Polynesian people had their origins in the Southwest Pacific. But from the Mormon point of view there is room also for an infusion of the blood of Israel from the Americas or elsewhere. The Book of Mormon itself says, "the Lord God has led away from time to time from the house of Israel, according to his will and pleasure. And now behold, the Lord remembereth all them who have been broken off" (2 Nephi 10:22).

A PEOPLE OF FAITH AND STRONG
BELIEF IN GOD

Among Mormons who are familiar with Polynesian Saints (Mormons) it is common to regard them as people of remarkable faith in the healing power of Priesthood administrations. Mormons commonly speak of the Polynesians as people of "simple faith." John H. Groberg, a former General Authority of the LDS Church, who is familiar with the islanders, has referred to them as people of "profound faith." Mormon lore is replete with stories of miracles of many kinds. Eric B. Shumway, former president of Brigham Young University-Hawaii, published a book titled *Tongan Saints: Legacy of Faith*, in which are recounted numerous first-person stories of spiritual healings, sacrifices for the church, miraculous escapes from death in accidents and terrible tropical storms, visions, warnings, and other gifts of the Holy Spirit. For many Polynesians the veil between mortal life and that on the other side is very thin. In some parts of Polynesia, for example among the Maori of New Zealand, some early European visitors reported spiritual beliefs that harmonized well with Mormon teachings concerning the nature of God. Mormon and Polynesian spirituality has been a natural match from the beginning.

Compared to the voluminous accounts of faith among the Polynesian people, fewer stories exist among the Melanesians and Micronesians—perhaps because the history of the church among those peoples is considerably shorter and they have consequently found fewer advocates. Time may change this perception. Those Caucasian missionaries who have labored among the Polynesians seem to have fallen within the same orbit of the miraculous. Undoubtedly Matthew Cowley, who in his later years served as an apostle in the LDS Church, is the best-known man of faith in Mormon Pacific history. During the late 1930s and through the years of the Second World War, he presided over the New Zealand mission of the church. His close associate Glen L. Rudd recounted this powerful incident:

> President Cowley did love to bless people. One time he blessed a little boy named Te Rauparaha "Junior" Wineera, who was born blind. His father said to President Cowley, "When you give him his name [giving infants their names is an ordinance in the LDS Church], give him his eyesight." President Cowley described that as a tough assignment. He blessed him, hemmed and hawed around for a while, waiting for the inspiration to come. Then it came, and he blessed him with the ability not only to see but also to hear. And he blessed him that over his young childhood, he would gradually overcome all the problems dealing with his equilibrium. The family did not know that this little baby was also deaf and that he had a problem gaining balance. Junior is in his sixties now [1997] and has superb vision. My wife and I have had our picture taken with him on various occasions. We both have glasses, and Junior, standing between us, has no glasses. He can read signs farther away than anybody I know. What a humble, sweet Maori man![4]

What Polynesian spirituality *was* in earlier times and what it *is* today are somewhat different matters. Hawaiian, Tahitian, Tongan, Samoan, and Maori Mormons of the twenty-first century are so completely incorporated into the mainstream of the church through standardized scriptures, printed administrative manuals, lesson manuals, magazines, and similar meetinghouse styles that it is difficult (except for language) to discern any difference between a Sunday school class in Chicago and one in Auckland, New Zealand, or Papeete, Tahiti. Still, they maintain a heritage of several highly esteemed cultural values, many of which they believe are in harmony with Mormon tenets.

Among Hawaiians (and other Polynesians, as well), three values are paramount: *Ke Akua*, God; *pule*, prayer; and *'ohana*, family. Other important values include: *ha'aha'a*, humility; *laulima*, working together; *ho'oponopono*, setting things right; and *lokahi*, unity. Closely related to all of these concepts is another cardinal value and virtue, the word and concept of *aloha*. Variations of this word are found throughout Polynesia. Visitors to Hawaii understand aloha to mean hello, goodbye, and love. All are correct, but it means much more. Speaking of the word aloha, a Hawaiian *kupuna* (literally a person of your parents' generation, but often used as simply a respected older person) said: "The *ha* in the word *aloha* is cherished by the Hawaiian people because it represents the 'breath of life' and the essence that is in all things and that is in tune with all things; it demonstrates that there is oneness with God." Another kupuna explained, "Aloha is a philosophical approach to living based on service rather than exploitation, giving rather than taking, selflessness rather than selfishness, conservation rather than wastefulness, respect rather than oppressing, love rather than hate."[5] Friends of mine at the Polynesian Cultural Center in Laie, Hawaii, speak of the Spirit of Aloha. To close friends they confide that to them it is the Spirit of Jesus Christ as expressed in word and deed.

Other values are emphasized among other island nations. In Tonga, *faka'apa'apa*, *foaki*, and *mateaki* are important. "*Faka'apa'apa*," writes Professor 'Inoke F. Funaki of BYU-Hawaii, connotes doing homage or obeisance—to show deference, respect, or courtesy. It also represents related dimensions such as *talangofua* (obedience) and *'apasia* (reverence). This value is considered uppermost in the socialization of children. Also very important . . . is the concept of *foaki* (giving, sharing, helping). . . . Finally, the concept of *mateaki* connotes loyalty and devotion, especially in fulfilling *fatongia* (obligation)." All of these values point a person toward "doing one's duty to God, king, and others."[6] All of these values and concepts harmonize well with basic tenets of Mormonism (and for that matter, with Christianity in general).

In *Aotearoa*, the "Land of the Long White Cloud," New Zealand, the Maori place great emphasis on the sacredness of the land, the *pa* or village, their sacred *wharenui* or houses, the *iwi* or tribe, and their genealogy. "Where are you from?"—that is, "from whom do you come?"—is very important. The Maori speak of having "a place to stand." In the Maori village at the Polynesian Cultural Center (PCC) in Hawaii stands a wonderful Maori house called *Te Arohanui o te Iwi Maori* (The Great Love of the Maori People)—a fully carved and traditionally decorated *wharenui* (large meetinghouse). Founded in 1963, the Polynesian Cultural Center, located in Laie, Hawaii, is owned and operated by the Mormon Church. It was created to provide employment for students at the Church College of Hawaii (CCH), Brigham Young University-Hawaii (BYUH), and to preserve and perpetuate the best of Polynesian culture. It is the most popular paid tourist attraction in Hawaii. Since the early 1970s it has hosted around a million visitors each year. In these graceful words Maori scholar and former administrator at the PCC Vernice Wineera, PhD, describes the spiritual essence of this place, the wonderful *wharenui*.

> The carvings in the house are representative of famous historical chiefs and heroes of New Zealand's Maori tribes. Because the PCC house is pan-tribal in its history, every Maori has a right to stand and speak within it. Every time I enter the beautiful *wharenui*, I am impressed with the realization that while up to a million tourists pass through it every year, they usually have no real understanding as to whose presence they are in. Powerful chiefs surround them and, from the vantage point of history and great *mana* [spiritual presence and power], gaze upon them from all four walls. Thus, hosts and visitors exchange gazes in the metaphorical body of *Te Arohanui o te Iwi Maori*. From a Maori point of view, it is as if sacred spaces, sites, and natural places have the ability to stand in both worlds—to exist in a *noa* (common) state while surrounded by the unknowing, non-belonging—but the concept also signifies sacrosanctity in the presence of the knowing, belonging *tangata whenua* (people of the place) and other Maori.
>
> Many tourists mistakenly believe that the Maori worship these carved icons of the tribes and culture. The respect the Maori afford these *taonga* [cultural treasures] is rooted in reverence for those people, now dead, who are the ancestors of all Maori. Thus, in every *wharenui* I have ever entered, it is the spiritual presence of these ancestors of the *tangata whenua* who, having lived, still live and thus confirm Maori identity. *Te Arohanui o te Iwi Maori* is imbued with the *mana* both of its craftsmen and of the chiefs and heroes of Aotearoa who reside permanently within it. "The Love of the Maori People" is a cultural treasure.[7]

The Maori acknowledge the presence of their dead ancestors and welcome them as part of their lives. Whenever greeting speeches are given and whenever formal occasions are held, ancestors are welcomed along with everyone else. One reason for the strong connection between Mormon missionaries and Polynesians was their shared view of life on both sides of the veil. Belief in life beyond the veil of death motivates many Polynesians to live lives of dedication to the values of the tribe, to the importance of the family, and to the memory of cherished ancestors, all of which are in conformity with the teachings and values of their Mormon faith.

From the early years of Mormonism in the Pacific Polynesian church, members desired to go to the temple. In the 1860s, Hawaiian Jonathan H. Napela (after whom the Polynesian and Pacific studies center at BYUH is named) was the first Polynesian to go to Salt Lake City to participate in LDS temple ordinances. He and thousands of others like him were driven by the belief and hope that through temple ceremonies they could be sealed as husband, wife, and children not only for time, but for eternity. Christ admonished, "whatsoever thou shalt bind [seal] on earth shall be bound in heaven"

(Matthew 16:19). But that is not all. Latter-day Saints believe vicarious ordinances for deceased ancestors may be performed in temples—baptisms, conferring of eternal blessings, marriages of couples, and sealings (bindings) of children to parents. The closeness many Polynesians feel for loved ones who have passed beyond the veil moves them to trace their genealogies and perform vicarious temple work for them.

A Temple-Building People

Close to the spiritual heart and values of Mormonism in the Pacific, and especially in Polynesia, is the temple. Since the first decade of Mormonism, Latter-day Saints have constructed temples in which to perform sacred ordinances for the living (particularly marriages for time and eternity) and for their dead ancestors (vicarious baptisms and sealings of families into eternal units). (Temple worship is discussed in chapter 14 in this volume.) Temple worship is considered the apex of Mormon belief and practice. When a temple is constructed in any part of the world, it is considered a manifestation that the church is firmly established there and that the members of the church are mature in their knowledge of and commitment to the church.

Polynesian Mormons have been favored with temples out of all proportion to their numbers. Currently there are seven temples in the Pacific area. Some history will provide context to this matter. Prior to migrating to the Great Basin of the American West in 1847, the Latter-day Saints constructed two temples—one in Kirtland, Ohio, and another in Nauvoo, Illinois. After the Mormons were established in the West, they constructed temples in four cities in Utah between 1877 and 1893. The next temple constructed and dedicated was completed in Laie, Hawaii, in 1919. Polynesian saints have long held that this temple was a sure indication that the Lord loved the Polynesians in a special way. Of course this is not possible to prove, but the physical presence of the temple in Hawaii was proof enough for thousands of island Latter-day Saints. A second Pacific temple was dedicated in New Zealand in 1958, and three more temples were dedicated in Samoa, Tonga, and Tahiti in the 1980s. Since then additional temples have been dedicated in Kona, Hawaii, and Suva, Fiji, the first in Melanesia. The vast distances of the Pacific have no doubt contributed to the need for relatively numerous temples in this realm.

Education and the Labor Missionary Program

On April 2, 1843, forty days before the Prophet Joseph Smith called Addison Pratt to serve a mission in the Pacific, Smith shared the following: "Whatsoever principle of intelligence we attain unto in this life, it will rise with us in the resurrection. And if a person gains more knowledge and intelligence in this life through his diligence and obedience than another, he will have so much the advantage in the world to come" (Doctrine & Covenants [D&C] 130:18–19).[8] Six weeks later, the Prophet returned to the topic, saying, "It is impossible for a man to be saved in ignorance" (D&C 131:6). Education, learning, seeking knowledge out of the best books, teaching diligently, and similar themes received great emphasis during the first decades of the LDS Church. If anything, that emphasis on education and learning has grown through the years and has been carried to the peoples of the Pacific since the earliest Mormon missionaries arrived there.

The educational undertakings of the LDS Church have contributed greatly to the economic, civic, spiritual, and moral uplifting of the island peoples. (For at least the last sixty years, when we use the term "peoples of the Pacific" we include significant percentages of nationalities and ethnic groups other than native Pacific islanders. This is especially true of Hawaii and New Zealand, but applies to some extent elsewhere as well.)

LDS educational efforts in the Pacific began in the mid-nineteenth century, almost as soon as the Mormons began settling the Great Basin. In 1851–52, when Louisa Barnes Pratt and her sister, Caroline Barnes Crosby (both missionary wives), found themselves among the illiterate children of Tubuai, in French Polynesia, they desired to teach them how to read and write so they could at least understand the scriptures. In Hawaii, Mary Jane Dilworth, another missionary wife, was motivated by similar concerns at about the same time. Other Hawaii missionaries operated tiny chapel schools on the major islands. When the Mormons acquired Laie Plantation in 1865, they almost immediately opened an elementary school. Various primary school efforts continued until the Territory of Hawaii took over the Laie Elementary School in 1927.

In New Zealand, LDS missionaries operated small chapel schools beginning in the 1880s. The government eventually provided good schools for all children, including the Maori, who made up the majority of Latter-day Saints, so these schools were closed. In 1913, the mission turned its attention and resources to the new Maori Agricultural College (MAC), a small residential high school for boys. Government-sponsored education made it unnecessary to operate the MAC after 1931. The MAC, as it was remembered by its alumni, served mostly LDS Maori boys.

The Samoan mission began in 1888. Soon thereafter the missionaries started rudimentary schools in many villages where small branches of the church were getting underway. The earliest of these schools were literally conducted under coconut trees. Soon more permanent schoolhouses were constructed of plaited palm fronds, but most buildings were temporary and makeshift. Educational materials—books, paper, pencils—to support the learning process were hard to come by. Mission presidents typically had few resources to share with the schools and their students.

In 1904, missionaries and members in Samoa created a residential school in a newly founded Mormon village called Sauniatu. Here, LDS students primarily from the island of Upolu were brought together to be taught not only the three Rs, but also appropriate Christian living. Boys and girls were housed in separate *fale* (Samoan- and Tongan-style houses), and adult chaperones who followed the traditional *matai* system (that is, the chiefly, patriarchal way) directed the students' activities during out-of-school hours.

Similar schools were organized at about the same time near Pago Pago, American Samoa, and on the island of Savaii. In 1926, a school named Makeke, meaning "arise and awake," was dedicated in Tonga.

Perhaps the most significant administrative reality until the 1950s was that the LDS schools were mission schools. The main problem with this was that every mission president's first responsibility was to proselytize the restored gospel. Finding time for running schools and staffing them with missionaries was a significant problem. Mission presidents were frequently torn by their realization that the schools were a blessing to their young church members, but that the missionaries also had other important proselytizing responsibilities.

Until the 1950s the "system" of church education developed without a master plan. Mission presidents, missionaries, and local members in each area had responded independently to immediate, local needs. During the 1950s, under the leadership of church president David O. McKay, leaders in Salt Lake City began to take responsibility for schools in the Pacific missions. McKay would oversee the radical transition from mission-operated to church-operated schools. Probably the most important development in the evolution of the administration of Pacific schools was the building of two church colleges: the Church College of New Zealand (CCNZ; actually a coed residential high school in American terms) and the Church College of Hawaii (renamed Brigham Young University-Hawaii Campus in 1974).

The man behind the creation of CCNZ was Elder Matthew Cowley. He had openly lamented the termination of the Maori Agricultural College in 1931 and unreservedly lobbied for a new school to take its place. Church leaders responded. Under instructions from church headquarters in Salt Lake City, mission president Gordon C. Young bought property for the new school in 1951. Progress was slow on the new school until the *Hui Tau* (all–New Zealand LDS conference) of April 1952. At that time, the NZ saints voted to support volunteer laborers with food and money until the school was completed. Within a few days of the Hui Tau, forty laborers reported to the building site. (A similar volunteer system had previously been implemented by mission president Emile C. Dunn in the construction of Liahona High School in Tonga.)

At the same time several influential persons from America came forward and created the first stages of what came to be called the Labor Missionary program of the church. The man who had the greatest ongoing influence was Wendell B. Mendenhall from California. With the support of President David O. McKay, he initially arranged for seven skilled craftsmen to go to New Zealand on construction assignments. These men became supervisors and teachers of crews of builders. They trained Maoris, Samoans, Tongans, and other volunteers to be carpenters, brick masons, cabinet makers, electricians, concrete workers, heavy-equipment operators, and so forth. What began in New Zealand eventually spread to all the LDS missions in the Pacific, including Australia and Japan. Hundreds of young men were called as full-time labor missionaries. Most of them learned trades that became their life's occupations. Between 1955, when the program became official, and 1965, when it ended, hundreds of chapels, schools, homes for faculty and mission leaders, mission office facilities, dormitories, auxiliary buildings, shops, sewer and water systems, and so on, were completed. On the list of important construction projects were the New Zealand Temple, CCNZ, the Church College of Hawaii, and the Polynesian Cultural Center. In a very real sense the buildings that were constructed by the labor missionaries changed the image of the church from that of a poverty-stricken organization to a prosperous, successful institution. Evidence of this was the rapid growth of the church during this constructive period and the years after. It is well to consider the Labor Missionary program an educational undertaking. Not only were the lives of the missionaries themselves changed and improved, but also their families were blessed and benefitted by the better incomes that their new occupations provided. Most of these men went on to be leaders in the church and in their occupations.

While the labor missionaries were busy creating new physical plants for the church, leaders of the church in Salt Lake City were engaged reconstructing the administrative organization of the entire Pacific education system. Mendenhall, whom President McKay had appointed chairman of the Church Building Committee in 1955, suggested that the schools be removed from the jurisdiction of mission presidents, and that the principals of the schools be responsible to the First Presidency of the church or whomever they designated. That separation was made in 1957. By 1959, all missionary teachers had been replaced with a professional force of trained teachers, many of whom were hired in America. Their salaries were provided from the general funds of the church, not the missions.

Before long the separate schools all over the Pacific were combined into a single system. To administer this system the First Presidency created in 1957 the Pacific Board of Education. Its first chairman was Wendell B. Mendenhall. The Pacific Board, which reported to the First Presidency, was both a policy-making and an administrative body. Besides formulating policy, it directly administered the Pacific schools of the church, hiring, firing, and supervising the administrative personnel, staff, and faculty for the system. The board tried to do all this without forfeiting the missionary spirit of earlier times. In 1961, board members wrote: "Teachers have been selected first of all for spiritual worthiness. . . . Each has assumed his [or her] appointment in the South Pacific in the spirit of a missionary."[9]

The Pacific Board of Education directed schools in the Pacific for eight years. In 1965, the Pacific schools were subsumed into the system that became the Church Education System, which continues to administer all LDS schools worldwide.[10] The Church College of Hawaii opened its doors in September 1955. It was President McKay's brainchild. He first visited Laie in 1921 and from that time on visualized a college to serve the young people of Hawaii and the Pacific. Before long the fledgling student body of 153 grew to hundreds and then gradually up to the 2700 students who study there today. What started as an institution that initially included primarily Hawaii students soon became a college for all Pacific islanders and then a place for many Asians and others. In 1959, CCH/BYUH gained accreditation as an institution granting two-year associate degrees, and was then expanded to a four-year liberal arts school that also emphasized business and education majors. BYUH is a fully accredited university.[11] The student body is international, but continues to serve the interests of its Pacific students. In 2011, students from over seventy-five nations studied there. BYUH alumni serve in positions in government, industry, business, and education in many nations.

CARRYING THEIR OWN LOAD

The history of the Latter-day Saints in Tonga stands out as an unusual example of growth under paradoxical conditions. LDS missionaries entered Tonga from Samoa in 1891. They had no success and the mission was closed from 1897 until 1907. Progress was slow during the early decades of the church there. During the early 1920s, the government passed a law making it illegal for Mormons to enter the country. This law was repealed in 1924, but the Tongan government restricted missionary entry visas to about a dozen at any one time.

Of this situation I wrote in 1986:

> There were only a little over one thousand members of the Church in Tonga in 1926. The mission seldom had more than a dozen missionaries assigned to it at one time. The value of mission property was still under thirty thousand dollars, there being only six permanent chapels. Although there were 481 members in Tongatapu, 202 in Ha'apai, and 397 in Vava'u, there were hardly enough Saints on any one island to justify a single ward. The average branch had only sixty members. From outward appearances it was not a stable mission. Yet by the 1970s, 19 percent of the population of Tonga was LDS—a greater percentage than the Church could claim in any other nation in the world.

> During 1922, 1923, and 1924, President [M. Vernon] Coombs called seventeen, nineteen, and thirteen local missionaries, respectively. His purpose was to compensate for Zion [Utah] elders who were not allowed in the country. He continued to call Tongans, usually married couples, after the exclusion law was repealed. He also called six to nine "home missionaries" every six months in Tongatapu and Vava'u, and fewer home missionaries in Ha'apai. This system continued on through the 1930s and until 1946. Then, because only the mission president, his wife, and three other missionaries were allowed in the country, the mission president started calling between twenty and forty local missionaries. After that, even much larger groups of local missionaries were called. The local missionaries communicated well with their own people, learned to teach and defend the gospel, and perhaps most important, strengthened their own testimonies of and commitment to the Church. And Tongan returned missionaries strengthened the local branches and districts.

> Because there were so few North American elders, local elders were called to serve not only as branch presidents but also as district presidents. . . . By the mid-1930s, the three districts were led by young men, all of whom were graduates of the Maori Agricultural College in New Zealand. Although the foreign missionaries were usually involved in the schools, during the 1930s and 1940s Makeke and the smaller schools generally had mostly Tongan teachers.

When World War II started, local Saints were already in charge of most activities and held most leadership positions. There was to be no transition from missionary church to local church.[12]

As the decades have passed since this early period, Tongan Mormons have continued to lead out in all phases of church leadership and missionary work in their own islands. The results today are impressive. In 2010, Tonga boasted the largest percentage of Latter-day Saints of any nation in the world—45 percent. Of an estimated population of 121,000 people, 55,173 were members of the Mormon faith. This success has been primarily because of the labors and service of the Tongans themselves. (It is noteworthy that the Samoan Mormon membership is not far behind—31 percent LDS in a nation of 220,000.)

THE MORMON PRESENCE IN THE PACIFIC

As of January 2011, there were 411,034 Latter-day Saints in the Pacific. They were distributed among twenty-one political entities: American Samoa (15,159 members), Cook Islands (1,853), Fiji (15,897), French Polynesia (21,245), Guam (2,140), Hawaii (69,872), Kiribati (14,927), Marshall Islands (5,093), Micronesia (4,193), Nauru (96), New Caledonia (1,949), New Zealand (104,115), Niue (284), Northern Mariana Islands (632), Palau (443), Papua New Guinea (18,336), Samoa (71,272), Solomon Islands (234), Tonga (58,805), Tuvalu (135), and Vanuatu (4,356). There were ninety-two stakes and twenty-seven districts that subsumed 977 individual units (wards and branches) of the church. There were ten missions and seven temples in the Pacific.[13]

For a period of almost seventeen decades the Church of Jesus Christ of Latter-day Saints has never faltered in its commitment to the peoples of the Pacific. Over time schools have been opened and then, because of changing local circumstances or church policy, terminated. In some areas branches of the church have been dissolved after many years of being in existence. Such closures almost always are in response to local demographic changes, such as migration, population shifts, and economic downturns. By and large the trend has been one of growth and development. All forms of church education continue to receive major financial support from church headquarters. For example, BYUH is undergoing a period of expansion from 2700 students to an eventual 5000. Physical facilities, too, are well maintained everywhere. The Polynesian Cultural Center from time to time receives allocations of millions of dollars to maintain and upgrade its facilities. New meetinghouses are constantly under construction.

Mormon missionaries are still walking the roads, the sidewalks, the trails, and the sandy beaches of the entire Pacific world. They continue to sail in small and fragile crafts to reach their appointed destinations. They continue to learn the languages of the people. They eat the local food. They still sit in the homes and huts of members and investigators of Mormonism to share their message of salvation. And whether they are missionaries sent from abroad or local young men and women, they usually develop a lifelong love for the people whom they serve.

NOTES

1. Sorenson and Johannessen, "Biological Evidence for Pre-Columbian Transoceanic Voyages," 238–97.
2. Oliver, *Polynesia in Early Historic Times*, passim. Oliver discusses the origins of the Polynesians extensively in his introduction and first several chapters.
3. Van Tilberg, *Easter Island*, 42.
4. Rudd, "Memories of Matthew Cowley," 21.
5. Wallace and Walk, "Hawaiian Values and the Gospel."
6. Funaki, "Reflections on the Legacy of Faith of the Tongan Saints."
7. Wineera, "Church and Cultural Foundations of the Polynesian Cultural Center," 112–13.
8. This section has been derived primarily from my own books *Unto the Islands of the Sea* and *Moramona: The Mormons in Hawaii*.
9. Pacific Board of Education, "Report to the First Presidency," 3.
10. Taylor, "Story of L.D.S. Schools," 2:174.
11. Britsch, *Moramona*, 176–87.
12. Britsch, *Unto the Islands of the Sea*, 448–50.
13. Statistics in this section are from *Deseret News 2012 Church Almanac*, 200–01.

BIBLIOGRAPHY

Britsch, R. Lanier. *Moramona: The Mormons in Hawaii*. Laie, HI: Institute for Polynesian Studies, 1989.

Britsch, R. Lanier. *Unto the Islands of the Sea: A History of the Latter-day Saints in the Pacific*. Salt Lake City: Deseret, 1986.

Deseret News 2012 Church Almanac. Salt Lake City: Deseret News, 2012.

Funaki, 'Inoke F. "Reflections on the Legacy of Faith of the Tongan Saints: Faka'apa'apa, Foaki, and Mateaki." In Underwood, *Pioneers in the Pacific*, 101–7.

Oliver, Douglas. *Polynesia in Early Historic Times*. Honolulu: Bess, 2002.

Pacific Board of Education. "Report to the First Presidency, 1 December 1961." Part II, p. 3. Copy in possession of the author.

Rudd, Glen L. "Memories of Matthew Cowley: Man of Faith, Apostle to the Pacific." In Underwood, *Pioneers in the Pacific*, 15–31.

Shumway, Eric B. *Tongan Saints: Legacy of Faith*. Laie, HI: Institute for Polynesian Studies, 1991.

Sorenson, John L., and Carl L. Johannessen. "Biological Evidence for Pre-Columbian Transoceanic Voyages." In *Contact and Exchange in the Ancient World*, ed. Victor H. Mair, 238–98. Honolulu: University of Hawai'i Press, 2006.

Taylor, Harvey L. "The Story of L.D.S. Schools." Bound typescript, 2:174, LDS Church Archives.

Underwood, Grant, ed. *Pioneers in the Pacific: Memory, History, and Cultural Identity among the Latter-day Saints*. Provo, UT: Religious Studies Center of Brigham Young University, 2005.

Underwood, Grant, ed. *Voyages of Faith: Explorations in Mormon Pacific History*. Provo, UT: Brigham Young University Press, 2000.

Van Tilberg, Jo Anne. *Easter Island: Archaeology, Ecology, and Culture*. Washington, DC: Smithsonian Institution Press, 1994.

Wallace III, William Kauaiwi'ulaokalani, and Richard K. Kamoa'elehua Walk. "Hawaiian Values and the Gospel." In Underwood, *Pioneers in the Pacific*, 92–95.

Wineera, Vernice. "Church and Cultural Foundations of the Polynesian Cultural Center." In Underwood, *Pioneers in the Pacific*, 109–19.

CHAPTER 35

....

MORMONS IN EUROPE

....

WILFRIED DECOO

1 MORMONISM BROUGHT TO EUROPE

....

1.1 Historical Survey

Mormon missionary work started in England in 1837. The emphasis on millennialism, continuing revelation, and "gathering out of Babylon," met the religious expectations of specific groups. By 1851, the United Kingdom counted 33,000 members, compared to the 12,000 in Utah. In the 1850s, more European countries followed. The response was mixed, with Protestant countries in the north yielding better results than the predominantly Catholic countries of the south. Converts were encouraged to gather to Zion: by 1900, some 91,000 members, mainly British and Scandinavian, had emigrated to the intermountain West.

By the end of the nineteenth century, immigration had slowed down. The church in Utah struggled during the stormy period over polygamy. In 1887, the Edmunds-Tucker Act dissolved the Perpetual Emigrating Fund Company, which had helped thousands of European immigrants. After 1890, a policy of accommodation with the United States government led the church to discourage converts to emigrate to Zion. However, missionary work in Europe continued. Countries with a Protestant background kept providing the best ground for conversions. But nearly everywhere the church had to face stiff opposition, fed by anti-Mormon publications. After the First World War, some countries, like Germany and Austria, witnessed noteworthy Mormon expansion. Others struggled. Emigration, in spite of church counsel, continued to drain the branches. At the outbreak of the Second World War, all European missions were closed and local congregations had to survive on their own.

The first decades after the Second World War proved fairly successful. Riding on a wave of pro-American sentiment and using insistent missionary techniques, the church was able to also expand in Catholic countries. However, superficial conversions by missionaries eager to obtain baptismal numbers also led to massive defections. Still, slow progress allowed for the organization of stakes and the building of temples as the crowning achievement. Since the 1990s, a major characteristic in western Europe has been the conversion of non-Europeans—refugees, temporary workers, and international students, in particular from Africa and Asia. In 2011, about two-thirds of new converts were not born in their country of baptism. It makes most local church units in western Europe multilingual and multicultural.

In the 1970s, the church took careful steps to establish a presence in countries behind the Iron Curtain—specifically Yugoslavia, Hungary, Poland, and East Germany, where a temple was built in 1985. The crumbling of communist regimes a few years later opened the gates for pioneering missionary work in other post-Soviet countries, with humanitarian and pedagogical projects as vanguards. But after the initial euphoria, the church, as a "foreign" entity, had to face the resurgence of nationalistic feelings and the power of reinstated national churches. Mormonism became viewed as part of a menacing invasion of alien cults. In the following years governments in nearly all of these countries enacted restrictive legislation to impede the spread of nonindigenous religions. Though the church, by carefully acting within the law, is able to function fairly normally in eastern European countries, the economic challenges encourage young members to emigrate to the United States.

In 2011, European membership stood at 486,000, of whom 186,000 (38 percent) reside in the United Kingdom. Sizeable numbers are found in Spain (47,000), Portugal (39,000), Germany (38,000), France (36,000), Italy (24,000), and Russia (21,000). Most other countries count less than 5,000 Mormons. These figures include all those who are on the rolls. The church does not disclose the number of people in attendance. The site www. Cumorah.com, which studies the data critically, reports an average activity rate in Europe of between 25 and 30 percent, meaning there would be about 130,000 active Mormons. It may be less, as the activity rate for the United Kingdom, which counts the largest number of Mormons, is reported at 18 percent. Some countries, like Portugal, are young and saw very rapid growth at first. In 1991, after sixteen years of missionary work, Portugal boasted 31,000 members. But many were "rushed converts" who did not stay. Today's activity rate is reported at only 12 percent. The situation is comparable in newly opened countries in eastern Europe: the original high activity rate, because it is first measured in small new units, shrinks over the years as the units grow but former converts disappear from activity. Overall for Europe, these data point at stagnation. The average of 9,900 European converts per year over the period 2001–11 barely succeeds in sustaining equilibrium.

1.2 Europe's Contribution to Mormonism

For obvious reasons the church is considered an American church, but it also has a significant European background that manifests itself in genes, in religious behavior, in culture, and in doctrine.

Genetically, the historic core membership can be traced to a European base. Not only were nearly all early American Mormons of English ancestry, but immigration brought tens of thousands of European converts to "Zion." In 1890, two-thirds of Utah's population consisted of immigrants and their children. New waves of European immigrants followed after each world war. Genetic studies illustrate the ancestry of Utah's white Mormon residents: 61 percent British, 31 percent Scandinavian, with Swiss and German for most of the remainder.

As to religious behavior, the church originated in an environment imbued with New England Puritan traditions. Though other major traits shaped Mormon identity and beliefs, the Puritan environment affected a significant part: simplicity in worship, the form of the sacrament, fasting and testimony giving, strict observance of Sunday rest, and the dynamics of church governance. These characteristics almost uniformly trace back to English Puritan origins, thus reflecting this local religious lifestyle in parts of England.

Culturally, in its broadest meaning, the "Mormon cultural region" in the American West was fashioned by numerous European immigrants, many of whom were experienced in architecture, engineering, manufacturing, education, or the arts. Most settled in urban areas in Utah where their impact was the most productive. Examples are numerous and well documented. Sometimes members were sent (back) to Europe to study certain disciplines, such as the 1890 "Paris Art Mission." Surprised visitors often recorded manifestations of an unexpectedly cultured environment to be found in the remote American West. Also, for decades after settling in, despite obvious Americanization, many European immigrants kept their national identities alive through clubs and societies, cultural events, small newspapers, ethnic restaurants, and specialty shops. Even today that heritage lingers on among descendants.

Doctrinally, the Book of Mormon asserts a perspective that intertwines America's destiny with divinely inspired input from Europe. Chapter 13 of 1 Nephi tells in prophetic mode how a man (Columbus), followed by Gentiles coming "out of captivity" (Europeans liberating themselves from oppression) arrive in the promised land (America). They bring the Bible to remnants of the House of Israel (Indians). This perspective is reinforced by the complex allegory of the olive tree, as described by Jacob, another Book of Mormon prophet: Gentiles, usually interpreted as coming from European nations, play a significant role in establishing the free nation where the gospel could be restored. It is also noteworthy that some of the most significant books on Mormonism, which structured and systematized Mormon theological thought in the early twentieth century, were written by three European immigrants, James E. Talmage, Brigham H. Roberts, and John A. Widtsoe.

2 PERCEPTIONS

The aspect of perceptions shows how various actors shape Mormon identities. Some of these perceptions are not unique to the European setting, but the examples are drawn from Europe.

2.1 Non-Mormon Europeans Perceiving Mormonism

2.1.1 *The Heritage of the First Century*

Since the 1830s, thousands of news reports, religious denunciations, and fiction have spread an overall negative image of Mormonism. News reports followed the trends of their American sources: mockery for the religious claims (which Europeans would see as examples of general American credulity), some sympathy for the plight of the persecuted Saints and their westward trek, and, finally, repugnance for the alleged despotism of church leaders and the "barbaric" practice of polygamy. Religious denunciation came from established churches fighting against Mormon missionary efforts. All this also fed into fiction. Dozens of novels, by popular authors such as Arthur Conan Doyle, Karl May, Balduin Möllhausen, and Emilio Salgari, mostly drew on the formula of the innocent heroine targeted for a polygamous marriage by one or more Mormon villains and the struggle of Christian heroes to free her. French authors, on the other hand, saw spicy gaiety in Mormon polygamy, as depicted by authors such as Jules Verne, Albert Robida, and Edouard Malortique. Mormon-themed popular trends continued into the twentieth century. British novelist Winifred Graham contributed to anti-Mormon persecution in the United Kingdom with her abduction stories of white female slaves. Her *The Love Story of a Mormon* was adapted to the screen as *Trapped by the Mormons*. Denmark capitalized on the theme with its own silent film, *A Victim of the Mormons*.

Another group of writings is academic, with France at the center. By the mid-nineteenth century, Auguste Comte's positivism had led to a renewed empirical study of human conduct, including religion. Though mostly agnostics, positivists were not against religion but were eager to prove its strictly human origins. Mormonism thus became a welcome study object as a potential new world religion based on "fraud." Scholars used as their main source the voluminous analysis of naturalist Jules Rémy (1860), who studied early Mormonism in Utah. In his *Histoire des origines du Christianisme*, Ernest Renan repeatedly refers to Mormon "analogue practices" nineteen centuries later. Eduard Meyer, German historian of early religions, drew the most explicit parallels with early Christianity and Islam in *Ursprung und Geschichte der Mormonen* (1912). The aim was to illustrate the natural genesis of all religions.

2.1.2 *Five Decades of Mainly Positive Perceptions*

From the 1930s up to the 1970s, the church in Europe enjoyed an encouraging period of outsiders' perceptions. Positive reports started to appear in the press, mainly thanks to the success of athletic and choral groups formed by missionaries. After the Second World War, missions reopened under the pro-American umbrella of liberation and the Marshall Plan. The church's welfare efforts to help ravaged Europe deserved public praise. The 1950s saw the construction of the first two European temples (in Switzerland and England) and an acclaimed tour of the Mormon Tabernacle Choir. In the 1960s, missions enhanced the Mormon image by missionary singing groups and teams playing baseball and basketball. American missionaries were deeply involved in leading the local units and became cherished friends of convert families. In the 1970s, the mammoth success of the Osmond brothers gave Mormonism a modern, upbeat aura. Still, emigration to the United States continued to appeal to converts. To a certain extent the church itself contributed to ending this era. Stricter mission rules, correlation, and managerial control reduced camaraderie, stifled creativity, and lessened local initiatives. The church in Europe became part of the retrenchment movement which Mauss identified.[1]

2.1.3 *Navigating the Anticult Movement*

Since the mid-1990s, the media have created a broad cult scare across most European countries. The tragedies at Jonestown and at Waco, and in the Solar Temple and Heaven's Gate groups had prepared this frenzy. The label of "destructive cult" became applied to many small and unfamiliar churches. Anticult associations began to thrive in this media wave. Established churches joined in. Targets became groups such as Jehovah's Witnesses, Scientology, and Mormons. Typically, critics confuse the institutional church with Mormon fundamentalists. Television documentaries on the church find marginal aspects more appealing than mainstream Mormon beliefs. Even for better-informed journalists, the image of the church as a powerful, corporate, conservative bulwark, with its bizarre founding, controversial history, and odd beliefs, is often too tempting not to deride it.

Governments of European countries, on the other hand, have been more tolerant toward the Mormon Church than toward Jehovah's Witnesses and Scientology. France, Belgium, and Germany conducted parliamentary investigations on cults, but Mormons were not retained as harmful. As to former communist countries, in the first phase of liberation from communist ideology, the call for democracy implied a genuine openness for pluralism. Next, however, a historically dominant church body, regaining its power, claimed its ancient role of unifying force. Overall, politicians are willing to cooperate with such an influential ally and advance ideological uniformity rather than an unruly diversity. The media found ample ammunition in the Western anticult movements to confirm the peril of foreign religions, which in turn influenced restrictive legislation toward minority churches. Overall, however, the Mormon Church, through its policies of entering a country legally and being upfront in its dealings with authorities, has had relatively few hurdles to overcome. In most European countries the church has therefore been able to obtain a form of legal recognition that is sufficient for its needs. Overall missionary work is freely allowed, with some exceptions, such as in Greece.

2.1.4 *Ignorance*

But perhaps the most dramatic finding about the perception of non-Mormon Europeans is ignorance. A 1993 church study, conducted by the Gallup agency, reveals that 95.8 percent of French people have no or almost no knowledge of Mormonism, in spite of seventy years of missionary work and a continuous Mormon presence in France. Only 5 percent have ever met a Mormon. When confronted with statements about Mormons, responses reveal overall misconceptions or ignorance.[2] There are no indications that things have changed significantly since then.

2.2 American Mormons Perceiving Mormonism in Europe

Because of their sheer number and impact, the perceptions of Americans are deeply ingrained in the collective consciousness, not only of American Mormons, but of European Mormons as well.

2.2.1 *Exceptionalist Perception: The Blood of Israel in Europe*

From the 1850s on, some church members disseminated a doctrine of ancient lineages, which was already familiar in Protestant circles. Populations around the world are privileged more or less thanks to their descent from biblical figures and tribes. Descendants of the tribe of Ephraim are said to be found among Anglo-Saxons ("British Israelism") and Scandinavians, a view that was later broadened to other parts of western Europe. This concept could easily permeate Mormon thought, reinforced as it is with the dispersion of Israel as depicted in the Book of Mormon. It also tied in with the assertion that "valiant" souls were to be born in choice times and places, where they would encounter the gospel. In the twentieth century, influential leaders taught this doctrine of literal blood lineage and exceptionalism. However, after the 1978 lifting of the ban forbidding the priesthood ordination of male members of African descent, and in view of the increasing internationalization of the church, official Mormon parlance broadened the concept to a universal relationship of all human beings with the House of Israel. But the perception of "the elect" and "divine destiny" of Europeans in their conversion to Mormonism is still alive as part of motivational discourse.

2.2.2 *Delightful Perception: Strong Members in an Idyllic Europe*

Mormon American sources provide a continual stream of positive information on the church in Europe (and in other parts of the world). Interviewed families tell how their church membership brings blessings and happiness. Leaders testify about success and growth. Historically this upbeat approach stems from a long tradition of self-defense against denigration from outsiders. Usually the publications also emphasize national or ethnic elements. European countries are depicted in the realm of tourist attractions of the old world. For American Mormons this portrayal ties in with the celebrated pioneer heritage of early Mormon converts. It is also a way to emphasize the international character of the church by highlighting cultural diversity. The church promotes this perception also through historical commemorations, where the youth is expected to "celebrate its country's heritage." But this kind of paternalistic approach often leads to folklorization and the creation of false authenticity. It is basically alienating, as people are confirmed in their alleged difference. This Mormon American input contributes to a Disneyesque perception of European countries where happy Mormon families also dwell.

2.2.3 *Dismal Perception: Materialistic and Immoral Europe*

The two preceding perceptions of Europe—exceptionalist and delightful—stand in stark contrast to the dismal perception that a number of American Mormons have of the old continent and the church's future in it. The reality is that the church is not grow-ing as expected and as promised. Comparisons with Mormon growth in Latin America since the 1950s and with Africa since the 1980s reveal that Europe is lagging far behind. Missionaries in Europe can hope to baptize, on average, one to two persons per year. Many of these converts are non-Europeans and most do not remain long in the church. So who is to blame? According to some American Mormons, the guilty party is Europe itself. They blame atheism, cynicism, materialism, nihilism, pornography, homosexual-ity, public nudity, and prostitution, as the main characteristics of Europe. All this, it is said, draws people's attention away from God and makes it impossible for Mormon mis-sionaries to have success. This dismal perception is fairly widespread among American Mormons, also judging from comments on Mormon blogs. Such negative evaluations are visibly tainted by the anti-Europeanism found among American conservatives, which also influences the views of American Mormons.

The three perceptions I identified stem from different traditions and concerns. American Mormons seem to wrestle with the place to be given to Europe in the world-wide expansion of Mormonism. Increase the efforts? Consolidate units to help them survive? Lower the number of missionaries in favor of more rewarding fields on other continents? Quietly leave the church in Europe in some kind of survival mode?

2.3 European Mormons: Identity and Self-Perception

2.3.1 The Diverse Profile of European Mormons

In 2011, the church claimed 486,000 members in Europe, a figure that includes all recorded baptisms. They form a widely divergent palette in terms of motivation, expe-rience, educational and cultural background, commitment, religious perception, and "standing" in the church. Also, mastery of English or not and access to Internet or not lead to vast differences in background knowledge about Mormonism. The high influx of non-European Mormon converts in western Europe is due to the fact that they are more easily reached. Uprooted, in search of a new community, open to a message of hope, and unafraid of missionaries, they more readily accept baptism. They also bring in oth-ers from their small social circle. Some become solid members, but many also fall away quickly. The influx of these converts creates peculiar challenges for the local units: tak-ing care of more people in need, facing issues with illegal immigrants, and providing constant translation. Immigrants integrate better if they stay long enough in the coun-try, learn the local language, and have abilities to serve in leadership positions.

2.3.2 A Minority Reaches the Family Ideal

Though family unity and happiness are focal points in Mormonism, only a minority of European Mormons seem to reach that ideal. Statistical data are not available, but expe-rience with any branch or ward will confirm that, on the whole, only about one-third to one-half of active members form fairly normal Mormon families. These figures translate into about 10 to 15 percent of the total membership. Family disruption can occur early in the conversion process if only one member or one part of the family decides to join the church. Converting to another church is, in most European countries, sensed as a major familial and sociocultural betrayal, in particular if the convert joins a so-called cult. The resulting drama is often severe. The ideal that a whole family joins, parents and children, sharing equal conviction, and remaining equally committed over their lifetimes, is a rare occurrence. It still leaves conflicts with grandparents and extended family. Next, in a Mormon family tensions arise when one partner lapses from activity—which is far from uncommon. Another hurdle is divorce, with the conflict over church membership as a factor. It leaves the divorced partner who remains active in the church in an often awkward position. Finally, many older teens or young adults turn away from activity. In Europe, the chances of such an outcome are high because children grow up in a non-Mormon environment, may have very few peers in the church, find partners outside the church, or may simply not want to devote their life to church service as they have seen their parents do. The pictures of large, multigenerational families and of temple weddings that adorn the walls and fireplace mantels in the homes of Utah (great-) grandparents are very rare in European homes.

2.3.3 *The Majority: 350,000 Mormons in the Margin*

"Inactive" members constitute the majority of Mormons in Europe—an estimated 70 to 80 percent of the total membership, which accounts for approximately 350,000 members. That ratio is comparable in other parts of the world outside the United States and Canada, where activity is slightly higher. The church counts these inactives as members and cares for them: retention and reactivation are core terms in church programs.

"Inactive" is a judgmental term. Dedicated Catholics can be called *pious* or *devout*, but others, even if only attending mass for a marriage or a funeral, are not labeled "inactive." Mormonism, on the other hand, requires a high level of involvement for members "in good standing": regular attendance, a calling in the organization, and holding a temple recommend, which also checks adherence to the Word of Wisdom and the payment of tithing. The church itself thus draws a line of demarcation which makes inactive members perceived as deficient. In the Mormon intermountain West, the "jack Mormon," often stemming from pioneer stock, often remains included in the Mormon-ethnic community and may still attend church for a family event. In other parts of the world, the "inactive" member is usually "out."

For France, Euvrard calculated that roughly 50 percent of new converts lapse from activity within two and a half years of membership.[3] For many, disengagement occurs after only after a few months or even weeks. These fleeting converts come typically from "quick baptisms" missionaries perform—often singles, expatriates, loners, including needy or unstable persons, who embrace the attention the missionaries give them. But many of these converts are easily disillusioned as self-centered expectations are not fulfilled. The dimension of required changes in life usually becomes clear only after baptism. Even if the conversion is genuine, the step from the religious discovery, with its spiritual excitement brought by missionaries into their own home, to attending the Mormon ward miles away, with often dreary talks and lessons, inadequately translated if the language is also a challenge, can be disappointing. For many converts there is also the gap to bridge between two totally different concepts of religion: from experiencing a rather mystical ritual as a bystander during a relatively short liturgical service, as practiced in traditional churches, to the long meetings and extended social interaction in Mormonism. The few Mormon ordinances are sober and restrained. Members have to create their own spirituality instead of receiving it as an exterior impulse, and some simply lack the gift for it. Add to these adjustments the pressure from non-Mormon family and friends or the longing for the convert's formal social life. Although the system requires the involvement of local members to ensure the integration of the new convert, often locals are already overburdened with tasks and the sheer number of problematic converts may prove unfeasible to handle with equal attention.

Another large group of inactives is mature members who become disengaged after years. For the Netherlands, van Beek counts about 40 percent of the inactives in that group.[4] There are those whose life events lead them away, such as divorce, (re)marriage, or acceptance of their homosexuality, and those who become disenchanted for a variety of reasons. Others fall prey to burnout after years of unselfish service. Though the *Church Handbook of Instructions* states that "members should not be asked to make excessive family sacrifices to serve or to support programs or activities," the needs of struggling units with many inactives often overrule that counsel. Problems with church history or doctrine can also cause defection. As disturbing information from anti-Mormon sources becomes more available, its effect increases. Problems with commandments, such as chastity, Word of Wisdom observance, or the payment of tithing play a role in certain cases, but they are seldom the sole cause of inactivity.

2.3.4 *The Relation with "America": How American Is the Church?*

In their efforts at internationalization, church leaders stress that the church is "not an American church," but a universal one. The correlation movement since the 1960s has tried to make the church "less American" by removing from church publications typical American items (for example, political references, affluent living style, US sports, food, activities, and the like) and by stressing the core message of the gospel. However, the church keeps strong American components—historical-geographical, ideological, and behavioral.

The historical-geographical component refers to the impact of Mormon history and location. Mormon converts everywhere in the world step into that history. Locations like Palmyra, the Sacred Grove, Cumorah, Kirtland, Jackson County, Haun's Mill, Nauvoo, Carthage, Winter Quarters, Martin's Cove, and This Is the Place, become part of their spatial religious consciousness. Even the physical experience of that history in the form of "Mormon historical tours" is offered to members abroad. Mormon tourism in America, with a sense of pilgrimage, is expanding. By restoring historic places as tributes to its past, the church itself is encouraging this tendency. Even as the church is internationalizing with the concept of multiple Zions in foreign countries, a fundamental America-oriented awareness remains part of the faith. In the context of their original culture, members take the countercultural step of converting to a unique "home-grown American religion."

However, the equation of "America" with "the United States" is not evident in this context. For converts abroad, the perception of Mormonism is obviously more at ease with the nineteenth-century tension between the church and the United States, rather than with present-day American patriotism and right-wing allegiance among Mormon US citizens.

Second is the ideological realm—that is, the relation between Mormonism and the "American way of life," understood here as the opportunities given to each individual for personal development and the pursuit of happiness. It is perceived as part of the American Dream, to which church authorities have proudly referred, especially in the 1960s and '70s, but also up to the '90s The rhetoric spills over into a sense of superiority and election, against the backdrop of America's messianic role in the world. It is interwoven with an abhorrence of socialism and communism. This belief in the power of individual talent and hard work to attain prosperity permeates the Mormon message. Most general authorities embody, from their former professions and their personalities, that very message. Members in the international church who are called to leadership positions tend to naturally adopt the same view and rhetoric. But in many countries, this highlighting of personal success runs counter to religious ideologies that revere abnegation and submissiveness. For converts from such realms, the adoption of Mormonism will thus require, at least mentally, a realignment to notions of self-actualization of the individual.

The third area pertains to elements in the behavioral realm. Wherever in the world the church has been established, white middle-class Americans were (and often still are) the organizers and first leaders of church units. Historically, this banner was borne primarily through thousands of missionaries, mainly from America's West. Next, Mormon American families living abroad, as well as scores of older missionary couples, also infuse local units with their behavioral patterns. Present-day missionaries, called from foreign lands, are immersed in a mission organization in which the interactions are shaped by Americans. Mission presidents, most still from the United States or Americanized, and visiting authorities, American or Americanized, disseminate through their function as role models particular behavioral patterns. Church-produced media contribute to the same dynamic. Typical behaviors include such things as the informality of social contact between genders and between ages; easiness in approaching strangers; the facial demonstration of assertiveness and commitment; the firm and somewhat longer handshake, accompanied by a smile and a direct gaze in the other's eyes; the "right" way to hug; making eye contact during interviews and meetings; a certain jovial looseness in conducting meetings; the presence and conduct of children during meetings; the advice on how to date at what age; the use of superlatives, extolling others as "wonderful" and "great," praising each child or youngster as "special"; and the homogenizing effect of dress and grooming standards on behavior. General Relief Society President Julie B. Beck (in the October 2007 Conference) praised Mormon mothers who "bring daughters in clean and ironed dresses with hair brushed to perfection; their sons wear white shirts and ties and have missionary haircuts." A final element is the corporate, managerial style of doing things. The tendency to call as ward, stake, and regional leaders, and hire as church employees, members who seem most fit, by personality, profession, and dress, to blend in the corporate, managerial style, reinforces such leaders to other members as role models.

Considering the three areas touched upon—historical-geographical, ideological, and behavioral—the church remains "American." Mormonism, in its expansion to other parts of the world, can thus aptly be called "an American world religion."[5]

2.3.5 *The Relation with the Home Culture*

2.3.5.1 *Estrangement from the Home Culture*

Mormons in a European country, like members throughout the world, live in a "home culture," with its distinctive manners and traditions. Though the church encourages involvement with society, the few surveys available for European members contradict this encouragement. According to Euvrard, 80.4 percent of French Mormons say that they are not engaged politically, and only 3 percent are members of a party.[6] It confirms my own survey among Belgian members.[7] Many converts disengage from social and political involvement. Some feel their unique religion supplants worldly organizations. Often church participation leaves them no time for other engagements. Indeed, in regions where the church is thinly spread, such as in Europe, travel distances are costly in time to attend meetings and activities, to visit members' homes, and to travel to a temple. With the addition of family home evening, scripture study, preparation of talks and lessons, and genealogical research, Mormonism shapes a way of life that easily fills the week outside school and work.

Church leaders are concerned about this tension between the exigencies of Mormon life and its feasibility in non-Mormon cultures. In 1980, the church instituted the three-hour Sunday block meeting schedule to reduce travel time and expense, and allow church members more time for home-centered Sabbath activities. The reality is, however, that supplemental meetings, plus one to two hours for travel, do not leave much of the Sabbath. In Europe, Sunday is a traditional day for visits with extended family, for recreation, and for all kinds of public activities and events. Dedicated Mormons have to reduce those familial visits, forfeit rest and leisure, and abandon most public activities and events, all of which tends to widen the gap with non-Mormon family and the rest of society.

Church leaders have often tackled the critical question of achieving balance between Mormon culture and home culture. Answers vary according to focus, compounded by the difficulty of defining "culture." If the focus is positive and optimistic, the tendency is to include everything about the home culture that is seen as appropriate and good. This inclusive approach stands in contrast with the antagonistic approach of the "culture of the world" as evil. That dichotomy of "us" versus "them" often prevails in the retrenchment rhetoric of talks and lessons. Van Beek concludes that by such an approach the church defines itself as a "counter-church," which leads to the construction of a polarized identity for the individual member.[8]

2.3.5.2 *What of the Home Culture Can Be Included in Mormon Life?*

I pointed earlier to the American penchant for identifying foreign countries through their exterior distinctiveness in folklore. There is a risk that permissible "cultural traditions" may be seen only in that realm. But many of these features incorporate a potentially gray zone. Can Mormon children in Finland, costumed as witches and wizards, participate in the beloved yearly trek through their neighborhood (at least as momentous as Halloween to American children), passing out willow twigs in exchange for candy or a few coins? But this activity always happens on a Sunday, thereby raising the issue of Sabbath observance. Can Sinterklaas, a figure dressed as a Catholic bishop, enter a Belgian or Dutch Mormon chapel to distribute the traditional goodies to the children in early December? Or the similar Mikulás in some eastern European countries? Can Mormons on Sunday, inasmuch as time after church permits, attend public activities such as family-oriented festivals and concerts? More delicate is the use of some religious traditions. Can former Anglican, Catholic, or Orthodox believers, who long for the cherished rites of Christmas Eve, organize a Mormon variant in the chapel (and use it for missionary purposes)? Can primary children enter the chapel on Palm Sunday carrying palm branches and singing an appropriate hymn, as is done in many Christian churches? The tendency is to refuse such incursions into Mormon territory, because they do not match predetermined standards of acceptability.

But there may be reasons to be more lenient and to establish helping criteria. For the individual and the family, a number of traditions, in particular for the Christmas and Easter periods, belong to a religious heritage that shapes their fundamental identity within the local community. Proscribing them creates voids that the church does not fill at present. Having church members participate in local traditions can signal an important message to the host society and its leaders. In some European countries the government looks at "foreign" religions with suspicion when they disengage from the surrounding culture by refusing to celebrate traditional feasts. Taking into account the range of cultural diversity often typical of a Mormon branch or ward in Europe with its immigrant converts from various foreign cultures, introducing these people to major traditions of the host society can help them better integrate. Integration of immigrants is high on the agenda of governments. A last argument—in some cases the most important—concerns non-Mormon family members. The conversion of a family member to this "American cult" is, in many countries, sensed by the rest of the family as a betrayal of the deepest cultural heritage. In cult investigations one of the key criteria for classification is the severance with family and society traditions. So there may be value in keeping certain local traditions alive in Mormon units, where non Mormon family members can feel at ease when invited.

2.3.5.3 *From Minimal Mormonism to Culture-Tailored Mormon Churches?*

A more sweeping approach that some Americans propose is to discard all Americanisms, define only the essence of Mormonism, and let each culture build around it according to their traditions.[9] The perspective of these American authors is well meant, but problematic for various reasons. What is Mormonism's most basic expression? What is the American cultural baggage that should be discarded? The church, as mentioned earlier, also contains undeniable American components. Perhaps we underestimate the value of the connections many members feel with (a portion of) Mormon American ethos. Perhaps we underestimate the sense of worldwide unity that comes from the style of "American" Mormon chapels and temples, where any Mormon can feel "at home" in whatever country. The cultural customization of Mormonism around a "core" in order to develop an idiosyncratic Mormon Church on a national or regional level is easier said than done. When we think that, for example, a Pacific, a Brazilian, or a Dutch Mormonism could emerge, we are probably identifying stereotypical features of those cultures, thus overlooking a myriad of local, social, and individual variations. Moreover, through conversions among immigrants, the church in many countries is already a cultural melting-pot.

However, some local customization within a rigid denominational church is not impossible. Since the 1960s, the Catholic Church has permitted such moderate developments, giving the national or regional leadership more latitude for initiatives and cultural adaptations and allowing local parishes a measure of leeway. Such creativity often injects renewed vitality into the local church. For the Mormon Church, the question of moderate and temporary inclusions of local cultural elements, within clear boundaries, remains a valid topic for exploration and experimentation.

3 THE FUTURE OF MORMONISM IN EUROPE

Despite challenges, Mormonism is implanted in Europe—in some countries with a presence uninterrupted since the 1840s and 1850s. The approximately 200 stakes and districts, some 1,300 meeting places, and a dozen temples, attest to that stable presence, even if the church remains a tiny minority. But how much growth can be realistically expected? Out of 800 million people in Europe, at least several million could be viewed as potential converts. The main problem is that the present missionary system reaches only an infinitesimal fraction of such a demographic and then only coincidentally. To alter this ratio, massive information campaigns and the teaching of large groups at once would be necessary.

If present variables remain the same, there is no reason to believe that the church in Europe will progress any differently than the past few decades. So any discussion about possible progress must propose changes within the church, weighing factors of attractiveness and repulsiveness to suggest different balancings in the realm of economics of religion. Though purely speculative, such analyses have value in their ability to generate discussion in a constant search for improvement. In the 1960s, the prospects of a fast-growing international church prompted the rise of the correlation movement, producing not only a coordinated curriculum that focused on general, noncontroversial doctrines, but also institutional streamlining and stronger management. However, both tendencies—doctrinal softening and institutional strengthening—might be partial causes of low interest in the church and of low retention. Would a reverse movement—doctrinal strengthening and institutional softening—yield better results? In other words, could Mormonism with a stronger and better-argued affirmation of its distinctive doctrines be more attractive for Europeans? Could it also be more viable if the institution lessened some of its demands?

4 CONCLUSION

A population pyramid of European Mormons shows a wide base with various layers of inactive members of different profiles, accounting for two-thirds to three-quarters of the total. Above them is a thinner layer of active members, some struggling, but all of them an engaged part of the community. Many of them are never married, divorced, or in part-member families. Over time, a number of them shift down to the lower layer. Meanwhile new converts, mostly non-European, trickle in. The tiny top of the pyramid is formed by the highly committed leaders of stakes and wards, always chosen from within strong Mormon families. They mostly set a tone of retrenchment. They do not always understand the challenges of members in the lower layers and seem to be unlikely voices for lenience in their interactions with general authorities. Within this small group at the top, dynasties of "birthright members" slowly emerge—who represent second-, third-, and even fourth-generation church members and who, through intermarriages, replicate the social pattern of similar families in Utah. We can expect that eastern European countries, where the process started more recently, will follow a similar trajectory in the coming decades.

Is there a European Mormon identity that parallels the fairly well-defined Utah Mormon identity? Yes, to the extent that active members are molded into a pattern of full commitment. Yes, to the extent that being a member gives one an ascribed status of "Mormon" in the non-Mormon society, with the sometimes problematic implications of that perception. Yes, to the extent that uniformity is a trademark of the church, meaning that everywhere in the world, Mormons hold church meetings in the same manner, according to a fixed schedule, sing from the same hymnbook, and attend lessons with the same manuals. The *Church Handbook of Instructions* details everything for worldwide application. The top-down structure with training sessions on each level guarantees this application. But, as van Beek points out, most European Mormons are also, or rather, Mormon Europeans, reflecting the wide array of their own social and cultural backgrounds.[10] It means that many active members develop plural identities to successfully navigate in three spheres: the official church realm, a self-defined Mormon sphere, and the surrounding society. At the same time, the church in Europe is fragmented because of the top-down structure and the language barriers. Unlike in the United States, mobility is almost inexistent.

The present set-up allows for survival of the church in Europe thanks to a kernel of dedicated members, the continuation of missionary work, and the rare addition of a temple, but it does not give any indication for substantial growth. Some fairly radical changes could improve the prospects, such as the suggested doctrinal strengthening and institutional softening, but without guarantees and perhaps with some backlashes. However, such changes are unlikely to even be considered, taking into account the conservative and cautionary approach on higher levels.

The critical remarks in this chapter should never overshadow appreciation for the sublime labors of thousands of European Latter-days Saints who, in spite of many challenges, remain faithful and, often for decades, render unending service in many capacities and circumstances. Their service is all the more noteworthy because, compared to well-established wards in the intermountain West, the demands of units with a relatively high proportion of people in financial, social, or psychological need are often staggering. They are complicated by a dearth of experienced leaders and the absence of professional Mormon services. Nevertheless, these dedicated members continue to serve, deserving their name of *Latter-day Saints*.

NOTES

1. Mauss, *Angel and the Beehive.*
2. Euvrard, "Socio-Histoire du Mormonisme en France," 472–76.
3. Ibid., 516.
4. Van Beek, "Mormonism, a Global Counter-Church?"
5. Eliason, *Mormons and Mormonism.*
6. Euvrard, "Socio-Histoire du Mormonisme en France," 459.
7. Decoo, "Mormonism in a European Catholic Country."
8. Van Beek, "Mormonism, a Global Counter-Church?"
9. For example, Sorenson, "Mormon World View and American Culture"; Mauss, "Can There Be a 'Second Harvest'?"
10. Van Beek, "Mormon Europeans Europeans or European Mormons?"

BIBLIOGRAPHY

Decoo, Wilfried. "Mormonism in a European Catholic Country: Contribution to the Social Psychology of LDS Converts." *BYU Studies* 24, no. 1 (1984): 61–77.

Eliason, Eric A., ed. *Mormons and Mormonism: An Introduction to an American World Religion.* Urbana: University of Illinois Press, 2001.

Euvrard, Christian. "Socio-Histoire du Mormonisme en France." PhD diss., École Pratique des Hautes Etudes, Paris, 2008.

Mauss, Armand L. "Can There Be a 'Second Harvest'?: Controlling the Costs of Latter-day Saint Membership in Europe." *International Journal of Mormon Studies* 1 (Spring 2008): 1–59.

Mauss, Armand L. *The Angel and the Beehive: The Mormon Struggle with Assimilation.* Urbana: University of Illinois Press, 1994.

Sorenson, John L. "Mormon World View and American Culture." *Dialogue: A Journal of Mormon Thought* 8, no. 2 (Summer 1973): 17–29.

Van Beek, Walter E. A. "Mormon Europeans or European Mormons? An 'Afro-European' View on Religious Colonization." *Dialogue: A Journal of Mormon Thought* 38, no. 4 (Winter 2005): 3–36.

Van Beek, Walter E. A. "Mormonism, a Global Counter-Church? (Part 2 and 3)." *By Common Consent.* June 19–20, 2009. http://bycommonconsent.com/2009/06/19/part-ii/.

CHAPTER 36

....

MORMONS IN ASIA

....

VAN C. GESSEL

FITS and starts characterize efforts by missionaries of the Church of Jesus Christ of Latter-day Saints to take their message of the restored gospel to the nations of Asia. As much as in any other region of the world—and more so than in many areas—rapid and often extreme changes in political climate, attitudes toward Western nations, and cultural clashes have scuttled initial attempts to send missionaries into various parts of Asia and led to an almost revolving-door approach to opening and closing nations to proselytizing work.

LDS Church headquarters in Salt Lake City made initial attempts to communicate their message to Asian peoples as early as the 1850s, scarcely twenty years after the establishment of the church in upstate New York, but none of those ventures was long-lived or met with anything that could be called sustainable success. The small cadres of missionaries sent to India, Siam, and Hong Kong in 1852 were withdrawn in 1856 with fewer than seventy converts to show for their labors. Two male missionaries arrived in China in April of 1853 and had fled by June, blaming their lack of success on internal strife and linguistic barriers, and it would be another ninety years before the church made a second attempt on the Chinese mainland. Apostle Heber J. Grant led the first contingent of elders to Japan in 1901, but for various reasons the mission was closed in 1924, able to boast only 137 individuals baptized.

Political upheavals throughout Asia, often tinged with at least a coloration of anti-Westernism, jeopardized all Christian missionary efforts at various times. Likely the most extreme response to the incursion of Western cultural influence (both spiritual and material) was the decision made in Japan in 1614 to expel all Western nationals—except Dutch traders who, more anti-Catholic than pro-Protestant, were interested in financial rather than heavenly rewards—and to obliterate all traces of Christian influence through brutal persecution and slaughter. One of the likely motivations behind the shogun's decision to expel the "barbarians" was the fear, fanned by the Dutch merchants, that the arrival of Catholic padres was merely the vanguard preceding a military invasion. That was not a totally unfounded fear, given what had been happening in other parts of Asia.

Yet, in one of those ironic reversals in the history of nations, it was, in fact, Western military action in Asia in the mid-1940s that prepared the way for the return of Latter-day Saint missionaries to Asian lands, including defeated Japan, war-torn Korea, and divided China. LDS servicemen who were part of the occupying armies in Japan or fighting forces in South Korea during and after the Korean War performed some of the earliest convert baptisms in those lands. The various attempts to create missionary inroads during the nineteenth century having ultimately failed, it was this "second coming" of LDS members—soldiers first, then missionaries—that led to the establishment of the church in Asian lands.

Still, Asia has been described by one historian as "the least fertile (with the exception of the Muslim areas) of all the major Christian missionary fields of the world,"[1] while another analyst has hypothesized an "invisible ceiling" that keeps conversion numbers for all Christian denominations frustratingly low in countries such as Japan.[2] The raw numbers certainly bear witness to these observations. Of the roughly three billion inhabitants of Asia in the early twenty-first century, somewhat fewer than one million are registered on the membership rolls of the LDS Church, and the Philippines is the only Asian country where a majority of the population professes one sect or another of Christianity. In addition to the significant political, historical, and economic challenges, religious and cultural beliefs, traditions, and practices that developed in Asia beginning many centuries before the time of Christ have created formidable barriers to the spread of His gospel there.

1 HISTORICAL BACKDROP

While the experiences of LDS missionaries in a number of Asian countries are remarkably similar, the situations in Japan, China, and Korea stand out as typical of the kinds of challenges and successes faced by those who brought to Asia the message of the gospel as restored through Joseph Smith. The case of Japan, in particular, merits close examination because of the multitude of difficulties that arose in the twentieth century.

1.1 The Late Arrival of the Latter-day Saints in Japan

Saint Francis Xavier of the Society of Jesus arrived on the shores of Kyushu Island in 1549. Catholic labors over the next sixty years or so, primarily among the military warlords and their vassals, produced as many as 300,000 converts to Catholicism (some sources claim more than half a million)—a larger percentage of the overall Japanese population than adheres to any sect of Christianity today. But eventually political distrust, questions of loyalties divided between feudal and heavenly masters, and other concerns led Japanese rulers to order the expulsion of all foreign missionaries and the torture and execution of any Japanese native who claimed allegiance to the outlawed religion. The blood of martyrdom and the humiliation of forced apostasy stained the lands of western Japan through the subsequent two and a half centuries of Japanese isolationism.

After Commodore Matthew Perry pried open the doors of the nation in the mid-nineteenth century, Catholic and Protestant missionaries returned to Japan and began preaching to the Japanese in 1873. This second honeymoon period was, however, short-lived, since burgeoning Japanese nationalism butted heads with growing Western racism in the mid-1920s. With the outbreak of the Pacific War, Christian missionaries who had not fled Japan were interned, and any churches that remained were closely scrutinized by the military police. Late in 1945, MacArthur's GHQ once again lifted the restraints on Christian missionary work, just as they had been rescinded seventy-two years earlier.

It was not until 1901 that the presiding authorities of the LDS Church decided to send its first missionaries to Japan. Apostle Heber J. Grant, accompanied by three missionary companions, reached Yokohama in August of 1901. But some Protestant missionaries, not at all eager to have Mormon rivals in the work, sparked an aggressively negative publicity campaign in the major Japanese newspapers long before Grant's arrival; meanwhile, Japanese leaders of a nascent women's rights movement were alarmed that if the practice of Mormon polygamy came to their country, it might scuttle their efforts to eradicate the widespread native practices of concubinage and prostitution. As early as 1890, a leading Japanese Christian periodical that focused on women's rights, *Jogaku Zasshi*, described Joseph Smith as a "slave to carnal passion" and labeled the practice of polygamy a "travesty of pure love and human feeling."[3] Even though the missionaries who arrived in 1901 countered that the LDS Church had officially abandoned polygamy in 1890, Grant's admission to a Japanese reporter that he himself had plural wives did nothing to quell the rumors that these newcomers intended to introduce the custom in Japan as part of their religious teachings.

The differences in religious heritage and culture—discussed in greater detail below—were a formidable obstacle to successful missionary labors, and when the mission was closed in 1924 with only 137 converts to show for its efforts, the mission president wrote to the church leadership that, "we haven't over five or six real Saints in the mission who are willing and ready to help carry on the work."[4] More than just the gulf separating LDS beliefs and practices from those of the Japanese, however, it was the rapidly deteriorating relationship between the United States and Japan that created an atmosphere hostile to the efforts of these missionaries from America. Japan had been riding the crest of a wave of nationalistic pride since the 1890s, and anti-American sentiment reached a fever pitch in 1924 when the United States Congress, in an outpouring of racial bigotry, passed the Asian Exclusion Act—clearly targeting the Japanese, who, thanks to earlier legislation, were ineligible for naturalization in the United States. The decision to close the LDS mission soon thereafter was motivated at least as much by the souring of national relations as by the lack of fruits from the missionaries' proselytizing labors.

Between 1924 and the end of the Second World War, the locus of missionary work shifted, with some modest success, to those of Japanese heritage living in Hawaii. The

first baptisms to occur in Japan after the 1945 surrender were performed by LDS servicemen, and the mission was reopened in the winter of 1948. After the return of missionaries to Japan, numbers of convert baptisms fluctuated dramatically, with increases
attributable primarily to infusions of greater numbers of missionaries and the opening
of new cities for their labors. One of the largest spikes in growth occurred between 1978
and 1982, in the wake of successful church sponsorship of a pavilion at Expo '70 in Osaka
and the dedication of the Tokyo Temple in 1980. The number of LDS members of record
in Japan at the beginning of 2010 was 124,041.

1.2 The Church in China

After the missionary trio who arrived in Hong Kong in the spring of 1853 reported a
disheartening lack of success, it was not until 1910 that Japan mission president Alma
O. Taylor was asked to visit China and report on the possibility of resuming the work.
But Taylor recommended against dispatching missionaries amidst the ongoing political upheaval. The next Chinese overture was made in 1921, when David O. McKay of
the church's presiding body, the First Presidency, visited as a part of a world tour to
assess church growth. President McKay dedicated China for the preaching of the gospel, described as follows: "They walked through shrines, pagodas, and temples fast fall-
ing into decay. Finally they came to a grove of cypress trees. A reverential feeling came
and a presence seemed to be upon them. They were sure that unseen holy beings were
directing their footsteps. There at Peking, in the heart of the most populous nation in
the world, undisturbed by the multitudes, they offered the dedicatory prayer, President
McKay being mouth."[5] His prayer included a petition that the bands of superstition con-
fining the Chinese people would be broken.[6]

A mission headquartered in Hong Kong was finally established in 1949, but eighteen
months later the outbreak of the Korean War forced its closure. A small company of missionaries returned to Hong Kong in 1955, where ongoing labors produced 24,114 convert baptisms by early 2010. In 1956, the first small company of missionaries was sent
to Taiwan, but it was not until 1965 that they had a Chinese translation of the Book of
Mormon available to teach prospective converts. An independent mission was established in 1971, and ongoing efforts produced over 50,000 members there by 2010. A temple of the church was dedicated in Taipei in 1984.

Spencer W. Kimball, who served as president of the LDS Church between 1973 and
1985, emphasized the need for the LDS people as a whole to prepare for a day sometime in the future when China might be opened to missionary work. In 1978, he stated,
"Nearly one billion of our Father's children live in China. . . . Six hundred and sixty million of them speak Mandarin Chinese. How many of us speak Mandarin Chinese?" The
following year, he told a group of church leaders: "We asked last conference for all members to pray with increased sincerity for peace in all nations and especially China, and
that we might make entry with our missionaries. Since then many people have been to
China and much interest has been shown. Let us ask our Heavenly Father to grant our

petition and permit this great neighbor, China, to join the great family of nations now bowing to the Lord Jesus Christ."[7]

As of this writing, activities of the church on the Chinese mainland under the communist regime have largely been limited to cultural and educational exchanges, many conducted by student performing groups and educators from church-sponsored Brigham Young University in Provo, Utah. As the People's Republic of China (PRC) began opening its doors to foreign residents, a number of LDS businessmen and government workers established residence in Beijing, Nanjing, and Shanghai, and the Chinese officials allowed worship services to be held for those with foreign passports. In 2010, talks between church leaders and Chinese officials led to what the church styled a "regularization" of its operations on the mainland, including permission for Chinese nationals who converted to the faith overseas and then returned to China to hold separate worship services, but not involving the possibility of sending missionaries to teach the gospel. The church remains highly hopeful that a day will come when they can preach their message "to every nation, kindred, tongue and people," but they are proceeding in their relationship with China with great caution and openness, respecting the wishes and sensitivities of the Chinese government.

1.3 Knocking on Korea's Doors

In many ways, the growth of the LDS Church in South Korea has followed a trajectory quite dissimilar to the pattern that has been common in other East Asian lands. Unlike China or Japan, where centuries of warfare and political interdiction have greatly restricted the importation of Christianity, Korea has had Catholic missionaries laboring with comparative freedom for nearly four centuries, with Protestant messengers following them in the mid-1800s. Nearly a third of the population of South Korea claims membership in one Christian denomination or another. In addition, the work of Christian missionaries in Korea has not been tainted by charges of imperialist intentions; in fact, the foreign missionaries were considered allies of the nationalist movement during the years of Japanese occupation of the peninsula.

Even with this fertile cultivation of the spiritual soil of Korea, LDS missionaries did not begin working there until 1956, first because of the Japanese appropriation of the land and then due to the outbreak of the Korean War. As with Japan, however, LDS servicemen were the first to teach their beliefs to the Koreans they interacted with. A separate Korean mission was established in 1962, and five years later the Book of Mormon was available in Korean.

1.4 Mongolia

The unusually rapid growth of the LDS Church in Mongolia makes the country an anomaly. Though geographically a part of Asia, lying closer to Beijing than to Novosibirsk,

Mongolia's sixty-seven-year status as a satellite of the Soviet empire provides at least the beginnings of an explanation of why the increase in convert baptisms in the country more closely resembles church progression in the Caribbean than it does the slower growth in other Asian lands. Nearly 3 percent of the 2.7 million people in Mongolia have become members of the LDS Church since missionary work began there in 1992, comparing favorably with an overall national number of 4 percent who belong to any Christian sect.[8] The comparative youthfulness of the population (nearly two-thirds are under the age of thirty), an adult literacy rate of 98 percent, and the fact that almost half of the population lives in urban areas, particularly the capital city of Ulaanbaatar, may also help account for the significant increases in convert numbers.

The first six retired couples called to serve as LDS missionaries in Mongolia were sent in 1992 to assist in policy planning for the country's university system, which had only recently been liberated from Soviet control. Although their assignment focused on educational and humanitarian assistance, they were also given permission to teach about their faith and to conduct congregational meetings. Following the baptism of two of the couples' students in 1993, a small group of young missionaries was sent later that year. The country was dedicated for the preaching of the gospel in 1993 by Elder Neal A. Maxwell, one of the church's twelve apostles, and became its own mission area in 1995. Within six years the Book of Mormon was available in Mongolian.

Humanitarian aid from the church continued to be administered to help relieve problems caused by subzero temperatures, droughts, and grass fires. In 2009, the first stake of the church was organized in Ulaanbaatar, and membership reached 9,239 at the beginning of 2010. Although the percentage of growth in membership has declined somewhat from a high of over 20 percent annually in 2003, it would appear that a spirit of political and spiritual liberation still fresh in the minds of the people, ongoing positive interactions between church leaders and Mongolian government officials, and what may perhaps be a more fertile religious heritage of Tibetan-style Buddhist Lamaism (rather than the Mahayana Buddhism that has permeated the rest of East Asia) have all contributed to the growth of the church in this particular Asian land.

1.5 South and Southeast Asia

With the conspicuous exception of the Philippines, the growth of the church in South and Southeast Asia is primarily traceable back only to the late 1960s or early seventies. Once again, much of the initial spadework was done by LDS servicemen stationed in various nations during the Korean and Vietnam wars. Thailand, with just over 16,000 LDS members in 2010, is the only Southeast Asian nation to claim membership in the five-digit range. Neighboring countries where missionaries are allowed to proselytize generally report numbers between 6,000 and 9,000 each.

The Philippines is unique, first because the population is approximately 80 percent Catholic, and therefore needs no introduction to the name or teachings of Jesus Christ. The ongoing presence of US military forces has facilitated the creation of servicemen's units of the church, and young missionaries have been laboring there in increasing numbers since 1961. With a member population of over 630,000, the Philippines stands out as a clear example of the comparative ease of teaching the LDS gospel in Asia to those who already have a belief in Christ.

2 CULTURAL AND SPIRITUAL CHALLENGES TO THE LATTER-DAY WORK

For centuries, Asian peoples have obtained spiritual guidance from the precepts of Hinduism, Buddhism, Confucianism, and a variety of folk religions. Consequently, beliefs about the purpose of mortal life, the idea of an afterlife, issues of individual agency and the individual's role in the social structure differ greatly from those in the Christian tradition.

2.1 Language

The comparative difficulties that most native English speakers have in attaining essential fluency in many of the Asian languages cannot be overemphasized. The three dominant languages of East Asia—Chinese, Japanese, and Korean—are classified by the Defense Language Institute of the US government as "Category IV" languages, meaning that they are the most difficult languages for native English speakers to learn, requiring as much as four times the amount of study hours to master as the Romance languages. LDS missionaries, their service limited to between eighteen and twenty-four months, face the stark reality that they seldom attain true functional proficiency in the language until a few months before they return to their homes.

An even more challenging communication issue is the absence of Christian vocabulary in the languages of Asia. Translators since the earliest period of interaction have been attempting to navigate a linguistic Scylla and Charybdis: do they appropriate and attempt to "convert" native religious terms by redefining them, which at best would provide a distant, potentially confusing approximation of what the missionaries were trying to teach? Do they create, essentially *ex nihilo*, new jargon that can only sound alien to Asian ears? Or do they simply give Asian pronunciations to Western terminology? Each of those approaches has been attempted, with attendant difficulties. In Japan, Xavier was so frustrated trying to find an appropriate word to describe the Christian God that he ultimately resigned himself to pronouncing "Deus" in Japanese phonetics. This stumbling attempt to introduce foreign vocabulary in Japanese pronunciation continues in the LDS Church today, where *baputesuma, bishoppu, endaumento, waado, suteeku,* and *hoomu tiichingu* (baptism, bishop, endowment, ward, stake, and home teaching) are standard terminology. As late as 2007, the characters used to transliterate "Mormon" in the title of the Chinese translation of the Book of Mormon were changed, since the original name could, through sound alone, be interpreted as "gate of evil." Apparently the linguistic existence of God in Asia is still open to debate:[9] Protestant sects in Japan today, as well as the LDS Church, attach an honorific ending (-*sama*, the superlative form of -*san*) to the indigenous Shintō term, *kami*, which encompasses all the animistic manifestations of spirit essence in the phenomena of nature and even, sometimes, humankind.[10]

The language barrier climbs to almost unscalable heights when it comes to translating Christian scriptures into Asian languages. Full translations of the Bible—undertaken by a variety of Protestant sects—into Chinese were not published until 1822, into Japanese in 1887, and into Korean in 1910. But the rapidity of linguistic change in these languages is often breathtaking, and the process of translation has had to be ongoing, with more and more colloquial versions appearing as the younger generations lose facility with the older forms of their languages. The first Japanese colloquial translation of the Bible did not come until 1955. A translation of the Book of Mormon into Chinese was not completed until 1966, while the Korean version was made available the following year. Because of the dramatic changes in the Japanese language over the course of the twentieth century, Alma O. Taylor's original 1909 translation of the Book of Mormon had to be almost completely revised in 1957, then again in 1995. And this doesn't even include the ponderous, seemingly unending challenge of coining appropriate vocabulary to communicate Christian concepts.[11]

2.2 The Differences in Religious Cultures

Because of the pervasive influence of Buddhism in Asia, the meaning of "religion" varies significantly from the traditional Christian sense of the term. If Christian worship can be broadly defined as "church"-centered, the religious climate in most Asian countries can perhaps best be characterized as "heart"-centered. The outward manifestation of Christian devotion in weekly congregational services has no Asian analog. There is, in essence, no such thing as a "church-going" Buddhist, Shintoist, or Hindu. In their spiritual lives, Asian people for the most part reject sectarian affiliations and are repelled by theological debates. It is common in much of Asia for individuals to stir up a syncretic soup they can sip in private—a mixture of what they see as the best from various religious practices that they blend together for individual consumption. The penchant of many Asian peoples to ignore the subtle distinctions between conflicting doctrines and to intermingle divergent beliefs and practices led the Japanese Catholic novelist Endō Shūsaku (1923–96), to use the term "mudswamp" to describe the spiritual climate of his country. In his powerful novel, *Silence* (Chinmoku, 1966), an apostate Catholic priest from the early seventeenth century argues: "This country is a more terrible swamp than you can imagine. Whenever you plant a sapling in this swamp the roots begin to rot; the leaves grow yellow and wither. And we have planted the sapling of Christianity in this swamp."[12]

In China, a traditional mix of folk religious observances and Confucian notions of social hierarchy has served as the primary spiritual guide for the people—which is still the case in Taiwan and, to a lesser degree, Hong Kong, but less so on the mainland since communism has emerged as the dominant philosophy of the ruling class. The Confucian vision of the ladder of social obligations has likewise planted itself in the Japanese and Korean psyches, though the Japanese edition muddied the waters in the late nineteenth century as the fabricated system of State Shintō replaced the local warlords with the image of an emperor ostensibly descended directly from gods who regarded the land of Japan as the finest of their creations.

It is not uncommon for Asians to identify themselves as atheistic but still be actively involved in seasonal practices that have traditional religious significance. Participation in Buddhist festivals, praying at shrines and temples and before small altars in the home, having marriages and funerals conducted by Buddhist, Shintō, or even Christian clergy—such customs indicate not only a highly eclectic ability to embrace differing traditions, but also a blurring of the distinction between being religious and being spiritually minded, as well as a very high correlation between religious and cultural practice.[13] One of the ongoing frustrations for Christian missionaries laboring in Asia is the involvement of their converts in cultural practices that have their origin in native religions. On the surface level, the offering of prayers on behalf of deceased ancestors might appear to be a religious activity, but there is also the likelihood that the supplicants may merely be engaged in a routine cultural rite that has no connection with their inner spiritual life. In much of Asia, religion *is* culture, and culture religion. Conversion to any brand of Christianity is, therefore, tantamount to severing ties with one's cultural identity; yet, due to the relatively weak social influence of the Christian churches in Asian countries, there is often little they can offer to the new member in terms of cultural and social institutions and practices that might fill the void. Interestingly, the varied menu of activities for adherents of all ages sponsored by local LDS congregations may be one of the most successful instances of a Christian group being able to offer mollifying substitutes for what seems to be taken away culturally and socially through conversion.

Two of the chief stumbling blocks to Christianity's success in Asia have been its assertion of a monopoly on saving truth and the sometimes ugly sectarianism between varied strains of Christian belief that have stained the reputation of the faith and often contradicted its fundamental precepts of charity and tolerance. Christianity's insistence on exclusive claim to the hearts, minds, and outward observances of all its adherents is problematic in the Asian mind, and the assertion of the LDS Church, grounded in modern scripture, that it is "the only true and living church upon the face of the whole earth," has the potential to raise even more hackles among Asians, who tend to interpret such claims as a rejection both of their spiritual and cultural heritages and an affront to their ancestors (Doctrine and Covenants [D&C] 1:30). They are quick to conclude that conversion to any brand of Christianity would be to abandon their heritage, betray their ancestors, and risk being regarded as somehow less than fully Asian.

The denominational wars in early modern times, even between rival Catholic missionary orders, looked to Asians too much like the colonialist battles being waged across the region. Competing claims on heavenly ordained authority, with the Catholics professing an unbroken line versus the LDS claim to a *restored* authority, have been of little interest to Asians, who don't acknowledge the authority of Christ in the first place. In some parts of Asia, denominationalism has been so unnerving to the local populace that converts themselves may hold to a belief in Jesus Christ and yet avoid or renounce affiliation with any particular sect: this is the case with the *mukyōkai*, or "non-church" Christian movement started in Japan in the late nineteenth century by convert Uchimura Kanzō (1861–1930). A number of Asian converts in the early twentieth century moved away from embracing Christianity as a religion but clung to its notions of individual freedom and justice in "Christian socialist" movements. Yet others chose to leave the church altogether, particularly young intellectuals who had wearied of the Western cultural imperialism that some missionaries seemed to package together with their doctrine, or who found the proscriptions on certain forms of behavior (particularly sexual morality) excessively restrictive in what they had initially thought was a "liberating" philosophy brought to their land.

It is difficult to pinpoint all the reasons why Asian people seem, judging from growth statistics, to be less interested, even apathetic toward, the message of salvation through Jesus Christ brought to them by LDS missionaries. One mission leader in Japan in the early 1950s put the blame on Japanese materialism: "The past year has been a prosperous year for Japan as a whole and we have noticed it in the attitude of the people. There has developed that spirit of indifference which always seems to come when there is an abundance of material things."[14] Absorption in material wealth and an expectation of earthly "blessings" for religious activity have often been identified as among the greatest stumbling blocks to the spread of the LDS faith in Asia.

One enormous challenge faced by both Catholic and Protestant ministers in Asia has been their doctrine—whether clearly articulated in their preaching or not—that the deceased ancestors of their potential converts have missed out on the chance for salvation because they did not accept Jesus Christ (and His church) during their mortal sojourn. Because of the prominent role that respect for ancestors and rituals designed to honor and bring comfort to their souls plays in virtually all Asian religions, efforts have been made by missionaries in more recent years to moderate that message, but the fact remains that a substantial proportion of the Asian population views conversion to Christianity as a betrayal of their ancestors and marks them as rebelling against age-old family traditions. The ways in which LDS theology may be able to break down this formidable barrier will be discussed shortly.

In addition, the feelings of a need for a godlike figure who atones for individual sins, thought by some to be a universal yearning, is conspicuously absent in Asian tradition, mythology, and religious practice. The "gods" of Asian cosmology, whether the bodhisattvas of Buddhism or the *kami* of Shintō, do not pay as proxies for the moral failings of the living; in the case of the former, having attained enlightenment themselves, they linger close to the world of delusion in order to *assist* others in following in their path; with the latter, their vaguely defined roles seem limited to enlivening the natural realm. As with so much Christian terminology, a word corresponding to "atonement" had to be coined from existing vocabulary; the translations—*shuzui* 贖罪 in Chinese, and either *aganai* 購い or *shokuzai* 贖罪 in Japanese—are dated words that mean "compensation, reparation, or indemnity," and as a verb, "to pay money to get something out of hock," or "to purchase the contract of one who belongs to another." Since the Asian traditions do not share the Judeo-Christian notions of vicarious sacrifice and the freeing of an enslaved people from bondage, it is not surprising that LDS missionaries and those of other Christian faiths struggle to communicate their core message in Asian lands.

Another significant obstacle to missionary success in Asia is the widespread, virtually dogmatic belief that organized religions are, at best, unnecessary to personal and national fulfillment and, in their worst manifestations, a palpable threat to public harmony and safety. The impact of Marxist philosophy, self-evident in China, is also pronounced in post–Second World War Japan, and religion has been regarded by many in the educated classes as a feudalistic throwback to irrational superstition. The Japanese distaste for religious groups has only mounted since the 1995 sarin gas attacks in Tokyo subways by members of the fanatical Aum Shinrikyō sect, one of scores of "new religions" that have cropped up in modern Japan, many of them attempting to link themselves into the native Shintō tradition but ultimately coming across to the public as fanatical and irrelevant. John P. Hoffmann points out that even the Sino-Japanese word for "religious group/sect" (宗教 Chinese: *zongjiao*; Japanese: *shūkyō*) carries connotations of disharmony and separation and an overt rejection of all other systems of belief.[15] Perhaps for this reason, consistently since the 1970s less than 30 percent of Japanese polled have described themselves as "religious." The erection of barriers between one's own group and the groups with which others affiliate—considered one of the defining features of Western-style religions—suggests an unwillingness to cooperate or negotiate, an almost diabolical separatism in most of the countries of Asia where the greatest social capital comes through "belongingness."[16]

2.3 Cultural Incompatibilities

This issue of "belongingness" is very important in understanding social and cultural practices in Asia. Whereas in much of Western society identity is defined using parameters focused on the individual, in those portions of Asia where Confucianism (and, in the case of Japan, also *bushidō*, or the "way of the warrior") has held sway, identity is linked powerfully and directly to the groups to which the individual belongs. Drawing on the work of the Japanese Christian psychiatrist Doi Takeo, Bruce C. Hafen postulates that the core of Japanese identity may be found in the concept of *amae*, variously translated as "dependence," "belonging," or even *Freiheit in Geborgenheit* ("freedom through emotional security").[17] Doi argues that Japanese derive both individual identity and personal satisfaction of needs through affiliation with a variety of groups and social organizations, making participation in any religious organizations unnecessary and, at times, a source of great conflict. He goes so far as to label *amae* the "essence of the Japanese concept of divinity." Consequently, the core hypothesis of LDS Christianity—that mankind was, in the beginning, "cast out" of God's presence but ultimately can be reunited (or once again be in a relationship of "belongingness") with Him and with loved ones through Christ's intercession—is absent in the founding conceptions of Asian philosophical and spiritual traditions. In a temporal sense, the LDS belief in man's premortal, mortal, and postmortal relationship with God is rendered irrelevant because of the remarkably effective ways in which Asian peoples cluster into groups of various kinds, care for one another, and meet each other's needs.[18]

The relatively small number of LDS converts in Asia, combined with the reticence of many Asian people to express personal feelings about faith or to try to persuade others to join them in their beliefs, has thus far prevented the church from creating a sufficiently powerful sense of group identity that it can rival or even take the place of existing secular associations. Some observers have suggested that a significant proportion of individuals who have been baptized into the LDS church come from those who were already marginalized within their society or who had weak ties to the kinds of groups that normally provide the required levels of "belongingness" in Asian society.

Those in Asia who meet with LDS missionaries feel a powerful sense of *obligation* toward them. Once a set of missionaries has gone to the effort of befriending a potential convert, the latter often will listen to the religious teachings out of gratitude, and in many contexts will agree verbally with what they are taught, whether they accept it or not, in order to avoid giving offense. Some even go so far as to be baptized out of these feelings of duty, whether it be for the spiritual guidance or even English conversation lessons they are receiving; few, of course, remain enthusiastically involved in the church or its activities.[19]

Geographically, historically, and emotionally, LDS converts in Asia are isolated from what might be called core LDS experience. The key events in LDS history—the First Vision of Joseph Smith, the inspired translation of the Book of Mormon, the organization of the church, the revelations and persecutions that followed, the pioneer trek, and the goal of building Zion *on the American continent*—are not only "foreign" to Asian members of the church, but, in some respects, are also an unspoken (and surely unintended) declaration of American supremacy when it comes to ownership of and identification with the LDS narrative. Even the links that are formed doctrinally and emotionally between LDS members in the West—the Israelite origins of the Nephite peoples, their own adoption into the House of Israel, and the prophesied destiny of the church to gather scattered Israel into one again in the last days—seem to exclude members in Asia. It should, therefore, not be surprising that some Asian LDS members have—unofficially—made claims that they are possibly of Nephite origin, often referencing a brief account in the Book of Mormon which describes a series of ships built by a "curious" man named Hagoth that are launched into "the west sea" around 55 BC, carrying large numbers of Nephite families from the American continent (Alma 63: 5–8). Even though the scriptural record says "[t]hey were never heard of more . . . and whither [they] did go we know not," some LDS members in Asia have expectantly conjectured that the ships could have navigated the Pacific and landed on their shores, linking them at least marginally with the Book of Mormon history that all LDS members across the world embrace as the word of God.

3 QUO VADIS?

Judging from the postconversion fruits brought forth by the hundreds of thousands of Asians who have remained faithful members of the LDS Church in their native lands, one cannot question the validity or strength of their devotion. Theirs is the onerous task of creating a religious culture and society that can accept, nurture, and socialize new members so that they can make the enormous transitions from their prior social niches and identify a comfortable spot for themselves in their new spiritual and cultural home. Of primary import is helping them understand that they have not traded away any portion of their "Asianness" by joining the church.

Evidence from recent studies suggests that the church and its missionaries are doing little to capitalize on the strong points of their doctrine and practice and the ways in which they differ from those of other Christian groups. The most prominent example is the LDS doctrine of salvation for the dead, revealed to Joseph Smith in 1842, which, along with other revelations to subsequent prophets, has made it clear that the gospel of Jesus Christ will be taught in the postmortal realm to all who did not have or take advantage of the opportunity to hear and embrace it during mortality. These teachings allow LDS missionaries to provide comfort and encouragement to Asian individuals who might have concerns about betraying their ancestors by joining a "foreign" faith, and would make allowance for the salvation of any deceased family members who chose to accept what the missionaries are teaching to their living posterity.

Since concern and respect for ancestors is a major component of most Asian belief systems, it appears that LDS missionaries could do more to emphasize and highlight this reassuring teaching of the church. Understanding of the doctrine provides an open link between present, past, and future for those who choose to take it, and encourages rather than hinders potential Asian converts in their desire to do something on this earth that will be of benefit to the spirits of their forebears. It is surely not hyperbole to propose that, of all Christian doctrines, this focus on working for the deceased has potential for broad appeal in many Asian lands, simultaneously helping those who will hear the message with a way to hold to some of their most heartfelt traditions while embracing new levels of spiritual enlightenment.

Few of the thick castle walls preventing LDS missionaries from making rapid progress in converting Asians to their message can be easily dismantled. The languages they have to master will not become any easier; the propensity of Asian people to be "spiritual" but not overtly "religious" will not change overnight; the materialism and strict social hierarchies by their nature resist change; and the broad divergence in cultural practices can at times seem like an affirmation of Kipling's "never the twain" declaration. Although in those parts of Asia where the church has established a solid foothold—the Philippines, Japan, Taiwan, Korea—the phenomenon of second- and sometimes even third-generation LDS membership is encouraging, it will still be many years before a clear sense of "LDS Asian identity" can be created as groups of "belongingness" within the church grow in size and influence. It bears remembering that, however far apart the beliefs of the Christian and Muslim worlds appear to be, they still share the monotheistic tradition of the Old Testament. Asia remains the largest and most populous region of the world where Christianity and its origins have as yet sunk no deeper than the roots of a eucalyptus, and the LDS affirmation of a "restored" Christianity cannot carry the same impact in lands where it was never found—or lost—in the first place. The messengers of the restoration will surely have to increase their understanding of the spiritual traditions of Asia and take to heart the Lord's admonition to His servants to "become acquainted with all good books, and with languages, tongues, and people . . . and a knowledge also of countries and of kingdoms" (D&C 90:15; 88:79). As they do so, and as the local members "enlarge the place of [their] tent . . . stretch forth the curtains of [their] habitation . . . and strengthen [their] stakes" (Isaiah 54:2), the Orient will doubtless become more and more scrutable to those who bear the gospel message.

NOTES

1. Britsch, *From the East*, 2.
2. Lee, *Clash of Civilizations*, 102.
3. Smith, "Translator or Translated?," 132. *Jogaku Zasshi* means "Journal of Women's Education."
4. Britsch, "Closing of the Early Japan Mission," 264.
5. Quotation from LDS Church President Spencer W. Kimball, in Gardner, "President Kimball Shares Missionary Vision with Leaders," 105.
6. Heaton, "China and the Restored Church."
7. Ibid.
8. In terms of percentage of LDS members to total population, Mongolia's .28 percent most closely compares internationally with numbers in the Bahamas (.26), Barbados (.21), Jamaica (.21), and Papua New Guinea (.28). Interestingly, the percentage also approximates the ratios in the United Kingdom (.24) and Wales (.27). Statistics taken from *Deseret News 2011 Church Almanac*.
9. Lively but inconclusive debates raged among Protestant missionaries laboring in China in the middle of the nineteenth century over the proper Chinese term to translate "God." The two chief candidates, *shin* (神) and *shang te* (上帝), were already burdened with centuries of native connotations that made either choice problematic.
10. I can't bring myself to agree with the conclusion of the good Reverend James Legge, who wrote regarding the proper term to translate God into Chinese: "There is *one truth* about it somewhere, for which trained and sanctified minds will not always, nor even long, grope in vain." Legge, *Argument for* 上帝 *(Shang Te) as the Proper Rendering of the Words Elohim and Theos in the Chinese Language*, iv.

11. See Morris, "Some Problems of Translating Mormon Thought into Chinese," for examples of the translation dilemma into Chinese. He notes on p. 80, for instance, that "the word currently being used for 'exaltation,' *ch'ao sheng*, is an old Buddhist term. The first verse of John, 'In the beginning was the Word,' uses *tao* for 'Word,' the very name of Taoism. This translation is eminently right, but it still produces confusion."

12. Endō, *Silence*, 237.

13. Hoffmann, *Japanese Saints*. Hoffmann first mentions this concept on p. 74 and elaborates on it in chap. 6.

14. Ibid., 32.

15. Ibid., 36–37, 74.

16. Ibid., 71.

17. Hafen and Hafen, *Belonging Heart*, 24.

18. Hoffmann, *Japanese Saints*, 70–73.

19. Britsch, *From the East*, 95–96.

BIBLIOGRAPHY

Boxer, C. R. *The Christian Century in Japan, 1549–1650*. Berkeley: University of California Press, 1967.

Breen, John, and Mark Williams, eds. *Japan and Christianity: Impacts and Responses*. Houndmills, UK: Macmillan, 1996.

Britsch, R. Lanier. *From the East: The History of the Latter-day Saints in Asia, 1851–1996*. Salt Lake City: Deseret, 1998.

Britsch, R. Lanier. "The Closing of the Early Japan Mission." In Neilson and Gessel, *Taking the Gospel to the Japanese*, 263–83.

Deseret News 2011 Church Almanac. Salt Lake City: Deseret News, 2011.

Elison, George. *Deus Destroyed: The Image of Christianity in Early Modern Japan*. Cambridge, MA: Council on East Asian Studies, Harvard University, 1991.

Endō Shūsaku. *Silence*. Trans. William Johnston. Tokyo: Sophia University Press, 1969.

Gardner, Marvin K. "President Kimball Shares Missionary Vision with Leaders." *Ensign*, 9, no. 5 (May 1979). http://www.lds.org/ensign/1979/05/news-of-the-church/president-kimball-shares-missionary-vision-with-leaders?lang=eng.

Hafen, Bruce C., and Marie K. Hafen. *The Belonging Heart: The Atonement and Relationships with God and Family*. Salt Lake City: Deseret, 1994.

Heaton, William. "China and the Restored Church." *Ensign* 2, no 8 (August 1972). http://lds.org/ensign/1972/08/china-and-the-restored-church?lang=eng.

Hoffmann, John P. *Japanese Saints: Mormons in the Land of the Rising Sun*. Lanham, MD: Lexington, 2007.

Lee, Robert. *The Clash of Civilizations: An Intrusive Gospel in Japanese Civilization*. Harrisburg, PA: Trinity Press International, 1999.

Legge, James. *An Argument for 上帝 (Shang Te) as the Proper Rendering of the Words Elohim and Theos in the Chinese Language*. Hong Kong: Hong Kong Register Office, 1850.

Morris, Robert J. "Some Problems of Translating Mormon Thought into Chinese," *BYU Studies* 10, no. 2 (1970): 173–85.

Neilson, Reid L. *The Japanese Missionary Journals of Alma O. Taylor, 1901–10*. Provo, UT: BYU Studies and Joseph Fielding Smith Institute for Latter-day Saint History, 2001.

Neilson, Reid L., and Van C. Gessel, eds. *Taking the Gospel to the Japanese, 1901–2001.* Provo, UT: Brigham Young University Press, 2006.

Ōno, Susumu. *Nihonjin no kami.* Tokyo: Shinchō Bunko, 1997.

Smith, Sarah Cox. "Translator or Translated? The Portrayal of the Church of Jesus Christ of Latter-day Saints in Print in Meiji Japan." In Neilson and Gessel, *Taking the Gospel to the Japanese,* 127–45.

PART VIII

MORMONISM IN THE WORLD COMMUNITY

CHAPTER 37

COMMUNITARIANISM AND CONSECRATION IN MORMONISM

J. SPENCER FLUHMAN

INTRODUCTION: THE COMMUNITARIAN VISION AND ITS DISCONTENTS

THE early Mormon communitarian formula was simple enough. In a move emblematic of his habit of simultaneously validating and assaulting traditional Christianity, founding prophet Joseph Smith bowed at the altar of the Bible and then altered it to fit his seeric vision. In what he viewed as an inspired expansion of Genesis, Smith extended its brief reference to Enoch and provided his infant Church of Christ a template for its leap into sacred time and space. God called Enoch's ancient holy city and people "Zion," his extended text read, "because they were of one heart and of one mind and dwelt in righteousness and there was no poor among them." The tripartite longing for a people characterized by unity, righteousness, and socioeconomic equality did not necessarily represent a radical departure from previous Christian communitarian experiments, but Mormon implementation of Smith's vision nevertheless proved controversial in the extreme. The text itself hinted at future trouble. First, if Enoch was one of Smith's model-analogs, and there is evidence he was, then Americans would have to reckon with a community led by an Old Testament–style prophet, not merely another enthusiastic frontier preacher. Second, if Smith's revisionist text was indeed scripture, an already crowded religious landscape now had a radically anti-individualistic voice to contend with. Third, if Zion named both a people and a literal holy *place* apart, Smith's vision was inescapably political at its core. Early Mormon communities, in other words, complicated already heated American contests over religion, authority, economy, and politics.[1]

Smith and the early Mormons hoped his Zionic ideals would salve proliferating divisions in American life, but they proved divisive, not only between Mormons and unbelievers, but bitterly so among Latter-day Saints themselves. Indeed, the means to Smith's visionary ends split the community in successive rounds. What emerges from the Mormon past is not a unitary set of strategies for realizing the goals articulated in the early texts and sermons. Rather, broad principles were themselves set in complicated relationships in documents deemed sacred by various groups, across decades and in diverse locations. From that unwieldy canonical effusion flowed an evolving and contested inventory of ideas and attempts to define a holy community. Though most Mormons across the spectrum of traditions tracing their roots to Joseph Smith would still assent to unity, righteousness, and socioeconomic equality as defining institutional goals, the fractious nineteenth-century ecclesiastical family was thoroughly bedeviled by the communitarian details.

In the early rounds of intra-Mormon wrangling over the parameters of the Zionic city, a central tension became clear. Future LDS Church president Wilford Woodruff recorded a memorable entry in his journal that marked his commitment to the Mormon project as he understood it. On the last day of 1834, Woodruff wrote: "Be it known that I Wilford Woodruff do freely covenant with my God that I freely consecrate and dedicate myself together with all my properties and affects unto the Lord for the purpose of assisting in building up his kingdom even Zion on the earth that I may keep his law and lay all things before the bishop of his Church that I may be a lawful heir to the Kingdom of God." This total devotion of self and property to the cause not only marked Woodruff as a loyalist during the disputes of 1837–38 and 1842–45, it anticipated his success among like-minded successors to Smith. Voicing his opposition to just this kind of complete commitment to Smith's directives, Warren Cowdery editorialized in the Mormon paper two and a half years after Woodruff's vow. After narrating the financial disaster that had rocked the Ohio LDS community, Cowdery questioned fellow Latter-day Saints' trust in Smith's economic direction. "If we give all our privileges to one man, we virtually give him our money and our liberties, and make him a monarch, absolute and despotic, and ourselves abject slaves or fawning sycophants." In Cowdery's mind, Smith had overstepped his role and brought the church into conflict with American liberty in the process. "Who does not see a principle of popery and religious tyranny involved in such an order of things?" Mormonism could scarcely hold together given such bitter differences over communal definition. At no point did Mormons resolve these fundamental paradoxes; rather, ongoing and often divisive engagement with them has long shaped the LDS communal experience.[2]

With tumultuous internal conflict nearly halving the community every few years, Latter-day Saints also found themselves at odds with nonbelievers. Mormon communal history existed in dynamic tension with broader narratives and developments, sometimes parallel and sometimes crosscutting. Clearly, Mormons hoped to redeem what they regarded as a society wracked with factions, hyperindividualism, and economic exploitation. By aggressively addressing those evils as they did, Mormons can be seen as swimming against strong cultural currents. They never transcended their received culture, however. Given their minority status and the power differentials that defined the nineteenth century, Mormons seemed inexorably pulled toward the centers of American life. In many ways, nineteenth-century Mormons seem tenaciously anachronistic, existing just behind the powerful, contested processes of capitalist elaboration and secularizing modernity. Moreover, because their economic activities were lashed so tightly with their controversial family arrangements, attacks on the latter could, and did, devastate the former. And Mormons ultimately found attractive opportunities closer to the centers of cultural power. The push of American courts, hostile federal officials, reform crusaders, and social critics was arguably matched by the pull of potential growth, cultural influence, and institutional coherence. Near the turn of the twentieth century, Mormon communitarianism was dramatically refashioned in the heat of national outrage and under the weight of the Saints' own modernist aspirations.

THE EBB AND FLOW OF EARLY MORMON COMMUNITY BUILDING

Against the backdrop of surging market elaboration and widespread valorization of politicoeconomic individualism in antebellum culture, Mormons can be cast as radical dissenters. Communitarianism was but another way that they stood apart, in their own minds, from a world ripening in iniquity. Early LDS communities were born in the shadow of Christian antecedents and developed in an age of communal experimentation. Their forms owed general direction to the broad expressions of Smith's revelations, but few, least of all Smith himself, indulged in rigidity or legalism with the details. Mormons mostly pulled back from communalism of property, unlike the Shakers, and were publicly sensitive to charges that they trafficked in a "common-stock" system. Also in distinction to other contemporary communal societies, Mormons mostly resisted shared living arrangements, preferring instead individual family dwellings. These moderate positions, however, are mitigated by the sheer scale of Brigham Young's efforts, discussed below, to hold back the capitalist tide and to remake the economy of the entire Great Basin region along the lines of Smith's early revelations.[3]

Early Mormons physically "gathered" together into new communities. The successive Mormon centers existed at the intersection of a millennial timetable and the hope for urban spaces wholly dedicated to righteousness. Joseph Smith's infant church was called to social order by an 1831 revelation instructing New York believers to join with those in Ohio. Subsequent revelations marked western Missouri as the eschatological center, the place for the holy city and a temple to be built for the returning Christ. A capital and satellite model was glossed with Old Testament language: a center place would be secured with outlying "stakes" to form the canopy of God's earthly kingdom (Isaiah 54:2). An 1833 city plat provided Smith's vision in brick-and-mortar terms: the "New Jerusalem" would evoke the ancient Israelite capital's centrality in sacred space. To drive the point home, streets in the Missouri city were to be named "Jerusalem Street" and "Bethlehem Street." Three concentric zones collapsed on a temple complex, which would function as the Mormons' *axis mundi*. In designing his city this way, Smith's vision captured competing impulses in antebellum culture. The farmer-prophet envisioned a city, not a hamlet. Its residential zone evinced a profound egalitarianism; lots were identical for those receiving a share in the new Zion. Even so, the temple anchored the city, and the Mormon priesthood, it was understood, would guide the community in its totality. This Zion mixed strong models of authority with pronounced leveling and populist protest against the market and churchly elites that, Latter-day Saints said, threatened to wreck the nation's righteous promise.[4]

As a cornerstone of the Zion-making project, Smith issued a revelation that set the community apart economically. Saints would "consecrate" their property for the poor's care and the work of the church. They would deed property to the church bishop and receive a "stewardship" over an allotment in return. Any surplus ("residue") would be kept in a "storehouse" for distribution to the poor. Many found the revelations' underlying logic compelling: all is God's, and human beings, as stewards, are accountable to the Maker for their use of His creative bounty. As it developed, the Missouri community received the most attention in terms of the revelation's property redistribution passages. Church leaders originally conceived of the revelation in terms of use rights only for individuals, with the church retaining ultimate ownership, but non-Mormon judges disagreed when ex-Mormons sued. In Ohio, Smith focused his efforts, at least between 1832 and 1834, on a management company he named the United Firm, which was given supervisory responsibility over both communities. The firm proved to be a microcosm of the broader struggle to realize the Zionic ideal. Members accused each other of wrongdoing, some found fault with Smith, and the firm's debts were inequitably settled, largely on the back of talented businessman Newell K. Whitney. After Smith implemented a series of local "high councils" to oversee the largest Mormon centers, economic direction was localized, too, and the firm was officially dissolved in 1834. (Ironically, Brigham Young adopted a code name for the firm, the "United Order,"— invoked by Smith to conceal members' identities in the published revelation—for his cooperative initiatives in the 1870s.) By 1836, church leaders had organized a bank but failed to secure a state charter; backed mostly by real estate and chronically short of specie, it had a brief and inglorious tenure. When it failed in the panic of 1837, hundreds of Ohio Mormons turned away, convinced that Smith was a fallen prophet. For many, the banking particulars were less at issue than the feasibility of Smith's holy-city model generally (Doctrine and Covenants [D&C] 42:1–10, 30–55; 104).[5]

After these abortive attempts at centralized economic control, official pronouncements in 1838 and 1841 adjusted the details but left the larger vision intact. An 1838 revelation formalized what had begun as a precipitous drop-off of initial consecrations after 1834. It stipulated that church members should give all their *surplus* property in an initial consecration and, thereafter, they would be required to "pay one-tenth of all their interest annually" as a "standing law." Since the surplus donation replaced the totalizing consecrations from earlier years, some commentators in retrospect marked this 1838 text as the end of the Law of Consecration in Mormonism. Some of Smith's eventual chief lieutenants in the church's apostolic quorum did not see things this way, however. When the northern Missouri center crumbled just months following the revelation, apostle Brigham Young, left to coordinate the flight from the state, invoked the law's principles and bound Latter-day Saints to donate all to support the removal of the ill and destitute (D&C 119:1–4).[6]

The subsequent Mormon capital in Illinois was less insulated than Smith's other Zions had been, but his truncated economic program still spawned division. At times, Smith preached against socialism and communitarian experimentation. At other times, he initiated reforms that pulled the community away from capitalist or industrializing priorities. While economic development in Illinois fell short of "systematic," leaders sporadically instituted cooperative measures to address the issues of settlement, labor markets, care for the poor and missionaries' wives, and some key community building projects—the impressive Nauvoo Temple not the least. An 1841 revelation required the temple's construction and, in addition, a hotel that might welcome dignitaries to the city. The call for the temple was not surprising, but the hotel marked an innovation, signaling both perhaps a less insular tone for the Illinois gathering (especially important after the Missouri disaster) and an acknowledgment that church building projects could provide needed employment for emigrating converts. Smith had imagined holy cities from the start, but some within and outside the church puzzled that the city's economy seemed distracted with the mere housing and feeding of the Saints; its industrial and manufacturing potential seemed perpetually untapped. Its agrarian orientation irked some prosperous Mormons. Once theological disputes and, especially, Smith's clandestine polygamy were added to the mix, some of Nauvoo's leading citizens fashioned a protest movement from their distaste for polygamy's scandal and their sense that Smith's economic and political direction amounted to tyranny. When dissenters published the first issue of a renegade paper, their concerns were clear enough. Along with charges of polygamy and political machination, they worried over their economic autonomy: they would "oppose the sacrifice of the Liberty, the Property, and the Happiness of the *many*, to the *pride* and *ambition* of the *few*." This line, of course, inverted the church leader's official narrative, which held that the restraint of personal ambition might rile the selfish, but it was a necessary prerequisite for the city of holiness (D&C 124:22–27).[7]

A COOPERATIVE ALMOST-KINGDOM
IN THE WEST

Brigham Young remained committed to Smith's vision. He and apostles Orson Pratt and Lorenzo Snow were its most vigorous defenders and they coaxed along less enthusiastic leaders after Smith's assassination. Young had cut his teeth as a leader during the evacuation crisis of 1838 and, in 1846, he drew on Smith's consecration ideals for yet another mass removal. The famed Mormon exodus tested community resources and patience, but Young and his fellow apostles, having successfully wrested ecclesiastical control from rivals, secured a gathering place at sufficient distance from other white settlers to enable them to build God's kingdom in peace, or so they thought. In the heady days of removal and early settlement, Mormon leaders planned a unified political, religious, and economic kingdom in imagined isolation. History exposed the separation fiction quickly: war with Mexico brought them again within the nation's political reach in 1848, thousands of Native Americans both enabled and impeded their plans, the California gold rush brought thousands of emigrants through the territory by 1852, and, by 1858, a federal army had set up camp between the two largest LDS settlements. The linking of the transcontinental railroad in Utah in 1869 formalized what should have been clear earlier: Mormons would face the problems of integration and adaptation sooner rather than later.[8]

Still, the Rocky Mountain Saints persisted in their temporal kingdom building until the end of the century. Though historians argue over whether it was politics or polygamy that propelled a final showdown with the federal government, the Saints' new economic cooperatives were deeply implicated in their tense relationships with non-Mormons, since antagonists routinely denounced centralized economic direction as a critical cog in the theocratic machine. Given both the realities of settlement in a sometimes unforgiving landscape and the threats Young perceived in "Gentile" (that is, non-Mormon) culture, in his own mind he had little choice but to press the Zionic vision with increasingly elaborate plans, eventually ranging well beyond anything Smith had implemented.

The kinds of informal, sporadic measures of the Illinois period continued to characterize Mormon efforts in the late 1840s and early 1850s. The famous Perpetual Emigrating Fund, hatched in 1849, offered a rotating source of credit to aid Mormons still gathering from the east and, eventually, from Europe. Despite its assistance to thousands of emigrants, the fund was hampered by indebtedness—over a million dollars' worth by 1880. Though unsuccessful as a business venture, the fund fulfilled its purpose of aiding the poor in their pilgrimage to Zion. In new settlements, Mormons fenced communally, supported community fields, irrigated by means of central church direction, donated surpluses to care for the poor, and deferred to church authorities to settle economic disputes. As congregational wards increasingly became the units of ecclesiastical administration, local LDS bishops "became in practice watermasters, fence supervisors, and bridge builders." Public projects, virtually indistinguishable from church projects for decades, gave the poor work opportunities. An ethic of sharing, saving, and avoidance of avarice was to keep the communities viable. No one was to take more land, timber, or water than he could use. Church leaders provided direction and correction in such matters. And since the church offered the most plentiful source of capital and authoritative advice on how resources might be allocated, non-Mormons in Utah found themselves often straining against powerful economic currents.[9]

The beginnings of more systemic and church-wide provisions developed in response to Young's sense of economic vulnerability. He feared the outbreak of gold fever and chafed at the presence of Gentile traders, sure that that their prices were exorbitant and their motives were foul. Defectors also frustrated him. In response, in 1854 he initiated an abortive program of consecration in which LDS property might be brought under centralized control. Consecrations were indeed recorded across the territory, but the fact that no property appears to have changed hands would make the move appear symbolic were it not for subsequent developments. With those in mind, the so-called consecration movement looks more like the first stirrings of Young's yearning to realize Smith's communitarian dream. The "Utah War" crisis derailed elaboration of the plan and Young was forced to put off additional innovations until the nation was distracted by the Civil War.[10]

In the 1860s, leaders put forward measures intended to increase self-sufficiency, weaken Gentile economic power, and insulate the Saints from corrosive elements of "eastern" society. To provide for the need for finished goods and unavailable staples, Young orchestrated a two-pronged plan: consumer associations and a boycott of Gentile merchants. Both were controversial. Young worried that if simply integrated into the national economy, Mormons would ever be at a disadvantage, forced to buy manufactured goods at a mark-up while letting resources bleed out of the territory. Early on, he restricted Mormons from trade altogether, but underestimated the consequences—he unwittingly had provided the gentiles sole possession of the field.

In the mid-1860s, he reversed course and attempted a Mormon monopoly of trade, which naturally sent non-Mormons into an uproar. LDS missionaries and converts had witnessed the success of a consumers' cooperative in Rochdale, England, and Mormon leaders seem to have taken their cue in part from English precedents. Lorenzo Snow established an extensive and successful cooperative at Brigham City in northern Utah. His goal, simply put, was for the community to manufacture all that it consumed. A cooperative store came first, in 1864, with a generous commodity dividend structure that made subscription attractive. A two-story tannery, a wool factory, sawmills, brick and adobe shops, a limekiln, blacksmith and furniture shops (all built by community labor), and community herds of sheep, cattle, and hogs followed. By 1874, Snow's dream was a virtual reality. The 400-odd families in the community were more or less self-sufficient; 372 shareholders owned the Brigham City Co-op. Its success was itself an eventual liability, however, as growth and its diversity of operations severely taxed community organizational and administrative resources. In 1877, chronic scarcities of cash, a crop nearly wiped out by grasshoppers, and a devastating fire in the woolen mill all took their toll. A year later, the US Collector of Internal Revenue levied a stiff penalty tax on the Co-op script. Never able to fully recover from the turbulent two-year reversal of fortune, the Brigham City experience nonetheless profoundly shaped Brigham Young's hopes for church-wide program.[11]

Four years after the inauguration of the Brigham City project, leaders in Salt Lake City established Zion's Cooperative Mercantile Institution (ZCMI) to secure manufactured goods at reasonable prices. Such an institution met with Young's approval because it tended, in his view, to check the covetousness of the few and to enrich the many. It also guarded church members from exploitation. Under the plan, individuals could buy stock in the institution, which would negotiate prices and offer goods through a central store in Salt Lake City, which then functioned as a wholesale distributer to branches throughout the territory. Since there was no restriction on the sale of shares (the wealthy could amass large holdings) and since voting rights were based on the numbers of shares owned, ZCMI bred less socioeconomic leveling than Young had hoped for, however. He capitulated on these matters to entice the most well-to-do Mormons to invest in the project's success. The institution achieved modest success for decades and, if the central store was more a joint-stock company, some of the retail stores veered toward a more cooperative framework.[12]

Against the backdrop of a national financial crisis in 1873, Brigham Young pushed ahead with even more daring arrangements in 1874. In a profusion of sermons, LDS leaders challenged Mormons with equal parts of the rhetoric of agrarian dissent (worries about speculation, credit manipulation) and the language of Mormon revelation (unity, care for the poor). Young had long been wary of the lure of Gentile mines and luxuries and, faced with reports that southern Utah communities were increasingly dependent on Nevada mining, he and other Mormon leaders reenvisioned cooperation. They dubbed the new system the United Order of Enoch or, simply, the United Order—admittedly amorphous terms invoked to describe a wide array of measures—and proposed a fundamental restructuring of the Mormon economy. Each urban ward or rural village would constitute an individual "order," bound by covenant to live piously and to pool both capital and labor. Local church authorities, or the boards they appointed, would provide centralized direction. Early talk seemed to jettison the notion of private property altogether; members would transfer property to the board and agree to assume those duties assigned to them. Disparities between rich and poor would evaporate. Simple living and renunciation of materialism would provide the excess capital needed to spur local production and, finally, insulate the Saints from dependency and ruin. As both a marker of the order's new realities and a symbol of its uniting of the sacred and temporal, individuals entering the orders were often rebaptized.[13]

Predictably, dissent issued immediately from both within and outside the church. Non-Mormons in Utah decried the enhanced controls against trade and charged Young with constructing an un-American monopoly. Others gleefully noted that not even all church leaders had put their property in the communal pot. Indeed, resistance seemed most pointed at the Mormon capital: though orders were organized in every Salt Lake City ward (that is, its twenty individual congregations), only one actually incorporated. The orders were more successful in the rural Mormon villages, but at the ecclesiastical and cultural center, the faith's intelligentsia and business leaders responded coolly to the new program. At one end of the spectrum came questions about the order's relationship to Smith's revelations. What of the early scriptural emphasis on individual "stewardships"? some asked. At the other end, dissidents coupled their outrage over the order with broader critiques of Young's leadership or of Mormonism's perceived hostility to individuality and free thought. A small but influential group of Salt Lake City elites had become mouthpieces for dissent in the late 1860s and they intensified their criticisms as the orders developed. Speaking to a crowd in Salt Lake City in 1874, leaders of the resistance denounced Young's "last swindle" to rapturous applause.[14]

In response to the criticism, Mormon leaders granted that times had changed since the 1830s, adjusted particulars to allow for privatization in some quarters, and gave local orders latitude in working out details. As a result, the orders varied in form and success depending on local circumstances. Few lasted more than a couple of years, but some could point to notable achievements. In St. George, site of the first order, the Mormons' first western temple stood as its crowning achievement, and, like ritual rebaptism, a telling symbol of their monism. The famed commune at Orderville in southern Utah enjoyed marked success for a few years and represented the far end of mid-century communitarianism: private property was abolished and members lived, ate, and worked communally until internal divisions and, especially, prosecution of polygamists forced restructuring. In modified form, the cooperative limped along until the end of the century. All told, the United Order movement numbered scores of local orders stretching from Idaho to Mexico.[15]

Despite Young's nagging suspicion that individualism had kept the orders from success, other developments ultimately doomed them. Most significantly, the hammer blows of federal resistance to Mormon power, ostensibly aimed at polygamy but nevertheless devastating to the church's economic activities, dictated the final end. Even earlier, though, Young's death and his successor's more market-friendly views had shifted the field. John Taylor, who had been born in England and raised in Canada, lacked Young's zeal for the orders and stressed that while the principles of cooperation remained in force, changing times would continue to necessitate adjustments. Taylor organized Zion's Central Board of Trade, with local boards throughout Mormondom, to coordinate major economic initiatives, but by the early 1880s it was clear that a fundamental transition away from the United Order had taken place. Rather than turn economic direction over to local ecclesiastical leaders, as Young had done, Taylor instead populated his board with leading LDS businessmen. His relative openness to broader markets and private initiative set the Saints on a course that was accelerated after the fiercest period of antipolygamy activism. Facing mounting debt and Saints unwilling to donate for fear of federal confiscation, Taylor's successor, Lorenzo Snow, famously instituted the "tithe," a standing one-tenth donation for all church members, as the means to rescue the church from financial ruin. By the 1920s, the church had largely recovered, but the "unifying cooperative ethic" of the previous century had unquestionably been stunted.[16]

The subsequent national financial crisis of the 1930s revived Mormon cooperation, but the details of that development show, dramatically, how fully (and quickly) the Latter-day Saints had acclimated to national norms. Early during the Depression, progressive-leaning members of the hierarchy had coordinated relief efforts in tandem with state and national agencies. With the death of ardent New Dealer Anthony W. Ivins, a counselor to church president Heber J. Grant, and the appointment of conservative J. Reuben Clark Jr., a new Security Program (later renamed the Church Welfare Plan) expanded grassroots relief efforts into a church-wide program of assistance. Grant and Clark, both deeply distrustful of Roosevelt and expanding federal power, ensured that the new program was defined apart from, and indeed in partial antagonism to, a rising welfare state. Mormons had deeply distrusted federal power since the 1850s, and the 1880s antipolygamy heyday had prepared the ground for the turn to the political right in the late 1930s. Mormon leaders had been leaning right, conspicuously ahead of the membership, since the 1890s, but Grant's antisocialist instincts anticipated rampant Cold War–era Mormon conservatism. With LDS luminaries like Ezra Taft Benson joining the anticommunist chorus with gusto, memories of the 1860s and '70s grew dim, to say the least. Where Brigham Young had railed against capitalism—he had fumed in 1876 about LDS educators who promulgated the theories of "[John Stuart] Mill and the false political economy which contends against co-operation"—leaders of the late twentieth century were almost uniformly conservative in their politics, as were most American Latter-day Saints. Only idiosyncratic or academic articulations of the older visions could be heard for long stretches of the late twentieth century. Though Mormon cooperation survived, and flourishes, in robust church welfare, education, and humanitarian aid programs, it does so firmly *within* the standing capitalist order.[17]

Echoes and Adaptations:
The Continuing Negotiation
of Mormon Community

The combination of polygamy and enclave economics pushed nineteenth-century Latter-day Saints onto sacred space and into sacred time, serving as they did as psychic and material thresholds into new forms of morality and community. But they had also accented their religious lives with separation and distinction. With the slow demise of both alienating elements, twentieth-century Saints had to reconceive of themselves and their relationship to the rest of the nation and world. Over time, a singular Mormon "people" became harder to conceptualize. The almost-ethnic tribalism of the previous decades seemed unfit for the forward-looking, integration-minded leadership at the turn of the century. Shorn of theocracy by force and choice, Mormons' "kingdom" talk changed. The once "holy nation" was spiritualized and merged with a stronger sense of the LDS movement as a "church." Mormon community more and more featured the congregational ward as its locus; in the first decade of the twentieth century, even the practice of the Salt Lake wards meeting for a common worship service at the famous Salt Lake Tabernacle had been replaced by individual ward services. "Gathering" too was spiritualized, and congregations of Mormons spread across the globe after the Second World War with little expectation that they would soon trudge to Utah en masse. The war's turmoil helped spur new forms of community action as well, as leaders struggled to meet European members' needs. Amidst the postwar rubble, an LDS humanitarian service was born.[18]

As might be expected, Mormons have dealt ambivalently with the variety, intensity, and extent of their ancestors' communitarianism. One thread of memory and interpretation has held a narrow view of the "law of consecration," defining it as the earliest Missouri arrangements only. A heading for one section in the current Doctrine and Covenants (section 119), for instance, narrates modern "tithing" as a *replacement* for the "law." In this construction, consecration was a failure. Accordingly, some historians have sometimes chided it as unworkably idealistic. Mormons, however, have put this interpretation to good use, wielding it as something of an LDS "jeremiad." In their sermonic tradition, consecration thus survives as a lever to urge Saints to greater commitment. The noble dream failed, modern Saints are told, because "we" (both "them" and "us") lacked sufficient faith and devotion. This narrative trend arguably started with Joseph Smith himself, who, on the heels of a failed attempt to recover lost land in Missouri, offered a revelation that promised that Saints would wait a "little season" for Zion's redemption, after the "army of Israel becomes very great." That "holding pattern" revelation formatted many later leaders' perceptions. Perhaps Zion and its socioeconomic egalitarianism await some future divine injunction and timetable (D&C 105:9–13, 26).[19]

As the twentieth century progressed, and as Latter-day Saints grew progressively conservative in their politicoeconomic outlook, consecration took on an increasingly eschatological hue. This abstraction or subversion of communitarianism could buttress the surging political conservatism, of course: with socioeconomic equality pushed ever toward the millennium, questions of social or economic justice and civil rights could be pushed to the margins as well. Corporate models, economic individualism, and capitalistic yearning could, and did, take firm root in such a setting. Stunningly, Joseph Smith's original vision could be almost excised in attempts to fit the past into the new frame. For example, in a recent adult Sunday school manual detailing Joseph Smith's teachings, the absence of any references to consecration is explained this way: "this book does not discuss such topics as the Prophet's teachings regarding the law of consecration as applied to stewardship of property. The Lord withdrew this law from the Church because the Saints were not prepared to live it."[20]

But another interpretative model has persisted alongside the failure thesis. Voiced most forcefully by recent church president Gordon B. Hinckley, it features pragmatism and continuity: "the law of sacrifice and the law of consecration were not done away with and are still in effect." This broader, more flexible, perspective acknowledges adaptability and change and helps modern Mormons makes sense of the prominent place consecration still holds in contemporary temple liturgy. (Recalling that liturgy, LDS scholar Hugh Nibley anticipated Hinckley: "The plain fact is that I have promised to keep a law, and to keep it now.") Perhaps Latter-day Saints, in their substantial commitments of time and resources, have been living the law all along to various degrees. Such a view of consecration might also make space for enhanced Mormon action on broader social, economic, and environmental issues. Where "church welfare" and "humanitarian aid" are well-developed components of institutional Mormonism, a recent adjustment to the church's working mission statement signals future possibilities. Whereas the church's mission had for decades been defined as a threefold endeavor to "preach the Gospel, perfect the Saints, and redeem the dead," the most recent edition of the church's official handbook added a fourth: care for the poor. Viewed at wide angle, Mormon history not only provides for, but demands, such an adjustment. And, as in the past, Latter-day Saints will likely rally around, and contest, such a development in their search for a community of unity, righteousness, and equality.[21]

NOTES

1. Faulring, Jackson, and Matthews, *Joseph Smith's New Translation of the Bible*, 105. When Mormon leaders chose code names to disguise their identities in select published revelations, Enoch was the only one immediately recognizable among the three names Joseph Smith apparently chose for himself. Whittaker, "Substituted Names in the Published Revelations of Joseph Smith," 103–12.

2. Woodruff quoted in Harper, "All Things Are the Lord's," 225; Cowdery, *Latter Day Saints' Messenger and Advocate*, July 1837, 538.

3. May, "One Heart and Mind"; Quinn, "Socioreligious Radicalism of the Mormon Church"; Taysom, *Shakers, Mormons, and Religious Worlds*; Foster, *Religion and Sexuality*.

4. See Parkin, "Joseph Smith"; Bushman, "Making Space."

5. Parkin, "Joseph Smith and the United Firm," 8–12, 33–38, 58–60; Hill, "Cultural Crisis in the Mormon Kingdom."

6. Leonard, *Nauvoo*, 142; Arrington, Fox, and May, *Building the City of God*, 41–42. Smith may have had other priorities in mind as well. See Givens and Grow, *Parley P. Pratt*, 175.

7. Leonard, *Nauvoo*, 123–72; *Nauvoo Expositor*, June 7, 1844.

8. Arrington, Fox, and May, *Building the City of God*, 42–43.

9. Ibid., 43–60 (quoted material on p. 51); Campbell, *Establishing Zion*, 25–39, 135–46; Alexander, *Mormonism in Transition*, 94.

10. Arrington, Fox, and May, *Building the City of God*, 63–78.

11. Ibid., 79–89, 111–33.

12. Ibid., 91–104; Arrington, *Great Basin Kingdom*, 293–322.

13. Arrington, Fox, and May, *Building the City of God*, 137–54, 158; Arrington, *Great Basin Kingdom*, 323–49.

14. Arrington, Fox, and May, *Building the City of God*, 137–58; quoted material in Walker, *Wayward Saints*, 282.

15. Arrington, Fox, and May, *Building the City of God*, 155–75, 265–94, 301.

16. Ibid., 311–26, 337 (quoted material on 337); Alexander, *Mormonism in Transition*, 180–211.

17. Mangum and Blumell, *Mormons' War on Poverty*, 93–156; Alexander, *Utah*, 329–33; Arrington, Fox, and May, *Building the City of God*, 340–50; Quinn, *Elder Statesman*, 377–424; quotation from Simpson, "Mormons Study 'Abroad,'" 796. As one example, iconic LDS scholar and ardent Democrat Hugh Nibley invoked Brigham Young to rebuke modern Latter-day Saints for their individualism and materialism. See Nibley, *Approaching Zion*; Nibley, *Brother Brigham Challenges the Saints*.

18. Shipps, "From Peoplehood to Church Membership"; Cohen, "Construction of the Mormon People."

19. Campbell, *Establishing Zion*, 137.

20. *Teachings of Presidents of the Church: Joseph Smith*, xiii.

21. Quoted in Harper, "All Things Are the Lord's," 213; Nibley, *Approaching Zion*, 388; Stack, "New LDS Emphasis." LDS apostle Henry B. Eyring recently reiterated this perspective in an LDS General Conference: "His [God's] way of helping has at times been called living the

law of consecration. In another period His way was called the united order. In our time it is called the Church welfare program"; Eyring, "Opportunities to Do Good," 22.

BIBLIOGRAPHY

Alexander, Thomas G. *Mormonism in Transition: A History of the Latter-Day Saints, 1890–1930*. Urbana: University of Illinois Press, 1986.

Alexander, Thomas G. *Utah: The Right Place*. Rev. ed. Salt Lake City, UT: Gibbs Smith, 2003.

Arrington, Leonard J. *Great Basin Kingdom: An Economic History of the Latter-day Saints, 1830–1900*. New ed. Urbana: University of Illinois Press, 2005.

Arrington, Leonard J., Feramorz Y. Fox, and Dean L. May. *Building the City of God: Community and Cooperation Among the Mormons*. 2nd ed. Urbana: University of Illinois Press, 1992.

Bushman, Richard. "Making Space for the Mormons." In *Believing History: Latter-day Saint Essays*, ed. Reid L. Neilson and Jed Woodworth, 173–98. New York: Columbia University Press, 2004.

Campbell, Eugene E. *Establishing Zion: The Mormon Church in the American West, 1847–1869*. Salt Lake City, UT: Signature, 1988.

Cohen, Charles L. "The Construction of the Mormon People." *Journal of Mormon History* 32, no. 1 (Spring 2006): 25–64.

Cowdery, Warren A. *Latter Day Saints' Messenger and Advocate* [Kirtland, Oh.], July 1837.

Eyring, Henry B. "Opportunities to Do Good." *Ensign* 41, no. 5 (May 2011): 22–26.

Faulring, Scott H., Kent P. Jackson, and Robert J. Matthews, eds. *Joseph Smith's New Translation of the Bible: Original Manuscripts*. Provo, UT: Religious Studies Center, Brigham Young University, 2004.

Foster, Lawrence. *Religion and Sexuality: Three American Communal Experiments of the Nineteenth Century*. New York: Oxford University Press, 1981.

Givens, Terryl L., and Matthew J. Grow. *Parley P. Pratt: The Apostle Paul of Mormonism*. New York: Oxford University Press, 2011.

Harper, Steven C. "'All Things Are the Lord's': The Law of Consecration in the Doctrine and Covenants." In *The Doctrine and Covenants: Revelations in Context*, ed. Andrew H. Hedges, Alonzo L. Gaskill, and J. Spencer Fluhman, 212–27. Salt Lake City, UT: Deseret, 2008.

Hill, Marvin S. "Cultural Crisis in the Mormon Kingdom: A Reconsideration of the Causes of Kirtland Dissent." *Church History* 49, no. 3 (1980): 286–97.

Leonard, Glen M. *Nauvoo: A Place of Peace, A People of Promise*. Salt Lake City, UT: Deseret, and Brigham Young University Press, 2002.

Mangum, Garth L., and Bruce D. Blumell. *The Mormons' War on Poverty: A History of LDS Welfare, 1830–1990*. Salt Lake City: University of Utah Press, 1993.

May, Dean L. "One Heart and Mind: Communal Life and Values Among the Mormons." In *America's Communal Utopias*, ed. Donald E. Pitzer, 135–58. Chapel Hill: University of North Carolina Press, 1997.

Nibley, Hugh. *Approaching Zion*. Ed. Don E. Norton. Salt Lake City, UT: Deseret, 1989.

Nibley, Hugh. *Brother Brigham Challenges the Saints*. Ed. Don E. Norton and Shirley S. Ricks. Salt Lake City, UT: Deseret, 1994.

Parkin, Max H. "Joseph Smith and the United Firm: The Growth and Decline of the Church's First Master Plan on Business and Finance, Ohio and Missouri, 1832–1834." *BYU Studies* 46, no. 3 (2007): 4–66.

Quinn, D. Michael. *Elder Statesman: A Biography of J. Reuben Clark*. Salt Lake City, UT: Signature, 2002.

Quinn, D. Michael. "Socioreligious Radicalism of the Mormon Church: A Parallel to the Anabaptists." In *New Views of Mormon History: A Collection of Essays in Honor of Leonard J. Arrington*, ed. Davis Bitton and Maureen Ursenbach Beecher, 363–86. Salt Lake City: University of Utah Press, 1987.

Shipps, Jan. "From Peoplehood to Church Membership: Mormonism's Trajectory since World War II." *Church History* 76, no. 2 (2007): 241–61.

Simpson, Thomas W. "Mormons Study 'Abroad': Brigham Young's Romance with American Higher Education, 1867–1877." *Church History* 76, no. 4 (2007): 778–98.

Stack, Peggy Fletcher. "New LDS Emphasis: Care for the Needy." *Salt Lake Tribune*, December 9, 2009.

Taysom, Stephen C. *Shakers, Mormons, and Religious Worlds: Conflicting Visions, Contested Boundaries*. Bloomington: Indiana University Press, 2011.

Teachings of Presidents of the Church: Joseph Smith. Salt Lake City, UT: Church of Jesus Christ of Latter-day Saints, 2007.

Walker, Ronald W. *Wayward Saints: The Godbeites and Brigham Young*. Urbana: University of Illinois, 1998.

Whittaker, David J. "Substituted Names in the Published Revelations of Joseph Smith." *BYU Studies* 23, no. 1 (1983): 103–12.

CHAPTER 38

MORMONS AND THE LAW

SARAH BARRINGER GORDON

WAR is sometimes called politics by other means.[1] We could say the same from the other end of the spectrum: law is politics by other means. We might extend the metaphor to say that lawyers are often tacticians, who battle through courts and legal arguments to accomplish political objectives. Bearing in mind the complex relations between law, politics, and violence, this history of law and lawyers begins with the Latter-day Saints' founding period, and continues through their migration westward and then to statehood. It will focus on the way lawyers functioned in Mormon experience in New York, Missouri, and Illinois, and then in territorial Utah, in their official roles as prosecutors and judges, but also as a defense bar, as a precursor to statehood. In the end, the development of a talented legal community made a difference to the history of the territory and the church that made the Great Basin its home. Lawyers affected Mormon Utah mostly through law and legal action, to be sure, not war and pillage. But even so, they made politics. For one thing, lawyers negotiated the settlement that led eventually to statehood for Utah, and then they settled in to run the state, just as they did across America.

There are four sections to this chapter. The first focuses on Joseph Smith, founding prophet of the church, and some of his many encounters with hostile (and sometimes friendly) legal systems from the 1820s to his death. After Smith's martyrdom in 1844, Mormons constructed a society virtually without professional attorneys. The second section talks about why and how this lawyerless world came about, and what the consequences were. The third section examines especially the 1870s, and the change in approach that brought lawyers into the picture both in Utah and in Washington, representing church interests as well as opposing them. The final section talks about the effects of this new legal community, which included Mormons as well as non-Mormons. In the end, Utah in 1896, when it was formally admitted as a state, looked a lot like other states. That is, lawyers in Utah had become central to politics and government there as elsewhere in America.

After statehood, Latter-day Saints had smart lawyers to call upon as they navigated the twentieth century, just as other groups did. In that sense, this chapter traces a pattern of growing legalism—with lawyers deployed strategically and often disastrously in the first period, prohibited from plying their craft in the second period, and then in the third period acting as defense counsel and prosecutors, and then finally negotiating a compromise, drafting a constitution, and assuming important posts in a new political jurisdiction in the last period.

There are many possible topics and ways of studying the legal history of Mormons and Mormonism that are not treated here—including the seating of Mormon apostle and senator Reed Smoot during the first decade of the twentieth century, prosecutions of the new polygamists of the twentieth and twenty-first centuries, the campaign against the national Equal Rights Amendment and for Proposition 8 in California, free-speech issues in Salt Lake City in the areas surrounding Temple Square, the rights of church employees, the role of lawyers in the modern church, and tax exemptions for church property, just to name a few.

This chapter, therefore, is one way of thinking about the relationship of law, religion, and politics in nineteenth-century Mormonism, rather than an attempt to cover the entire field. It is helpful to focus distinctly on the pre-statehood period, in part because careful attention to the role of law and lawyers changes the way we think about the early church and Utah during the formative territorial period. This perspective qualifies the standard "Americanization of Utah for statehood" story that we have seen in the works of leading historians in the field; it also complicates the story. Lawyers initially were not welcome in Utah; their craft was widely condemned among Mormons for distorting the truth and sowing conflict among the Saints. Eventually, lawyers were key to the negotiations that brought resolution to the long and painful contest over polygamy and Mormon claims to self-governance in Utah. In that sense, Brigham Young was right, lawyers *were* dangerous to Zion—whether they were Mormon or not. They helped undo the most controversial tissues of difference that separated Mormons from "Gentiles," as all non-Mormons were called. Lawyers on both sides of the divide over Mormonism found common ground as they litigated in the 1870s and '80s. So this chapter documents a "legalization of Utah for statehood," a refinement of prior work, based on research into the role of lawyers in bringing change to the Great Basin Kingdom in the late nineteenth and early twentieth centuries.[2]

The New Dispensation
and its Legal Troubles

During his short life, Joseph Smith was involved in many legal conflicts, including well over 200 lawsuits, whether as a defendant, witness, or plaintiff. He also presided over courts and government, particularly as mayor of Nauvoo, Illinois, an office that included responsibilities as justice of the peace and presiding judge of the municipal court of Nauvoo. Three major cases provide some background for Smith's legal world, and for the ways secular law and lawyers affected the early church. Ultimately, the legal system did more than just harass the Prophet, it betrayed him and led to his death at the hands of a lynch mob in 1844.

For almost twenty years before his martyrdom, Smith received a series of lessons in the power and limits of law and legal action. Among the most important early cases was a complaint brought against Smith in 1826, which claimed that he had been hired by a Pennsylvania man to locate a long-lost Spanish silver mine along the banks of the Susquehanna River using certain stones "by which he could discern things invisible to the natural eye." The nephew of the Pennsylvania treasure seeker charged that Smith had defrauded his gullible uncle. A local newspaper also reported that Smith had been tried as a "disorderly person," who was known as a "glass-looker, pretending to discover" hidden treasure. Smith's seer stones were recognized tools among the many diviners and cunning folk of his era who sought hidden truths of the spirit as well as of the earth in millennial and perfectionist religious movements.[3]

Smith himself took the witness stand at trial. He readily admitted that he had a stone that could reveal "hidden treasures in the bowels of the earth," but denied making a profession as a diviner.[4] The man who hired him was also vigorous in Smith's defense; he was certain that Joseph had powers to divine. The defendant, in other words, challenged the complaint on the grounds that there was no "pretending" about him, he was a true seer. The outcome of the trial was not included in the records, and scholars disagree about the likely outcome. From a modern legal perspective, the nephew (who had not been harmed, as far as we know) would not have had standing to complain that his uncle had been defrauded by Smith.

Other charges of disorderly conduct against Smith were brought after the publication of the "Golden Bible" and the organization of the church in early 1830. This time, the complaint was that he caused "an uproar by preaching the Book of Mormon" and claimed "angelic visitations," all in an effort to get money from those who came to hear him. Smith was acquitted after a trial that lasted two full days, but was immediately rearrested and apparently charged with casting out a devil, only to be acquitted once more. In both trials, Smith had "legal" counsel, two non-Mormon farmers "well versed in the laws" who claimed that the accusers were simple bigots.

Charges of fraud followed the Prophet to Ohio, where in early 1837 Smith and other Mormon leaders established a rogue bank after their request to create a legal one had been denied by the state legislature. The Kirtland Safety Society Anti-Banking Company was ill-considered and ill-timed, and its notes were by definition fraudulent. They were also worthless, it turned out, because the Panic of 1837 engulfed the Kirtland Safety Society as it did many other banks. Smith was charged criminally and sued for debt in civil court. Of ten judgments against him, three were satisfied in full, three in part, and four not at all. Smith complained about "malicious and vexatious law suits," but this incident tarnished his reputation among some followers as well as non-Mormons. When the Prophet left Ohio for Missouri in 1838, he was bankrupt and his opponents had come to believe that he regarded himself as above the law. Smith and those who went with him went from the frying pan into the fire.

In October 1838, Missouri Governor Lilburn Boggs capped a crescendo of mutual antagonism between Mormons and Gentiles with an order to drive the Saints from the state or "exterminate" them. Boggs had learned that Mormons had engaged in a battle with what they mistakenly thought was a mob of anti-Mormons, but in fact was a contingent of the state militia. One soldier had died in the confrontation, giving his opponents fuel for charging the Prophet with serious crimes indeed. Four days later, and one day after seventeen Mormons had been ambushed and murdered by a mob in Haun's Mill, Joseph Smith was arrested for treason. At their arraignment, the judge held that there was enough evidence to proceed, and Smith and a handful of other Mormon leaders spent the next six months in jail awaiting trial. Scholars have argued that Smith might plausibly have been charged with inciting larceny and receiving stolen goods, and also possibly encouraging arson and insurrection, but not treason. Smith was determined to fight back against his enemies; he advocated attacking the homes and property of anti-Mormon vigilantes, and taking their property to the bishop's storehouse, where it would be distributed to Saints who had been victimized by mobs. "[The Prophet's] angry rhetoric stirred the blood of more militant [followers]," concluded one recent biography.[5]

Smith had not himself taken part in any violence, however. It was also clear that Boggs extermination order had gone too far and the treason charge was unsubstantiated. It became a profound embarrassment to Missouri around the country. When Smith escaped from jail and fled to Illinois, therefore, Missouri officials were saved from a growing scandal. They could conveniently label Smith an outlaw, while Mormons concluded that Gentile law was irredeemably corrupt.[6]

In the new Mormon city of Nauvoo, Smith received a charter from the Illinois state legislature that granted substantial rights of self-government. There, Smith served as mayor, justice of the peace, and presiding judge of the municipal court. Lilburn Boggs of Missouri, however, had not forgotten his old enemy. When in 1842 Boggs was attacked and shot several times through a window in his home, he concluded that Smith must have ordered his assassination. Missouri issued an extradition order for Smith, to which the Mormons responded by issuing a writ of habeas corpus they claimed was valid under the Nauvoo city charter. According to the Mormons, the writ also allowed the municipal court to investigate the merits of the extradition warrant, truly a vast increase in local legal power in contravention of the traditional understanding of the writ. This sophistry outraged many around the country, and once again charges of fraudulent manipulation of the law were leveled against Mormons in general and Smith in particular.

When the prophet went into hiding to avoid arrest, the situation became dire indeed. A new Missouri governor, however, eventually assured all concerned that he did not want to stoke the controversy, and Smith surrendered to federal officials in late 1842. Federal District Court Judge Nathaniel Pope found the extradition order was invalid not on the merits, but because it did not allege that Smith had committed a crime in Missouri. However sound the legal reasoning, "the feeling [outside the Mormon community] persisted that Joseph had once again ducked through legal loopholes, and this rankled his enemies." The fact that he had many outstanding debts and tried to declare bankruptcy at this time also added to the claim that Smith had manipulated the legal system to his own advantage at the expense of others.[7]

Over the succeeding months, Smith's growing political, religious, and military power exacerbated the sense that he viewed himself as above the law. Smith himself, although he had once contemplated studying law, became a candidate for president of the United States in 1844, with a platform that reflected his dislike of the profession after long experience as a defendant in legal proceedings: "Like the good Samaritan, send every lawyer as soon as he repents and obeys the ordinances of heaven, to preach the gospel to the destitute without purse or script."[8]

The most dangerous phase of this debate over law arose within the Mormon community, when a group of influential Nauvoo residents became openly critical of the Prophet in early 1844. They charged him with personal and political immorality, especially for his practice of polygamy; this dissenting group also planned to start an opposition newspaper. The situation devolved into a series of lawsuits and criminal complaints against the dissenters, including assault, perjury, gambling, insulting city officials, and resisting arrest. Despite all this, the newspaper, called the *Nauvoo Expositor*, was finally published in early June. It was so critical of Smith that he called it "a greater nuisance than a dead carcass." When the city council obligingly enacted an ordinance giving the mayor the power to suppress dangerous libels, Smith ordered the Nauvoo marshal to destroy the press and burn all copies of the offending publication.

As one leading study put it, "the destruction of the *Nauvoo Expositor* was the death-knell for the legal sanctuary the Mormons had created in Nauvoo."[9] Although some scholars have defended Smith's right under law to "abate" the *Expositor* as a nuisance, most agree that the freedom of the press was the paramount legal standard. The Sedition Act of 1798, which made criminals of Republican opponents of the first Adams administration (especially troublesome newspaper editors), unleashed a torrent of criticism of government authoritarianism when conservative Federalists revealed their distrust of freedom of speech, press, and the right to free political opposition. After they learned of the destruction of the press in Nauvoo forty years later, non-Mormons in areas surrounding Nauvoo drew on this legacy to create an uproar. The outcry was so virulent that the Illinois governor openly doubted his ability to control the state militia if Smith did not surrender. Smith, who first went into hiding across the Missouri border, eventually turned himself in when his wife Emma wrote to him that the entire population of Nauvoo was in danger of being attacked and the governor finally assured Smith that he would guarantee his safety. Yet after Smith was in custody in nearby Carthage, Illinois, the governor left a local anti-Mormon militia in charge of the jail. Within hours, a group of men with blackened faces stormed the small structure, murdered Joseph and his brother Hyrum Smith, and wounded one other Mormon.

The subsequent investigation of the lynching resulted in indictments against nine men, of whom five stood trial. All were acquitted; by now, Mormon witnesses so distrusted the legal system in general and Carthage in particular, that they went into hiding to avoid subpoenas. This time, instead of escalating the violence into civil war, the Saints retreated far away, taking themselves into the wild vastness of the western frontier.

When Joseph Smith had gone into hiding in late June 1844, he and his brother planned to escape to the Great Basin in the Rocky Mountains. After his death, Smith's successor Brigham Young led the Saints on a remarkable exodus—westward to the refuge that Smith had already chosen. There in the Great Basin, Mormons finally found the freedom to build a society from the ground up. Lawyers were not part of the picture.

ORDER WITHOUT LAWYERS

Latter-day Saints were a deeply law-bound people from the earliest period. At the same time, they shared their dislike of lawyers with many other Americans, then and now. But especially in Utah they took antilawyerism to new heights, and often mixed in disdain for significant parts of the American legal system, including the common law. Brigham Young's distrust of lawyers is important to the unfolding story, as well as to his eventual and reluctant encouragement of a profession that Young had long despised, to positions of significant power. This part of the story is a tale of "order without lawyers," drawing an analogy with the work of legal theorists who argue that it is possible to have well-functioning communities without the presence of law.[10] In other words, they argue that the formal rule of law is often a hindrance to communities that develop effective self-governance. In many senses, they are arguing against official processes and those who administer them—in other words, they think that many aspects of life would be better without lawyers.

Brigham Young would have agreed with these scholars. And indeed the order without law movement draws unconsciously on utopian ideas that Young shared with other religious leaders in the heady decades of the early nineteenth century. Building on the opening claim of this chapter, John Humphrey Noyes, leader of the Oneida Perfectionists, put it this way: "we hate lawsuits as we hate war." Brigham Young, too, was deeply opposed to litigation, and especially to the common law. Lawsuits between Mormons were strongly discouraged. Young condemned litigation as an evil "that opens a wide door, when indulged in, for the admission of every unclean spirit." In other words, going to secular law marked a spiritual failure that threatened the entire community.[11]

Among the first acts of the Mormon-controlled Utah territorial legislature was the passage of a statute that included prohibition of actions to collect lawyers' fees. This provision echoed a seventeenth-century Massachusetts statute, but also went far beyond anything the New England Puritans had designed. Local Utah courts were also forbidden to cite legal precedent or apply the common law. In particular, legal technicalities were to be avoided at all costs. Any legal representative who was found not to have pursued the "truth" of the matter in his representation of a client was subject to disbarment, a fine of $100, and imprisonment. Even then, Mormons were encouraged in the strongest terms not to use these courts, but to bring their disputes to the local bishop, who would resolve the disagreement, or send the parties on to the ecclesiastical courts—a ghost court system run by the church that handled the nuts and bolts of internal dispute resolution throughout the territorial period and beyond.

Litigation between Mormons and non-Mormons was handled by the local probate courts, whose jurisdiction was extensive. Usually, probate courts decide questions of wills and estates, guardianship, and the like. In Utah, the Mormon-controlled territorial legislature granted probate courts the power to hear all criminal as well as civil cases. Probate judges were elected to four-year terms—in many cases, the local bishop and judge of the ecclesiastical court was also the probate judge. These courts also drew up jury lists for federal as well as local courts in the territory.

The probate courts were designed to function without the presence of lawyers, and to rely only on common sense, rather than on legal technicalities. As Brigham Young put it, lawyers were "pettifoggers" whose "specious . . . pretenses," and "servil[ity]" kept them hostage to "the musty rubbish of ages gone." One contemporary observed about his Mormon brethren: "Their [peculiar] judicial economy was after the patterns of the New Testament rather than after the patterns of Blackstone. It was this which made Mormon rule so obnoxious to Federal judges and Gentile lawyers. Federal judges could not possibly find their vocation in a purely Mormon commonwealth, nor could Gentile lawyers reach the pockets of the people."[12]

The extraordinary powers of the local courts were matched by Mormon control of the political system, which united church and state as a means of building the Kingdom of God in anticipation of the Millennium. Once again, Mormons' attempt to establish a separate and utopian society triggered charges of partiality and deception from outsiders. Mormon control of judges and juries, and their dislike of lawyers, led non-Mormons to conclude that they could not hope for justice in Utah's probate courts. They complained that yet again Mormons had used legal loopholes to evade law by which other Americans were bound. In particular, federal legislation designed to extend the civil law to Utah was frustrated by Mormon claims to self-government in the territory. For example, the legislative mandate for selection of all juries through the probate courts guaranteed that no jury, even those empanelled in the federal courts for the territory, would enforce antipolygamy laws. Federal judges sent to Utah, as well as non-Mormons in the territory, complained long and loud about the futility of attempting to enforce federal laws. By the late 1860s, even the federal judges acknowledged that an 1862 federal statute that outlawed polygamy was "a dead letter" in Utah. Mormons replied that they viewed the law as unconstitutional, so that lack of enforcement was evidence of the law's fundamental invalidity, rather than their lawlessness.

For twenty years, the Mormons had the best of this argument. And some scholars have claimed that the law dealt by the probate courts was rough, but also roughly fair. But lawyers were always and passionately opposed to this system. They included ambitious young men who came to Utah during or after the Civil War hoping to build lucrative careers in mining law after the discovery of silver. Instead, they found themselves a despised microminority within a larger and also embattled non-Mormon community in Utah in the 1860s.

Even more important, territorial officials who were hired by the federal government and charged with governing Utah found themselves frozen out. Their livelihoods depended on persuading Washington that they and legal process—rather than the army (politics by military means)—were the best way to save Utah and its benighted inhabitants from the clutches of religious fanaticism and violent oppression. These federal officials were natural conduits for antipolygamy: their presence in the territory reflected anti-Mormonism in the east, and bolstered criticism of Mormon polygamy and other departures from the law and practice in the rest of the country, and broadcast their complaints back to Washington, and so on. The order without lawyers that Mormons had hoped to create looked more and more to the outside world like a society gone badly wrong. Something had to give.

Lawyering Up

Gradually, it became evident to Mormon leaders that defense of Zion required legal expertise. Pressure from Congress and territorial judges, including revocation of the incorporation of the church, indictments of Brigham Young and other Mormon leaders for lewd and lascivious cohabitation, legal proceedings against Mormons for polygamy and the Mountain Meadows Massacre, and the complex litigation surrounding Young's estate after his death in 1877, all contributed to the development of a legal strategy to defend the church. Lawyers soon followed, both Mormon and eventually non-Mormon, as debates over Mormon distinctiveness and religious rights flowed into legal channels.

The president of the church himself recognized that many of his own difficulties were legal. By the early 1870s, Brigham Young had been arrested, sued for alimony by an estranged plural wife, his adopted son John D. Lee had been excommunicated and was under investigation for his part in the Mountain Meadows Massacre, and the jurisdiction of the probate courts and their powers to control jury selection had been sharply reduced by federal legislation. These setbacks occurred as Young lost some of his edge to old age. His opposition to lawyers had long deterred young Mormon men from pursuing careers in the law. Now, he began to relent. In the early 1850s, Young said openly, "we have no use for lawyers," whose study of the law led them to "forsak[e] the Gospel." By the mid-1870s, however, Young began to call for talented young men to enter the legal profession, so that they could defend the Kingdom of God against those who would undermine it by the deployment of a hostile legal system.

The career of Franklin S. Richards illustrates the potential and perils created by Young's conclusion that a coterie of loyal Mormon lawyers was needed to defend the Saints in court. Richards recalled sixty years later that Young took him aside as a very young man and advised him to study law, so that he could represent Latter-day Saints when they were attacked by the legal weaponry of those outside the faith, especially the federal government. After he read law "alone," Richards was admitted to the bar in 1874. He was the first fresh Mormon face among a growing non-Mormon legal community. Richards served as general counsel to the church for thirty years, and was perennial co-counsel on briefs to the United States Supreme Court, often appearing at oral argument as back-up to whichever high-profile lawyer had been hired to argue the case in Washington. Richards' law firm defended prominent Mormons accused of crimes related to polygamy at trial and on appeal in Salt Lake and Ogden. He was apparently retained by the church to appear for these defendants, which if true would create an interesting conflict of interest. The church opposed promises by church members to obey antipolygamy laws in return for light or suspended sentences, but individual defendants may have wished to avoid prison terms by making such promises.[13] If the lawyer who represented them counseled against such pleas, then he acted against their interests this is a well-known ethical quandary.

Indeed, his work on behalf of polygamous Mormon men required Richards to walk a tightrope, ethically and legally. Richards himself never took a plural wife. Instead, he quietly but consistently opposed continuation of polygamy, a practice that clearly deterred the economic development of the territory and prevented its admission to the union as a state. Yet, Richards was so successful at mediating between Mormons and federal officials that he eventually became the law partner of former prosecutor Charles Varian, who was widely attacked by the Mormon press in the 1880s as a virulent anti-Mormon.

Other Mormon lawyers followed similar professional paths. Gradually, these young lawyers built an articulate and successful defense bar. Joseph Rawlins hung his shingle in the 1870s, and handled many complex and delicate matters for the church, including polygamy defense work and parts of the long and bitter litigation surrounding the estate of Brigham Young. Rawlins, who was also a monogamist, took the leading role in the establishment of the influential Democratic Club of Utah in 1884. Several other young lawyers were prominent members of the club, among them Richards and others whose names appeared frequently as defense counsel in the flood of polygamy prosecutions that dominated the life of Utah territory by the mid-1880s. The club's initial platform included this statement: "We firmly repudiate the idea that any citizen is under obligation to take his political counsel from those whose avowed purpose is a continued violation of law." That is, this organization, which included leading young Mormon lawyers, departed sharply both from the admonition, commonly attributed to Brigham Young's successor as church president and his advisers, that polygamy must be defended at all costs. Instead, this political club endorsed obedience to law as the means to advancement.[14]

Yet another exemplary lawyer from outside the Salt Lake area was Samuel Thurman, the leading lawyer in Provo, who by the early 1880s was an up-and-coming young attorney within the Mormon fold. He was a member of the territorial legislature from 1882 to 1890. He was also a Democrat (rather than a member of the Mormon People's Party) and a monogamist, quietly resisting both the political and marital structures of an older generation of Mormon leaders. No doubt because of these attributes, Thurman served as the US Attorney for Utah from 1892 to 1896, the first time in forty years that a Mormon had held the post. By the 1880s when Thurman's career took off, he and other astute Mormon lawyers had begun attending formal law schools in the East, working across religious barriers (Thurman was the law partner of future Supreme Court Justice George Sutherland for several years) and working hard to achieve statehood for Utah.

SETTLEMENT

Ironically, the prominence of these young lawyers within their profession was achieved through defending in court a practice that they eschewed in their private lives. Like the trained professionals they were, however, Thurman, Richards, and their co-counsel crafted plausible legal arguments in defense of their polygamous clients. They had some impressive wins, forcing prosecutors and judges to craft new and far less devastating methods and legal strategies. Yet most of the lawyers in this story did well, Mormon as well as non-Mormon after 1880. The careers of two older lawyers, who shared the limited legal work in the territory before the advent of aggressive federal enforcement, demonstrate far much the professional environment for lawyers had improved. Both Aurelius Miner and Zerubabbel Snow were trained as lawyers before the exodus to Utah. Together, they represented the legal talent of the Latter-day Saints. Both had faded from view by the 1880s; Miner especially was despised by the federal judges sent by Washington to enforce the law in Utah, and eventually was found guilty of unlawful cohabitation in 1885 and served six months in prison. He was then disbarred from legal practice, although his professional biography does not mention his conviction.

Aside from a few incidents such as Miner's conviction, the legalization of Utah was swift and successful. Utah went from a territory where lawyers' influence was banned in 1850, to a place in which lawyers called many of the shots, all in the space of about thirty-five years—a generation, in other words. In his study of the territorial Southwest, the historian Howard Lamar remarked on generational differences in Utah in the late 1880s. He argued that the Latter-day Saints, who had begun in the 1830s with youthful and physically powerful men at the helm, were now governed by much more seasoned and undeniably old men. Wilford Woodruff, for example, was eighty-two when he became church president in 1889. George Q. Cannon was twenty years younger, and was far more modern than Woodruff. But it was the next generation, with promising lawyers such as Richards, Rawlins, and Thurman, who were forty-somethings in the 1880s, who ushered in an age of professional specialization, a far cry from the frontier "jacks of all trades," as Lamar put it.[15]

Lamar's focus on change across generations can be extended to the way that the legal profession marked the men of this third generation as thinkers and actors in Utah. Lawyers managed reconciliation in the territory, helping craft a workable framework for government in the early 1890s. What they eventually settled on was a draft constitution that closely tracked the structure of government in other states. These constitutions were the product of lawyerly thinking, and placed lawyers frequently in positions of power. The pattern is familiar to students of American history: the historian John Murrin studied late-colonial Massachusetts and found a roughly parallel track for legal culture there and for the triumph of legalism, with its embrace of formality of argument and procedure, clearly defined standards and precedents, and so on. At the national level, moreover, twenty-six out of forty-four presidents have been lawyers; 45 percent of Congress currently is composed of lawyers.

When the constitutional convention convened in Salt Lake City in 1894 to draft the document that would finally admit Utah into the Union as a state, Utah's leading lawyers were there. There members of the Mormon defense bar met with prosecutors and judges who had sent Mormon polygamists to jail and had excluded all Mormon men from jury pools. Together, they buried the ideological and religious differences that had been so divisive only two decades earlier. As a group with a shared vocabulary and shared goals, these men figured prominently at the convention, replicated the basic structures of other American governments, and resolved the fundamental question that had so dominated Utah history. Thus they ended the battle that had created the bench and bar, and brought lawyers to power.[16] Polygamy, they concluded, would forever be a felony in Utah.

If lawyers and the legal profession were the beneficiaries of the long and bitter antipolygamy campaign, there were also clear losers, even though we often don't remember their losses. The focus of the campaign against polygamy gradually yet steadily excluded women. In the 1870s and even in the early 1880s, women's organizations could realistically be considered the vanguard of antipolygamy activism. Women such as Ann Eliza Webb Young "divorced" Brigham Young and then went on a spectacularly successful nationwide lecture tour, and Angie Newman campaigned for an "industrial Christian home" for escaped plural wives. Ann Eliza was a sensation when Brigham Young flaunted his power and polygamy. And Angie Newman argued strenuously that women should have a refuge from patriarchy. They gradually found themselves sidelined over the course of the 1880s.

Once prosecutions began in earnest, both women lost their public following. Ann Eliza Young's career collapsed in the 1880s, and she fell into such obscurity that even her place and date of death are unknown. Angie Newman was outraged to learn that the Industrial Home that she had fought for and which was supposed to temper male-dominated justice with woman's mercy, was in fact turned over to men the moment it was built. (Utah's three territorial judges and federal prosecutors, all lawyers, made up the board, together with Territorial Governor Caleb West, also a lawyer.) Within three years, it became not a refuge but a poor house, and after only over six years, it closed on the unanimous recommendation of its all-male governing board.

Another group of women also lost from the shift to law as the primary vector for antipolygamy. As is often the case in criminal trials, the purported victim gradually faded from public view. The actors in polygamy prosecutions (both defense and prosecution) were exclusively male. It was men who accused, tried, and defended other men. By no means should we minimize the suffering of Mormon men who were sent to prison for living their religion. But the battle against polygamy had begun under the banner of women's place in a democratic society—women's interest in monogamy, the respect for women that was essential to an American state, and so on. And it was defended in the early days on many of the same grounds—on the superiority of polygamy and its capacity to ensure a husband for every woman, on motherhood, and on the duties of men to wives.

The prosecutions of the late 1870s through the early 1890s exposed women to the law, not only because their husbands were incarcerated. Women were called upon to be witnesses in countless cases. They struggled to be loyal and faithful, yet also to tell the truth. Often they failed to manage these contradictory mandates. Dozens of women were prosecuted for perjury; hundreds more perjured themselves out of desperation. Almost 200 women were also prosecuted for fornication, a crime typically reserved for prostitutes and the odd serving girl who got pregnant on the job. In territorial Utah, women who were understood in their communities as upstanding and chaste faced such charges. They have been left out of the historical scholarship and even contemporary accounts, an oversight that no doubt reflects the shame of the fornicator label at the time, but that should not be replicated through historians' focus on men alone.

Last in our list of those screened about by the legalization of Utah is the army. It was a constant presence in the background, and sometimes in the foreground, such as in the Utah War of the late 1850s. Most of the time, Mormon defendants and territorial officials avoided violence. Both sides had strategic interests in avoiding the armed intervention that would surely follow outright violence, but they fought a deadly serious conflict in the courts. Mormons, of course, knew well after the Utah War and the Mountain Meadows Massacre, and even more certainly after the Civil War, that open rebellion or even sustained rhetorical challenge to the national government could not be a winning tactic. Mormon defendants and the church as a whole were committed to a policy of resistance that fell just short of provoking martial law.

Territorial court personnel had a related interest. They strove to deploy law rather than war as the means of political change, because their jobs depended on the perception that the court system was the most effective means of dealing with defiance of federal legislation in territorial Utah. All legal processes channel violent behavior into confined spaces, controlled by the state. In that sense, lawyers presided over a bloodless war against Mormons in the late nineteenth century.

In the process, the professional bar created connective threads between Saints and Gentiles, establishing political as well as legal avenues for cooperation. Even as lawyers on both sides they fought bitterly over "the Raid," which saw some 3,000 indictments of Mormon men and several hundred of Mormon women, they developed a unifying professional ethic. In the end, law and government in Utah followed well-worn paths. Reconciliation and eventually statehood were negotiated and implemented in ways similar to other American jurisdictions. The "fusion" movement, as the conciliators were known by the late 1880s, was dominated by lawyers and integrated groups such as the Democratic Club, and included young and middle-aged Mormons and non-Mormons more interested in developing the territory and achieving statehood than in squabbling over polygamy. In 1887, this group supported a proposed constitution for Utah that included a provision outlawing bigamy and polygamy. B. H. Roberts, a polygamist who had fled prosecution in the late 1880s, future congressman-elect, and historian of the church, noted disdainfully in his history the "murmurings and complainings among the people" that reached a critical level in the late 1880s. He also lamented the growing "number of those who were willing, against the general policy of church leaders, to promise obedience to the antipolygamy laws for the future and thus escape punishment."[17]

When Wilford Woodruff's Manifesto appeared in 1890, it was one product of feverish negotiations between Mormon leaders and members of the Senate Judiciary Committee, which was considering a drastically punitive bill that would have disfranchised all Mormons and abolished the territorial legislature. But even as Congress debated the most draconian action yet for Utah, there were signs in the territory itself that the war of laws was all but over. The Manifesto came as no surprise to lawyers Franklin S. Richards and Samuel Thurman, or even, it seems, to leading federal judges and other legal officials who had led the prosecution of polygamists but were just as eager as others to resolve the stand-off. All were poised to take advantage of the phenomenal growth in economic activity that the end of the war would bring: development of the territory had been artificially slowed by concentration on the one great issue. Richards soon introduced the motion that officially dissolved the People's Party, to which all good Mormons had belonged: he then joined Thurman and Rawlins in the Democratic Party.

As the professional history of lawyers put it in the early twentieth century, "the fields of brilliant achievements in the arenas offered by law" had captured local sons of Utah, as well as drawing ambitious young lawyers from outside the faith. There they worked to rationalize and organize a familiar form of government, and then settled in to run the new state of Utah after its admission in 1896. Quietly but inexorably, lawyers assumed their traditional dominance, a process that completed "the legalization of Utah."

NOTES

1. Von Clausewitz, *On War*, 1:24.
2. See, for example, Larson, *"Americanization" of Utah for Statehood.*
3. Smith, *Biographical Sketches of Joseph Smith the Prophet*, 91–92.
4. Testimony reprinted in Brodie, *No Man Knows My History*, 427.
5. Bushman, *Joseph Smith*, 371.
6. Quinn, "Culture of Violence in Joseph Smith's Mormonism," 23–25; Hartley, *My Best for the Kingdom*, 29, 42; Madsen, "Joseph Smith and the Missouri Court of Inquiry," 116–22.
7. Thurston, "Boggs Shooting and Attempted Extradition," 55. Smith's petition in bankruptcy listed his debts at $73,000, including almost $5,000 for a promissory note to purchase a steamboat from the federal government. After much negotiation and proposals from both sides in late 1842 and early 1843 for settlement that would have had Smith paying off the federal debt in full over several years, the case nonetheless remained unresolved when Smith was murdered in 1844, and eventually his property was sold in 1852 to pay the federal note (valued at $7,870.23). Oaks and Bentley, "Joseph Smith and Legal Process," 773–79.
8. *General Smith's Views*, 7; Poll, "Joseph Smith and the Presidency," 17–21.
9. Firmage and Mangrum, *Zion in the Courts*, 113.
10. Ellickson, *Order without Law*; Woodward, *Lobster Coast*.
11. Noyes quoted in Robertson, *Oneida Community*, 292; Weisbrod, *Boundaries of Utopia*, 115–22; Young speaking in 1852, quoted in Bancroft, *History of Utah*, 440n1.

12. Young quoted in *Latter-day Saints Millennial Star* [Liverpool], May 19, 1852, 216; Tullidge, *Life of Brigham Young*, 200.
13. On the conflict over such promises, see Whitney, *History of Utah*, 3: 358–59.
14. Rawlins was alienated from the Church by the mid-1880s, Rawlins, *Unfavored Few*.
15. Lamar, *Far Southwest*, 399–400.
16. *History of the Bench and Bar of Utah.*
17. Roberts, *Comprehensive History of the Church of Jesus Christ of Latter-day Saints*, 6: 217.

BIBLIOGRAPHY

Alexander, Thomas G. "Charles S. Zane: Apostle of the New Era." *Utah Historical Quarterly* 34, no. 3 (Fall 1966): 290–314.

Alexander, Thomas G. "Federal Authority versus Polygamic Theocracy: James B. McKean and the Mormons, 1870–1875." *Dialogue: A Journal of Mormon Thought* 1, no. 3 (Autumn 1966): 85–100.

Allen, James B. "The Unusual Jurisdiction of the County Probate Courts in Territorial Utah." *Utah Historical Quarterly* 36, no. 2 (Spring 1968): 132–42.

Arrington, Leonard J. "The Settlement of the Brigham Young Estate, 1877–79." *Pacific Historical Review* 21 (1952): 1–20.

Backman, James. H. "The Early Church and the Legal Profession." J. Reuben Clark Law Society, 2004. http://www.jrcls.org/publications/perspectives/backman%20early.lds.attorneys.jan9.04.pdf.

Bancroft, H. H. *History of Utah, 1540–1887.* San Francisco, CA: Bancroft, 1890.

Bentley, Joseph I. "The Legal Trials of Joseph Smith." *Encyclopedia of Mormonism.* Ed. Daniel H. Ludlow. 4 vols. New York: Macmillan, 1992.

Brodie, Fawn M. *No Man Knows My History: The Life of Joseph Smith.* 2nd ed. New York: Alfred A. Knopf, 1995.

Brooke, John L. *The Refiner's Fire: The Making of Mormon Cosmology, 1644–1844.* New York: Cambridge University Press, 1994.

Bushman, Richard L. *Joseph Smith: Rough Stone Rolling.* New York: Alfred A. Knopf, 2005.

von Clausewitz, Carl. *On War.* Trans. J. J. Graham. 3 vols. London: Kegan Paul, 1918.

Driggs, Kenneth. "'Lawyers of Their Own to Defend Them': The Legal Career of Franklin Snyder Richards." *Journal of Mormon History* 21, no. 2 (Fall 1995): 84–125.

Ellickson, Robert C. *Order without Law: How Neighbors Resolve Disputes.* Cambridge, MA: Harvard University Press, 1991.

Firmage, Edwin B., and Richard Collin Mangrum. *Zion in the Courts: A Legal History of the Latter-day Saints, 1830–1900.* Urbana: University of Illinois Press, 1988.

General Smith's Views of the Powers and Policy of the Government of the United States. Nauvoo, IL: John Taylor, 1844.

Gordon, Sarah Barringer. *The Mormon Question: Polygamy and Constitutional Conflict in Nineteenth-Century America.* Chapel Hill: North Carolina University Press, 2002.

Gordon, Sarah Barringer. "The Twin Relic of Barbarism: A Legal History of Antipolygamy in Nineteenth-Century America." PhD diss., Princeton University, 1995.

Hartley, William G. *My Best for the Kingdom: History and Autobiography of John Lowe Butler.* Aspen, CO: Aspen, 1993.

Heimberger, Ron. *Brother Brigham's Book III: Lawyers and the Law*. Springville, UT: Cedar Fort, 1996.

History of the Bench and Bar of Utah. Salt Lake City: Interstate Press Association, 1913.

Lamar, Howard R. *The Far Southwest, 1846–1912: A Territorial History*. New Haven, CT: Yale University Press, 1966.

Larson, Gustive O. *The "Americanization" of Utah for Statehood*. San Marino, CA: Huntington Library, 1971.

Madsen, Gordon A. "Joseph Smith and the Missouri Court of Inquiry: Austin A. King's Quest for Hostages." *BYU Studies* 43, no. 4 (2004): 93–136.

Oaks, Dallin H. "The Suppression of the *Nauvoo Expositor*." *Utah Law Review* 9, no. 4 (Winter 1965): 862–903.

Oaks, Dallin H., and Joseph I. Bentley. "Joseph Smith and Legal Process: In the Wake of the Steamboat Nauvoo." *Brigham Young University Law Review* 1976, no. 3 (1976): 735–82.

Oaks, Dallin H., and Marvin S. Hill. *Carthage Conspiracy: The Trial of the Accused Assassins of Joseph Smith*. Urbana: University of Illinois Press, 1975.

Pascoe, Peggy. *Relations of Rescue: The Search for Female Moral Authority in the American West, 1874–1939*. New York: Oxford University Press, 1993.

Poll, Richard D. "Joseph Smith and the Presidency, 1844." *Dialogue, a Journal of Mormon Thought* 3, no. 3 (Autumn 1968): 17–21.

Quinn, D. Michael. *Early Mormonism and the Magic World View*. Salt Lake City, UT: Signature, 1987.

Quinn, D. Michael "The Culture of Violence in Joseph Smith's Mormonism." *Sunstone*, October 19, 2011. https://www.sunstonemagazine.com/wp-content/uploads/sbi/articles/164-16-38.pdf.

Rawlins, Joseph L. *"The Unfavored Few": The Autobiography of Joseph L. Rawlins*. Ed. Alta Rawlins Jensen. Carmel, CA: Author, 1956.

Roberts, Brigham H. *Comprehensive History of the Church of Jesus Christ of Latter-day Saints: Century 1*. 6 vols. Salt Lake City, UT: Church of Jesus Christ of Latter-day Saints, 1930.

Robertson, C. N. *Oneida Community: The Breakup, 1876–1881*. Syracuse, NY: Syracuse University Press, 1972.

Smith, Lucy Mack. *Biographical Sketches of Joseph Smith the Prophet, and His Progenitors for Many Generations*. Liverpool: Orson Pratt, 1853.

Thurston, Morris A. "The Boggs Shooting and Attempted Extradition: Joseph Smith's Most Famous Case." *BYU Studies* 48, no. 1 (2009): 5–56.

Tullidge, Edward W. *The Life of Brigham Young*. Salt Lake City, UT: Star Printing, 1877.

Weisbrod, Carol. *The Boundaries of Utopia*. New York: Pantheon, 1980.

Whitney, Orson F. *History of Utah*. 4 vols. Salt Lake City, UT: G. Q. Cannon, 1892–1904.

Woodward, Colin. *The Lobster Coast: Rebels, Rusticators and the Struggle for a Forgotten Frontier*. New York: Penguin, 2005.

CHAPTER 39

MORMONISM IN THE AMERICAN POLITICAL DOMAIN

NOAH R. FELDMAN

POLITICO-RELIGIOUS CONFLICT AND THE GEOPOLITICS OF SPACE

CONSIDER the history of Mormonism and American politics through two distinct, equally important lenses.[1] The first focuses on the interaction between American political institutions and Mormon religious beliefs and practices. Broadly speaking, this is a story of government repression, religious response, and eventual, gradual resolution. Shaped powerfully, though not exclusively, by plural marriage and its aftershocks, the story can be encapsulated in a single fact. The Republican Party, which once condemned Mormonism alongside slavery as one of the "twin relics of barbarism,"[2] nominated the grandson of a polygamist for the presidency in 2012. The historical story that moves from condemnation to acceptance forms an important chapter in the annals of bigotry, toleration, and socioreligious change. The lens for understanding the story focuses our attention on ideas, practices, and legal-political institutions.

The second lens for understanding Mormonism and American politics refracts the geopolitics of space. From the time that Brigham Young brought the refugee Mormons to the new Zion in Utah, Mormonism became inextricably linked to the settling, pacification, irrigation, and economic development of a major portion of the American intermountain West.[3] If the history of American politics must be understood generally in the light of the dual projects of territorial expansion and political integration, Mormonism played an important and, in a sense, unique role in those dynamics. Alone among important post-Puritan American settlers, Mormons organized themselves into a political order that was simultaneously religious and geographic-territorial. Once it was organized into a territory and then a state, Utah was no longer officially a religious entity. Yet the state's official seal, which bears the Mormon religious symbol of the bee-hive, serves as a concrete reminder that a religio-political enclave can exist and function politically without the formal recognition of the state.[4]

The history of Mormonism as a religio-political movement, developing land while simultaneously interacting with the federal US government, itself constitutes a story of tension, partial strategic accommodation, and eventual resolution. Put simply, the genius of moving the bulk of the Mormon community to a new and previously neglected settlement zone was that it gave Mormonism bargaining power relative to the anti-Mormon trends in American political life. If Mormons could successfully settle, irrigate, and develop, they could become the major force in a state that would, by consti-tutional symmetry, become a political entity like other existing states.

Yet in becoming a state like others, Utah would also become (at least for a time) a state unlike others—unlike in its distinctive religious and cultural composition. As Utah became the only state closely associated with a particular organized religious move-ment, Mormonism would become the only American religion with a plausible claim to its own American homeland. In Utah, Mormons would both be free from anti-Mormon prejudice and also have a base of strength from which to negotiate a decline in anti-Mormonism in the general American polity. Over the course of a century and a half, this model of negotiated political development worked. In the process, it shaped both Mormonism itself and American politics more broadly.

Can the two lenses on Mormonism in American politics—one focused on politi-cal ideas and religious practices, the other on constitutional geopolitics and land development—be brought together into a single, unified perspective? To do so poses significant methodological challenges, yet it is the desideratum for a comprehensive study of Mormonism and American politics.

In this chapter, I will try to sketch the argument for the two lenses of analysis and offer a preliminary sketch of how they might be aligned. I am conscious that, unlike the other contributors to this volume, I am not a master of the voluminous historical archives that mark the royal road to the history of Mormonism.[5] Nevertheless, as a student of US con-stitutional history, particularly with regard to religion, I have inevitably engaged with the most distinct and remarkable example of religio-constitutional development that America has ever seen. I therefore hope that this synoptic picture will be understood as a suggestion for future research, not at all as a definitive word on the topic.

THEOCRACY AND INSULARITY

Joseph Smith and his followers would have encountered discrimination and hostility in nineteenth-century America even if Smith had never adopted the principle of plural (or "celestial") marriage. There were two reasons for this inevitable hostility. First, the Mormon community was not only a religious community but also aspired to function as a political one. As early as the 1831 settlement of Independence, Missouri—and more fully in Nauvoo, Illinois, established in 1840—Smith sought to organize the Mormon community into a simulacrum of a political state. His political vision extended not merely to his own role as a leader but to a broader and capacious organization of the community into a kind of shadow state or government.[6]

Although such organization by religious groups was not wholly unprecedented in American history—the Puritans, after all, had done something similar—it was highly unusual during the nineteenth century. Inevitably, the apparent organization of the religious community into a competing political entity would have elicited skepticism, hostility, and perhaps even hatred from American society at large.

Second, the Mormon community favored an economic insularity. Certain enterprises were directly owned by the Prophet (although this practice seems to have reached its fruition later in Utah under Brigham Young).[7] Mormons who owned their businesses themselves preferred to do business with other members of the church. As their communities grew and were increasingly successful, this insularity was sure to provoke resentment from outsiders.

In early nineteenth-century America, the market became the dominant mode of economic organization. That fact was highly significant for public reception of Mormon practices. Of course, Mormons were hardly unique in their preference to do business within the community. But other communities that experienced success in conjunction with a preference for keeping business within also encountered hostility and discrimination on these grounds.

An attack on Smith by a mob in Kirtland, Ohio, in March of 1832, long before plural marriage was introduced or made public, encapsulates the combination of political and economic hostility. Ezra Booth, a former Mormon who had renounced his membership, incited the riot with a series of inflammatory letters in the *Ohio Star*.[8] One of his letters declared that Mormonism had one aim: "the establishment of a society in Missouri, over which the contrivers of this delusive system, are to possess unlimited and despotic sway."[9]

Yet beyond these reasons for hostility toward the Mormon community loomed what became far and away the dominant rhetorical component of anti-Mormon sentiment in nineteenth- and early twentieth-century America: plural marriage. From the time that Smith declared the principle openly to the time, some three-quarters of a century later, when the church formally changed its stance on the practice, no other religious practice received comparable attention and disapprobation in American life. This opposition to polygamy played an important role in US political history; undoubtedly, it also played the central role in shaping political relations between Mormons and the broader American public.[10]

Although, as I shall argue in this chapter, geographic and economic factors also played a meaningful role in shaping this relationship, I do not wish to advance the argument that the fight over polygamy was strictly epiphenomenal. There is every reason to believe that the rhetorical opposition to polygamy in nineteenth-century America was sincere in its motives. That opposition included some forms of religious bigotry; and it certainly opened the door to more bigotry. Yet, at the same time, the opposition to polygamy was part of normative nineteenth-century American Protestantism. It also played a role in galvanizing early American feminism.[11]

The political features of the opposition to polygamy included, at first, organized public outcry against the Mormons and their church. It was a lynch mob that killed Joseph Smith—and it is crucial to recognize that, in nineteenth-century America (and beyond), lynching and mob activity were recognizable elements of collective, even coordinated political action. Although lynching was the most extreme manifestation of mob activity, the phenomena of public protest, mass marches, and what is sometimes called "politics out of doors" were fundamental to American political culture.[12] The mobs that threatened and harassed Mormons and shaped the move of the Mormon community from Independence, Missouri, to Nauvoo, Illinois, must be understood as products of organized *political* opposition.

THE MORMON QUEST FOR AUTONOMY

If Gentile hostility to plural marriage was the leading driver of political relations between the Church of Jesus Christ of Latter-day Saints and the American polity, it was the response of the church that made that relationship especially complex, important, and fascinating. The church could have responded to the legal and extralegal repression that it encountered by knuckling under and accepting the impossibility of proffering a deviant strand of family and sexual relationships in an America deeply committed to a single, normative version of sexual regulation. That it did not do so is the single most significant fact of the first seventy-five years of Mormon political life in America.[13]

In essence, the strategy adopted by the Mormons was not to stand and fight but to flee. In this endeavor, they were able to draw upon the rich tradition of religious symbolism that had inspired the Puritans themselves when they founded the Massachusetts Bay Colony in their famous "errand into the wilderness." If, for the Puritans, North America represented the farthest reaches of human civilization, the Mormons' goal was to go as far west as was necessary to establish their own polity.[14]

In the first instance, Nauvoo, Illinois, proved to be not far enough. In a sense, its location was too desirable to establish a community that would be free from governmental interference. Despite Smith's attempts to project independence—or perhaps, rather, because of them—Nauvoo came under the political authority of the state of Illinois.[15] Within the boundaries of that state, it was impossible to establish an alternative legal framework that would be outside the reach of laws against polygamy. What was needed was not simply greater distance but the possibility of creating an independent political state.

In the Utah territory, then still unorganized and, indeed, formally still a part of Mexico, Brigham Young found such a place. Young rejected California because it was already too populated.[16] But people per se were not the most fundamental problem with the Californian option. The real problem was the impossibility of autonomous political authority where a substantial population of non-Mormons already existed.

Once again, it is necessary to invoke the threat of government prosecution for polygamy to explain the appeal of creating a new political space. Without the principle, it might still have been desirable for the church to possess its own political authority; but given that state laws expressly outlawed and criminalized a crucial component of the practice of the Mormon religion, there was ultimately no substitute for political independence. The legal dimension of the formalized suppression of Mormonism was therefore central to the construction of a distinctive Mormon polity in Utah.

Here the historical process of geographical expansion and settlement throughout the United States enters our story. Why were Utah and the intermountain West available as space free of political control? How could Brigham Young plausibly believe that he could create there a polity that would be distinctively Mormon?

In Europe, of course, as on the settled East Coast, every place where one might set foot fell under the specific sovereign control of a political entity. In the literal sense, Utah in 1847 was also controlled by a sovereign. It had been part of Mexico, which was in the process of ceding it to the United States as part of the aftermath of the Mexican-American War. But political sovereignty had not yet been fully and formally established in Utah, and for a distinctly American reason. Ultimately, all areas of the continental United States had to come under the control of not only the federal government but also of a state government. (The sole exception, Washington, DC, was specifically delineated in the Constitution as occupying this unique status.[17]) Utah would first become a US territory—but then it would eventually become a state.

Indeed, just a few years after the Mormons reached Utah, the famous Supreme Court decision of *Dred Scott v. Sandford* established the constitutional principle that any territory controlled by the federal government must ultimately come under the control of some duly constituted state.[18] This constitutional reality may not have been fully adjudicated before *Dred Scott*, yet it was presumably understood intuitively by Young and his followers, who did not aspire to remain in a federally administered territory indefinitely. It meant that the community of Deseret that they intended to found would eventually have to become a state or part of a state. Of course, it was precisely belonging to a state that had been the problem for Mormons in Missouri and Illinois. What Utah promised—what the dream of Deseret embodied—was the creation of a new state of the United States.[19]

Creating a state was no small aspiration. Founding new states through self-organization was not an unimaginable or unique event in the history of American expansion.[20] What was wholly original was the idea of forming a new state that was itself specifically connected to, managed by, and, in effect, controlled through the auspices of a church.

There was no necessary constitutional prohibition to make this impossible. The establishment clause of the US Constitution made the establishment of religion unconstitutional—but only for the federal government. Its language specified that "*Congress* shall make no law respecting an establishment of religion." [21] It was not until the adoption of the Fourteenth Amendment, in the aftermath of the Civil War, that it became possible to imagine the Bill of Rights applying to the states.[22] Thus in the 1850s it was conceivable to imagine a de facto established religion coming into existence within the context of Utah.[23]

But an established religion was not Deseret's most important feature for the Mormons. What they needed was a state government *sufficiently controlled by Mormons that its laws would not prohibit polygamy*. Once again, the distinctive constitutional structure of the United States was absolutely crucial to the plan. The states, not the federal government, have authority over family law. At the national level, there was and would always be a substantial majority intolerant of polygamy and happy to see it criminalized. In an individual state, however, things might be different—provided that Mormons made up the majority.

American federalism allowed distinctive social and legal practices to continue at the local level by insulating them from federal control. Indeed, the Mormons had a clear precedent upon which they could rely: the "peculiar institution" of slavery. Slavery might be unpopular with the American population measured as a statistical whole, but it retained constitutional protection because it was within the domain of the individual states and majorities in the southern states wanted it. It was therefore more than simple bigotry when the Republican Party, in a series of political platforms, named slavery and polygamy as "the twin relics of barbarism."[24] The Republicans were pointing to undesirable social practices that were nevertheless protected by the constitutional structure of federalism.

From the Mormon standpoint, then, federalism appeared to be the *deus ex machina* that would save the community from the profound unpopularity of its religious beliefs. It was not to be. Had Deseret been admitted as a state alongside California in 1851, this brilliantly ambitious plan might have succeeded. Instead, it was organized into the territory of Utah.[25] As a territory, it came under direct federal control—and had to go through a series of congressionally mandated steps before it could become a state. For Mormons, this process posed a dual problem. First, the federal government could make demands upon the LDS Church in exchange for statehood. Second, in the run-up to the actual grant of statehood, Congress could exercise its authority over territories to pass laws that related to issues ordinarily reserved to the states. Thus, it was Congress, not a state legislature, that passed the key statutes outlawing polygamy and then outlawing any organization that advocated polygamy—namely, the LDS Church itself.[26] The only way in the US system that Congress could pass laws relating to marriage was if those laws applied to a territory, not a state—and Utah was such a territory.

It was nevertheless not altogether unreasonable for Mormons to imagine they might be able to gain some protection from the courts even when this federal legislation regarding marriage came into effect. After all, advocates of slavery in the territories had sought and received constitutional salvation from the US Supreme Court, which, in *Dred Scott*, had overturned the Missouri compromise outlawing slavery in the US territories north of the 36°30′ line. *Dred Scott* specified that Congress lacked the authority to prohibit slavery in the territories insofar as slaves were private property whose masters could bring them anywhere without forfeiting their ownership rights.[27] It thus subjected Congress's territorial control to limitations derived from individual rights conferred by the US Constitution.

The Mormon attempt at a similar claim came about in the 1878 case of *Reynolds v. United States*, in which the Supreme Court considered whether the right to free exercise of religion in the First Amendment rendered unconstitutional Congress's prohibition on polygamy in the Utah territory.[28] In *Reynolds*, the court decided not to extend the same protection to polygamy that it had earlier extended to slavery. The times were different. The Civil War was in the past. What was more, while slavery had enjoyed a regional (white) constituency, polygamy was appreciated nowhere but in Utah. The court decided that the free exercise of religion did not extend to a person's choice of whom to marry. This decision set the course for an inevitable conflict between the principle of polygamy and the Mormons' aspiration to control their own political space.

What happened next shaped the relationship between Mormonism and American politics for the next 125 years. Faced with a choice between exercising political authority within Utah by abandoning polygamy or resigning itself to a permanent status of outlawry, the church, painfully, opted for the former. The process took decades, and it entailed several stages, including the secret preservation of polygamy in the hopes of its maintenance.[29] Ultimately, however, the power of the United States government was too great.

THE UTAH COMPROMISE

Yet that is not the whole story. In addition to the stick with which the federal government beat Mormons over polygamy, there was also a substantial carrot. That carrot was the promise of a state more or less under Mormon control. It was this component of Mormon political life that would eventually emerge as most unusual seen in comparison with the rest of the United States. The reason for its emergence was, to be sure, historically contingent. As I have suggested, the LDS Church sought refuge in Utah largely in order to avoid prohibitions on polygamy. But once that goal was no longer attainable, the trajectory of Mormon political independence shifted.

Now the reasons for establishing quasi-autonomous political control were different. They were connected to the capacity of the church to sustain itself, grow, and spread its message to the world, to produce a homogeneous set of cultural practices in a distinctively sanctified space. The new Zion would no longer protect the distinctive religious principle for which it was intended, but it remained a new Zion nevertheless.

After all, the population of Utah was already overwhelmingly Mormon. The political class was primarily Mormon as well. Wealth was, over time, increasingly concentrated in the hands of leading Mormon families. Enormous wealth was also concentrated in the church, controlled by a president who could exercise near total control over that wealth pursuant to the 1851 charter of incorporation granted to the LDS church by the general assembly of Deseret.[30]

Had the federal government wished to do so, it could probably have insisted on the redistribution of the church's wealth and perhaps even the reduction of the power of the president before agreeing to recognize Utah as a state. Indeed, in 1862 and 1867, Congress passed laws specifically revoking the church's charter of incorporation.[31] Yet Congress did not attempt to expropriate the church or redistribute wealth in Utah, and for reasons that deserve some analysis.

The prevalent ideology in the United States at the time was in no way hostile to the accumulation of great wealth by individuals. Seen from the standpoint of the Gilded Age, Brigham Young or his successor presidents were a species of robber barons—clever entrepreneurs who had gotten to a place first and cornered its market.

Indeed, the resemblance of the Mormon Church to a business corporation, sometimes remarked upon negatively by the church's critics in the twenty-first century, may actually have been an advantage in the late nineteenth. Corporations, after all, were familiar things. Over the second half of the nineteenth century, the American for-profit corporation had shown itself to be the greatest engine for the amassing of wealth ever conceived. To the extent that the church's control over the state of Utah approximated corporate control, Utah resembled other states, such as the mining states of Montana and Colorado, in which corporate interests dominated. For the affairs of a state to be very much in the hands of a small number of businesspeople was relatively normal. Progressives eagerly criticized such arrangements, but the arrangements themselves were familiar enough not to have blocked the accession to statehood of those states in which they existed.[32]

This new circumstance brought into play in a different way political dynamics that had already been created by Brigham Young. These dynamics had to do with the imperative of settlement—and the politics of water.

THE POLITICS OF WATER

Settling every spot of the American continent between the two oceans was not an inevitable component of the American secular religion of manifest destiny. Early explorers considered the intermountain West as an unconquerable desert. Brigham Young was almost unique in imagining the possibility of creating a large and functioning urban-rural community on the banks of the Great Salt Lake. But once Mormons settled Salt Lake City and began to use irrigation techniques to a high degree of effectiveness, the appeal of settling desert regions more broadly grew apace.[33]

No doubt, as Leonard Arrington argued in his influential *Great Basin Kingdom*, the Mormons enjoyed significant advantages in making the desert bloom. First, they had the motivation: there was, after all, nowhere else for them to go. Second, the Mormons had the morale to do the job. Deep commitment to religious belief told them that their presence was divinely ordained; and if God willed it, then surely it was no dream. Third, when it came to laying out systems of irrigation, the Mormons enjoyed a substantial organizational advantage. By their nature, irrigation and water management are public goods. If they lie in the hands of individuals who do not pay attention to the interests of the whole, they can easily fall into the trap known as the "tragedy of the commons." By virtue of its organization, its capacity to collectivize or distribute property, and its capacity to take into account the interests of the whole, the economic-religious engine of the Mormon Church was uniquely well placed to engage in the process of making the desert habitable and, indeed, arable.[34]

At first, Brigham Young seems to have counted on his ability to organize and add value to land as a basis for negotiating with the federal government over the question of polygamy.[35] After all, the Mormons had something that the federal government very much wanted: they had the capacity to turn empty space into organized political space. As it turned out, the federal government was unwilling to take the deal—because it did not need it. By the time Congress acted decisively against polygamy, settlement in the intermountain West had begun in earnest. If the Mormons had ceased to exist as a religious group in the 1870s and 1880s, Utah still would have been settled—just not by Mormons.

Indeed, it is fair to say that, in an uncoordinated and probably unplanned fashion, the federal government took tremendous advantage of the LDS Church. After all, Young and his followers had built up Utah partly in the hopes of trading their successful accomplishments for religious independence and freedom from antipolygamy legislation. The federal government allowed them to believe this for long enough to settle the Utah territory. When the job that no one but the Mormons could have done was nearly complete, the federal government told the church that it could not have the very thing that it wanted. By then, it was too late for the Mormons to pull up stakes. Had they done so, it would not have been a result uncongenial to the federal government.

Of course, from the opposite standpoint, the LDS Church arguably should have anticipated that, when push came to shove, the federal government would find a way to deny it the religious independence that it sought. Such, after all, had been the fate of slavery. Though it had taken a war to do it, slavery became illegal despite the constitutional protections that it had once enjoyed.

The federal government of the nineteenth century was consolidating its power over a vast expanse of territory and a growing population. As Mexico, the Native American tribes, and the recalcitrant, independence-seeking South had all learned, the United States did not eschew the use of force to establish control. In 1898, this growing economic and military juggernaut would use force abroad to expand its empire into the Pacific. Compared to other formidable (and defeated) opponents, the Mormons were unlikely to hold their ground against the American government. This realization was, no doubt, part of the Mormons' entirely rational decision to accept the conditions that the United States was offering.

But to see this purely as a story of federal domination would be too simple. The federal government was prepared to accept a Utah that maintained some—though not all—of the features of the utopian idyll of Deseret.

FORGING A DEMOCRATIC UTAH

Congress still had to reckon with the religious character of the Mormon community before it would grant statehood. One crucial feature was the question of democracy: could the Mormons participate in ordinary democratic politics? Were they, in the language of the nineteenth century, capable of acting as citizens, of making meaningful choices among competing political parties and candidates?[36]

The specter of communal decision-making and bloc-voting were not far from the minds of critics—and for both good and bad reasons. Throughout the century, the great model of collective voting as a threat to democracy was the Catholic community in the United States. Beginning with the rise in Irish immigration after the great famine and continuing through the contentious anti-Catholic political season of 1875–76 (when the Blaine Amendment was introduced in Congress), anti-Catholic sentiment and rhetoric focused on this threat. In its essence, it could be stated simply: Protestantism amounted to voluntary choice in religion; democracy permitted voluntary choice in politics. The two went together hand in glove. If Catholics, with their submission to authority and skepticism of civil liberties, could be construed as a threat to democratic politics, Mormons were no less vulnerable.[37]

Mormonism in the late nineteenth century had not fully embraced democracy as a mechanism of governance. Internally, its leaders were selected not by vote but by divine sanction. Once in office, its president possessed power that was formally unchecked. There might have been complex, cross-cutting lines of allegiance among family lineages, but the organizing principle was still kinship rather than voting. Decisions came from above.[38]

Externally, when the Mormon community had possessed political autonomy, it had not always used democratic means to exercise its power. Nauvoo had been organized along quasi-monarchical lines. Elections in Deseret were few and did not seem to follow the familiar forms of electoral competition.[39] Contemporaries might have been justified in wondering if a Mormon state would really behave democratically.

Fortunately for the Mormons, Congress's interest in democracy was more formalistic than substantive. Two political parties had to be shown to exist. According to stories that are difficult to validate but which bear symbolic value, Mormon leaders assigned church members to parties almost at random.[40] The Republican Party was deeply unpopular after its decades of open anti-Mormonism, but the Mormons needed representation in each party to prove that they could adapt to the democratic form of government.

What remained in place after the adoption of democratic forms in Utah was the dominant position of the church hierarchy in matters political and economic. Consensus-style politics became the norm for a century or more. Deference to leading families in the political realm continued to exist in the state for a similar period of time.[41] It is fair to say that in no other US state has a similar situation existed in the modern era.

Not only does the church influence politics more in Utah than does any other church anywhere else in the United States, but the overlap between influential church families and key political players is also far more extensive. Reinforcing this insularity is the importance of kinship-network politics, an anomaly in a country that is largely characterized by diffuse (if not anomic) family relations. The Mormon emphasis on genealogy and family, in the realms of both theology and practice, is the obvious explanation.

MAKING THE DESERT BLOSSOM

Why did this situation persist? Once again, the answer lies in the way the LDS Church has been able to work itself into the political power structure in the United States at large. Elected politicians from Utah, mostly Mormon, were able to participate in coalition building that entrenched the existing political structure as a normal feature of American politics. Once such coalitions developed, it became undesirable and even impossible for any outside political player to break them apart.

More importantly, as the state grew and developed, it became a regional leader in the establishment of a diversified economy in the intermountain West. Water remained at the core of this growth. Over the last several decades, historians have come to agree that the story of the region generally is the story of water.[42] Once necessary to support agriculture, the water now supports urban and suburban populations. Utah led the development of water use, and it led the establishment of a political constituency committed to keeping water flowing.

Of course, the connection of Utah's Mormons to their land—and to the water that they have brought to it—is far more than economic. The residents of Utah developed their own distinctive sense of topography and history that corresponded in a complex way to their religious commitments and beliefs.[43] No less than Israeli Zionism, Mormon Zionism can be understood as deeply interwoven with the story of making the desert bloom. In both cases, a biblical trope drawn primarily from the book of Isaiah (though also elsewhere in the Hebrew Bible) and connected with the notion of divine grace and providence dominates the scene.

Such religious beliefs, however, must also be juxtaposed with the broader American commitment to the development and peopling of the continent. Even now, many decades after the completion of the settlement process, American ideology remains closely connected to the idea of enabling settlement throughout the continent, even in otherwise inhospitable locales, and even at considerable expense to taxpayers in other domains. To put it perhaps a bit too simply, there is generally in American politics a close relationship between the ideology of settlement and the politics of water—even now that the ideology goes largely unacknowledged.[44]

Ideology and politics feed on one another, and each in turn is nourished by the economic interests that depend on the provision of water and the maintenance of the population. My purpose here is neither to rehearse this familiar analysis nor even to point out that the distinctive Mormon ideology of settlement and water is an important historical and contemporary link in this chain. It is, rather, to suggest that the history of the relation between Mormonism and American politics would be wholly insufficient if it did not pay attention to this dimension of settlement and water use. The vested interests that benefit from existing structures need not be major corporate interests. They can include ordinary householders; and they also include, centrally, the LDS Church and Mormon individuals (at least those in Utah) taken as a distinct political interest.

THE HARD LESSONS OF 2008

How, if at all, does this story end? How will the relation between the LDS Church and American politics emerge in the future? To glimpse the beginnings of an answer, one must look to the political crisis created within Mormondom by the failed presidential bid of Mitt Romney in 2008 and the changes it wrought, both in the church and in Romney, over the next several years.

If it seems overstated to speak of a crisis after 2008, that is only because by cultural style and organizational opacity the senior leadership of the LDS Church does not advertise crises. Romney was almost certainly the strongest Republican candidate in 2007–08. He was defeated in the primaries in no small part because former Governor Mike Huckabee of Arkansas, himself a Baptist minister, drew direct attention to Romney's religion, and that in unflattering terms. Romney's campaign responded with a public speech meant to put the issue to rest. As a conservative Republican candidate, Romney could not claim his religion was irrelevant to his program of government or his character. He had no choice but to argue that his religion was terribly important—but that anyone who asked him about its particulars was deploying a "religious test" in violation of the spirit of the Constitution.

The argument was weak, and the strategy failed—at a cost not merely to Romney but to the LDS Church as a whole. It seemed ironic that a church so devoted to missionizing was caught out by its inability to explain its beliefs and practices in a way that would satisfy the general public. But the problem lay deep within Mormonism's origins as a mystery religion that preserves a range of beliefs and rituals for the initiated only.[45] Romney had himself been a missionary and a bishop in his local stake. He was, in principle, the perfect figure to explain his faith. But norms of reticence coupled with concern about public perceptions made the task almost impossible.

In the aftermath of this debacle, the general authorities of the church seem to have made the tactical decision to devote the church's considerable resources to a public political fight focused on a single issue—same-sex marriage. The strategy culminated with the passage of California's Proposition 8, which reversed a California court decision authorizing the practice. LDS funds and organization played a major role in the undertaking.

Many observers considered this strategy to be risky if not downright irresponsible. The long-term trends in public opinion made it clear that same-sex marriage would ultimately obtain public approval. In the meantime, Proposition 8 and others like it were vulnerable to reversal by the courts. (Indeed, the United States Court of Appeals for the Ninth Circuit struck down Proposition 8 as unconstitutional.[46]) Either way, the LDS Church would find itself on the losing side of a major political battle.

But that was not the only oddity about the church's choice of political skirmishes. By focusing on an issue connected to marriage, the church opened itself to the charge of hypocrisy and failure of historical memory. It was, after all, the same church that for many years had struggled against the oppressive insistence of the state that marriage may only be between one man and one woman. Critics of the church's stand would argue that it was precisely a guilty conscience over plural marriage that caused the church to insist so stridently that marriage must be the same for all. Public opposition to same-sex marriage assured that Mormonism's polygamous past would constantly appear before the public eye.

In retrospect, however, the strategy may have been more effective than it appeared at the time. Liberals indeed roundly criticized the church for the position that it had taken. But this criticism, even when it invoked polygamy, distracted public attention away from the church's substantive religious beliefs, which had been the subject of such strong evangelical critique. Evangelicals, for their part, could not help but agree with the church's position, even if they did not make any great effort to unite with the church against same-sex marriage. The intent might have been to create alliances with evangelicals. But even if that effort failed, the overall effect was to soften the harsh tenor of evangelical attack on Mormonism.

When Mitt Romney ran again for president in 2011–12, evangelical candidates in the race refrained from direct attacks on Mormonism. The person who eventually emerged as Romney's most serious challenger, Rick Santorum, was a Catholic who, though close to evangelicals, was not one of them. Santorum never launched a major attack on Romney's faith. Then, when Romney clinched the nomination, evangelicals found themselves in a double bind. They might not want to vote for a Mormon, but their alternatives were to stay home or to vote for the incumbent president, Barack Obama.

Obama also did not make an issue of Romney's religion. The political logic was simple: not only might some Democratic voters object to the bigotry, but Obama's own religious background had also been the subject of major controversy in 2008 and beyond, both because of his association with Rev. Jeremiah Wright, an African American preacher whose belief commitments grew out of Black liberation theology, and because of the persistent (and erroneous) rumor that he is a Muslim. Obama had much to lose by bringing up the topic of religion.

The upshot was that in 2012, the same Republican Party that had once denounced Mormonism as a relic of barbarism fielded a Mormon presidential candidate—and his religion played no very major role in the campaign. This represents a stage of normalization for the relationship between Mormonism and American politics. Bias may continue, and Utah's distinctive political culture, with close ties between church leaders and political leaders, will persist in some form for some time. But the relationship will increasingly look less distinctive and unique compared to that between other major religious traditions and the political life of the United States.

NOTES

1. Thanks to Ranch Kimball for conversations emphasizing the importance of water resources, to Melissa Proctor for guidance on all matters LDS and for helpful substantive suggestions, to Nate Oman for his valuable comments, and to Ariel Berkower for excellent research and editorial assistance. Errors great and small are my own.
2. Gordon, *Mormon Question*, 1. I owe an enormous debt to Gordon's book, as will be evident throughout; Gordon is the first writer to point to the connection between federalism and Mormon political development, and in this essay I am building on a foundation she has laid.
3. Arrington, *Great Basin Kingdom*, 22–28; Alexander, *Great Basin Kingdom Revisited*.
4. Durham, *Desert between the Mountains*, 158 describes Mormon traditions surrounding honeybees and beehives, which symbolize industry and cooperation.
5. Feldman, *Divided by God*, 99–110; Feldman, "What Is It About Mormonism?"
6. Bushman, *Joseph Smith*, 163–76, describes Smith's establishment of a Zion in Independence; 410–14 discusses the Nauvoo charter.
7. Arrington, *Great Basin Kingdom*, 6–35.
8. Bushman, *Joseph Smith*, 168–69.
9. Ibid., 178.
10. Gordon, *Mormon Question*.
11. Ibid., xx.
12. Wilentz, *Rise of American Democracy*; Kramer, *People Themselves*.
13. Flake, *Politics of American Religious Identity*.
14. Gottlieb, *America's Saints*, 12–13, notes contemporaneous comparisons between the Puritans and the Mormons, including Ralph Waldo Emerson's description of Mormonism as the "afterclap of Puritanism."
15. Durham, *Desert between the Mountains*, 118–23.
16. Arrington, *Great Basin Kingdom*, 40.
17. US Constitution, art. 1, § 8, cl. 17.
18. Dred Scott v. Sandford, 60 U.S. 393, 446 (1856).
19. Durham, *Desert between the Mountains*, 158.
20. Morgan, *State of Deseret*, 7, compares the formation of Deseret to the attempts to organize Texas, Franklin (a proto-Tennessee), Oregon, and California.
21. U.S. Constitution, amend. 1 (emphasis added).
22. Gordon, *Mormon Question*, 77–78. Of course some writers (and one Supreme Court justice) still believe the establishment clause should not be incorporated under the Fourteenth Amendment. See Elk Grove v. Newdow, 42 U.S. 14, 33 (2004) Thomas, J. concurring; Amar, *Bill of Rights*, 36–39.
23. Morgan, *State of Deseret*, 13, explains that civil and religious rule in Deseret were not "separate and distinct" but rather "dual aspects of a single authority"; Oman, "Preaching in the Court House and Judging in the Temple," 157, delineates the structure of the LDS court

system and argues that the courts are crucial to an understanding of the nature of total-izing political authority in Deseret.

24. Gordon, *Mormon Question*, 55–65. Gordon broadly deserves credit for demonstrating the relation between the polygamy question, federalism, and slavery; Mason, *Mormon Menace*, 111–13, links postbellum white Southerners' fondness for states' rights to their refusal to recognize the statehood of Utah, which, they realized, would grant polygamy a toehold in the American legal system.

25. Morgan, *State of Deseret*, 67–91, on the process and politics. On the extraordinary "ghost government of Deseret" which existed between 1862 and 1870, and consisted of the elected members of the territorial legislature meeting separately in the "General Assembly of Deseret," without congressional sanction, see 91–119.

26. Gordon, *Mormon Question*, 149–54, 164–66.

27. Dred Scott v. Sandford, 60 U.S. at 450–52.

28. Reynolds v. United States, 98 U.S. 145 (1878).

29. Flake, *Politics of American Religious Identity*.

30. Arrington, *Great Basin Kingdom*, 30; Morgan, *State of Deseret*, 185–87.

31. Djupe and Olson, "Latter-day Saints," *Encyclopedia of American Religion and Politics*, 251. Church of Jesus Christ of Latter-day Saints v. United States, 136 U.S. 1.

32. Arrington, *Great Basin Kingdom*, 129–30.

33. Gottlieb, *A Life of Its Own*, 204–05.

34. Arrington, *Great Basin Kingdom*, 52–53. Worster, "Kingdom, the Power, and the Water," 25, 33. Worster acknowledges Arrington's account of Brigham Young's quasi-collectivism over natural resources, yet also describes Arrington as subscribing to the "irrigation myth."

35. Gottlieb, *America's Saints*, 46–47.

36. Gordon, *Mormon Question*, 93, 95, 172.

37. Feldman, *Divided by God*, 64–85, 99–110.

38. Morgan, *State of Deseret*, 12, speaks of "democratic forms," emphasizing that in Utah elections prior to 1870, "the people voted not on a choice of alternatives but on whether to sustain the decisions of leaders in whom they had faith." See also 34. Bushman, *Joseph Smith*, 153. Bushman, by contrast, writes that "[i]n a democratic time, the Mormons emerged as the most democratic of churches, rivaled only by the Quakers." If this proposition is true (and what of American Presbyterians, Methodists, and even Episcopalians?), it must be so only relatively speaking. Bushman himself, in the same paragraph, calls the church's ministry "authoritarian" as well as democratic.

39. Gordon, *The Mormon Question*, 26, 93.

40. See, for example, G. A. Prince and W. R. Wright, *David O. McKay and the Rise of Modern Mormonism* (Salt Lake City, UT: University of Utah Press, 2005), 334; Benjamin Borg, "The Hidden Moderate Utah: The Political History of the War within the Mormon/Republican Relationship," *The Hinckley Journal of Politics* (2012), 37, available at http://epubs.utah.edu/index.php/HJP/article/viewFile/666/509. See also Richard Lyman Bushman, speaking at the Pew Forum Faith Angle Conference, May 14, 2007, transcript entitled "Mormonism and Politics: Are They Compatible?," available at http://www.pewforum.org/2007/05/14/mormonism-and-politics-are-they-compatible/ ("The People's Party was dissolved and Mormons were instructed to join one or another of the national political parties. They were sometimes assigned: 'You become a Democrat; you become a Republican'. There are Democrats in Utah to this day who are Democrats only because their great-grandfathers were told they should be.").

41. Gottlieb, *America's Saints*, 66–94 details the history of church's involvement in American politics.
42. Reisner, *Cadillac Desert*.
43. Farmer, *On Zion's Mount*.
44. Reisner, *Cadillac Desert*.
45. Compare Feldman, "What Is It About Mormonism?"
46. Perry v. Brown, 671 F.3d 1052 (9th Cir. 2012).

BIBLIOGRAPHY

Alexander, Thomas G. *Great Basin Kingdom Revisited: Contemporary Perspectives*. Logan: Utah State University Press, 1991.

Amar, Akhil Reed. *The Bill of Rights: Creation and Reconstruction*. New Haven, CT: Yale University Press, 1998.

Arrington, Leonard J. *Great Basin Kingdom: An Economic History of the Latter-day Saints, 1830–1900*. Urbana: University of Illinois Press, 2005.

Bushman, Richard L. *Joseph Smith: Rough Stone Rolling*. New York: Alfred A. Knopf, 2005.

Djupe, Paul A., and Laura R. Olson. *Encyclopedia of American Religion and Politics*. New York: Facts on File, 2003.

Durham, Michael S. *Desert between the Mountains: Mormons, Miners, Padres, Mountain Men, and the Opening of the Great Basin, 1772–1869*. New York: Henry Holt, 1997.

Farmer, Jared. *On Zion's Mount: Mormons, Indians, and the American Landscape*. Cambridge, MA: Harvard University Press, 2008.

Feldman, Noah. *Divided by God: America's Church-State Problem*. New York: Farrar, Straus and Giroux, 2005.

Feldman, Noah. "What Is It About Mormonism?" *New York Times*, January 6, 2008.

Flake, Kathleen. *The Politics of American Religious Identity: The Seating of Senator Reed Smoot, Mormon Apostle*. Chapel Hill: University of North Carolina Press, 2004.

Gordon, Sarah Barringer. *The Mormon Question: Polygamy and Constitutional Conflict in Nineteenth-Century America*. Chapel Hill: University of North Carolina Press, 2002.

Gottlieb, Robert. *A Life of Its Own: The Politics and Power of Water*. San Diego: Harcourt, 1988.

Gottlieb, Robert, and Peter Wiley. *America's Saints: The Rise of Mormon Power*. New York: Putnam's, 1984.

Kramer, Larry D. *The People Themselves: Popular Constitutionalism and Judicial Review*. New York: Oxford University Press, 2004.

Mason, Patrick Q. *The Mormon Menace: Violence and Anti-Mormonism in the Postbellum South*. New York: Oxford University Press, 2011.

Morgan, Dale L. *The State of Deseret*. Logan: Utah State University Press, 1987.

Oman, Nathan B. "Preaching to the Court House and Judging in the Temple" *BYU Law Review* 2009, no. 1 (2009): 157–224.

Reisner, Marc. *Cadillac Desert: The American West and Its Disappearing Water*. New York: Viking, 1986.

Wilentz, Sean. *The Rise of American Democracy: Jefferson to Lincoln*. New York: Norton, 2005.

Worster, Donald. "The Kingdom, the Power, and the Water." In Alexander, *Great Basin Kingdom Revisited*, 21–38.

CHAPTER 40

MORMONS AND
INTERFAITH RELATIONS

RICHARD J. MOUW

THE topic of interfaith relations loomed large for Mormonism from the movement's very beginnings in the early decades of the nineteenth century. Indeed, it was precisely the diversity of conflicting religious beliefs, so clearly on display among the denominations during that period in western New York state, that motivated Joseph Smith to launch his own spiritual quest. As he put it in one of his accounts of the First Vision: "In the midst of this war of words and tumult of opinions, I asked myself, what is to be done? Who of all these parties are right; or, are they all wrong together? If any one of them be right, which is it, and how shall I know it?" And when he had the opportunity to ask the Son of God himself "which of all the sects was right," he received the rather blunt answer "that all their creeds were an abomination in his sight."[1]

For Joseph Smith and his early followers, the primary religious "other" was traditional Christianity, with its assortment of denominations and revivalist groups. This meant that the dominant approach to other religious perspectives was a polemical one, as Mormons engaged in a sustained effort to establish their claim to be the only legitimate receivers of a "restored gospel." This polemical posture continued throughout the nineteenth century, as the church expanded its reach to other parts of North America, as well as to the British Isles, western Europe, and Australia—all of them cultural contexts for the most part shaped by mainstream Christian traditions.

A strong emphasis was placed during this period on the contrast between Mormonism's recovery of pure gospel teachings and the "apostasy" of traditional Christianity. Potential converts were confronted with the need to make an urgent decision for truth and against error. As Joseph Smith articulated the warning in 1843, all who rejected the restored gospel with its continuing divine "oracles" would be consigned to "the damnation of hell."[2] Here he echoed the verdict delivered in the Book of Mormon: "O the wise, and the learned, . . . and all those who preach false doctrines . . . and pervert the right way of the Lord, wo, wo, wo be unto them, saith the Lord God Almighty, for they shall be thrust into hell!" (2 Nephi 28:15).

The near-exclusive focus on differences with traditional Christianity was bound to change when Mormonism spread beyond Christendom. In the mid-nineteenth century, Brigham Young articulated a plan for the expansion of the church to Asia, with an immediate focus on India. That effort failed to materialize, however, with the result that direct contacts with non-Christian religions never occurred to any significant degree until the expanded missionary outreaches in the early twentieth century. In 1901, Heber J. Grant established a permanent Mormon presence in Asia, with the founding of a mission to Japan, and from this point on, it was necessary for Mormon missionaries to the non-Christian world to possess at least a minimal knowledge of the cultural-religious environments to which they were being sent. Over the next decades, then, the requirements for a knowledge of interfaith realities increased in the church's educational efforts, both in the missionary training program and in Brigham Young University's curricular offerings.

Toward a Friendlier Face

The question of how a specific religious group understands the beliefs and practices of other faith communities has important connections to how that group is in turn seen by others. This has been especially true for Mormonism, which has elicited unusually negative responses on the part of other faith traditions. A key factor here is the strong LDS commitment to evangelization activity. Unlike other religious communities, where missionary work is often expedited mainly as a career choice for professionals, the ambitious mission program of the LDS has been a right-of-passage assignment for its young members, with Mormon men in their late teens and early twenties (and, increasingly in recent years, young women as well) being sent on one- to three-year assignments to various destinations for full-time evangelization efforts. The high visibility of Mormon missionaries in communities in North America and around the world has caused ongoing friction with other religious groups, who see their own constituencies as targets of Mormon "proselytizing."

Even as the LDS missionary program continued to expand, however, Mormonism began to show a friendlier face to those of other persuasions, with church leaders initiating efforts to form cooperative relations with non-Mormons, joining local and national interreligious councils, and encouraging their constituencies to participate in local community projects. A growing interest in interfaith dialogue accompanied these cooperative efforts, particularly as the LDS support for academic pursuits produced a Mormon scholarly subculture that has become increasingly active in the larger intellectual community. In 1972, Brigham Young University established the Richard L. Evans Chair of Christian Understanding, for the "promotion of understanding among people of different religious faiths through teachings and other activities centered in Jesus Christ and his teachings." In the mid-1990s, "Christian Understanding" in the title was dropped in favor for "Religious

Understanding," with the express purpose of expanding the scope to non-Christian religious perspectives.

Opposing Forces

While much goodwill has been gained by these and other activities in recent decades, Mormonism still occupies a somewhat awkward presence in the world of interfaith relations. Two groups in particular, Jews and evangelical Christians, have nurtured some ongoing antagonism—and in some cases overt hostility—toward the LDS.

Mormonism's relationships with the Jewish community have been complicated by several factors. Mormonism is, in fact, strongly philo-Semitic, a natural expression of the Mormon conviction that the Book of Mormon provides detailed information about an ancient migration of a segment of Israelites to North America, whom Mormons see as their immediate spiritual forebears—and reinforced by Mormon prophetic teachings about an eventual Jewish acceptance of Jesus as the promised Messiah. And while LDS philo-Semitism is undergirded by some teachings that are unique to Mormon thought, Mormonism's basic theological understanding of its relationship to ethnic Judaism does not differ greatly from the views of many mainstream Christians, who see Gentile Christianity as having been—following the apostle Paul's teaching in chapters 9 through 11 of his Epistle to the Romans—"grafted onto" Israel. A particular point of irritation for Jews regarding Mormonism, though, has been the Mormon habit of referring to all non-Mormons as "Gentiles," thus implying a special "Jewish" identity for the LDS.

Far more serious for relations with the Jewish community, however, is the LDS practice of "baptism for the dead." Jewish groups have protested the vicarious baptisms by Mormons of both Nazi leaders and Holocaust victims. In response to the Jewish protests, LDS genealogists have worked diligently to purge the names of such persons from their lists of potential baptisms, but not with complete success—a matter that has caused continuing friction between the two communities.

No group has shown a more sustained and aggressive opposition to Mormonism, however, than evangelical Protestants. Joseph Smith was raised in a religious environment dominated by evangelical revivalism, and much of his early polemic was directed toward evangelicalism in particular. The evangelicals of his day responded with equal fervor, denouncing his claims to new revelations from God as Satanic in origin. And while the harsh tones of early Mormon denunciations of traditional Christianity have largely subsided, the overt hostility toward Mormonism continues in many evangelical quarters.

In good part, the strained relationship between Mormons and evangelicals stems from the fact that both groups are strongly committed to evangelization, which often puts them at direct odds with each other in missionary contexts. Furthermore, each can boast of members who have "converted" from the other camp, and there are instances on both sides of the divide where the conversion narratives depict the converts' previous allegiance in terms of Satanic deception. Furthermore, the restorationist themes in Mormonism are often matched by the evangelical claim to be the most faithful present-day defenders of "the faith once delivered to the saints."

While mainline Protestants, Catholics, and the Orthodox have shared some of the concerns that have characterized the evangelical attitude toward Mormonism, these other Christian groups have not been nearly as active in their opposition to Mormon thought and practice. Evangelicalism's special brand of active hostility toward Mormonism has been stimulated by an active evangelical "countercult" movement, which has produced a fairly large body of anti-Mormon literature. A key figure in this regard has been the late Walter Martin, a popular speaker and author, whose many writings, especially his book *The Maze of Mormonism* (1962), have had a major impact on evangelical understandings of Mormon teachings and practice.

The countercult movement has employed several strategies to discredit Mormonism's claims to be the sole possessor of a "restored" gospel. The most extreme has been the approach of Ed Decker and Dave Hunt in their 1982 film *The God Makers*, with a book of the same title, in which they allege Mormonism's direct ties to Satanism and the occult.

More characteristic of the countercult approach, however, is the effort to discredit Joseph Smith's claim to have discovered the long-buried golden plates from which he was able to transcribe the Book of Mormon. Various historical investigative paths have been explored in the hopes of demonstrating plagiarism or some other form of fraud.

In 1998 two evangelical scholars, Carl Mosser and Paul Owen, authored a lengthy essay in a journal published by the Trinity Evangelical Divinity School. The title of their essay, "Mormon Scholarship, Apologetics, and Evangelical Neglect: Losing the Battle and Not Knowing It?" signaled the authors' main contention: that countercult activists seemed ignorant of the significant scholarship being done within the Mormon community, not only the sophisticated apologetic work done by the Foundation for Ancient Research and Mormon Studies (FARMS), established in 1979, but also other wide-ranging historical studies done by LDS scholars, with many of their works published by secular university presses. The fact that "the sophistication and erudition of LDS apologetics has risen considerably while evangelical responses have not," Mosser and Owen argued, means that evangelicals cannot simply continue to rehearse their standard criticisms of Mormonism.[3]

As if in direct response to the Mosser–Owen essay, two scholars—one evangelical and the other LDS—published a book together in the same year that embodied the very kind of new critical engagement that Mosser and Owen called for. Craig Blomberg, an evangelical New Testament scholar at Denver Seminary, and Stephen Robinson, a religion professor at Brigham Young University, issued their book *How Wide the Divide? A Mormon and an Evangelical in Conversation.*[4] Blomberg and Robinson had spent several years meeting together in dialogue about key differences between the two faith perspectives, and in their book they recorded their friendly discussions of their differences, as well as exploring areas of common theological commitment. Published by the prominent evangelical InterVarsity Press, their book was chosen as a 1998 "Book of the Year" by *Christianity Today*.

The interaction between Blomberg and Robinson soon became the inspiration for an ongoing dialogue between Mormon and evangelical theologians, meeting for semian-nual discussions jointly convened by Brigham Young University and Fuller Theological Seminary. This conversation has in turn generated a number of other dialogue events, bringing together college students from both traditions, as well as public conversations between local LDS and evangelical congregations—and, significantly, increased friendly contacts between the LDS leadership and representatives of evangelical denominations and organizations.[5]

In this new stage in evangelical–Mormon relations, the focus has shifted away from questions about historical "fact," such as the existence of the golden plates and alleged inconsistencies in various early Mormon testimonies and reports. The newer focus has been on key theological questions, such as the nature of religious authority, the doc-trine of the Trinity, the person and work of Christ, "divinization," and the relationship between grace and "good works." These discussions between two communities whose past relations have been extremely hostile are seen by many as a highly significant devel-opment in the world of interfaith relations.

Indeed, the very fact of Mormon intellectuals and church leaders engaging in give-and-take dialogue with counterparts representing traditional Christianity should be enough to put to rest the depiction of contemporary Mormonism as a "cult." The leadership of the Jehovah's Witnesses or Christian Science or Hare Krishna do not typi-cally engage in leisurely theological dialogue with representatives of other religious traditions. Nor do such groups sponsor world-class universities, with faculty members possessing earned doctorates from premier graduate studies programs, including major divinity schools. Nor do such groups seek out conversations where they can explore possible commonalities with the teachings of long-standing religious bodies.

The LDS Church has established itself as a significant religious group with a develop-ing theological perspective and a creative engagement, not only with interfaith dialogue, but also with the larger issues of society, politics, and culture. An important question for continuing discussion with evangelicals and others in the broader Christian com-munity is how to understand Mormonism's relationship to the Christian tradition as such. Historic Christianity is itself theologically pluralistic, embracing a variety of doctrinal strains. Can that pluralistic mix be understood as diverse enough to include Mormonism as yet another strand of "Christian" thought and practice?

Jan Shipps is one non-Mormon scholar who has explored the question of Mormonism's theological placement in great detail. A historian, and a Methodist, who has devoted much of her career to the study of the development of Mormonism, Shipps was the first non-Mormon to be elected president of the Mormon History Association. In her major study of Mormonism, *Mormonism: The Story of a New Religious Tradition*, published in 1987, she argued that Mormonism should be seen as having a continuity-discontinuity relationship to traditional Christianity in a manner not unlike Christianity's relation-ship to Judaism. In a later work, *Sojourner in the Promised Land: Forty Years among the Mormons* (2000), she went further in the direction of depicting Mormonism as within the broad Christian movement.

TAKING WORLDVIEWS SERIOUSLY

It should at least be clear by now that the assessment of Mormonism's relationship to traditional Christian thought cannot be done adequately by the kind of doctrinal "check-list" approach that has often been utilized by the countercult movement. It is not sufficient for understanding Mormon theology simply to point out that Mormons deny the Trinity, that they affirm the Virgin Birth of Christ while construing it differently than standard Christian formulation, that their doctrine of the atonement pays undue attention to Gethsemane, and so on. This check-list approach to Mormon doctrines treats these and other teachings as discreet doctrinal emphases. In contrast to this approach, Mormon theology can be rightly understood by others only after giving Mormonism the opportunity to lay out the complex fabric of its overall understanding of basic questions.

The "check-list" approach is a simplified version of a more sophisticated methodology in the study of religious perspectives, one that makes primary reference to an inventory of beliefs or conceptions that are assumed to be common to various religious perspectives. As Stephen Neill—a missionary theologian and a founding bishop of the Church of South India—observed in his study of world religions, this "comparative religions" approach can be misleading. When we take, for example, the idea of the deity and lay various conceptions side by side, we fail to see, said Neill, that we are abstracting those ideas from other ideas with which they are interconnected. In so doing, we detach the ideas in question "from the living experiences which has given rise to them," thereby draining them of their vitality, because we ignore "the living fabric of the religion from which the idea has been somewhat violently dissevered."[6]

When applied to the study of Mormonism by traditional Christians and Jews, the use of this comparative approach has frequently failed to do justice to the inner coherence of Mormon thought. It might be informative on one level, for example, to warn ordinary members of an evangelical congregation that the Mormon missionaries who ring the doorbell believe that God has a physical body, or that they deny "creation *ex nihilo*," or that they do not endorse the notion of salvation "by grace alone." But those warnings by themselves do not properly engage the more basic and complex LDS understanding both of the human predicament and of how the "opening of the heavens" in the nineteenth century revealed the salvific remedy for that predicament.

To probe the broader context in which various doctrines and practices function for a given religious perspective is to focus on larger worldview questions. Brian Walsh and Richard Middleton have summarized the basics of a worldview in terms of these four questions: Who am I? Where am I? What's wrong? What is the remedy?[7] Or, to expand a bit on those simple queries: a worldview will offer a conception of human nature, a more general account of the nature of reality in general, a conception of the human predicament, and a prescription for solving at least some of the key problems associated with the human predicament—all of this often embedded in a complex narrative.

Mormon scholarship in recent years has given some careful attention to these kinds of questions as they relate to a narrative-based worldview, which must be articulated in order to understand the unique teachings of Joseph Smith and others. How, for example, are we to understand the phrase, often cited by Mormon leaders, that the members of the Godhead and human beings are "of the same species"? In what sense is this intentional rejection of the traditional Judeo-Christian insistence on an unbridgeable ontological gap between Creator and creature? How does this help in fleshing out the Mormon version of the potential "divinization" of the human person? And so on.

Not only are worldview sensitivities essential for an in-depth grasp of what might otherwise be seen as highly idiosyncratic Mormon claims, but those sensitivities are also crucial for an accurate understanding of other religious traditions. These sensitivities have in fact begun to operate in LDS treatments of other religious perspectives, as is evident, for example, in a textbook on world religions authored by four Mormon scholars—a volume widely used in LDS circles in Institute classes, university courses, and missionary training programs. The book, *Religions of the World: A Latter-day Saint View*, summarizes in some depth the basic tenets of variety of religious worldviews.[8] Significantly, the tone of the book's treatment of those perspectives is positive throughout. While common themes are singled out for discussion and similarities are identified, nuances are also explored, with attention to different strands of thought within the various religious traditions.

The authors of *Religions of the World* not only present detailed accounts of the teachings of world religions, they also offer some important reflections on how the very fact of a plurality of religious perspectives can be viewed theologically from an LDS perspective. And in these explorations they do look for commonalities between Mormon teachings and various elements in other religious systems.

To acknowledge the dangers—of the sort that Bishop Neill points to—of the comparative religions approach is not to give up on the search for at least some commonalities among religious perspectives, as long as the effort to identify common themes is made only after paying careful attention to the unique worldview character of a perspective in question. Indeed, the Christian tradition has long explored and debated the proper framework for finding and assessing commonalities in the variety of religious expressions. In part, those explorations have been motivated by a passionate interest in the question of whether salvation is limited only to those communities that embrace the teachings and practices of the Christian faith.

THE SCOPE OF SALVATION

The question of eternal salvation has figured prominently in the ways evangelicals and other traditional Christians have assessed Mormonism's relationship to Christianity. The idea of salvation is, admittedly, a complex one, but it certainly includes the element of eternal destiny. To be "saved" is to have been placed in a proper relationship to God, which, in turn, is to be assured of "eternal life." Thus, an important question about the LDS for traditional Christians is: are Mormons, *qua* Mormons, "saved"?

The fact is that Mormonism poses the same kind of question in the other direction. Are traditional Christians "truly Christian" even if they do not possess the fullness of the restored gospel? And what of persons in other religious traditions? What is necessary from a Mormon point of view for a non-Mormon to avoid eternal damnation?

LDS teachings about the afterlife offer more hope than is typical of traditional Christianity for those who have not accepted the claims of the gospel in this life. To be sure, the highest heaven, the "celestial kingdom," is reserved exclusively for those who have submitted to the ordinances of the restored church, including those who accept the opportunity to do so in the afterlife. But there are lesser "degrees of glory"—the "terrestrial" and "telestial" realms—available to those who will be assigned to one or the other on the basis of works performed in their lifetimes. As for hell, only those who have been persistently unrepentant sinners will occupy the place of perdition.

Recent theological discussions of the possibilities of salvation for those who have not embraced Christianity have identified three schools of thought on the subject. The *pluralistic* view allows for many different paths to salvation, with Christianity being only one of many such paths. The *exclusivist* position sees salvation as restricted to those who put their faith in Christ as "*the* Way." A third approach is the *inclusivist* option, which sees Christ as the only true Savior, but allows for the possibility that persons who have not put their faith in Christ might nonetheless be beneficiaries of his atoning work. The authors of *Religions of the World* utilize this framework, placing Mormonism in the inclusivist camp. And this does seem to be the obvious choice, given the LDS teaching that persons who have not submitted to the Mormon ordinances, while being excluded from the celestial realm, can nonetheless avoid perdition by being granted admission to, for example, the terrestrial kingdom.

The primary focus of the *Religions of the World* volume, however, is not on how one achieves salvation as such, but on how to understand the teachings of other faith communities in their own terms. With this clearly in mind, the authors utilize the inclusivist label also with an eye to questions of religious truth. For support, they cite the views of Orson F. Whitney, who served as one of the Quorum of the Twelve in the early decades of the twentieth century—a time, as we have already noted, of the beginnings of the LDS's global missionary outreach. Because the gospel "embraces all truth," Whitney wrote, Mormons can explore the larger world of religious thought and practice with the conviction that "[n]o righteous principle will ever be revealed, no truth can possibly be discovered, either in time or in eternity, that does not in some manner, directly or indirectly, pertain to the Gospel of Jesus Christ."[9] Thus Mormonism rejects both the relativism that characterizes the pluralistic approach, but also the exclusivist denial that truth can be found in other religious perspectives.

EXPLAINING COMMONALITIES

Christian theologians have usually not been content merely to acknowledge the presence of truth in other religions. They have also offered theological explanations about what makes the capacity for genuine insights into moral and spiritual matters possible without the direct aid of "special revelation." In most of the classical Christian traditions these explanations have been seen as necessary in the light of what is often labeled "the noetic effects of sin." Given the traditional understanding of the fall into sin as fostering in human beings a spirit of rebellion against the revealed will of God, to what degree did this rebelliousness affect the "natural" human capacity for grasping truth about God's design for human life?

One widely held view is that God, out of a divine desire not to allow human sinfulness to destroy the fabric of created life, issued a "prevenient grace," a kind of universal moral-spiritual "upgrade" that freed the human spirit and will from the most devastating effects of sin. On this view, unredeemed human beings have the capacity not only to discern basic moral truth, an ability often linked to a notion of "natural law" or "general revelation," but they also have the ability actually to choose in favor of the good. And even when these depictions of continuing moral and spiritual capacities are viewed with some suspicion, as in several strands of Calvinism and Lutheranism, there is still often an acknowledgment that the worst tendencies of human fallenness are held in check by the possession in sinful human beings of the remnants of "the image of God" that was originally invested in human nature (Genesis 1:26–27).

Mormon perspectives on the noetic capacities of unredeemed humanity do not fit neatly into this larger theological discussion. Part of this is due to the ambivalent attitude toward the fall in much of Mormon thought. On the one hand, there are certainly affirmations of the fall as a tragic act of rebellion against God, as portrayed in Alma 42:9: "the fall had brought upon all mankind a spiritual death as well as a temporal, that is, they were cut off from the presence of the Lord." At the same time, the kind of emphasis seen in the Pearl of Great Price, where Eve declares joyfully that were it not for the fall humans "never should have known good and evil" (Moses 5:11), has encouraged Mormon thinkers to argue that the fall was also a necessary step toward human maturation. Given this endorsement of a positive aspect of the primal act of rebellion, it is not surprising that Mormonism does not pay as much attention as traditional Christian theology to sin's "noetic effects."

The authors of *Religions of the World* conclude their study of specific world religions with a helpful overview of what they see as the options for a Mormon understanding of a general moral and religious knowledge. Some of these options fit nicely into the more general theological approach of the Christian tradition. For example, the authors make use of the traditional Logos doctrine, based on first chapter of the Gospel of John, regarding Christ "the true Light, which lighteth every man that cometh into the world" (John 1:9), pointing out that this view is endorsed in Doctrine and Covenants 84:45–46 and 88:12–13. In this vein, the authors suggest that "the Spirit of Christ" has been at work throughout the human race, inspiring, for example, ancient Greek and Roman philosophers, artists in Asia, and religious teachers such as Buddha and Confucius.[10]

The Mormon authors also point to the reality of a shared human condition in which people everywhere experience—beneath the particularities of their time and place—common anxieties and hopes, giving rise to similar practices and symbolic representations. Here too there is a strong connection to a widely accepted Christian view that religion arises out of fundamental human yearnings, as expressed by Augustine in his much quoted prayer at the beginning of his *Confessions*: "Thou hast made us for thy-self and restless is our heart until it comes to rest in thee."[11]

The authors also discuss an option that has had some currency in the Christian past, but is no longer given much attention in mainstream Christian circles, namely, the idea of a *prisca theologia*, a pure original theology that, while corrupted as it was transmitted throughout history, continued to be "remembered" in fragmented and imperfect ways. In the older Christian versions of this perspective, there was much reliance on the scatter-ing, after the Great Flood, of the offspring of Noah to various parts of the earth, carrying with them elements of truths and principles that had been directly revealed before the Flood to godly patriarchs. Versions of the influence of a *prisca theologia* are still occa-sionally taught, especially in the evangelical world, where books are written, for example, that claim to find references to Old Testament narratives and imagery in Chinese written characters. But an increasing reluctance on the part of many Old Testament scholars to treat the Noah stories and other ancient narratives as straightforwardly "historical" has meant a diminishing of the attractiveness of a *prisca theologia* as an explanatory device.

The LDS authors of *Religions of the World* observe that the device—they call it "dif-fusion"—has been commonly accepted in Mormon circles. But they make it clear that they see it as having only a limited explanatory function. While it is quite possible that migrating groups might well have taken with them "the original principles and ordi-nances of the gospel" that had come to them by direct revelation, this factor "fails to cover much of the ground" in accounting for widespread religious similarities. More is required, in the form, for example, of a "polygenetic view—that religious beliefs and rituals have arisen spontaneously and independently in various countries but have gen-erally followed uniform patterns of development."[12]

The one LDS option for understanding shared concepts and symbols among various religions that is not at all likely to elicit agreement on the part of traditional Christians is tied to the Mormon belief in the premortal existence of human spirits. The *Religions of the World* authors make the case here by citing the views of past church authorities, particu-larly Joseph Fielding Smith and Orson F. Whitney, who taught that since there is only a "thin veil" that separates human beings from the spirit world from which they came, indi-viduals often experience "echoes of eternity" that are in reality "glimmers" of something once directly experienced in the spirit world. Much of what is often thought of as the prod-dings of "conscience," the *Religions of the World* authors suggest (following the argument of Truman Madsen), is rightly understood as the remembering of that premortal past.[13]

AN IMPORTANT VOICE IN THE DIALOGUE

The use by contemporary Mormon scholars of premortal existence in discussing shared moral-religious knowledge is an interesting case in point for assessing Mormonism's overall role in the present day interreligious context. On the surface, it is easy for tra-ditional Christians to dismiss the notion of a premortal spirit world as simply another example of the way in which a "cult" will set forth teachings that distinguish it from more mainline expressions of religious belief. But a dismissal of that sort would be too easy in this case. As Terryl Givens has shown in his impressive study of the concept of premortal existence, the idea has a long philosophical and theological history, with some major Christian thinkers—Augustine of Hippo heading the list—having wrestled seriously with the idea often with considerable sympathy for it, even when they ultimately reject it.[14]

The attractiveness of premortal existence has much to do with the way it addresses a conviction that has been shared by many philosophers and theologians, namely, that a thoroughgoing empiricism does not adequately explain the contents of our moral and religious consciousness. Our human sense of right and wrong, our conceptions of the divine, and even our basic convictions about truth and beauty cannot be explained—so the argument goes—simply in terms of what we have *learned from* experience. There must be some sort of content that we *bring to* our lives as human beings. This was at the heart of Plato's contention, set forth in the *Meno* and illustrated by Socrates's famous geometry lesson with a slave boy, that "all learning is remembering (*anamnesis*)." For Plato this meant that our learnings in this life are made possible only by the possession of ideal standards that we have gained in a premortal encounter with eternal Forms.

As Givens shows, Augustine, in addition to attending to this "learning" aspect of premortal existence, was also puzzled by the Christian contention that all human beings are complicit, from the very beginnings of our mortal life, in the guilt incurred by Adam and Eve in their rebellion against the divine will—a teaching summarized in the popular formula "In Adam's fall we sinned all." How, Augustine queried at one point in his theological journey, could this be the case unless a newborn child has already *done* something that incurs this guilt prior to birth?

To be sure, there are other ways of accounting for the sense that we bring content, whether guilt or knowledge, to our moral and religious lives. Theologians have often explained our shared complicity in Adam's rebellion, for example, by utilizing a notion of collective guilt that is not unlike the notion, promulgated well beyond theological circles, that present-day white Americans are responsible for their ancestors' racism. Or they have posited a sovereign divine decision simply to impute Adam's guilt to all of his descendants. And the view that we come "equipped" with, say, a concept of duty or a sense of the divine has often been set forth in terms of a doctrine of "innate ideas."

However we ultimately assess the merits of these arguments, we should at least acknowledge them as attempts to address important concerns. And the theological versions of the arguments have an advantage over the purely philosophical approaches in that they provide a larger narrative framework for understanding the point being made. A doctrine of "innate ideas" by itself, for example, leaves many genuine questions unanswered. If the human mind comes equipped with, say, an idea of a divine being, or of a conception of duty or virtue, how did the "equipping" come about? It is precisely this kind of question that the Mormon notion of a premortal spirit world addresses, along with the traditional Christian teaching that God has designed all human persons in such a way that they bear the divine image. And these explanations are embedded in narrative-worldview schemes that flesh out what otherwise might seem to be an arbitrary positing of an "equipment," without offering any explanation of how the "equipping" came to be.

Of course, it is possible to avoid these doctrines and their supportive narratives simply by refusing to acknowledge that there is anything about our moral-religious consciousness that requires explanations of this sort. But there are many in the world of religious thought who oppose that move precisely because they worry about the skepticism and relativism that it fosters. For those who share these worries, it is increasingly obvious that on many of the basic issues of life we are faced in our times with a fundamental decision: Are we *creators* of truth and goodness or are we *discoverers* of that which comes to us from a source that is beyond our own feeble capacity fully to comprehend?

For those who see ourselves on a journey of discovery, on the lookout for cognitive and moral markers that are not of human making, the dialogue among ourselves about how best to discern these things is an urgent task. That dialogue will surely require debate about what we are convinced within our respective worldviews are matters of eternal importance. But it will also necessitate, in ways that we have failed to sustain in the past, the exploration of shared convictions about human flourishing in a world whose deep and complex woundedness will only be made worse by strategies shaped by skeptical and relativistic mindsets.

However the representatives of the "major" religious traditions view Mormonism's past, it is a clear fact of contemporary life—and one to be celebrated—that the Mormon community is continuing to clarify its perspective on the basic issues of life. And it is doing so with increasingly robust intellectual resources and a demonstrated capacity for service to the common good. Mormonism has not only earned the right to be given an important role in interfaith conversations—those conversations will be greatly diminished if the Mormon voice is not heard.

NOTES

1. Smith, *History of the Church of Jesus Christ of Latter-day Saints*, 1: 18–19.
2. Smith, *Teachings of the Prophet Joseph Smith*, 272.
3. Owen and Mosser, "Mormon Scholarship, Apologetics, and Evangelical Neglect," 181.
4. Blomberg and Robinson, *How Wide the Divide?*
5. *Standing Together* is one such organization that works to build bridges between LDS and Evangelical communities. In 2007–9, *Standing Together* hosted an annual National Student Dialogue conference that brought together LDS and Evangelical college students for two days of interfaith dialogue. For more information see: http://www.standingtogether.org/.

   Additionally, the *Foundation for Interreligious Diplomacy*, which seeks to cultivate "religiously bi-lingual diplomats," has undertaken various initiatives to promote goodwill between members of different religions. Chapters have been formed for Mormon, Evangelical, Mahayana Buddhist, Shia Muslim, and Sunni Muslim communities for the purpose of cultivating diplomatic practices within each tradition better dialogue between religious traditions. For more information see http://www.fidweb.org.

6. Neill, *Christian Faith and Other Faiths*, 3.

7. Walsh and Middleton, *Transforming Vision*, 35.

8. Palmer et al., *Religions of the World*.

   More recently, Paulsen and Musser's book *Mormonism in Dialogue with Contemporary Christian Theologies* represents an interfaith project that explores comparisons between LDS theology and several of the leading Christian theological voices of the twentieth century.

9. Whitney, "Gospel of Jesus Christ," 26.

10. Palmer et al., *Religions of the World*, 249.

11. Augustine, *Confessions and Enchiridion*, 13.

12. Palmer et al., *Religions of the World*, 247.

13. Ibid., 248–49.

14. Givens, *When Souls Had Wings*, 99–127.

BIBLIOGRAPHY

St. Augustine. *Confessions and Enchiridion*. Trans. Albert C. Outler. Grand Rapids, MI: Christian Classics Ethereal Library, 2006. http://www.ccel.org/ccel/augustine/confessions.iv.html.

Blomberg, Craig L., and Stephen E. Robinson. *How Wide the Divide? A Mormon and an Evangelical in Conversation*. Downers Grove, IL: InterVarsity Press, 1997.

Foundation for Interreligious Diplomacy. http://www.fidweb.org.

Givens, Terryl L. *When Souls Had Wings: Pre-Mortal Existence in Western Thought*. New York: Oxford University Press, 2010.

McDermott, Gerald, and Robert Robert. *Claiming Christ: A Mormon-Evangelical Debate*. Grand Rapids, MI: Brazos, 2007.

Neill, Stephen. *Christian Faith and Other Faiths: The Christian Dialogue with Other Religions*. New York: Oxford University Press, 1961.

Owen, Paul, and Carl Mosser. "Mormon Scholarship, Apologetics, and Evangelical Neglect: Losing the Battle and Not Knowing It?" *Trinity Journal* 19, no. 2 (Fall 1998): 179–205.

Palmer, Spencer J., Roger R. Keller, Dong Sull Choi, and James A. Toronto. *Religions of the World: A Latter-day Saint View*. Rev. ed. Provo, UT: Brigham Young University, 1997.

Paulsen, David L., and Donald W. Musser, eds. *Mormonism in Dialogue with Contemporary Christian Theologies*. Macon, GA: Mercer University Press, 2007.

Shipps, Jan. *Mormonism: The Story of a New Religious Tradition*. Urbana: University of Illinois Press, 1985.

Shipps, Jan. *Sojourner in the Promised Land: Forty Years among the Mormons*. Urbana: University of Illinois Press, 2000.

Smith, Joseph, Jr. *History of the Church of Jesus Christ of Latter-day Saints*. 7 vols. Edited by James Mulholland, Robert B. Thompson, William W. Phelps, Willard Richards, George A. Smith, and B. H. Roberts. Salt Lake City: Deseret News Press, 1902–12; 2nd ed. Salt Lake City: Deseret, 1951.

Smith, Joseph, Jr. *Teachings of the Prophet Joseph Smith*. Ed. Joseph Fielding Smith. Salt Lake City: Deseret, 1976.

Standing Together. www.standingtogether.org/.

Walsh, Brian J., and J. Richard Middleton. *The Transforming Vision: Shaping a Christian World View.* Downers Grove, IL: InterVarsity Press, 1984.

Whitney, Orson F. "The Gospel of Jesus Christ." *Elder's Journal* [Southern States Mission] 4, no. 2 (October 15, 1906): 26. In Palmer et al., *Religions of the World*, 11.

CHAPTER 41

··

MORMONS AND MUSLIMS

··

DANIEL PETERSON

THROUGHOUT its history, especially in the nineteenth century but continuing even today, Mormonism, as taught and practiced within the Church of Jesus Christ of Latter-day Saints, has been compared by Western commentators to Islam—most enthusiastically by those with an agenda hostile to both. Books bearing titles like *The Mormon Prophet and His Harem* (1868) and *Mormonism: The Islam of America* (1912) have sought to discredit Mormonism by linking it with Christendom's traditional geopolitical and ideological archrival. As the eminent British Islamicist H. A. R. Gibb once observed, Muhammad has been labeled a "proto-Mormon."[1]

More respectably, the prominent American sociologist Rodney Stark, who is not a Latter-day Saint, has argued that Mormonism represents "that incredibly rare event: the rise of a new world religion"; the Latter-day Saints, he asserts, "stand on the threshold of becoming the first major faith to appear on earth since the Prophet Mohammed rode out of the desert."[2]

For this very reason, the famous Berlin historian of religions Eduard Meyer undertook the serious comparative effort that resulted in his *Ursprung und Geschichte der Mormonen* (1912). "Mormonism," wrote Meyer, "is not just another of countless sects, but a new revealed religion. What in the study of other revealed religions can only be surmised after painful research is here directly accessible in reliable witnesses. Hence the origin and history of Mormonism possess great and unusual value for the student of religious history."[3] And, indeed, Islam and Mormonism do manifest common theological features, most of which they also share with their Abrahamic religious cousins generally (that is, with Judaism, and with other Christian sects): They believe, for example, in a personal God who purposefully created the universe and intervenes in its history, which proceeds in a linear fashion toward a cosmic consummation wherein all will be physically resurrected and brought to judgment.

Both believe in prophets, and those prophets are, with only two major and a few minor exceptions, held in common. For both Islam and Mormonism, Adam and Eve were created by God and placed in the Garden of Eden. Noah and his family were saved from a punitive flood in order to preserve a righteous remnant of the human race. Abraham was chosen by God to become "the father of the faithful" and the ancestor of prophets. Moses confronted Pharaoh, received the law at Sinai, and led the Children of Israel in the wilderness. Jesus, too, is venerated by both Islam and Mormonism, although, as will be discussed briefly below, in different ways.

Both Islam and Mormonism rely upon a canon of authoritative scriptural texts. They are, both, accordingly, religions strongly oriented toward textual interpretation, and are "people of the Book" (Arabic *ahl al-kitab*).

Moreover, the so-called Five Pillars of Islam—testimony (*shahada*), prayer (*salat*), almsgiving (*zakat*), fasting (*sawm*) during the holy month of Ramadan, and pilgrimage (*hajj*)—find varying degrees of analogy in Mormon emphasis on vocal professions of faith, daily prayer, tithes and offerings and welfare contributions, regular monthly twenty-four-hour fasts, and temple attendance. (Latter-day Saint temples, like modern Mecca, are closed to those outside the faith, and both temple worshippers and pilgrims to Mecca dress in white.)

Historically and sociologically, too, parallels definitely exist. Perhaps the most striking is the division that occurred in both communities following the death of their founding prophets, with Islam's Sunni–Shi'i split echoed in the rift between those who followed Brigham Young to the Great Basin, by far the largest group, and those who remained behind in the Midwest (most notably, but not limited to, the Reorganized Church of Jesus Christ of Latter Day Saints, now known as the Community of Christ). In both cases, disagreement centered on the question of succession. Shi'ites and "Reorganites" insisted that the right to lead the community rested with the founder's nearest male relative, while their respective opponents, much more numerous, deemphasized that hereditary principle if they didn't altogether reject it. But it isn't altogether clear that even the surprisingly specific historical resemblance of the schism between Sunni and Shi'i Islam to that between Utah Mormonism and its much smaller Midwestern sibling represents anything more than coincidence; other indisputably poor and superficial comparisons have also been adduced.

The polygamy practiced by Joseph Smith, Brigham Young, and many other nineteenth-century Mormons, for example, is and has always been an obvious-seeming similarity, and, for transparent reasons, has drawn a great deal of titillated attention. Indeed, it's almost certainly what first inspired the comparison. But the parallels here are, in many respects, far more apparent than real. For instance, whereas polygamy in Islam continued a commonly accepted practice of Arabian society, Mormon plural marriage was a dramatic and highly controversial innovation in America and the West. Moreover, while marriage is a contract in Islam, and marriage and families are encouraged, marriage doesn't play the central role in Islamic doctrine that it plays in Mormonism, where it is essential for the highest degree of blessing in the hereafter. "He it is," says the Qur'an, addressing humanity and speaking of God, "who made you from a single soul and made from it its mate that he might dwell in tranquility with her" (Qur'an 7:190). "And," the Qur'an declares, "we placed in the hearts of those who followed [Jesus] compassion and mercy and monasticism, which was their innovation. We did not prescribe it for them" (Qur'an 57:27). These are affirmative statements, but they do not approach the centrality of marriage as it figures in the Mormon scriptural canon:

> For behold, I reveal unto you a new and an everlasting covenant; and if ye abide not that covenant, then are ye damned; for no one can reject this covenant and be permitted to enter into my glory.
>
> And again, verily I say unto you, if a man marry a wife by my word, which is my law, and by the new and everlasting covenant, and it is sealed unto them by the Holy Spirit of promise, . . . Ye shall come forth in the first resurrection; and if it be after the first resurrection, in the next resurrection; and shall inherit thrones, kingdoms, principalities, and powers, dominions, all heights and depths . . . and they shall pass by the angels, and the gods, which are set there, to their exaltation and glory in all things, as hath been sealed upon their heads, which glory shall be a fulness and a continuation of the seeds forever and ever.
>
> Then shall they be gods, because they have no end; therefore shall they be from everlasting to everlasting, because they continue; then shall they be above all, because all things are subject unto them. Then shall they be gods, because they have all power, and the angels are subject unto them.
>
> Verily, verily, I say unto you, except ye abide my law ye cannot attain to this glory. (Doctrine and Covenants [D&C] 132:4, 19–21)

Many observers, and not merely those of the Victorian period, have found it irresistible to compare the Mormon concept of eternal marriage, linked with a plurality of wives, with Muslim notions of the *houris*, the paradisiacal virgins who will wait upon the blest.[4] Further, the tangibility of the Muslim and Mormon conceptions of heaven—or, to use a more loaded word, their sensuousness—has often been adduced as a similarity between the two faiths. But, once again, the comparison is superficial. In the Qur'an, the *houris* (whose origin is unclear) represent the pleasures of paradise for the saved. The Qur'an depicts heaven as a garden beneath which rivers flow, a glorious place where the saved relax after their mortal trials. They will dwell in "gardens of Eden whose portals are open to them. Therein they will recline, calling for abundant fruit and drink" (Qur'an 38:50–51). "They will recline upon carpets whose interior is of brocade, and the fruit of the gardens will be near at hand" (Qur'an 55:54). "For them there is a foreknown provision of fruits while they are honored in gracious gardens, seated opposite one another upon thrones. A cup will be passed around to them, crystalline, from a spring fountain, delicious to those who partake. Free from bad effect, they will not be intoxicated by it" (Qur'an 37:41–47).

The Mormon concept of eternal marriage, by contrast, promises righteous husbands and wives and children a continuation of their mortal kinship beyond death, along with the possibility, at some unspecified future point, of yet more spiritual children ("a continuation of the seeds forever and ever"). "That same sociality which exists among us here," taught Joseph Smith, "will exist among us there, only it will be coupled with eternal glory, which glory we do not now enjoy" (D&C 130:2). There is no emphasis on pleasure nor even on relaxation, but rather on furthering the salvific work of God.[5]

On the other hand, as illustrated in the lengthy quotation above from Doctrine and Covenants 132 ("then shall they be gods"), there is, in Mormonism, a strong association of temple marriage with the doctrine of exaltation or human deification. While this is plainly redolent of the ancient Christian teaching of *theosis*, and while it has some parallels in teachings on the margin of Muslim thought, such a doctrine is utterly foreign to mainstream Islam.

Another point of frequent comparison is the claim by both Muhammad and Joseph Smith to be postbiblical prophets. Usually enough to satisfy those making the comparison—and, for many Evangelical Protestant critics, enough to *damn* both men—this parallel can actually be pursued further. Both Islam and Mormonism seem to take what might be termed a "dispensational" view of human history, which is seen as a repeating cycle of prophetic revelations followed by periods of apostasy. They differ, however, in that Muhammad is seen as the "seal of the prophets" (*khatim al-nabiyyin*), which is typically taken to mean that he is the last of them (Qur'an 33:40). "No prophet or apostle will come after me," Muhammad is reputed to have declared in his so-called Farewell Sermon, whereas Latter-day Saints regard Joseph Smith as the founder of a new and continuing line of modern prophets.[6]

As postbiblical prophets, both Muhammad and Joseph Smith produced new books of purported scripture—respectively, the Qur'an and the Book of Mormon (and the Doctrine and Covenants and the Pearl of Great Price). Both the Book of Mormon and the Qur'an provide a sacred history for an area largely or even altogether ignored by the Bible. But the two books are quite different in various ways, as well. Whereas, for instance, the former claims to be the narrative history of several ancient peoples (with some sermons and letters included), the Qur'an is a collection of discrete revelations received at different points during Muhammad's life. Short narratives play, at most, an occasional and subordinate role.[7] Moreover, while, for Islam as for Judaism and mainstream Christianity, the scriptural canon is closed, in Mormonism the canon remains open.

Muslims and Mormons are both often said to deny the doctrine of the Trinity. But this alleged similarity masks enormous differences. Islam emphasizes the unity of God (*tawhid*), and denies the deity of Christ. Moreover, since at least the earliest decades after the death of Muhammad, mainstream Muslim thought has come to espouse the view of God sometimes called "classical theism," affirming divine incorporeality, impassability, omnipotence, and omniscience. Mormonism, which insists upon the divinity of Christ, worships a "Godhead"—some Mormon authorities have even used the word *Trinity*—of Father, Son, and Holy Ghost. But Mormonism rejects Nicene ontological Trinitarianism in favor of a "social" model of the Trinity in which, while the three persons are perfectly united in love and will, they are otherwise distinct (see Chapter 17, this volume). Two members of the Mormon Godhead—the Father and the Son—are corporeal, with tangible bodies of flesh and bone, whereas the Holy Ghost has a spiritual body of determinate form. For that reason, Mormonism is often accused by its critics of "tritheism."

The one absolutely crucial difference between Islam and Mormonism, already alluded to immediately above but worthy of special emphasis, is that the Qur'an denies the deity of Christ and ascribes no redemptive role to either Jesus or Muhammad. By contrast, Mormonism teaches that "Jesus is the Christ, the Eternal God, manifesting himself unto all nations."[8] "There is no flesh that can dwell in the presence of God," says the Book of Mormon, "save it be through the merits, and mercy, and grace of the Holy Messiah" (2 Nephi 2:8). We can be saved only by "relying alone upon the merits of Christ" (Moroni 6:4), for "there shall be no other name given nor any other way nor means whereby salvation can come unto the children of men, only in and through the name of Christ, the Lord Omnipotent" (Mosiah 3:17).

Despite these and other fundamental theological differences, Mormons have historically manifested a markedly sympathetic attitude toward Islam and Muslims. The unjust persecutions of his followers led Joseph Smith, for example, to become a passionate advocate of religious tolerance, even—explicitly—for Muslims (though in antebellum America tolerance toward Islam was largely a matter of abstract theory since there were, as yet, virtually no Muslims on the continent).[9] In the late 1830s and early 1840s, he had an opportunity to demonstrate the sincerity of his commitment to religious freedom when he and his followers established Nauvoo, which would eventually become the second largest city in the state of Illinois. "We wish it . . . to be distinctly understood," he remarked,

> that we claim no privilege but what we feel cheerfully disposed to share with our fellow citizens of every denomination, and every sentiment of religion; and therefore say, that so far from being restricted to our own faith, let all those who desire to locate themselves in this place, or the vicinity, come, and we will hail them as citizens and friends, and shall feel it not only a duty, but a privilege, to reciprocate the kindness we have received from the benevolent and kind-hearted citizens of the state of Illinois.[10]

And those sentiments were embodied in the city's legal system.

William Law, a leader of the church at the time, reported that "As to the city ordinances we have passed all such as we deemed necessary for the peace, welfare and happiness of the inhabitants, whether Jew or Greek, Mohammedan, Roman Catholic, Latter-day Saint or any other; that they all worship God according to their own conscience, and enjoy the rights of American freemen."[11] Mormon theology provided a sturdy basis for such tolerance. "While one portion of the human race is judging and condemning the other without mercy," Joseph Smith taught,

> the Great Parent of the universe looks upon the whole of the human family with a fatherly care and paternal regard; He views them as His offspring, and without any of those contracted feelings that influence the children of men, causes "His sun to rise on the evil and on the good, and sendeth rain on the just and on the unjust." He holds the reins of judgment in His hands; He is a wise Lawgiver, and will judge all men, not according to the narrow, contracted notions of men, but, "according to the deeds done in the body, whether they be good or evil," or whether these deeds were done in England, America, Spain, Turkey, or India. He will judge them, "not according to

what they have not, but according to what they have," those who have lived without law, will be judged without law, and those who have a law, will be judged by that law.[12].

In his famous Farewell Sermon, the Prophet Muhammad advised Muslims that "all mankind is from Adam and Eve—an Arab has no superiority over a non-Arab," unless it be by "piety and good action."[13] A strikingly similar concept appears in the Book of Mormon: "Behold," said the prophet Nephi, "the Lord esteemeth all flesh in one; he that is righteous is favored of God" (1 Nephi 17:35). Accordingly, Mormon teaching has historically advocated not only tolerance but appreciation for sincere adherents of other faiths, expressly including Muslims.

In September 1855, Jules Rémy, a French newspaper correspondent, attended services in the Bowery, forerunner to the Salt Lake Tabernacle, during which two speakers addressed the audience positively, "from the sacred pulpit," about Islam. Incredulous, Rémy asked "who could have seen a person educated in Protestantism become the apologist of Mohammadanism in the 19th century?"[14] The speakers were almost certainly the Mormon apostles George A. Smith, a cousin to the slain prophet Joseph Smith, and Parley Pratt, whose comments about Islam and Muhammad were strikingly favorable by Christian standards of the day.

Speaking on September 23, 1855, Smith, who had been reading Islamic history, said of Muhammad that "there was nothing in his religion to license iniquity or corruption; he preached the moral doctrines which the Savior taught; viz., to do as they would be done by; and not to do violence to any man, nor to render evil for evil; and to worship one God."[15] Continuing, he declared that "this man descended from Abraham and was no doubt raised up by God on purpose to scourge the world for their idolatry." Then, expanding his focus to the Arabs and Muslims as a whole, he observed that, "just as long as they abode in the teachings which Mahomet [that is, Muhammad] gave them, and walked in strict accordance with them, they were united, and prospered; but when they ceased to do this, they lost their power and influence, to a very great extent."

His sympathy is unmistakable, and very many serious Muslims would strongly agree with his moral diagnosis of their historical decline. "It is a difficult matter," Smith went on, no doubt thinking of his own cobelievers as well as of Muslims, "to get an honest history of Mahometanism translated into any of the Christian languages. . . . It is a hard matter . . . to get an honest history of any nation or people by their enemies."

Embarrassed at having given the congregation essentially a classroom lecture, Smith confessed that "history is a natural theme with me." But Parley Pratt was so enthused at Smith's remarks that he immediately jumped up to continue the topic:

> My brother, George A. Smith, has wished us to excuse his Mahometan narration, but I would feel more like giving a vote of thanks to the Almighty and to His servant for so highly entertaining and instructing us.
> . . . We may think that: Mahometanism, compared with Christianity as it exists in the world, is a kind of heathenism, or something dreadful, and the other we look upon as something very pretty, only a little crippled; and for my part, I hardly know

which to call the idolatrous side of the question, unless we consider Mahometanism Christianity, in one sense, and that which has been called Christianity, heathenism.

Mahometanism included the doctrine that there was one God—that He was great, even the creator of all things, and that the people by right should worship Him. History abundantly shows the followers of Mahomet did not take the sword, either to enforce their religion or to defend themselves, until compelled to do so by the persecutions of their enemies, and then it was the only alternative that presented itself, to take up the sword and put down idolatry, and establish the worship of the one God.

Once again, the sympathy is striking, and especially so given Pratt's place and time. "I should rather incline, of the two," he continued,

to the side of Mahomet, for on this point he is on the side of truth, and the Christian world on the side of idolatry and heathenism. . . .

Mahometan history and Mahometan doctrine was a standard raised against the most corrupt and abominable idolatry that ever perverted our earth, found in the creeds and worship of Christians, falsely so named. . . . I am inclined to think, upon the whole, leaving out the corruptions of men in high places among them, that they have better morals and better institutions than many Christian nations. . . . I think they have exceeded in righteousness and truthfulness of religion, the idolatrous and corrupt church that has borne the name of Christianity.

The remarkably liberal character of these comments can perhaps best be put in perspective by comparing them to the famous May 1840 public lecture given in Edinburgh by Thomas Carlyle, one of the premier English-speaking intellectuals of the mid-nineteenth century, regarding Muhammad and Islam.[16] "Here for the first time in a prominent way," observes the eminent twentieth-century historian of Islam W. Montgomery Watt, "was it asserted that Muhammad was sincere and the religion of Islam basically true."[17] Just fifteen years later, though, from a pulpit in the isolated and only recently settled Great Basin desert of the United States, a pair of high-ranking Mormon leaders, drawn not from the intellectual elite but from the American frontier working class, were saying something rather far along similar lines.[18]

Undoubtedly the most significant expression of Mormon attitudes toward Islam came on February 15, 1978, when Spencer W. Kimball—sustained by faithful Latter-day Saints as a "prophet, seer, and revelator"—and his counselors in the First Presidency of the church issued an official statement regarding the church's position toward other religions generally. The statement reads:

Based upon ancient and modern revelation, The Church of Jesus Christ of Latter-day Saints gladly teaches and declares the Christian doctrine that all men and women are brothers and sisters, not only by blood relationship from mortal progenitors, but also as literal spirit children of an Eternal Father. The great religious leaders of the world such as Mohammed, Confucius, and the Reformers, as well as philosophers including Socrates, Plato, and others, received a portion of God's light. Moral truths were given to them by God to enlighten whole nations and to bring a higher level of

understanding to individuals. The Hebrew prophets prepared the way for the coming of Jesus Christ, the promised Messiah, who should provide salvation for all mankind who believe in the gospel. Consistent with these truths, we believe that God has
given and will give to all people sufficient knowledge to help them on their way to
eternal salvation, either in this life or in the life to come.[19]

With this attitude, Mormons have found it congenial to live and work with Muslims.
The official Latter-day Saint Charities organization, for instance, has cooperated on
numerous occasions with Islamic Relief Services in disasters and humanitarian crises,
including the tragic December 26, 2004, tsunami in the Indian Ocean (in the aftermath of which, among other things, Latter-day Saints distributed copies of the Qur'an
to stricken Muslims who requested them). Brigham Young University's former World
Family Policy Center, previously known as NGO Family Voice but now off campus and
independent, has collaborated with representatives of Islam and of the Vatican in promoting and defending certain principles related to families at the United Nations and
elsewhere. Moreover, because of many shared moral values, prominent Muslim families in the Middle East and other predominantly Muslim regions, wanting American
educations for their children but fearing the moral climate (as they see it) prevalent on
American college campuses, have felt comfortable sending their sons and daughters to
study at Brigham Young University in surprisingly large numbers.

Significantly, though, for a group as notoriously missionary-minded as the Church
of Jesus Christ of Latter-day Saints, there is, out of deference to Muslim concerns about
(and rules against) conversion, no Mormon proselytizing program that directly targets
Muslims. While Muslim conversions have occurred, such conversions are not actively
sought by the church and, in many cases, are actively discouraged. Most predominantly
Islamic countries are altogether off limits for Latter-day Saint missionaries, and even
where such missionaries are permitted, they have commonly focused their efforts on
Christians and other non-Muslims.[20]

Latter-day Saints typically regard missionary efforts as urgently important, but they
do not believe that those who do not hear and accept their message in this world will be
damned. Believing, as they do, in postmortem evangelization, they can afford to be optimistic about the eternal prospects for their non-Mormon neighbors.

Interestingly, there is support in the Qur'an for a similarly serene attitude toward
non-Muslims, in verses that tend to resonate with Latter-day Saints:

Those who believe, and those who follow Judaism and those who follow Christianity
and the Sabians, whoever believes in God and in the Last Day and does works of
righteousness—they have their reward with their Lord, and no fear shall come upon
them, neither shall they mourn. . . .

And they say "None shall enter Paradise except he be a Jew or a Christian." . . . But,
no, whoever submits his face to God and does good, he has his reward with his Lord.
No fear shall come upon them, neither shall they mourn.

The Jews say "The Christians base their faith on nothing," and the Christians say
"The Jews base their faith on nothing," while they're both studying the scriptures.

They speak as people who don't know. But God will judge between them on the Day of Resurrection concern that on which they used to differ.

To each [community] there is a direction that it follows, so vie with one another in good deeds. (Qur'an 2:62, 111–13, 148)

If God had willed, he would have made you one people. But, in order to test you in what he gave you [he did not]. So compete with one another in doing good. You will all return to God, and he will inform you concerning the things in which you differ. (Qur'an 5:48)

These verses make it almost impossible not to think of Gotthold Ephraim Lessing's 1779 German Enlightenment play *Nathan der Weise*. The centerpiece of the work is the Ring Parable (*Ringparabel*), narrated by Nathan when asked by the great leader of the Muslim Countercrusades, Saladin, which religion is true. An heirloom ring with the magical ability to render its owner pleasing before God and humankind had been passed for many generations from each successive father to the son he loved most. But when it came to a father of three sons whom he loved equally, he had promised it (in "pious weakness") to each of them. Later, desperately seeking a way to keep his promise, he had ordered two replicas to be made that were indistinguishable from the original, and, on his deathbed, he gave a ring to each of them.

The brothers quarreled, of course, over who owned the *real* ring. However, a wise judge admonished them that it was impossible to tell at that time which one was real, that it couldn't even be ruled out that all *three* rings were replicas, the original one having been lost at some point in the past. He told them that to find out whether one of them had the real ring it was up to them to live in such a way that their ring's powers could prove true, to live a life pleasing in the eyes of God and humankind rather than expecting the ring's miraculous powers to take care of everything.

Absent missionary efforts, one important manifestation of Mormon outreach to the Muslim world is Brigham Young University's Middle Eastern Texts Initiative (METI), which publishes dual-language editions of important writings from the classical period of Islam. Impelled by a perceived both academic and general need for such translations and, in a time of tension between the West and the Islamic world, by a desire to send a Latter-day Saint message of respect for Islam and Muslims, METI issued its first volumes in the late 1990s. At the time of writing, roughly twenty-five volumes have appeared, published by Brigham Young University Press and distributed by the University of Chicago Press. A few of the volumes represent eastern Christian authors, and a subseries focuses on the medical works of the great Arabic-writing rabbi, jurist, and philosopher Moses Maimonides, but far and away most of METI's attention has been devoted to Muslim authors, including such illustrious names as al-Ghazali, Ibn Sina (Avicenna), and Ibn Rushd (Averroës), as well as such relatively lesser known but important authors as Suhrawardi, Qadi 'Abd al-Jabbar, and Mulla Sadra.

Writing already in 2006, in his *Islamic Philosophy from Its Origin to the Present: Philosophy in the Land of Prophecy*, the prominent Irano-American intellectual historian Seyyed Hossein Nasr remarked that "what is needed for Islamic philosophy is something like the Loeb Library for Greek and Latin texts where the text in the original appears on one side of the page and the English translation on the opposite page. Fortunately during the last few years Brigham Young University has embarked upon such a series."[21] The standard foreword appearing in each Islam-related METI book reads as follows:

> Islamic civilization represents nearly fourteen centuries of intense intellectual activity, and believers in Islam number in the hundreds of millions. The texts that appear in [the Islamic Translation Series] are among the treasures of this great culture. But they are more than that. They are properly the inheritance of all the peoples of the world. As an institution of The Church of Jesus Christ of Latter-day Saints, Brigham Young University is honored to assist in making these texts available to many for the first time. In doing so, we hope to serve our fellow human beings, of all creeds and cultures. We also follow the admonition of our own tradition, to "seek . . . out of the best books words of wisdom," believing, indeed, that "the glory of God is intelligence."

Meticulously produced and deliberately priced relatively low, the METI volumes are intended not merely for academic researchers but for classroom use and, perhaps, even wider distribution, with the goal of enhanced understanding and better relationships between people of different faiths and cultures.

In the early days of Islam, Muslim, Christian, and Jewish scholars worked side by side to render the great texts of ancient Greek science, mathematics, medicine, and philosophy into Arabic, an effort that contributed mightily to the rise of classical Islamic civilization and that is often referred to in historical treatments under the term *bayt al-hikma*, "The House of Wisdom." Today, in front of the building that houses METI's personnel and operations, an upright stone bears the name of Brigham Young University and, in Arabic, *bayt al-hikma*. While at first glance a rather grandiose title, it's perhaps not wholly inappropriate, as, this time, Christian, Muslim, and Jewish scholars are cooperating to translate the great texts of the classical Islamic period into English.

It is not an unfitting symbol for the way in which Muslims and Latter-day Saints, building upon common ground despite differences, are increasingly able to work together.

NOTES

1. Gibb, *Mohammedanism*, 16.
2. Stark, "Rise of a New World Faith," 18, 19. Compare Stark, "Modernization and Mormon Growth," 13–23.
3. Meyer, *Ursprung und Geschichte der Mormonen*, 2. (This and all other translations in this chapter are mine.) For a critical evaluation of Meyer's work on the Latter-day Saints, see Lyon, "Mormonism and Islam through the Eyes of a 'Universal Historian,'" 221–36. Nibley, "Islam and Mormonism," 55–64, draws on Meyer's analysis.

4. On the *houris*, see, for example, see Qur'an 37:48–49; 38:52; 52:20; 55:56; 56:22–23, 35–38.

5. Visiting Salt Lake City in 1860, the great Victorian explorer Sir Richard Francis Burton, who knew "oriental" polygamy well (and was fascinated by it), was struck, and probably disappointed, by the distinct lack of sensuality apparent in Mormon Utah. See his *City of the Saints*.

6. Muhammad, "Farewell Sermon," 80.

7. The Qur'an is actually more appropriately compared to the Doctrine and Covenants, which, along with certain letters and other documents, contains revelations received by Joseph Smith (as well as, in a few cases, by his successors in the presidency of the church).

8. The specific phrase comes from the title page of the Book of Mormon, but the doctrine is a principal theme throughout the book and the rest of the Latter-day Saint canon.

9. For a fuller treatment of this subject, with references, see the transcribed lecture by Peterson, "Mormonism, Islam, and the Question of Other Religions."

10. Smith, Rigdon, and Smith, "Proclamation to the Saints Scattered Abroad," 277.

11. Law, "Much Ado about Nothing," 832.

12. Smith, "Baptism for the Dead," 759.

13. Muhammad, "Farewell Sermon," 80.

14. Cannon, *Writings from the Western Standard*, 51.

15. George A. Smith's and Parley Pratt's remarks occur in *Journal of Discourses* 3: 31–41. Two much later but still notably favorable treatments of Islam, published in the official magazine of the Church of Jesus Christ of Latter-day Saints, are Mayfield, "Ishmael, Our Brother," and Toronto, "A Latter-day Saint Perspective on Muhammad." (Nibley, "Islam and Mormonism" is rather less positive.)

16. Carlyle, *On Heroes, Hero-Worship, and the Heroic in History*, chap. 2.

17. Watt, *What is Islam?*, 1.

18. Peterson, *Muhammad*, is a sympathetic modern biography by a Latter-day Saint scholar.

19. Cited in Britsch, "I Have a Question," 48.

20. Latter-day Saint proselytizing missionaries currently serve in parts of Africa, in Indonesia and Malaysia, and in a few other largely Muslim areas. In the latter part of the nineteenth and the early twentieth centuries, Mormons sought converts in Turkey and Palestine, and a small mission functioned in Iran until the Islamic Revolution of 1978–79.

21. Nasr, *Islamic Philosophy from Its Origin to the Present*, 24.

BIBLIOGRAPHY

Britsch, R. Lanier. "I Have a Question: What is the Relationship of the Church of Jesus Christ of Latter-day Saints to the Non-Christian religions of the world?" *Ensign*, 18, no. 1 (January 1988). http://www.lds.org/ensign/1988/01/i-have-a-question?lang=eng.

Burton, Richard Francis. *The City of the Saints*. Ed. Fawn M. Brodie. New York: Alfred A. Knopf, 1963.

Carlyle, Thomas. *On Heroes, Hero-Worship, and the Heroic in History*. London: Longman's, Green, 1906.

Cannon, George Q. *Writings from the Western Standard*. San Francisco, CA: Cannon, 1864.

Gibb, H. A. R. *Mohammedanism: An Historical Survey*. New York: Oxford University Press, 1970.

Journal of Discourses. 26 vols. Reported by G. D. Watt et al. Liverpool: F. D. and S. W. Richards et al., 1851–86; reprint, Salt Lake City: n.p., 1974.

Law, William. "Much Ado about Nothing." *Times and Seasons* 3, no. 17, July 1, 1842: 831–32.

Lyon, James K. "Mormonism and Islam through the Eyes of a 'Universal Historian.'" *BYU Studies* 40, no. 4 (2001): 221–36.

Mayfield, James B. "Ishmael, Our Brother." *Ensign* 9, no. 6 (June 1979). http://www.lds.org/ensign/1979/06/ishmael-our-brother?lang=eng.

Meyer, Eduard Meyer, *Ursprung und Geschichte der Mormonen*. Halle: Niemeyer, 1912.

Muhammad, "Farewell Sermon." In *Speeches in World History*, ed. Suzanne McIntire and William E. Burns, 79–80. N.p.: Infobase, 2010.

Nasr, Seyyed Hossein. *Islamic Philosophy from Its Origin to the Present: Philosophy in the Land of Prophecy*. Albany: State University of New York Press, 2006.

Nibley, Hugh. "Islam and Mormonism—A Comparison." *Ensign* 2, no. 3 (March 1972). http://www.lds.org/ensign/1972/03/islam-and-mormonism-a-comparison?lang=eng.

Peterson, Daniel C. "Mormonism, Islam, and the Question of Other Religions." Paper presented at the FAIR Conference, Sandy, UT, August 5, 2011. http://www.fairmormon.org/perspectives/fair-conferences/2011-fair-conference/2011-mormonism-islam-and-the-question-of-other-religions.

Peterson, Daniel C. *Muhammad: Prophet of God*. Grand Rapids, MI: William B. Eerdmans, 2007.

Pratt, Parley P. "Mahometanism and Christianity" [September 23, 1855]. *Journal of Discourses* 3: 38–42.

Smith, George A. "The History of Mahomedanism" [September 23, 1855]. *Journal of Discourses* 3: 28–37.

Smith, Joseph. "Baptism for the Dead." *Times and Seasons* 3, no. 12, April 15, 1842: 759–61.

Smith, Joseph, Sidney Rigdon, and Hryum Smith. "Proclamation to the Saints Scattered Abroad." *Times and Seasons* 2, no. 6, January 15, 1841: 273–77.

Stark, Rodney. "The Rise of a New World Faith." *Review of Religious Research* 26, no. 1 (September 1984): 18–27.

Stark, Rodney. "Modernization and Mormon Growth: The Secularization Thesis Revisited." In *Contemporary Mormonism: Social Science Perspectives*, ed. Marie Cornwall, Tim B. Heaton, and Lawrence A. Young, 13–23. Urbana: University of Illinois Press, 1994.

Toronto, James A. "A Latter-day Saint Perspective on Muhammad." *Ensign* 30, no. 8 (August 2000). http://www.lds.org/ensign/2000/08/a-latter-day-saint-perspective-on-muhammad?lang=eng.

Watt, W. Montgomery. *What Is Islam?* New York: Longman's Green, 1968.

Index